SEX WORK IN POPULAR CULTURE

Sex Work in Popular Culture delves into provocative movies, TV shows, and documentaries about sex work produced in the last fifteen years – a period of debate and change around the meaning of sex work in North American society. From Oscar-winning films to viral YouTube videos, and from indie documentaries to hit series – many of which are made by women – the book reveals how sex work is being recognized as real work and an issue of human rights. Lauren Kirshner shares how popular culture has responded by producing the dynamic new figure of a sex worker who challenges tropes and promotes understanding of the key issues shaping sex work.

The book draws on labour and feminist theory, film history, current news, and popular culture, all within the context of neo-liberal capitalism and the rise of transactional intimate labour. Kirshner takes us from erotic dance clubs to porn sets, illuminating the professional lives of erotic dancers, massage parlour workers, webcam models, call girls, sex surrogates, and porn performers. Probing how progressive popular culture challenges stereotypes, *Sex Work in Popular Culture* tells the story of sex work as labour and how the screen can show us the world's oldest profession in a new light.

LAUREN KIRSHNER is an assistant professor of English at Toronto Metropolitan University.

Sex Work in Popular Culture

LAUREN KIRSHNER

UNIVERSITY OF TORONTO PRESS
Toronto Buffalo London

© University of Toronto Press 2024
Toronto Buffalo London
utorontopress.com

Printed and bound by CPI Group (UK) Ltd, Croydon, CR0 4YY

ISBN 978-1-4875-0786-2 (cloth)   ISBN 978-1-4875-3711-1 (EPUB)
ISBN 978-1-4875-4863-6 (paper)   ISBN 978-1-4875-3710-4 (PDF)

Library and Archives Canada Cataloguing in Publication

Title: Sex work in popular culture / Lauren Kirshner.
Names: Kirshner, Lauren, author.
Description: Includes bibliographical references and index.
Identifiers: Canadiana (print) 20240357639 | Canadiana (ebook) 2024035768X |
    ISBN 9781487548636 (softcover) | ISBN 9781487507862 (hardcover) |
    ISBN 9781487537111 (EPUB) | ISBN 9781487537104 (PDF)
Subjects: LCSH: Sex work. | LCSH: Sex workers. | LCSH: Sex in popular culture.
Classification: LCC HQ118 .K57 2024 | DDC 306.74 – dc23/eng/20240404 | 306.74 – dc23

Cover design: Eric C. Wilder
Cover image: etraveler / Shutterstock.com

We wish to acknowledge the land on which the University of Toronto Press operates. This land is the traditional territory of the Wendat, the Anishnaabeg, the Haudenosaunee, the Métis, and the Mississaugas of the Credit First Nation.

This book has been published with the help of a grant from the Federation for the Humanities and Social Sciences, through the Awards to Scholarly Publications Program, using funds provided by the Social Sciences and Humanities Research Council of Canada.

University of Toronto Press acknowledges the financial support of the Government of Canada, the Canada Council for the Arts, and the Ontario Arts Council, an agency of the Government of Ontario, for its publishing activities.

Contents

List of Illustrations   vii

Introduction: A New Sex Worker in Popular Culture   3

1 Working It: Popular Culture, Feminism, and Sex Work   23

2 Dancing to an American Dream: Dignifying Erotic Dancers' Labour in "Road Strip," *P.O.P.*, *Magic City*, *Afternoon Delight*, and *Hustlers*   47

3 Massage Parlour Mothers on Prime Time: How the Fallen Woman Became a Mompreneur on *The Client List*   85

4 Twenty-First-Century Peep Show: Feminist Entanglements in *Cam Girlz*, *Cam*, and *Teenage Cocktail*   117

5 Sex and Entrepreneurship in the City: Building Intimate Business in *The Girlfriend Experience*   151

6 Sexual Healing: Sex Surrogate Care Workers in *The Sessions* and *She's Lost Control*   183

7 Hardcore in the Big Apple: *The Deuce*'s Feminist Sex Work Epic   213

Curtains: From Victimhood and Vice to Sex Workers' Rights   253

Acknowledgments   271

Filmography   273

List of TV Series   279

Notes   281

Bibliography   337

Index   369

Illustrations

0.1 Opening scene from *Hustlers*   4
0.2 *New York* and *New York Times Magazine* covers   11
1.1 Margo St. James   24
1.2 Scenes from *Klute*   26
1.3 Pop culture headlines   41
2.1 Erotic dancers in the Snack Pack in *P.O.P.*   66
2.2 Scene from *Afternoon Delight*   73
2.3 Scene from *Hustlers*   76
3.1 Billboard advertisement for *The Client List*   86
3.2 Massage parlours in 1970s popular culture   89
3.3 Fallen women behind bars   97
3.4 Mentoring at the massage parlour in a scene from *The Client List*   103
3.5 Railing against whorephobia in a scene from *The Client List*   109
4.1 The Mutoscope and the peep show   120
4.2 Webcam models featured in *Cam Girlz*   129
4.3 Scenes from *Cam*   139
4.4 Scenes from *Teenage Cocktail*   147
5.1 Books about call girls   154
5.2 Kissing as a transaction in scenes from the film *The Girlfriend Experience*   161
5.3 An embrace in a scene from the film *The Girlfriend Experience*   171
5.4 Refusal to repent in scenes from the TV series *The Girlfriend Experience*   180
6.1 Scene from *Masters of Sex*   189
6.2 Cover of *Surrogate Wife* and scene from *My Therapist*   190
6.3 Scene from *The Sessions*   195
6.4 Scenes from *She's Lost Control*   203
7.1 Uncovering a forgotten history in scenes from *The Deuce*   219
7.2 Candy on the street in a scene from *The Deuce*   221

7.3 Candy behind the camera in a scene from *The Deuce* 229
7.4 *Red Hot* in a scene from *The Deuce* 233
8.1 Scene from *Pleasure* 258
8.2 Scene from *Tangerine* 262
8.3 Scene from *Good Luck to You, Leo Grande* 267

SEX WORK IN POPULAR CULTURE

Introduction: A New Sex Worker in Popular Culture

In the 2019 film *Hustlers*,[1] inspired by a real-life scandal at a New York City erotic dancing club, a rookie dancer named Charity meets Ramona, played by Jennifer Lopez, in a spectacular opening scene where she watches the seasoned pro dance to Fiona Apple's song "Criminal." Poised, self-possessed, and with abs so etched they look airbrushed on, Ramona climbs, spins, whirls, and drops on the brass pole to Apple's unrepentant lyrics: "Right or wrong, I don't suffer for my sins." Later, Ramona takes Charity under her wing and teaches her how to hustle. As Ramona says, "This city, this whole country, is a strip club. You got people tossing the money and people doin' the dance." A sex worker caper and a critique of capitalism in sequins and stilettoes, *Hustlers* shook audiences off their high horses by showing how all workers, in one way or another, are dancing for the dollar.

Hustlers is part of a new wave of sex work popular culture that is today everywhere you look. Pole-dancing studios promising to help women get fit offer deals on Groupon, porn star memoirs crown bestseller lists, blockbuster films bring undressing acts to the Oscars, and actresses win Emmys for playing ladies in red. In the hit HBO series *The White Lotus* (2021–), two sex workers gamely conclude season two by strolling off into the sunset. Similarly, in the film *Poor Things* (2023), the sex-positive heroine trades carnality for cash in a delicious carnival for the senses, a role that earned Emma Stone an Academy Award. The 2015 viral Twitter saga by A'Ziah (Zola) King, a twenty-year-old erotic dancer turned author, also captivated millions. Her namesake, Émile Zola, wrote *Nana* (1880), a famous novel about a sex worker who perishes for her sins.[2] Yet, in the 2020 film adaptation of King's story, *Zola*, the titular character is portrayed as a proud, unapologetic pro. From celebrity tweets to magazine cover stories, social media to street activism, sex work has become a site of limitless curiosity for the public, a well of inspiration for creators, and a subject of renewed feminist debate, marking a seismic change from the twentieth century, when the

Figure 0.1. *Hustlers*, a movie about sex work, stigma, and inequality, opens with Ramona (Jennifer Lopez), an unrepentant and proud erotic dancer, captivating the crowd with her stagecraft.

public image of sex work was usually buffeted by myths and buoyed by prurient interest. Not so today.

Things have changed quite a bit since the first blockbuster I ever saw about a sex worker. Dim the lights, cue the VHS, and grab the microwave popcorn: *Pretty Woman*, standard 1990s sleepover fare starring Julia Roberts and Richard Gere, was about a beautiful street sex worker with shampoo-commercial red hair who meets a rich banker when he gets lost one steamy evening on the wrong side of LA. What starts with some friendly directions back to his hotel becomes a night to remember, budding a romance that climaxes with a classy makeover and ends with a marriage proposal. A combination of "Cinderella" and "The Ugly Duckling," it was a fairy tale that appealed to the perennial girlhood wish for transformation – and it delivered. For in the end, the glass slipper – erm, thigh-high stiletto boot – fit.

But it was the 1990s spectacle *Jerry Springer* that introduced me to a far less romantic image of the sex worker. Characterized by flying chairs, flowing confessions, and shocking paternity tests, the notorious talk show frequently featured sex workers as guests. I can still picture them careening onto stage in stretchy leopard-print dresses, yelling expletives scarcely heard through the audience's jeers and boos. I found them intriguing and attractive, though I knew I wasn't meant to. The show portrayed them as dangerous women, plunking them down next to "good" women (wives) who accused them of "stealing their men," suggesting sex workers' treachery and appalling lack of sisterhood. Sex workers, through their clothes, language, and on-stage antics, were marked as "Other," the quintessential bad girls, broken and traitorous. Even episode titles drove this point home, depicting sex workers as betrayers ("You Slept with My Stripper Sister!"), greedy manipulators ("Strippers Milking It"), and violent ("High End Stripper Smackdown"). In sum, the popular culture of my 1990s youth taught me that sex workers were either (a) romantic heroines rehabilitated by the handsome, rich men who rescued them, or (b) overly hair-sprayed harlots who could wreck a home faster than the time it took to toast a Pop-Tart.

Though I couldn't know it then, that dual imaginary was built on the over 1,400 films and 300 TV shows featuring sex worker lead characters produced since 1896.[3] From sun-kissed epics like *East of Eden* (1955) to valentines like *Breakfast at Tiffany's* (1961), gritty dramas like *Taxi Driver* (1976) to comedies like *Irma La Douce* (1963), sex workers have long been a fixture on screen because they are such compelling and controversial figures, embodying both desire and danger, power and vulnerability. In fact, more actresses have won Oscars for playing sex workers than for any other role.[4] Yet, for over 100 years, the US has also criminalized and stigmatized sex workers, incarcerating and shaming them for their work.[5] During this time, popular culture contributed to this stigmatization by recycling stereotypical images of the sex worker as a fallen woman or a femme fatale, her amorality, fragility, and disposability her main features. While some sex workers on screen were certainly dynamic, many more were symbols of danger, vanquished virtue, and the wrong side of town, a silky and smoky repository for the taboo that presented audiences with the opportunity to vicariously experience what in real life we condemn – our free pass into synthetic sinfulness. As Helga Hallgrimsdottir, Rachel Phillips, and Cecilia Benoit rightly observed, media depictions of this era did not emphasize the "work" aspect of the sex work industry.[6]

I learned this firsthand while at university, when I got to know a few women who did sex work. Their stories were nothing like the ones I saw on screen. This was in the mid-2000s, when popular culture as a whole had become more sexualized. Lad mags were deifying fake tans and breast implants on size-0 frames, and the "girl power" being proselytized on MTV was typified by midriff-baring tops and belly button rings. The Pussycat Dolls climbed the pop charts, and *Moulin Rouge!* (2001) brought the brass rail to the Oscars. Media about "cool" sex work flooded the big and small screens, coinciding with the internet's explosion of sex, from the voyeurism of *Girls Gone Wild* to alt porn epitomized by the Suicide Girls, who blended sex and the rhetoric of empowerment (and some pretty gorgeous ink) as effortlessly as the flavours in Neapolitan ice cream.

To pay her tuition, one friend of mine got a job at a big box sex shop downtown, a heavily air-conditioned emporium that sold a ton of edible underwear. I sometimes visited her at work, and as I perused the aisles of overpriced kitschy schoolgirl costumes, Rampant Rabbit vibrators (discussed during brunch tête-à-têtes on *Sex and the City*), and toys modelled after porn star parts, it became clear to me that we'd entered an age when the *idea* of sex work made a mint for corporations. Yet, real-life sex workers were still being held in contempt. Popular culture was missing the bigger picture. The sex workers I knew weren't jubilant like Vivian Ward in *Pretty Woman*. No silver fox in a Maserati waited to whisk them away after work. They took the subway home. They were articulate about the perks and pitfalls of their jobs, worried about getting arrested, wore jeans when not at work, and challenged most every popular culture stereotype. It bothered me that stories like theirs – stories of ordinary sex workers – were being muted in favour of the two most common pop culture images then seen on screen: the market-friendly glamour girl and the exploited victim. Most upsetting, these depictions all but buried the movement for sex workers' rights against criminalization and stigmatization.

In the last decade or so, however, North American culture has, in conjunction with changing economic conditions and tremendous social and political debate, begun to shift. From the legislative level down to the level of the street, there has been a push to start appreciating sex work as legitimate work instead of seeing it as a criminal act. My goal with this book has thus been to analyze sex workers in popular culture in this time of social change. To that end, I've immersed myself in films, TV series, and documentaries of the past fifteen or so years. I've sat in packed city theatres and empty suburban multiplexes. I've streamed blockbusters on Netflix and Vimeo and sleeper hits on Kanopy and

Crave. I've tracked down obscure films on DVD and VHS, and I've clocked hundreds of hours in front of my TV watching all stripes of paid sex in the most unsexy way: with a pencil and a notepad. From it all, I've learned that a new representation of the sex worker in popular culture has emerged – a dynamic figure who reflects changing attitudes about sex and work and feminist ideas about empowerment.

In the pages to come, I argue that in a new context of rising activism by sex workers for recognition and labour rights, economic shifts brought about by post-Fordist and neo-liberal capitalism, and the normalization of transactional intimate labour, popular culture is now taking an active role in constructing new, dignifying images of sex worker entrepreneurs that contrast with criminalizing and stigmatizing portrayals of the past. These new images highlight the "work" of sex work, inviting us to glean new insights into the hidden labour processes of a clandestine job while building understanding for the sex worker's wide-ranging struggles, from stigmatization to precarity. While some scholars have dismissed contemporary pop culture portrayals of sex workers as tawdry advertisements for the sex industry, I argue that popular culture about sex work is increasingly a contested field where new stories are being told and feminist debates about this work are playing out.

Employing feminist theories of sex work, labour theory, and the methodologies of feminist media studies, I examine how popular culture portrays six different sex work professionals: erotic dancers, massage parlour workers, webcam models, call girls, sex surrogates, and porn performers. By foregrounding these women's agency and skills, underscoring their work as a means of achieving economic mobility, and challenging the anti–sex work position espoused by conservative patriarchal ideologies and prohibitionist feminists, popular culture's new representation of the sex worker distinguishes sex work from trafficking, emphasizes women's bodily autonomy and choice, and implicitly contributes to the movement to destigmatize sex work. While women have historically been the least likely beneficiaries of capitalism, and earlier popular culture framed sex workers as passive victims of the capitalist system, pop culture's new sex worker chooses and benefits from her work. Yet, far from the glamourama lady in red, she is an ordinary woman with bills to pay, kids to clothe, rent to make, and lights to keep on. She is a mother, a student, a wife, a sister, a best friend, and a woman who hustles.

Along the way, we visit erotic dance clubs, ritzy hotels, feminist porn sets, suburban bedrooms, and massage parlours through stories told from sex workers' points of view and often directed by women and shot in ways that challenge the male gaze. The new sex worker in popular culture acts as a flashpoint for issues relevant to all women under patriarchal capitalism, from precarious work to bodily autonomy. She poses a threat to the double standard faced by women – on the one hand valued for their sex appeal, and on the other denigrated for monetizing it – and she has opened new avenues for the representation of the most marginalized of women workers and one of the most stereotyped on screen. The new sex worker wants respect, not rescue.

Yet, even as the new sex worker smashes stereotypes, she also sometimes gets intertwined with a post-feminist sensibility that equates entrepreneurship with empowerment, emphasizes freedom as realizable through the market alone, and elides deeper examinations of the challenges women face under patriarchal capitalism. At times, her "businesswoman" ethos swaps one ideology – patriarchy – for another: neo-liberalism. The new sex worker pronounces herself a feminist and a sexually empowered woman, but her individualist actions can undermine feminism's focus on collective empowerment and deflect from the collective struggle for sex workers' rights. Furthermore, she is predominately young and white, and thus in no way representative of the heterogeneity of sex workers in North American society. Even so, the new sex worker is far more dynamic, realistic, and progressive than those that came before her. By asking the viewer to regard without condescension how and why sex workers do their work, popular culture is making significant strides that are worth examining.

With this reading of film, TV, and documentaries – through a labour lens and within and against the grain of social changes associated with post-Fordism and neo-liberal capitalism – I explore how popular culture circulates ideas about sex workers beyond the binary question – is sex work good or bad? – made famous by the so-called feminist sex wars beginning in the 1970s. While the most publicly visible feminism today is still linked to an ironclad idea that sex work is constitutive of patriarchy and the sex worker its victim,[7] the new sex worker in popular culture shows us that there is much more to this picture. By conversing, massaging, teaching, performing, marketing, and empathizing, the sex worker being represented by pop culture today is an *entrepreneur*: she uses what Catherine Hakim calls her "erotic capital" as a strategy for making her way in the world, in a corner of the market where women are more successful than men. Thus, I depart from feminist scholars who view sex work as an automatic expression of women's victimhood. Indeed, for some, any movie that does *not* depict sex work as a brutalizing experience is judged as distorting the "real" experience of sex workers. *Pretty Woman*, for instance, has been criticized for failing to represent the "hopelessness" and "drug use" of the sex worker's life,[8] while Molly Haskell called one of the best sex worker films ever made, *Working Girls* (1986), "a feminist fantasy," declaring that no woman could exit sex work with her "soul intact."[9]

In contrast, I don't assume that sex workers are exploited victims, nor do I interpret popular culture as always being complicit with capitalist patriarchy. Rather, I shed light on new popular culture that paints a more complex picture of women who choose and benefit from sex work, the material conditions underlying these women's choices, and the potential consequences – social, economic, and legal – within a post-Fordist, neo-liberal, capitalist world. To borrow a phrase from Arlie Hochschild, these sex workers "do not accommodate passively."[10] Accordingly, I move away from theorists who read more labour-focused popular culture about sex workers as mystifications of the "real" experiences of sex workers. I take up Angela Jones's call for "critiques of neo-liberal feminism" to also explore "the potential benefits of such ideologies for the feminist subjects who adopt them."[11] In doing so, I contribute to feminist media studies by considering the role popular culture plays in destigmatizing sex workers by portraying the *work* of sex work, a hitherto understudied area. At the same time, I examine how popular culture portrays how race, gender, and class intersect to shape the often inequitable and oppressive conditions of sex work and sex workers' experiences.[12]

Contexts: Selling Sex Today

The last decade or so serves as the historical framework for this book's interpretations of popular culture, for it saw more changes in the economic, political, legal, news media, and labour movement environments around sex work than ever before. During this time, post-Fordist capitalism drove a shift from standard to increasingly non-standard employment relations, and the full-time work that once defined America's economy has been supplanted by jobs that are part-time and contractual.[13] At the same time, neo-liberal discourses continue to cast all workers as "entrepreneurs" within a precarious global gig economy, where everyone has to hustle to survive. The sex industry today is paradigmatic of these wider economic changes, a multibillion-dollar colossus encompassing erotic dance clubs, massage parlours, escort agencies, brothels, peep shows, and pornographic film companies – not to mention content creator websites like OnlyFans.[14] From downtown streets to suburban plazas, roughly 3,500 strip clubs across the US employ 400,000 performers who gross over $3 billion annually.[15] Almost 5,000 massage parlours net $1 billion a year,[16] the global sex toy market (whose sales spiked during the peak of the COVID-19 pandemic) is valued at $28.64 billion,[17] and in 2020 the webcam modelling industry earned $6.86 billion.[18] According to one Urban Institute study, the sex industries in New York City and Atlanta are more profitable than their drug and gun trades combined.[19] And on top of all that, internet pornography accounts for 30 per cent of all data transferred on the Web, with recent figures revealing that its profits exceed in one year more than the collective profits of Hollywood, the NBA, the NFL, and the MLB.[20] Simultaneously, American culture at large has become more sexually liberal and liberated, and support for once-marginal sexual practices and identities has grown, helping to normalize erotic professionals, from "sugar babies" to "girlfriend experience" call girls who fashion intimacy into just another transaction in a marketplace of sexual commodities.[21]

At the same time, the sex workers' rights movement has been growing, with added strength coming from allies who have used their institutional weight to declare sex work a human rights issue. In the last decade, the Joint United Nations Programme on HIV/AIDS (UNAIDS), the World Health Organization, and the prestigious medical journal *The Lancet* have aligned themselves with the decriminalization movement.[22] In a 2015 watershed event, Amnesty International formally backed sex workers in their fight for decriminalization, citing how the fear of criminal prosecution drives sex workers underground, where they become more vulnerable to violence. As one Norwegian sex worker put it, "You only call the police if you think you are going to die."[23] Tawandah Mustafah, Amnesty International's director of policy, wrote that sex workers are receiving "no, or very little, protection from the law," which "interferes with … [their] human rights."[24] Some municipal and federal governments are also moving towards decriminalization. Sex work has already long been decriminalized in Australia and New Zealand, and Belgium became the first European country to do so in 2022. Also in 2022, following the lead of Baltimore and Philadelphia, New York City announced that it would stop prosecuting sex workers and reverse prostitution charges going back thirty years, signalling a monumental shift in the US criminal justice system's approach to sex work.[25]

The news media's approach is changing too, breaking from a past when it regularly linked sex work to trafficked women, disease, organized crime, public nuisance, child abuse, and violence.[26] Capturing this change, one journalist writing in the *Daily Dot* declared 2015 the "year sex work dominated in the news" and observed that "journalism about sex workers was generally respectful, even laudatory."[27] In March 2016, *New York* magazine asked, "Is Prostitution Just Another Job?," ultimately answering in the affirmative and rallying support for decriminalization.[28] A few months later, *New York Times Magazine* ran its first-ever cover story on sex workers, sympathetically portraying their battle for civil rights.[29] A cascade of respectful, nuanced stories that centred sex workers as the experts on their labour followed in high-profile publications such as *Vanity Fair*, *The Independent*, *The Telegraph*, *The Atlantic*, the *Huffington Post*, and *Vice*. And the trend has continued. Recognizing media's complicity in sensationalizing sex workers, the International Journalists' Network recently published a list of recommendations for reporting on sex work,[30] and in 2023, one *New York Times* writer noted how "sex work" was becoming the preferred term over "prostitution," even far outside the "academic, activist and progressive strongholds" where it originated: "It's now commonly used by politicians, the media, Hollywood and government agencies."[31]

Public figures are also supporting sex workers, stirring mass audiences and galvanizing record support. In 2015, the actress and comedian Margaret Cho posted her most personal tweet ever: "I was a sex worker when I was young," she wrote, "it was hard but well paid. There's no shame in it."[32] At the 2017 Women's March in Washington, DC, writer and transgender activist

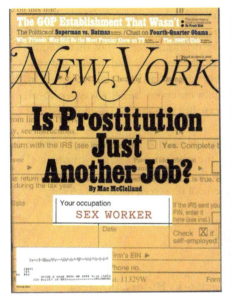 

Figure 0.2. The news media is publishing empathetic and nuanced stories that centre the voices of sex workers and trade condescension for respect.

Janet Mock implored a crowd of 500,000 to support "the sex worker fighting to make her living safely."[33] Meanwhile, sex workers have themselves been organizing through collective action in watershed cases. In 2012, erotic dancers won a federal class-action lawsuit against their employer for $13 million of unpaid back wages.[34] In 2016, the Retail, Wholesale and Department Store Union (RWDSU), the largest retail labour union in the US, welcomed sex shop workers into its ranks, and in 2021, the Canadian Union of Public Employees (CUPE), the largest Canadian workers' union, enthusiastically opened its doors to sex workers.[35] When the dancers at the Star Garden Topless Dive Bar in Los Angeles went on strike in 2022, the story garnered international media coverage.[36] Similarly, when renowned sex worker activist and writer Carol Leigh died that same year, national newspapers that once ignored the cause she had spent her life championing celebrated her as a feminist icon. All the while, sex worker activist organizations, such as the International Union for Sex Workers (IUSW), the Sex Workers Project, and the Red Umbrella Project, continue to organize for political change at the local, state, and national levels with campaigns that trumpet their main message: whether or not one approves of sex work morally, criminalizing it forces women to conduct their business underground, denies them access to legal and labour rights, and increases their stigmatization.

These labour movements for sex workers' rights have coincided with shifting public opinion about sex work. In a US national poll in 1981, just 30 per cent of respondents thought sex work should be decriminalized,[37] but that number has been steadily rising. In 2012, 38 per cent of Americans said they would support decriminalization; in 2016, that number had jumped to 44 per cent, and by 2020, it was at 52 per cent.[38] As Gayle Rubin observes, "sex is always political. But there are historical periods in which sexuality is more sharply contested and more overly politicized. In such periods, the domain of the erotic life is, in effect, renegotiated."[39] It is these renegotiations over the past fifteen years or so that have shaped popular culture's representation of the new sex worker, recognizing and dignifying her work, tacitly contributing to the decriminalization of her labour, and challenging stereotypes that have played out on screen for over a century.

From the Clam to the Ferrari: Sex Work's History on Screen

To fully understand the new sex worker in popular culture, it's useful to first look back at who she was to measure how far she's come. Indeed, today's pop culture fascination with sex work is not a new phenomenon. When the Lumière brothers toured Russia in 1896 to promote their new movie projector, they brought with them a troupe of singer–sex workers from Paris. The women's dancing and singing was so seductive, wrote one observer, that even those leery of the new technology came out to take a look.[40] Film-makers soon put undressing women on film as a lure for a green movie-going public. France's *Le Coucher de la Mariée* (1896) made a splash with its ringside view of a bride disrobing for her ablutions, and *Birth of the Pearl* (1901), a voyeur's take on Botticelli's *The Birth of Venus*, portrayed a nude woman (actually in a flesh-coloured body stocking) emerging from a huge clam.

But for much of the twentieth century, Hollywood traded this whimsy for a more ideological approach, scripting sex workers into one of two casts: that of the fallen woman or the femme fatale. While sex worker characters certainly varied, the most common were representative of the disreputable "Other" woman – "the whore" played in contrast to the reputable "virgin" wife.[41] Unsurprisingly, men wrote and directed 95 per cent of the movies about sex workers produced in the twentieth century.[42] As Nickie Roberts wryly notes, "if prostitution truly is the world's oldest profession, then men writing about it is certainly the second oldest."[43] From the hapless streetwalker to the canny businesswoman, the fallen woman to the flashy courtesan, sex workers have been imagined by male writers into many forms, but most often they served as foils for patriarchy's idealized woman.[44] On top of sex workers rarely being portrayed as capable mothers, their sexual frankness, financial autonomy, and flouting of monogamy cemented their status as the "abnormal" women in society.[45] Gerda Lerner identifies this division between "respectable" and "disrespectable" women the foundation of patriarchy.[46]

Scholarship on sex work in popular culture in the twentieth century has revealed the pervasiveness of this "virgin–whore" binary. In their 1994 study of sex workers in American cinema, Elizabeth Hirschman and Barbara Stern found that sex worker characters conform to one of four typologies: the good-punished, the good-unpunished, the evil-punished, and the evil-unpunished. Yet despite these characterological differences, the sex worker characters die in more than three-quarters of the films Hirschman and Stern analyzed, while no male characters do, even if the men have committed crimes, including murder.[47] Far more wide-ranging, Russell Campbell's comprehensive *Marked Women: Prostitutes and Prostitution in the Cinema* (2006) examined the representation of sex workers in 300 global films produced between 1896 and 2005 and similarly showed how the screen "symbolically contains" the sex worker's threat to patriarchy by restricting her to rigid typologies and story arcs that most often lead to a finale of marriage or death.[48] Campbell explained the outsized number of films depicting the death of sex workers as revenge fantasy, wherein the sexually liberated woman is punished for "the disturbance she causes; socially, by defying patriarchal authority; psychologically, by arousing male anxiety about the female as threatening Other."[49] Scholars have also examined the opposition Hollywood films and television constructed between the "bad" sex worker and the "good" wife, the former exaggerating the latter's banality, and the latter exaggerating the former's venal nature.[50] Lisa McLaughlin has likewise argued that television's sex workers functioned "primarily within the terms of restrictive binary oppositions."[51]

There have been some exceptions, however, to these sex worker stereotypes on screens both big and small. In films of the 1920s, for example, sex workers were sometimes strong, independent, and well-rounded characters who initiated sex without being punished, as in *Sadie Thompson* (1928) and *Rain* (1932). Likewise, in *Shanghai Express* (1932), Marlene Dietrich played an unrepentant sex worker who lives happily ever after out of wedlock.[52] In his comprehensive *Prostitution in Hollywood Films* (1992), James Parish identifies a number of such films with complex sex worker characters from this era, which rode the tailwinds of feminism's first wave until several Hollywood sex scandals sent studios, fearing draconian censorship, in search of a reputation manager.[53] They found him in Will Hays, a former US postmaster general who became first president of the Motion Picture Producers and Distributors of America (MPPDA) and the architect of a set of moral standards – the Hays Code – which subjected all scripts to an approval process: only those that received a "Purity Seal" were greenlit for production. Section 2 of the Hays Code, concerning prostitution, stated that "impure love" could not be made to "seem right and permissible" nor be "detailed in method and manner,"[54] forcing film-makers to find alternative ways of representing sex work on screen. From 1934 until the late 1960s, Hollywood euphemized sex workers as chorus line or dance hall girls, whose characterizations were, for the most part, thin and moralizing.

The suspension of the Hays Code in the late 1960s brought sex workers to screen in new and versatile ways, though their labour largely remained hidden inside Pandora's box – or a velvet one, as in *Breakfast at Tiffany's*, which gilded sex work with a luxury look from a touchably safe distance. *Cactus Flower* (1969) and *Irma La Douce*, which launched the careers of Goldie Hawn and Shirley MacLaine, respectively, introduced the cheeky sex worker gamine who would come of age with *Pretty Woman*'s Vivian Ward. Despite no longer being consigned to death or marriage, these sex worker heroines were still fantasies. As Meryl Streep pithily put it at the 1991 Screen Actors Women's Conference, Hollywood was making too many films about "hooking. And I don't mean rugs."[55] Yet, while white sex workers on screen gained dimensionality, sex workers of colour continued to be sexualized as submissive, tempting seductresses and compliant lovers for white men.

In the 1990s, virgin–whore typologies were left in the dust by movies about empowered erotic dancers and gutsy call girls who shucked big bucks for the studios. These new sex workers strutted in power suits – some even drove Ferraris – and were "one of the guys" now, the goals of feminism seemingly won, and sex work and capitalism copasetic. At first blush, these liberated ladies seemed strong: they didn't beg their fathers, or the Holy Father, for forgiveness. Instead, they knelt before the altar of capitalism in features that linked the commodification of sexuality to empowerment and treated sex work as just another business. "We both screw people for money," says banker Edward to sex worker Vivian in *Pretty Woman*. That film notably transformed Hollywood's portrayal of sex work by replacing the persistent image of the victimized sex worker with one of a likeable pro, yet it also sidelined the labour of sex work and the workers' struggles. Touting what Rosalind Gill has usefully termed a "postfeminist sensibility,"[56] an anaemic feminism linked to self-objectification and the mall, such films turned sex workers into karate-chopping concubines who fought patriarchy with their pulchritude one trick at a time and treated sex as a fast route to empowerment.[57]

The glamourization of sex work in the post-feminist pop culture of the 2000s has also been richly explored, with several scholars critiquing the "porno chic,"[58] "raunch culture,"[59] "ho chic," and "self-objectification"[60] infused in many sex work films, television shows, and documentaries of this era that focus on individual liberation through self-improvement and market transactions that take the "we" out of feminism.[61] With its celebration of women's entrepreneurship, popular culture of this period tended to respond to social inequality with neo-liberal remedies or "defiant assertions of individualism."[62]

This sex worker type comes at two costs: first, she glamourizes sex work as an always-empowering experience, and second, she does not, as Catherine Roach has noted, lead to greater social acceptance of or increased rights for sex workers.[63] Actually, as Marina Della Giusta and Laura Scuriatti point out, her appropriation of sex work aesthetics "puts back into circulation the dichotomy of the virgin/whore ... and defines women in relation to their bodies."[64] Similar issues have shaped documentary films that link sex work with a feminism of pluck and individualism – a genre Jane Arthurs calls "docu-porn"[65] and Karen Boyle terms "docu-soap."[66]

In sum, from the early twentieth century to the turn of the millennium, Hollywood has largely produced and circulated simplistic stories about sex workers that propped up patriarchal stereotypes and accorded with the economic and political status quo. I am reflexive about this history when critiquing popular culture that rehashes tropes without addressing the structural conditions – classism, racism, and sexism – that may motivate women into sex work in the first place and that elides the intersecting social inequities and oppressions shaping this work. This neo-liberal sex worker story, to use a phrase from Juno Mac and Molly Smith, risks losing "sight of the fact that sex work is gendered."[67]

Danger, Violence, Stigma: The Stakes

Popular culture's ideas about sex workers matter because they shape how real-life sex workers may be perceived and treated. *Ideas* perpetuated in religious doctrines about sex workers being morally corrupt have resulted in the execution of women in this occupation throughout history. *Ideas* propagated by prohibitionist feminists about sex workers being universally victimized led to generations rejecting the notion that sex workers could speak for themselves. The ideas communicated about sex workers by popular culture today similarly intersect with real-world political, labour, and legal movements that have the power to either support sex workers in practising their trades with dignity, safety, and the full protection of the law, or repress them within the existing paradigm that denies them their civic rights and subjects them to shame, harassment, and serious danger, including violence and even death. Stuart Hall explains this well with his term "signification spiral," which describes the escalating process by which marginalized groups are associated with characteristics of deviance that "increases the perceived threat of an issue through the way it becomes signified."[68] In other words, criminalizing representations of sex workers begets more such images, creating a contemptuous spiral that comes to pass in society as truth. For this reason, as Catherine Hakim notes, sex workers are habitually "regarded as victims, drug addicts, losers, incompetents, or as people you would not wish to meet socially."[69] These images separate sex workers from "respectable" women by stigmatizing them, a term Erving Goffman coined from the Greek to refer to the social process that marks someone apart as "bad" and "amoral,"[70] and which begins when "we believe the person with a stigma is not quite human."[71]

The film critic Molly Haskell once wrote that "in cinema the stakes for women are especially high."[72] For sex workers, the stakes are even higher. Though current and former sex workers are all around us, most are closeted about their work for fear of arrest, employment sanctions, or social stigmatization, and those who do speak up assume great risk.[73] Unlike our understanding of other workers with whom we have regular contact, our dominant ideas about sex workers derive almost exclusively from popular culture, giving it a disproportionate power to shape our perceptions about them – to dehumanize or humanize, criminalize or normalize, denounce or dignify, build stigmas or break them.[74]

Today, between 1 and 2 million sex workers in the US sell their services without legal, labour, or civil rights, leaving them vulnerable to violence and social stigmatization.[75] Ironically, sex workers are often framed as threats to public safety who must be monitored and exposed. Sheriff department websites across the US will often publish mug shots of women arrested for prostitution along with their full names,[76] John TV, a website run by a reactionary conservative sex work prohibitionist, posts videos of sex workers and their clients being ambushed in cars, and in 2012, the gossip website The Smoking Gun outed Suzy Favor Hamilton, a celebrated former Olympic runner, as a sex worker, resulting in a campaign of public humiliation and Hamilton's suicide attempt.[77] News media has long associated sex workers with disease, child abuse, violence, sex trafficking, objects of filth, and public nuisance, and women employed in diverse sectors, from teaching to journalism, have been fired from their jobs when their pasts as sex workers came to light.[78] These examples of stigmatization are fueled by the idea that sex work "spoils" a woman's identity, to use Goffman's term. In turn, this "spoilage" underwrites the contempt of individual sex workers and normalizes the violence against them at large.

More sex workers are murdered in the US than in any other nation, and their murders routinely go unsolved.[79] Between 1970 and 2009, 22 per cent of all serial killer victims in the US were sex workers; in the last decade, that number rose to 43 per cent.[80] Perpetrators who choose sex workers as their victims do so tactically, assuming that these women's deaths will be unlikely to receive media attention or justice. A glaring example of this was brought to light by the 2020 Netflix documentary *The Ripper* about convicted mass murderer Peter Sutcliffe. Known as the "Yorkshire Ripper," Sutcliffe's first three victims were sex workers, whom the West Yorkshire Police Department repeatedly disparaged and differentiated from his "innocent" victims. This bias even bled into the perpetrator's 1981 trial, where prosecution noted that "some [victims] were prostitutes, but perhaps the saddest part is that some were not."[81] After the film was released, the police department formally apologized to the families of these women. A similar situation was exposed by another Netflix film, *Lost Girls* (2020), about law enforcement's botched investigation into the disappearances of Shannan Gilbert and four other sex workers, whose families "begged the police" to find their loved ones for over a decade. Even after their bodies were found on Gilgo Beach on Long Island,[82] these women were all but blamed for their fates, as when the chief of police called it "a 'consolation' that the killer was 'selecting from a pool' of women 'willing to get into a car with a stranger.'"[83] Since DNA evidence led to the 2023 arrest of the suspect, the film has helped to highlight law enforcement's negligent response to these sex workers' murders and that of others more widely.

Despite increased attention and police apologies, the violence against sex workers – and, in particular, sex workers of colour – is unending. This was seen most recently at the height of the COVID-19 pandemic, when anti-Asian racism and historical xenophobia resulted in an upswing of violent attacks. In 2021, six women of East Asian descent were murdered in three separate massage parlours in Atlanta, and the year prior a massage parlour worker of Asian descent was killed in Toronto by a seventeen year old inspired by "incel" (involuntary celibate) ideology. While violence against sex workers is inseparable from violence against all women, sex worker safety depends upon calling out the misogyny that drives the treatment of sex workers' jobs as a priori explanations for their fates.

While popular culture does not make or uphold the laws that criminalize sex workers in real life, nor does it unilaterally inspire misogynist men to hate and hurt them, depictions in pop culture are significant since what we see on screen can cast long shadows on sex workers' lives – or become a resource for their empowerment. In this regard, I see popular culture as "a cultural forum" for our debates about sex workers in society and our "deepest dilemmas."[84] I align myself with third-wave feminist media scholars and interpret popular culture as a means for both upholding society's dominant ideologies and challenging the status quo in the service of "subordinated and disempowered" ideas and groups.[85] For this reason, popular culture about sex workers also matters to sex workers.

A crucial part of the research for this book thus involved connecting with a diverse group of sex workers to understand their impressions of popular culture. I interviewed six sex work professionals, including an escort, an erotic dancer, a massage parlour worker, a webcam model, a call girl, and a sex surrogate. These women – Ava-Lynn, Leyla, Michelle, Tracy, Sophie, and Vera[86] – ranged in age from twenty to fifty-five years old and came from Canada, the US, and Europe. It should go without saying that six women cannot represent all sex workers, but their diverse cultural and class backgrounds, work experiences, and consumption of popular culture in the 1980s, 1990s, and early 2000s – the oldest watching films in cinemas and the youngest streaming videos on Netflix – made their impressions extremely valuable for me. All the women save for the youngest described feeling burdened by the weight of pop culture's mischaracterization of and myths about sex work, describing how distorted a picture *older* popular culture in particular gave the public about real-life sex workers. The eldest, Ava-Lynn, recalled watching *Pretty Woman* in the cinema while she was working as an escort and it "pissing her off" because of its depiction of a sex worker marrying a client. "None of us want to do that!" She couldn't recall a single movie that didn't glamourize sex workers or make them seem pathetic.

It made sense that younger sex workers saw things differently. Vera, in her late thirties, told me about how she discovered sex surrogacy in a TV documentary. "It got me interested," she said of the work she now does professionally. Sophie, the youngest at nineteen, recalled watching TV movies with sex workers who were smart and capable. But when I asked her if these movies ever portrayed any of the risks or challenges of sex work, she was unable to think of one that did. "Actually, they made it look too fun and easy," she admitted. Sophie said she likes working independently as a call girl because having only a few clients who pay her well allows her to retain her identity as a "regular student." At the same time, she acknowledges that her fear of getting outed and stigmatized keeps her from being honest about her work with her family, and her friends who do know worry about her. "I didn't see any of *that* on TV." What resounded in my interviews was that the contours of popular culture have changed, increasingly depicting sex workers as a heterogeneous group, humanizing them, and leaving judgements aside – yet there are still important elements being left out. Sex workers' perspectives on popular culture matter most, as their lives are affected by what is on screen, and for this reason I open most chapters with an epigraph from one of the women I spoke with to centre their perspectives and to signal my respect for their time, words, and experiences.

~~Prostitute~~ → Sex Worker: Terminology and Scope

As you will have already noticed, throughout this book I use the terms "sex work" and "sex worker," both coined by sex worker activist and writer Carol Leigh in 1978 to challenge the historical connotations of criminality bound up in the word "prostitute" and to underscore the centrality of labour processes and economic motivations involved in the sale of sexual services.[87] As Leigh later said, "This invention was motivated by my desire to reconcile my feminist goals with the reality of my life and the lives of the women I knew. I wanted to create an atmosphere of tolerance within and outside the women's movement for women working in the sex industry."[88] Focusing on the labour performed by women in the industry – rather than on their subject positions as "prostitutes" – united women on a platform that highlighted connections between sex work and other forms of waged work.[89] The term "sex work" also played a foundational role in reframing the feminist debate on sex work by legitimizing sex workers as the authorities on their own work. This is the language used by the international sex workers' rights movement and by the sex workers I have come to know personally. Not to be confused with sex trafficking, a crime involving manipulation, coercion, and often violence,[90] "sex work" refers to the "payment of money for sexual services between two *consenting* adults,"[91] and the women in the popular culture explored ahead are consenting adults who have chosen their work.

They are also indoor sex workers – erotic dancers, massage parlour workers, webcam models, call girls, sex surrogates, and porn performers – who comprise most of the sex industry today, an estimated 80 per cent.[92] I focus particularly on what Elizabeth Bernstein describes as a growing number of middle-class sex workers who incorporate emotion, performance, and authenticity into their work,[93] and who are advantaged by higher pay, stable workspaces, the ability to screen clients and implement safety measures, and lower rates of criminalization and arrest – conditions that make their work more amenable to entrepreneurship.[94]

Now, a word on scope. The heaps of sex work popular culture that has appeared in the last decade or so required me to draw parameters, which I did by focusing on the films, TV shows, and documentaries watched by massive audiences – that is, those produced by major networks (such as CNN and Lifetime) and aired in prime-time spots, those appearing on popular video hosting platforms (such as YouTube and Vimeo) with substantial views, and those that received much critical acclaim. Borrowing Raymond Williams's useful definition of popular culture – that which is "well-liked by many people"[95] – I essentially focus on the *most popular* popular culture, because its massive consumption reveals the zeitgeist of what popular culture is revealing about sex work today. If popular culture, as bell hooks reminds us, is our "primary pedagogical medium for masses of people" and "where the learning is,"[96] these shows and films are our classroom. In confining myself to American popular culture of the past fifteen or so years, I take to heart Haskell's contention that "decades are artificial divisions, full of contradictions, particularly in film where there is always a partial lag."[97] Many films and TV shows offering nuanced images of sex work appeared before the last decade. However, in the new climate I earlier outlined in this introduction, sex work in popular culture has come into view in ways previously unseen and has much to teach us about the world's oldest profession today.

What's Ahead

In chapter 1, "Working It," I explore how feminism, popular culture, and labour intersect to set the stage for my subsequent chapters. While the imaginations of creators and genre codes shape popular culture's content and form, I maintain that feminist thought has had the most enduring impact on popular culture about sex work. It is therefore crucial to understand its conceptualizations of sex work and its main themes. I put into conversation feminism's prohibitionist, empowerment, and labour paradigms with an especial focus on the last two, through which I read popular culture throughout this book. With this labour perspective in mind, I move into the twenty-first century to explore the nexus of neo-liberalism and precarious labour and its impact on the commercialization of intimacy. Finally, I explore five types of labour that form the theoretical core of this book. Overall this chapter provides the "key" for reading popular culture about sex work today by showing the relationship between theory, politics, and popular culture, allowing us to appreciate its real-life stakes.

In chapter 2, "Dancing to an American Dream," I examine the documentaries *Power of Pussy (P.O.P.)* (2012), *Magic City* (2015), and "Road Strip" (2014), and the films *Afternoon Delight* (2013) and *Hustlers* (2019), which elevate erotic dancing to a neo-burlesque art and portray performers as canny strivers using their "erotic capital" while rejecting the low wages of "McJobs." In "Road Strip," single mothers provide for their families by spending weeks on the road, while *P.O.P.* and *Magic City* explore a famous Atlanta club where dancers train in an informal stripping sisterhood. These personal portrait documentaries privilege the dancers' experiences as they build careers, but the money isn't easy to earn, and the relationships between the dancers and their clients are unequal, a theme taken up by both *Afternoon Delight*, which queers *Pretty Woman*, and *Hustlers*, which is, as far as I know, the first sex worker vigilante movie that pits erotic dancers against Wall Street bosses.

Chapter 3 examines the TV movie *The Client List* (2010) and its follow-up series of the same name (2012–13) about single mothers who become massage parlour entrepreneurs – "mompreneurs" – during the 2007–8 financial downturn. Massage parlour workers are typically portrayed as "social problems"[98] and sex worker mothers as "fallen women,"[99] but both the film and the series, at least at first, elevate these mothers into agential breadwinners and

Introduction: A New Sex Worker in Popular Culture 21

heroines. At the same time, they celebrate what Sharon Hays calls "intensive mothering"[100] by framing massage parlour work as a viable way for single mothers to achieve prosperity, regardless of structural inequalities. While scholars have begun exploring the long-standing taboo of motherhood and sex work,[101] popular culture about it in the context of twenty-first-century neo-liberalism remains underexplored, and this chapter focuses on this new area of study.

Chapter 4, "Twenty-First-Century Peep Show," centres on webcam models and their creative entrepreneurship in the documentary *Cam Girlz* (2015) and the feature films *Teenage Cocktail* (2016) and *Cam* (2018). Part of a multibillion-dollar industry, webcam models work in digital rooms and earn "tokens" they convert to cash, run businesses, and describe what they say is the empowering nature of their work. Framing webcam modelling as an alternative to low-wage jobs and as an opportunity to become entrepreneurial, *Cam Girlz* validates webcam models' "authenticity." At the same time, webcam modelling becomes an escape from perilous conditions in *Teenage Cocktail*, where two lesbian teenagers use camming to earn the money they need to escape their homophobic town. While unity rules *Teenage Cocktail*, fragmentation fuels *Cam*, a thriller that personifies precarity through the story of one model's ambition, which pushes her into a terrifying labyrinth of doppelgängers and identity theft. Set in bedrooms, in the crush of long nights, this chapter investigates the tension between sex work, precarious labour, technology, and capitalism.

In chapter 5, I examine *The Girlfriend Experience* (2009) film and TV series (2016–21), which capture the zeitgeist of transactional intimacy under neo-liberal capitalism through stories of call girls who sell simulated romantic affairs. While the most iconic call girl film, *Breakfast at Tiffany's*, euphemized sex work, the gritty vérité of *The Girlfriend Experience* (both the film and its spin-off series) lays bare the extensive "backstage" work of producing "the girlfriend experience," a blend of sex and intimacy that becomes the women's winning business model. Yet, far from the blithe and mysterious Holly Golightly, who approached her work with the levity of her name, these call girl heroines are hustlers with crushing student debt who stage romantic dates through often alienating emotional labour that leaves them feeling ambivalent. While prohibitionists view call girls as patriarchy's dupes, the film and series are too smart for glib conclusions. As they normalize sexual labour's congruencies with other precarious and embodied service work, they free transactional intimacy from the closet of amoral things and show its relationship to neo-liberal capitalism.

Chapter 6, "Sexual Healing," delves into the little understood world of sex partner surrogates – professionals who use physical touch and intimacy for healing and who guide their clients towards more fulfilling erotic lives – through the award-winning and critically acclaimed films *The Sessions* (2012) and *She's Lost Control* (2014). The films validate sex surrogates as skilled care workers who enhance the mind as much as the body and recognize the therapeutic role they play in facilitating sexual well-being, an intrinsic part of a good life. While the films celebrate sex surrogates who bring their clients healing and bliss, they also ask: What happens when relationships with clients deteriorate or become dangerous? *She's Lost Control* in particular shows how the criminalization of sex work isolates and imperils sex surrogates, while both films call for sex workers to be destigmatized and their services recognized as life enriching.

Chapter 7 focuses on *The Deuce* (2017–19), David Simon and George Pelecanos's epic TV series about porn during its golden age in the 1970s and 1980s as seen through the eyes of its women creators and performers. Set in the eponymous New York City neighbourhood remembered today as a seedy subterrain of porn cinemas dominated by men, the show goes beyond that surface to recover the lost story of a feminist community of sex and porn workers who challenge stigma, racism, police corruption, and patriarchy in a visually stunning critique of work under neo-liberal capitalism. But *The Deuce* is not a simple tribute to sex worker "empowerment." Rather, it examines the structural conditions that impel women into porn, highlights the uphill battle performers face in a voraciously profit-driven industry where misogyny and racism endure, and intercedes into the feminist sex wars. Through the stories of a porn auteur, an actress, and a sex work activist, *The Deuce* adopts a non-judgemental stance to ask: Can a feminist porn-maker succeed in a capitalist patriarchy?

The value of examining the new sex worker in popular culture rests in how she unearths and registers shifting social attitudes about sex work – informed by labour and feminism – today. She offers a long-overdue window into sex work, grounded in inclusive feminism based on tolerance, not discrimination and moralization, and while she sometimes shores up neo-liberal and post-feminist discourses of "choice," she offers a vital new lens for thinking about sex work in the twenty-first century. She reveals the struggles sex workers face, challenges the myth that sex work is not real work, troubles the assumption that all sex workers are victims, and dismantles the belief that sex work is incompatible with feminism. At her most enlightened, she shines a light on patriarchy's double standards, not just with respect to sex workers but all women – *"Be sexy." "Don't be a slut." "Assert yourself." "Don't be so demanding." "Be independent." "Don't act like a man."* – and she exposes the hypocrisy of punishing women for selling what men expect to get for free. Taking us into dance clubs and condos, bedrooms and hotel suites, popular culture's new sex worker reveals changing social attitudes about the world's oldest profession today. While prohibitionist feminists have long used the sex worker as a metaphor for the oppressed woman,[102] and media scholars have long viewed her as a victim, the *new* sex worker in popular culture is a proud pro – and a feminist.

# 1 Working It: Popular Culture, Feminism, and Sex Work

[If I made a movie about sex work] I would do a feminist movie. I would love to do a big budget feminist movie. Where you can understand and care about these women, but without seeing them as goddesses.
– Ava-Lynn, former escort

The conventional social criticism, of course, says that "these are bad women, fallen women, degraded and victimized" … many working girls, however, have chosen their jobs and do not feel like victims. Women in the sex industry have been so reviled on both sides that there must be a way in which we can establish a dialogue which is not against women who work in this way.
– Lizzie Borden, director of *Working Girls* (1986)[1]

My whole life is a feminist experience. Sex work enhanced my feminism. I am also empowered from money.
– Carol Leigh (aka Scarlot Harlot), sex worker and activist who coined the term "sex work" in 1978[2]

In the late 1960s and early 1970s, three events changed the lives of sex workers forever. The first was the 1969 US Supreme Court decision to legalize pornography, which expanded the industry from its base in 16 mm films – loops screened in seedy bookstore booths and backrooms – to a multibillion-dollar enterprise that put blockbusters like *Deep Throat* (1972) on glittering 42nd Street marquees. The second was the women's rights movement. Women's political self-determination, which began with the right to vote in 1918, grew during *Roe v. Wade* (1973) and expanded through the movement's demands for equal rights in the professional and personal realms. This coincided with the articulations of sex-positive feminism, located at the intersection of sexual expression and women's emancipation. In the 1970s, women became more

Figure 1.1. Margo St. James, the charismatic founder of COYOTE, the first sex worker activist organization, poses in front of an X-rated movie theatre. "It's well past time for whores to organize," she said, heralding in a new era for sex worker self-representation.

sexually subjectivized, the taboo around pre-marital sex diminished, and casual sex became less risky due to the availability of birth control. Along with these changes came the neo-liberalization of the economy and the rise of precarious service work.

At the same time, the sex workers' labour movement was born. The first advocacy organization, COYOTE (Call Off Your Old Tired Ethics), founded in 1972 by charismatic sex worker activist Margo St. James, argued that sex workers chose their jobs, were capable of self-representation, and deserved a platform to discuss sex work beyond the one-dimensional radical feminist gender model.[3] St. James reserved a particular animus for hypocritical prostitution laws and double standards around women's sexual conduct: "It's perfectly legal for a woman to have sex with anyone as long as she chooses ... but the minute five cents changes hands – then boom! She's a whore, and she goes to jail. It's ludicrous."[4]

St. James's comment raised the headiest issues of feminism – including women's work, money, bodily autonomy, and sex – which were also rippling through popular culture at that time. In 1971, Carole King released her majestic album *Tapestry*, the single "It's Too Late" a strident feminist ballad about a woman leaving a man; *The Mary Tyler Moore Show* entered its second season with Mary still single, working, and happy; and Gloria Steinem, at the National Women's Political Caucus, extolled feminism as a revolution against inequality and prejudice. Yet sadly, sectarianism had already deeply fractured the feminist movement, and one of its most public bête noires was the meaning and impact of sex work.

On one side, there were the radical feminists. They argued that sex work was degrading to women and complicit with patriarchy, maintaining that women who claimed to have consented to doing sex work were, as Andrea Dworkin put it, "counterfeit female sexual revolutionaries."[5] Kate Millett, so famous as a feminist public intellectual that she was featured on the cover of *Time* magazine in 1970, characterized a woman's choice to engage in sex work as a "psychological addiction, built on self-hatred" in her bestselling book *Sexual Politics*.[6] On the other side, there were the labour and sex-positive feminists. They argued that sex work was legitimate work deserving of the same employment and legal protections as other forms of labour under capitalism. Speaking to the *San Francisco Examiner*, Margo St. James dismissed the radical feminists' position as a mothballed dogma that conveyed the idea that "women who are sexual are 'bad.'"[7]

The feminist "sex wars" and popular culture collided with the 1971 release of *Klute*, an arterial enquiry into the daily labour of New York City call girl Bree Daniels. The part of Bree was played by Jane Fonda, who spent time with sex workers while researching her role and, as a result, played the part with astonishing empathy and depth. Peripherally a murder mystery, *Klute* is really a character-driven story of a complex woman who loves her job and feels a quiet power in turning sex into a transaction while at the same time worrying about her life's direction. At one point, Bree asks her therapist, "Why do I still want to trick?" Her therapist answers: "Because you're successful as a call girl." When Fonda won the Academy Award for Best Actress in 1972, there was some expectation that she would weigh in on sex work during her acceptance speech.[8] Was it exploitation and connected to patriarchy? Or was it empowering and just a job? On stage, Fonda took hold of the award and spoke into the mic: "There's a great deal to say, and I'm not going to say it tonight. I would just like to really thank you very much."[9] Then, she walked off stage. No easy answers.

Yet, *Klute* did stake a position, albeit quietly. In one scene, Bree travels alone at night to a deserted Manhattan warehouse for a date with a regular client. She rides a caged elevator that opens on an upper floor of what is unmistakably a garment factory. In the dim light we see the cutting tables, gigantic bolts of cloth, and rows of sewing machines that take on a haunted look without their operators sitting behind them. Wearing a sequined evening gown and black

Figure 1.2. *Klute* shunned sex worker clichés with Bree Daniels (Jane Fonda), a smart, complex sex worker who sidesteps all stereotypes. Roger Ebert called her "the call girl who does not, for once, have a heart of gold."[10]

feather boa, Bree cuts a remarkable figure in this drab space. As she strides past the sewing stations, her relative glamour makes us imagine the women who work there by day, stitching clothes for strangers, doing alienated labour on fashions they could never afford to buy for themselves. It reminds us of the factory work most women were consigned to a generation earlier – work that was gruelling, poorly paid, and often dangerous. Bree tells her therapist that "tricking" gives her a sense of "control" over her life, and we see why at the end of Bree's date with the factory owner, who treats her kindly. The money she collects from an hour of work – spent drinking sherry, listening to old records, and having sex – exceeds what her client's garment workers probably earn in a week. Despite Bree appearing almost regal as she exits the factory, *Klute* never suggests that sex work is glamorous, but the film does recognize it as real work that, for some, can be better than the alternative.

This chapter thus explores the "great deal [there is] to say," as Fonda put it, about feminism, sex work, and labour, providing the theoretical foundation for this book as a whole. New popular culture about sex work is subversive. To understand why that is, we first must appreciate the historical social construction of sex work and its relationship with contemporary feminist theories about sex work. To that end, this chapter examines the three dominant feminist positions on sex work: the prohibitionist, empowerment, and labour paradigms. Prohibitionists argue that the sexual objectification of women is the root of women's oppression in society. Accordingly, they view sex workers as "victims" of patriarchy and call for their rescue and for the total abolition of prostitution.[11] The empowerment paradigm, on the other hand, holds that the oppression of women is rooted in the patriarchal control of women's sexuality, which forces women to be sexually passive while permitting men total sexual freedom.[12] To smash this double standard, the empowerment paradigm argues that a woman must move from sexual object to sexual subject outside traditional gender roles.[13] Accordingly, sex workers are viewed as feminist radicals who use their sexuality for freedom and pleasure, and to challenge patriarchy. Finally, the labour paradigm – less invested in the sexual dissidence of the empowerment perspective – focuses on securing legal and employment rights for sex workers, viewing sex workers as labourers who have agency and make decisions within the constraints of class, sexuality, and gender.[14] Overall, its goal is to centre sex worker voices as "legitimate sources of knowledge about their work."[15]

The feminist labour perspective that guides this book has a long, rich history, but often it has been sidelined by the more publicly recognizable, state-aligned prohibitionist position. But, as I will demonstrate, a labour perspective provides the most compelling explanation for why women engage in sex work, and it imagines the clearest path forward to achieving the safety, self-determination, and legal and civic rights that sex workers have long been denied. Having thus established the superiority of the labour paradigm in light of the failure of the prohibitionist legislative model for sex workers, and having contextualized sex work under neo-liberal capitalism today, the final section of this chapter will introduce five labour concepts for understanding popular culture images of sex workers in the twenty-first century.

Contexts: A Brief Social History of Sex Workers

Stories about sex workers have been told for thousands of years. Though these stories have varied considerably in both content and form, it is fair to say that most have contributed to sex workers' infamy and, in many cases, were used as justification for the barbarous punishments sex workers received. In the Middle Ages, for example, if a woman was found guilty of prostitution in the city of Toulouse, she was marched naked to a river and placed in a cage called an *accabussade*, which was then submerged underwater. Whenever her thrashing stopped, the cage was pulled from the river and the nearly dead woman revived. This process was repeated three times before the woman was finally carried off to jail or hospital – and similar stories circulated all across Europe.[16] In the Victorian era, the sex worker's very body became a symbol of grotesque ruin, as in Émile Zola's famous 1880 novel *Nana*, in which the eponymous character is described as a "ferment of destruction" between whose "plump thighs Paris was being destroyed."[17] Even the burgeoning field of criminology contributed to the narrative of sex workers as moral degenerates. In 1893, Cesare Lombroso, father of the pseudo-science of eugenics, published *La donna delinquente: La prostituta e la donna normale* (Criminal woman: The prostitute and the normal woman). In this infamous book, he described how he measured the body parts of hundreds of sex workers and argued that foot length and thigh circumference could determine a woman's moral bankruptcy.[18]

But despite this emphasis on punishment and morality, sex work has always been a *labour* issue. In nineteenth-century New York City, for example, sex workers were commonly factory girls from poor backgrounds trying to improve their lives. "For many, prostitution was not far removed from viable 'respectable' alternatives," writes Marilynn Wood Hill, "and thus it was taken up by a relatively broad group of women … to establish their independence."[19] So common was sex work that until the twentieth century the idea of "prostitutes" constituting a distinct occupational group was unheard of. Instead, as Carole Pateman notes, "they were seen as women who offered services as part of the laboring poor, casual workers who drifted in and out of prostitution based on their needs and other available work."[20] In the 1880s, sexologist Havelock Ellis interviewed sex workers in London's East End and confirmed these economic motivations and episodic work patterns: "She was earning 18 shillings a week in an umbrella factory," he said of one such women, "[and] she occasionally took to the street near one of the big railway stations."[21]

Dr. William Acton, a shrewd observer of Victorian era prostitution, argued that the Industrial Revolution had forced women into a bleak position, and sex work – provided it occurred in a safe, reputable house – could reasonably be considered a better, safer, and easier alternative: "If we compare the prostitute at 35 with her sister, who perhaps is the married mother of a family, or has been a toiling slave for years in the over-heated laboratories of fashion, we shall seldom find that the constitutional ravages often thought to be necessary consequences of prostitution exceed those attributable to the cares of a family and the heart-wearing struggles of virtuous labour."[22] Likewise, the physician William Sanger recognized that sex work often arose out of "sheer need."[23] In his colossal *History of Prostitution* (1858), which includes interviews with over 2,000 sex workers and explores their labour conditions, payment structures, and motivations, Sanger condemned the Church for its beliefs and the State for its laws, both of which had left sex workers "banished, scourged, branded, executed ... held up to public opinion as immoral ... [and] denuded of their civil rights."[24]

The Feminist Scene behind the Screen

In the twentieth century, feminist scholars profoundly impacted public opinion on sex work, deepening theorizations with questions about causation, harm, agency, and resistance.[25] In what ways does sex work link to larger gender inequalities? How does patriarchal capitalism and sex work intersect? Do the benefits women find in sex work correct women's disadvantages under capitalism, or reinscribe them? Would decriminalization increase sex workers' safety? How might sex work be viewed as a transgressive act? And if sex work is rooted in patriarchy, can sex workers be feminists?

The relationship between sex workers and the Western feminist movement is long and troubled, going back to the mid-nineteenth century when the values associated with idealized femininity – such as nurturance and maternal care – became enshrined within the first-wave feminist movement. Out of this came what Laura María Agustín refers to as "the rescue industry" and its reformers, who viewed sex workers as women who had "lost their virtue" and tried to rescue them – whether this help was sought or not.[26] Most feminists and their allies rejected the idea that a woman would choose sex work. This prejudice plunged Charles Dickens into scandal after he helped a wealthy feminist, Lady Burdett Coutts, establish a rescue home for fallen women in London in 1858. After reading an anonymous article written by a sex worker in *The Times*, Dickens wrote to the editor asking for her name so he could send her to the rescue house. Dickens's letter was printed, but, embarrassingly, he had not read to the end of the sex worker's article. It turns out the writer was upset with "do-gooders" like Dickens who interfered with her work and criticized the condescension of rescuers like him: "You the pious, the moral, the respectable ... why stand you on your eminence shouting that we should be ashamed of ourselves? ... What if I am a prostitute? What business has society to abuse me?"[27]

The novelist and feminist philosopher Mary Wollstonecraft, writing in 1790, had called sex work the more honest alternative to "legal prostitution" – that is, marriage.[28] Socialists took up this view and were the first to challenge dominant conceptions of sex workers as victims. In *The Origin of the Family, Private Property and the State* (1884), Friedrich Engels argued that marriage was socially sanctioned prostitution and that a married woman "differed from an ordinary courtesan only in that she does not hire out her body, like a wage worker, but sells it into slavery once and for all."[29] For Engels, monogamous marriage was a symptom of the capitalist system's "bourgeois social order, where chastity is proscribed and adultery punished ... for women but not men."[30] In the footsteps of Engels, author and activist Emma Goldman declared sex work a logical choice in a society that exploits workers: "We must rise above our foolish notions of 'better than thou' and learn to recognize the prostitute as a product of social conditions. Such a realization will sweep away the attitude of hypocrisy and ensure a greater understanding and more humane treatment."[31] Goldman had an especial insight into sex work, having laboured as both a factory worker and a sex worker. Noting that factory workers earned a pitiable $6 a week, Goldman understood sex work as "the direct result, in many cases, of insufficient compensation of honest labour."[32] Goldman thus saw sex work as a variant on marriage, writing that "it is merely a question of degree whether [a woman] sells herself to one man, in or out of marriage, or to many men."[33]

Feminist thought has ineluctably shaped popular culture, and popular culture has long borne the traces of these feminist debates. As Rosalind Gill writes,

> Feminism is now part of the cultural field. That is, feminist discourses are expressed within the media rather than simply being external, independent, critical voices. Feminist-inspired ideas burst forth from our radios, television screens, and in print media in TV discussions ... indeed it could be argued that much of what counts as feminist debate in western countries today takes place in the media rather than outside it.[34]

To be fair, the salacious storylines and titillating images of popular culture sometimes made the politics harder to suss out, and film-makers were hardly consciously using their works to proclaim a feminist position, though they did anyway. But today, the new sex worker in popular culture decisively aligns with the feminist empowerment and labour paradigms and challenges the prohibitionist position. An exploration of these paradigms will enhance our understanding of the popular culture ahead – and the ideas it both draws from and challenges.

Oppression: The Prohibitionist Paradigm

The prohibitionist paradigm – sometimes called the "oppression" paradigm[35] – is composed of academics and anti–sex work advocates who oppose sex work and all measures to regulate it through decriminalization and legalization. While their position dovetails with many religious and conservative groups, prohibitionists reject sex work not on the basis of any sort of moral or religious objection but because they see it as the dominant tool of patriarchy.[36] Borne out of a critique of gender inequality, prohibitionists argue that patriarchy oppresses women by subordinating them to the sexual needs of men. Kathleen Barry calls sex work "the foundation of women's oppression … normalized."[37]

Prohibitionists hold that sex work is both the cause and perpetuator of women's oppression because it turns women's bodies into commodities that men buy through the "male sex right."[38] When men hold this "sex right," they argue, women become disposable objects upon which men "act out their sexual dominance."[39] They contend that even though women have won greater labour and reproductive rights in the past three decades, the sex industry has at the same time expanded to reinstall its continued sexual and economic exploitation of women. Further, patriarchal society teaches women that sexual objectification is normal, even "empowering," while men use the sexual objectification of women to earn huge sums of money with which they can lobby the media to produce positive stories about the sex industry.[40] The notion that women "choose" sex work, prohibitionists posit, is illusory, imbedded in "non-choices" structured around exploitation.[41] They argue that as long as women are educationally and economically marginalized, the sex industry will have a ready pool of employment from which to draw. They shun terms like "sex work," which suggests its legitimacy as labour, and use terms like "slave" and "survivor" and "exploited women" instead.[42]

Prohibitionists view sex work as "rape that is paid for,"[43] seeing it as inherently violent and dangerous.[44] They often assert that abuse, degradation, and humiliation are intrinsic and intractable features of selling sex and typically portray sex workers as inevitable victims of physical assault and rape.[45] As Margaret Baldwin puts it, "basic to the john's sexual experience is the eroticized disregard of the woman."[46] For Andrea Dworkin, a sex worker is "the literal reality of being the dirty woman."[47] Violence against sex workers was a recurring theme in much of the popular culture of the twentieth century, yet the murder of sex workers in films and TV shows was rarely explored as a systemic issue, as it is by prohibitionists, or even part of the main plot. Instead, their bodies were regularly used to shock audiences, suggest seediness, or illustrate the pathology of a deranged man. Often the first time we saw a sex worker on screen, she was already dead.

For prohibitionists, sex work is a dehumanizing experience due to the link they posit between a woman's sexuality and her sense of self.[48] Numerous films have portrayed sex work leading to suicide,[49] such as *The Downward Path* (1900), where a sex worker dies by drinking poison, *Waterloo Bridge* (1931), in which a sex worker jumps to her death in the Thames, and *Money on the Side* (1982), which begins with three California women opening a call girl agency and ends with one severely beaten and another hanging herself. Inflamed by panic over "white slavery," many early Hollywood films also focused on threats to young women's virtue and women's inherent frailty.[50] Prohibitionists perpetuate this theme by asserting that women with pre-existing mental illnesses and unresolved traumas are more susceptible to entering sex work, having been taught that their bodies are a site of pain and exploitation.[51] They even portray sex work as *causing* mental illness.[52] Hollywood has produced miles of film in this vein, frequently depicting straitjacketed or traumatized sex workers on screen. In *Nuts* (1987), for example, a psychologically fragile call girl who murders one of her clients in self-defence fights for her right to be declared mentally competent against the advice of her lawyer and family who want her to plead insanity. While the film exposed some of the prejudices against sex workers, it also portrayed them as femme fatales. "What do you want to do?" asks the prosecuting attorney. "Put her back into the streets to see who she kills next?" *Nuts* further suggested that trauma, not money, motivates women to enter sex work. Even *Pretty Woman* took up this theme, with Vivian confessing, "When I was a little girl, my mama used to lock me in the attic when I was bad," effectively cementing trauma as the leading cause for women to turn tricks.

That said, films centring on sex work, trauma, and violence are not necessarily simple or sensationalistic, as was the case with Patty Jenkins's *Monster*, the riveting 2003 film based on the life of Aileen Wuornos, a sex worker who was executed in 2002 for the murder of six men who paid her for sex, all of whom she testified had tried to rape her. While Wuornos's life story – marked by traumas, poverty, and high turnover outdoor sex work – does align with many of the prohibitionist stereotypes of the universal sex worker, Jenkins portrays her as much more than a mere victim or a femme fatale. Through the dazzling performance of Charlize Theron, who won an Oscar for the role, Wuornos emerges as a dynamic character, a drifter with longings as deep as her wounds.[53] So too with the documentary *Streetwise* (1984), which focuses on youth on the streets of Seattle, Washington, with several of them engaging in sex work. The film was inspired by Mary Ellen Mark's startlingly beautiful portraits of some of these young people, including Tiny, who was just thirteen when filming began. While the documentary highlights the dangers of sex work – the Green River Killer was a presence during this time – it does not sensationalize violence nor depict it to emphasize the bodies or pathologies of sex workers. Instead, it suggests how criminalization makes those like Tiny more vulnerable to exploitation and predation, as they cannot comfortably seek protection from the police. Prohibitionists argue that murdered sex workers are not victims of rogue psychopaths but rather evidence of the sanctified hatred of women in patriarchal society.[54] *Streetwise* would probably agree, but the film parts ways with the prohibitionist criminalization model, which it shows to be part of the failing status quo.

A prevailing notion among prohibitionists is that sex work is a dehumanizing industry that objectifies women. In *Fire Down Below* (1957), sex worker Irena confesses: "I'm no good. I'm all worn out … I've been debased. I look in the mirror and I say, 'What a lie.' ... The face looks like the face of a human being." In *Eyes Wide Shut* (1999), a sex worker lies on the floor motionless after overdosing on cocaine as people step over her to get to the bar. "Maybe she got her brains fucked out," one cynical passerby drawls. In *Leaving Las Vegas* (1995), Sera laconically tells her customer, "For five hundred bucks you can do pretty much whatever you want ... you can fuck my ass ... you can cum in my face." *Pretty Woman*, generally remembered as an upbeat romance, actually opens with a dead sex worker on the sidewalk surrounded by a gawking crowd.

Prohibitionists reject that sex work is real work – the selling of a service or one's time – and view it as the commodification of the entire self. Consequently, they deny that sex workers have professional skills or that sex work can be a "neutral" work experience.[55] They rebuff, too, that sex work can be financially rewarding and assert that cash earned from it is "demeaning."[56] Taking a hard line against engaging in dialogue with sex workers, prohibitionists have been known to exclusively invite "reformed sex workers" to their debates from activist groups such as WHISPER (Women Hurt in Systems of Prostitution Engaged in Revolt) and Women Survivors of Pornography, perceiving practising sex workers as "too victimized, and too prone to false consciousness to be able to represent themselves objectively."[57]

Considering these critiques, prohibitionists oppose measures to decriminalize sex work, arguing that slackened laws will put women at greater risk and do little to curtail violence, improve working conditions, or end trafficking,[58] which they wrongly conflate with sex work,[59] as seen in films from *Traffic in Souls* (1913) to *Taken* (2008). In consonance with this perspective, the US government views sex work as exploitation and considers criminalization – especially of the "buy" side, as in the "Nordic model" – the only way to protect women.[60] Prohibitionists' goal is to end sex work and forge a new system of power that privileges women's experiences; until then, their goal is to remove women from prostitution and heavily criminalize male buyers of sex.[61]

Power and Pleasure: The Empowerment Paradigm

Drawing inspiration from liberal feminism, the empowerment perspective – often referred to as "sex-positive" feminism – asserts that sex work can foster opportunities for self-expression beyond traditional gender roles, with the potential to "change the balance of power in society."[62] Empowerment paradigm feminists argue that the oppression of women is rooted in the patriarchal control of women's sexuality, which hypocritically forces women to be passive while permitting men total sexual freedom. This group seeks to smash rules that label women as "sluts" and that expose them to social stigma.[63] Against sexual puritanism, empowerment feminists consider sex work a tool of "reappropriation" and see women's sexual autonomy and participation in the sexual realm as a foundational aspect of feminism.[64] Accordingly, they embody Carol Queen's definition of "sex positivity," "the cultural philosophy that understands sexuality as a potentially positive force in one's life."[65] Hollywood films spanning the decades such as *Baby Face* (1933), *The Happy Hooker* (1975), and *The Best Little Whorehouse in Texas* (1982) affirm sex workers who challenge gender roles and trespass sexual mores. They embody the goal articulated in the manifesto of the International Committee on Prostitutes' Rights (ICPR) "to affirm the right of all women to determine their own sexual behavior."[66]

Sex positive feminists argue that sex work can provide women with economic independence and a sense of agency over their bodies and choices. They believe that by supporting the rights and choices of sex workers, society can challenge the stigmatization of all sexual women and the criminalization of sex work. In her 1981 essay "Lust Horizons: Is the Women's Movement Pro-Sex?," feminist writer and cultural critic Ellen Willis censured prohibitionists for marginalizing sex workers, just as nineteenth-century patriarchal society had done when dividing women into "virgins" and "whores."[67] The empowerment paradigm challenges the idea that sex work perpetuates the objectification of women's bodies. It contends that what may *appear* like submission may not in fact *feel* that way for a woman who views sex as a realm of play and power. Essentially, someone who may seem commodified may actually be a savvy participant in a performance of sexuality. In the HBO series *The Deuce*, one erotic dancer puts it well: "I like the dancing. I'm a feminist dancer. I know that sounds, you know, like a pacifist executioner or something, but I see [the work] as an avenue to explore sexual dynamics."

This paradigm also asserts that selling sex can feel empowering. In her book *Live Sex Acts*, Wendy Chapkis articulates this liberatory terrain through interviews with sex workers who identify as "politicized whores," describing how they challenge the "male sex right" by selling sexual services to men who had expected to get them for free.[68] Similarly, Eva Pendleton notes that "the act of making men pay ... reverses the terms under which men feel entitled to unlimited access to women's bodies."[69] Simone de Beauvoir likewise viewed the paid sexual transaction as subversive in how "the money has a purifying role ... for to make the man pay ... is to change him into an instrument."[70] In the empowerment paradigm sex work is thus a provocative rearrangement of the marriage contract and the male sex right wherein women reap its financial benefits.

Some empowerment feminists emphasize that sex work can be a means for women to explore and choose a radical lifestyle that has been traditionally off-limits to them.[71] Belle Knox, a women's studies major at Duke University, rejected the patriarchal proviso that if women are smart, they "cannot also be sexual."[72] She paid her tuition by acting in pornographic films and saw her career as a form of asserting sexual freedom: "Feminism means I can take ownership of what I enjoy sexually ... because feminism is not a one-size-fits-all movement.... I'm an ambitious young woman. I'm a student at Duke. I'm a slut who needs to be punished."[73] In *Crimes of Passion* (1984), Kathleen Turner plays a successful fashion designer who finds subversive fulfilment in her seditious nighttime roleplay. Equally, feminist pornographer Anna Arrowsmith discovered her vocation one night while walking home through London's red-light district: "What I felt suddenly was not anger, but envy; that men had their sexual desires catered to in every way – from prostitution to magazines to films.... I knew then that it was much more productive to spend my time creating something that allowed women to explore their sexuality than it was to thwart men's freedoms."[74] Many subjects in the chapters ahead describe sex work as offering them an arena in which to express their sexual autonomy, a right they had been previously denied.

Viewing sexual conservatism and feminist prohibitionism as complicit in women's oppression, the empowerment paradigm supports the decriminalization of sex work and sees it as a key step in reducing the stigma associated with such work and the sexual-based shaming of all women. Much of the popular culture in the coming chapters expresses empowerment ideas; at the same time, only some critique the material and structural conditions that often lead women into sex work, and even fewer champion the causes of the sex workers' rights movement. The labour paradigm fiercely does both.

Work and Rights: The Labour Paradigm

Less focused on the pleasure-seeking politics of the empowerment perspective, the labour paradigm calls for the decriminalization of sex work and the recognition that sex workers deserve legal and labour rights like other workers under capitalism.[75] While it concedes that women face oppression in patriarchal society at increased levels and must make decisions within the constraints of race, class, sexuality, and gender, it considers sex workers as agents trying to transcend those conditions.[76] The goals of the labour perspective are to reduce the stigmatization of sex workers, place sex workers at the centre of the decriminalization debate, make distinctions between sex work and sex trafficking, reconceptualize sex work as legitimate labour, and ultimately decriminalize sex work.[77] In opposition to prohibitionism, it seeks to make it easier for sex workers to function within capitalism by articulating a "rights-based frame to counter the 'victim frame' that conflates sex work and trafficking."[78]

The labour paradigm is the lens through which I read popular culture, paying especial attention to its key themes of sex worker agency, stigma, skills, and safety. On screen, the portrayal of sex work as labour was for a long time quite rare. A turning point was *Working Girls* in 1986. Directed by Lizzie Borden, the film was unique in its refusal to pathologize, romanticize, or reduce sex workers to "types," focusing instead on their labour at an establishment in New York's

Upper East Side through the eyes of Molly, a lesbian call girl and aspiring photographer. Borden's attention to detail captured the minutiae of Molly's workday: shopping at the drugstore, fielding phone calls, counting cash. The sex was neither glamorous nor traumatizing, just a repetitive routine of Vaseline, paper towelling, condoms, and washing up. When asked about her unusually nuanced sex worker characters, Borden said, "I just treated prostitution as a job, as work, like any other."[79] In this spirit, the labour paradigm provides a public platform to advocate for more nuanced theories of sex work beyond the one-dimensional radical feminist gender model, particularly by exploring how sexual labour fits within the framework of capitalism.

This book's dominant theme, rooted in the labour paradigm, is that women choose to enter sex work primarily for economic reasons, seeing advantages in it over other options.[80] As Rachel West, spokeswoman for the US Prostitutes Collective (US PROS) has emphasized, "Prostitution is about money, not about sex."[81] The labour perspective highlights this and other reasons women engage in sex work, including the promise of high wages; the potential to earn a substantial income in a short time (leaving more time for creative pursuits or other vocations); barriers to other forms of employment due to age, location, immigration status, or other personal factors; flexible scheduling (especially convenient for mothers); disenchantment with "straight" jobs; the need to pay tuition; curiosity or a wish for adventure; the desire to meet interesting people, challenge social norms, confront economic sexism, or experience a sense of empowerment by being paid for sexual services; or simply because they like sex work and are good at it.[82]

In *Working Girls*, Molly describes sex work as giving her more "time, independence, and flexibility." New popular culture similarly tells stories of diverse women choosing sex work to escape from low-wage jobs, often in retail and restaurants where being overworked is the *carte du jour*. In *Cam Girlz* (2015), Sarah describes working double shifts at a pizza restaurant in the blast of a hot oven that leaves her little time to see her infant daughter. Her account stresses sex work as a path from low-wage into higher-wage precarious work. Likewise in *The Girlfriend Experience* (2016–21), Christine, a law student, becomes a call girl to achieve a middle-class lifestyle that's becoming ever more elusive to her generation. These sex workers, to one degree or another, benefit from their work, despite facing numerous risks and challenges.

A central argument of the labour paradigm is that the greatest threat to the safety, health, and well-being of sex workers is not the work itself but its criminalization. The most widely applied framework internationally, criminalization prohibits both the buying and selling of sex and certain activities associated with it.[83] More recently, Sweden, Norway, the UK, and Canada, have implemented the "Nordic model," a framework in which people may sell sexual services but not purchase them. This model is vocally supported by prohibitionists who believe that criminalizing the "buy" side (almost exclusively men) will reduce the demand for sex work, allowing for the eventual "rescue" of sex workers.

A decriminalization framework, on the other hand, allows – but does not regulate or license – all consensual sex work between adults. The labour paradigm makes a compelling case for decriminalization in four parts. First, it contends that since most women sell sex for economic reasons, criminalizing sex work does not act as a deterrent but rather burdens these women with added financial hardships through bail costs and lawyer fees and makes it harder for them, once they have criminal records, to find work outside of the sex industry, should they wish to. Second, it underscores the difference between sex work and sex trafficking, the latter being a crime and the former being victimless. Third, the labour perspective argues that sex work is a transaction between adults, not a public safety issue; therefore, the policing of sex work places a huge financial burden on the justice system that could be better allocated towards investigating actual crimes. Finally, it maintains that the greatest risk to sex workers is not the work itself but the laws that compel them to work in secret to avoid arrest. This increases their vulnerability to exploitation and rape, assault, robbery, and murder; reduces their ability to use safety measures and harm reduction strategies, making it harder to report violence committed against them; perpetuates the public image of them as deviant; impedes their ability to be entrepreneurial (e.g., to register as a business or open a bank account), and blocks their right to organize for better conditions through collective action and unionization.[84] Amnesty International has stated that "the policing of sex work exacerbates stigma, compromises access to resources, justifies violence, and is steeped in racial disparities."[85] While prohibitionists highlight how some sex workers are victimized by clients as proof that sex work should remain illegal, the labour paradigm points out that if violence against women is cause for criminalizing an entire practice, then the high number of women abused by their husbands would be grounds for outlawing marriage.[86]

The popular culture ahead gives vivid shape to the labour paradigm, highlighting the benefits sex workers find in their labour along with the challenges they face, including stigmatization and criminalization. Importantly, it asks: Whose interests do these laws serve? It rails against the conflation of sex work and trafficking and takes focus off trauma stories to spotlight sex workers who choose their work. As Jacqueline Comte notes, "for many women in the Western world, it is not lack of work skills or the need for survival that leads them to ... sex work, it is rather because they find advantages in doing so, compared with other work opportunities."[87] And while "sex work is a dream job for only a few,"[88] as Lola Davina writes, the popular culture ahead explores their good reasons for choosing it.

To be sure, the less labour-focused, more neo-liberal portrayals at times overemphasize the agency of sex workers. As some observers have warned, placing "choice" at the foundation of feminism fails to address the climate of systemic gendered oppression in which many women, every day, act.[89] Yet, there is good reason for popular culture to sometimes embrace what might *sound* like the rhetoric of choice feminism. Patriarchy has long used the discourse of the sex worker's "abnormality" to abuse her and to rationalize her criminalization. Meanwhile, prohibitionists have engaged with sex workers only as saviours or moral superiors (under the banner of saving sex workers from themselves). Kathleen Hanna, the lead singer of Bikini Kill, captures this tendency well with an anecdote about attending a talk by Andrea Dworkin in the late 1980s:

> I stepped to the mic during the question period and told [Dworkin] I was paying my way through college by stripping and that I thought the law would actually hurt me and not help me. She told me, in front of a packed lecture hall, that I was misguided, would be haunted forever by being a stripper, and that it would ruin my life.[90]

Clearly it did not, and Hanna would later channel her contempt for Dworkin's position into the song "Jigsaw Youth" with the lyric, "I can sell my body if I wanna."

Bearing this double-barrelled weight of assumed victimhood, sex workers have understandably felt compelled to make simplified, strident arguments – even to deny the existence of oppression within the sex industry, bar none – in order to assume the mantle of credibility and speak. Melissa Gira Grant aptly describes this double bind:

> When the public is groomed to expect a poor, suffering whore, it's appreciable why some sex workers who do come out would take pains to provide a counter-narrative: to never look like a prostitute. They are asked only to talk about how empowering it all was or about how much of a survivor they are. They have to convince audiences how much they have their shit together.[91]

Along the same lines, writer and former erotic dancer Lily Burana describes the pressure she felt to be unequivocally rosy about her work. Looking back on this defensive stance, she writes: "Sure, I want to show the world that strippers can be capable, thinking, feeling people, able to set boundaries, care for other people and ourselves. But taken too far, such emphasis on the positive casts me as a Paglian caricature – all triumph and no clue."[92]

The best of sex work popular culture today shows us how structure *and* agency bear on sex worker's lives. Elizabeth Bernstein sums up this need for balance well, writing that we must recognize that while sex work may sometimes be rooted in inequitable social conditions, it may also "constitute an attempted means of escape from even more profoundly violating social conditions."[93]

Ronald Weitzer's "polymorphous paradigm" usefully conceptualizes sex work according to the hierarchies already present in it, considering "victimization, exploitation, agency, job satisfaction, self-esteem and other dimensions as variables [rather than] constants."[94] This requires us to "think about sex work as involving a continuum of occupational experiences" and to "make use of language similar to that used when discussing other types of labour in late modern capitalist societies … particularly service work."[95]

Understanding the "work" of sex work and the nuances of a polymorphous perspective necessitates a deeper look at the political-economic circumstances under which it emerges. As Nina Power reminds us in her perceptive study of neo-liberal feminism, *One-Dimensional Woman*,

> No discussion of the current fortunes of women can take place outside of discussions of work. The inclusion of women into the labor force has brought about unprecedented changes in the way we understand the "role" of women, the capacity of women to live independent lives and the way in which women participate in the economy more generally.[96]

Indeed, within media studies the intersection of work, class, and sex continues to be a neglected area, and scholarship as it relates to sex work has been largely concentrated in ethnographies of call girls,[97] erotic dancers,[98] webcam models,[99] and sex surrogates.[100] Ethnographies illuminate the realities of sexual labour, but an examination of how popular culture represents this work is needed. As Lisa McLaughlin points out, feminist media studies must interrogate how the "experience of labour varies not only by class but also by virtue of one's location along dimensions that include gender, race, ethnicity, nation, sexuality, ability, and generation."[101] Eileen Boris, Stephanie Gilmore, and Rhacel Parreñas similarly urge us to focus on "the labour processes of sex work," as these reveal the exploitation sex workers face but also their tactics to exert "control over their labour."[102] To understand popular culture about sex workers, then, we must also look at the labour environment of which sex work is a part.

Hustling in Every Way: Work under Neo-liberal Capitalism

Sex work is – and has always been – a labour issue rooted in the subordination of women in patriarchal capitalism. After all, before the invention of the spinning wheel in the thirteenth century, women had three options for survival: become a wife, a nun, or a sex worker.[103] Of course, sex workers are the original hustlers, but the last decade or so that forms the backdrops for the popular culture in this book saw many changes in the economic environment around sex work that merit a closer look. According to Ava Carrarra, "to understand how sex work has changed requires thinking through how both our labour conditions and the political economy of the industry has been transformed."[104] It follows, then, that to understand popular culture about sex work, we need to first probe how sex work is shaped by broader shifts under neo-liberal capitalism.

New popular culture paints a vivid picture of neo-liberalism, a philosophical doctrine and political-economic ideology that promotes "free-market fundamentalism," the idea that humans reach their potential through what David Harvey calls "entrepreneurial freedoms" within an economic and governmental system that privileges unregulated markets, individual property rights, individual liberty, and free trade.[105] So imbedded is neo-liberalism into our way of life that Georges Monbiot argues that "we seldom even recognize it as an ideology."[106] Introduced in the 1970s, neo-liberalism replaced Fordism, which had governed American life since the early twentieth century and supported a large welfare state, trade and financial regulation, and standard employment relationships (i.e., full-time jobs with benefits).[107]

Post-Fordist neo-liberalism, which rose during Thatcherism and Reaganism, shrunk the welfare state, encouraged privatization and deregulation, transferred power to corporations and banks, and introduced free trade policies.[108] In turn, corporations supersized their bottom lines by offshoring jobs, resulting in the North American economic base shifting from manufacturing to the sale of services, sending workers from the factory to the call centre, the coal mine to Costco. These new service jobs demanded new forms of affective labour, turning the production of feelings into a professional obligation, especially for women.[109] As Nicole Cohen points out, the precarious service jobs created in the wake of neo-liberalism's ascent rely "heavily on communication" and draw on "workers' communicative, cognitive, intellectual, and affect capacities in more intensified ways."[110] In short, post-Fordist neo-liberalism restructured how governments, corporations, and people work, while promising prosperity and equality for all.

Yet, since the 1970s, the income gap between the 1 per cent and the rest has widened, and workers have endured plummeting wages and the rise of the bleak new coinage "downward mobility."[111] The emotional and financial strain of chronic precarity is hard to overestimate, and overburdening oneself with gigs for fear of having none is not uncommon, especially in sectors dominated by women – such as retail, food service, and health care – where long hours are often followed by sudden layoffs.[112] A 2023 study found that 8 million Americans held multiple part-time jobs involuntarily, a 44 per cent increase since 2007.[113] At any given time, millions of Americans are searching for new part-time work in anticipation of their current (and multiple) part-time jobs ending.

Working It: Popular Culture, Feminism, and Sex Work

Figure 1.3. New popular culture highlights how sex work shares many features (and inequalities) with other forms of service work in the gig economy, revealing the congruencies between sex workers and all women service workers under capitalism.

A 2016 study found that 25 per cent of part-time workers live in poverty.[114] Yet, braced by neo-liberal ideologies, gig work continues to be framed as "opportunity" under the celebratory banner of "entrepreneurship."

Sex work and the gig economy are connected. As Bernstein notes, the growth of the gig economy has wrought "profound transformation in the erotic sphere."[115] As more women face the prospect of low-paying McJobs, sex work emerges as an enticing way of earning more money in fewer hours, with more control. Sex work and gig work also share many characteristics. Both are precarious, involve emotional labour, and require workers to constantly search for new gigs in anticipation of their current gigs ending, "a full-time job on top of your full-time job," as one webcam model told the *New York Times* in a 2021 story titled "Jobless, Selling Nudes Online, and Still Struggling."[116] In the past decade, students have turned to sex work due to rising tuition and crushing debt.[117] During the COVID-19 pandemic, women who lost their jobs after retail stores were shuttered entered the sex industry in unprecedented numbers.[118] The adult subscription platform OnlyFans, launched in 2016, saw new sign-ups increase by 75 per cent as women laid off from retail jobs took up nude modelling to keep the lights on.[119] Much of the popular culture in the coming chapters portrays women turning to sex work to escape stressful and precarious low-wage gig work and, in its non-judgemental tone, suggests a new understanding that everybody in neo-liberal capitalism, in one way or another, has to be a hustler. The new sex worker in popular culture is, by and large, a resilient, hard-working, smart, scrappy, resourceful, and multifaceted woman. But as she manages debt, uncertainty, low-wage gigs, and a broken social safety net by becoming resourceful, she augurs popular culture's tendency to reframe poverty as opportunity, what Rosalind Gill and Akane Kanai describe as neo-liberalism's tendency to "call forth ... subjects who are 'creative,' 'flexible,' and 'positive' ... when rights to employment and social safety nets are continually under attack."[120] In many ways, popular culture's new sex worker is neo-liberalism's ideal subject: an "entrepreneur" in a service-based economy in which hustling is the new norm. Nonetheless, by drawing our attention to the *work* of sex work – its labour processes – popular culture supports her vital transformation from an outcast into a dignified professional.

Working It: Showing the Labour of Sex Work

Examining sex work popular culture today *as work* is important because work has historically been invisible in popular culture, especially women's work. In its early days, TV treated work as a shadowy place the male hero strode to and from wearing a hat and with a rolled-up newspaper under his arm, while women's unpaid work in the home was framed as her life's calling, as suggested by her gleaming chrome appliances.[121] By depicting women as domestic servants, media normalized their natural place in society as unwaged workers in the invisible economy of the home, not as wage-earners in the formal capitalist economy. This is why films that showed women's labour in *detail* – whether in or outside the home – were so rare and subversive.[122] As Pauline Kael, the *New Yorker*'s first film critic, wrote in 1971, "Work is rarely treated in films. It's one of the peculiarities."[123] That changed in the 1970s and 1980s with Mary Tyler Moore, Murphy Brown, and Angela Bower becoming TV's iconic working women, yet one analysis of prime-time television between 1957 and 1986 still found that only 24 per cent of women characters had identifiable jobs, and even fewer were seen working at them.[124] And the labour of sex work remained hidden in popular culture's closet of amoral things, which augured its outlawed status. But as Ann Lucas rightly observes, "prostitution is more than a set of signs and symbols about gender, sexuality, or power"; it is "a rich site in which to explore the meaning of work."[125] While popular culture once foregrounded the glitz of the "frontstage" show, in this book I show how new movies and TV shows explore, validate, and dignify the sex worker's "backstage" labour across five distinctive areas: entrepreneurship and erotic capital; emotional labour; aesthetic labour and display work; body work; and care work.

First, the new sex worker in popular culture is an *entrepreneur* whose services blend sex, performance, intimacy and self-commodification, the "process of assigning market value to goods that previously existed outside the market."[126] Leveraging her attractiveness, emotional intelligence, and performance and interpersonal skills, and self-promoting through branding, from sleek websites to social media to curated wardrobes, she builds her client base while controlling her schedule, managing her environment, and freeing herself from oppressive management. Many identify as creative entrepreneurs,[127] and some even describe their performances as art and expressions of "authenticity." This portrayal is not entirely rosy, however. She also confronts less glamorous aspects of sex work entrepreneurship, such as vulnerability to economic exploitation, the challenge of "turning off" her work persona, and the feast-or-famine nature of precarious work that often makes her reluctant to decline gigs, even when on the brink of exhaustion.

In addition to selling sexual and emotional experiences, the new sex worker entrepreneur in popular culture embodies economist Catherine Hakim's theory of *erotic capital*, which proposes that women can strategically use a constellation of personal qualities – including beauty, sex appeal, charm, energy, humour, and self-presentation – for economic mobility. Drawing upon Pierre Bourdieu's concept of cultural capital, which posits that taste (and consumption patterns) reinforce existing class hierarchies and divisions,[128] Hakim argues that erotic capital is self-made, not class-bound, serving as an equalizing strategy for "erotic dancers, burlesque artists, lap dancers, call girls, night club hostesses, and waitresses."[129] While Hakim's theory overlooks some of the limitations of erotic capital, which I address in the following chapters, it vividly highlights how patriarchal ideology and prohibitionist feminism have marginalized this form of capital by telling women that if they are smart they "cannot also be sexual."[130] The new sex worker in today's popular culture unabashedly monetizes her erotic capital from a position of dominance, but she also faces stigma for these perceived transgressions, revealing enduring biases against sex workers and sexual women.

Additionally, the new sex worker in popular culture engages in *emotional labour*, Arlie Hochschild's concept for the obligatory performance of "feeling" women service workers undertake, where "the emotional style of offering the service is part of the [very] service itself."[131] Hochschild's theory exposed the gendered expectation that women perform relentless cheer, for which they are not paid, through "surface acting" (faking smiles) and "deep acting" (drawing on memory and imagination to block unpleasant feelings and please the client). What makes these performances harder to pull off under the altered conditions of neo-liberal capitalism, Hochschild argues, is the consumer's distaste for (and ability to recognize) "phoniness" and their parallel desire for the "unmanaged heart," or "spontaneous 'natural' feeling."[132] To meet this demand, workers draw even more from "its opposite – the managed heart" – and performances of "worked up warmth."[133] While Hochschild's theory critiqued the patriarchal expectation that women perform cheeriness for men for free ("Smile for me, honey!"), the new sex worker in popular culture *is* actually paid for the smile she puts on.

Yet, the hazards of emotional labour are real, and sex workers guard against them by drawing on one of three emotion management strategies: identifying "wholeheartedly" with their work; identifying "cynically" with their work; or developing a "healthy estrangement of self from role" while valuing one's skills as "an illusion maker," which Hochschild identifies as the most protective tactic.[134] While prohibitionists argue that the high demands and risks of sex work make disassociating a job requirement, the new sex worker in popular culture adopts these emotion management strategies to deliver her services and to retain personal boundaries. That said, her emotional labour places her at risk of "alienation,"[135] and in the coming chapters we explore how burnout can lead to the erosion of boundaries, and to some unsettling high-stakes climaxes.

While the new sex worker increases her control through boundary-setting, she also regulates her professional life by investing in her appearance through *aesthetic labour*, her observance of "certain dress codes, hairstyle rules, and clothing prescriptions,"[136] and *display work* to become "overtly sexualized ... for sale ... [and] on display."[137] Once upon a time, popular culture put its sex workers in gaudy costumes, linking licentiousness to fishnets: "By your dress, attitude, and make-up, the prostitute indicates her trade," says the pimp in Jean-Luc Godard's sex work classic, *Vivre sa vie* (1962), indicating the sex-sartorial heuristic. The new sex worker in popular culture, however, does not have "the look" but is seen in jogging pants and in sequins and spike heels equally. In the coming chapters, sex workers engage in aesthetic labour as they stage masquerades of ideal femininity through conspicuous consumption and costuming. While this "production" of femininity is an integral part of crafting the new sex worker's personae and power, it's also exhausting, making it a double-edged sword.

Next is *body work*, the labour Carol Wolkowitz describes as the "intimate, messy contact with the (frequently supine or naked) body."[138] From assessing the body to adjusting it, adorning the body to massaging it, body work is central to sex work but far from exclusive to it; many fields, including massage therapy, personal support work, barbering, and practical nursing, draw on body work practices.[139] In conceptualizing sex work as a form of body work, popular culture invites us to consider the congruencies between sex work and other forms of body work and plays an important destigmatizing role. While body work is highly gendered, with a history of being devalued and marginalized, new popular culture treats it as a vocation, showing the contributions sex workers make to their clients' lives as they massage, stroke, hold, rub, cradle, and caress to provide pleasure, comfort, and education with stamina, grace, and strength.[140]

Finally, we turn to *care work*. While scholars have traditionally classified care work as labour exclusive to the family unit and the home, in the twenty-first century it is increasingly clear that care work "is no private issue."[141] Sex work is increasingly seen as a form of care work. Indeed, physicians have recognized sex work as a "helping" profession for over 100 years,[142] and the therapeutic alliances between sex workers and clients with disabilities is widely known. Guided by scholarship on "intimate labour,"[143] "relational work,"[144] and "care work" – the labour of helping others "develop [to] their fullest human capacities"[145] – I explore in the coming chapters the new sex worker as a care worker. Unlike popular culture's classic sex worker "nurse" type – an Oedipal fantasy, half mother, half sexpot – the new sex worker is not a titillator but a teacher-like figure.

Finally, in addition to showing the *work* of sex work, I also attend to how popular culture registers the occupational distinctions present in the sex industry, a subject that has received surprisingly little attention from media studies scholars. Following Weitzer, who argues that sex work must be understood according to its existing stratifications,[146] I examine popular culture not according to typologies but with respect to sex work occupations in all their diversity. More than twenty-five types of sex workers were identified by Christine Harcourt and Basil Donovan in their groundbreaking thirty-year longitudinal study.[147] From street-based sex workers to massage parlour workers, phone sex operators to webcam models and sex surrogates, sex "work experiences vary widely from one stratum to another."[148] Currently, no studies of popular culture images of sex work examine the differences in representations according to sex work type, a blind spot considering the radically different work experiences of sex workers according to the location of their work and its social and legal status. By examining the new sex worker as she appears in the context of six distinct types of sex work labour, I show how popular culture interprets the occupational diversification and experiences of sex work today.

Infused with respect for sex work and a feminism that recognizes her choice, the new sex worker in popular culture is a complex figure who challenges monolithic feminist narratives and castigates the commonest (and most morally soaked) screen stereotypes: the naive hooker with the heart of gold and the hardened harlot David Thomson aptly describes as the "bitter old woman sitting alone, counting her money."[149] Her presence on screen, guided by an inclusive feminism, registers shifting political, social, and economic values and places women's self-determination at the centre of the story. By getting into the *work* of sex work, popular culture's new sex worker is not a concept, a threat, or a moral lesson but rather a woman with dignity who goes to work.

2 Dancing to an American Dream: Dignifying Erotic Dancers' Labour in "Road Strip," *P.O.P., Magic City, Afternoon Delight,* and *Hustlers*

I don't want to tell the story of an exploited girl ... or the girl who started out as a stripper and made it to Hollywood or like or anything like that. That's been done and that's not real life. What is real life are the girls who you can tell are sitting there making a list of the stuff they have to do tomorrow while grinding on some guy's lap and thinking, "Tomorrow I have to take my kid to daycare."
– Leyla, erotic dancer

It is difficult to be a stripper and resist internalizing the negative stereotypes, i.e. they are abused, come from broken homes, abuse drugs and alcohol, lead violent lives, and are forced into the sex industry out of desperation.
– Debi Sundahl[1]

The stigma is starting to come off the word "stripper."
– Diamond, *Magic City* (2015)

"The image that is portrayed in TV and movies, that strippers are prostitutes or crackheads, or don't care about themselves ... you get that stigma," says Gigi Maguire in the documentary *Power of Pussy (P.O.P.)*. Gigi, an erotic dancer-turned-entrepreneur, is the owner of Pole Fan Addicts, a dance studio with shiny blonde wood floors, gleaming brass poles, and mirrored walls. Gigi opened her studio after a decade of saving money from dancing at Magic City, a thriving Atlanta club. Younger erotic dancers now train at Gigi's studio, perfecting their climbing, inversions, and spins, moves that require endurance, athleticism, and sensuality. Like Gigi, they take pride in their work. "This is our power, what you use to get the independence you need," Gigi says, pointing to the pole. To uninitiated audiences, the pole is a stage prop, but *P.O.P.* makes it into a symbol of economic mobility. The climb is steep, and so is the drop, but the financial rewards are potentially life changing for Gigi and her fellow dancers.

Today, erotic dancing is worth $6 billion annually in the US and involves an estimated 70,000 dancers – and uncountable audiences.[2] From the truck stop tavern with a makeshift stage to the VIP-only club where the cash flows like the Cristal champagne, there are more erotic dancing clubs per capita in the United States today than in any other country. What is it about stripping and the stars and stripes? According to Lily Burana, erotic dancing's "American-ness" stems from the nation's perennial tension between puritanism and capitalism, the ambivalences that pivot on "access and denial, the vacillation from awe to dismissal."[3] Thomas Edison's 1896 film *Fatima's Coochee-Coochee Dance* exemplifies this tension: a two-minute reel of a disrobed belly dancer flailing her hips, it became the first case of film censorship in the US, forcing Edison to conceal Fatima's mid-section in the second print.[4] By far the most visible outpost of the sex industry, erotic dancing also lies on a boundary of respectability: legal, visible, and taxable, yet stigmatized, storied, and taboo.

In the last number of years, erotic dancing popular culture has increased as part of what Brian McNair calls "stripper culture."[5] From Cabaret Barbie (with her fully "posable" body), to skyscraper heels on couture runways, to MAC Cosmetic's 2015 appointment of Blac Chyna, a former dancer, as its spokesperson, erotic dancing's imagery, tools, and techniques are big business. Yet, this sexual labour remains a divisive issue, especially in feminist thought. While sex-positive feminists argue that erotic dancing is an empowering subversion of compulsory female docility, radical feminists assert that it teaches women that their bodies are their most valuable assets and prioritizes the titillation of men over the dignity of women. As one former dancer wrote in *Ravishly*, erotic dancing is "a depressing, unhealthy cesspool … [and] for most women, it's a damaging dead-end."[6] Media scholars, too, have critiqued popular culture for glamourizing erotic dancing, especially documentaries that prize sensationalism over telling stories with substance. But in the last decade or so, popular culture starring subversive dancers who take pride in their stagecraft has begun telling new stories about this labour.

In this chapter, we delve into five of the most remarkable, exploring the work lives of talented dancers who use their "erotic capital" to establish a foothold – in six-inch heels – in a crumbling economy. With gravitas and style, the documentaries "Road Strip" (2014), *Power of Pussy (P.O.P.)* (2012), and *Magic City* (2015), and the feature films *Afternoon Delight* (2013) and *Hustlers* (2019) give dancers the spotlight to challenge myths and correct misconceptions in dynamic stories about striving, struggling, and sometimes thriving in an unequal society. Taking us backstage into bustling clubs in Los Angeles, Atlanta, and Manhattan, the films dignify erotic dancing by linking it to burlesque, a skilled art form that also attracted working-class women with dreams of economic mobility a century ago. Drawing parallels between erotic dancers and burlesque artists, the films focus on the work of professional erotic dancing today, from the long hours choreographing and practising routines to exhausting hustles for lap dances, as well as the dancers' personal lives, which share little with their stage personae.

While sometimes overstating the empowerment of "erotic capital" and downplaying its liabilities, these films reveal the challenges and rewards of erotic dancing through the dancer's own eyes and share several common aims: to correct the devaluation of erotic dancing labour; to counter the stigmatization of dancers; to increase understanding of what dancers do; and to highlight the inequalities between "those with the money and those doing the dance," turning the strip club stage into a metaphor for inequality under capitalism. I begin this chapter by situating erotic dancing within its history of burlesque and working-class culture, then look to its historical portrayal on screen before moving on to examine the relationship between sex work and the documentary form. This will prepare us to then look at popular culture's new erotic dancer and her uptake of these rich themes in new stories of hustling in heels for the American Dream.

Contexts: From Burlesque to the Bump 'n' Grind

To appreciate the novelty of "Road Strip," *P.O.P.*, *Magic City*, *Afternoon Delight*, and *Hustlers*, we need to first understand erotic dancing's origins in burlesque, one of the more lucrative entertainment industry opportunities working-class women pursued at the turn of the twentieth century. Burlesque is a form of musical theatre dating to the mid-nineteenth century that drew on elements of vaudeville, minstrelsy, and the music hall, and included dancing, singing, comedic skits, colourful lighting, live music, and ribald humour and teasing nudity that captured the zeitgeist of an era and its audiences' tastes and fantasies. Burlesque was controversial: conservatives saw it as profane and perverted, while literary luminaries from T.S. Eliot to Hart Crane were besotted by it. They wrote poems celebrating the dancers' talents and allure, recognizing their performances as both art and craft.

Burlesque, the forebear of stripping, was aspirational from its very roots. As Rachel Shteir notes in her illuminating history of striptease, burlesque's pioneering producers were strivers with accents, outcasts seen as outré by the rarefied uptown set.[7] The Minsky Brothers, enterprising Russian Jewish immigrants, bought a tenement on the Lower East Side in 1901, leased the first floor to a Yiddish theatre, and transformed the upstairs into a makeshift burlesque playhouse.[8] Early patrons were mostly poor, Jewish immigrants who rode up six floors in a freight elevator to see "derrieres, a bit of tit, all of their thighs."[9] Knowing their audiences lived in sunless tenements, burlesque producers sought to create spectacles in the aesthetics of the American Dream, with its cornucopia of consumer delights and quixotic wonders, like at Carroll's, in 1910, where shows were filled with "bubbles, marble statues, rainbow lights, mosaic glasses, friezes of metal, bars of gold, subterranean fog, feathers, chandeliers, and bejeweled ruffles."[10] And that was just the opening act. These sensorial spectacles provoked awe and stimulated audiences' class fantasies of bettering themselves in the land of opportunity.

Women entertainers at the turn of the century also saw in burlesque an opportunity to realize the American Dream in spite of economic disadvantages. Many early burlesque performers came from the working class. Facing restricted professional and educational opportunities, they relied on their allure and entertainment skills to carve out independent lives for themselves. As Shteir points out, "by presenting a sexual self outside of the realm of ordinary experience, women could overcome their working-class origins and make it ... striptease was one of the only ways out of the grueling demands of housework and the toil of the sweatshop, monotonies that reformers, being mostly men, generally only theoretically understood."[11] For performers who longed for a career and to become financially independent, but who lacked the right social connections, business canny, and formal training to go uptown, burlesque beckoned, which is what made it "radical in the sense that it allowed women to climb the economic ladder."[12] Burlesque performers drew on their "erotic capital," an economic resource comprised of qualities including sexual attractiveness, liveliness, charm, and social presentation. According to Catherine Hakim, erotic capital was "crucially important [for] certain occupations ... [including] strippers, burlesque artists [and] erotic dancers."[13] For example, Gypsy Rose Lee, today a burlesque icon, escaped the drudgeries of factory work by turning her erotic capital into a career; by the 1940s, she was earning $2,500/week.[14] As she put it, the stage was her one opportunity to "hurl herself ... into the American Dream."[15] While burlesque had become a more explicit striptease by the middle of the twentieth century and was simply "stripping" and lap dancing (which was more hands on) by the 1980s, erotic dancers and burlesque artists share many qualities: their economic motivations, their strength and agility, their dancing talents, and their canny understanding of the desires of the audience and how to balance the art of revelation and concealment.

The visual attractions of striptease made it a natural subject for film-makers, and erotic dancers have been making moves in popular culture for more than a century. But until recently, they have for the most part been statuary moulded by the male gaze, continuations of patriarchy's preoccupation with disrobing beauties. The focus was on the frontstage, as viewed by the male audience, leaving the women's stories out. Early cinematic portrayals of striptease, as Belinda

Smaill argues, rarely explored dancers' lives or talents in any real way; rather, women's bodies were bait for the box office, training audiences to associate moving pictures with titillation.[16] Dancers' bodies were usually filmed from the male audience perspective, which heightened the impression of the dancers' passive availability. In their heyday after the Second World War, striptease films like *A Night at the Follies* (1947) and *Striptease Girl* (1952) offered little exploration of the inner lives of erotic dancers – or artistry. On show instead was a "staging of … a fantasy about female erotic life"[17] revolving around bare skin and extreme characters. Through the 1950s, Hollywood churned out erotic dancer gold diggers, starlets, and lost girls, framing them as "a morally corrupting force."[18] Even as erotic dancing clubs became popular in US cities in the early 1960s, clear-eyed movies about dancers were in short shrift. Exploitation films about "girls who went wrong" took up the virgin–whore dichotomy with a vengeance. Emblematic of the genre was *Girl in Trouble* (1963), a story of a rebellious teenage girl who runs away to New Orleans and gets work at an erotic dance club where she is exploited, the film ending with her *mea culpa*: "I have committed the most terrible of sins. It never would have happened if I had been wiser at the start." This and other similar films carried moralizing messages about women's naiveté and rationalized – in the age of women's liberation – the imperative for women to be kept at home, in the control of men.

The 1990s reality TV boom cemented erotic dancer stereotypes with shock and humiliation talk shows disguised as makeovers and helpful interventions.[19] The "making over" of the individual from an "unruly" subject to a neo-liberal ideal was a core trope of the tabloid talk shows centred on "transforming 'at risk' individuals into successful managers of their lives and futures."[20] The most "authoritarian" of these formats portrayed incorrigible or helpless individuals and then "tamed" them with the help of experts or audiences, who were invited to weigh in with advice or abusive jeers (hello, *Jerry Springer*). These shows, packaged as benevolent and for the public good, did not probe the structural causes (e.g., racism, classism, and sexism) of its guests' difficult realities but rather profited by framing disenfranchised people as damaged goods, including erotic dancers who were represented as both petty and dangerous. That said, aspirational strivers ruled in *Flashdance* (1983), where welder Alexandra performs at a club by night and dreams of becoming a ballerina by day, *The Players Club* (1998), in which a budding writer strips to save money for journalism school, and the notorious *Showgirls* (1995), in which penniless Nomi Malone works at a seedy club called The Cheetah while hustling for a plum part in a big Las Vegas show. In these films, erotic dance clubs were hangouts for perverts, and escaping them was the goal for the wise-beyond-their-years heroines. Plus, most were shot from a male point of view and rife with gratuitous and questionable sex (such as the underwater blowjob in *Showgirls*). And, of course, the tartan-skirt stripper aesthetic of the 1990s, aided by Britney

Spears's midriff-baring outfit in the music video for her bubblegum anthem, "Baby One More Time," elevated the virgin–whore dichotomy to fashion iconography, inspiring legions of young women to don schoolgirl stripper Halloween costumes.

But mostly, the screen visualized erotic dancers as eye candy and disposable props. In *Grand Theft Auto V* (2013), part of one of the bestselling console video game series of all time, players step into the shoes of "Michael," who, when not robbing banks, tricks dancers into having sex with him for free.[21] Another video game, *Leisure Suit Larry: Magna Cum Laude* (2004), invited players to become a college student with "16 erotic dancers conveniently at his disposal."[22] On the small screen, *CSI: Crime Scene Investigation* (2000–15) featured erotic dancer victims (with camera-ready cleavage) in chalk outlines, while *The Sopranos* (1999–2007) made Tony's strip club Bada Bing! the setting for mob meetings, where the only erotic dancer with a wisp of a storyline is Tracee, who is later murdered while pregnant in one of the show's more gruesome homicides, the camerawork emphasizing her beauty and gory demise. Similarly, in the video game *Mafia II* (2010), gunned down dancers in lacy lingerie bleed to death in stylized multi-angle sequences. With TV shows, movies and video games of the 1990s and early 2000s perpetuating the image of dancers as damaged and victimized women, it is unsurprising that a 2007 public opinion poll found that 30 per cent of respondents believed that erotic dancers had below average intelligence, 55 per cent thought erotic dancing was an unacceptable job, and 73 per cent saw the industry as exploiting women.[23]

While erotic dancer stereotypes ruled fictional pop culture, the documentary, or the "creative treatment of actuality,"[24] stood apart as this occupation's surprisingly solid advocate, which warrants some explanation. In the twentieth century, the most popular documentary style was the expository mode, also known as the "social issues" documentary. Developed by John Grierson in the 1930s, this approach focused on narrating stories about social issues. Content was stressed over form, and objective knowledge emphasized over personal experience and memory. Attention was placed on the "issue." Common themes included poverty, welfare, sexism, and violence. Most films had a narrator – a male "voice of reason" – who would introduce a social problem and, by film's end, offer solutions.[25] Individual subjects primarily illustrated a thesis and appeared as "types" rather than as rounded people. By the end of the twentieth century, this form, progressively seen as heavy-handed, was replaced by "infotainment" as the new documentary form of choice, with a brash, no-holds-barred tone (of which *Jerry Springer* and other tabloid shows were exemplary).[26] But in the early 2000s, sex work documentaries also began to enter prime-time space on cable channels, like HBO's *G String Divas* (2000) and *Cathouse* (2002) and Showtime's *Family Business* (2003–6), all featuring "real-life" accounts of women doing sexual labour that were far from sensational.

Jane Arthurs usefully coined the term "docu-porn" to describe this slew of non-fiction media that appeared in the 2000s. These documentaries tended to celebrate women in the sex industry for their economic success and personal empowerment and gave sex workers an opportunity to speak about their labour outside of the rigid framework of tabloid talk shows. Yet despite the potential of the documentary form to act as a catalyst for the adoption of new beliefs and values that can foster social change,[27] Arthurs critiqued docu-porn's sexually charged imagery for co-opting "empowerment into the familiar relations of voyeurism"[28] and for downplaying sex workers' ambivalent feelings about their work.[29] These drawbacks notwithstanding, docu-porn had two major redeeming features: it complicated binary feminist thought on sex work (Is it good or is it bad?), and it portrayed sex workers as ordinary women, chipping away at the "rigid boundary between 'us' and 'them.'"[30]

While docu-porn remains a useful term, documentary as a genre has become more sophisticated in the past decade, and the erotic dancer films I examine in the next section illustrate this depth. They metabolize a vocabulary of respect and rights to explore erotic dancers' triumphs and ambivalences, using interviews and observational camerawork to tell stylish stories about entrepreneurship and stagecraft. While the expository documentary was focused on issues, these are "personal portrait" documentaries, which focus on people and stress subjectivity. This documentary form, as Bill Nichols notes, is especially useful for highlighting the "performative aspects of sexuality,"[31] and such films mark a growing regard for erotic dancers as professionals more widely speaking. Today, in fact, the US Bureau of Labor Statistics recognizes erotic dancers as professionals in a category with ballet dancers and choreographers.[32] Taking up this more labour-focused perspective are films such as *The Wrestler* (2008), *Afternoon Delight*, *We're the Millers* (2013), and *Hustlers*, the TV series *Beyond the Pole* (2018–21) and *P-Valley* (2020–), and the documentaries *League of Exotique Dancers* (2015), "Life as a Truck-Stop Stripper" (2014), *Magic City*, *P.O.P.*, and "Road Strip," episode six of *This Is Life with Lisa Ling*, which tell true stories that highlight dancers' entrepreneurship and economic motivations, depicting a career that takes talent and practice to pull off.

"Road Strip": Erotic Dancers as Travelling Entrepreneurs

Journalist Lisa Ling opens "Road Strip" (2014) with a powerful declaration: "What people don't understand is what difficult labour this is." Serving as a defence of erotic dancers and an ode to their unsung work, the hour-long episode featured in season one of the CNN series *This Is Life with Lisa Ling*, which took viewers on a "gritty, breathtaking journey to the far corners of America."[33] Focused on marginalized subcultures and social issues through the stories of ordinary Americans, season one also included episodes on gay rodeo performers, painkiller addicts in the Mormon Church, and women working in the male-dominated oil fields of South Dakota.[34]

"Road Strip" played an integral role in establishing the series' non-judgemental, sex-positive, overtly feminist tone. Utilizing the personal portrait documentary form, it dismantles stereotypes that devalue pole work. The dancers, in allyship with Ling, are both the episode's star attraction and its narrative voice. Chyna, Iman, Chanel, Sarah, and Antonia – in their twenties and thirties – are mothers, creative writers, and college students who spend a considerable part of their dancing careers on the road, working "guest spots" at clubs in different cities, aiming to earn in just a few intense nights what would typically take much longer to make locally. While the documentary challenges the taboo of erotic dancing, it also offers a sober analysis of the demanding, stigmatized, and precarious nature of this work.

The opening montage, showing the dancers packing their suitcases, saying their goodbyes to loved ones, and driving away from their family homes, vividly portrays the determination, sacrifice, and motivation of these erotic entrepreneurs. "On the weekends they drive six hours to cash in on a once-a-year business opportunity," Ling explains, highlighting the unusual labour process. Contrasting with the familiar image of the erotic dancer working shifts at her local club, "Road Strip" is about itinerant dancers. They travel to cities where large numbers of men converge – Myrtle Beach, South Carolina, for golf tournaments, or Hurley, Wisconsin, for RV rallies – with a common goal: "to make as much money in the least amount of time" to bring home to their families. One vibrant segment of the episode even explores the history of burlesque, drawing explicit parallels between these striving dancers and their hustler forebears, including the iconic Gypsy Rose Lee. "What these women share," Ling notes, "is the drive to be successful."

Sex work documentaries are often criticized for hyperfocusing on women's bodies, leading some scholars to argue that they are just another way – albeit through an "educational" pretence – of objectifying women.[35] That "Road Strip" wants to do the sex work documentary differently is evident in its non-sensationalistic camerawork and Ling's assertive narration, which celebrates the dancers' talents, opinions, and entrepreneurship, not their bodies. With this focus on the dancers' identities, "Road Strip" exemplifies the personal portrait documentary mode, a style that is adept at spotlighting "a marginalized sexual experience or identity."[36] Unlike the expository social issues documentary that predominated in the twentieth century and tended to carry a moral "message," the personal portrait form gives its subjects the space to narrate their lives free of judgement. Bill Nichols highlights that this form is "most vividly displayed in relation to issues of sexuality and gender,"[37] making it exceptionally suited for the episode's goal: to challenge the patriarchal shaming and stigma that has long haunted erotic dancers. "Road Strip" contends that these professionals are not victims but entrepreneurs with ambitions that extend beyond the club. They are hard-working women focused on "the bottom line." As Ling says:

> One thing is present in all of them: ambition. For some women, stripping allows them to make more money than other day jobs. Some dancers use the money to put themselves through school … others take advantage of the flexible schedule, like mothers who want to spend more time with their children.

Entrepreneurship involves assuming risk to single-handedly establish a business. Today, the trope of the female entrepreneur is popular on the big and small screens, aligning with Catherine Rottenberg's description of neo-liberalism "normatively constructing and interpolating individuals as entrepreneurial actors,"[38] a concept that extends beyond traditional boundaries. For example, one financial analyst on LinkedIn praises the similarities between entrepreneurs and erotic dancers:

> I told her I worked in finance. She told me she was a stripper. I asked her the same questions I would ask a startup CEO and her answers were smarter and more authentic than any CEO I'd ever interviewed. The pure economics of her business are a thing of beauty: predictable cash-flows (less than 5% variability from forecast), high barriers to entry (most women won't strip), low cyclical sensitivity (when times are tough, men need strippers more).[39]

Similarly, in a Q&A with the *This Is Life with Lisa Ling* team, the producer of "Road Strip," Heidi Burke, describes how this "new type" of entrepreneurial erotic dancer inspired her to make the episode:

> The idea [for making "Road Strip"] came from an online article that a dancer wrote about her own experience traveling to a booming oil town to make money. These dancers were an entirely new type.… We had never seen anything on these entrepreneurial women … before and wanted to capture what this lifestyle was like.[40]

The erotic dancers of "Road Strip" are entrepreneurs of erotic capital, yet they're motivated not so much by the stage's bright lights as by what it allows them to escape: the drudgery of low-wage jobs. Like burlesque artists at the turn of the twentieth century, these performers are drawn to the stage mostly by economic factors, implicitly linking factory work of a century ago to the call centre gig work of today. In voice-over, Ling highlights the profession's benefits – from high income to scheduling flexibility to more time with one's children. By exploring their motivations and multifaceted lives, Ling broadens our perspective, moving us beyond the narrow stereotype of the dancers' mere sexualization at the club.

Whereas "docu-porn" tends to portray sex workers on stage, in various states of undress, "Road Strip" emphasizes the women's identities outside of the club. Several interviews take place in the dancers' rented homes on the road, showing the performers cooking meals and connecting with their kids after a hard day of work. "Goodnight, Monkeyhead!" comes one child's squeaky voice through the mother's speakerphone. These domestic scenes underscore the many roles the dancers play on stage – and off. In one interview, twenty-one-year-old Iman, a single mother to a three-year-old girl, sits in the kitchen of the rented home she shares with other travelling erotic dancers when on the road. She wears jeans, a sleeveless T-shirt, and minimal make-up. She articulately describes her plan to dance until she reaches the age of thirty; then, she intends to invest and live off the proceeds of real estate while focusing on giving her daughter "a good life." Chyna, another erotic dancer, wants to open her own housecleaning business one day and envisions expanding it nationwide. Seasoned dancer Antonia explains how in one night of dancing she earns what would otherwise take two weeks of full-time work to make, enabling her to devote more time to her true vocation of writing. In *Spent*, the memoir she published in 2014, Antonia further describes how dancing helped her and other dancers she knows raise their standards of living, pay tuition, rear kids, and launch creative careers, providing "a way forward. Despite the circumstances, the women I work with are resourceful and clever."[41]

"Road Strip" challenges the idea that erotic dancers are exploited women as it explores how single mothers, aspiring writers, and college students find financial stability and the sense of empowerment that comes from succeeding in – and benefiting from – a male-run industry. Rather than simply critique neo-liberal capitalism, "Road Strip" is interested in how women manoeuvre within it to create opportunities. As Ling says, "It can be lonely being an erotic dancer, but the cold hard cash keeps them in the game."

Aesthetic Labour and Display Work: Advertising on Stage,
Selling on the Club Floor

The most compelling aspect of "Road Strip" lies in its respect-building for the talents, resilience, and hard work of erotic dancers. Focusing on their aesthetic labour, display work, and emotional labour, the documentary aligns with Ling's central argument that "a good erotic dancer is skilled in many art forms that go beyond taking off her clothes." It skillfully explores display work, including the pole moves that require acrobatic agility, steely confidence, theatrical flair, knowledge of sightlines and blocking, impeccable timing, and the ego strength to handle the scrutiny of an audience that may critique as much as it enjoys. This work, both physically and mentally demanding, is performed in settings designed for men, creating an inherently uneven power dynamic. "Road Strip" challenges perceptions, however, by adopting the dancers' perspectives, revealing that the view from the stage is not what it seems from the floor.

In her singular Marxist-feminist analysis of erotic dancing, Chris Bruckert breaks down the labour processes of the dancers according to the club's distinctive areas: backstage, frontstage, and the floor and booths where dancers perform private shows.[42] Bruckert's spatial categorization helps us map out how "Road Strip" depicts labour across all three spaces.

The first place we visit is backstage, specifically the dressing room (or "locker room"). This area is both privileged and private, off-limits to clients and male managers. It's the only area in the club where dancers can fully be "off" after sets or while preparing for them. It's a sanctuary. But the dressing room, we learn, is not a tranquil place but rather a construction site where dancers build their sexual allure and become personified fantasies using the tools of their trade, from cosmetics to wigs to costumes. This aesthetic labour includes the grooming practices of adopting "certain dress codes, hairstyle rules, and clothing prescriptions."[43] Watching dancers engage in aesthetic labour quickly effaces the valorized fantasy of "natural" beauty. Shots of countertops strewn with flat irons, wigs, make-up tubes, and compacts remind us of Simone de Beauvoir's adage that "women are made, not born."

A dancer's popularity rests upon her personality, appearance, age, stage presence, and dance skills, but equally important is that she fit the mould of an established type. As Dahlia Schweitzer notes, the most successful erotic dancers are "conceptually ... a physical manifestation of an idea resident in the minds of men."[44] Yet "Road Strip" challenges the radical feminist idea that dancers are handmaidens of patriarchy because they *appear* to be conforming to male fantasies. As Ling suggests, their aesthetic labour empowers them to monetize the looking men have always expected to do for free. As the camera tracks dancers using tools to exaggerate the features most associated with idealized femininity – stiletto heels to make legs appear longer, gloss for poutier lips, and push-up bras and implants for rounder and higher breasts – "Road Strip" lays bare the performance of femininity, dignifying the dancers' canny construction of it.

In addition to looking sexy and personifying fantasies, dancers must also master the art of pole dancing. This display work requires them "to incorporate and execute (in very high heels) their own eclectic mix of ballet, jazz, acrobatics, aerobics and posing."[45] They not only need to choreograph shows that abide by the conventions of the form, which typically involves nudity by the third song, but they must also, like burlesque performers, reach that climax in a lateral, artful, even narrative way to avoid boring the audience. (Lili St. Cyr, one of burlesque's early stars, described her stripteases as "mini pieces of theatre."[46] In her avant-garde act titled "Suicide," she portrayed a heartbroken woman disrobing for a bath and submerging in a tub illuminated to simulate water, with the stage then fading to black to signify her death.) This imaginative blend of nudity and narrative at the core of dancing, according to Debi Sundahl, challenges the "insulting misconception ... that anyone ... can strip. It takes practice and talent to be able to pull off an entertaining and truly erotic performance."[47] As dancers use their bodies as both text and illustration, they weave stories, ideally inspiring patrons to buy lap dances. While some dancers in the documentary are seasoned pole professionals, others, like Chyna, are novices facing a steep climb. That is, up the brass pole that soars from the stage floor to the ceiling and is the lion's share of the erotic dancer's work.

"Road Strip" dignifies "pole work" through live-action sequences that showcase the dancers' elan, strength, and endurance. It uses zooms to focus on Chyna, Iman, Chanel, and Antonia as they climb the pole. John Berger, in *Ways of Seeing*, discusses how Western art often sexually objectifies women by depicting them in full-frontal nudity, giving viewers a sense of total ownership over the woman's body.[48] Similarly, Karen Boyle has critiqued the docu-porn genre for its voyeuristic imagery,[49] which caters to the male gaze. "Road Strip," however, emphasizes craft and technique with unsensational camerawork from the dancers' perspectives. Chyna, as Ling points out, is new to the stage and learning "how to make her body entice." After months of practice, she performs a stage show set to saxophone music; she twirls, hoists, flips, climbs, and opens her arms in balletic V-shapes reminiscent of a gymnast's elegance and risky moves. The camera captures this, focusing not on full-frontal imagery but on close-ups of non-erogenous body parts mid-move – an arched leg, a fingertip, a smile. At the same time, artistic close-ups of the environment – beer glasses, cigarette embers, and other dancers moving about the floor – convey Chyna's perspective. *She* is doing the looking.

Erotic dancing is, undeniably, a pantomime of idealized femininity that dancers present as authentic, despite the arduous aesthetic labour involved in manufacturing it. Heidi Mattison aptly describes this illusion: "Nothing was what it appeared. Most of these women took multiple names, matching their multiple personalities. Image, reality, manipulation, it was a sea of deception."[50] Prohibitionists view the adoption of stage names and the donning of costumes as detrimental to a sex worker's psyche, "hollowing [her] out."[51] In contrast, "Road Strip" considers these performance tactics strategic tools that empower, rather than harm, dancers. It helps dancers to compartmentalize their private and work lives and detach from the unpleasant parts of their jobs, gaining control over them. Furthermore, in a world where women are still called "uptight" for rejecting unwanted sexual advances (like catcalls), some dancers find empowerment in turning this attention to their advantage by monetizing it.[52] In this vein, "Road Strip" suggests that dancing can challenge patriarchal dictates that demand women hide their sexuality to avoid being labelled as "sluts." As Muriel Dimen observes, patriarchy has historically deprived women of a sense of "sexual at-one-ness," which is necessary to self-esteem.[53]

Sarah, a younger dancer, describes how developing and performing her stage persona ("Clara") has helped her overcome insecurity stemming from the bullying she experienced as a teenager when she was called "ugly." Of her leggy, exhibitionistic, sparkly G-string–wearing alter ego, she notes, "Clara doesn't have stage anxiety." In "Road Strip," dancers display, monetize, and control access to their sexual performances, achieving what Eva Pendleton calls "fundamental sexual restructuring."[54] The documentary as a whole suggests that if patriarchy trains women to please men and look pretty, erotic dancing is simply a frank acknowledgment of this role, repurposed for profit – which is why it remains taboo. Antonia encapsulates this sentiment: "I think it's hot and empowering. Our culture tells us that it is bad and degrading, but I don't subscribe to that. Our bodies are gorgeous, and our sexuality is beautiful."

"Road Strip" portrays agential dancers who choose and benefit from their work, yet the documentary doesn't glamorize or glorify their gigs, nor their industry. The dancers are especially candid about their occupation's biggest challenges: the long hours, the sadness they feel being on the road away from their families, and the precarity endemic to sex work – how they never know whether a night's hustling will reap hundreds, or nothing. With its focus on the personal, the documentary doesn't delve into the economics of erotic dancing, but it's worth noting that the industry has changed over the last two decades, advantaging club owners, not dancers. Before the 1970s, erotic dancers were classified as employees of the burlesque houses at which they worked. They belonged to unions, paid dues, and collected lost wages when on strike. The rise of pornographic film, and later home video, however, phased striptease out, and by the mid-1970s, burlesque clubs across the US were mostly shuttered for triple-X fare.[55] When the early 1980s recession hit and the offshoring of jobs reorganized the North American economy, more workers shifted into service sector jobs, and options for working-class women declined, as did wages. Meanwhile, the burlesque club was replaced by the strip club. Between 1980 and 2000, dancing in North America went from a unionized job to a service sector gig,[56] a change that had devastating effects on dancers: it meant that they had no sick leave, vacation time, health insurance, or job security, and if customers were inappropriate, dancers had no official recourse for addressing those harms. Today, most erotic dancers don't belong to unions, nor do they receive pay from the clubs where they dance. Troublingly, although these clubs classify dancers as independent contractors, they often treat them like full-time employees by scheduling their shifts and, in some cases, obligating them to perform for free – or worse, charging them for the privilege of performing.[57] The stage is where dancers primarily earn their money. The performers' on-stage acts serve as advertisements for the private lap dances they try to sell off stage, sometimes their only source of income in the club.[58]

Pretending Interest, Feigning Desire: Erotic Dancing and Emotional Labour

"Road Strip" doesn't candy coat the hard work of selling lap dances as its camera tracks the women perambulating the club. "That's kind of the goal here, to get men into private rooms, because that's where the money is made," Ling explains, as we watch dancers striking up conversations, which, like the rest of the work in the club, is harder than it looks. The quick thinking and emotional intelligence demanded of sex workers led Camille Paglia to describe them as "superb analyst[s]."[59] Similarly, "Road Strip" pays careful attention to this labour to challenge the misconception that erotic dancing is a deviant occupation. It implicitly draws on scholarship that emphasizes the skills of the dancers, particularly the interactions between them and their customers that "mirror respectable negotiation in mainstream culture."[60] In just a moment or two, dancers must capture the customer's attention, read his needs quickly and accurately, and make him feel uniquely desirable, all while subduing her own feelings of boredom and irritation. This is emotional labour to the nth degree, and we watch dancers do it as Chyna jokes with a customer and Antonia whispers into the ear of another, performing the physical gestures of friendliness and flirtation Arlie Hochschild calls "surface acting."[61] Were that enough to sell a dance, dancers would rejoice, but the documentary shows that it takes a sense of personal connection and the customer feeling uniquely special, as though the dancer has chosen him, to sell. To meet this need, service workers engage in "deep acting" – method acting to rouse positive feelings – as though "an imagined happening is really happening now."[62] Customers at erotic dancing clubs place a high premium on "realness" and often ask dancers to "drop the routine," a request dancers oblige by bringing forth yet another act.[63] Despite knowing that illusion is the métier of the club, some customers visit strip clubs and buy time with dancers because they are looking for companionship and to "be treated as a special person."[64] To accommodate this need, the dancer will "muster up ... a believable performance."[65] The routine is all part of late capitalism's intimacy economy, where, as Hochschild argues, there is an "unprecedented value on spontaneous 'natural' feeling," or the "unmanaged heart."[66] Such is the irony of the erotic dancing club, "Road Strip" shows, where illusion is queen and authenticity a most valuable commodity. These performances of feeling impact the dancers, and "Road Strip" lets us decide what those impacts are by showing us the interactions.

Showing rather than telling is a hallmark of the personal portrait documentary form, representing a departure from the expository "social issues" documentary that predominated in the twentieth century. The expository mode placed the narrator in the role of judge and orator and proceeded rhetorically to argue a point to a conclusion. Individual subjects were often used to illustrate the thesis; as individuals, they were seldom explored. "Road Strip" challenges this heavy-handed approach, typifying what Bill Nichols describes as the personal portrait documentary's tendency to "implicitly live out the underlying issue without even identifying it."[67] "Road Strip" critiques power dynamics more through observational camerawork than through exposition, aligning with the personal portrait documentary style. Particularly, it looks at how performing feelings places workers at risk of what Hochschild calls "alienation" from themselves.[68] In scenes where dancers interact with customers, "Road Strip" implies that high earnings can sometimes lead to alienation, often without a pay-off. While some dancers work at upscale venues in big cities – Antonia at the Playboy Club, where she can earn triple digits nightly – others struggle to make a living at clubs outside of urban centres, despite doing intensive emotional labour. In one scene, at a mostly deserted rural Minnesota bar, Sarah struggles to find buyers for her $25 lap dances. Growing desperate, she lowers her price to $10, and with still no takers, she approaches a man at the bar: "One dollar? You can't even buy a soda pop for one dollar," she entreats. When he shrugs and turns away, she moves to the next man, her pitch growing more desperate: "Will you give me a dollar to see my boobies?" A close-up of Sarah's strained face vividly portrays her frustration, making narration unnecessary. While Sarah would be unlikely to give the man who just rejected her the time of day in her real life, in the club, it's her job to pretend to like him, and this disconnect between feeling and feigning at work, the episode suggests, is troubling, especially for Sarah, who describes pegging her self-confidence to the audiences' adulation, meaning that rejection is more than just a financial loss.

"Road Strip" also suggests that erotic dancers may feel obligated to downplay their intelligence and pretend naiveté to credibly embody the stereotypically docile feminine role for which customers show a preference. The repression of intelligence is part of what led Hochschild to argue that women service workers are often expected to play *contradictory* roles; in her examination of the hiring preferences of airline companies, she found that the ideal flight attendant candidate is a smart woman who "can also cope with being considered dumb."[69] In one scene, Chyna sits on a customer's knee, bantering with him while also unfurling her subtle sales pitch for a lap dance. Deciding to satisfy his request for "realness," in a moment of "dropping the act," Chyna tells her customer about her goal of one day opening a large-scale cleaning business. Knowing that her career as a dancer has a limited timeframe, she has sketched out her next move and explains her business idea with real enthusiasm. After making this "real" disclosure, the customer looks at her, wearing a dumbfounded expression, and suggests she forget about her idea and stay "right here" (presumably on his lap and certainly in the club). The camera's focus on Chyna's tight smile in response to this condescending dismissal of her agency – and identity beyond the club – highlights how at odds her performance of submissiveness is with her independence.

Thus, "Road Strip" ends by proposing that erotic dancers must strike a deal with themselves to play to the fantasy of femininity to fill their bank accounts but suggests that this credit comes also with a debit of authenticity. It complicates any pretence of erotic dancing being always empowering and invites the viewer to consider how dancers, like other precarious workers, hustle without any guarantees of dignity or pay. These are the sacrifices of life on the road and the tension these strong women feel in an industry where, to the untrained eye, chasing opportunities may look like submissiveness, but is not.

Power of Pussy (P.O.P.): **An Erotic Dancing Sisterhood**

The representation of Black dancers in popular culture outside of music videos used to be rare, but women of colour have worked the stage since the burlesque era. "I wasn't really naked. I simply didn't have any clothes on," quipped the American burlesque star Josephine Baker at the height of her career in the 1920s.[70] Baker, born to a St. Louis domestic worker, shattered barriers by achieving fame at the Folies Bergères in Paris. There, she a created a commercially viable persona that blended titillation and irony, captivating audiences with her graceful movements and sparkling stage routines. Baker danced her way to financial security and made art with her body and voice. Today, famous rappers from Cardi B to Blac Chyna openly discuss their past careers as erotic dancers, yet popular culture's portrayal of the erotic dance club remains predominately represented by white performers. "Just Google 'stripper' and what do you see?" asks Ivy Downer. "A sea of blonde hair, blue eyed women with huge breasts in 10-inch heels. Strippers of color are poorly portrayed in the industry." Yet, as Downer also notes, "the momentum has recently grown for stripper visibility, especially for women of color."[71]

Exemplifying this momentum and visibility, *P.O.P.* is an independent documentary made in 2012 by Artemis Jenkins, an Atlanta film-maker. Uploaded on YouTube in four parts, it follows four Black dancers at Magic City, a renowned club in Atlanta. The thirty-nine minute film, which went on to get millions of views, follows the professional lives of a close-knit troupe of dancers who support each other by practising and performing in a collective called the Snack Pack, which is managed by entrepreneur and former dancer Gigi. Taking a vérité approach and set to original music by local rap and hip hop artists, *P.O.P.* is about performance, ambition, and power, and its candid interviews and sizzling live-action sequences highlight the talents of dancers, from novices to pros, giving them the stage to shatter stereotypes and showcase their work. *P.O.P.* is about women who proudly use their erotic capital for economic mobility but, like "Road Strip," also explores how potentially big rewards come with big challenges.

Magic City is a nationally famous hub for Atlanta's thriving hip hop and rap music scene. A gathering spot for recording industry insiders and hopefuls, the VIP seats closest to the stage are where the executives scoping for new artists sit. The dancers at Magic City play a major role in supporting these artists' shots at fame. As *P.O.P.* shows, aspiring musicians give Magic City's disc jockeys their demo tapes to play during the dancers' stage shows, which become make-or-break testing grounds for new music: if a dancer can bump, pole climb, twerk, and grind to it, the song likely has traction, and the artist behind it may get signed to a label. The synergies between erotic dancers and hip hop artists are at the heart of *P.O.P.* The club is a creative industry incubator where ambitious hip hop and rap artists put their best songs forward, erotic dancers perform innovative, sensual, and acrobatic shows, and music industry moguls make deals. Music is an intrinsic part of the personal portrait documentary, according to Bill Nichols, and in *P.O.P.*, music is a constant backdrop. The thumps, crackles, samples, and grooves mixed by Atlanta artists harmonize with the dancers' performances to suggest the creative synergy between Magic City's erotic dancers and musical artists.

Ambition and agency are leitmotifs of *P.O.P.*, and class mobility is a goal all the dancers share, hitching their hard work to a hoped-for future of economic stability. *P.O.P.* portrays its star, Gigi, as a symbol of class mobility and the American Dream – or at least a dream in the making. Tall and toned, with mermaid hair, Gigi is a single mother who saved the money she earned from dancing for ten years to amass the capital to open Pole Fan Addicts, a training school for new dancers and a pole fitness studio. Now, younger dancers who aspire to Gigi's level of success and professionalism – and income – can train with her. Like the performers in "Road Strip," the women in *P.O.P.* don't wax poetic about dancing being a path to tinselled success; rather, they describe it as an escape from the penury of double shifts, bad bosses, and the precarity of work in fast food restaurants and retail, where the wages are low and the treatment demoralizing.

Naturally, the money is better at the club, but *P.O.P.* doesn't romanticize the stage as a final career stop; for many it is just another stepping stone from struggling to something modestly better. Virgo, a member of the Snack Pack, says that people sometimes overemphasize the "choice" to strip: "My situation was, I didn't have any money. I came from nothing. Stripping was a way out." Far from celebrating erotic dancing as a cure-all for racialized class inequality, *P.O.P.* offers a more realistic picture of women choosing this work in conditions not of their own making. Another dancer, Cali, says, "You have to make a bean. You have to make shit happen in your life … [and] I have something a lot of other girls don't have … the will to survive. I am fighting for it." Gigi discloses that she wouldn't want her daughter to become an erotic dancer; nevertheless, she's pragmatic about her job. Simone is similarly practical: "If you're going to do it," she says, "you got to learn how to do it right." In their wish to transcend their working-class origins, the dancers in *P.O.P.* share with burlesque artists not only an economic goal but also a wish to be taken seriously as artists, not just as women who take off their clothes.

Erotic dancing is a form of display work – the presentation of sexualized body capital in exchange for wages.[72] *P.O.P.* is an eagle-eyed dissection of this – but the work *behind* the stage show. This backstage work has usually remained hidden, an erasure that Ivy Downer says has led to "serious misunderstandings about what stripping entails and what kind of labour it requires."[73] *P.O.P.* corrects this misunderstanding passionately. As Gigi says:

> There is a difference between a stripper and an entertainer.... A stripper is going to get on stage, two step, booty shake, and get naked, … [but] an entertainer is going to work the pole, give you a show, and you'll be so amazed at the show you aren't even going to realize that you didn't see no titties or coochie because she didn't take her clothes off. But you wouldn't even care because the show you saw is so much better.

While "Road Strip" was about individual dancers performing solo on stage, as per the convention, *P.O.P.* exposes an extremely unique arrangement: dancers who work collectively in the Snack Pack, a self-organized erotic dancing sisterhood. Composed of four dancers, the Snack Pack meets regularly at Pole Fan Addicts to train under the mentorship of Gigi, using the synergies they create to polish their shows and sharpen their technical prowess. It is notable that all the performers have experience in professional dance or athletics. "When you have a background in technical dance, it helps your stage presence," Gigi explains, "because you already have that form and that tightness in the technique. You put two and two together and create what we've done with strip." Collectivity and sustained collaboration between sex workers is rarely seen in popular culture, which is why P.O.P.'s Snack Pack is so original. Jenkins's live-action sequences at Gigi's studio showcase the knowledge sharing and support that stirs this women-only space, where dazzling nighttime shows are built on strenuous daytime practice and where dancers motivate each other and develop their stagecraft, choreographing and critiquing collectively.

Close-up camerawork captures the Snack Pack's spins, inversions, climbs, flips, and other advanced pole moves, such as the "trapeze hang," the "advanced Z-seat," the "double stargazer," the "rainbow," and the "rubber double elbow," making appreciable how technically demanding this work is. The women climb the poles, cling by crossed legs, clench their abs to perform upside down sit-ups, and run their hands along their own bodies sensually. Heels on the floor, they "pop their butts," bending at the waist, gripping their haunches, and vibrating. These sequences never feel voyeuristic. Rather, they capture the frisson of the form, treat the dancers' work respectfully as a vocation, and distance the dancers from the stereotype of victimhood. In one scene, Snack Packers move on the pole, one dancer upside down, the other balanced on her, legs pumping. "That's 'riding a bicycle,'" Simone says. The dancers rearrange; now one grips the pole with her thighs and holds her partner aloft, lifting her up and down as though she's featherweight. "That's the bench press," she says, as the dancers melt into their next move. "No shade to girls who get up there and do the two step stripper stroll, [but] we are doing way more." P.O.P. de-sexualizes the women's bodies by circling back to the craft, connecting it to their lifelong talents, and framing pole work as a natural continuation of their innate interests. As Virgo says with a grin, "I know how to climb the pole because I used to climb trees a lot."

The film draws our attention to how the Snack Pack also provides erotic dancers with much-needed solidarity in a male-centred business, where women are paid to commodify themselves inside the club – and often stigmatized outside of it. In this regard, Gigi not only teaches dancers how to use their bodies to entice but also how to manage the emotions that come with the stigma of their jobs. Gigi is an entrepreneur, but her business is also driven by personal experience: she remembers well the anxiety she felt as a rookie dancer without any formal training or a manual for pole moves. "When the club hires you, they put you on the floor. There is no training.... If you don't have someone to show you the ropes and key insight, it can be a disaster. A lot of people get blindsided, they get shocked and say that's not for me," Gigi explains. She remembers how that steep learning curve made her debut more challenging than it would have been with support from other dancers. This support is crucial, as the stigmatization erotic dancers experience is often be far more damaging than the challenges inherent to the work itself.

Figure 2.1. Erotic dancers in the Snack Pack practise in *P.O.P.*, where sisterhood and stripping go hand in hand.

Like "Road Strip," *P.O.P.* scrutinizes the stigma erotic dancers regularly face through the intimate form of the personal portrait documentary, which allows the dancers to describe and respond to this discrimination. Several performers say their families view them as "sluts" and "prostitutes" and lament how strangers assume they are threats or want to steal their husbands. They describe being denigrated by people who have never bothered to ask them questions or try to understand what they do and why. The effect of sequencing these interviews after exploring the dancers' motivations and talents compels us to look closely at our own biases about why we perceive dancers differently than other women in the entertainment industry. One dancer describes doing "honest work," adding jokingly, "we don't even dance on Sunday!" while lamenting the public's assumption "that erotic dancers are hos, doing it with everybody." With these interviews, the film critiques patriarchy's double standard, which encourages women to passively receive the male gaze, but then shames them for using – monetizing – that very same erotic capital to make ends meet.

In defending the agency of women who choose pole work for economic mobility, *P.O.P.* challenges the prohibitionist characterization of erotic dancers as victims as well as the good girl–bad girl binary that roots it. The film's very title – *Power of Pussy* – draws on sex-positive feminism and saucily mocks the hypocritical conditions of patriarchy that urge women to conceal their sexuality (or performances of it) lest they be labelled "sluts." And while the dancers' entrepreneurship definitely caters to the male gaze, the documentary itself draws its strength from giving the male gaze the cold shoulder as it keeps returning to the economic imperative that drives these performers. Furthermore, *P.O.P.*'s portrayal of agential Black erotic dancers seems to imply that by staging lucrative shows within a supportive community, the members of the Snack Pack are working against the disadvantages they face in society. *P.O.P.* frames erotic dancing not as vice but as a job and an art form; it makes visible the existence of Black erotic dancers in a mediascape that has tended to overrepresent white strip culture; it portrays Black erotic dancers not as victims but as skilled, talented, smart, and self-possessed strivers driven by entrepreneurial gusto; and it represents the club as a space of symbiotic sisterhood wherein erotic dancers enjoy supportive friendships. In these ways, *P.O.P.* offers a refreshing new image of erotic dancers that repairs stereotypes. As Gigi says, "I want people to appreciate us, instead of holding us in a negative light. I got my confidence from dancing."

Magic City: The Glamour, Cash, and Aspiration

Magic City, a documentary commissioned by *GQ* in 2015 and directed by the celebrated creator Lauren Greenfield, received much acclaim when it was released on YouTube and was watched by millions. In her previous film, *The Queen of Versailles* (2012), Greenfield investigated the pursuit of the American Dream under neo-liberal capitalism, its elusive (and infrequent) attainment, and conspicuous consumption. At only twenty minutes, *Magic City* is a quick, lush look at erotic dancing, a whirlwind of music and moxie that dignifies dancers and their display work. The film features plenty of close-ups, unsurprising considering its funder, but Greenfield's camerawork is never voyeuristic. Her film is a compelling and dauntless portrait of hard-working women who hope to find on the stage a path to prosperity. At the same time, it points out the limits to erotic dancing as a sustainable way to achieve that dream.

Like *P.O.P.*, the eponymous *Magic City* takes place at Atlanta's bustling club and portrays the fertile interchange between aspiring rap artists and erotic dancers, who both share the goal of becoming wealthy and eminent. Greenfield's observational camerawork inside the club and her off-site interviews with hopeful rap stars and erotic dancers highlight the synergies between these two groups of enterprising performers. "The money's green, and this is what it's all about," says rapper Future in the opening scene, auguring the documentary's main themes: creative entrepreneurship and the pursuit of what one artist refers to as his "American Dream." For music artists, Magic City is an audition suite with a possible doorway to stardom. The DJs make or break careers: "If your record isn't playing in Magic City, it isn't cool in the streets," says one aspiring rapper. The erotic dancers perform to these potential hits and are instrumental in deciding whether a song sinks or soars. "The dancers are like the A & R [artists and repertoire] people. It's like Motown was in the seventies, with groups on every corner," one DJ explains, alluding to the community that produced the iconic sound in Detroit, "same in Atlanta, except it's rap."

Several now-prominent rap artists – including Future – were discovered at Magic City. Their stories inspire still-undiscovered artists to hustle under the club's glamorous mirror balls. Unlike these hopefuls, however, the dancers aren't seeking fame and fortune but simply a way to make ends meet. Virgo, in her twenties, describes growing up poor; Simone, the same age, is trying to save for college. *Magic City* frames the pursuit of money as the motivator of the music artist and dancer alike. In one scene, the manager of the club wryly notes, "It's chicken wing bones on the floor, cash everywhere, and money, the American Dream." A dancer named Secret says she made $15,000 in her first week on stage. Visually, the documentary features so many images of cash that it becomes a character unto itself and invites the viewer to imagine earning and spending such sums. Close-up shots lit by baby pink and violet footlights show the erotic dancers on stage as men throw wads of dollar bills, making clear that the earning, spending, and flaunting of cash is the engine that drives Magic City – and capitalism. At the end of the night, the dancers climb on stage in sequined bikinis to collect their cash, dragging heavy bags stuffed with the bills they scoop up. One dancer describes walking on thick piles of cash like "a plush carpet" as another hoists a cash-stuffed bag over her shoulder and jokes that she's "Santa Claus." Opulent panning shots of the stage covered in rugs of bills suggest a cushion against poverty. One erotic dancer climbs the pole, shakes her hair down, and wiggles her bum: "My money-making move," she explains. These sequences show off the women's bodies, but on their own terms, vibrating with the power and purpose of dancers who tactically use their bodies as tools, leaving no doubt that their work is entrepreneurship. "It's like a corporation," a dancer explains as the camera pans the stage covered in cash that is hers at the end of every night.

Apropos the personal portrait documentary form, which "stress[es] subjectivity and experience" and assigns "enduring worth to specific moments,"[74] *Magic City* uses rich, colour-saturated vignettes set inside the club to evoke opulence. Panning shots of the club's lush, jewel-toned interiors evoke aged liquor and velvet, leather and smoke, and suggest a world of opportunities for dancers and music industry hopefuls alike. The opening shots particularly showcase this panache, with *Magic City*'s elegant-looking white stucco exterior and neon pink sign whose sensual cursive spell out "Magic City" like a beacon. A white horse-drawn chariot drives by, followed by a BMW, suggesting the collision of old wealth and self-made prosperity. Taking us inside the club, the camera captures the velvet banquettes, gold-accented tables, and shiny floors as men in tailored tuxedos mingle and watch the dancers on the stage. Backstage, meanwhile, dancers up next prepare for the male gaze with cosmetics, costumes, clip-on locks, heels, and eyelashes – costumes of ideal femininity. With these images, *Magic City* suggests that erotic dancing is a world in which money is free-flowing and glamour ubiquitous.

But at a deeper level, *Magic City* suggests that there is subversive power in cannily using the male gaze and the appearance of submission for economic mobility, especially for women whose bodies have been historically objectified by racist discourses that enrich white hegemony. While the short film doesn't explicitly address white supremacy, nor how colonialism and slavery link to current racial, class, and gender inequalities, *Magic City* implies a particular power for Black erotic dancers in monetizing the male gaze. As Kimberly Foster writes, "for too long Black women have practiced a politics of containment wherein we have been instructed to conceal our bodies for fear that they will work in service of imperialist white supremacist capitalist patriarchy. But fear and shame do not encourage resistance."[75] The dancers in *Magic City* see their performances as tools, expressions of their ambition, and hedges against containment. As the dancer Diamond remarks, "Being average has never been an option for me. My goal is to become a bigger entertainer." One of the DJs adds: "The erotic dancers are the movie stars." But the documentary never loses sight of the purpose that drives these dancers every time they put heel to stage.

Despite its support of erotic dancers, *Magic City* questions whether the brass pole is a viable way out of low-paying jobs, professional dead zones, and double shifts that leave no time to see one's children. More than the other documentaries, it raises the possibility that few of the dancers in the club will leap from its stage to financial stability, let alone stardom. While the interview subjects in *Magic City* express typical visions of what "making it" would look like – nice homes, stable lives for their children, financial freedom – even these modest ideals don't match the reality of many dancers. The club manager suggests that the savviest dancers will earn as much as possible, as quickly as they can, and then "get out." Sadly, he says, some "get addicted to the pole." He ponders the divide between the fantasy of the American Dream in the club and the workaday reality of most dancers – and Americans: "People have a hard time separating reality from entertainment. But there is a line, a *thick* line."

While *Magic City* remains reserved on whether its dancers achieve a version of the American Dream or not, it does confirm the lavish lifestyles of the male DJs whose songs they dance to. In a later scene, a rising star DJ named Esco, who is about the same age as many of the dancers, takes the documentary crew to his home, a hilltop mansion with a glimmering topaz swimming pool and clear panoramic view of the Atlanta skyline. While the camera follows Esco around his impressive property, it never travels into the interiors of the dancers' homes, an elision that points to a gendered class division between Magic City's DJs and the dancers. Esco has connections to other powerful DJs, recording artists, and record company executives as well as an already lucrative career, but the erotic dancers still clock in every day, and their futures are uncertain. Intelligently, *Magic City* destigmatizes and dignifies the labour of erotic dancers yet suggests limits to this "empowerment." In one scene, an aspiring rapper throws dollar bills on a dancer who undulates below him. "It's not about money," he calls out over the music, "it's about power! I could throw this money on her ass and I don't even care! She doesn't even care! It's a rush."

In keeping with the personal portrait documentary form, *Magic City* doesn't critique the social power relations of this charged moment in which a man pays a woman to silently act out the role of compliant sexual object below him while he stands above her, holding the mic – and the money. However, it tacitly asks us to consider that perhaps such men are willing to support women in roles that draw on the rhetoric of sexual empowerment, but only if they do not contest the unequal balance of sexual power in the club, and in society. Nonetheless, these erotic dancers know *why* they're acting out these roles and what they're getting out of playing them, and that's the parting message of *Magic City*, a documentary that challenges the stereotype of erotic dancers as "sluts" or "hos," as lamented by Gigi, but makes clear that erotic dancing is not always a path to prosperity.

Afternoon Delight: Flipping Stripper Stigma … with Sapphic Love

The term "afternoon delight" entered our lexicon in 1976 through a song by Starland Vocal Band, whose sly coinage referred to an indulgent, probably secret, act of midday sex. *Afternoon Delight*, the 2013 film written and directed by Joey Soloway, has a few sweet tricks up its sleeve too. It tells the story of Rachel, a woman in her late thirties, who takes a trip to a strip club with her husband to try to rekindle their dull marriage. Instead, sparks fly when Rachel gets a lap dance from McKenna, a young performer who becomes Rachel's muse and, later, lover. By turns incisive, daring, and bold, the film is all about challenging stereotypes. While "Road Strip," *P.O.P.*, and *Magic City* validate the labour of erotic dancers by exploring their talent and hustles, along with the inequality between men and women in the strip club, *Afternoon Delight* takes up the feminist debate between prohibitionists, who argue that all sex workers are victims, and sex positivists (in this case erotic dancers), who say they choose their jobs. In the film, equally focused on work, desire, and division, a shaky allyship is staged through the unusual relationship between Rachel and the erotic dancer McKenna.

When the film opens, Rachel's life is *tidy*, but she feels crushed by the demands of conventional motherhood and is a blocked aspiring writer who spends her days doing banal volunteer projects at her son's school instead of writing. At home, she and her workaholic husband have lost their spark, and the trip to the erotic dancing club becomes a bit of a desperate attempt at rekindling it. Alas, the lap dance Rachel receives leaves her confused, aroused, and somehow feeling responsible for the young woman she assumes is a victim and hates her job. So, she returns the next day on the pretence of buying coffee at a nearby snack truck and befriends McKenna. When McKenna is later evicted, Rachel invites her to move in to her family's home.

The movie is, essentially, a send-up of *Pretty Woman*, where a middle-aged, upper-class man "rescues" a younger, working-class sex worker. While Rachel initially does try to "save" McKenna, *Afternoon Delight* is far from a fairy tale. By queering sex work's most famous Cinderella story, Soloway's film questions the prohibitionist credo to "save" sex workers as Rachel tries to shed her biases and assumptions about who erotic dancers are. The film is, at its roots, an astute critique of feminists who see themselves as saviours of "gullible lost girls," or of more benevolent sounding offers to "help" erotic dancers, the sex industry's most visible "victims," by handling them like fixer-uppers. As one journalist wrote of erotic dancers in the *Globe and Mail* not long ago, "I've never been into a strip club … [because] I'd likely end up talking the ladies into attending night school or walking my dog for a nominal fee."[76] While the feminist-as-saviour trope goes back to the nineteenth century, *Afternoon Delight* stops it in its tracks with its smart erotic dancer heroine who has no interest in walking a dog for a nominal fee.

Solway, who would go on to helm the TV show *Transparent* (2014–19), here channels Ellen Willis's critique of prohibitionists who marginalize sex workers by separating women into categories of respectability, just as nineteenth-century patriarchal society did. McKenna disdains the saviour mentality: "I hope you're not a Captain Save-a-Ho," she tells Rachel, after seeing the very different world in which she lives: an LA enclave where SUVs sit in front of two-car garages and lawns sparkle with bright green affluence. The film, by turns incisive and witty, personifies the sex wars with an almost-love-story that cuts through sectarianism and disrupts binary thinking on sex work. It does this through Rachel and McKenna's very different perceptions of sex work. With her assumptions about sex worker victimhood, Rachel represents prohibitionist feminism; with her pragmatism and sex positivity, McKenna embodies the empowerment and labour perspectives. Soloway develops their relationship brilliantly, turning neither woman into a caricature. Initially, Rachel sees McKenna as a charity case, and her reason for inviting her to move in is "to help her." Yet Rachel also revels in the carnal excitement of living vicariously through McKenna's subversive job and enmeshes herself into it by interviewing her for an article she is ostensibly going to write:

> RACHEL: So, you've been a sex worker … How long have you been doing … sex?
> MCKENNA: Two years. I started when I was twenty.
> RACHEL: You told me you were nineteen.
> MCKENNA: Yeah, I tell all my customers that. The barely legal thing – it turns them on.
> RACHEL: What does it mean to see other people as customers?
> MCKENNA: Doctors have customers, psychiatrists have customers, people that work in stores have customers. A lot of people in this world have customers.

While Rachel denies that she's a "Captain Save-a-Ho" – a male customer who self-appoints himself to rescue sex workers who don't want to be rescued – she privately does see herself as McKenna's "one opportunity to get out of being a sex worker." As a comfortably middle-upper-class woman, Rachel can't imagine why a woman would want or *need* to strip, and she assumes that McKenna must feel degraded by her job. Rachel's husband concurs: "Strip clubs are sad," he says, "they make me the opposite of horny. They make me angry." At the same time, Rachel, we later learn, is a sexual assault survivor, which colours her views on men's access to women's bodies, paid or not. In any case, from her place of economic privilege, she makes it her job to "save" and "rehabilitee" McKenna.

Afternoon Delight, in essence, is the story of an odd couple. It's funny and thought-provoking in equal measure. And its tension comes from the collision of the two women's assumptions about each other. McKenna sees Rachel as a thwarted woman. Rachel sees McKenna as a lost girl. Yet very quickly, it becomes clear that McKenna is happy and it's Rachel who needs saving – from her creatively dead, sensually bereft, intellectually disconnected life. Inspired by McKenna's stories, Rachel tells her husband that she's going to help McKenna straighten out her life by "setting up a blog … maybe we can co-write it," but this is just a pretence to transfuse her very stuck life with McKenna's carnal

Figure 2.2. Take a walk on the wild side: Rachel's (Kathryn Hahn) creativity and sexuality is catalyzed by her relationship with McKenna (Juno Temple), an erotic dancer, in *Afternoon Delight*.

energy, and pretty soon Rachel begins looking to McKenna as her muse and experiences an awakening: she stops going to dull PTA meetings, rediscovers her creative interests, starts writing, and masturbates for the first time in decades. One afternoon, McKenna rubs lotion on Rachel's feet, an initially sweet gesture that turns into more as McKenna unbuttons Rachel's nightgown. "Just breathe," McKenna whispers, as Rachel's eyelids flutter in a shock of blissful abandon.

As noted, *Afternoon Delight* flips the script on the commonest gender dynamic in the sex worker movie: that is, of an upper-class man deciding to rescue a working-class sex worker and "finding himself" along the way. *Pretty Woman* and scores of other films, from *Waterloo Bridge* to *WUSA* (1970) to

Leaving Las Vegas, are vehicles for male self-actualization in which the Mary Magdalene sex worker figure sacrificially dies for the hero – or marries him. *Afternoon Delight* scraps saviour and victim roles for a relationship between equals with no sacrifice on either side; McKenna gets a beautiful home to live in, a friendship, a spicy affair, and family comforts, while Rachel develops the capacity for self-examination and drops her narrow-minded notions about sex work. *Afternoon Delight* is also remarkable for being a rare sex worker movie portrayal of a lesbian affair. While the screen has traditionally turned sex workers into fantasies for the male gaze, *Afternoon Delight*'s camera captures McKenna through Rachel's sapphic lens and makes their affair – which is really of the mind, save for a few physical encounters – the film's locus of pleasure. In fact, aside from the lap dance for Rachel, McKenna never dances in the film, and she makes clear that her professional empowerment on the stage comes not from giving men visual pleasure but from the money she earns from them.

That said, no fairy tale takes shape in Soloway's film. In the end, Rachel is not strong enough to dismiss the social stigma attached to sex workers, publicly assert her sexual desires and queer identity, and truly support McKenna's choices. As sexual tension between Rachel and McKenna build, they kiss. Soon after, Rachel goes with McKenna on a "date" and plays the part of a sex worker. She pretends to be a call girl, dressing up and using a fake name, and watches McKenna have sex with a client, a turning point in which she begins to accept her own attraction to women. At the same time, seeing McKenna perform heterosexuality for pay makes Rachel realize how much of a performance her own marriage has been. While Rachel began trying to save McKenna, she is now living vicariously through her, wishing both to be her and to be *with* her. However, this fantasy has limits. Trouble arrives when Rachel's friends begin asking her about the nature of McKenna's job and probing Rachel's relationship with her. Too embarrassed to admit the truth, Rachel tells her friends that McKenna is her new live-in nanny, not a sex worker. Also, Rachel's fantasies of being a sex worker and her bisexual desires unsettle her, and so she begins distancing herself from McKenna and rejecting the intimacy they shared. Soon after, Rachel has a breakdown and accepts that she's been unhappy in her marriage for a long time. The film ends shortly after she (at least temporarily) separates from her husband, her future uncertain yet ambivalently hopeful. While the sex-worker-cum-love-story almost always gets tied up with a bow – death or marriage – *Afternoon Delight* ends with a proud sex worker who has changed not a whit.

Afternoon Delight deftly dismantles preconceived notions about erotic dancers. It illustrates Rachel's evolving perspective on sex work, showing her initial biases gradually melting away through a newfound understanding of her own desires and identity. Through McKenna's strength, self-determination, and influence on Rachel, the film challenges one-dimensional feminist characterizations of sex work. The stirring lap dance from an erotic dancer that kicks off the film is, finally, a spark for a whole life transformation. With this ending, *Afternoon Delight* rejects the prohibitionist feminist credo to "save" sex workers and dismisses the myth that erotic dancers are "victims." One of the film's final scenes illustrates this perfectly as Rachel drives past the club where she and McKenna met. We see McKenna outside, laughing and talking to friends. She looks like she's thriving. Rachel begins to slow down, in "Captain Save-a-Ho" mode once again, but then drives on, having realized – as we do – that McKenna doesn't need to be saved. *Afternoon Delight*, in the end, is a film about projection, where Rachel's fantasy of saving a sex worker ends with Rachel being saved *by* a sex worker from a life of inauthenticity.

Hustlers: Erotic Dancer Vigilantes

"Road Strip," *P.O.P.*, *Magic City*, and *Afternoon Delight* validate the labour of erotic dancers, yet with their focus on subjectivity – relationships and professional skills – they remain mostly mute on the unequal distribution of wealth in capitalism, and on how capitalism may propel some women into the erotic dance industry. This was especially the case during the hardscrabble years following the 2007–8 financial crisis, when erotic dancing was a necessity for some women. Lorene Scarafia's feature film *Hustlers* (2019) addresses this inequality in the form of a revenge story about erotic dancers who flirt with vigilantism by scamming Wall Street bankers.

Based on a true story and Jessica Pressler's award-winning *New York* magazine article with the bold title – "The Hustlers at Scores: A Modern Robin Hood Story: The Strippers Who Stole from (Mostly) Rich, (Usually) Disgusting Men and Gave to, Well, Themselves"[77] – *Hustlers* opens in 2005 as single mother Destiny, a twenty-something Chinese American, starts dancing at a Manhattan club under the wing of an older dancer named Ramona. Mutually exploitative relationships find a perfect diorama in the club, where everybody, from the banker to the dancer on his lap, is hustling – until the American – and then global – economic crisis destroy the dancers' business. Against a backdrop of foreclosures, evictions, spiking unemployment, and nosediving incomes, the dancers learn of how the greed of Wall Street bankers and CEOs perpetrated the crisis, then had their companies bailed out by the State, receiving massive severance packages while millions of working people were fired and lost their homes. They have a class awakening and come to see the world in two categories: the *haves* who make the economic decisions, and the *have-nots* who

Figure 2.3. Ramona (Jennifer Lopez) takes rookie dancer Destiny (Constance Wu) under her wing in *Hustlers*, an ode to female friendship meets the vigilante story meets the sex worker caper.

live out the consequences. In the film's opening, recently unemployed Destiny pawns her grandmother's necklace to buy groceries.

Ramona, also a working-class woman of colour, views her clients – Wall Street bankers – as "the motherfuckers at the top. CFOs, CEOs, corporate raiders." She devises a scam to "even the score" by fraudulently overcharging their credit cards. By targeting the financial industry's most visible ambassadors, Ramona, Destiny, and a group of dancers militantly, and later somewhat self-deceptively, rationalize their heist. Unlike the performers in the documentaries discussed earlier who see a future for themselves and try to dance their way to the American Dream, the dancers in *Hustlers* decide the American Dream is rigged and proceed to play by its rigged rules in pursuit of their own prosperity.

Hustlers is an unusual film about sex workers in how it replaces the velvet of accommodation – the tried-and-true formula of getting ahead by being sexy and *nice* – with a sledgehammer of revolt by way of a scam. It is, however, far from didactic. With its breathless script, distinctive characters, and lush camerawork that makes even sweat beads as photogenic as sequins, it is fun to watch. But beneath its slick pole moves it is an overt underdog vs. power elite story reminiscent of rare sex workers in films like *Baby Face*, where smart and sexy women claw their way to the top by using sex and scams to seize the privileges of the elite. Its self-confident script asks: If the richest men at the helm of corporations build fortunes by exploiting workers, making and often breaking rules with impunity, what would happen if the situation were reversed, and an underclass of women workers chose to exploit and profit off these men?

Hustlers portrays erotic dancers who commit crimes, but it does not present them as criminals. That is the film's rabbit trick. Against the virgin–whore binary, *Hustlers*' characters are complicated. So is the world in which they live. The film weaves their transgressions into a social context, and while never glorifying them, makes sense of them and garners the women empathy. This is in part due to the film's structure. Narrated by Destiny retrospectively as she gives an interview to a female journalist on the beat for *New York* magazine, *Hustlers* privileges an erotic dancer's point of view while making appeals for acceptance directly to the audience. Aware of how the news media perpetuates stereotypes about sex workers, Destiny, before the interview, tells the journalist: "I want to make sure you're not writing a story about strippers being criminals. Because that's what everybody does. I was doing a job as honest as anyone. It's things like these that add to the stigma and perpetuate it." As Destiny speaks to the journalist, the film speaks to the audience, asking us to suspend our own stereotypes about erotic dancers and to consider a more complex story.

Like "Road Strip," *P.O.P.*, *Magic City*, and *Afternoon Delight*, *Hustlers* challenges stereotypes by shifting the narrative and visual focus from the dancers' bodies on stage to their real lives off-stage. The opening scene does this brilliantly as it takes us backstage, where dancers – who range from their late teens to their forties – talk about their personal lives and kvetch about problems as they unwind from their sets, shedding their stage personae as fast as their spangled G-strings and dispelling myths about innate sexiness. As one dancer undresses, making no effort to be graceful, or cater to the male gaze, she holds her platform heel high above her head and proclaims, "I like being on my couch! In some natty pajamas, with my ice cream … no make-up, and for damn sure not with these on!" before tossing the absurd shoe that customers find sexy onto the floor. By delineating between her on-stage persona and her private self, she draws attention to the aesthetic labour for her on-stage role and her total disavowal of that labour once she is off the stage. In even more titillating scenes *Hustlers* dispels myths. Ramona's striptease, the aesthetic centrepiece of the film, establishes her unrepentant use of erotic capital. As she pole-spins and climbs to Fiona Apple's sultry hit "Criminal" – a song whose female narrator denies wrongdoing despite admonitions from her critics – Ramona's sexualized showboating twinned with the song's rebellious lyrics flouts the history of women's bodies being controlled and shamed by men and challenges the very criminalization of sex work. She is proud, not sorry, about using her erotic capital for economic mobility.

But far from a love letter to the erotic dancing industry, *Hustlers* shows how dancing is an option for some multi-racial working-class women in a precarious gig economy. The dancers have few economic privileges, and many are women of colour, including Destiny and Ramona, who are first-generation Chinese American and Puerto Rican American, respectively, and single mothers. Before dancing, both worked in other service industries, which were inflexible and exploitative. In Ramona's case, the gig economy, with its precarity puffed as "flexible opportunities," turns out to be hostile to her childcare responsibilities. When she asks for an earlier shift so she can pick her daughter up from school, her indifferent boss replies, "Am I the father? Then why should I give a shit? Isn't there a babysitter or nanny?" At the club, however, Ramona sets her own schedule and makes more money, without the indignity and hassle of begging her male boss for consideration. *Hustlers* tells similar stories of dancers who make rent, buy food, and pay college tuition with their dancing earnings. One dancer calls her gig "the green brick road." Tellingly, Destiny enters the club for the first time to the song "Control" by Janet Jackson, with its fierce lyrics about a woman taking control of her life. While *Hustlers* portrays erotic dancers as precariously employed, it does so without provoking pity, showing them using their erotic capital to earn money and care for their families. Erotic dancing may not be the best job, it argues, but it is a better job than what is on offer elsewhere.

Hustlers' inciting incident is the financial crash, in whose wake business in the club plummets. Ramona describes the dire situation: "2008 happened. People didn't want to spend money anymore." In montage, *Hustlers* shows dancers dejectedly circling the empty club while the few remaining customers parsimoniously nurse drinks and watch free stage shows instead of buying lap dances. In this way, the film is sympathetic to the link between poverty and the gig economy by showing how erotic dancers are precarious workers who lack the protections of standard employment relations. *Hustlers* spotlights how the owners of some erotic dance clubs take advantage of precarious performers during lean times, compromising their pay, safety, and satisfaction to increase their own profits. By continuing to charge dancers a fee to perform on stage, even when the club is empty, the owners compel the dancers to become sources of free entertainment in hopes of selling lap dance. But after having to "tip out" the hosts, the DJ, and house Mom, many of the dancers go home indebted to the owners. The club management's response to the financial crash is not to implement support for the dancers, but to remove "the cameras from the champagne room" to tacitly encourage the dancers to sell sexual services. Simultaneously, management hires newly immigrated "Russian models" who, according to Destiny, "give blowjobs for $300 a pop." While club management employs undocumented women to artificially drive prices down, matters are made worse by stingy customers opportunistically taking advantage of the desperation they sense on the part of the dancers by demanding lower cost "services."

Hustlers shows men treating Destiny and Ramona in degrading ways. The behaviour of some exemplify what Carole Pateman calls the "male sex right" to possess women's bodies as "commodities in the capitalist market."[78] While Destiny does not offer sexual services during a lap dance, a customer tells her not to be a tease (the very definition of a lap dance!) and commands her to stroke him. When she declines, he becomes aggressive. On top of these provocations, some customers, high on cocaine, are belligerent and unpredictable, insulting the dancers by drawing on degrading sex worker stereotypes about their so-called damaged psyches. Without other job prospects or management support, the dancers feel they have no choice but to cater to aggressive clients who believe that their wealth entitles them to treat erotic dancers with contempt.

In a less inventive film, this would be the end of the story – the confirmation that erotic dancers, despite finding some benefits in their jobs, are finally the victims of a sex industry in bed with patriarchy. But in *Hustlers*, this is where the script is flipped. When a wealthy customer promises Destiny $300 for a lap dance and then cheats her, leaving her with small change, Ramona and Destiny have an awakening. They connect this theft (of a working-class sex worker's payment for service by a wealthy man) to the exploitation of all working-class people under patriarchal capitalism. They see in their entitled customers the personification of arrogant investment bankers and Wall Street traders whose bullish tactics in part led to the financial crash. Speaking on behalf of all racialized, precarious women, Ramona laments how CEOs earned huge bonuses after the bailout, while ordinary working women like herself lost jobs and descended into poverty.[79] Ramona's class consciousness and analysis boils into anger and takes shape as a revenge plot that she outlines for the other dancers:

> We gotta think like these Wall Street guys. You see what they did to this country? They stole from the country. Hard-working people lost everything. And not one of these douchebags went to jail. That's what's paying for their blowjobs. The fucking retired firefighter's fund. We can't dance forever. What are you going to do? Go back to minimum wage? This game is rigged. It does not reward people who play by the rules. You either stand in the corner or get in the ring. They would do this anyway. Nobody gets hurt.

While erotic dancers in popular culture are typically portrayed as accommodating sex objects, and in the more progressive documentaries discussed earlier, as ambitious women who use "deep acting" to hide their true feelings and cater to male customers' demonstrated preference for niceness, *Hustlers*' erotic dancer characters not only feel but act on the most taboo female emotion: *anger*. In her now-classic work, *The Dance of Anger*, Harriet Lerner writes that women are often "discouraged from the awareness and forthright expression of anger," and that "women who openly express anger at men are especially suspect" and seen to be "unladylike."[80] But in *Hustlers*, female working-class anger against rich entitled men erupts. Angry that their business has been upended, disgusted by their treatment by men, and contemptuous of a system that allows the richest to become richer, the dancers concoct a scheme they consider retributive, a feat of DIY chemistry and method acting they call "fishing." In short, it works like this: posing as single women out on the town, they target rich men in upscale bars, get them drunk, take them to their club, drug them with a mixture of ketamine and MDMA, and defraud their credit cards. When the men awaken from their stupors they are, save for some mild headaches, unscathed – that is, until they check their credit card statements.

In scenes that combine the drug-making imagery of *Breaking Bad* with the textured close-ups of The Food Network, *Hustlers* shows the dancers building a well-oiled heist machine. They keep meticulous records, beautify themselves to catch the "biggest fish," and cook blue crystals of MDMA on a baking sheet in Ramona's kitchen, drugging themselves first to figure out the perfect dose that will inhibit men but not harm them. Eventually, as their heist becomes more profitable, they hire other dancers on a freelance basis, train them, and, like a corporation, rake in most of the profit. Destiny, the moral compass of the film, expresses misgivings as their thefts mount, but Ramona insists that the swindled money is reparation. While sceptical of Ramona's questionable form of justice, Destiny takes comfort in the idea that their marks are so rich that the sums they extort won't be noticed, and she is swept up in the delight of suddenly seeing a balance in her bank account after a life of poverty.

How do the dancers persist with their scheme? In a clever twist on the impact of stigma, *Hustlers* shows how the women's heist succeeds in part because they functionalize the stigma of sex work by *reversing* it. "Nobody is going to know," Ramona says of their scheme. "What? Are they going to say 'I spent $5,000 at a strip club'?" In the traditionally stigmatizing erotic dancer tale, sex workers ooze shame, hide their work, and live smaller lives in fear of exposure and public humiliation. In *Hustlers*, however, they can sustain their scheme for so long because none of their marks go to the police, given that doing so would expose them to scrutiny and moral consternation, especially married men with children in gated communities. *Hustlers* thus shows the women using their stigmatized status as a shield. By committing their crimes from within the taboo space of the club, they achieve temporary impunity, not unlike the bankers who hid their exploits within an opaque banking system.

As a title, *Hustlers* sets the stage for an exploration of the thin line dividing business and crime under capitalism and suggests that practices defended by corporate capitalism's doctrines would be outright criminal in civic life. In a blunt, sometimes cartoonish way, it asks what the difference is between the hustle of bankers who sell complex financial products and the hustle of erotic dancers who also sell intangible products – dances, smiles, affection, and attention – with unpredictable outcomes. "You're just another deal to them. And that's all they are to you. It's business. And it's a more honest transaction than anything else they did that day," Ramona tells Destiny. To reinforce the parallels between hustlers, the film intercuts scenes of dancers on the stage with traders on the Dow Jones floor to question the difference between one hustler who society reviles and another it venerates. According to the *Cambridge Dictionary*, the word "hustler" has three unique definitions: a person who seizes opportunities through calculated ingenuity; a person who manipulates for her own gain; or a sex worker. *Hustlers*' dancers could be described by all three definitions, and the bankers by two, and that is what makes the story so rich. As Ramona sums up:

> There's really nothing I can say to make sense of what went down. But everybody's hustling. This city, this whole country, is a strip club. You got people tossing the money and people doin' the dance.

But what is vexing about *Hustlers*, ultimately, is how its dancers attain empowerment by aping the crony capitalist practices of the men they stiff. Ramona and Destiny's swindling of male bankers is rooted in a critique of capitalism, but rather than address capitalism through political action, they Frankenstein their antagonism into a scheme they pass off as a feminist strategy while the audience wonders how or if it advances feminism for the 99 per cent. In this regard, *Hustlers* embodies "post-feminism," or feminism's collusion with neo-liberalism, in its emphasis on rugged individualism in the marketplace as opposed to coordinated collective political action by and for the majority of women.

To compete with the men they loathe, the dancers emulate the very behaviour of these men. They take on the merciless tactics of their Wall Street customers, ultimately using a bait and switch – with chemicals, not financial instruments – to profit. In this way, the film asks the viewer to consider if there is a difference between a hustler with an MBA and a hustler in a G-string. Both are salespeople who sell intangibles in a world of capitalist greed run amok. But by the end of *Hustlers*, following the real-life story, the men of Wall Street get back to business, while the women who hustle get arrested, charged with fraud, and dispossessed of their earnings. Destiny pleads guilty in exchange for testifying against Ramona, thus breaking their feminist solidarity. Ramona, meanwhile, gets five years of probation and sixteen weekends at Rikers Island. As justice is served according to the rule of law, the film ends with a pang, and it is this denial of a happy ending that gives *Hustlers* its scrappy power, its insight into the dignity of the women doing the dance and also the inequality that drives them.

Heels Too High, Night Too Long: The Limits of Erotic Capital

"Road Strip," *P.O.P.*, *Magic City*, *Afternoon Delight*, and *Hustlers* convey new, positive, and destigmatizing images of sexual entrepreneurs who draw on their erotic capital as a strategy to make a living and climb the economic ladder. They suggest that erotic dancing is a craft, an empowering subversion of compulsory female docility, a way of capitalizing on men's entitlement to look at women as sex objects, and a viable career and/or stepping stone for women who are not born with the privilege of other forms of capital. They remind viewers that erotic dancers are hard-working mothers, students, friends, and dynamic people, not victims or objects. At the same time, these films' relative muteness on the limits of erotic capital as an economic strategy warrant some exploration.

First, these stories perpetuate the idea that a woman's primary value in the market lies in her being sexually attractive to men.[81] Of course, this value is both fleeting and shaped by extrinsic social factors from age to matching up with beauty ideals associated with youth.[82] Erotic dancers start losing whatever erotic capital they've cultivated quickly, giving a dancing career a short expiration date. While the films suggest this limit, they resist scrutinizing an industry in which every worker's value begins to plummet from her debut. Nor do they address how difficult it can be for dancers to shift from the stage to other jobs. The story of life after erotic dancing is an important one taken up by the reality TV series *Beyond the Pole*, which takes place entirely off stage, but the show unfortunately failed to attract an audience and was cancelled after two seasons.

Moreover, these films skirt the well-documented racism within the erotic dancing industry. True, the portrayal of successful Black erotic dancers in *P.O.P.* and *Magic City* challenges their historical absence in popular culture and the prohibitionist notion that the sex industry is totally pernicious for women of colour. But these depictions might lead one to assume that we live in an age of inclusive, safe, and lucrative spaces for Black erotic dancers, even though that is not really the case. In 2007, for example, a Houston erotic dancing club was sued by the US Equal Employment Opportunity Commission after asking Black waitresses and dancers to stay home when a high-spending, racist customer was due to arrive. In 2021, dancer in Washington, DC, sued her club for frequently and unjustly turning her away upon arrival for her shifts. This was particularly distressing as she often spent up to three hours in preparatory aesthetic labour, only to be told that there were already "'too many Black girls working' that night."[83] This not only wasted her time but also caused her financial hardship and psychological distress. Some clubs even forbid DJs from playing rap or hip hop music, a tactic purportedly used by racist managers to disincline Black customers from visiting.[84] Because of the persistence of racism in the industry, Black women and women of colour frequently work harder but receive less respect and lower pay.[85]

Furthermore, these films and documentaries at times portray erotic dancing as a solution to the low wages, gendered wage gap, and lack of state support for working-class women, especially single mothers. While the dancers on screen seem generally pleased with their work, supplementing low wages earned elsewhere in the service economy with dancing is a necessity for others off screen, making the empowerment of erotic dancing appear less promising compared to the benefits and steady pay of full-time jobs, scarce as they are in the gig economy.[86] Moreover, these narratives often resist class inequality through neo-liberal "common sense" in how "we govern the self," rather than through collective feminist struggles.[87] Similarly, just as the theory of erotic capital prioritizes "self-improvement" over critiquing "systemic power relations,"[88] these dancers are often portrayed as trying to cope with the world rather than seeking to change it.

Of course, there are collective solutions to the problems in erotic dancing that these works highlight. The beacon documentary *Live Nude Girls Unite!* (2000), which received less mainstream circulation than the films discussed in this chapter, chronicles the struggles to form the first-ever labour union for erotic dancers at San Francisco's Lusty Lady in the 1990s. *Live Nude Girls Unite!* places collective action alongside sex-positive feminism, creating a valuable bridge between sex worker labour organizing and neo-liberal "valorization of personal power through sexuality."[89] In many ways, the documentary prefigured the organizing efforts of erotic dancers today, who are mobilizing with increasing strength. For example, in 2022, performers at the Star Garden Topless Dive Bar in Los Angeles went on strike after club managers failed to respond to a petition demanding increased safety measures and an end to racist practices within the club.[90] While the films and documentaries in this chapter are not activist in this sense, mum as they are on a politics capable of confronting capitalism's reigning neo-liberal ideology, they do more than just entertain; they engage in a subtle yet vibrant form of resistance by shifting the perspective to the personal stories of erotic dancers as seen through their own eyes, both on and off stage.

In doing so, they chip away at stereotypes about erotic dancers that have been portrayed on screen since the turn of the twentieth century, starting in films, then in talk shows, and later in video games – caricatures of female helplessness marked by stereotypes and eroticized violence. In stark contrast, "Road Strip," *P.O.P., Magic City, Afternoon Delight*, and *Hustlers* showcase the labour, talent, skill, tenacity, and resilience of erotic dancers, implicitly connecting them to a history of burlesque and the women who found a way on stage of leveraging their erotic capital for class mobility. While these portrayals might seem apolitical in the strictest capital "p" sense of the word, their contribution lies in enriching our understanding of the complexities of dancers' experiences in personal stories of climbing, if not to the American Dream, then at least towards something better than they had before.

3 Massage Parlour Mothers on Prime Time: How the Fallen Woman Became a Mompreneur on *The Client List*

If I could make a movie about sex work, I would love to weave a tapestry that really shows everything ... because that's how I feel about it ... how it helped my life. How it helped me.... How it helped me with my son.
– Michelle, massage parlour worker

Mothers involved in sex work [have had] their lives, perspectives, material conditions, and voices ... neglected and ignored for far too long.
– Rebecca Bromwich and Monique Marie DeJong[1]

Success [under neo-liberalism] is defined as facing obstacles with resilience, initiative, and creativity, one's aspirations being "limited" only by one's own hunger, drive, passion, and execution.
– Catherine Rottenberg[2]

In the winter of 2012, soon after the word "mompreneur" entered the English dictionary and unemployment in the US hit 9 per cent, a plucky billboard appeared high above Sunset Plaza in Los Angeles. It pictured actress Jennifer Love Hewitt wearing an impish smile and a lacy leather bustier, while male mannequins clad in business suits dangled precipitously as if risking their lives in their lusty climb towards her. The billboard was for Lifetime's new series *The Client List*, and the press release that followed promised a show "in line with [the network's] commitment to bringing viewers envelope-pushing content." That pledge, along with the show's tag line – "simply irresistible" – certainly primed viewers for an R-rated spectacle of raunch and risk. But when the series aired a few weeks later, viewers met heroine Riley Parks, whose main interests were not in scandal or sex but rather the business of sex work and mothering. For two seasons, *The Client List* followed Riley – massage parlour entrepreneur by day, super mom by night.

Figure 3.1. The billboard advertising *The Client List* promised raunch and risk. The show delivered much more, with a story about a sex worker mother struggling during the financial downturn.

While the show's pilot brought in an ample 1.2 million viewers,[3] topping the TV movie that inspired it, male reviewers approached it like a wet T-shirt contest. *Variety* lauded Jennifer Love Hewitt's relatability, "no small feat with that body,"[4] while *Slate* predicted that the viewer's husband would "find himself mildly titillated by … Riley's cleavage."[5] The *New York Daily News* summed it up as "delicious trash."[6] To be sure, the show's many plunging teddies, bouffant hairdos, and occasional soap operatic writing made it easier to pink-slip, but in doing so, critics missed what was historic about *The Client List*: it was the first major network prime-time series to feature a sex worker mother heroine. A figure of ill-repute – known as the fallen woman – the sex worker mother has long lived in the shadow cast by her counterpart, the idealized mother, the latter linked to asexuality, while the former is scorned and seen as incapable of mothering. But on *The Client List*, based on real-life events, the so-called fallen woman leaves the shadows and drives a minivan to T.J. Maxx on a streak of reinvention as a sexual entrepreneur.

Sex work and motherhood are rarely spoken of in the same breath, but upwards of 60 per cent of sex workers are mothers.[7] Sex worker mothers, assumed to be harming their children and incapable of mothering, have been roundly scorned throughout history,[8] their outlaw status traceable to the virgin–whore dichotomy and its division of women into categories of "respectability." This binary deepened in the nineteenth century when public discourse, novels, and art took up the fallen woman with a passion and plotted onto her one of two ends: death or religious redemption. While fallen women may seem part of a distant past, a woman's sexuality continues to be a defining feature of her perceived fitness for motherhood, which explains why sex worker mothers are among the most stigmatized of all women and sex workers.

The Client List, the story of single mothers who become massage parlour entrepreneurs during the financial crisis of 2007–8, challenges this stigmatization, offering a new lens through which to view sex work and motherhood. What is especially interesting, though, is how the film and TV series diverge. While the film ultimately gilds the virgin–whore binary, the series challenges it by reconfiguring the fallen woman into a massage parlour entrepreneur – a "mompreneur." In doing so, it posits harmony between the sex worker and the mother, sheds light on her struggles, and rallies for her rights. It also introduces the business of transactional sex without moral judgement, taking an intimate look at one woman's enterprising hustle and the connections between it and the gig economy. At the same time, the series makes what Sharon Hays calls "intensive mothering"[9] the sex worker mother's price of admission into society, and choice, individualism, entrepreneurship, and Victoria's Secret push-up bras her main tools for grabbing at the brass ring. It also leaves out the story of how one in every two new businesses in the US fails and how 41 per cent of single mother-led families live below the poverty line.[10] Together, both the film and the series probe our deepest biases about mothering, sex, and respectability.

I begin this chapter with an overview of the massage parlour industry within its historical framing to establish a context for *The Client List*'s representation of this line of sex work. I then move on to explore popular culture's historic portrayal of the massage parlour, as well as motherhood, to clarify what makes *The Client List* a novel representation of both. With this in place, I move on to examine *The Client List* film, showing how it takes up prohibitionist and patriarchal ideas, which the series, with style and seriousness, would go on to dismantle.

Contexts: In the Bawdy Rub

To understand the significance of *The Client List*'s massage parlour mother we need to look back at the massage parlour, the fallen woman, and popular culture about both. Massage parlours are in-call establishments where attendants sell nude massages and manual masturbation. Established in the US for over 100 years,[11] they grew in number and popularity in the early 1970s when returning GIs who had enjoyed massage on furlough in Asia brought the demand back with them.[12] The massage parlour workers who "stroke, knead, vibrate," as the *Village Voice* euphemistically reported in 1972,[13] existed in a legal grey zone between licit entertainment and illicit vice; major North American cities licensed the establishments in which they worked but not the sexual services they sold. That said, the carnal poetry of the parlours' very names left little doubt as to their offerings, from Lady Strawberry, Delilah's Den, Neptune's Health Spa, and Charlie's Angels dotting Toronto's Yonge Street to Sugar Shack, Honey Haven, Danish Parlour, Love Machine, and Sensitivity Meeting Room in New York's Times Square, their facades painted with Jayne Mansfield-esque blondes and bubbly carnival lettering advertising "$10 Completes."[14] This laissez-faire approach changed in the mid-1970s, however, as political campaigns built on "tough on crime" agendas placed parlours in their crosshairs,[15] leading to mass shutdowns, while conservative news media stoked public outrage by framing massage parlour attendants as flashy ne'er-do-wells and threats to the community. In one national magazine story from 1977, the writer's disdain for parlour workers practically drips off the type: "Call her Josie. In the work-a-night world of commercial sex real names don't matter.... Josies ... run to a type: young, undereducated, flashily attractive, greedy, and, like most whores ... lazy as sin."[16] The news media's stereotyping of parlour workers "served to mobilize a moral panic"[17] and paved the way for more demeaning images in popular culture.

Massage parlour workers in movies came in three types: promiscuous bon vivants, dodgy villains, and buxom victims. *Mme. Olga's Massage Parlor* (1965), a black-and-white low-budget thriller, combined all three in a lurid tale about a wolfish parlour madam who tortures her female workers "in a variety of brutal ways" – as the poster promised – and conjured a hellish workspace ruled by sadomasochistic relations between women (read: no feminist solidarity here!). Released shortly after *The Feminine Mystique* (1963), Betty Friedan's call for female emancipation from domesticity, the film's "machines that destroy the very soul of beautiful women" and "innocent, helpless girls" in chastity belts reflected a real fear of women's sexual agency and celebrated their containment. *Massage Parlor Murders!* (1973), persisting with themes of women's victimhood, told the story of massage parlour workers in Times Square being terrorized by a serial killer who's never apprehended, reducing these workers to mere prey. With no less nudity, the soft-core cuckolding fantasy *Massage Parlor Wife* (1975) tracked an unfaithful wife moonlighting as a massage parlour doyenne and ended with a ménage à trois. But perhaps the most widely seen massage parlour worker was in Stanley Kubrick's 1987 war epic, *Full Metal Jacket*, in which a Vietnamese body rubber says to an American GI, "Me so horny, me love you long time, baby. Me sucky sucky, me love you too much," her only lines in the film that would go on to become an oft-repeated racist punchline.[18]

How the Fallen Woman Became a Mompreneur on *The Client List*   89

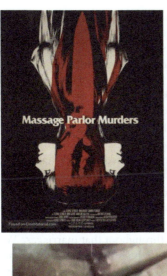

Figure 3.2. In the 1970s, massage parlours stirred moral outrage, influencing popular culture focused on violence or happy endings, featuring two types of sex workers: the compliant and the dead.

While these salacious images banked dollars for movie studios, they papered over the stories of ordinary massage parlour workers from Toledo to Times Square working under the crush of stigma behind beaded curtains in scruffy second-floor firms fronted by red neon. Women whose shoulders ached and who got blisters from shifts worked in heels, women who packed sandwiches to save money, counted cash on break, loved the big tippers, loathed the cheapskates, and rode the bus home exhausted yet relieved to have not seen a cop, the cloying smell of body oil baked into their skin. Women who chose this work for its income and flexibility, its power to buy shoes, fruit, and roller skates. Yet, the films of this era obscured this labour and erased the fact that massage parlour workers were also mothers.[19]

Mother work and sex work have long been considered antithetical, yet they are both constructed in a one-dimensional way "that re-inscribes and maintains a patriarchal social order."[20] Traditionally, a woman's valuation rested upon her virginity at marriage and her fidelity throughout that marriage.[21] Women who were seen to transgress this expectation, be it through desire or rape or coercion, were stigmatized as "defiled" and ostracized.[22] In the nineteenth century, as the Industrial Revolution elevated a new middle class that defined social roles ever more by gender, discourses of ideal motherhood enshrined her into the public imaginary as the sacrificing asexual angel in the house – associating respectable motherhood with the domestic sphere and sexual purity – while casting the disreputable "whore" as her opposite, the apocryphal anti-mother. As Lucy Bland notes, "Behind the veneer of the dominant nineteenth-century ideal woman – the domestic 'angel in the house' – lurked the earlier representation of sexualized femininity: the Magdalene behind the Madonna."[23] This binary was fortified by the field of medicine, and married women were commonly advised by physicians to abstain from sex for all but one day a month, while husbands were encouraged to have sex every four days, guidance that tacitly sanctioned men's associations with sex workers, although they "affected in public to deplore" these women.[24]

This binary between respectable mothers and disreputable sex workers also reinforced patriarchal capitalism by enshrining economically dependent women into the invisible economy of the home as unwaged workers. By denouncing her opposite, the economically independent "whore" – later softened into the fallen woman – patriarchal discourses entreated women to strike what Carole Vance has aptly described as "the traditional bargain women were forced to make with men: if women were 'good' (sexually circumspect), men would protect them; if they were not good, men could violate and punish them."[25] The virgin–whore binary foreclosed on the possibility of women – but especially mothers – being complex individuals with libidinous *and* nurturing drives – to be, in short, complex people equal to men. In *The Dialectic of Sex* (1970), Shulamith Firestone sums up the virgin–whore binary well as it relates to motherhood: "Those who resemble the mother are 'good,' and consequently one must not have sexual feelings towards them; those unlike the mother ... are sexual and therefore 'bad.' Whole classes of people, e.g. prostitutes, pay for their lives with this dichotomy."[26]

The dichotomy between sex worker and mother finds its most potent figuration through the fallen woman, who can be traced to the earliest documents in English and denotes an unmarried woman who becomes pregnant out of wedlock, violating the virgin–whore dichotomy. Although Victorian novels and paintings treated her sympathetically,[27] she seldom rejoined society, lost and almost never regained custody of her children, and frequently died from venereal disease or suicide, her death symbolically reinforcing the virgin–whore dichotomy and the impossibility of a sex worker raising a child. As Joanna Brewis and Stephen Linstead note, drawing on the earlier work of Maggie O'Neill, the death of the fallen woman served to "draw boundaries around 'respectable' female sexuality as well as demonize prostitutes."[28] The fallen woman reinforced patriarchal prohibitions against women's sexual expression and illustrated the consequences of women's sexual agency. Fallen women were sexual deviants, the foil to the asexual mother.

Today, the legacy of the fallen woman is observable in the figure of the sex worker mother, who is roundly characterized as an unfit parent and, like the fallen woman, has her sexuality scrutinized as evidence of her unfitness for parenting.[29] A 2016 Salvation Army fundraising campaign poster epitomizes this enduring taboo against sex worker mothers. The ad featured a black-and-white image of a boy sitting on the ground in a filthy-looking room, his knees pulled to his chest and his head bowed in dejection. The caption read as follows:

> I know now that my mother was a prostitute. She'd bring "clients" to our house and lock me in the bathroom while she did what she did. I hated that bathroom. There was no way out. The window was busted but up way too high. The toilet stinking of strangers. One day I found Mum's old razor. Tried it against my skin. Pressed harder. Until the blood came ... I was 5.

Backlash from sex workers' rights organizations eventually got the ad pulled, but its messaging spoke volumes about the stigmatized status of sex worker mothers – namely, the assumption that they neglect and abuse their children – and how, as parents and people, they routinely see their "lives, perspectives, material conditions, and voices" demonized and dismissed, which has life-changing consequences.[30] Sex worker mothers are more likely to have their children removed from their care, even when no evidence of neglect or abuse is found, and within clinical settings often conceal or minimize their involvement in sex work for fear of losing custody of their children.[31] Sex workers who do lose custody of their children often experience guilt, depression, and grief, and many report their children feeling ashamed of their work – "losing respect for them" – and even cutting off relations with them.[32] In a tragic irony, the sex work women engage in to provide for their children is often used against them as evidence of their negligence and inability to mother.

Author and sex worker mother Juniper Fitzgerald learned this first-hand after publishing the first-ever children's book about sex work in 2017, *How Mamas Love Their Babies*. Called "wonderful" by MSN and "a political statement that flows from passion and love" in a starred *Publishers Weekly* review, the public reaction to the book was nonetheless swift, fierce, and condemning. Fitzgerald describes how her

> desire to destigmatize sex-working mothers came at a price: I received death threats, strangers have called Child Protective Services on me … [and] I'm not alone – the juxtaposition of sex work and parenting makes a lot of people uneasy.… This punishing stigma will continue to flatten the full personhood of *all* mothers until we eradicate the racist, sexist, ableist, classist, and heteronormative cultural perceptions of what constitutes the perfect mother.[33]

With few exceptions, popular culture helped maintain the binary between "good" asexual mothers and "bad" libidinous sex workers. In the mid-twentieth century, idealized mothers on big and small screens, such as June Cleaver, Lucie Arnaz, and Edith Bunker, had the sex drives of lampshades, while their husbands flaunted theirs giddily. Meanwhile, sex worker mothers were painted as unmaternal wenches, ranking somewhere between witches and homewreckers in terms of likeability. This binary loosened in the later twentieth century, when sexy mothers started appearing on screen, but they were often divested of maternal qualities and treated as comic relief, like Peggy Bundy on *Married … with Children* who pranced around in leopard leggings and talked openly about sex but was so bad a cook that she bungled even the Jell-O to a roaring laugh track. Such characters reified the virgin–whore binary by making clear that a woman cannot be sexual *and* maternal – and if she tries, she's apt to fail at both.

Today, however, there is a new frankness around maternal sexuality in popular culture. As Elizabeth Podnieks argues, mothers on TV and in film negotiate new "roles and identities."[34] Reality television, ever pressed for more extreme subjects, embraces unconventional motherhood through shows such as *16 and Pregnant*, *Jon & Kate Plus 8*, and *Pretty Wicked Moms*, whose exaggerated, sometimes depraved, extreme formula pivots on calling out bad mothers and approving of self-sacrificing ones. Shows featuring mothers who are "unabashedly sexual, idiosyncratic and seriously deleterious in her caretaking skills" are rife,[35] while series like *Weeds* and *Workin' Moms* feature mothers who buck traditional images of chaste domesticity while competently caring for their children. At the same time, popular culture portrays massage parlour workers non-judgmentally in films such as *Feel* (2006) and *Inherent Vice* (2014), and documentaries such as *Happy Endings?* (2009). *The Client List* embodies all of the conflicts bound up in motherhood and sex work in a story about a mother who finds security, control, and a source of quiet pride in her taboo work – at least until she becomes Texas's most notorious sex worker.

Beauty Queen to Body Rubber: *The Client List*'s Fallen Woman

The Client List (2010), the first prime-time TV movie about a massage parlour mother, launched with a splashy ad campaign combining the taboo of family values and sex. On the poster, star Jennifer Love Hewitt clutches a leopard print duvet, her smile, like the Mona Lisa's, as inscrutable as the film's tag line: "A mother will do anything for her family." Given the setting – a small town in Texas – and the taboo of the storyline, the film seemed poised for a Petri-dish fallen woman story, but *The Client List* is a craftier three-for-one. That is, three films for the price of one, fit together like a Mrs. Potato Head toy: the feet of a fallen woman, the body of a neo-liberal Southern belle, and the brain of a born-again preacher. To be fair, none of this emerges until the third act, which is part of the film's appeal. With its character-driven narrative told from a sex worker mother's point of view, it is a seemingly sympathetic story of a mother's resolve to save her family at any cost. So, when we see the price she pays for it, we almost believe she deserves it – and then remember it's not 1844.

The story, like all melodramas, begins behind a white picket fence. The Hortons seem to have it all: husband Rex works in the booming construction industry, and Samantha, blessed with beauty and intelligence, adores being a stay-at-home mother to their two children. But when the financial downturn hits, Rex loses his job, leading to their house being remortgaged and then sent into foreclosure, forcing Samantha into the blighted job market just as the Great Recession starts rumbling. Samantha, a registered massage therapist, applies to many positions without success before finally securing a gig at Kind Touch Health Spa, a strip mall nail and beauty shop. Not long after, she discovers it's actually a brothel, but she decides to keep the job anyway – "for my family," Samantha says. The film, based on a true story, captures in this premise how job loss compels mothers into sex work, but not without anxiety.

The panic attack Samantha has on her first day of work feels raw and authentic. Coping with the stress of her new job, including figuring out how to handle customers and manage her own feelings while fearing everything that could go wrong, is a common, anguishing experience for novice sex workers. Alas, the film doesn't explore this. Instead, Samantha's anxiety is linked to her religious beliefs, as symbolized by the bobble-head angel toy on her truck's dashboard to whom she confesses her sins each night as she drives home from the parlour. Her *mea culpas* reassure the audience that she does feel bad about sex work, and her contrition distances her from the venal siren (who *chooses* sex work and enjoys it, flouting family values). Thus, *The Client List* gets off the ground with sex work streaked with tears of maternal sacrifice.

Despite its fallen woman set-up, the film's first act, its most sensitive, portrays something that was once left off screen: sex workers who are friends with each other. The film traces Samantha professionalization with her colleagues in intimate scenes. The women, without savings or family wealth to fall back on, share an economic motivation: some chose sex work over low-paying gigs; others, facing unemployment, like Samantha, took the best they could get; others still are moonlighting in sex work while waiting for passion projects to pay off. Jacie, the parlour's owner and an aspiring novelist, has done the math: "Sex work pays a whole lot better than writing!" Tanya is building her tattooing business, and Sugar, at nineteen, is buying vocal lessons she hopes will help land her a spot on *American Idol* and launch a singing career. They agree that massage parlour work is "better than waitressing," their most likely alternative, since it is better paying and more reliable seeing that people's spending habits on taboo activities often remain stable during economic slumps.[36] Thus, Samantha's colleagues are confident about their job security: "We were worried when the economy tanked, but it turns out that this is the most recession-free business!" As Samantha rises on wings of entrepreneurship, the film frames sex work as a problem-free industry. So, by the time the fairy-tale flick of sex work is mentioned – Jacie announces, "My favourite movie is *Pretty Woman!*" – the film's second act is well underway, leaving the fallen woman story in the dust.

Part two of *The Client List* is about transformation as Samantha becomes a parlour pro, and Love Hewitt is so likeable as an actor that she can make even folding small white towels look interesting. The massage parlour is portrayed as a well-greased enterprise where women exercise free choice, enjoy their work, and reap financial rewards without incurring any physical stress or suffering any stigma. Yet, as it legitimizes the parlour's lock-in-key fit with capitalism, the film also treats sexual labour coyly, skirting the issue of what Samantha actually *does* in those frangipani-scented rooms. It is a far cry from the *Texas Monthly* article on which the film is based, which satisfyingly zeroed in on the economy of an enterprise where handies are handled with Taylorized efficiency:

> The madams rented out the massage rooms to the girls between the hours of ten and six for $30 per half-hour session, with the prostitutes keeping any tips for "extras" (oral sex was $60, straight sex was $100, and anal sex was $150, while other combinations and varieties were negotiated on a case-by-case basis). "Out-calls,"

since they were riskier, were more expensive, ranging from $150 per half hour to $1,000 for the whole night.[37]

Just as Samantha's sexual activities at the spa remain elusive, so too do the socio-economic factors that first led her to sex work, and foreclosure on her home (unethical lending practices like subprime mortgages) and a job search in the desertified economy (the economic crash of 2007–8) fade away like flaws under pore-perfecting BB cream as the movie pays tribute to the post-feminist ideal of the sexy body as the cure for social problems.

As we have seen, Catherine Hakim's theory of erotic capital argues that sex workers leverage their allure tactically using femininity as an economic strategy. But *The Client List* makes Samantha's sexiness intrinsic to her identity, establishing a binary between the sexes in which men are valued for their stoicism and women for their looks and loquaciousness. Samantha believes her former "Miss Bixby" high school beauty queen status gives her entitlements: "In America … a girl this pretty ain't supposed to be poor!" When her six-year-old daughter balks at getting braces, she says: "Your Mama's gonna tell you something true: no matter what a girl chooses to be, life is far easier for a girl if she is pretty!" Women characters regularly link their appearances to their limited life options: "My Mom says I was too fat to get a husband!" and "My Mom said I was too pretty to be a lawyer!" The film thus explains Samantha's success as a massage parlour worker through her "feminine" qualities alone, validating a woman's self-definition through sex appeal to men as the apogee of empowerment.

Consequently, the film goes fuzzy when it comes to showing the actual labour – the skills that massage parlour workers possess, like business savvy, intelligence, humour, and patience – and treats sex work instead as a carefree, sartorial adventure, with scenes of a lingerie-clad Samantha massaging her clients' carved obliques. Occasionally, Samantha plays therapist, yet even this emotional labour is minimized as an expression of her natural female compassion as a mother (at one point she even bakes her client cookies *on her own time*). In fact, Samantha's life revolves around being nurturing to men as a sex object and being nurturing to her kids as a mother, these roles being depicted as a woman's most natural. And while it's refreshing to see sex workers and clients transacting without the animus presumed by prohibitionists, Samantha's clients – Calvin Klein model types – suggest that sex workers only sell services to men they are attracted to in real life. (In one ethnography, massage parlour workers described their clients as "ordinary schmucks."[38]) Meanwhile, all of the fun Samantha's having strips her of her saving grace as a sex worker mother: her martyrdom.

The transition from neo-liberal success story lacquered with maternal pride into the film's third act occurs when Samantha takes herself on a mini shopping spree. It is a seemingly minor plot point, but for the fallen woman an elephantine infraction. As Russell Campbell reminds us, the only socially permittable sex worker mother type embodies "altruistic devotion to others … [and] engages in prostitution not to benefit herself."[39] As quickly as Samantha can tap her Amex card, the film snips her angel wings and turns her sweetness to cynicism and self-involvement. "Men are simple," she tells Jacie mockingly, "'I'm *horny*, I'm *thirsty*, I'm *hungry*.'" She stops baking cookies for clients and instead mocks them: "What they want is for me to lie to them," she seethes. "Wives lie to their husbands for free, and I lie to them for money!" She picks up a drug habit, her relationship with her family nosedives, and from here on, with the subtlety of a coffee table–size painting of Jesus, the film links sex work with sin. Driving home high on cocaine, Samantha makes loopy confessions to the angel on her dashboard, while her colleague, Sugar, proclaims, "God is always watching," quits sex work, and joins a Pentecostal church, invoking Christianity as a sex worker's best bet for redemption.

Samantha's fall comes in the form of a police raid on the parlour where she is arrested and charged with felony prostitution. When her face is broadcast on the local news, her family learns that she was not, in fact, performing sports massages. This reveal commences the film's new fallen woman story. Like Victorian paintings that portray fallen women as suicides on riverbanks or looking out from behind prison bars, *The Client List*'s climactic image is of Samantha in a jail cell, dressed in an orange state-issued jumpsuit. "I wish I could crawl into a ball and make it all go away," she sobs. When Samantha later faces her husband at home, he finalizes the shame she feels. "I see you as a whore now," he says. Her mother, too, heaps on the scorn: "I must have raised you wrong," she says. "Thank God your father is dead." The "father" is Samantha's husband, her clients, and the criminal justice system, which gives her a thirty-day jail term that the film treats as justified. The image of Samantha in orange behind bars, separated from her children and condemned by the "father," fortifies the conservative idea that sex workers ruin families. In fact, Samantha's sex work *supported* hers, but the fallen woman has long served an ideological purpose: to be the vessel of men's displaced guilt about purchasing sex, while society "holds her ordeal to be necessary."[40] Some 200 years of fallen women later, it's plus ça change.

The feminist Gerda Lerner called the division between "respectable" and "disrespectable" women the foundation of patriarchy.[41] For historian Nickie Roberts, the "patriarchal division of women into either whores or good mothers is one of the biggest lies about prostitution."[42] Yet, the fallen woman also carries hope for redemption. In the film's conclusion, Samantha trods down this path by taking a waitressing job at a flyblown truck stop. Wearing an old-fashioned frilly uniform, she buzzes between tables, repeating her old mantra with a twist: "Waitressing's not so bad!" Despite the unlikelihood of her new job paying the

How the Fallen Woman Became a Mompreneur on *The Client List*   97

Figure 3.3. Fallen women behind bars: sex worker mothers, the picture of sin and despair, in *A Mother Deposits Her Child at Foundling Hospital* (1855) by Henry Nelson O'Neill and *The Client List* (2010).

bills, her family is pleased. "You screwed up," her mother says, "but you cleaned up your mess." Thus, as we watch Samantha scrub tables and scrape plates in a traditionally female job that requires her to literally take orders from men, *The Client List* suggests that Samantha is "cleaning up" her act by resuming her proper role as asexual mother. Yet, while the film mostly condemns sex work, it contradictorily prizes the sex worker's skills, as in one late scene when a group of local women barge into Samantha's house and demand she teach them what is rumoured to be her top-notch fellatio technique. She obliges, and the carnal knowledge that condemned her to ill repute becomes her key to redemption in the film's earnest denouement of female solidarity around an expertly deep-throated banana.

The Client List validates the patriarchal double standard that encourages women to use their erotic capital in the marriage market yet punishes them when they monetize it outside of marriage. It concomitantly subdues in Samantha the most taboo female emotion – anger – as she shows no contempt for the hypocrisy of a system that awards her a tiara at prom for being beautiful, yet punishes her for making men pay for access to it. "It's amazing what you'll say yes to," Samantha later says. "I know it's no excuse! I thought I was saving my family, but it was actually the worst thing!" Samantha's male clients meanwhile continue their lives of upstanding citizenry, and prostitution laws that punish women exclusively are treated as sacrosanct.

The film's final image is of Samantha and her family at an indoor amusement park, an overtly Rockwellian ending that suggests redemption – that is, if Samantha continues to play the one-dimensional role of wife and mother that assures the restoration of the virgin–whore binary. Amid the arcade games and children playing, Samantha's husband smiles at her and says, "You look nice," reinforcing her looks as her primary value. How the family will pay the back-mortgage payments – what compelled Samantha into sex work in the first place – remains a mystery as economics are sidelined in a moral ending that understands sex work, finally, as the outcome of a confused woman's poor choices. Ultimately, Samantha's suffering and redemption in *The Client List* furnishes a cautionary tale that exemplifies the enduring taboo against sex worker mothers and one of popular culture's enduring anti-feminist grifts: the fallen woman story reconstituted as the neo-liberal success story. While giving men an easy pass, it holds mothers responsible for children while simultaneously condemning them for the work they do to provide for their families, an anti–sex work slam dunk.

Sexy Mama: Massage Parlour Mompreneurship on *The Client List* TV Series

Angels, abs, and brimstone turned out to be a winning combination, and Lifetime reprised *The Client List* as a series in 2012, again starring Love Hewitt. Yet, while the movie was a red-hot cautionary tale, the TV series was more thoughtful, less judgemental, and overtly supportive of sex workers. Lifetime hinted at this more progressive approach before the pilot aired, noting that *The Client List* "falls in line with our strategy to expand … unapologetic programming that will surprise audiences."[43] The series dignified sexual entrepreneurs and took viewers inside a sex workplace rarely seen on TV. Whereas the film relished in the sex worker mother's fall, the show elevated her, without buffing away the challenges of her work.

The series' more realistic perspective is indicated immediately as the pilot opens in the wake of the Great Recession, in a spiral of job cuts, home foreclosures, and economic decline unparalleled since the Great Depression.[44] When Riley (Love Hewitt) loses her job as a registered massage therapist (RMT) at a country club, she joins the legion of the unemployed, but the inciting incident deepens when her husband abandons the family, thrusting her into the role of sole breadwinner in the ruined job market. After being rejected from massage therapist gigs, Riley unsuccessfully seeks out minimum wage jobs (on which she couldn't support her family) and is unable to apply to many others due to scheduling conflicts with her childcare responsibilities. With these setbacks, *The Client List* exposes the constraints single mothers face before they decide to leave licit labour markets for illicit ones as some did during the financial downturn.[45] By the time Riley secures a job at a spa called The Rub, the audience is rooting for her.

Riley's agency is a strength of the series as a whole. In an interview, Love Hewitt identified Riley's "choice" as her defining characteristic: "Riley is someone who is in control of her choices ... she's in control of the spa, she's in control as a mother, and even though life continues to throw her difficult[ies] ... she always handles it really well."[46] Indeed, earning enough money to raise children on a single income is a motif that comes up constantly in the narratives of single mothers who decide to do sex work after considering the likeliest other option: double shifts at menial jobs leaving no time to see their children. This is evident as Riley weighs the risks and benefits of sex work against her responsibilities as a single mother, and this deliberation – and absence of moral judgement about her decision – is what makes the series so different from the film. After learning that her spa offers two tiers of service – therapeutic massages (which pay poorly) and sexual massages (which are lucrative) – Riley at first chooses to offer only non-sexual massages in a bid to remain a "respectable" mother. "I want a job I can be proud of," she tells The Rub's owner, Georgia. Yet, in a reversal of expectations – and the standard sex worker narrative – Riley's *non-sexual* massage work turns out to be demoralizing; in montage we see her clients treating like a servant, speaking to her with contempt, and rarely tipping her, while the physically grueling labour leaves her drained each night with no energy left to spend quality time with her children.

As Riley kneads and pounds for a pittance at a low-paying and time-consuming job that clashes with her goal of maximizing her time with her children, the series forces us to question our assumptions about what makes a job "respectable" – its moral status or the actual experience of the worker – and builds empathy for her situation. In fact, when she decides to start offering sexual massages, the series explicitly takes up the labour position by showing how sex work offers Riley (and women like her) greater control, higher income, and scheduling flexibility, which she finds especially important.[47] Whereas the film ultimately condemned Samantha's decision to engage in sex work as an error of judgment, the TV series frames Riley as an intelligent hustler who weighs the pros and cons and makes an informed decision – and in doing so, builds respect and empathy for her.

One of the show's equally refreshing qualities is how it validates Riley's labour as a massage parlour worker as she learns the ropes of commodifying sexual encounters. As a rookie sex worker, Riley is nervous, uneasy, proud, embarrassed, curious, and sometimes ambivalent, and the series paints a rich picture of her new career without sugar-coating the more vexing moments, which she is helped through by her colleagues. Showing camaraderie between sex workers is rare in popular culture, where the commonest groups tend to be generic (blurs of fishnet-clad women on street corners), or sadistically sexually charged (as in *Mme. Olga's Massage Parlor*, where the torturer is another sex worker), or carceral (huddled women in jail cells) and reinforce the trope of the defective and criminal sex worker without allies. In contrast, *The Client List* series portrays Riley's allyship, relationships, and solidarity with other massage parlour workers. They find understanding and empathy within their community that is unavailable elsewhere, supporting one another and sharing knowledge and survival skills.

The Client List draws on what we know now about precarity. Riley's colleagues at the spa are ordinary (not fallen) women who choose sex work as their best option, not because they see it as a dream job. Over two seasons we meet around a dozen colleagues who are distinctive, daring, vulnerable, and interesting, and who make appreciable the diversity of drivers for women in sex work and their diverse life histories. Included among these are Selena, a thirty-something equestrian with a Shania Twain swagger who hopes to one day buy a horse farm, and Nikki, a working-class college student and math whiz who aspires to a STEM profession and explains her motivation frankly: "Tuition's expensive." The shows paints a prismatic picture of diverse colleagues – including women of colour and women across the age spectrum – who share a wish for stability in an economy where standard employment relations and social safety have been eviscerated. Unlike the movie, where submissiveness was the high-water mark of feminine success, Riley and her colleagues don't want to be admired for their beauty or docility. In fact, the spa's owner, Georgia, emphasizes how a woman's industriousness and intelligence trumps her sex appeal: "I got all of this," she says, gesturing around her at the massage parlour she owns, "because of this," she says, pointing to her head, "not this," she finishes, pointing to her breasts. While Riley's preference was to keep her original job at the country club, the series lauds her resourcefulness and adaptability and suggests that she and her colleagues have made sound decisions to step outside the licit economy into illicit and lucrative sex work.

The show also considers how massage parlour work, as more than just a temporary escape from low-wage jobs, offers some women a chance to transcend structural barriers, secure middle-class lifestyles, and even become part of the owning class. It embodies this idea through The Rub's owner, Georgia, one of the show's most compelling characters. While portrayed as a white woman in the film, Georgia is depicted as a Black woman in the series, signifying *The Client List*'s intention to tell a different story about sex work, starting with the diverse women in it. Georgia is smart, stylish, and dynamic, and her characterization as a successful Black entrepreneur exemplifies the leveraging of erotic capital to transcend race- and class-based inequalities.[48] That said, the show elides the broader societal racism reflected within the sex industry. Specifically, it is mum on the objectification of Black women, what Patricia Hill Collins situates in the discursive construction of white women as submissive asexuals and Black women as "sexually aggressive Jezebel[s]," a dichotomy that rationalizes abuse and perpetuates white supremacy.[49] Today, Black women remain far more likely to be arrested for prostitution and may encounter lower pay and discrimination, harsh realities the series does not grapple with. Even so, *The Client List* creates in Georgia a truly original sex worker character whose success troubles the prohibitionist credo that all women of colour in the sex industry are victims. Moreover, it emphasizes Georgia's intelligence as the primary source of her power, steering clear of objectification. In an interview, Loretta Devine, who plays Georgia, shared how she had previously been cast as "a lot of mothers" but could transcend these restrictions in her role as an entrepreneur who "oversees twenty or more women in a business that is thriving."[50] The series also portrays Georgia's wisdom and success extending to younger sex workers, particularly through her mentorship of Riley, who looks to Georgia as a model of strength to emulate as she becomes a sexual entrepreneur.

Fallen Woman Rising: Building a Sex Business

The incompatibility between sex work and mothering was at the heart of *The Client List* film, in which fallen woman Samantha "cleans up her mess" by exiting the massage parlour industry. Taking a very different tack, the series suggests that sex work and mothering need not conflict when Riley becomes the owner of The Rub, buying it from Georgia who decides to retire but remain in Riley's life as a friend and mentor. While the film made Samantha into a cautionary figure whose downfall illustrated the irreconcilability of sex work and mothering, the series harmonizes and blends the roles of mother and sex worker by transforming Riley into a massage parlour mompreneur.

Mothers, of course, have long engaged in sex work and also operated businesses, but the seamless combining of mothering, sex work, and business is part of a new twenty-first-century zeitgeist. By harmonizing Riley's roles, *The Client*

List makes Riley's ascent to the owning class its most strident endorsement of massage parlour mompreneurship. A portmanteau of "mother" and "entrepreneur," *mompreneur* is defined in the *Oxford English Dictionary* as "a woman who sets up and runs a business in addition to caring for young children."[51] The term first appeared in 2006 with the launch of the website Mompreneurs Online, a networking forum for women that saw traffic of up to 7 million visitors a month.[52] Since then, mompreneurship as a concept has appeared in magazines, websites, books, and academic articles, and the concept and practice's meteoric rise can be explained by the internet's affordances to run businesses from home, the rising numbers of single mothers, and the overall growth of business opportunities for women.

Traditionally, mompreneurship and sexual work are not linked, but *The Client List* suggests how they share many of the same motivations: a wish to work independently and to earn more money than one would at another job, allowing more time with one's children,[53] a desire to balance work and family,[54] a wish to choose one's own hours, as well as more "classic" entrepreneurial motivations, such as a "desire for independence and control, the need for challenge, improved financial opportunity, and the identification of a business opportunity."[55] Riley's mompreneurship asks us to reconsider the taboo against sex worker mothers by highlighting sex work's congruencies with other forms of entrepreneurship. By tracing her career from worker to owner/mompreneur, *The Client List* shows that sex work establishments can be safe, comfortable, and convivial workplaces where women can achieve economic mobility.

In this vein, *The Client List* reveals the *labour* of massage parlour work. It does so first by taking us into The Rub and depicting it as a professional workspace. While the stereotypical setting for massage parlour work, as in many 1970s films, was rife with images of exploitation – seedy-looking red-lit bars festooned with bedraggled people and alleyways where broken needles and condoms floated in puddles of urban flotsam – The Rub is in a suburban strip mall. Its genteel exterior helps it stay under the radar, while its interior is professional and elegant, its Rothkoesque art, blooming orchids, and neatly folded linens making it resemble a five-star spa or an upscale dermatologist's office. Staff wear buttoned-to-the-neck uniforms, and client history forms on clipboards stack the reception desk, where a sleek computer with a streamlined booking system offers clients a professional welcome. The Rub's sophistication makes it easy to forget that Riley and her colleagues are, in the eyes of the state, criminals, and this is exactly the show's point: by stripping the massage parlour of the imagery of sin and stigma, *The Client List* suggests its congruency with other embodied personal industries. It normalizes the massage parlour in a post-Fordist economy where services comprise the bulk of the GDP – 57 per cent – and daily life is increasingly marked by such smooth transactions between willing adults.[56]

Figure 3.4. Entrepreneurial mentoring at the massage parlour on *The Client List*: Georgia (Loretta Devine) teaches Riley (Jennifer Love Hewitt) how to run a smooth operation.

With full body rubs with sweet almond oil payable by credit card, *The Client List*'s vision of personalized tap-your-credit sex is emblematic of late capitalism's reshaping of the romantic affair into what scholars today call transactional intimacy.[57] According to Eva Illouz, transactional intimacy has several features: first, it takes place outside of settings traditionally associated with monogamous sex (i.e., the bedroom in the home), yet in spaces that are nevertheless "permissive"; second, an attitude of instrumental rationality guides these affairs, stripping them of transgressive elements; and third, such transactions are carried out by people "who are most proficient at switching between sexual pleasure and forms of economic activity."[58] *The Client List* embodies transactional intimacy, from The Rub itself – a beautiful, "permissive" setting – to the parlour's professionalized labour processes (intake forms, credit card payment, uniforms) to its staff, who abide by a strict code of conduct same as any paraprofessional working closely with other people's bodies (for example, it is forbidden to date clients). Riley herself epitomizes the entrepreneur who is "proficient at switching,"[59] as being a mother *and* a sex worker form the basis of her character. If motherhood can be said to be a performance, sex work is too, the series suggests, as it shows Riley's massage work coolly coexisting with mothering. In fact, adding to her skills in body work, display work, and emotional labour, Riley sometimes exploits her image as a mother as a value-add.

Managing, Kneading, Costuming, Listening: Parlour Labour

As *The Client List* illuminates massage parlour mompreneurship, so it opposes prohibitionist claims that sex work is *not* work. Sheila Jeffreys, for example, has argued that "youth and inexperience are the most highly valued aspects of a girl inducted into prostitution."[60] Seeking to highlight the hard and soft skills sex workers employ that go well *beyond* sex, *The Client List* reveals Riley engaging in activities common to all entrepreneurs: bookkeeping, ordering stock, paying bills, balancing budgets, managing staff, marketing, and making business plans. Far from the fallen woman wishing for rescue, Riley applies herself to transforming The Rub into an even more profitable enterprise and sees sex work as a vocation. And by treating her work as a vocation, *The Client List* shows the *work* of massage parlour work, particularly body work, display work, and emotional labour.

The series centres on Riley's body work narratively and photographically and validates this professional work, shoring up how body work includes "stigmatised occupations such as sex workers."[61] Close-ups of Riley pounding, kneading, and caressing her clients' bodies with documentary detail take her point of view and make her skill, strength, and stamina appreciable As a trained massage therapist, Riley uses her knowledge of physiology to relax and relieve her clients' pain. Her RMT credential distances her from sex, as does the show's vagueness around her services; it's not until season two, when she jokingly calls herself "an expert handler," that we learn what she does (a delayed revelation that suggests a desire to invoke sex without committing to it, like the TV film). Yet, this coyness opens space to gently explore Riley's professionalism and sheds a positive light on the body work that sex work involves. As Julia Twigg et al. observe, many of the "most positive cultural associations of body work, including touch as comforting or healing, are also seen as feminine, drawing on deeply entrenched patterns in relation to motherhood."[62]

Riley's job is also to produce visual pleasure, and her display work involves lingerie, make-up, and costumes ranging from French maid outfits to nursing frocks. She uses these costumes to cater to her clients' fantasies, but just as erotic dancers tactically employ stage names and costumes to source courage and confidence, Riley uses her tools to build a massage parlour persona that is separate from her private life. Or as she puts it, leaning over her client with a grin: "I can be whoever you want me to be." While prohibitionists – and *The Client List* film – view the performances inherent to sex work, like stage names and costumes, as harmful to a sex worker's psyche, linking it with disassociation, Riley's display work martials her "deep acting" skills. As she morphs from French maid ("Is somebody teeklish?") to geisha, cheerleader to hula girl, Riley, a master of compartmentalizing, uses display work as a strategy to build distance between her work persona and mother self, as evidenced by the Moulin

Rouge-esque costumes she wears at The Rub and the jeans and sweatshirts she dons at home. "Making guys fantasies come true is our part of our job," she explains to a colleague. "The other part of our job," she adds, "is letting the guys *know* that this is *just* a fantasy." Costumes play a huge part in this boundary setting.

Interestingly, Riley's most requested role – nurse – revolves around maternal nurturing. You will recall Arlie Hochschild's notion that emotional labour often looks like "mothering … silently attach[ing] itself to many a job description."[63] In one session, wearing a nurse's uniform, Riley whispers to her client, "Relax, Mama's gonna take care of you." As a sex worker mother, Riley understands the taboo of breaking the virgin–whore dichotomy and cannily exploits this forbidden dyad, invoking the oedipal drive in her oil executive clients for big tips. While the film made Samantha's work an expression of her preoccupation with sexiness and "natural" nurturing – to the absurd point of baking cookies for clients – the series characterizes Riley's work as the exchange of professional skills for payment, and her "mothering" acts at work are wholly separate from her private life of mothering. Mothering does not "silently attach" itself to her job; rather, it is built into the fee up front.

The show also explores Riley's emotional labour, both as a professional tool and a burden. Managing her tone and body language and selecting the perfect words of reassurance at just the right moment comprise a vast portion of her job and shore up what scholars have argued for decades: that as much as erotic services, parlour attendants sell affection, conversation, advice, and a listening ear.[64] Numerous scenes show Riley interacting with her vulnerable clients including the divorced, the widowed, the late-in-life virgins, and those struggling with sexual dysfunctions. The show goes to great lengths to humanize these men – sometimes to near comic degree: there is the man whose Jumbotron marriage proposal is savagely rejected before a crowd of 20,000 at a baseball game; the awkward computer programmer seeking Riley's support as he musters the courage to ask out his long-time crush; and the rodeo stuntman who entrances thousands yet fails to interest women in real life.

By showing Riley's emotional services – comfort, validation, and advice – being sought and purchased in excess of sexual ones, the series challenges the claim that men who buy sex do so to act out their misogyny, an idea summed up by Andrea Dworkin's legendary remark that male sexuality is "the stuff of murder, not love."[65] Rather, the show explores how paid sex encounters offer the privacy and anonymity that allow for self-disclosure under the guise of a "manly" activity. At times, the series treats the massage room as a therapy office and a confessional booth, but this intimacy is a burden for Riley, too. Arlie Hochschild argued that emotional labour places workers at risk of losing the parts of themselves they subjugate to please their customers.[66] At times, Riley's clients' high needs and the strain of trying to fulfil them send her to the edge of exhaustion, and her occasional stress meltdowns and frustration with annoying, dull, and demanding clients add a level of veracity among the many otherwise idyllic scenes starring far-fetched (and muscle-etched) Herculean clients.

But Riley also finds significance in her work and identifies strongly as a helping professional, activating Clare Stacey's contention that some sex workers find emotional labour a meaningful experience, especially those who have autonomy, as Riley does.[67] Thus, when former clients get in touch to say they're now in romantic relationships thanks to the confidence they developed with her, Riley feels a great sense of professional pride, as she explains to her best friend:

> This may be hard for you to grasp, but I'm not ashamed. I know you'll find this hard to believe, but I like my job. Something happens in those rooms. I help them with their problems. Sometimes it gets physical, but for the most part, it's much more important than that.... I feel like I really made a big difference.

As well as offering relational rewards, aesthetic and emotional labour may come with personal pleasure and satisfaction.[68] In fact, the show suggests that in the wake of her torpedoed marriage, Riley's performances, which blend her identities as a sexual and maternal woman, serve as an outlet for exploration of her sexuality and an opportunity to claim the sexual agency that her conservative upbringing and early marriage denied her – in short, a chance to break the virgin–whore dichotomy and its expectations of chaste motherhood. The series critiques the double standard that permits men to act freely on their sexual impulses while upbraiding women as "sluts" for the same behaviour as Riley wears costumes and flirts with clients who compliment her and return for repeat visits (often becoming regulars), renewing her self-confidence and challenging the patriarchal edicts that link motherhood with asexuality. The series doesn't judge Riley for being curious, uninhibited, and adventurous, and it recognizes that wearing a nurse costume or a frilly French maid dress may *look* like objectification but feel empowering. While the fallen woman suffers for her sexual agency, and certainly never gets pleasure from it, Riley uses her sexuality to build a business, explore herself, and stabilize a life for her children.

Intensive Mothering and Whore Stigma

The fallen woman first appeared in a 1795 poem called *Matilda; or, the Dying Penitent* by George Reynolds, who tenderly describes Mary Magdalene's onerous trials and death as a "final ascent on angel's wings towards heaven."[69] A maternal martyr who never gets to see her children grow up, the fallen woman was depicted as an incapable mother. She frequently died to illustrate sex work's incompatibility with mothering and the virgin–whore binary or, occasionally, underwent a tar-and-feathering of redemption like Samantha in *The Client List* film. In the spin-off series, however, Riley's massage parlour mompreneurship supports her maternal role. She is not only what Donald Winnicott calls "the good enough mother"[70] but is in fact a selfless, devoted mother who epitomizes what Sharon Hays calls the "intensive mother."[71] Put another way, she is the mother who *does it all*. While building a thriving massage parlour, she also treats motherhood as an all-consuming practice: she drives her kids to school, cooks, is active in their school lives, and is frequently doing leisure activities with them, reading to them, and tucking them in at bedtime. Numerous interior shots of Riley's home show the extent to which her life is organized around motherhood: lunchboxes line the counter, dolls and toy trucks perch on chairs, and little pairs of running shoes sit by the front door, everything just *so*. Despite her illegal job and taxing work schedule, Riley strives and succeeds at maintaining the family's household and routine and assures her children that they are loved and safe: "I'm here for you. That's what we do. We're a family."

As a preternaturally devoted mother and a massage parlour mompreneur, Riley epitomizes Hays's "intensive mother."[72] A late-twentieth-century invention that has taken full flight today, the intensive mother, according to Hays, emerged in late capitalism in response to the conflicting demands mothers faced: to be, on the one hand, individualistic and to act according to the logics of the marketplace; and on the other hand, to be unselfish and nurturing – not *too* careerist – and to devote themselves *wholeheartedly* to their children. According to Hays, this is "the cultural contradiction of motherhood,"[73] which leaves mothers who want to meet the expectations of ideal motherhood with only two options: forgo a career in the marketplace and assume the role of the stay-at-home mother, who cooks, sews, cleans, and provides round-the-clock nurturance to her husband and children; or be a professional *and* a homemaker by becoming an "intensive mother" who is "expected to juggle both roles without missing a beat."[74] But being everything, for everyone, comes at a high cost, and Hays argues that intensive motherhood dictates that if a mother wishes (or must) "participate in the larger world … she must then pay the price of an impossible double shift."[75] The double shift is core intensive mothering, without recognition or hope for a day off.

On *The Client List*, Riley epitomizes the intensive mother and clocks an "impossible double shift." She works at The Rub – seemingly seven days a week, at least at first – *and* she works tirelessly at home, responsible for all domestic duties from food preparation to cleaning to driving. Yet, rather than critique this wrenching double shift, *The Client List* normalizes it, suggesting that intensive mothering is Riley's key to success and how a sex worker mother may become respectable. In other words, a particularly intense form of intensive mothering is the price Riley pays for her transgressive job, illustrating the reality of how sex workers may feel compelled to conform to gender norms to counterbalance the stigmatization of their work.[76]

Yet, given that intensive mothering is a burden on all mothers, not just sex workers, we can also regard Riley's double shifts as a challenge to the stereotype of the neglectful sex worker mother that originates in the virgin–whore binary. *The Client List* melts the binary between virgin and whore, wedding these historically opposed roles precisely by portraying Riley as an intensive mother, her work providing her children with a high standard of living that would be impossible to replicate on the wages of a poorly paid service job. Earning enough money to raise children on a single income is a motif that comes up constantly in the narratives of sex workers, and providing their children with a stable life is a primary motivator for women to enter sex work. Riley uses her high pay to buy her children necessities and luxuries – from clothes and braces to karate lessons and bikes – and to maintain a new-looking car and pay the mortgage on the family home. Nothing better illustrates the series' support for the sex worker mother than the framed photograph of her children that Riley keeps on her desk at The Rub, symbolizing the harmony of her massage parlour mompreneur and mother identities.

For all of the karma points Riley's intensive mothering racks up, however, *The Client List* paints a vivid picture of how the threat of losing custody of her children contributes to her marginalization and vulnerability, experiences that are common to all sex worker mothers. The show also leaves no doubt that criminalization imperils sex workers (and their children) by exposing them to harassment from police, public scorn, and stigma, which leads to their increased isolation and feelings of chronic stress. Given that sex work still carries a one-year prison sentence in the US, this stress is very much well-founded. In season one, an undercover police officer comes into The Rub; his session with Riley is friendly. Days later, however, the same officer stops Riley on the highway under the pretence of giving her a speeding ticket (when she was not in fact speeding) and threatens to expose her. "Does your family know what you do for a living?" he asks menacingly, before implying that she owes him a sexual favour in exchange for his silence. The series highlights how criminalization increases Riley's vulnerability at the hands of this bullying officer, who wields his power predatorily knowing that she will not report him since doing so would implicate herself. These threatening encounters highlight how criminalization and the fear of being revictimized prevents sex workers from accessing police support and criminal justice, leaving them vulnerable to financial extortion, manipulation, and violence. Ironically, Riley has this encounter despite paying the police kickbacks to secure protection for The Rub – which is hardly guaranteed.

Riley's experiences are exemplary of whorephobia, the disgust, discrimination, aggression, hostility, and negative attitudes directed at sex workers. Gail Pheterson calls it the "social and legal branding of women who are suspected of acting like prostitutes."[77] A central feature of whorephobia, or whore stigma,

How the Fallen Woman Became a Mompreneur on *The Client List*   109

Figure 3.5. *The Client List* rails against whorephobia, highlighting its intention to shame, marginalize, and humiliate sex workers like Riley.

is its intent to marginalize, shame, and humiliate, as Riley learns one afternoon when she is confronted by a scene of terrifying vandalism: the word "whore" has been spray-painted across the side of her vehicle. This is the first time Riley faces whore stigma concretely, and she breaks down in tears, first of shame, then of anger, as she realizes she has no legal recourse for responding to this crime as going to the police would be self-incriminating. With Georgia's help, Riley scrubs the slur off, but this public denigration erodes her confidence. The scene stands in contrast to the film, in which the incarcerated Samantha is tasked with "cleaning up her own mess" as a latter-day fallen woman; in the series, two sex workers clean up the mess of an anonymous misogynist who stirs our indignation.

Whorephobia also causes sex workers to internalize negative stereotypes perpetuated by media, police, and religion, the commonest being that sex workers are diseased, criminal, dangerous, exploited, victims of abuse, and untrustworthy.[78] These are particularly significant for women, as most languages have words like "slut" and "ho" but no pejorative male equivalent, leading women to want to distance themselves from such labels and their consequences. Knowing that friends and family would judge her harshly and even cut off contact if they knew about her work, Riley, like many sex workers, chooses to keep her occupation secret and engages in behaviour modification, such as monitoring her speech and inventing fictional jobs as covers. Yet, given the central role work plays in an adult's life, keeping hers hidden is a burden that isolates her. As Riley puts it: "The work is fine, but leading a double life gets lonely." Later Riley breaks down and describes the impact of whore stigma: "I'm a single Mom … my husband left me … I lie to my friends and family about what I do. I lie to everyone about everything, and I hate it." Whorephobia also places sex workers at a higher risk than the general population for stress, low-self-esteem, depression, substance use, family estrangement, and even suicide.[79] Furthermore, disclosing one's status as a sex worker is not a remedy, as one cannot predict the response they will get – if it will be loving and accepting, or judging and disgusted.

The series illustrates this when Riley decides to tell her best friend, Lacey, about her secret work. It's a huge risk, but Riley knows her friend to be a tolerant person and their friendship to be one based on unconditional love and understanding, qualities that Riley hopes will transcend the shock and taboo of her secret. Sadly, Lacey is appalled by Riley's disclosure and manifests her own whorephobia as a visceral disgust for her friend: "I'm going to be sick," she says, demanding that Riley leave her car, which confirms Riley's worst fears about her job and reinforces her internalized whorephobia. Lacey, having been raised to think of sex worker mothers as fallen women, struggles to reconcile the image she has of Riley as a caring mother with the stereotypes of sex workers she's grown up with. Her visceral response to Riley illustrates how deeply rooted whorephobia is.

At the same time, the series suggests that people can and do reconsider their stereotypes based in whorephobia. This happens a few days later when Lacey apologizes to Riley, having come to understand that Riley's job supports her but does not define her. Even so, Riley internalizes her friend's initial rejection. She dreams that her husband returns to the family and in disgust calls her a whore. Later, the dream repeats, but this time she talks back, shouting, "You left me! It's the only way I could make money!" which signals her growing self-regard and refusal to internalize whorephobia any further.

Nevertheless, whore stigma erodes even the most confident sex workers' self-perceptions. Riley's feisty colleague, Selena, who is single and childless, is resigned to the conclusion that no decent men will date her because of her work: "You think I buy into the fairy tale? How can I even hope for it? With our jobs? The secrets? I'm not marriage material."[80] Selena's certainty that her job has marked her as "damaged goods" in the dating and marriage market might seem alarmist, but a cursory glance at Reddit, a discussion hub that's the world's sixth most popular website, shores it up. In response to variations of the question "Would you date or marry a former sex worker?," hundreds of commenters have chimed in with an almost unanimous "no," their sentiments ranging from the frank ("Automatic deal breaker for me") to the misogynistic ("Say no to a ho" and "Why would I trust a sex worker?").[81] That Selena's clients – and the Reddit commenters, perhaps – are happy to buy services from a sex worker but ashamed to know her in real life speaks to the endurance of the virgin–whore binary and illustrates how patriarchy continues to connect a woman's sexual life to her respectability. It also speaks to how whore stigma is enduring, flexible, and porous. We see this in *The Client List* film, where virulent whorephobia sends Samantha to jail while the men who bought services from her walk free. Yet while Samantha suppresses the most taboo female emotion – anger – and admits to doing "the worst thing," Riley acts on hers and begins defending herself and retaliating against some unethical police officers and the owner of an erotic dancing club who threatens to expose her.

Whorephobia is contextual, too. Chris Bruckert and Colette Parent note that whore stigma is "shaped by … the intersection of sex worker stigma … with other identities."[82] Riley's intersectional identity as a sex worker and a single mother places her at a seismically greater risk for whorephobia. As a result, secrecy becomes her way of life, and the steps she takes to keep her work and home lives separate become all-encompassing: she has multiple cell phones, hides money to avoid making suspiciously large deposits at the bank, screens her clients to ensure they will exercise discretion, uses a pseudonym, and deliberately chooses to run her business far away from her home. While whorephobia is a social process, not a legal one, the series reveals how related and mutually reinforcing they are, and Riley's worst fear is stigmatization bringing her into contact with the criminal justice system. What if the graffiti on her car had drawn scrutiny? What if the police raid her spa? What would she tell her children if she were to be arrested? While Riley is never unlucky enough to lose her children, *The Client List* shows how that ever-present threat erodes her quality of life.

Without ever being heavy-handed, the series makes a pretty definitive argument against the criminalization of prostitution, showing how the criminal justice system imperils Riley's well-being and burdens her with innumerable challenges. While prohibitionists argue that prostitution laws exist to protect women, *The Client List* suggests that it harms them, a contention supported by the numbers. As previously mentioned, women sex workers in North America, for example, comprise 97 per cent of all prostitution arrests, proving that the law almost unanimously targets and punishes women.[83] Furthermore, the pervasive fear of arrest creates a further safety risk as sex workers who are assaulted at work are unlikely to report this violence to law enforcement for fear of being arrested themselves. *The Client List* gestures to this irony when Riley's office is broken into. Naturally, Riley does not contact the police but instead a local judge who is, ironically, one of her most loyal customers.

For Georgia, who is of an older generation, it is obvious that sex workers "need to operate in the shadows," as she tells Riley. Georgia is less inured to whorephobia than she is pragmatically resigned to it, having learned to operate her business with kickbacks to the police among other workarounds. The irony is that Georgia kept her business running for decades by paying the very institution that enforces the laws that punish her. With Georgia and Riley, the series asks us to have empathy for sex worker mothers and to question our prejudices against them that are applied to women exclusively. While *The Client List* never implies that sex work is a panacea for Riley's problems, it does emphasize her agency to choose it. Yet, the show's focus on individual choice is also its weakness.

Mompreneurs with Boundless Agency ... and Buns of Steel

Riley's financial peril during the crash of 2007–8 becomes an opportunity to reinvent herself through one of neo-liberalism's most cherished ideals – what David Harvey calls "entrepreneurial freedoms."[84] Her transformation from a fallen woman into a massage parlour mompreneur thus becomes proof of her resilience and the virtues of entrepreneurship. By pulling herself up by her bootstraps, the series suggests that irrespective of structural inequalities, single mothers can use their pluck and wits to grab at the brass ring. But behind *The Client List*'s rosy picture of mompreneurship lie the widespread inequalities neo-liberalism has exacerbated, from the end of standard employment relationships to rolled back social welfare programs.[85] Thus, while *The Client List* reconfigures the fallen woman into a feisty mompreneur, it mutes how neo-liberalism demands more from women for less and glamourizes entrepreneurship as the cure-all for inequality.

After the financial crash, the greatest blows were dealt to women who already held the most precarious and low-paying jobs. In 2008, the unemployment rate in the US hit 9.3 per cent,[86] and women were earning 67 cents for every dollar earned by men. Yet, the series only passingly bears witness to these inequalities and what, in part, they stem from: the end of standard employment relations (like Riley's old job at the country club, which paid well and came with benefits). Instead, it reframes the black hole of precarity into a bright star for reinvention as Riley rises as a mompreneur. But Riley's meteoric success in sex work leaves out mompreneurship's less photogenic angles, like out how one of every two new businesses in the US fails and how 41 per cent of single mother–led families live below the poverty line.[87] It also skims over the economic privations that compel so many women into starting their own businesses in the absence of other options – what Nora Caplan-Bricker describes as the "ugly constraints that force many women ... into experiments that easily flop."[88] By transforming Riley from a struggling single mother into a successful business owner within a year, *The Client List* suggests that mompreneurship is a workable strategy for economic mobility for any single mother with pluck and neglects to imagine the supportive role the state must often play – whether through daycare programs, student loans, or other forms of assistance – for those women like Riley who were using food stamps, not feather boas, to survive the Great Recession.

On top of papering over gendered inequalities and hyping the promise of mompreneurship, the show also endorses a vision of motherhood freighted with unreasonable expectations and normalized under neo-liberalism.[89] Mothers who "do it all" – sexy, hard-working careerists with fresh blowouts and buckets of time to have babies and baby their husbands, without breaking a sweat or a nail – began appearing in popular culture in the early 2000s. While this image was positive in how it decoupled ideal motherhood from the traditional image of the domestic asexual angel at the hearth, it problematically suggested that embodying perfection in the home *and* at work was the new normal, which, as Lynda Ross rightly notes, "essentially reinforces the conception of motherhood as a test of a woman's psychological adequacy."[90] *The Client List* also at times romanticizes Riley's self-sacrifice, which is the fallen woman's hallmark. A long-time aspiring singer, she foregoes an opportunity to perform for a record company executive interested in signing her band after she receives a phone call from her daughter who has had a nightmare and wants her to come home. In another episode, she stays up into the early morning hours to bake cookies for her daughter's school fundraiser rather than buy store-bought ones, as that would be less than perfection. In these and other incidents, Riley's self-sacrifice is treated as basic and emblematizes what Susan Douglas and Meredith Michaels call the "new momism."[91] Building on this idea, Julie Wilson and Emily Chivers Yochim describe this as a turn to a "highly romanticized and yet demanding view of motherhood in which the standards for success are impossible to meet."[92] While showcasing its progressiveness in transforming the fallen woman, *The Client List* also reveals its complicity in perpetuating a new stereotype.

A part of the new momism pivots on maternal sexiness, and *The Client List* reminds us of how, even in such a labour-focused show, the sex worker's "MILF" body is still the currency that is traded for audience approval. The show's usually female point of view shifts noticeably during massage room scenes when the cinematography indulges in screen-filling cleavage and pin-up style shots, an oft-repeated visual motif that links motherhood with yet another male fantasy: king-sized curves. Looking sexy is an especially important site of "empowerment" under neo-liberal post-feminism, and its beauty ideals are highly rigid.[93] As a buxom, glossy haired sylph, Riley typifies post-feminist's poster woman, the "yummy mummy," popularized by *The Yummy Mummy's Survival Guide*, a self-help bestseller that advises mothers on how to be full-time fashionistas, expert homemakers, and career women while looking smoking hot in a sheath dress.[94] As Lynda Ross observes, yummy mummy discourse (like the discourse of intensive mothering) demands "perfection on all fronts."[95] Riley's yummy mumminess also reproduces a widespread double standard in popular culture wherein out-of-shape fathers get affectionately teased for their "dad bods" – or even lusted after because of them – while mothers are seen as having "let themselves go."[96] Riley's yummy mumminess also adds a caveat to the show's entrepreneurial proposition: single mother sex workers *can* thrive in the financial downturn, but only if they are in their twenties or thirties, conventionally attractive, and work double shifts.

Riley's pluck and success reflect what Lisa McLaughlin describes as the tendency of "realist narratives [to] place responsibility ... on 'individuals [rather than] political dimensions.'"[97] And as Rosalind Gill and Akanae Kanai note, "as employment and social safety nets are continually under attack, media are increasingly implicated in calling forth subjects who are 'resilient,' 'creative,' 'flexible,' and 'positive.'"[98] In *The Client List*, the massage parlour momepreneur is a phoenix rising from the ashes of the financial downturn with grit and determination, working double shifts in high heels and driving a minivan with freshly baked cookies in the passenger seat. Riley's individualistic ascent mutes how feminist progress is made through collective action for structural changes. Riley's solo rise emblematizes the ambivalence Elin Diamond, Denise Varney, and Candice Amich describe in liberal feminism wherein "hardworking women entrepreneurs are celebrated ... as triumphal examples of postfeminism even as female poverty and income inequality increase."[99] *The Client List* movie particularly ignores inequality and, moreover, blames single mothers for their struggles as it restores the virgin–whore binary through a new fallen woman story. More progressively, the series challenges the fallen woman/sex worker mother stereotype, but it also suggests that irrespective of structural inequalities, single mothers like Riley can seize control of their lives by becoming entrepreneurial, looking sexy, and making choices.

The Client List series ended abruptly after two seasons, just after Riley's estranged husband returned to town and discovered her secret life. "I can explain," she says, before the scene cuts on a cliffhanger. That explanation was supposed to arrive in season three, which never came to pass because of a disagreement between executive producers over, of all things, how to accommodate Love Hewitt's real-life pregnancy. According to Deadline and E! News, Love Hewitt wanted her real-life husband (who plays her estranged husband on the show) to be the fictional baby's father; the show's producers, however, preferred the fictional baby's father to be Riley's brother-in-law, a wholesome local cop whom Riley grows close to during her husband's absence. In any case, the show folded because the creators could not figure out how to handle a *pregnant* sex worker mother, who, it would seem, visually and symbolically, proved too subversive for even prime time. Nevertheless, *The Client List* deserves a medal, or at least a #1 Mom mug, for transforming the fallen woman into a sex worker momepreneur. With its sassy and binary-breaking makeover of one of the most taboo sex worker figures, the series announced, with the boldness of its billboards, that sex work in no way determines a woman's fitness for motherhood.

 **4 Twenty-First-Century Peep Show: Feminist Entanglements in *Cam Girlz*, *Cam*, and *Teenage Cocktail***

> *I've worked for the last two years, six to eight hours a day, seven days a week. I can take breaks, but every break I take, I don't make money. The best thing about my job is the admiration and the attention.... If I got a job working at H&M, I would make a lot less! [If I could make a film about webcam models] I think I would first show what everyone finds interesting – how she got into it.... I would film her thoughts. How she feels during it, how the users treat her ... and sometimes seriously funny things happen.... Your dog or cat suddenly jumps into the picture or someone farts. I would record all of that ... so that the viewers see, experience, and even feel the positive as well as the negative sides.*
>
> – Tracy, webcam model

> *People think we're just dumb sluts or something. But you need intelligence and drive, and you have to be an entertainer. There are large groups of women who do this as a choice and feel empowered by it.*
>
> – Ceratonin, webcam model in *Cam Girlz* (2015)

In March 2015, a twenty-one-year-old woman known only by her screen name "LillSecret" was asked to leave a public library branch in Windsor, Ontario, after being caught exposing her breasts to a computer she was using to live stream to a website called Chaturbate.[1] Viewers around the world watched and tipped LillSecret "tokens" for her public peep show, which, unlike Janet Jackson's famous 2004 Super Bowl flash, was seen by relatively few. Nonetheless, LillSecret's job made headlines the next day. The story had low newsworthiness but was pure click-bait gold, as the vitriolic reader comments showed: "She is a morally degenerate member of society" one comment on *CBC News* online read, while another suggested that "anyone this exhibitionistic has a mental health problem."[2] One reader offered this inflammatory yet inexact analogy: "She's in the same category as a man who plants a hidden cam in a ladies' toilet." She even received death threats. To be sure, the flashing was audacious, and using the public library computer was enterprising to say the least, but the outrage was disproportionate and boring. The more interesting story, which went unexplored, was *why*. One possibility was that LillSecret, like most young women, was trying to get by in an economy that had failed her. That year, as for the previous five, her hometown of Windsor was Canada's "most unemployed city."[3] In any case, the outrage for LillSecret's not-so-secret job spoke volumes about the public's disdain for webcam models, the newest, and arguably most misunderstood, category of sex worker.

In the last ten years or so, public as well as feminist debates have increasingly focused on webcam models, erotic performers who live stream nude shows through the internet for payment. Blending the interactivity of peep shows with the image-rich raunch of porn, webcam modelling is the fastest growing sector of the sex industry, generating profits of over $3 billion a year, or one-third of all adult entertainment revenues.[4] On any given day in 2019, some 20,000 webcam models were titillating and vibrating in virtual rooms for over 60,000 unique customers who paid them with virtual tokens exchangeable for US dollars. During the COVID-19 pandemic, traffic to webcam model websites increased by 75 per cent.[5] Prohibitionist feminist critics of the camming industry have condemned it as nothing more than a new form of porn with digital bells and whistles still governed by the male gaze. In an article published on the popular online *Feminist Current*, one writer describes webcam models as "masturbatory tools" and "things whose value lies primarily in their ability to provide erections."[6] These condemnations, as well as those directed at LillSecret, share a common oversight: they fail to acknowledge how the webcamming industry is reshaping the power dynamics of porn by eliminating the middle men and providing women performers with a degree of power, profit potential, and control over their labour processes and content rarely seen in other occupations in the sex industry.

The documentary *Cam Girlz* (2015) and the feature films *Cam* (2018) and *Teenage Cocktail* (2016) aim to tell this story by taking a day-in-the-life approach to exploring the labour of webcam models in all their diversity. The models range in age from eighteen to over sixty and include women of colour, teens, lesbians, wives, and those who describe themselves as "fat." Set mostly in bedrooms, the films are sensitive to each woman's story and take up their points of view to explore both their motivations and the challenges of their work, including the strain of feigning authenticity and the pressure to always be working that pushes some beyond their limits. Nevertheless, the films portray webcam models as empowered entrepreneurs who build brands and say they self-actualize in the creative aspects of their work. Moreover, they present webcam modelling as an escape from low-wage jobs and as a form of entrepreneurship in which women exercise control and make media, which sometimes verges on subversive performance art.

Yet, with their focus on empowerment through individualistic entrepreneurship rather than collective action, these films sometimes embody what Rosalind Gill calls a "postfeminist sensibility."[7] *Cam Girlz* in particular endorses a sexy body as a site of personal empowerment and largely ignores webcam models in less affluent countries, whose experiences are less than camera-ready. *Cam*, on the other hand, digs a bit deeper by cleverly personifying the alienation of emotional labour through a dizzying story of a webcam model's doppelgänger. *Teenage Cocktail*, most profoundly, is a subversive queer love story about teenage webcam models; the film's curiosity about its characters' desires, drives, and inner worlds exchanges plastic discourses about empowerment for a sweet tale about sex worker labour and solidarity – with a twist.

I begin this chapter by contextualizing the work of webcam modelling historically (as a modern digital peep show), technologically (as enabled by the internet and the Web), and economically (as a fast-growing subset of the contemporary pornography industry). After contextualizing the emergence of the cam-girl phenomenon, I then highlight four ways that *Cam Girlz* represents webcam modelling as an empowering form of work and creative expression, probing the film's "postfeminist sensibility" before turning to how all three films take up a labour perspective by shifting focus away from their subjects' so-called transgressions to their inner struggles, their victories, and their hopes.

Contexts: From Peep-Show Booth to Mega Broadband Business

Webcam modelling is a digital peep show. Its origins date to the late-nineteenth-century Mutoscope, a wooden box inset with a magnifying glass through which the viewer peered to watch short loops of sexually oriented films.[8] In *What the Butler Saw* (early 1900s), for example, a woman undressed while the viewer ostensibly "spied." Mutoscopes inspired a moral outcry. An 1899 letter in the *New York Times* called them "vicious and demoralizing" because they were "exhibiting under a strong light, nude female figures."[9] By the mid-twentieth century, the film box peep show was replaced by live peep shows consisting of an enclosed booth facing a curtained barrier; when the viewer deposited coins into a slot, the barrier would rise to reveal a naked woman sitting or dancing on the other side of the partition.[10] The film and live peep show both offered viewers time-limited spectatorship and used a coin system and a glass screen, yet neither offered interactivity, both were physically awkward to use, and you never knew what you might step into.

Figure 4.1. The Mutoscope was the conceptual prototype for what would eventually become the peep show and, later, webcam modelling.

The introduction of residential broadband in the 1990s brought an array of graphic and sexually oriented websites into millions of households across the US that would change both the sex industry and consumers' relationship to it. For example, in 1999, only 3 million homes in the United States had high-speed internet; in 2006, over 60 million did. While the first sex worker website, alt.sex.prostitution, had launched in the 1980s, the first online escort agency went live in 1994, and the first independent call girl website in 1996.[11] As the internet began providing people with free, private, and comfortable access to pornographic images, live peep shows began losing their appeal and gradually faded away, becoming sticky relics in downtown adult stores before eventually disappearing completely. From porn sites to sex worker web pages, the internet became a wonderland of explicitness and raunch, where anyone with access to a computer was just a few keystrokes away from viewing whatever fleshy fascinations they could conjure. The ubiquity of sexually graphic imagery on the internet, as Elizabeth Bernstein notes, eliminated "the biggest obstacles to the buying and selling of sexual services: shame," and it "shifted the boundaries of social space, blurring the differences between underworld figures and 'respectable' citizens."[12] This shifting of space was also literal: while the threat of being seen exiting a porn cinema caused many would-be fans to stay home, the internet's affordance of anonymity emboldened consumer demand for digitized sex productions, spurring the growth of inventive forms of digitized peep shows.

It was during the internet's growth spurt that the first cam girls built websites, but in the early 1990s these sites had nothing to do with the sex industry. In her insightful history of the cam-girl phenomenon, Theresa Senft notes that the genre's trailblazers were young women who began building personal websites consisting of text written in the conceit of journal entries, images, message boards, and live-streamed video.[13] These early cam-girl websites were not business-oriented but more akin to adolescent forays into self-exposure, experiments into the possibilities of harnessing technology to practise trying on and presenting an authentic self to the world, and bids for attention and kinship.[14] Message boards on the sites invited visitors to comment and fostered interactivity between creators and their audiences. Furthermore, early cam-girl websites constituted a digital feminist subculture, where cam girls often discussed the personal and political issues that touched their lives. By discussing their private lives through a public forum, cam girls made the personal political and developed an aesthetic that placed a premium on "authenticity." The homemade websites, the unedited and raw quality of the live videos, and the connections women forged with one another drew voltage from the 1990s DIY movement that included zine culture and punk rock and celebrated authenticity and anti-consumerism.[15]

Setting was also important. Because cam girls tended to be college students or teenagers still living in their parents' homes, they broadcast by default from their dorms or bedrooms, settings that accentuated the "authenticity" of their shows. With their stuffed teddy bears, posters of New Kids on the Block or Soundgarden, and ceiling glow stars visible in the frame, these cam girls not only presented themselves but also a private slice of their lives as seen through their authentic habitats. When webcam technology and high-speed internet dovetailed to allow for video streaming in the mid-1990s, some creators added a live element to their websites. In 1996, Jennifer Ringley, who became a cam girl of international renown, began broadcasting the first live webcam show on her website, JenniCam, from her dorm room at Dickinson College.[16] At the height of its popularity, JenniCam drew 100 million viewers a week.[17] Invoking her commitment to broadcast authenticity, Ringley said she wanted to "show people that what we see on TV – people with perfect hair, perfect friends, perfect lives – is not reality – I'm reality."[18] To that end, one day in 1997 Ringley had sex with her boyfriend on camera. As Theresa Senft points out, this was a decisive moment of "blurring life, art and porn."[19] For the millions of viewers who tuned in, what made Ringley's product so appealing was its marked difference from pornography. While traditional pornography fetishizes disembodiment, Ringley's broadcast felt like "reality."[20] Galvanized by Ringley, other cam girls began offering erotic shows and monetizing their sites, setting in motion the growth of a full-fledged cam-girl industry.[21]

The earliest feminist scholarship on cam girls – by now known as webcam models – was largely condemnatory and drew implicitly on Laura Mulvey's theory of the "male gaze" to portray webcam models as teenage flaunters who subverted feminist gains by objectifying themselves into a state of "to-be-looked-at-ness."[22] One scholar called them "exhibitionists who position a cam on themselves to titillate young boys."[23] To be sure, webcam models display themselves and give male viewers the power to "buy" services and "watch," but what early detractors neglected to consider was how webcam modelling's production mode and digital form changed the power dynamics between both industry and worker and spectator and performer by shifting authorial control into the webcam model's hands. First, while Hollywood actresses are hired by producers, commanded by directors, and aestheticized by lighting and make-up experts, webcam models are more autonomous, since they produce, direct, and design their own productions and turn a profit from their own media images. Second, the looking relations were also different. In porn, female performers traditionally don't look into the camera, but webcam models are free to engage in other activities while on camera (like painting their fingernails, doing homework, performing non-sexual theatrical acts, etc.), which destabilizes the subject-to-object gaze Mulvey proposed. As Michele White has argued, by actively looking back at viewers, webcam models refute some of the submissive aspects of being looked at as an object.[24] Furthermore, by broadcasting from their bedrooms and emphasizing their feelings, cam girls remained within girl culture's historically circumscribed position within the private space, but they also subverted the use of that space by making it public and marketable.[25]

Today, thousands of models live stream their productions on the world's four largest camming websites: ImLive.com, CamsCreative, CamSoda, and Chaturbate. Audiences range from zero to in the thousands, depending on popularity, and the model chooses which acts she performs, posting the available sex acts or spinning a wheel, each act linked with a price.[26] As Paul Bleakley argues, the control cam girls have over their labour processes is a source of agency, and webcamming may provide some women with an opportunity to become "entrepreneurial amateurs" and "take control of the adult entertainment business in a revolutionary form of sexual feminism."[27] Angela Jones also notes webcam models' agency on a concrete level: they set their own schedules, decide which acts to engage in, choose how much to charge, and can block and ban customers from their virtual rooms.[28] As of late, the cultural industries have picked up and cashed in on the webcam model phenomenon, producing and circulating a number of documentary and feature films about their lives and labours in the digital economy. Although the personal, creative, and subversive origins of webcam modelling may seem invisible in today's camming industry, many of these films are tying it back to its origins in stories of women who see webcam modelling as a path to economic mobility, a form of creative entrepreneurship, and a subversive, feminist expression of their authenticity – and even art.

Cam Girlz: A Day in the Life of Sexual Entrepreneurship

Cam Girlz (2015) is a personal portrait documentary in which thirty-seven webcam models from the US literally and figuratively take to the screen to represent themselves and their labour. With its high production values, smooth electro-synth soundtrack, and sensitive close-ups, *Cam Girlz* is quite stylish. It is also quite intimate. Set mostly in bedrooms, the documentary takes a "day-in-the-life" approach. Through interviews and observational vignettes, it creates a viewing experience that is immersive and attentive to each story. For director Sean Dunne, the goal was to make "a film about women who challenge the establishment and societal norms."[29] It was also to challenge the prohibitionist assumption that webcam models are exploited women, and to show them in all their professional dynamism. As Dunne writes, "I was blown away by how intelligent, well-rounded and business savvy they were. It felt unexpected, they were very much empowered by this work."[30] Visually and rhetorically, Dunne weaves this perspective through *Cam Girlz*, maintaining that webcam modelling is legitimate work. This is suggested right from the opening montage, which shows webcam models starting their workdays by setting up their video equipment. With technical precision, they unravel power cords, clip cameras onto tripods, plug in computers, tweak lighting, apply make-up, fasten bras, select costumes, and prepare backdrops for their shows. By showing the women's workaday routines, *Cam Girlz* establishes webcam models as professional performers and webcam modelling as both a business and a media production. As one model, Sophia, says, "We're normal people. It's just a job."

Historically, harmonious depictions of family life and sexual labour have seldom been seen together in popular culture; instead, sex workers have been portrayed as being in violent and toxic relationships and coming from (and creating) broken homes. (We saw this in the previous chapter, where Samantha is stigmatized for being a massage parlour mompreneur.) *Cam Girlz*, however, opens by showing webcam models enjoying quality time with their families. One model watches television with her partner; another kisses her son and husband goodbye as her laptop sits open, waiting for her; Princess Hunny, with blue hair, tattoos, and glasses, plays video games with her boyfriend and shows off her pet rats; several models stroll through nature, pick flowers, and picnic.

By opening with images of webcam models' professional and personal lives, *Cam Girlz* establishes its premise: that women in this occupation, like other workers, seek and achieve a balance between their home lives and careers. With these domestic scenes of girlfriends, wives and mothers, pet owners, and outdoor enthusiasts, the film asserts that these women's jobs do not define them. It seems like an obvious point, but it's the first portrayal I've seen of an ensemble cast of sex workers who are not engaged in sexual activities when the cameras start rolling.

Equally original is how the film challenges the predictable form of docuporn, particularly its characteristic stiff on-camera interviews with sex worker subjects who, in part because of this formality, tend to paint overly rosy pictures of their work. There are no on-camera interviews in *Cam Girlz*. Instead, Dunne recorded audio interviews with the models he then layered over footage of them at work to "bring the audience into as intimate a space as we possibly could."[31] This innovation of form allows for more spontaneity, resulting in a purer form of documentary offering unparalleled access to the models' labour processes.

Cam Girlz portrays webcam modelling labour in four key ways. First, it represents this labour as a way for women to escape low-waged and exploitative service jobs and enter more empowering and autonomous work. Second, it depicts webcam modelling as a way for women to become mini media companies unto themselves where they practise as creative entrepreneurs. Third, it depicts webcam modelling as medium for creative and subversive sexual performances capable of countering pornography's dominant visual codes as well as a way in which webcam models can express their authenticity. Finally, it frames webcam modelling as a catalyst for women's sexual self-discovery and as a means for women to renew their self-confidence.

Webcam Modelling: An Escape from Precarious, Low-Wage Service Work

The allure of webcamming rests principally in its high pay and low barrier to entry, requiring only a computer and a camera. Without any up-front joining fees or onerous hiring processes, one can start immediately. The income is potentially high, with top earners netting from $10,000 to $75,000 a month, and, most significantly, it is legal, safer than in-person sex work, and allows models to work from home.[32] *Cam Girlz* validates how webcam modelling has offered women an escape from the poorly paying, exhausting, and sometimes even exploitative service jobs that are so widespread under neo-liberal capitalism. Models describe webcamming as a safe harbour from a storm of bad jobs, nasty bosses, and debt. One young mother, Bell, sits in her living room with her squirming toddler on her lap. She describes how as the manager of a pizza restaurant, on-her-feet work in the blast of a hot oven, she often worked double shifts to make ends meet: "Before camming I was at work more than I was at home. My house was actually just ... a bed." Now, she works half the time for double the pay. Another model describes the relentless bullying she endured from her boss at a psychologically damaging job that led to a stress breakdown. "I hated my job. I would cry on the way to work. I would cry on my way home. I was miserable." Crystal Cat, a model in her twenties seen wearing pink lingerie, describes how webcam modelling allowed her to quit her $10 an hour waitressing job and move into a safer neighbourhood. "We do this by choice," she says. Sophia, from her bedroom with her black cat snoozing beside her, explains how webcamming allowed her to complete her undergraduate degree debt-free, without working full-time; now, she plans to pursue graduate studies to become a therapist.

Thus, *Cam Girlz* represents webcam modelling as a way out of mediocre, low-wage jobs and towards high-paying work that enables women to achieve some measure of financial independence. The film highlights the vocational pride models take in their work and the entrepreneurial spirit that drives them, revealing the holes in the exploitation narrative. While prohibitionist feminists argue that sex workers choose their work from "non-choices," *Cam Girlz* emphasizes that, as independent contractors, webcam models set the terms of their work. "I'm in complete control of everything," says Violet October, a twenty-something model with wavy, violet-coloured hair. "I never wanted to work a normal job. I wanted to be my own boss. I didn't want my tattoos and coloured hair to hold me back."

While some models concede the possible conflict between men paying them to perform specific sexual acts and their purported agency, they insist they are in control because they can, at any moment, simply log off. Webcam models also cite the safety of their work relative to other sex work jobs. "There is a very large group of women who do this for a living, as a choice. And feel empowered by it," says one model, as the digital sound of coins dropping into her account can be heard tinkling in the background.

It's Just My Business: Webcam Modelling as Creative Entrepreneurship

Cam Girlz represents webcam modelling as a positive opportunity for women to engage in entrepreneurship and gain greater economic control over their lives. The women in *Cam Girlz* use phrases like "camming is my business" and mention entrepreneurial techniques such as "marketing to build a fan base." They describe their interactions with viewers as transactions and consider the services they sell as goods, while also regarding themselves as products. "You are selling yourself. At the end of the day, you are a product," says Pinki Pixie, who wear cat ears and performs from her bedroom decorated to look like a gameshow set. Like "Road Strip," which celebrated its erotic dancers' business savvy, *Cam Girlz*'s focus on women's agency draws from neo-liberal discourses of entrepreneurship and an ethos of self-reliance: "That's what being entrepreneurial is – depending on yourself. I'd rather have that than depend on someone else." Other models describe liking the control entrepreneurship gives them over their work: "It's my own time, my own rules. It's like I have my own business," says Lana Rose, a Latinx woman in her twenties. Many describe the benefits of being "your own boss" and having "no one control me." Others discuss the personal satisfaction that comes with becoming an entrepreneur: "It's just so empowering for me. I never thought I would be able to run my own business and manage my time the way I want to."

Cam Girlz's portrayal of this ambitious group of webcam models challenges the oppression paradigm's conception of sex work as a last resort for traumatized women. These models, on the contrary, are inventive, driven, and passionate, and almost all of them identify as creative entrepreneurs. The term "creative entrepreneur," which has only emerged in the last fifteen years, describes a new kind of worker within twenty-first-century capitalism who is flexible, creative, and self-employed, and who produces and sells creative products and commodities on the open market outside of any institutional structure.

In *Cam Girlz* we see webcam models assume the roles of producers, directors, production designers, marketing experts, and performers all at once. They build their personal brands by inviting clients into their personal worlds and use creative entrepreneurship to connect with audiences. Webcam models are selling intangible commodities – performances, images, time, and services – but *Cam Girlz* emphasizes the extent to which they understand that their clients desire "authentic experiences"– what Arlie Hochschild calls the consumer's greatest wish in late capitalism stemming from a growing weariness with "phoniness."[33] *Cam Girlz* shows webcam models crafting online personae and participating in social media activities that accentuate their "authenticity" and help them build relationships with viewers. Many webcam models maintain Instagram, X (formerly Twitter), and Facebook pages to connect them to fans. Furthermore, some sell their phone numbers for offline texting and, for a fee, will write a viewer's name on a piece of paper and post it in their room, a signification of that viewer's status in the performer's private "world."[34]

As directors and production designers, webcam models also craft their sets and stages with intent to build strong personal connections to their audiences. The webcam models in *Cam Girlz* seemingly draw on the legacy of the 1990s cam girls and broadcast from their bedrooms where they create "displays" of authenticity to meet viewer demand and make money. "Display work" is labour in which "the primary exchange of bodily capital is for the purpose of visual consumption, either in image, video or direct contact for a wage."[35] In *Cam Girlz*, the models' bedrooms appear curated with personal effects that suggest the model's backstory and characteristics: books (studiousness), stuffed animals (youth and innocence), a ukulele (creativity, folksiness), and knickknacks (whimsy). Some webcam models even have cats curled up near them. Through this entrepreneurial display work, webcam models give viewers imaginative access to their private, "authentic" worlds. As a result, webcam modelling presents as more authentic than and different from traditional pornography.[36]

Cam Girlz also represents webcam models doing display work through their web pages, which come to function as supplemental marketing tools. As Rosie, a Black model with freckles who performs in a bikini, says, "Marketing is important for building a fan base." Webcam models post their measurements, photographs in different fashion looks (swimwear, evening wear, sportswear), personal writings (brief autobiographical narratives), and inspirational quotations. Like the DIY cam-girl websites of the 1990s – or the earlier *Playboy* centrefold questionnaires in which models furnished answers about their favourite foods, hobbies, and dreams in their own purported (usually very girlish) handwriting – these web pages blend the personal with the mercantile and give the viewer further imaginative access to the model's private world. As *Cam Girlz* shows, webcam models are also directors who make decisions as to how they will appear on screen. While the webcam models perform in their literal bedrooms, they simultaneously perform in "virtual" bedrooms in which they interact with clients through live video, text, and audio. It is in these virtual rooms that models sell a range of live services, from the overtly sexual (erotic dancing, using sex toys, masturbating) to the more niche and fetishistic (slurping noodles, applying make-up) to the everyday and companionate (conversation). The variety of erotic acts that webcam models offer is vast, but *Cam Girlz* emphasizes that models choose which acts they will perform to accord with their own comfort levels, and they set their own prices by posting lists of available sex acts. In Pinki Pixie's bedroom we see a list of offerings, which include the following:

Gold Shows
- Ice show – tease
- Shower – voyeur
- Panty modelling
- Oil show
- Lotion show
- Spanking show

Website
- Ice
- 100 spanks
- Hot & cold (ice + wax)
- Messy BJ (toy)
- French maid
- Bound orgasm

Clips4Sale
- Floor scrubbing
- Tooth brushing
- Nose blowing
- Getting dressed
- E-cig
- Sleeping

As *Cam Girlz* shows, the premium placed on acts not typically associated with sex work, like "floor scrubbing," "tooth brushing," and "nose blowing," reflects the extent to which customers want (and will pay for) intimate access to what Hochschild calls "spontaneous 'natural' feeling."[37] When the model has collected the set price from viewers, she will perform the show. *Cam Girlz* represents these performances and creative entrepreneurship as a source of satisfaction for webcam models who feel that their work reflects their authentic selves. Ultimately, it is the goal of every webcam model in a public room to entice users to "take her private" (to a virtual private room), where her fees increase steeply and she earns most of her income.

Webcam Modelling as Counter-Porn Performance Art

Cam Girlz represents webcam modelling as a creative form of self-expression in which women subvert the visual codes of traditional pornography. Pornography, in general, abides by two visual codes: fragmentation – the convention of close-ups of women's body parts, suggesting her use value in a sexual sense alone – and submission, which links women's arousal to violence.[38] The most extreme examples of this coding occur in pornographic simulations of rape, the variations being that the woman either succumbs to the man's force and begins to enjoy her rape, or she continues to resist and suffers through it. Either way, in such images, women are fragmented to orifices and objectified.[39] In *Cam Girlz*, webcam models reverse these visual codes by mounting shows that emphasize wholeness and agency, creativity and choice.

In *Cam Girlz*, we see webcam models reconfiguring the visual codes of traditional pornography as they stage spectacles showcasing their theatricality, artistry, audacity, and creative control. Many models push the boundaries of porn by combining the playfulness of the peep show with DIY cam-girl aesthetics. They adopt personae, craft narratives, and use props, costumes, choreography, and music to disrupt the conventions of pornography, at times elevating it into performance art. In these shows, the sexual act is an encore, not the main act. Webcam model Aella's stage persona is a Pierrot: she performs in striped shorts, a white blouse, a red beret, and white pancake make-up, miming perfectly the staccato movements of the sad clown as she opens her umbrella, simulates hearts exploding from her chest, and plays *chansons* on the accordion. For Aella, subverting viewers' expectations about what constitutes porn motivates her to make "every second of what I [do] on camera … interesting. Anything that I thought was unexpected, I wanted to do…. I've always had the tendency to want to make everything I do special." Given that most women on the platform will perform sexually explicit shows, Aella's subversion is also an entrepreneurial strategy of doing, in her words, "something that would set me apart."

Some models' performances directly challenge the audiences' expectation of graphic sex and nudity. Veronica Chaos, a skilled ventriloquist, has animated conversations with a puppet modelled on Beetlejuice. Her own costume is equally fantastical: a red ball gown, scarlet lipstick, and a black *Great*

Feminist Entanglements in *Cam Girlz, Cam,* and *Teenage Cocktail* 129

Figure 4.2. A dancing Pierrot, a human mermaid, and an intimate conversation partner are just a few of the unconventional roles and stage acts of webcam models featured in *Cam Girlz,* exemplifying the performers' creativity as well as the pressure they feel to put on a novel show in a highly competitive industry.

Gatsby-esque wig, a decadent look that conjures 1980s prom queen meets Dadaism – and the result of hours of aesthetic labour. Veronica is uninterested in titillating men. She sees webcam modelling as an opportunity to practise her performance art with a live audience (which is larger than most for performance art shows). Another model, Ceratonin, uses lime green–coloured lights and steam to transform her bathroom into a marine-hued mermaid's paradise; like an X-rated Esther Williams – the 1950s movie star who wore mermaid costumes and performed in water – she performs from her bathtub, her show drawing in equal parts from striptease and performance art. These iconoclastic images challenge the idea that webcam models are being objectified. As Veronica explains, "I like the performance aspect of it. I like the idea of creating something very sexual, but also something very terrifying and bizarre." Similarly, Aella describes how her performances reveal her authenticity as an artist: "The thing about being a cam girl is that it reflects something essential about who you are and then comes back to you tenfold. It's a mirror."

Some webcam models in *Cam Girlz* take things a step further by wearing costumes that boldly – and sometimes even aggressively – reject traditional notions of idealized femininity. One model wears a space suit and goggles; another a taco costume; yet another a plastic horse's head and a knapsack. Though it might seem that few viewers would pay to see a dancing astronaut or a gyrating taco, these "erotic" acts make sense in view of Hochschild's assertion that, in late capitalism, the consumer wants "authenticity." Seen in this light, these offbeat costumes, marked as they are with the imprimatur of their quirky creators, *feel authentic*. And, of course, at a certain point both the space suit and the taco costume will unzip, the horse head will pop off, and more sexually explicit shows will begin. So, while webcam models reconfigure the visual codes of pornography, the paying audience still gets, in the end, what they want. As we watch *Cam Girlz*'s webcam models undermining the codes of pornography by staging creative scenes for men who pay them, it is clear that these women are not victims of a one-way objectifying male gaze.

"I'd Never Had an Orgasm": Sexual Self-Discovery on Screen

Women engage in emotional labour to manage negative feelings in service work, yet, according to Angela Jones, some webcam models "claim sexual agency and reject emotional labor by emphasizing that their orgasms are authentic."[40] Some of the subjects in *Cam Girlz* connect their sexual labour to personal empowerment, drawing on sex-positive feminism's enthusiastic articulations of sexual agency. While prohibitionists argue that sexual expression is immaterial to the goals of feminism, the empowerment paradigm asserts that patriarchy operates through the repression of women's sexuality, and that only by ending their sexual repression will women be truly liberated. As Dorothy

Allison writes, "Not addressing these issues reinforces the rage and fear we all hide, while supporting the status quo of sexual oppression."[41] A feature of sex-positive feminism, then, is the open discussion of female sexual pleasure in all forms and the renunciation of sexual repression.

Many webcam models describe their work as the catalyst that burnished their sexual repression – even shame – into self-acceptance and provided them with the capacity for pleasure. Webcam model Amelia Twist admits: "I'd never had an orgasm before camming. My first one was on camera." Several others emphasize that they had little to no sexual experience before becoming webcam models and suggest that their work gave them a kind of sex-positive re-education, allowing them to transcend the sexual repression that once defined them. Many describe growing up in sexually repressive families under religions dogmas that censured sexual exploration, particularly for women. Taught to shun their sexual impulses and forgo personal pleasure, they learned to feel ashamed of their bodies. Aella explains: "I was raised in a very Christian family. It was very repressive. I didn't know I had a vagina until I was eleven years old. So, I kind of had to grow without my own sexuality. I was raised to think sex was dirty." These raw admissions in voiceover are juxtaposed against images of these women twirling around poles, handling vibrators, and performing stripteases that seem to confirm their accounts of transformation. Another model, Sweet Potato, describes how performing for audiences has enlarged her understanding of her own body's potential for sexual pleasure: "Camming helped me discover what I like about myself." Bell sums it up: "I knew nothing about sex [before camming]."

A further strength of *Cam Girlz* is its body positivity and rejection of rigid Western beauty ideals. The webcam models are diverse: from eighteen years old to sixty and including women of all colours and sizes – thin, voluptuous, and fat. Several models assert that working in the industry has increased their self-confidence and describe how validation – in the form of compliments and tips from clients – has repaired their poor body image. Marissa Frost, who performs on her secluded sundeck in a Batman T-shirt, Marvel comic underwear, lemon yellow garters, and with a 1960s hairdo, says her husband left her because of her "looks." While she turned to webcam modelling for financial reasons, it provided the unexpected benefit of rebuilding her shattered confidence through clients who not only appreciate her fuller figure but actually prefer it over slimmer forms. Several models who identify as "plus size" call the work "liberating." In these vignettes, *Cam Girlz* critiques popular culture's fat shaming of heavier women and commends webcam modelling as a professional area in which performers do not have to "look like an ideal woman," as Sweet Potato says. *Cam Girlz* further suggests that in addition to transforming many of these women's relationships to their bodies, cam work has also improved the models' psychological well-being. "The world confuses me a lot," says Princess Hunny, who self-identifies as being on the Autism spectrum. She credits camming with teaching her how to "read" people.

Popular culture rarely portrays women over the age of sixty unless with diminished capacities.[42] Khyla, one of the documentary's most interesting subjects, is a sixty-year-old webcam model who turned to the work after suddenly becoming a widow: "My husband died on me, he had a massive heart attack. I couldn't eat or sleep. I wasn't doing real good," she says. Wearing leopard print lingerie, Khyla lies in bed in the pose of a mermaid on a rock, one knee lifted, her toes pointing gingerly, while her grey, wavy hair falls down one shoulder. Khyla explains why she enjoys her job:

> It validates me, that I've still got it, that I still feel good about myself. The thing is, I don't want to start looking for someone new. I just want to be with him. With these guys, I get a sense of that connection. I just wanted to feel that connection again. There is a unique category of men looking for older women. Camming turned my life around.

In its celebration of Khyla as a beautiful, sexual woman in the prime of late-middle age, *Cam Girlz* offers a good reminder of the myriad reasons women choose sex work and an original image of a mature sex worker. Yet, as we listen to Khyla talk about her personal, emotional reasons for webcam modelling, we wonder if economic factors do not also compel her. Yet, in *Cam Girlz*'s obeisance to a narrative of personal empowerment, the pitfalls of webcam modelling get left off the screen.

The Post-Feminist Problem: What Cam Girlz *Leaves Off Camera*

Cam Girlz's strength lies in challenging assumptions about sex worker victimhood. Yet this is also one of the film's weaknesses, for as it spotlights its feisty subjects it reveals what Rosalind Gill calls the "profound relation between neo-liberal ideologies and postfeminism" and the "normative notions of femininity" that post-feminism promotes.[43] Over the last twenty years, scholars have described feminism's shifting focus from collective action to individual empowerment as the neo-liberalization of feminism. The problem with this reappropriation, as Kalpana Wilson rightly argues, is that it "permits little scope for any talk about power."[44] The webcam modelling industry, too, adopts "at the micro level" ideas that "mirror these macrostructural economic and political policies."[45] In 2015, the CEO of one of the largest webcam modelling sites, Chaturbate, celebrated the webcam model as a symbol of freedom and autonomy:

> A lot of college girls cam their way through school, and a lot of single mothers are now able to provide for their families comfortably and spend more time with their children. It's very empowering. They're in control of what they do. And if anything gets too uncomfortable, they can just close the laptop and walk away.[46]

In a similar fashion, *Cam Girlz* portrays the models' work exclusively through a lens of "personal empowerment," which it defines as individualistic acts in line with capitalism. Only passing attention is paid to the low-paying jobs the women fled for webcam modelling, and no mention is made of the capitalistic interests underpinning these bad jobs and the widespread inequality they help to perpetuate. Absent also is critique of the webcamming industry, including how the profits are divided, the models' non-existent bargaining power with the corporate websites on which they rely, and the degree to which models are vulnerable to piracy and doxxing.[47] In this regard, *Cam Girlz* typifies the personal portrait documentary, which, as Bill Nichols notes, subordinates "the political in favour of ... [representing] the subject as a self-contained, self-determining entity."[48]

One of post-feminist media's defining features is its preoccupation with the female body as the font of a woman's value and identity. *Cam Girlz* validates models who link their sexiness to their self-esteem and synonymize their bodies with the self: "They see me naked, they see me sad, they see me happy, they see the real me," says one model. Another feature of media's post-feminist sensibility, according to Gill, is the celebration of sexual assertiveness as an index of one's empowerment.[49] *Cam Girlz* emphasizes this sexual assertiveness as not only empowering but transgressive. As one model says proudly, "If I can be a thousand peoples' dream girl, then fuck yeah." Ariel Levy has argued that women's complicity in their own sexual objectification is one of neo-liberal feminism's greatest coups.[50] True, when *Cam Girlz*'s subjects speak about their sexual desire and satisfaction ("I had my first orgasm on camera") as an index of their empowerment, we root for them, yet when their orgasms are all directed at men who pay for them, we rue the commodification of something so private and singular. What happens to women's personal pleasure when it is sold to men on demand? Maybe nothing. But the question lingers.

This is especially the case when models engage in sadomasochism by request, the most popular act being spanking, especially hitting one's own buttocks with a wooden paddle. The dissonance between the models' purported empowerment is stark as we watch their flesh swell with bruises and welts. In another scene, while a voiceover talks about "authenticity" and "empowerment," one model holds another by a dog collar and yanks: "She's pretty when she's humiliated and drooling," she says. Of course, suggesting that the models' performances of BDSM unequivocally harms them promotes a view of women as docile and forgoes the possibility that some feel rewarded by this work. But when work results in bloodletting, and when the order for it comes from men, unexamined comments about empowerment start to wear thin. *Cam Girlz*'s personal portrait form – which forgoes critique – accentuates the dissonance between the images of submission and the models' proclamations about empowerment.

The term "emotional labour" is never used in the film, but the models clearly cope by adopting the strategies Arlie Hochschild has theorized.[51] Some see their work as cynical performance: "This is a business relationship. My clients are a font on a screen," says one model, Ginger. Others see the value of their jobs and acknowledge their skills "positively [as] requiring the capacity to act."[52] Hochschild theorized this method as the most critical for avoiding burn-out and maintaining separation between role and self. Some webcam models, however, identify "wholeheartedly" with their roles, describing their on-camera personae as "authentic," "real," "an expression of myself," "really real," and "not acting." *Cam Girlz* celebrates this blurred line, portraying claims of this work being authentic and an expression of self as examples of these women's self-actualization. Yet this blurring can have negative consequences, according to Hochschild, who warns that women service workers who over-identify with their roles, who melt self and work role, who essentially deny that they are "performing" at all, are vulnerable to what she calls withdrawal into "a robotic state," where they lose "access to (true) feeling ... a central means of interpreting the world around us."[53] This collapse, Hochschild cautions, can lead to "widespread trouble."[54]

Emblematizing this "trouble," Pinki Pixie describes how her work led to a stress breakdown:

> This job can definitely encourage you to become bipolar. On good nights I won't sleep, but on bad nights I curl up in a ball and wish I didn't exist anymore. After seven days of working eight hours a day and seeing hardly any results, I had a kind of nuclear atomic meltdown. Trying so hard and putting everything I had into it and failing, I just kinda cracked. I'd been barely sleeping, waking up to panic attacks, dreams of camming every single night, and it's exhausting ... my dark moments get pretty dark. But I'm a super optimistic person. I'm of the mindset that the last week and a half sucked but things will get better.... Not only do I want to do it for the money, but I want to prove it.

Here, *Cam Girlz* seems finally prepared to explore the personal costs of crushing emotional labour under neo-liberal capitalism and how it is accentuated in work without guaranteed income. "Even when I'm not on, I'm working literally 24/7," Pinki continues. "If you really wanna do good at it, you have to live and breathe it for a while." We wish Pinki would say *more* here, about how it feels to "curl up in a ball" and wish to stop existing after an eight-hour shift entertaining men. Her admission, however, is quickly glossed over by her peppy declaration about being "a super optimistic person," returning the film to its narrative nucleus about women finding opportunities in entrepreneurship.

Double Trouble: A Webcam Model Lost, and Found, in *Cam*

While *Cam Girlz* only touched on the strain of isolated, precarious emotional labour, this issue is at the heart of *Cam* (2018), a smart, creepy movie about the blurry line between role and self and the challenge of switching off when the show is done. Part sleep deprived fever dream, part Hitchcockian noir piloted by an eerie lookalike, *Cam* subverts genre expectations and uses mirrors, doubles, and sleights of hand to build to a climax that champions sex worker dignity. It may also be the first sex work movie to use a doppelgänger to personify the hazards of over-identifying with one's work and getting lost in it.

Writer Isa Mazzei, who would go on to pen *Camgirl* (2019), a memoir that offers an insider's view of the camming industry, brings a similar sex-positive labour focus to *Cam*, whose driving force is an ambitious twenty-something year old named Alice. Where she lives and what exactly she is like remain mysterious, but that is the film's point: Alice's life *is* work. With her goal of breaking into the top fifty on her camming site, she forgoes sleep and a social life. She is close to reaching her goal until her account is mysteriously hijacked by a doppelgänger who steals her identity, sending Alice on a search for answers that peaks in a violent showdown. Summarized like that, the film sounds like a 1970s sex worker exploitation flick a la *Massage Parlor Wife* that ended on bended knee of one sort or another, but *Cam* flouts the past and is one of the more inventive films about sex work of late that is not about victimhood. Dispelling myths that sex workers need to be saved, *Cam*'s heroine fights for her right to choose her work, which the film treats coolly, as a business.

Infused with a labour perspective, *Cam*, at heart, is a tribute to sexual entrepreneurship. When we first meet Alice, she's in her dark bedroom, before her laptop, wearing a negligee, and performing for her audience. In the harsh glow of her laptop, her dancing is sensual, but the bags under her eyes are visible. As the producer, anchor, director, and stage manager of a twenty-four-hour network starring herself, Alice's goal to crack the top fifty on her camming site impels her to work hard to create new content and new roles to engage her audience. One night she's a barely legal teen on a bed of giant teddy bears, ready to lift up her little kilt. On "Date Night" she's a smoky siren eating steak and listening to Vivaldi. Sometimes her prop is simply a dildo. From planning shows to managing her online persona, building her sets to beautifying herself with scalding showers, tweezing, exfoliating, and costumes – Alice is a workaholic who spends more time in her roles than as herself. But the money is great. While Alice's mother, a hairdresser, works all day on her feet for minimum wage, Alice live streams lucrative shows from a bed of pillows, the film suggesting that webcamming is her path to class mobility.

At its core, *Cam* is about the work of producing authenticity, which is Alice's bestselling product. She makes each customer feel uniquely special by becoming a human rolodex of emotional responses, catering to each client's moods and needs based on the details she remembers of their lives, while at the same time peppering her acts with little self-disclosures. She tells her viewers when she has "to pee" and laments how she's "no good at doing make-up." (Her make-up looks professional.) With the canniness of a salesperson and the sincerity of an ingénue, Alice drops a personal anecdote here, asks a question there, creating what seem like "authentic" relationships with the dozens of men who pay her, while actually playing multiple characters and wearing costumes according to her clients' various and often conflicting daily requests. Her workdays, thus, are a carousel of performances and verbal code-switching, as she morphs from bubbly teeny bopper (in a varsity jacket with red silky sleeves) to trenchant femme fatale (lace teddy). Yet, whether she's talking dirty or telling a lonely teen about her love of cats, toying with or spinning the wheel to determine her next titty flash, it is noticeable that Alice's acts share an accommodating character based on simultaneous self-expression and denial: she must be clever without being threatening, sexy without being intimidating, sweet without being prudish, creative without being expressive, and permissive without being pathetic. It's an emotionally exhausting juggling act of pretending with the added expectation of passing the phoney off as reality.

Yet, authenticity on its own isn't enough in a saturated market where attention spans are short and new models are constantly joining the site. Fans are fickle and want to see something new. Something shocking. Thus, Alice takes extreme measures. In one scene, she holds a sabre above her chest, the tip pressing into her sternum. "Do it!" one fan types into the chat window. "Let's see the blood!" Alice plunges the sword into her chest, blood spurting from the wound, and a curdled moan escapes her lips before her eyes flutter closed as she collapses to the floor. Her audience, for once, is stunned and silent, sated in their desire for realness. Moments later, Alice pops up. The wound, it turns out, was latex, the sword, plastic, the blood, red-coloured corn syrup from a Halloween store, but it all *looked* real, and the *ching ching ching* of digital coins in the sidebar confirms the audience's approval: upping the ante on authenticity, even violently, sells. Another successful day at the office.

But *Cam* shows us that the difference between the faux and the authentic is becoming increasingly imperceptible, not only in Alice's online world but in the offline world too. Alice's clients believe they have real relationships with her, twinned souls as emojis on the screen. In one scene, Alice and a client go to a kitschy Mexican restaurant, a strip mall spot where nachos are bathed in Cheez Whiz, mariachi Muzak blares, and sombrero-wearing waiters who speak no other Spanish greet customers with a "Hola!" Looking delighted, Alice's date says, "Wow, this place is so authentic!" In *Cam*, the line between the real and the fake is disappearing fast, and personal relationships can be bought on demand in a hyper-capitalized, commodified world, where manufacturing feelings and performances is the standard of service work, and simulation a prized skill.

Alice's performances recall the inventive models in *Cam Girlz* whose shows toyed with the codes of fragmentation and submission, raising the porn aesthetic into theatrical spectacle (in a taco costume in one memorable case). Alice's faux *harikiri* spectacle and necro-sexpot roles remind us of how sex work is what Melissa Gira Grant calls "demonstrating a skill within a set of professional boundaries."[55] The problem is that Alice *has* no professional boundaries.

Cam argues that the work is more than demanding – it is exhausting. But it's also precarious. Without sick days, holidays, or eligibility for employment insurance, Alice's precarity in a hyper-competitive industry not only demands that she up the ante but also erase all boundaries between private and work time. And she does. In fact, there is no separation between Alice on and Alice off. While getting her nails done, she texts fans; while texting fans, she uploads new photos; when asleep, she dreams up new ideas for future shows. The film is shot in an icy blue and purple palette, as if the sun is being suppressed and it is permanently midnight, underscoring how there is no time *off* and not *enough* time. Like the famous 1936 Chaplin film *Modern Times*, in which manufactured goods fly off the assembly line too quickly for the worker to service, Alice struggles to keep up with the demand – or rather, the pressure to make sure that the demand doesn't dip – while handling clients who want more than a single human can offer. It's not long before Alice finds herself logging in at all hours, obsessively, as she pushes herself to work harder on less sleep (for fear of missing the chance to snag a new fan). When her rank dips inexplicably, she despairs: "What am I supposed to do? Not sleep?" she says. Then, something peculiar happens: the line between herself and her on-screen persona dissolves completely.

In a neo-liberal age, precarity and the compulsion to work around the clock is the new norm. But *Cam* desensitizes and exaggerates this new way of life to make us pay attention to the alienation it produces. It does this by altogether dissolving the line between Alice's online persona and her private life to launch the film's creepy turn: the arrival of the doppelgänger. One day, Alice finds herself locked out of her account; at the same time, she notices a new webcam model, Lola, on the site. What's most troubling is that Lola, while looking identical to her, is a slightly better version of her, the springy gig worker on speed, the ideal neo-liberal subject who works longer, faster, and better, without breaking a sweat. Unable to get back into her own account, Alice watches her doppelgänger rise in the site's scoreboard as her own rank drops and she begins to feel as though she no longer exists. The rest of the film follows Alice on a disturbing journey to get her identity back.

Of course, her doppelgänger never existed. Like Borges and Poe, who used doubles to suggest the uncanniness of modernity and the fragmentation of self under the automation of capitalism, giving spectral form to the humanly repressed and the unspeakable, *Cam* is about the disintegration of the self under neo-liberal capitalism when the boundary between work role and private self is totally erased. It uses the double to represent the loss of control, numbness, and fragmentation Arlie Hochschild posited as occurring when women service workers identify "wholeheartedly" with their roles, placing them at risk for what she described as "burnout" and withdrawal into "a robotic state" where they lose "access to (true) feeling," which leads to "trouble."[56] While *Cam Girlz* only briefly touched on burnout before resolving it too rosily (recall Pinki's "I'm a super optimistic person"), *Cam* personifies Hochschild's "trouble" through the doppelgänger, a hellish personification of the ideal neo-liberal subject who takes responsibility for herself and displays ghoulish resilience through workaholism.

Cam's doppelgänger also reveals a further risk: webcam models' loss of control over their own images in an age of digital piracy and surveillance. With its twisty plot turns, *Cam* evokes how webcam models literally lose control of their images when they are unlawfully recorded by clients who may later put these pirated videos on porn websites, meaning that for a one-time fee, webcam models effectively give away their images for perpetuity. With Alice's doppelgänger, *Cam* suggests that as an unregulated industry, webcam modelling leaves workers vulnerable to exploitation, and companies that profit off models' labour take no responsibility for their well-being or intellectual property rights; meanwhile, given webcam models' marginal power as precarious workers, there is little recourse a model like Alice can take against a large website once her image has been recorded. And given that one's identity is increasingly constituted by one's online images, Alice's loss of control over her own online image puts her at great risk of stigmatization and loss of future employment.

Cam, you will recall, was written by Isa Mazzei, a Berkley graduate and ex-webcam model. Initially, Mazzei set out to make a documentary. It is a good thing she didn't. The decision to personify emotional labour burnout with a doppelgänger is brilliant. And by encasing this story in the unexpected form of a labyrinthine noir thriller, *Cam* gets audiences to drop their preconceptions and root for a heroine who just happens to be a sex worker, using symbols and sleights of hand, not ideological slogans, to support sex workers' rights. These features make it unique as a sex work film. Yet, like overt activism, *Cam* starts by recognizing sex work as a choice that offers Alice income, independence, potential creativity, and some satisfaction, at least before Lola shows up. But with its balanced look at work with big payoffs and huge pitfalls, the film is far from cautionary. Mazzei is one of the few out sex workers who has written a wide release film about a sex worker, and she has advocated passionately about the need for "more authentic portrayals [of sex workers] in mainstream media."[57] Her insider knowledge and lived experience infuses *Cam* with a dignity she herself did not always get as both a sex worker and a writer. In an interview with *Vice* in 2018, Mazzei describes shopping her script around Hollywood

Feminist Entanglements in *Cam Girlz, Cam,* and *Teenage Cocktail*   139

Figure 4.3. Working nine to five isn't an option for Alice (Madeline Brewer), a twenty-something webcam model in *Cam*, a movie that blurs the line between self and role and personifies exhausting emotional labour. Later, Alice experiences the shattering impacts of "whore stigma" – the fear, hatred, and contempt for sex workers – when her house is defaced by graffiti.

and producers asking her crass and belittling questions about webcam modelling and sex while expressing doubts that she – a former sex worker – could write a film.[58] Mazzei's indignation is inscribed into the film in its brilliant examination of sex worker stigmatization.

Stigmatization is a process that works by intimidating a person into conformity and compliance or into accepting the abuse that maintains their abuser's authority. It also produces shame, as in movies where public shaming sends the sex worker, after her fall, into bowed-headed repentance. *Cam*, however, is a treatise against stigmatization that begins by showing the full effects of it. Alice is repeatedly ignored, dismissed, or threatened because she is a sex worker. When her account is hacked, she contacts the website's tech support line but is dismissed by the male operator for "being hysterical." When she goes to the police for help, the officers feed their own prurient curiosity: "What's the weirdest thing you've ever done?" one officer asks her. The questions toggle between proposition and threat before shifting to victim blaming: "If you don't want this, get off the internet."

Stigmatization also impacts Alice's personal life. Her brother's friends learn that she is a webcam model, out her in a particularly humiliating way at a public event, and chase her out of her mother's home with whorephobic jeers; later, they spread the news throughout the community with the intention of further isolating her. At one point, "whore house" is spray-painted across the front of Alice's mother's home, a public attack meant to humiliate and intimidate Alice into stopping her work by causing her family reputation loss. But Alice does not internalize whore stigma nor submit to her detractors, and she vows to keep working. In this regard, *Cam* makes Alice into a formidable force of indignation against moral majority harassers as she intensifies her efforts to stop her double, regain her identity, and return to work. Alice refuses to hide in the shadows.

The traditional ending for a sex worker film was once death or marriage, the graveyards for rogue women. Were *Cam* made even just twenty years ago, it might have ended in this way, signalling that sex work is unsustainable and sex workers unworthy of civic participation without redemption first. *Cam*, however, turns this cobwebbed trope on its head. Not contrite, nor in wedding whites, nor dying, Alice, in the end, defeats her doppelgänger and assumes her identity again. The film climaxes when Alice and Lola go head-to-head on the webcam site in a performance death match wherein the winner gets "whatever she wants." The paying audience, of course, judges. When her doppelgänger starts outperforming her, Alice panics and resorts to her most popular show – her faked suicide – and its violent antics. She smashes her face against her keyboard, eventually fracturing her own nose. It shocks, the bloods looks real (because it is), the coins flow in, and Alice "wins." The prize she demands is the doppelgänger's password, which she uses to delete her profile, thereby killing her menace and restoring herself to unity. While the act is violent, it is also transformative, like a caterpillar destroying its chrysalis to become a butterfly. Whereas the old story insisted that sex workers need saving, *Cam* portrays Alice as a sex worker who saves herself and fights for her right to exist.

The film's last scene suggests exactly such a new beginning, with Alice sitting in a swivel chair in a warmly lit salon as her hairdresser mother combs her freshly dyed hair for her re-launch on the camming site. The warm palate of this finale stands in stark contrast to the cold blues and violets of the earlier scenes in which Alice primped furtively in her dark bedroom, her career in the closet and a huge source of stress and shame. *Cam*'s final image of Alice sitting under the warm orange lights represents her newfound freedom to be out as a sex worker without consequences and solidifies her transformation. And with Alice now having the support of her mother, *Cam* shows a fledgling solidarity between a sex worker and an ally.

The film ends explicitly on this note of choice as Alice debuts as "EveBot" on the camming site. Starting at position 16,600, it will be a long climb to the top fifty, but Alice looks eager. "Hey, guys," she says into her camera, as *Cam*'s own camera zooms in on her smiling face, her nose bearing the scar from the death match in which she killed her doppelgänger. In an interview with *Subvrt* magazine, Isa Mazzei said that she wanted *Cam*'s viewers "to be rooting for [Alice] to go back to sex work."[59] Mazzei characterizes Alice's re-entry as empowering, and in a chic 1960s mini dress and updo, Alice certainly looks like she has her sass back. But what is she returning *to*?

Presumably, she will face the same threats as before – overwork, identity fragmentation, burnout, harassment, piracy, and clients who pay her most generously when she conflates sex and violence. Alas, Alice's own critique of her industry is absent as she returns to it, and in this regard, the doppelgänger loses some of its symbolic frisson as it comes to rest, finally, as something vaguely creepy rather than a brilliant personification of emotional labour burnout. *Cam* keeps the viewer waiting for an overt critique of capitalism, the rabbit to be pulled from the hat – that is, the doppelgänger to be explained as an apparition of exhaustion and overwork, thus solidifying the film's argument. Instead, *Cam* wobbles, building points for two arguments at once: it is both a treatise against precarious labour and a defence of it, though it ultimately ends as a straight-up valentine for the right to return to work that is exhausting and precarious. In this regard, *Cam*'s ending seems to trade in the post-feminist message that *any* choice that *any* woman chooses, even the simulation of sexual violence, is feminist.

Further, all this violence, from Alice's fake suicide scene to her fracturing her nose, is hard to square as "performance" when it bears such a striking resemblance to violence against women in real life and even elsewhere in the film itself. Two of the film's male characters, both clients, are exceptionally creepy: one assaults Alice (while muttering "I've had girls like you to try to scam me before"), while the other promises help but tricks her. Hearing Alice voice her thoughts about her industry, and knowing how she interprets her work, would offer some assurance that she is performing, not disassociating, as she re-enters it. Yet, since *Cam* plays out on the level of allegory, where it finally stands remains as ambiguous as Alice herself by the film's end, where Alice's accomplishment is a return to the status quo.

On the other hand, the film's final image of the scar on Alice's nose may also suggest that Alice is simply playing the role that offers her the greatest benefits in neo-liberal capitalism, in precarity, in post-feminism, where a young woman's self-sexualization, self-discipline, self-promotion, and self-objectification are her best hedges against being broke. In comparison to *Cam Girlz*, whose outro images were of webcam models unplugging their computers, signalling the end of the workday and the barrier between "role" and "self," *Cam* concludes with Alice's assumption of a new role with the same old risks. Whether or not Alice will be able to build a barrier between her role and self this time remains to be seen. *Cam* takes seriously the pressure that haunts precarious workers and the risk of over-identifying with one's role, yet as Alice regains her identity, the film celebrates a sex worker who demands to be seen, fights for it, and wins.

Coming Out on Camera: *Teenage Cocktail*'s **Sex Work Bildungsroman**

While *Cam* explored the alienation of performing authenticity, *Teenage Cocktail* (2016) puts a sweet twist on the sex worker film with a story about webcamming as a road to self-actualization. Directed by John Carchietta, the film follows two queer seventeen-year-old girls, Jules and Annie. In love but stuck in a homophobic town, they hatch a plan to run away to New York City. It's a hopelessly romantic and impractical plan, but we root for them. And while their scheme doesn't come to fruition, their journey is a gleaming Bildungsroman that channels sex positivity by flipping the script on the typical teen sex worker film.

Movies about teenage sex workers are rare, but not new. They first appeared as B-grade flicks in the late 1960s. As the second-wave feminist movement galvanized women to pursue pleasure in their private lives, the teen sex worker film reactively preached against young women's sexual exploration and self-determination with its themes of the frightful city and bodily restriction. A common plot involved a disobedient, barely legal teen running away from home, ruining her reputation, and being saved by a father or a male love interest who ferries her home to safety. Of course, teenage girls are vulnerable, socially and economically, but these films were not critiques of patriarchy and its main tool – sexual violence – but rather bodice-rippers laced with moralistic maxims that projected patriarchal anxiety about women's freedom.[60] They portrayed teenage girls as Fabergé eggs – valuable and pretty objects best kept behind glass – yet objectified their bodies and "transgressions." The 1966 film

Little Girls, its tag line reading, "Little girls who have grown faster than their minds," epitomizes this erotic doublespeak in which sexy images celebrated what the story condemned. Its poster featured an image of a teenage girl with cherubic cheeks, watermelon breasts, and a plush mouth puckered into an O suggesting both her credulity and oral facility. The film told the story of four teenage girl runaways who are kidnapped by a pimp and forced into a sado-masochistic lifestyle before being rescued and disciplined by the police and their fathers for being bad girls.

The teen sex work film's history of having it both ways – titillate and condemn! – is what makes *Teenage Cocktail* so remarkable. A Bildungsroman, a queer love story, and a sex-positive fairy tale, it shuns these sexist and heteronormative conventions. It also flips the script on the very concept of authenticity in a commodified world. While *Cam Girlz* and *Cam* explored the exhausting hustle of faking authenticity, *Teenage Cocktail* is all about how camming launches (and funds) a *real* love story. Indeed, one of the greatest pleasures of the film is its depiction of a relationship between teen girls that revolves around activities *apart* from boys. So common is the "boy crazy" trope that in 1985 the artist and writer Alison Bechdel developed a tongue-in-cheek test to determine a story's feminist chops in her long-running comic *Dykes to Watch Out For*. Now known as the Bechdel test, it asks two questions: (1) Does this work feature at least two female characters who discuss a matter other than boys or men? and (2) Do these female characters have names? *Teenage Cocktail* passes the Bechdel test with flying colours in a story of taboo love and the pursuit of authenticity.

In Bildungsroman fashion, the film opens with the girls under pressure to conform. The setting is an unnamed American town where school buses roll by on lonely rural roads and school is a blur of banality. Seventeen-year-olds Jules and Annie meet by chance in the library. Extroverted and self-possessed, Jules exudes a devil-may-care attitude; Annie is shy and introspective. As opposites they attract, and Jules becomes Annie's id, the sexual impulse she's bent on repressing. As their friendship develops, so does their attraction to one another. Annie's mother, however, is set on repressing her daughter's sexuality, and Annie internalizes her mother's homophobia. By focusing the first third of the story on the young women's lives *before* they become sex workers, *Teenage Cocktail* invests in them as full human beings while credibly establishing the conflict that sex work is to solve. While Annie feels suppressed by her family, Jules feels trapped by their small town. She shares with Annie her fantasy of escape:

> Bright lights, big city, it's the only thing I ever wanted. See these waitresses here? All of them went to our high school. They're all stuck here. In New York, anything can happen. I need that excitement. You should come with me.

Annie is tempted but scared. She hasn't yet accepted her sexual interest in women, and, for all their innuendo, she and Jules have not even kissed yet. But there is no turning back, and their relationship intensifies: they give each other matching tattoos, devise a secret handshake and mantra – "one dream" – and live in a giddy cocoon world of secret plans and inside jokes and teenage ardour. In the real world, they fake straight. One night, they go on a double date, and the boys they are with dare them to kiss. They say it's "for the boys," but the camera shoots the kiss with the zeal of a Hollywood close-up, moving between their perspectives with fast cuts and finally becoming a dizzying drunk swirl that captures their infatuation. Having reached a turning point, they decide that happiness is possible only if they run away to New York City.

Teenage Cocktail steers away from conceptualizations of webcam modelling as a moral outrage and builds understanding for why Jules and Annie choose it. How else could two not-yet-legal teens earn enough money to get to New York? In answering this question, the film recognizes that while sex work may sometimes be rooted in inequitable social conditions, it may also, as Elizabeth Bernstein notes, "constitute an attempted means of escape from even more profoundly violating social conditions."[61] Jules shares a secret with Annie: she clandestinely webcams from her bedroom. Does Annie want to join her? Annie is sceptical and a bit scandalized, but Jules reassures her that it's not gross, and emphasizes the easy money. "I don't do anything bad. I don't even take off my clothes," Jules says. She persuades Annie to try it, promising that if she feels uncomfortable, they will stop. The young women's queer relationship thus becomes the catalyst for sex work, flipping the script on the teen sex worker film where girls are naive and asexual. Though inexperienced, Annie and Jules know what they want.

Like *Cam Girlz* and *Cam*, *Teenage Cocktail* dignifies webcam modelling. In montage it shows the young women preparing for the camera using imagery that evokes Halloween pageantry and slumber party giddiness, imbuing the exhausting shift work planning, decorating, costuming, and performing of shows with humour and eroticism. In the hands of a less nuanced film-maker, Jules and Annie's performances on camera would look like soft-core porn a la *Little Girls*. But in *Teenage Cocktail*, the focus is on the labour and its relationship to the girls' identity formation as they explore themselves and each other as queer women. In fact, their "performances" spark their coming out through their most popular act: their lesbian show.

Women performing lesbianism for men is so very 1990s, and girls casually kissing girls "because I liked it" is the stuff of early aughts pop songs. But this simulated sapphic ardour came with the compulsory look back to the camera, the audience, the authenticity finally resting within the desire for a male audience to approve. *Teenage Cocktail*'s greatest coup is flipping this script. This is where webcam modelling becomes truly subversive. As Jules and Annie perform lesbian shows for their male audiences, who assume they are putting on an act, they are living authentically, for the first time, and seizing an opportunity to suspend their default heterosexuality by using their shows as a safe space to act on desire long repressed. In other words, they are getting paid by men to serve their own needs. The image challenges prohibitionist characterizations of sex work as self-abnegation as it shows Jules's and Annie's identity formation being catalyzed on camera as they transform from compulsorily heterosexual objects to authentic sexual subjects by embracing their queer identities. Ironically, the lesbian acts that make them exquisitely vulnerable in the world become a lucrative business on camera. As the young women use the patriarchal form of porn to rebel against sexual repression and repurpose the male gaze as a pretence to live out their authentic lesbian identities, *Teenage Cocktail* presents camming as a feminist act extraordinaire.

Teenage Cocktail's point of view works against the typical teen sex worker film by centring on its heroines' inner lives. Emphasizing Jules and Annie's subjectivity was a priority for director Carchietta, who hired an almost all-female crew and took an approach where "collaboration [...] is everything."[62] The visual difference is striking. *Cam Girlz* and *Cam* centred on sexual displays and nudity, whereas *Teenage Cocktail* has none: "I never once thought any kind of nudity belonged in the picture. It just wasn't necessary," Carchietta said.[63] The absence of nudity shifts visual weight from the characters' desirability as sexual objects onto Jules's and Annie's desires as sexual subjects, and the camerawork and lighting, from close-ups to the use of red and pink filters, a valentine-coloured palette, expresses the eroticism and authenticity of their lesbian love through their own eyes.

This difference also shapes the sex acts they perform on camera. In *Cam* and *Cam Girlz*, masochism and sexual violence were commodified, without comment from the models, reinforcing pornography's number one creed: that women are aroused by their own submission, or, at the very least, enjoy its simulation. Jules and Annie do not perform sexual violence, nor do they orgasm from their interactions with men. Mostly, they are bored by men, as suggested by the grey interface of the website and the dull, pixilated faces on the screens. Whereas *Cam Girlz* emphasized, and sometimes overstated, webcam models' control, and *Cam* personified the total loss of it, *Teenage Cocktail* occupies a middle ground, where agency is tempered by structure. As such, the film never loses sight of the young women's motivation: money. In its most memorable scene, the girls playfully toss bills around Annie's bed, awestruck by their earnings. Just as in *Magic City*, where soft rugs of cash on the stage floor scooped up after each show symbolized for the dancers a cushion against poverty, the cash Jules and Annie earn is a cushion against inauthenticity, helps builds their viability as a lesbian couple, and encourages them to push forward with their plan to run away to New York City.

But the film is also astute enough to flag how whorephobia threatens the life Jules and Annie are trying to build. When students at their school learn of their work and out them as "sluts," they face the ridicule of the community. Like Alice in *Cam*, however, this only ups the ante for them, and they intensify their work by placing an ad online offering full-service sex. When they get hired by a man for the night, their hubristic headlong dive into their date suggests their teenage delusion of invincibility but also their desperation. The evening is a double performance where everyone is playing a role. Jules and Annie wear ostentatiously sexy clothes and don new names, impersonating glamourous 1980s sequined and eye-shadowed call girls, and their host, a man dressed in a tuxedo, is actually a pool cleaner impersonating the rich homeowner who is abroad. But nobody knows this, and the evening proceeds in a mechanical fashion as both sides ape their roles. While Jules finds the novelty exciting, Annie is uneasy: "I don't even know what I'm doing anymore," she says. "This doesn't feel right." Nevertheless, they leave with the money. We never learn whether Jules and Annie sleep with the man, but either way, Annie's discomfort underscores how sex work carries risks and, for some women, will just feel wrong.

In movies about teen sex workers, men are traditionally aggressors and women their victims, but *Teenage Cocktail* climaxes through the girls' own agency. Unbeknownst to Annie, Jules has secretly photographed their client asleep and emailed him the photo with an extortion demand for $10,000; if he does not comply, they – minors – will go to the police. Jules's action is greedy, and criminal, to be sure, but she also believes that their client is rich and rationalizes milking him as a tax for his transgression. Moreover, that sum is everything for their New York City dream. However, the email does not reach a rich man but a working-class pool cleaner, whose wife sees it first and, realizing what has happened, leaves with their children. His life come undone, the enraged pool cleaner goes out to find Jules and Annie for revenge. *Teenage Cocktail* ends in a high-speed chase and a showdown in a supermarket, a send-up that nuances what has otherwise been a sex work cakewalk. At the film's finale, the enraged client knocks Jules out and begins to strangle Annie, and it seems poised to end, like so many others, with the girls' death. However, *Teenage Cocktail* reverses the norm when Jules strikes the pool cleaner, releasing Annie to safety. With this ending, *Teenage Cocktail* suggests the limits of transactional sex for two inexperienced young women in a world that still criminalizes sex work. It is far from an idyllic ending, but it is also far from the typical teen sex worker tale. No saviour men, no repentance, no guilt.

The threats of stigmatization, homophobia, familial rejection, violence, and internalized whorephobia loomed large over Jules and Annie throughout the film and threatened to break them apart, but *Teenage Cocktail* ends with its heroines walking arm in arm in their town, still bonded. "I'll never let you go,"

Feminist Entanglements in *Cam Girlz, Cam,* and *Teenage Cocktail*   147

Figure 4.4. Jules (Fabianne Therese) and Annie (Nichole Sakura) explore their lesbian desires on camera in *Teenage Cocktail*, a queer love story where webcamming becomes the young women's path to plan and fund a new life.

Jules says to Annie. "I'm gonna take care of you and protect you," Annie replies. The close-up of their faces as they speak their mantra in unison – "one dream" – crystallizes their commitment to each other in a finale that places queer love at centre stage. Free of the moralistic message that sex work damages a woman psychologically, Annie and Jules resume their life in this overtly sweet ending, suggesting that sex work neither defines a woman, nor warrants a sad ending on screen. While *Teenage Cocktail* follows two teen sex workers who lose control, it ends with a toast to their solidarity.

Empowerment and Authenticity: The Product That Flies off Shelves

All three films explored in this chapter go beyond the simple characterization of sex workers as either criminals or victims by portraying young, entrepreneurial women who harness their sexual performances and authenticity as creative entrepreneurs. Through the personal portrait documentary, *Cam Girlz* represents webcam models escaping low-wage service jobs, exercising control, and reconfiguring the traditional visual codes of pornography in performances they say empower them with creativity, agency, and pleasure. That said, *Cam Girlz*'s extolling of webcam modelling's "entrepreneurship" at times sounds like corporate brochure sloganeering for camming platform corporations, as it mostly elides the impacts of precarious emotional labour, of which camming is a paragon. Its focus on a privileged group of Americans likewise leaves out models living outside of the most profitable industry centre where exploitation has been noted. Muted also is the racism prevalent in the US camming industry, where the lion's share of remuneration goes to white women and which, as Angela Jones found, rewards Black models who "adopt a look that adheres to a traditional feminine white aesthetic" including chemically straightened hair and coloured contact lenses.[64] *Cam*, on the other hand, inventively uses a doppelgänger to embody what Hochschild called the "trouble" of over-identifying with one's work role. At the same time, Alice's return to an industry whose practices remain unchanged makes no challenge to corporations that earn millions while investing little into worker pay, safety, and satisfaction.

Both *Cam Girlz* and *Cam* epitomize popular culture's tendency to celebrate entrepreneurial subjects whose unbridled agency draws from neo-liberal discourses of individualistic empowerment. Yet, "empowerment" was never meant to refer to individual acts. Coined by social worker Barbara Bryant Solomon in the 1970s, it described "an ethos" of collective action to encourage marginalized communities to implement their own collective strategies for solving problems.[65] *Cam Girlz* and *Cam* invoke the concept of empowerment without identifying the source of the inequality that power redresses. They are exemplary of the "feminist entanglements" of post-feminist media. As the films humanize webcam models as "creative" entrepreneurs, the story of why women work longer hours, with less security, for lower pay is left off camera, and the films remain within a framework that is copacetic with capitalism. *Teenage*

Cocktail, meanwhile, flips the script of the teen sex worker tale with its story of camming as a path to queer self-definition and solidarity.

What the three films share is a focus on how authenticity and sex work can coexist – and the limits of this. While *Cam Girlz* and *Cam* represent the emotional labour of simulating authenticity, what Arlie Hochschild calls the "unmanaged heart," in *Teenage Cocktail*, Jules and Annie take risks to chase the real thing. As a trio, with their attention to webcam models' labour and their refusal to scold women for profiting from these performances of sexuality, the films enrich the feminist conversation on sex work and move it away from the sort of moralistic uproar caused by LillSecret in that Windsor public library.

5 Sex and Entrepreneurship in the City: Building Intimate Business in *The Girlfriend Experience*

A woman would probably say, "Why do you do this to yourself?" I like the powerful feeling of it. I can choose my schedule. They help me financially.... [But] it's kind of tough sometimes, keeping the personal and work separate.... I kind of build a character for myself. I give different information so it helps keep a distance.... If I could make a movie about a sex worker, you would see me as a normal student. I really work hard for school. I go out often with friends. Then you would realize this girl is a sex worker sometimes. This would be the point. That you can do this job and respect yourself.
– Sophie, call girl

Men were not paying for sex.... They were paying to act out a fantasy.
– Roberta Victor, call girl[1]

What fascinated me was telling the story that hasn't been told, which is the girl who was wanting to do this and wasn't coming from an abused background. She has a lot going for her and decides to do this.
– Riley Keough on Christine, the call girl she plays in *The Girlfriend Experience* (2016–21)[2]

In the last couple of decades or so, as the sex industry has breached the borders of red-light districts, sexual services have diversified to include trysts that euphemize the transaction and metaphorically melt the clock. Today, sex workers go on dates, spend the night, and keep track of everything from their clients' proclivities to their pets in their roles as ideal girlfriends through the popular "girlfriend experience" (GFE), which wraps an affectionate service in the fantasy that it is not store-bought. Put another way, while paid sex is often assumed to be a quick and dirty act, and intimacy once drew its meaning from its opposition to the marketplace, neo-liberalism's credo of "everything is for sale" has ushered in "a brave new world of commercially available intimate encounters that are subjectively normalized for sex workers and clients alike."[3]

This chapter explores popular culture's GFE call girls and the work that underpins their commodification and sale of intimacy. It delves into how the shift from a Fordist to a post-Fordist economy – in which competition, consumerism, and individualism are king – has compelled call girls to become entrepreneurs and asks: How has the transactional nature of intimate relations in neo-liberal society brought about a new, more rounded, nuanced, and sympathetic image of the call girl in twenty-first-century popular culture?

I take up this question as I examine Steven Soderbergh's feature film *The Girlfriend Experience* (2009) and its spin-off television series of the same name that ran for three seasons (2016–21). Together, they capture the zeitgeist of transactional neo-liberal capitalism and the proliferation of a new sex worker commodity: the girlfriend experience. Unlike the stereotype of the cold, clock-watching pro, these GFE call girls dine, kiss, cuddle, banter, listen, soothe, and converse in their roles as professional proxy girlfriends. *The Girlfriend Experience* dignifies this work from the call girl's perspective, pulling back the curtain to reveal her hidden backstage work as an entrepreneur who turns herself into a brand, targets clientele, and creates intimate emotional encounters that entail "authentic" feelings. Yet, far from idealizing this work as a cakewalk in Louboutins, *The Girlfriend Experience* probes the labour of self-commodification and reveals its fault lines – the anomie, stress, burnout, and alienation – aspects the film and series deglamourize. In this regard, *The Girlfriend Experience* makes the call girl a metaphor for neo-liberal capitalism's endemic precarity, where exhausting hustles are trumped up as empowerment, and individual entrepreneurship is often a facade for a grind without a safety net. I begin this chapter with a brief history of the call girl and popular culture's representations of her work, and then offer a close reading of *The Girlfriend Experience*'s stories about the life and labour of women who work as call girls in a neo-liberal, capitalist society.

Contexts: Actresses of Authenticity

To fully appreciate the novelty of *The Girlfriend Experience*, it's useful to briefly look back at the business and history of the call girl's labour. The term "call girl" emerged in the early 1960s, brought about by loosening prostitution laws, an increase in disposable income, a spike in global travel, and the rise of telephone communications.[4] While "call girl" originally named a sex worker reachable by telephone, by the mid-1960s she was synonymous with "classiness" and the performance of feelings, and tales – some apocryphal, some grounded in reality – cast her as deal-closing arm candy for the male bourgeoisie's charge account dinners. At the same time, call girl scandals, like the undoing of British cabinet minister John Profumo as a result of an affair with a so-called call girl, ignited call girl mania, siring memoirs, pop sociology tomes, and pulp novels that professed to illuminate her secret, gold-plated world where sex, intimacy, and capitalism were said to be enjoying their first ménage à trois

Yet, call girl entrepreneurs were new only in name. In ancient Greece, *auletrides* were higher-ranking sex workers and ingenious self-promoters who adorned the bottoms of their sandals with nails that imprinted licentious messages on the sand like "follow me," an early marketing gambit.[5] *Hetaerae*, or courtesans, were famed intimacy experts who lived independently and handled their own finances, privileges the average Greek woman was denied.[6] Phryne, one of the most famous *hetaerae* of Classical Athens, was immortalized in a poem by Rainer Maria Rilke and in paintings that celebrated her allure. In late-nineteenth-century Paris, "the glamour period of the brothel" began, exemplified by Le Chabanais, opened in 1878 by Madam Kelly; the establishment was so successful, Madam Kelly was able to sell shares in it.[7] Across the ocean, the entrepreneurial Everleigh sisters, who Karen Abbott describes as a "20th century amalgamation of Martha Stewart and Madonna,"[8] built an empire around sex and intimacy. From modest means, they "decided that creating a fantasy for others was better than pretending to live in one,"[9] and they opened the "most richly furnished house of courtesans in the world" according to the *Chicago Tribune* in 1901,[10] featuring a ballroom with golden friezes, $650 gold spittoons, and themed rooms where the club's "butterflies" could entertain customers.[11] Posh addresses like the Everleigh mansion gave call girls privileges relative to other sex workers as well as greater control over their labour – and often repeat business.

Today in the twenty-first century, call girls comprise a major part of the sex industry and, apropos neo-liberal capitalism's demand that workers become entrepreneurial, often self-identify and operate as entrepreneurs, sharing many features with other sole proprietors: they market themselves, set their rates, prefer referrals, screen and vet their clients, manage their schedules, field phone calls, arrange transportation, and promote and sell their services on social media.[12] Because they control the means of sexual production (their time, personalities, and bodies) and choose when and where to offer sexual services (and sometimes collect the full profit from their labour), call girls tend to be conceptualized as the least exploited sex workers, as they are owners and workers combined. Indeed, call girls are frequently distinguished from other sex workers by virtue of the control they exercise over their own labour processes.[13] Call girls interviewed by Ann Lucas in Los Angeles and New York, for example, described the importance of "the business side of things," with one seasoned pro noting that "if you stay in the business over time, you're forced to become more entrepreneurial."[14] The terms call girls use to describe their roles vary,

Figure 5.1. Martinis and mischief: call girl mania of the 1960s sired memoirs and pop psychology books claiming knowledge of the inner world and professional life of the storied call girl.

from escort to companion, but generally they are more likely to have regular clients and are among the higher earning sex workers.

Now that we've defined what a call girl is, it will be useful to explore a few concepts central to the work she does: namely, performativity, conspicuous consumption, and the commodification of intimacy. *Performativity* refers to the practices and roles sex workers adopt to establish control and professional boundaries as well as the ways in which their work is "a form of mimetic play, an overt assumption of the feminine role in order to exploit it."[15] Call girls construct and play many feminine roles for their clients: beauty queen, therapist, lover, interlocutor, cheerleader, listener, and illusionist. Fast readers of character, shape shifters, and empaths who know how to make a client feel uniquely desirable, call girls create little pieces of theatre by the hour, weaving sexual fantasies into live-action encounters using the hotel room or the condo as the stage. Call girls are performers, and numerous memoirs by call girls emphasize acting as their métier and use words like "fantasy," "make believe," "actress," and "illusion" to describe the work they do.[16] In her ethnography of New York City call girls, Martha Stein likewise stressed that to

> switch roles quickly is the core of the call girl's work. Men don't come to her hoping to find a relationship with a real woman, but with a three-dimensional embodiment of a fantasy woman. They pay her for the opportunity to satisfy their desires with a partner, undiluted by intrusion of an unpaid partner's own desires and personality.[17]

More recently, writer and former call girl Maggie McNeill wrote that a call girl

> is a kind of entertainer; she is there to provide a kind of interactive show for you. It is, ultimately, an illusion; it no more matters how she "really" feels, or what she "really" likes, or whether she is "really" excited, than it matters that Penn and Teller aren't "really" making things vanish or appear or transmogrify into something else.[18]

For some, a key part of this illusion involves performing as members of a social class to which they do not belong but to which their clients frequently do. In *The Call Girl: A Social and Psychoanalytic Study* (1959), the first comprehensive study on the subject, Harold Greenwald wrote that "call girls are the aristocrats of prostitution. They exude the aura of a ballet dancer or an art student, in any case, a girl from a good background."[19] For many call girls this involves projecting "the kind of front that gives you a respectable address."[20] Preparing this performance of "classiness" requires call girls to engage in *conspicuous consumption*, the idea that the things we publicly consume, wear, and display send messages to others about the social groups to which we belong – and do not belong. Specifically, Thorstein Veblen argued in his 1899 classic, *The Theory of the Leisure Class*, that people were "conspicuous" in their consumption to try to craft and project middle- and upper-class identities,[21] buying products and experiences associated with what Pierre Bourdieu later called "taste" through things like "cosmetics, clothing or home decorations ... to assert one's position in social space."[22]

Conspicuous consumption, then, can be understood as an entrepreneurial strategy for attracting wealthy clients by appearing to already belong to their class and social world. For example, call girls employed by Cachet, a venerable agency in 1980s Manhattan, abided by a strict sartorial code: girls were to wear high-quality undergarments, garter belts, and sheer stockings – no fishnets or patterns – and instructed to carry theatre programs or briefcases to their assignations.[23] One of France's most famous madams, the subject of the 1977 movie *Madame Claude*, was herself "perfectly coiffed and Chanel clad" and apparently "obsessed with fixing" the call girls in her employ to exude an air of refinement by dressing them in "Saint Laurent clothes ... Cartier watches ... Winston jewels ... Vuitton luggage" and sometimes making them over with help from plastic surgeons.[24] In her study of millennial call girls in New York City, Elizabeth Bernstein observed strategic "deployment of cultural and educational capital" and in on case "a faked French accent."[25] In sum, call girls conspicuously consume to project an image of the class they are targeting as clients, and they signal their taste through markers including clothing, comportment, manners, elocution, culinary appreciation, and knowledge of current events.

Yet, while performing classiness may initially attract clients, call girls sustain long-term clientele by simulating intimacy through tremendous emotional labour. Martha Stein wrote about this in her trailblazing ethnography, *Lovers, Friends, Slaves … The Nine Male Sexual Types*, which she based on hundreds of hours spent watching sixty-four call girls have over 1,200 encounters with clients through peepholes and doors left ajar in a New York City brothel. In her conclusion, Stein wrote that call girls devoted the lion's share of their time to providing their clients not with sex but with emotional support, leading her to term these encounters "psycho-sexual transactions."[26] As intimacy experts, the services call girls sell include caressing, kissing, hugging and other non-sexual acts of affection, and, of course, conversation and companionship.

More recently, Bernstein has described how intimacy is now "for sale and purchase as readily as any other form of commercially packaged leisure activity."[27] Unlike the married couple whose non-commodified intimacies are socially understood to be a sign of their monogamous love, call girls sell physical and emotional intimacy by the hour, payable by cash or credit card. From a meaningful stare across the table that suggests a deep knowingness ($1,500 an hour), to the recollection of the name of your childhood dog (gentleman only), to a tingle-inducing touch of fingers tracing up your spine (overnights possible on request), moments once reserved for non-commercial relationships have entered the marketplace and represent the uberization of intimacy and the delivery of the heart, bubble wrapped.

Nothing illustrates the commodification of intimacy better than the call girl's production and sale of the "girlfriend experience" (GFE). Ronald Weitzer has called it "a kind of relationship … rather than just sex."[28] As opposed to the "porn star experience," where clients try out sexual acrobatics gleaned from adult films, a client buying a girlfriend experience seeks companionate affection, empathy, and warmth from a call girl, who plays the part of cheerleader, admirer, confidante, friend, and lover all at once.[29] While she sells sexual services and companionship, her job is to gild her service in authenticity. Thus, her task is twofold: first, to provide a commercial service, and second, to act as though her attraction to the client is sincere.[30] The term "bounded authenticity," coined by Bernstein,[31] helps explain the similarity between these encounters and a stage play, where "bounded" refers to a play's temporality when the actors and the audience work together to suspend disbelief to believe the fiction is real.[32] The call girl's production of authenticity embodies Arlie Hochschild's contention that in late capitalism women service workers must "be a better actor."[33] Or, as Holly Golightly famously put it in *Breakfast at Tiffany's*: "I'm the most real phony around!"

In mid-twentieth-century films, call girls came in three types: the euphemized sophisticate in silk gloves who was never seen at work yet had a charge account at Bergdorf's, the strident businesswoman with the cracked voice who had seen it all, and the unruly call girl whose death at the film's end reinforced the virgin–whore dichotomy. Famous movies starring call girl–like figures such

Building Intimate Business in *The Girlfriend Experience*   157

as *The Blue Angel* (1930), *Of Human Bondage* (1934), and *BUtterfield 8* (1960) used these formulas. But some call girls in the pre–Hays Code era, as Molly Haskell notes, were permitted to succeed "without being stigmatized as unfeminine or predatory,"[34] as in *Shanghai Express* (1932), in which a call girl played by Marlene Dietrich lives happily ever, yet such films were later rare.[35] Usually, stiff moral standards curtailed the dignification of the call girl's work, as in *Baby Face* (1933), where call girl Lil uses sex, wit, and charm to climb in New York high society – that is, until the censor board required MGM to change the film's ending, in which Lil was rich and happy, to make clear that that a woman's choice to engage in sexual capitalism "left her in no better a position."[36] MGM complied, and the film ended conventionally with wedding bells. That said, Lil's climb, powered by erotic capitalism – and without tears about vanquished virginity – repudiated moralists, especially in one scene where she directs her invective straight at them: "I know what the world thinks. Everyone blames me! No one knows the truth. I was all alone here, no family, no friends. I was working hard, earning my own living!" Still, her nuptials furnished the moral value of the story in the end. When the Hays Code was finally dropped in the 1960s, films could drop their moral baggage, and bubbly call films like *Irma La Douce* (1963), *Cactus Flower* (1969), and *Breakfast at Tiffany's* (1961) galvanized full-fledged call girl heroines, although explicit reference to their work was rare.

Breakfast at Tiffany's, the most popular of the bunch, deserves brief pause. Released in 1961, Blake Edwards's film is set in New York City and revolves around an effervescent glamour girl, Holly, her lifestyle, and her mysterious job. A mid-century masterpiece in screenwriting, set design, directing, and acting, including a noteworthy role for a dapper orange tabby, the Gershwin-scored film in swinging sixties pastels dealt with themes of identity as Holly reveals herself as a complex woman of her own invention, running from a past life as one Lula Mae Barnes, married off at fourteen. But it appeared when the Hays Code still forbade depictions of "impure love" on screen, so it euphemized Holly's job, her work from nightfall to twilight (in evening gowns) a stand in for sex work. But Truman Capote, on whose novel the film was based, confirmed Holly's job to *Playboy*, calling her "an escort" who received "a check" for "going home for the night" with "expense account men."[37] The movie won three Oscars and was deemed "historically significant" by the Library of Congress, and Holly's signature style – tight turtleneck, black cigarette pants, and ballet flats – is still invoked as the quintessence of elegance, with *Marie Claire* noting in 2014 that "no character [is] more synonymous with glamour than Holly Golightly."[38] *Breakfast at Tiffany's* was made at a time when real-life call girls were getting booked on Rikers Island,[39] so its portrayal of a deep, likeable, and smart call girl was progressive. Yet, it was perhaps acceptable to audiences precisely because it euphemized sex work, concealing the story of a struggling call girl into an American Dream set in emeralds.

While *Breakfast at Tiffany's* was an upbeat and positive depiction of an escort, other films associated call girls with disorder, mental illness, and moral decay. *Agony of Love* (1966), billed as "An Adult Venture Into a Woman's Inner Most Being," was about a neglected wife who secretly rents an apartment and starts working as a call girl; the film climaxes with a car chase and her death. In the iconic *Belle de Jour* (1967), Catherine Deneuve plays an addled housewife who becomes a call girl for reasons she can't quite pinpoint, yet she knows that she'll "have to atone for it one day." Similarly in *BUtterfield 8*, Elizabeth Taylor plays Gloria, a sumptuous raven diva with a quick tongue and a confident frankness who is involved with a married man; while the film opens on a rebellious note – with Gloria scrawling "No Sale" in red lipstick on a mirror – it ends conventionally with her death in a car wreck, in sadistic slow motion. Xaviera Hollander's 1972 bestselling sex-positive memoir, *The Happy Hooker: My Own Story*, was all about building a Manhattan sex empire and becoming a sex entrepreneur,[40] but while the book was both saucy and generous on the business details, its 1975 screen adaptation treated sex work more as a hobby and way of meeting rich men. Martini, please!

In the 1980s, Hollywood retooled the call girl into a girl Friday for blue-chip sharks, with a focus on drawing parallels, however far-fetched, between sex workers and white-collar businessmen. Emblematic is *Pretty Woman* (1990), in which Edward analogizes his work as a banker with Vivian's as a sex worker: "You and I are such similar creatures, Vivian. We both screw people for money." In *Risky Business* (1983), *Night Shift* (1982), and *Dressed to Kill* (1980), brainy call girls help young, middle-class white men build businesses and get rich, while their own economic and legal status remains unchanged.[41] These films glamourized sex workers alongside the ruling class, forgetting that the former is frequently arrested for servicing the latter. In any case, Reaganite conservatism and prohibitionist feminism inflected films like *Money on the Side* (1982), where a call girl hangs herself, and *Nuts* (1987), in which Barbra Streisand plays a call girl on trial for the murder of her client. While both credibly highlighted the possible unpleasant aspects of sex work, their "sex work is dangerous" credo lacked the nuance of *Klute* (1971) and *Working Girls* (1986), which, without gloss or brimstone, portrayed smart call girls working under neo-liberal capitalism without reducing them to victims of it.[42]

In the twenty-first century, savvy call girl entrepreneurs who create intimate experiences for their clients began appearing in films, such as *The Girlfriend Experience* (2009), *A Perfect Ending* (2012), and *The Escort* (2015), and in TV shows, such as *House of Cards* (2013–18), *The Killing* (2011–14), *The Girlfriend Experience* (2016–21), *Law & Order* (1990–), *Shiva Baby* (2020), and *Strut* (2021–), a television comedy about a shy twenty-something year old who starts here own escort agency with two friends.[43] These new works are different from those of the past because they are often told from the call girl's point of view and shun the *fare du jour* of death and mental disturbance, and of glamourization, too. *The Girlfriend Experience* film, in particular, offers a provocative representation of the call girl as an entrepreneur of transactional intimacy.

Making Authenticity in Manhattan: Steven Soderbergh's *The Girlfriend Experience*

Set in late 2008, in the wake of the Wall Street and global financial collapse, *The Girlfriend Experience* (2009) is the story of "Chelsea," an entrepreneurial call girl who sells the GFE to clients for $2,000 an hour. Filmed in five-star hotels, swanky restaurants, and town cars, it trails Chelsea through Manhattan over a period of several days as she sees clients, shops, grooms, meets with experts whom she hopes will help her expand her business, and audio records a diary for a journalist writing a story about her. At the end of the film, trouble ensues as her carefully separated personal and business lives converge. The film portrays her as a rational woman with conflicting feelings about her job, which she chose as an alternative to worse jobs during hard economic times, and as entrepreneur who is trying to make her way under neo-liberal capitalism.

The Girlfriend Experience foregrounds the call girl's financial motivation with its setting: late 2008 New York as the US is sliding into financial ruin. The timing is poor for any business expansion, but Chelsea has plans to "take her business to the next level." As a poised twenty-something call girl with a designer wardrobe, shiny espresso hair, and flirtatious feline eyes, Chelsea is excellent at her job and sees it as her path to financial independence: "I didn't want to depend on my parents' money. That's more than half the reason I started doing this job in the first place." Chelsea is a white and privileged middle-class call girl who chooses her clients, sets her rates, works only a few days a week, lives in a chic Manhattan apartment, and says she generally likes her work ("Lucky for me he's attractive, so that helps, and I enjoy myself"). Her ambition is to parlay her earnings into the start-up capital she needs to open her own luxury clothing boutique. Moreover, as the global economy crashes and unemployment and low-paying precarious work spikes in a post-Fordist gig economy, she sees sex work as the least exploitative and most rewarding form of service work she can do.

Stylistically, *The Girlfriend Experience* is an homage to Godard's 1962 *Vivre sa vie*, the New Wave vérité classic that mined the anomie of capitalism through the eyes of a Parisian call girl. Like Godard's mirthless opus, the film portrays capitalism as system where no feeling or experience lacks a price tag, even the most intimate. To reveal this chilly world, Soderbergh abandons the intimacy-building devices of narrative cinema – plot, backstory, and character development – for vérité strategies like fragmentation, improvisational dialogue, a distanced camera, a storyline with lots of white space, and real time. Yet, while *Vivre sa vie*'s call girl was an outsider – a pariah used by men – who dies by suicide in a grim final indictment of transactional intimacy, in Soderbergh's revision half a century later the call girl is part of Manhattan's crème de la crème, totally in sync with twenty-first-century neo-liberal capitalism, and her product – transactional sex and the "authentic" encounter – so ubiquitous and normalized that, most unusually for a film about a call girl, there is almost no sex on screen. Instead, the film focuses on the labour that precedes and follows the sex act, deploying the eminently curious vérité form to explore Chelsea's emotional labour in two settings: "backstage," where she prepares for her dates, and "frontstage," where she creates intimate experiences of authenticity for her clients while balancing the "acts" that Arlie Hochschild refers to as "surface" and "deep acting."

The Girlfriend Experience's opening scene is a meticulous study of Chelsea's performance and highlights her ability to enact "a clear separation of self from role."[44] It begins in a chic SoHo restaurant with exposed brick walls, Edison bulb light fixtures, and humming dinnertime chatter as Chelsea and her client, a handsome French banker, sit at a candlelit table absorbed in a cozy-looking conversation. The camera focuses on Chelsea's face as she "surface acts" to perform interest and build intimacy.[45] She leans forward and smiles, as if drawn by her client's magnetism; she plays with her hair as if piqued by sexual interest; she arches an eyebrow as if moved to flirtation. Chelsea also "deep acts," working up "authentic" feelings for this synthetic situation. A person is said to be "authentic" when their actions reflect their innermost thoughts, feelings, and values.[46] Chelsea is dedicated to creating the *impression* of authenticity while maintaining what Hochschild calls a "healthy estrangement of self from role." She takes pride in her skills as "an illusion maker"[47] and works hard to foster frisson by employing Konstantin Stanislavski's technique that encourages an actor to enter a scene by using their own personal memories as a resource to feel "an imagined happening is *really happening now*."[48] Chelsea's authenticity is convincing. The appetizers come, the Pinot is corked, the conversation becomes zingier, and by the time she and her client exit the taxi at his hotel, her arm entwined in his, they look like a couple on an early date that's going exceptionally well. The real-time unfolding credits Chelsea as a talented performer, and, with the first act over, roses fly onto the stage.

Not really, though, for Chelsea's job is to conceal the act and the stage and maintain the fantasy that her authenticity comes from her beating heart. Just as a knockoff purse is sold as the "real thing" to a customer who knows it isn't, the GFE is transacted between Chelsea and her client who cooperate

Figure 5.2. Kissing is part of the service on offer – and paid for by cash – in *The Girlfriend Experience*.

with a mutual suspension of disbelief. Thus, while her client understands that he is buying her pretence, he nevertheless judges its credibility, and their shared awareness of and involvement in the fantasy becomes, ironically, an act of bonding. Soderbergh exaggeratedly draws on the visual vocabulary of romance to emphasize the artifice built into Chelsea's double duty of suspending disbelief and deep acting to ensure her client has a good time. She curls up on the couch, kicks off her heels, and sends him doe eyes, as if testing to see if her affections will be reciprocated; he puts on some jazz and pours them red wine. Their bodies draw closer. Their fingers curled around the wineglass stems is a stock romantic shot, and as blues notes fill the sultry-lit room, they embrace and, finally, kiss.

Call girls are likely to engage in affection, and many report kissing, hugging, and caressing their clients, though some may use diversionary tactics to keep kissing to a minimum.[49] Simone de Beauvoir even noted that the call girl "reserves for her lover the kiss on the mouth."[50] Similarly, it is conventional in Hollywood films for sex workers *not* to kiss (we can think of Vivian Ward's "I don't kiss clients" in *Pretty Woman*), but Hollywood loves its smoochy close-ups, so Soderbergh slows things down for an extra-long spell to emphasize Chelsea's deep acting and five-star girlfriend experience. Western culture has long defined the kiss as the most emotionally consummate act. From Auguste Rodin's sculpture *The Kiss* (1882) to Robert Doisneau's iconic photograph of the lip-locked couple outside the Hôtel de Ville (1950), it is the visual marker of intimacy, bar none.[51] Given that paid sex is usually framed as intimacy's antithesis, the kiss is one of the rarest sights in a sex worker film. Again, working against the sex work movie trope, *The Girlfriend Experience* skips the sex for the post-coital conversation, in which Chelsea's client confides, solicits advice, and talks about his innermost feelings. Chelsea is endlessly patient and spends the night, and her role-playing continues the next morning as she and her client sip lattes and read the *New York Times* in matching bathrobes on a green rooftop overlooking Manhattan. So committed are Chelsea and her client to this performance that neither break character even when he gives Chelsea an envelope of money he euphemizes as a "gift." Businesses pay workers; lovers give each other "gifts."[52] It's only when finally alone in her chauffeured car that she finally drops the act and counts the cash like the entrepreneur she is. The marathon girlfriend experience is shown in vérité to dignify Chelsea's work as she exits the stage.

The Girlfriend Experience also emphasizes the emotional labour GFE call girls do. Chelsea sees a dozen clients but sleeps with only one. With the rest she plays the part of supportive girlfriend, creating "bounded authenticity" for the lonely, the stressed, and the commitment-averse who want affection without the risk or responsibility of a real relationship. Chelsea's clients are wealthy blue-chip men who store gold bars in vaults; in Chelsea, they store their feelings. Hobbled by the financial crisis, many feel fearful and impotent and look to her as a sounding board and therapist. Some admit that buying GFE services feels less taboo than therapy. "I'm feeling so stressed out. I should probably see a shrink, but it's more fun to see you," one client says. Others vent, lament, and cry, but the narrative focus remains on Chelsea, completely. The film is clear that as Chelsea performs she maintains emotional boundaries that imbue her performances, while convincing, with the low-fi energy of a Rothko painting, an emphatic presence whose dominant expression is absence. She is curious (but never probes), complimentary (but never obsequious), sympathetic (but never pitying), and affectionate (but never smothering). Counterintuitively, Chelsea's remoteness builds intimacy for her clients because it allows the focus to remain on them. Indeed, her clients say they value her because she "knows them" and is "real."

Of course, her clients do not know the real "Chelsea" (whose name, we learn, is actually Christine), and their illusion rests upon her concealment of her labour, which is what keeps them coming back (and for real-life call girls as well). As Hochschild notes, "to show that the enjoyment takes effort is to do the job poorly."[53] Lynne Pettinger found that on escort review websites, the most positive reviews are for call girls who seem "real" and seem to be enjoying themselves (and who appear to have real orgasms).[54] Conversely, clients give low scores to call girls who seem fake, rushed, or disinterested. *The Girlfriend Experience* highlights the tactics Chelsea uses to meet the demand for the "unmanaged heart." Yet, just as the film itself conceals the division of labour behind it, Chelsea's performances "on stage" conceal the work required to make them feel so lifelike. Soderbergh, savvy to this, takes us behind the curtain.

Websites, Waxing, and 24/7 Availability: The Backstage Labour of the GFE Call Girl

While *The Girlfriend Experience* foregrounds the frontstage, it even more so offers a behind-the-scenes look at running a GFE call girl business. Chelsea is an entrepreneur whose self-employment enables her to produce, market, and sell services free of looming management or a potentially sexist boss who takes liberties with a precarious employer–employee relationship. But running this business independently is a hustle, and throughout the film Chelsea's entrepreneurship is explored and dignified by scenes that emphasize her digital marketing practices, conspicuous consumption, and aesthetic labour: she creates marketing plans, communicates with clients online, conducts meetings, sets schedules, rents space, fields phone calls, arranges transportation, shops, primps, picks up dry cleaning, pays taxes, and keeps financial records.

Building a customer base is challenging for any business, but even more so for an illegal one, making the call girl's marketing plan a delicate and dangerous art. As Ann Lucas notes, call girls are attentive to how they produce and promote themselves through personal branding,[55] and *The Girlfriend Experience* shows Chelsea attentively targeting clients through the internet. Soderbergh himself emphasized this: "The super high-end GFEs work totally on their own.... This is something the internet really makes easy."[56] Chelsea, out of necessity, manages what seems like a 24/7 marketing campaign. In fact, the film's inciting incident is a new call girl threatening Chelsea's high-ranking position in the GFE call girl market, prompting her to double down on marketing. Whereas call girls once relied on print ads and telephone lines (making them vulnerable to arrest), in the 1990s they began capitalizing on internet adult sites such as Eros, Backpage (until 2018), Craigslist (until 2018), and Slixa to publicize their images and communicate and connect with prospective clients.[57]

The Girlfriend Experience represents this side of Chelsea's business in a scene with a web developer who specializes in marketing for call girls. The openness of their meeting – with their matching Macbooks sharing table space in a chic Midtown café – and the detached and clinical way he assesses Chelsea's website, eyes narrowed as he scrolls, suggests how business-like her business really is, and how it can be scrutinized and optimized like any other commodity: "We can improve these photos. I can make these a lot more high-class. They need to be top quality," the web developer tells her. He also advises her to "improve her logo" and "make the overall aesthetic of the website much more high-class." Like many digital media entrepreneurs contending with a cluttered online market for various searchable services, Chelsea's main concern is achieving search engine optimization (SEO) for her website so that it appears first in searches for "Manhattan GFE call girls." The developer's suggestion is for Chelsea to get herself on the biggest escort review websites: "The more links there are, the better the SEO will be." At the mention of "review websites" her face becomes noticeably strained.

Escort review websites are user-aggregated spaces where clients anonymously rate and leave comments about sexual service providers in the style of restaurant reviews.[58] Ever since the launch of The Erotic Review and Punternet in the 1990s, call girls have been publicly evaluated according to appearance, performance, personality, apartment, location, and even parking.[59] In *The Girlfriend Experience*, managing and marketing herself online costs Chelsea a lot of money, but it also causes stress. The competition is also so fierce that she decides to hire this digital media expert on a monthly retainer of $1,500, since she fears bad reviews of her work. For Chelsea, the internet and review websites are a double-edged sword: key to bringing in new clientele, but also a form of surveillance and source of judgement that pressures her to go the extra mile to prevent clients from leaving negative reviews. Moreover, the anonymity of these sites provides a cozy home for disgruntled clients who may leave nasty reviews to undercut her carefully crafted online image and destroy her business. This stress motivates Chelsea to control the aspects of her business that she can through aesthetic labour and conspicuous consumption.

Cashmere, Silk, and Gold: Conspicuous Consumption and Aesthetic Labour

Given that her success and marketing is based on her appearance in photos and in real life, one of Chelsea's main business strategies is aesthetic labour. Throughout the film, Chelsea engages in aesthetic labour to achieve a beauty standard expected by clients and shops for designer clothes, cosmetics, and grooming goods, embodying Simone de Beauvoir's axiom that beauty is a performance "achieved through training."[60] In one scene, she wakes up in a posh hotel room beside a client, scampers to the bathroom, and proceeds to comb her eyelashes *one by one* before returning to bed to feign an "I just woke up like this" yawn. Chelsea's aesthetic labour is less about looking sexy (although that matters) than achieving a sophisticated look congruent with the tastes and preferences of the social class of clientele she wishes to attract: rich Wall Street bankers. She does this through conspicuous consumption of products branded to signify wealth and high-class status, and she invests an enormous amount of time and energy into her appearance and wardrobe to augur her own economic mobility. Even the name she chooses for her professional GFE persona – Chelsea – conjures the Manhattan neighbourhood of exclusive shops and bistros.

Chelsea's identity is so tied to her appearance that her diary voiceover narrations throughout the film are almost exclusively descriptions of her outfits:

> I met with Philip on October 5th and 6th. I wore a Michael Kors dress and shoes with La Perla lingerie underneath and diamond stud earrings. We met at 7:30 at the hotel for a drink downstairs. He liked my dress but didn't go into detail why.

And she meticulously records her life according to her sartorial decisions:

> On October 25th, I met with Dennis.... I put on a Kiki de Montparnasse corset, panties, and gloves. The shoes were basic Zara.... On October 28th I met Dan. I wore a vintage black cashmere sweater, Ernest So jeans, and Pour La Victoire boots.

These voiceovers and the film's vast imagery of boutiques, jewellery, hairdressers, cosmetics, perfumes, handbags, sunglasses, and mirrors habituate Chelsea in a world where identity is formed and reinforced through consumerism, and personal empowerment through exhausting grooming and consumption of branded products. Through Chelsea, the film exemplifies what Rosalind Gill has described as a core quality of post-feminist media culture, wherein "the body is simultaneously presented as a woman's source of power and as always unruly, requiring constant monitoring surveillance, discipline and remodelling (and consumer spending) in order to conform to ever-narrower judgments about female attractiveness."[61] In this regard, Chelsea seems to be an ideal post-feminist subject for whom shopping to look good, and looking good for others, feels like "empowerment." Yet given the primacy of appearance in her business, it's no wonder that shopping and looking good is Chelsea's pastime and, later, her neurotic obsession. Seen in this light, her incantation of designer labels begins to seem less like blithe consumerism and more like an uncanny form of prayer, the label dropping conferring on her a much-needed form of security in a competitive industry at a time when precarity is the status quo.

In this regard, Soderbergh draws our attention to Chelsea's precarity in a saturated market, aligning her with actresses and models whose careers also depend on maintaining a high-def image of perfection. (A sex worker not projecting the right look is one of the more memorable and painful scenes in *Pretty Woman*, in which working-class Vivian is rebuffed by snobby clerks in a designer clothing store who cattily judge her on her inexpensive-looking clothing before her client swoops in to give her a "makeover" to suit his own class preferences.) By transforming shopping and grooming – commonly thought to bring women pleasure – into a professional requirement, a business expense, and a hustle and grind, the film shows how taxing the work of looking good is, and how looking good is a way of managing the stress of precarity. As Ashley Mears notes, precarious workers whose appearances are central to their jobs manage "uncertainty" by engaging in "the ongoing production of the body and the self, necessitating that they are 'always on' and unable to walk away from the product."[62]

As the film goes on, we see how this precarity makes searching for new work Chelsea's *other* full-time gig, placing her on a treadmill of servicing clients and searching for new ones – aesthetic labour, conspicuous consumption, and marketing – that speaks to how precarity has intensified for entrepreneurial sex workers, and many other gig workers, under neo-liberal capitalism. Indeed, Chelsea makes herself available twenty-four hours a day to answer inquiries from potential clients and, with her smartphone in hand and her new website always open for business, she can never truly switch off her GFE persona.

The Girlfriend Experience refuses to pass moral judgment on Chelsea's life and work, however. In fact, it normalizes it by suggesting a congruence between it and other forms of precarious work under neo-liberal capitalism's credo of remaking oneself to "service people." For example, Chelsea's work has many similarities to that of her boyfriend, Chris, a personal trainer to elite bankers. The film uses a parallel structure and title cards between images of them at their respective workplaces – Chelsea talking with clients in hotel rooms, Chris training out-of-shape financiers in fitness clubs – to emphasize how both do work that involves physical proximity, sweat, emotion, exertion, and helping their clients self-actualize as their personal cheerleaders. Chelsea's performances are bounded by the revolving doors of posh hotels, and her boyfriend's by the doors of the gym. As Chelsea clinks glasses with a client and says how "she enjoys talking to him," Chris encourages his client sweating away on a Nautilus machine: "Way to go! You're doing great!" Both good-looking and charismatic, they both undertake considerable aesthetic labour and conspicuous consumption to appear as walking advertisements for the embodied services they sell.

At the same time, their clients' desires for "authenticity" force Chelsea and Chris to perform rhetorical acrobatics to hide their transactional relationships in the guise of "relationship building." When Chris tries to sell a client another package of training sessions, he invokes their personal connection – "I don't think our relationship should end so soon" – and in an even fainter sales pitch after a date ends, Chelsea lingers by the door waiting, but not asking directly, for her "gift." By revealing the similarities between Chelsea and Chris's work,

The Girlfriend Experience shows how the production of intimacy is a new norm under neo-liberal capitalism, where becoming, being, and serving as an entrepreneurial subject is not only virtuous but increasingly mandatory. The film underscores Chelsea's fit with neo-liberal capitalism as she strides confidently through hotels, cafés, boutiques, and art galleries; far from Godard's pariah call girl in *Vivre sa vie*, she is part of society precisely because her work pivots upon its central values.

The Girlfriend Experience dignifies Chelsea's work, but it does not glamourize or glorify it. Instead, it exposes the hardships of repetitively producing and performing improvisational pieces of theatre that prop up her clients' egos. When doing this work, Chelsea must hide her frustration, boredom, and even contempt behind a smile, which stays fixed on her face despite what she actually thinks. Chelsea's strategic concealment of her own thoughts and feelings with a permanent smile is fitting, however, given her job is to "be who the client wants her to be." So, she smiles when her clients drone on, she smiles when they are inept, and she smiles when they turn brusque at the ends of dates, coldly pushing "gift" envelopes into her hands. Clearly, a cost of Chelsea's work of repeat and return performances engineered to make her clients happy is a form of alienation from herself.

For a performer, the end of a show brings release and a sense of accomplishment, but a performer who cannot leave the stage will lose their sense of connection with their authentic self, and they may ultimately change how they feel inside to match who they play on stage. As Hochschild reminds us, melting the crucial separation between one's role and one's private self leads to "numbing ... [and] when we lose access to feeling, we lose a central means of interpreting the world around us."[63] This is what happens to Chelsea. When the film opens, Chelsea has a clearly delineated private (backstage) self and work (frontstage) self, but without an exit from the stage and feeling compelled by her clients to always "be on," she starts to identify wholeheartedly with her role that is so core to the fantasy she sells.

The Girlfriend Experience also highlights the toll a call girl's work may take on their own intimate relationships. This manifests in Chelsea's withdrawal from her romantic personal relationship to her partner, Chris, which increasingly resembles the alienating transactional relationships she has with clients. They are a disconnected couple. A shot of Chelsea waking up in a hotel room with a client is intercut with one of Chris starting his day in their apartment, alone; scenes of Chelsea dining with her clients are interposed with images of Chris jogging, again alone, suggesting their very separate and disconnected lives. The stress of always having to connect with clients disconnects Chelsea from Chris, and her after-work routine of crashing onto the couch and zoning out by watching TV and poring over astrology books figuratively suggests Chelsea's residence in another universe far away from Chris's. The film doesn't blame

Chelsea's work for her personal intimate relationship's eventual failure but correlates it with the labour pains and numbing psychological effects of doing emotionally intensive service work. Having invested their affect into building authentic "intimate relationships" with strangers at work, both Chelsea and Chris simply have no emotional energy left to invest in each other.

Moreover, *The Girlfriend Experience* contemplates the social alienation of working as a call girl. To play her servile role, Chelsea must identify with it "wholeheartedly," mastering the art of what Hochschild calls "pulling the two [of ourselves] closer together either by changing what we feel or by changing what we feign."[64] As the film progresses, we see that Chelsea has feigned to such a degree that when not on stage, she has no life. We never see her socializing; her relationship to her family is non-existent; her boyfriend is a prop; and she is never seen with the same client twice. This, coupled with the film's fragmentary style, which precludes any social relationship development, is exactly the point. Chelsea's choice to do sex work, though rewarding from a financial perspective, leaves her socially isolated and seeking more fulfilment than her transactions offer. After one appointment, Chelsea tells her driver, "[The client] didn't even kiss me goodbye. It was very strange. It was a very awkward departure. I mean, he's never done that before," voicing a latent expectation that their transaction be more than it is. Caught on a sleep-work-spend merry-go-round, her days a miasma of beauty appointments, dry cleaning drop offs, and performances with strangers she pretends to know, Chelsea retreats into somnambulism and becomes alienated from herself and everyone around her.

The Girlfriend Experience furthermore probes the hazards call girls face when working with and through sleazy and corrupt intermediaries. Throughout the story, Chelsea alludes to sex industry gatekeepers who treat her like nothing more than an object to be transacted. Late in the film, on the advice of her web developer, Chelsea meets with an industry "expert," a self-styled web 2.0 Svengali who runs a popular review website and claims to help call girls become successful by increasing their online presence. The "expert," who operates under the moniker the "Erotic Connoisseur," is an opportunistic pervert who preys on ambitious women like Chelsea by writing fake reviews in exchange for sexual favours. The meeting, which takes place at a warehouse where porn is shot, plays out the Hollywood "casting couch" trope where the high-powered producer preys on the ingénue's hopes and anxieties about the exchange value and symbolic currency of her persona. The expert slickly brags about his star-making capabilities for other call girls and insults Chelsea's status to establish his credibility: "Cara is twenty years old. Fell off the turnip truck. When I put up the reviews, she was so in demand. You think you know what upscale is, but I'm offering you upscale demand." Then he flatly asks her for sex: "A review copy, if you will," he says smugly, implying that if she doesn't comply, he will write negative reviews and damage her reputation.

This overt attempt at blackmail triggers Chelsea into a panic attack, and she retreats to the washroom where the "expert" can be heard in voiceover ordering her to "clean her vagina with a Q-tip." This humiliating scene, in which an industry intermediary uses degradation and the threat of reputation loss in a bid to extort sex, makes Chelsea's earlier comment that she needs to wear "thick armour" in her business an understatement. Sex industry power imbalances and class divisions between male owners/intermediaries and female service providers are magnified here, highlighting how sex workers in existing unregulated black and grey markets where they are denied legal rights leaves them vulnerable to exploiters like the "Erotic Connoisseur." Although Chelsea refuses to cater to this man, the scene shatters the control she claimed as her work's greatest perk and reveals the sex industry's bigger structure – and the patriarchal power it perpetuates. Furthermore, it reminds us of call girls' vulnerability to industry exploiters who operate with impunity and asks us to consider how, if Chelsea's work were decriminalized, she would be empowered to go to the police, a labour union, or simply reach out to friends for the support she badly needs. Sex work's criminalization and stigmatization prevent Chelsea from getting that protection and support, and she instead faces men who control capital and regard women's bodies as commodities that are bought and sold.

Stuck on Stage: The Costs of Self-Commodification

While *The Girlfriend Experience* explores the individual, interpersonal, and social troubles call girls may experience on and off the job, it doesn't suggest that sex work itself is responsible for these problems. Rather, it indicts neo-liberal capitalism's demand that humans should and can reach their full potential and freedom through "entrepreneurial freedoms"[65] and, by doing so, makes the hazards of Chelsea's own choice of business and labour process emblematic or symptomatic of the wider political economy system that shapes it. While neo-liberals champion individual entrepreneurship and competition as the gilded path to achieving their financial dreams, *The Girlfriend Experience* gives the lie to this fantasy by showing the stress, atomization, alienation, and loneliness it may cause. The reward, the film suggests, is consumerism, but sweeping shots of Chelsea walking by shop windows on empty Madison Avenue at dusk imply this is empty compensation. While *Breakfast at Tiffany's* call girl Holly Golightly was rewarded by the jewels she got in exchange for her doing her job, in *The Girlfriend Experience*, the gems have stopped glittering.

The Girlfriend Experience doesn't make Chelsea's alienation unique to sex work, though. Rather, it suggests that sex work's criminalization and stigmatization are what compel Chelsea into secrecy, which prevents her from reaching out for the emotional support she needs. Lacking support, she is fragile, and her boundaries begin to break down. By film's end, she breaks the cardinal rule of her enterprise by acting on romantic feelings for a client and seeing him outside business hours for free. His appeal? He's the first (and only) person in the film who asks Chelsea questions about *herself* and does emotional labour *for her*. She ends her moribund relationship with Chris and leaves for the Hudson Valley by train for a weekend rendezvous she won't have to contrive. As she sits on the train wearing casual clothes, the camera focuses on her relaxed, smiling face, and for the first time all film the audience sees she is *not* at work – she is not being paid or preparing to be paid for pretending to be someone else. Tellingly, her obtrusive sartorial voiceovers abruptly stop as she leaves for the city in anticipation of a weekend of authenticity and intimacy with someone who understands her and wants to know the real her.

But the finale of *The Girlfriend Experience* undercuts this fairy-tale promise. Chelsea's client/lover phones to say "I've been thinking about you non-stop" before telling her that he is not coming, now or ever, calling her by the wrong name before hanging up. A consummate consumer of the GFE, Chelsea's lover has pumped the brakes on the border of their bounded relationship, realizing that he prefers the control of paying to be in a show in which Chelsea ensures he is the star, free to walk off stage at any time, over the real thing. It's a shattering moment. For Chelsea, it confirms that her performance has a higher value than her authenticity, and she regrets relinquishing control, breaching her boundaries, and misjudging her client's sexual fascination for an interest in "the real her."

A tracking shot of Chelsea returning home by train captures green patches of farmland flashing through the window, a suggestion of authenticity, before giving way to the grey cubist blocks of the city of artifice, tears trailing Chelsea's cheeks as she clutches her iPhone. At this breaking point, a voiceover interrupts. It is the repugnant "Erotic Connoisseur" reading the savage review he has posted on his website about Chelsea, no doubt punishing her for refusing him "a review copy" of sex:

> With her smoky eyes, dark, straight hair, and perky little body, Chelsea would appear to have the goods to satisfy the guy or girl next door. Alas, Chelsea seems bent on marketing herself as a sophisticated escort. With her flat affect, lack of culture, and her inability to engage, Chelsea couldn't even dazzle Forest fucking Gump.

The Connoisseur's brutal review gives expression to the misogynistic objectification to which sex workers are continually subjected. After all of the effort, time, and money she has invested into trying to "take her business to the next level," this nasty review will be devastating since Chelsea is a freelancer in a hyper-competitive business where demand is uneven and where her reputation lives and dies on the strength of anonymous reviews.[66] So, she returns to the city and tries to re-establish herself – and the value of her product.

Figure 5.3. Everything is for sale in *The Girlfriend Experience*, even authentic intimacy. The embrace looks real, and may even feel real for both parties, but the transaction still abides by the ticking clock.

In *The Girlfriend Experience*'s denouement, Chelsea visits a Hasidic jeweler client at his Manhattan diamond store for a lunch hour intimacy quickie. He greets her by name and takes her to his cluttered back office where she strips to her bra and underwear and they embrace. The slow-moving scene is smash-full of contradictions: he is bear-like, she is bony; he is clothed, she is nearly naked; their embrace looks loving, yet they are virtual strangers; he is at his own workplace, yet she is the one who is working. A menorah sits behind them on a windowsill suggesting tradition, family, and community – a contrast to their connection, which is commodified, transactional, and individualized. Noticeably, neither disengages after he reaches orgasm, a lingering that suggests their mutual yearning for connection that eludes them in their daily commodified lives. Her client then softly begins to weep. Shot in a warm, yellowy light, the camera focuses on their entwined bodies, suggesting that this was more than a cut-and-dry transaction and that the tears might as well be both of theirs. Yet, even in this moment of mutual vulnerability, a wall clock above them noticeably ticks, counting down the minutes of the appointment, reminding the viewer with a subtle wink that this embrace, however intimate and authentic it looks and may even be, was bought and paid for in cash.

It is fitting that *The Girlfriend Experience* climaxes with a tenuous embrace in a diamond store where everything is for sale. One of capitalism's biggest coups was manufacturing a synthetic twin for everything grown by nature. Sugar was rebooted as aspartame, the breast uplifted by the gel implant, cotton retooled into rayon, and socializing redefined by social media. Yet, the scene suggests that there remain some things that can't be faked. Authentic intimacy, like a diamond, forms through a deep organic process requiring an investment of time, heat, pressure, and energy. The process may yield a flawless AAA stone, or not, as nature makes no promises. Manufactured intimacy, like the GFE, is like a cubic zirconia produced in a lab where the growth rate is accelerated, the energy inputs minimized, and the risk of failure eliminated by design. The process promises the product's shape, lustre, and value, and as a consequence of being manufactured, the stone is guaranteed perfect, yet it is not real, and it will scratch and crack under pressure. In *The Girlfriend Experience*, Chelsea is an entrepreneur who understands how to manufacture her product perfectly and excels at marketing and selling it. And while she and the buyer know it is counterfeit, the quality of the simulation, as judged by male clients online and off, is more important than its authenticity. Whereas *Breakfast at Tiffany's* euphemized sex work with its showcase of diamonds, *The Girlfriend Experience* puts Chelsea's late capitalist anomie into the jewellery store window for all to see.

Law Student to Sex Scandal Call Girl: *The Girlfriend Experience* TV Series

In the ads for *The Girlfriend Experience* series, which premiered in April 2016, the network Starz described the show as being about "transactional sex." Based on Soderbergh's film, season one revives the Chelsea/Christine character, this time a hard-working law student and intern at a prestigious Chicago firm and, later, a part-time call girl. Shot in steely blues and textured in chrome, glass, and pinstripes, *The Girlfriend Experience* portrays the hollowness of neo-liberal capitalism, where individualism, competition, and consumerism are king and anything, even the simulation of love, can be bought and sold. With its sleek camerawork and star-studded cast (Christine, the heroine of season one, is played by Riley Keough, Elvis's granddaughter), *The Girlfriend Experience* takes us from the conference room to the client's penthouse with its non-judgemental exploration of high-end sex work. But it's also about whore stigma, misogyny, and hypocrisy, and it shifts between the worlds of corporate law and sex work to ultimately suggest their congruence. The show's message is that sex workers are normal women who make choices and weigh out their options, and it demonstrates this as Christine parlays knowledge she has picked up in law school to professionalize as a call girl, ultimately deciding that sex work is more satisfying than litigating for the Fortune 500. Normalizing sex workers and challenging tropes was a goal for the show, as Riley Keough later said in an interview: "What fascinated me was telling the story that hasn't been told, which is the girl who was wanting to do this and wasn't coming from an abused background. She has a lot going for her and decides to do this."[67] While the series aired for three seasons, I focus here on season one, which dealt with a rich array of sex worker issues and set the tone for the seasons that followed.

The TV series opens by introducing Christine before she has become a call girl. Early scenes show her studying at the college library and working at a part-time job to pay her tuition while also interning at a law firm, Kirkland, to gain "experience" she hopes will propel her into a lucrative legal career. When Christine loses her part-time job, however, she faces eviction and panics. A solution comes by way of Avery, her best friend, a call girl for the caviar set who suggests Christine dip a toe in by visiting her at a posh hotel. The women don plush bathrobes and make a game of phoning room service to order absurdly overpriced items: "What's your most expensive bottle of champagne?" they quip. "$700? What's your most expensive bottle of wine? $900? Can we get both?" and pay with Avery's client's credit card. The scene unfolds with slumber party giddiness, but her zero balance bank account looms large as Christine is initiated into the work of being a call girl.

Early on, then, the TV series depicts sex work not as a plum job, but as a mode of easing one's burdens in a gig economy. That we meet Christine *before* she becomes a call girl builds our understanding of how, like most women who choose to engage in sex work, economic factors lead. For Avery, sex work is better than a retail gig that pays an unliveable wage. It also suits her, as she tells Christine: "It's not something I want to make into a career. But I enjoy it. I like meeting new people, I enjoy sex, and I only do it a few times a month … I get off on it. The rush. All the attention. Knowing he likes me." *The Girlfriend Experience* explores the factors a woman weighs when deciding to engage in sex work according to her history and needs, and her comfort around transactional sex.

Initially, Christine worries that selling sex will feel unsettling or psychologically damage her. "And you have to fuck [them]?" she asks tentatively. Avery confirms: "Yeah, and *fuck*." Christine looks in the mirror – an appraising look, as if to ask, "Will I?" – before the scene jumps ahead to her astride a client mumbling rote dirty talk and then cuts again to a shot of the two young women exiting a hotel the next morning. Christine's first trick is over fast, but its brevity is not a glossing over. The scene dispels any moral judgement of sex work and also drops any pretences of call girls living the high life. Actually, nothing has changed – except Christine now has rent money. Movie images of turning one's first trick often involve strong feelings of regret, but the series troubles the idea that sex work is life changing – or even uniquely unpleasant – and raises the point that if women have unsatisfying sex for free all the time, why not get paid for it? After their night, the young women look tired, like service workers finishing a shift, but nobody is traumatized. Christine has simply found a way to earn money through sex in a society that provides young working people with fewer and fewer options to make their way.

From here on in, *The Girlfriend Experience* centres on Christine's development as a call girl, becoming a veritable wikiHow on her business and, like the film, trades the lurid for the logistical, signalling that sex work is worthy of being understood as labour. To break into the industry, Christine meets with Jacqueline, a manager/madam who offers insight into how call girls navigate the grey market of sex. With her skirt suits and chignon, Jacqueline resembles a financier and, we later learn, once was one. "I have a business to run. I have to judge pretty quickly," she tells Christine at their meeting, which unfolds like a job interview. She takes Christine on and begins investing in her as a product for upper-class clients at $2,000 an hour. She moves Christine into a swanky apartment whose sleek interiors fit the image she is cultivating as "Chelsea," Chicago's newest GFE call girl. While prohibitionists have argued that adopting pseudonyms is psychologically harmful for sex workers, *The Girlfriend Experience* portrays it as protective: by anonymizing herself, Christine draws firm boundaries between herself and the persona she is paid to perform.

The Girlfriend Experience acknowledges that sex work *is* different from other jobs yet highlights how misogyny and exploitation is hardly confined to it. For example, after her internship interview, the male bosses at Kirkland speak behind Christine's back mockingly but hire her because she is "usable." When working as an intern for experience, not pay, the male associates drop heaps of work on her desk and bark orders. When doing sex work, Christine is paid for her time and performances; at the law firm, men expect women to serve them, sometimes even with sex, for free. When Christine finds out that Erin, a senior law associate, was asked by her male superiors to sleep with a corporate client to secure his business, she is disgusted at the double standard (no male partner has ever been asked to do the same), and she comes to understand how men's accumulation of wealth frequently depends upon the free labour of women, not only in the household but also at a paid job. Much like the dancers in *Hustlers* have an awakening of class consciousness, Christine's observations of old-boy-chummy patriarchy in the corporate workplace strip what remains of her sexual propriety. *The Girlfriend Experience* reveals the exploitation in the "straight" economy and makes sense of why Christine turns to sex work, which offers her more money, power, and control. Fortunately, some of the knowledge she has gleaned from the world of corporate law becomes indispensable to her production as a "classy" call girl.

Intimacy: A Timeless and Recession-Proof Product

Christine's warm smile, sultry eyes, and sexy voice are but a few of the tools in her GFE kit. She is adept at reading her clients' emotional temperatures and deep acting to meet their needs. For a widowed businessman who feels powerful when caring for the weak, she plays a forlorn Lolita; for the monologist who likes to hear himself talk, she's a silent sounding board. For the fragile, she is motherly; for the dominant, who loves power, she is a deferential daisy blooming just for him.

Yet, in even the most intimate-seeming encounter, the price sticker sometimes shows. Christine's date with a lonely widower is interrupted by a call from Jacqueline, who needs the client's credit card number in order to charge it. As the client reads out the digits, Christine makes notes on her phone about his personal triumphs and tragedies he's just shared so she can use them to build more intimacy when they next meet. Some might argue that Christine's taking on of a traditionally subservient role in performances of sweetness to stroke a man's ego is perpetuating patriarchy, but, actually, Christine is challenging it by getting paid for doing what women have always been expected to do for free.

That said, *The Girlfriend Experience* explores how real feelings can and do develop amid this dissimulation, and even seasoned call girls risk becoming emotionally attached to their clients, as one storyline centring on Christine's relationship with a soft-spoken widower businessman demonstrates. The depth of her attachment is clear one afternoon on his yacht when she loses sight of him in the waves and panics. It turns out he's fine, but when he later does die, Christine is devastated and resolves to harden her boundaries. When a client confesses that he's been borrowing money to see her and asks her to temporarily reduce her rate, she refuses: "This is a business to me," she tells him. The series emphasizes the imperative to keep work and life, business and pleasure, transactional intimacy and personal attachment, separate. In fact, it stresses the consequences for call girls who do *not* through Christine's friend, Avery, who falls in love with a client who later spurns her, leading to her having a nervous breakdown. Toughened to these risks, Christine firms up her boundaries in all areas of her life and starts to see all relationships as transactions.

In this respect, *The Girlfriend Experience* series makes Christine into an unusual female heroine: a sex radical of sorts, who rejects social proscriptions of passive femininity, refuses to peg her self-esteem to external validation from men, and is disinterested in romantic relationships and marriage with children. Always frank in her business dealings, she skips the accommodation women are trained to serve up alongside assertiveness – to shield themselves from being seen as too aggressive – and embraces her freedom to ask for what she wants. As fiercely individualistic in her private sex life as she is in her work, she prefers negotiating terms up front. In the pilot episode, for example, she goes to a bar and locks eyes with a handsome stranger across the room. She strides up to him and, without missing a beat, says, "I want to fuck you." At his apartment, they undress dispassionately and, at Christine's insistence, waive foreplay. "Stand over there and masturbate," she commands, and they bring themselves to climaxes. Goal achieved, she gathers her things. "Do you want my phone number?" he asks, looking confused as she demurs and marches out. A little rude, sure, but refreshing.

Christine's sexual iconoclasm might lead one to read her as a post-feminist for whom raunchy sexual display passes for feminist empowerment. Rosalind Gill describes this quality as part of a larger shift in media culture from a past of portraying women "straightforwardly objectified" to a present where women are presented as "active, desiring sexual subjects who choose to present themselves in a seemingly objectified manner because it suits their liberated interests to do so."[68] But far from being a "female chauvinist pig" – a term memorably coined by Ariel Levy – Christine seems to enjoy sex, boldly so, and not for an audience or to prove that she's a "cool girl." The series uncouples the sexual woman from "badness" and asserts that a woman can enjoy casual sex without it being symptomatic of a psychological wound. She is a sex-positive character, and her boldness makes her compelling. And yet, Christine's life at large is a lonely one, characterized by Wi-Fi-enabled autoeroticism. She frequently uses a pornographic live streaming website to watch men masturbate while she does the same, clicking "next" when bored in what seems to be an endless live stream of mechanical jerking and ejaculating. Even still, Christine's preference for autoeroticism is never pathologized, just coded as a natural idiosyncratic expression of sexual desire in her transactional world, where market logics increasingly melt into private sex.

Christine, with her diamond-strength individualism, repudiates the fallen woman stereotype, yet one of the weaknesses of the show is that her uber-ambitious, detached persona never cracks to reveal a more conflicted person underneath. Not that every sex worker *needs* to be complicated. But the existence of competing drives is human and the basis for dramatic tension and emotional intensity, and so we want to know: What drives her? Is it just the money? (If so, by a certain point she's saved quite a bit, so it must be more than that.) Is the risk worth it? Is sex work changing her – or not? Alas, none of these questions are answered, and, in a gaping way, Christine remains inscrutable, a flat character performing on the frontstage, an instrumental expert whose only goal is making money. As she tells her sister, embodying the transactional credo of her world: "I just don't like spending time with anyone unless things are being accomplished." Her few personal connections include one with her boss and sometime-lover, law partner David, who can boost her pay or help her climb.

Indeed, Christine spends more time in her GFE call girl persona than as herself, and she gradually experiences Hochschild's "separation from the self" and separation from meaningful social relations, leaving her socially isolated. Is this what Christine wants? Or is it a result of the fact that she spends more time pretending in her role than living her own life? In the film, Chelsea finds this anomie and solipsism agonizing, but Christine is inured to it, as underscored by the many mirrors in the series, reflecting back Christine's only connection and ally: herself. As for feminist solidarity, there is none. At one point, a client's wife begs her to stop seeing her husband. "I'll pay you $10,000 to stay away. $20,000," the desperate woman cries. Christine coldly negotiates the best deal for herself and is emotionless as she takes the cash from the devastated woman, this fee simply another successful transaction. Yet, these scenes don't judge or portray her as the cold and heartless call girl; rather, they suggest that her way of navigating life is a new norm – an expression of business relations under neo-liberal capitalism, as bloodless as she sees it at the law firm.

But the TV series also suggests a salient difference between Christine's venture and those undertaken by so-called legitimate businesses: Christine is honest about what she sells, while the male lawyers who head the firm where she works are frequently liars. By contrasting Christine's candour with the subterfuge of her colleagues, *The Girlfriend Experience* highlights the irony of sex work's criminalization. Christine's boss, David, abuses his power by instigating a sexual relationship with Christine, dangling the promise of a full-time job when she graduates. Other colleagues likewise engage in unethical practices with impunity to boost billable hours and keep money flowing into the firm.

Of course, corporate law and sex work are ineluctably different, the former venerated and the latter criminalized, and *The Girlfriend Experience* does not crow that "sex work is work like any other." It recognizes how criminalization and the threat of exposure raises the stakes and compels Christine to live a double life and take numerous precautionary measures, including using a separate phone and apartment for business and using a pseudonym to stay under the radar. Nevertheless, the series carefully explores how, despite her privileges, Christine remains as vulnerable to whore stigma as other sex workers.

The Attachment That Ruins a Career: Whore Stigma Revenge Porn

Whore stigma is rooted in the long history of women being publicly humiliated for violating the prevailing patriarchal codes and norms governing female sexual expression. Over 150 years ago, Hester Prynne's forehead was branded with the letter "A" in *The Scarlet Letter* to mark her transgression, and in our time, sex workers are still outed, shamed, ridiculed, and excoriated in focused takedowns that teem with misogyny. This is illustrated infuriatingly by the story of the former Olympian Suzy Favour Hamilton, who was exposed as a Las Vegas call girl in 2012 by the tabloid website The Smoking Gun, triggering a public scandal and a career tailspin. Both Nike and the Walt Disney Company cut sponsorship ties, and Hamilton, harassed by online misogynists and trolls, fell into a suicidal depression.[69] Her castigation exemplifies how women are held to standards of sexual behaviour that are never applied to men. Case in point: at the time Hamilton's career crashed for the "crime" of working as a call girl, the actor Charlie Sheen – who in 1995 admitted under oath to hiring call girls at least twenty-seven times through Hollywood madam Heidi Fleiss – was TV's highest paid actor.[70]

The Girlfriend Experience smartly probes the hypocrisy of these sexual conduct rules in a storyline about whore stigma and revenge porn. When one of Christine's clients dies and leaves her money, his children assume the inheritance was manipulated and try to strong-arm her into forgoing it by threatening to expose her as a call girl: "Everyone will find out what you really do for a living – your friends, your family, your law professors," they tell her. Christine's worst fears come to pass when a sex tape recorded by a client without her consent is emailed to her boss. On it, she performs fellatio and, at her client's request, says, "I like having sex for money." Through what her boss speciously claims was a technical glitch, he forwards the video file to 100 associates. The violation of Christine's privacy and the exposure of her life as a call girl is ruinous. Her male colleagues trade the video like a baseball card and openly mock her as her boss does nothing to curtail this toxic work environment. Within hours, the whole firm has seen the tape. The lack of compassion for Christine's victimization and the ease with which her colleagues stigmatize her as a "whore" speak to the extent to which whore stigma is mobilized, even in seemingly liberal-professional workplaces.

Revenge porn, a sexually explicit video made and shared without consent for the purpose of humiliating and stigmatizing the person who appears in it, is one of the most virulent misogynist tactics of the digital era. It is classified as "non-consensual pornography" in the US and as "image-based sexual abuse" in the UK, where it is now illegal.[71] None of Christine's legal colleagues come to her defence, and her boss takes no responsibility for circulating the video. In fact, his only comment is to blandly suggest that Christine "go home," effectively blaming the victim. The harrowing sequence highlights the vulnerability of all sex workers to public humiliation and draws attention to how sex workers' lives continue to be defined by their sexual history in ways that men's lives are not. Christine's agonized response is used by her colleagues as evidence of her instability, highlighting how, as Arlie Hochschild notes, women's feelings are discounted in two ways: "by being considered rational but unimportant or irrational and hence dismissable."[72]

This is the climax of the first season, and it is a lonely one. Outed as a call girl and humiliated by revenge porn, Christine's legal career is over. This transforms sex work – formerly a choice – into her means for survival. It is here that Christine's veneer cracks, like Chelsea's did in the film, and she longs for real intimacy, not the counterfeit sort she sells. It is in this state of emotional exhaustion that she relinquishes her boundaries and develops personal feelings for a client who validates her. Also like Chelsea in the film, Christine is excited about the prospect of being seen as a unique individual. A scene at her client's penthouse unfolds like a date, beginning with her client giving her a bracelet and serving dinner. Yet what begins romantically ends with an abrupt tone change as the warm light turns icy. After finishing in bed, her client drops a box of Kleenex on her and says, "It's best you leave." The alienating moment in which Christine lies on the rumpled bed is shot in polar blue light, and, ironically, she wears the bracelet he just gave her, a token of his affection, the glittering jewel that, in the end, like Chelsea's counterfeit jewels, is a fraud.

On Christine's next date, a sweaty millionaire too high to have sex has nevertheless hired five escorts to sit on the couch and talk to him. Prescription pill bottles litter a table the call girls sit around like dolls. When Christine and the others prepare to leave, the client takes stacks of bills from a safe and pays each $1,500 an hour. The wealth is less astounding than the emptiness in this lavish suite, where strangers gathered around a table of drugs becomes the new intimate experience. The emotional and spiritual vacuity in a setting of extreme privilege focuses the tension on Christine's life too: paid well for work she finds easy, there is no shame in being a call girl, but this moment, as she sits mannequin-like, watching a millionaire snort drugs and pass out, is not self-actualizing. Serving up no false rosiness about sex work being empowering, the series recognizes the unequal power between young, financially struggling call girls and older, wealthy male clients. The men have the capital to transform their own lives, buy experiences, and consume, while working-class women like Christine make the best of a lopsided situation by exploiting their erotic capital, yet the gnawing feeling this creates is written all over Christine's face: she wants more than this.

Yet, here's the difference between the scene and what prohibitionist feminists claim is sex work's deep-down degradation. While Andrea Dworkin called sex workers "duped women," Christine is far from credulous: she understands the unequal power between rich lawyers, clients, and landlords on the one hand, and herself, a sex worker, on the other – and it angers her. This anger launches an uncharacteristic finale in which she makes a bold power move. Surprisingly, considering the news media's history of stigmatizing sex workers, Christine decides to use the media to her advantage and reaches out to journalists to tell her story of the revenge porn. Only one journalist from a local paper responds.

The interview starts insipidly: "Christine, tell me, why did you decide to become a sex worker?" It's prurient, and we know the answer: money, and because she enjoyed it. And how else can a twenty-one-year-old woman make that much money? But Christine senses, in the journalist's tone, the expectation for a different answer – about being abused, about having low self-esteem,

Figure 5.4. Revenge porn and a humiliation campaign reveals the stigmatization of sex workers, but Christine's (Riley Keough) refusal to repent in *The Girlfriend Experience* is a small victory against it.

about being forced, these reasons being what Melissa Gira Grant describes as the sex worker's standardized and socially scripted *mea culpas* "the public is groomed to hear."[73] But Christine challenges the virgin–whore binary underlying the journalist's very question: she states that she chose to become a call girl because she wanted to, and that being a call girl should in no way determine people's estimation of her character or capabilities as a law student.

> CHRISTINE: As a woman, it's difficult to be seen as a sexual person and a competent professional at the same time.
> JOURNALIST: Unless sex is your profession. You did say you like to get paid for sex.
> CHRISTINE: I like sex. I was role-playing. Is that a problem?

Her answer at first feels deflective, yet Christine's refusal to express contrition for her work is a bold repudiation of the compulsory story in which a sex worker justifies her actions (like a criminal) and begs for absolution (like a fallen woman). Christine's refusal to tell this compulsory sex worker story shines a light on how different sexual standards are applied to men and women, particularly how men are rarely asked to justify their sexual proclivities (but often celebrated for them), like David, her boss at the firm, a Lothario who also makes fraudulent business deals but is never sanctioned. Christine's all-out refusal to repent for anything challenges capitalist society's shaming of sex workers for transacting as the ruling class does, but transparently.

Emboldened by her fall, not silenced by it, Christine sues Kirkland for circulating the video and causing punitive damage and wins a settlement. Her victory suggests justice for victims of revenge porn and also implies that for sex workers, there may yet be justice through legal change. Nevertheless, the toxic masculine work environment disenchants Christine with law, and at the show's climax she leaves university to professionalize as a full-fledged call girl entrepreneur. The series frames her work, in the end, as a more honest gig than corporate law as it is practised under her former boss, a view Christine sums up in their final meeting:

> Everybody is paid to be everywhere. It's called an economy. I fucked people, but I didn't fuck people over like you did.... And I'm selling, but at least I'm honest about what I'm selling, and they know exactly what they are buying.

While prohibitionists cite the commodification of women in the sex industry as proof for why sex work should be abolished, *The Girlfriend Experience* argues that far from being a unique arrangement, sex work simply crib notes from patriarchal capitalist society. While whorephobia and revenge porn threaten Christine's career and well-being, rather than leave sex work she doubles down to become more successful and decides to expand her business as a call girl.

All That Glitters: Transactional Intimacy's Less Glamorous Side

The Girlfriend Experience film and TV series represent a neo-liberal capitalist society in which sex work is entrepreneurship. They portray how the cynical relationship building tactics of modern business have been shifted to the business of transactional intimacy, of which Chelsea and Christine are masters. Nonetheless, they both dignify and normalize call girls by representing them as ordinary working women trying to survive, even as they rue what neo-liberal capitalism does to people.

Non-judgmental to the end, both the film and series leave us not with conclusions, but questions. What are Chelsea's and Christine's plans beyond their GFE entrepreneurship? How will they face aging in an industry where youth and novelty is queen? Do they have an exit plan? Who would they call if they were arrested? Who could help them if they were jailed? Who can they be honest with about their lives? Noticeably, Christine and Chelsea are not in solidarity with other call girls: there is no sign of activism or action against prostitution laws, no disruption to the status quo, nor demand for change. Quite the reverse, the film and series suggest that it is wisest (and safest) for Christine and Chelsea to remain atomized. And while winning a lawsuit presages some progress, Christine remains a cipher. Chelsea, a more well-rounded character, reckons with the risks of alienation and emotional burnout and how her self-commodification mirrors the logics of capitalism. While both film and series critique what neo-liberal capitalism demands of people in the twenty-first century, neither presents an alternative to this system and elide existing sex worker activism that continues to grow in the US and beyond.

So, in the absence of collectivity, in a society ruled by capital – and male corporate – interests, the status quo reigns, and Chelsea and Christine seek to even the score as cynically as the system they see no hope in changing. Both women hold themselves to a high beauty standard and achieve it. With their symmetrical faces, low BMIs, and gorgeous hair and wardrobes, they are sexual subjects, agents, apolitical, and embody third-wave feminism's most avowed value: to be desirable.

In this regard, *The Girlfriend Experience* highlights how the call girl's acceptance in broader society may continue to be conditional on performing a traditionally "feminine" role that reinforces patriarchal capitalism. When Christine and Chelsea try to break from these restrictive roles to become more complex – and sometimes, angrier – women, to want *more*, the consequences are swift and severe: in Chelsea's case, personal humiliation, and in Christine's, public humiliation and the end of her law career. So, Chelsea and Christine choose to return to the status quo to assure their success.

Whereas popular culture once painted call girls as outsiders and unstable women and rarely showed their work, *The Girlfriend Experience* dignifies their labour and explores its challenges that come at an emotional cost. Chelsea and Christine understand this work and excel at it in a world where self-commodification and precarity are increasingly normalized. In these stories, call girls are not outsiders but entrepreneurial insiders, and their freedom to walk through elegant hotels, conduct meetings in airy cafés, and operate businesses underscores their role within the neo-liberal social order.

6 Sexual Healing: Sex Surrogate Care Workers in *The Sessions* and *She's Lost Control*

> *People want help with their sexuality ... especially if [they] have suffered trauma or pain.... As surrogates we technically live in a legal no man's land. A surrogate has never been prosecuted, but there really is no legal support for us.... If I could make a movie about women surrogates, I would really want to show the arc of the intimacy and some of the personal struggles that clients bring.*
>
> – Vera, sex surrogate

"I'd never heard of a sex surrogate," said Helen Hunt, referring to the character she played in *The Sessions* (2012), for which she received an Oscar nod. "I'd never seen anything like it."[1] Perhaps the least known sex worker, sex surrogates are sexual guides, troubleshooters, and healers. Specialized in clients whose sexual challenges have negatively impacted their lives, sex surrogates teach, coax, caress, kiss, whisper, encourage, instruct, and provide educational experiences to those who have faced barriers to achieving what Tracey De Boer calls "sexual inclusion."[2] Formally called surrogate partner therapy, its inventors, the sexologists William H. Masters and Virginia E. Johnson, claimed it to have an 85 per cent success rate.[3] However, by the 1980s, moral conservatism, the HIV/AIDS epidemic, and ethical issues around the legitimacy of curative sex had all but shuttered it.[4]

In the last ten or so years, however, sex surrogacy has appeared widely in popular culture. Memoirs written by sex surrogates have been published, sex surrogates have spoken on talk shows, and stories about sex surrogates have been featured in magazines as well as in feature films, TV shows, and documentaries including *Shortbus* (2006), *The Sessions*, *She's Lost Control* (2014), *Grey's Anatomy* (2005–), *Masters of Sex* (2013–16), and *This Is Life with Lisa Ling* (2014–22), to name just a few. In this chapter, I examine two feature films that galvanized public awareness about sex surrogacy and increased its respectability as a practice: *The Sessions*, based on the true story of sex surrogate Cheryl

Cohen-Greene's therapeutic relationship with her client, poet Mark O'Brien, and *She's Lost Control*, about a graduate student sex surrogate who loves her work, even when it becomes unsafe to do it. Both films attracted sizeable audiences and critical acclaim. *Newsday* called *The Sessions* "a funny, tender, and mostly un-sentimentalized movie about physical and emotional triumph,"[5] while the *New York Times* praised it for being a "profoundly sex-positive film."[6] The *Los Angeles Times* called *She's Lost Control* "a quiet triumph, a true herald of a distinctive and necessary voice in cinema."[7] Sex surrogacy, once a controversial and little-known medical experiment, has entered the limelight. As Cheryl Cohen-Greene wrote in her memoir, published the same year *The Sessions* was released, "Whereas prostitution is one of the world's oldest professions, surrogacy is one of the newest."[8]

The Sessions and *She's Lost Control* delve into the often misunderstood role of the sex surrogate, dignify her care work, and explore her process with clients whose disabilities and dysfunctions have impaired their intimate lives, often leading to increased isolation and feelings of powerlessness. Burnishing away stereotypes of tawdry, transactional sex with stories of vulnerability and anguish, triumph and grit, the films portray sex surrogates as professionals enriching their clients' lives by facilitating experiences that foster personal growth and the confidence that comes with being seen as a sexual person. Told mostly from the sex surrogates' points of view, with a focus on their labour practices, the films portray practitioners who treat their work as vocations, showing the professionalism and precision that guides the therapeutic process as they consult with referring therapists, create treatment plans, teach and practise emotion management techniques, facilitate exercises, take clinical notes, invoke boundaries, and prepare their clients to take their new skills into non-commercial relationships, the ultimate goal of the surrogacy relationship. Eagle-eyed dissections of complex relationships, the films shift our attention from sex surrogacy's moral status to its impacts and ask: What role does sexual intimacy play in a human life? And how might sex workers contribute to and enrich people's lives? While physicians, the disability rights movement, and indeed all sex workers have argued for the social value of sex work for almost a century, the films illuminate it as they hold up sex surrogates as emissaries of the erotic world.

I begin this chapter by contextualizing sex surrogacy as a form of care and body work, noting the emotional labour it demands and its relational rewards, before moving on to examine how *The Sessions* and *She's Lost Control* represent sex surrogates as care workers and, finally, the powerful case both films make for why sex surrogacy – and sex work in *all* forms – should be decriminalized.

Contexts: Healing Sex

Sex workers have long been associated with healing. In the Stone Age, women were seen as the incarnations of goddesses and took on roles as priestesses, forging a vital mode of communication between the community and the "cosmic source."[9] Out of this worship emerged the tradition of ritual sex, in which women acting as fertility deities copulated with men to win the favour of the gods, increase fertility in the community, and bless crops. Later the process was formalized and taken into temples. This harvest sex ritual was seen as so integral to the survival of the community that laypeople were eventually replaced by professional performers – the first sex workers in history. Their work was seen as a contribution to the community rather than a hedonistic act.[10] Without a competing narrative, early sex workers were revered until religion and patriarchy wrote a new story. Yet despite its later stigma, some physicians regarded sex work as care work. In a 1929 address, the esteemed British physician Dr. William J. Robinson argued that "the profession of prostitution must be declared perfectly legal and legitimate; nay, it must be judged as an occupation of public utility."[11] Trailblazing researcher Martha Stein, who observed hundreds of interactions at a brothel through peepholes, concluded that conversations surpassed time engaged in sex and "relieve[d] psychological tensions," leading her to declare sex work "restorative and therapeutic" and the sex worker "a paraprofessional sexual therapist."[12]

The formal concept of sex surrogacy, or surrogate partner therapy, was developed by the American gynecologist William Masters and his later collaborator, sexologist Virginia Johnson, during their experiments into treatment methods for "human sexual dysfunction" at the University of Washington in the 1950s and 1960s. They introduced the concept of sex surrogacy to the world in their 1970 book, *Human Sexual Inadequacy*, which ushered in a new way of looking at – and solving – human sexual problems through a medical lens.[13] Masters and Johnson had become household names four years earlier with the publication of *Human Sexual Response* (1966), a book that was to popular studies of human sexuality what Betty Crocker was to baking; it was a bestseller. Unlike the era's other famous sexologist, Alfred Kinsey, who had confined his research to questionnaires, Masters and Johnson observed thousands of couples and individuals, ranging from eighteen to seventy years old, engaging in self-stimulation and intercourse in a laboratory and measured their responses physiologically with video cameras, medical equipment, and custom-made instruments, most famously, a glass dildo nicknamed "Ulysses," which calibrated the female orgasm internally.[14]

Despite its rousing subject matter, *Human Sexual Response* was not prurient, its respectability earned through its abstruse writing style and administrative language, which took the flush out of fornication. Furthermore, the book emphasized that the research was not about *increasing* peoples' sexual pleasure but serving the functionality of the family: "The Foundation's therapeutic program for relief of sexual dysfunction is fundamentally a process of marital-unit education," they wrote, referring to the Reproductive Biology Research Foundation (later, Masters and Johnson Institute) they founded in 1964.[15] Masters and Johnson argued that men with sexual dysfunctions stood the greatest chance of recovery not by undertaking theoretical exercises alone or by talking with therapists, but by working directly *in coitus* with a partner, preferably a spouse. As Masters noted, "I have emphasized that a cooperative sexual partner is indispensable."[16] For men without a spouse, Masters and Johnson conceptualized the sex partner surrogate.

Today, sex surrogacy follows a similar model. Clients connect to sex surrogates through referring therapists. In relationships lasting several weeks or months, sex surrogates guide clients through tailored sensory exercises and structured discussions that encourage the frank exploration of sexual desires, anxieties, memories, and values before moving on to hands-on exercises focused on mutuality, how to give and receive sexual pleasure, and building emotional intimacy.[17] The goal is to equip clients with the confidence to pursue sexual relationships in the future, outside of a commercial exchange.[18] Both client and sex surrogate continue to meet regularly with the referring therapist for feedback. Therefore, sex surrogates can be understood as one "part of a three-way therapeutic team" that includes the therapist, the sex surrogate, and the client.[19] Yet under US law, sex surrogacy is identical to and therefore *is* prostitution.

But sex surrogacy has always flown a flag of status and legitimacy compared to other forms of sex work due to its origins in and links to medical science. As Yitzchak Binik and Marta Meana note, sex surrogacy has "experienced no serious criticism or competition from other professionals and little societal opposition, the exception being of some religious groups."[20] Yet some may wonder why Masters and Johnson's "invention" of sex surrogacy was needed, given the existence of "healing" sex workers since antiquity. As Thomas Szasz points out, sex workers have long worked with men with disabilities, and the "invention" of "sex surrogacy" speciously claimed "superiority [over] prostitutes … by asserting that they are professionals whose practice is based on science … whereas their competitors are quacks."[21] Ironically, in the mid-1950s Masters had hired 118 sex workers in the employ of St. Louis brothels for his initial research, recognizing that their knowledge of arousal techniques could be useful in his research into male sexual dysfunction.[22] His consultations with sex workers led to the development of ideas presented in *Human Sexual Response*, in which sex workers are credited for "techniques for support and control of the human male" that proved successful in "direct application."[23] Yet, a decade later, when single men sought treatment at their clinic, Masters and Johnson rejected the idea of hiring sex workers to be their partners, writing that "to use prostitutes would have been at best clinically unsuccessful and at worst psychologically disastrous."[24]

Masters and Johnson thus conceptualized "surrogates," stressing they needed to be volunteers.[25] However, the number of women willing to do therapeutic exercises leading to sex with men they barely knew while wired to machines and watched in a lab was limited. The role of sex surrogate was thus eventually broadened to include the paid professional. In other words, sex workers got a new name and a new degree of respectability. The discursive transformation of sex work (and sex workers) into sex surrogacy (and sex surrogates) exemplifies how "prostitution itself has an internal hierarchy,"[26] and how our cultural understanding of sex work depends upon four factors: (1) the discourse framing the sex act (in this case, medical research/science); (2) the goal (nuclear family functioning); (3) the status of the person supervising the acts (a physician); and (4) the setting in which it takes place (a university lab).

The Showtime series *Masters of Sex*, a period drama about Masters and Johnson's work from the 1950s to the 1970s, a heady time of sexual revolution, brilliantly focalizes the tension between sex surrogacy (the new medical treatment) and sex work (the oldest profession) through Betty DiMello, a hardscrabble brothel worker presumably based on one of the women Masters employed in the 1950s. Betty resents Masters's academizing of the sex work at which she is expert, and the tension between the two characters, and what they represent – Betty's working-class lived experience and on-the-job knowledge of sex work and Masters's middle-class academic pursuit of it – is played out in a restaurant scene in which they meet to discuss Masters's research findings. The scene pays tribute to Betty's wisdom while critiquing the academic redefinition of the work she's been doing for years, giving Betty the final zinger:

> MASTERS: (*Running his pen down a clipboard.*) So … number four was the slowest … taking ten minutes … and number five achieved no arousal at all.
> BETTY: (*Eating a ham sandwich. Shrugs disinterestedly.*)
> MASTERS: The last client … how long did he stay in the plateau stage?
> BETTY: For fucking ever!
> MASTERS: I have eleven minutes.
> BETTY: (*Sounding bored, gulping her drink.*) Well, you're the expert.
> MASTERS: Your napkin, actually, goes in your lap –
> BETTY: From a man standing in a closet watching people hump all night …
> MASTERS: It's work.
> BETTY: Oh really?
> MASTERS: Client nine … I have your climax lasting nine seconds.
> BETTY: I was faking.

MASTERS: (*Looking confused.*) You didn't have ... an orgasm?
BETTY: You're serious?
MASTERS: I'm serious. You *pretended* to have an orgasm? Is that a common practice among prostitutes?
BETTY: It's a common practice for anyone with a twat. Women fake orgasms, almost all of them. (*Drinking beer.*) Although I haven't checked my clipboard lately.

Masters's condescending tip for Betty on how to hold her napkin at the very moment she claims her authority and questions his underscores the show's smart uptake of the class dimensions of sex surrogacy itself (i.e., an upper-class physician empowered to define the world's oldest profession to a practitioner of it).

While there *are* differences between the labour of sex workers and sex surrogates, the similarities are notable. Both sex workers and sex surrogates sell sexual and emotional labour in a commercial exchange. Both work according to a particular process, adapting their style according to their clients' needs. Both serve clients who, for whatever reason, are unable or unwilling to find an outlet for their needs outside of a commercial exchange. A body of research has also found that sex workers are likely to have clients with disabilities, and to provide clients with emotional nurturing and education. In fact, "men with physical and sensory impairments are a core group of clients that visit commercial sex workers."[27] Sex surrogacy's discursive separation from sex work, however, served a protective function against stigma. The publication of *Human Sexual Inadequacy* galvanized the practice of sex surrogacy, and by the early 1970s hundreds of sex surrogate groups had been established across the US,[28] with the first memoir by a sex surrogate, Valerie X. Scott's *Surrogate Wife: The True Confessions of a Sex-Therapist*, appearing in 1972 in pocketbook form with an enticing pink cover fit for a drugstore book carousel. In 1973, the International Professional Surrogates Association (IPSA) was formed. A whole cottage industry of popular culture dealing with sexuality – from desire to dysfunction – then followed, especially books aimed to reach a dual market of readers: those intent on titillation, and those who wanted advice from legitimate professionals. A publishing boom quickly followed with books such as *Everything You Always Wanted to Know about Sex (But Were Afraid to Ask)* (1969), *How to Become the Sensuous Woman* (1971), *Male Sexuality: A Guide to Sexual Fulfillment* (1978), and *Becoming Orgasmic: A Sexual Growth Program for Women* (1976).[29] By then, sex work and sex surrogacy had been firmly differentiated as separate occupations without any overlap.

Sex surrogacy's origins as a medical intervention separate from sex work guided early popular culture about it. In what is probably its screen debut, the film *My Therapist* (1983) starred Marilyn Chambers as sex surrogate and PhD student Kelly, whose no-nonsense disposition, though offset by her tight tops, made clear that sex surrogates were professionals. "Here with me in sex surrogate therapy," Kelly tells one recalcitrant client who keeps trying to take off

Figure 6.1. Sex worker Betty DiMello (Annaleigh Ashford), on *Masters of Sex*, looks amused as she explains her work to Dr. Masters, including a faked orgasm.

his pants, "we learn certain exercises to help a man overcome his sexual dysfunction. Now, the first exercise begins with full frontal nudity. Do we begin the exercise, or do you go home?" *My Therapist* also stressed sex surrogacy's clinical code with Kelly's workplace being the "Sex Therapy Clinic," ascetically decorated like a vintage doctor's office, while the film's alternative title, *Love Ya Florence Nightingale*, an allusion to the famously altruistic British nurse, underscored the sex surrogate's contributions to the greater good. Yet, the film's sexualized tone and nudity two minutes in made its star, a national name since starring in *Behind the Green Door* (1972), the first X-rated movie in the US to get a wide release, into even more of a lusty object. The sensitive *Private*

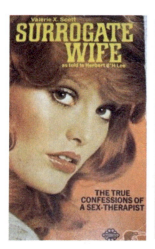 

Figure 6.2. The memoir *Surrogate Wife: The True Confessions of a Sex-Therapist* helped put sex surrogacy on the map as a therapeutic practice. Likewise, the professional-looking "Sex Therapy Clinic" in *My Therapist* suggests the sex surrogate's status and competence, yet the quick cut to her nudity makes a less convincing case.

Practices: The Story of a Sex Surrogate (1985) homed in on the labour of sex surrogacy but was not widely seen, while the absorbing Academy Award–winning short documentary *Breathing Lessons: The Life and Work of Mark O'Brien* (1996) elegantly narrativized sex surrogacy from the perspective of the male client, but dealt only passingly with surrogate Cheryl Cohen-Greene's experience. Yet, what these films did bring to the fore was the care work sex surrogates do.

This trend has continued in the last decade as scholars have identified "care work"[30] and the related areas of "intimate labour"[31] and "relational work" as key components of sex surrogacy.[32] As Emma Dowling notes, care work "is no private matter,"[33] and it employs what Douglas Haines calls "an affective outlook and a set of practices."[34] Increasingly, care work has "the connotation of being physically or emotionally close, private, sexually intimate, or caring,"[35] with its therapeutic goal being to help others "develop [to] their fullest human capacities" and live satisfying lives.[36] In *The Sessions*, the practice of care work, and the professional role of sex surrogates, are elevated to a necessary therapeutic service.

"I Don't Want Your Return Business": The Sex Surrogate Care Worker in *The Sessions*

The Sessions (2012), an Academy Award–nominated film directed by Ben Lewin, is a character-driven story with the talkiness of a stage play and the intimacy of a novel. Based on true events recounted in Mark O'Brien's long-form 1990 magazine article, "On Seeing a Sex Surrogate," the film spans three months in 1988 when sex surrogate Cheryl Cohen-Greene (played by Helen Hunt) worked with O'Brien in bedrooms and hotel rooms, sessions that would change both of their lives. O'Brien, a childhood polio survivor, a poet, a disability rights activist, and a journalist, was largely confined to a life-saving iron lung, a respirator that encased his entire body and breathed for him. "It's big and yellow and ugly," O'Brien wrote of it, "but it works."[37] Immobilized for up to twenty hours a day, O'Brien's opportunities for intimacy throughout his life had been severely limited. *The Sessions* tells the story of the six sessions with a sex surrogate that changed that, a process through which he came to see himself as a sexual and sensual being, worthy of love. "She put her hand on my chest," he says in the film. "No one had ever done that. The act of affection made me weep."

In her spirited 2012 memoir, *Intimate Life: Sex, Love, and My Journey as a Surrogate Partner*, Cheryl Cohen-Greene writes: "I have had over 900 sexual partners.… Often, I ask the audience what words come to mind when they hear this figure. Here are a few of the most common: whore, skank, slut. Well, I'm none of those."[38] With this sex-positive declaration, Cohen-Greene goes on to explain her vocation: helping clients overcome sexual anxiety and challenges in one-on-one encounters that put a new spin on sex work. *The Sessions* uses the first meeting between Cheryl and Mark to establish the sex surrogacy relationship and to highlight its differences from other types of sex work. The scene takes place in a bedroom where Mark lies prostrate on a bed, having been lifted and arranged there by his attendant who now waits in the living room. Cheryl enters and greets Mark warmly. Overcome by nerves, Mark blurts out, "Your money's on the dresser." Cheryl, in a firm tone, informs Mark that she is not "a prostitute," so he doesn't have to pay upfront. "Shall we start again?" she ask. Cheryl then explains their unique relationship and her role:

> Although the aim is for us to have sex, I'm not a prostitute, and you don't need to pay me up front. I've nothing against prostitutes, but there's a difference.… The difference between me and a prostitute is that I don't want your return business. I'm here to help you learn about your sexual feelings, so you can share them with a future partner.

By drawing a distinction between Cheryl's work and the Hollywood stereotype of sex work, *The Sessions* discursively distances her relationship with Mark from the commercial sex exchange associated with brevity and lust. By highlighting that she is not "a prostitute," Cheryl is certainly "borrowing respectability" from sex surrogacy's medical origins. Yet, with Cheryl's emphasis through language on sex surrogates' pedagogical approach (e.g., "I'm here to help you communicate") the film is also cleverly rebutting the prohibitionist assertion that sex workers have no skills. As we've seen, Sheila Jeffreys, for example, has argued that "youth and inexperience are the most highly valued aspects" of a sex worker.[39] In direct contrast to this, *The Sessions* leads with an assertion of sex worker knowledge and wisdom, establishing what will become a relationship of tutelage and a new frame through which to regard sex surrogacy as a healing intervention.

The Sessions does this by portraying Cheryl working according to guidelines, emphasizing sex surrogacy as a healing, client-centred practice. As the IPSA notes, "the surrogate participates with the client in structured and unstructured experiences that are designed to build client self-awareness and skills."[40] At their first session, Cheryl outlines what sex surrogacy is, explaining that they will have no more than six sessions; that theirs is a professional relationship; that she has a family she will not speak about; and that she will keep the focus on Mark. The boundaries Cheryl establishes exemplify what Arlie Hochschild calls the strategy of positing "a healthy estrangement, a clear separation of self from role"[41] and underscores the professional approach she takes predicated on technique, not titillation.

One foundational idea behind sex surrogacy is that sex is primarily a mental act. As such, the film makes Cheryl's first goal to set the petrified Mark at ease. Having never been alone with a woman in a potentially sexual context, he trembles in bed. "Mark, just take a deep breath," Cheryl says, closing her eyes and modelling deep inhalation, "and let go," she finishes, exhaling through her mouth. The film unfolds this meeting scene in real time to highlight Cheryl's control. She speaks with the warmth of a caring friend but with the judiciousness of a skilled teacher. She uses well-selected words and disarming gestures to modulate the emotional intensity of their conversation, and she intersperses her medical questionnaire with personal remarks: she compliments Mark's shirt and cologne, and when she learns he can maintain an erection, she suggests that he should be proud of himself: "Do you know how many men there are on this planet who would give anything for a natural erection?" At the end, she says, "You did great." *The Sessions* shows how Cheryl pivots between evaluating Mark, reassuring him, asking him questions, and building his confidence, which are all part of her repertoire of skills as a care worker.

Body–Mind Connection: The Sex Surrogate as Body Worker

In relationships lasting several months, sex surrogates use structured exercises, practice, and guided conversation to help clients become more at ease in their bodies, connect to their sexuality and desires, give and receive pleasure, and build emotional intimacy towards the goal of pursuing fulfilling relationships outside of a commercial exchange.[42] This care work frequently involves body work as well. Body workers, according to Talli Rosenbaum, Ronit Aloni, and Rafi Heruti, use their own bodies to "model sexual comfort and confidence."[43] While the Hollywood sex worker stereotype embodies a strutty exhibitionistic confidence, Hunt imbues Cheryl with quiet poise, which denotes her therapeutic goal and her self-assurance. Her style is also understated: she wears plain shirts, a loose skirt or jeans, and flat shoes, her underwear is beige and practical, and her face is make-up free. Notably, the camera's point of view (POV) in the first nude scene in the film is hers, and never voyeuristic. It puts you in her shoes as she strips, sinks onto the edge of the bed, and runs her fingers along Mark's arm. The camera challenges the male gaze by unconventionally shooting her in profile against a very un-erotic background (a wall unit filled with pottery and books). This female POV strips the scene of its titillating elements and distances Cheryl from the stereotype sex worker object, turning her into an embodied subject and accentuating her power as a self-assured body worker.

Body workers are experts at "assessing, diagnosing, handling, treating, manipulating, and monitoring bodies,"[44] and sex surrogates use tactile exercises to instill confidence in their clients. A lifetime of being marginalized for his physical differences has left Mark ashamed of his body, and out of touch with it. For this reason, Cheryl starts their process with "body awareness" exercises. Masters and Johnson described initial exploratory touching, which they termed "sensate touch," as vital to this therapeutic relationship, noting that "clothing should always be removed prior."[45] Cheryl begins by unbuttoning Mark's shirt: "I don't want to hurt or injure you in any way," she says, tracing her fingers down his chest. She explains that she will touch every part of his body: "If something feels good, tell me. If something feels ticklish or bothers you, let me know. I don't want you to tolerate anything." It is through Cheryl's adroitness at facilitating body awareness exercises that *The Sessions* portrays the extent of her expertise as a body worker. She runs her fingers through Mark's hair – "You have soft hair. It's nice to the touch. Do you like it?" – and Mark's fluttering eyelids and shyly materializing smile show the stirring effects of this touch, as do close-up, real-time shots of Cheryl's fingers gently rubbing Mark's earlobe, a remarkably visceral sight. When Mark develops an erection he panics, having learned to associate arousal with imposition and inappropriateness, but Cheryl reassures him that his reaction is a normal response to sexual stimuli and nothing to fear. As Cheryl moves from emotional labour, to care work, to body work, normalizing Mark's urges and reactions, *The Sessions* dignifies the range of her skills and impact.

On many occasions, *The Sessions* portrays Cheryl's care work verging on epiphany-inspiring therapy. In a later session, she places a naked Mark before a full-length mirror. "OK, Mark," she says. "This is your body." Mark grimaces, reluctant to even look. Having spent his lifetime living in a body that is *handled* but never *touched*, objectified and prodded by doctors, carried and wheeled by caregivers, and tethered to life-preserving machines, Mark has learned to see his body as an encumbrance, his sex as futile, his lungs as "paper bags." At 4'7", he weighs around sixty pounds and is embarrassed by his frailty.[46] Yet, encouraged by Cheryl's directive, he looks into the mirror. In the documentary *Breathing Lessons*, O'Brien reflects on this long-delayed moment of reckoning: "I was surprised I looked so normal, that I wasn't the horribly twisted and cadaverous figure I had always imagined myself to be." *The Sessions* credits Cheryl's work as the catalyst in transforming Mark's shame into tenuous self-acceptance. It recognizes that Cheryl is doing work that no other professional – doctor, nurse, personal support worker, or therapist – much less a friend or family member, could do for Mark.

Yet, *The Sessions* stages Cheryl's care and body work most vividly when she and Mark have sex for the first time. Mark is petrified of sex. As a bookish virgin, he has prepared by reading books on human physiology, which have given him the unfortunate idea that he will hurt Cheryl by having penetrative sex with her. Mark's sexual neuroses about penetration injury would appear to be rooted in the traumatic memory of contracting the poliovirus as a child, a foreign body literally invading him and causing irreparable injury. The prospect of encountering another foreign body – Cheryl's literal body – triggers a trauma response of being that helpless child, and he panics. To relax him, Cheryl uses a visualization exercise and instructs him to close his eyes. "Picture yourself as a six-year-old boy at the beach [before he contracted polio].... Describe some of your feelings," she whispers. Having intuited that Mark's trauma has manifested as sexual shame, Cheryl hopes that by inviting Mark to connect to an earlier part of himself that is untouched by trauma and pain, he will also reconnect to, and have empathy for, the little boy inside him who did not ask for his life to be irreparably changed by polio.

Mark follows Cheryl's voice to startling and cathartic ends, a reverie the film shows from his point of view through a montage illustrating his mental journey back to his own childhood as a boy with a 1950s crew cut and glittering blue eyes, to a scene of summertime gaiety – and mobility. A young Mark runs along a beach with his sister squealing with pleasure as his feet slap the wet sand. "I feel very exhilarated … the wind and the wet sand beneath my toes," Mark, the adult, says, as the boy in his memory propels himself with ecstatic bursts of energy. "Do you really feel like him?" Cheryl asks. "Can you really picture him? … As you are now …? … And are you mad at him? Do you blame him for getting polio? Was it his fault?" Tears well up in Mark's eyes, and in a cascade of sensuous images – the smooth inner swirl of seashell, a cat's whiskers, lapping sea waves and gulls – Mark orgasms. It is a remarkable sequence of sexual ecstasy and emotional catharsis. And with it, *The Sessions* validates Cheryl as a healer.

Sex Surrogate Care Workers in *The Sessions* and *She's Lost Control* 195

Figure 6.3. *The Sessions* emphasizes the clinical approach sex surrogates take to their work: Cheryl Cohen-Greene (Helen Hunt) transcribes clinical notes after a session with Mark O'Brien.

While *The Sessions* depicts Cheryl's work as nurturing, it never suggests that she is a quasi-mother, a girlfriend, or a sex worker "nurse," the last being a stock sex worker figure, as Russell Campbell points out, that reductively proposes that sex workers' nurturance is intrinsic to their caring "female" qualities.[47] The film stresses that Cheryl's effectiveness is grounded in her professional skills and her emotion management strategies, as well as in her ability to separate her work and private selves. Wendy Chapkis has argued that because sex workers receive payment and think of affect as a "job," they gain "greater control": because "emotion was no longer something that simply happened to them, they felt practiced in also creating and controlling it."[48] In *The Sessions*, Cheryl uses emotion management techniques to maintain boundaries. For example, at the end of their first session, a clearly enchanted Mark says, "Tell me something about yourself. Anything." Cheryl responds that her private life is off limits. By keeping the focus on Mark, Cheryl guards against transference and countertransference, the process by which personal feelings enter a therapeutic relationship and place it at risk.

The Sessions also illustrates Cheryl's professionalism by frequently showing her working in her home office. While the stereotypical Hollywood sex worker is rarely gifted with intellect or even meta-cognition, nor even portrayed reading a book, *The Sessions* represents Cheryl as a serious and thoughtful clinician who reads and writes. Her home office is filled with books and writing pads and looks like the study of a physician or a therapist. On her large desk are notebooks and pens, a fax machine, an open appointment calendar, and a tape recorder she uses to dictate her clinical notes that she later transcribes. Following each of her sessions with Mark, Cheryl sits at her desk in the glow of her lamp and speaks into her tape recorder, noting his progress and challenges: "[Mark] cannot masturbate. Has only the occasional kissing experience ..." As she speaks, the camera significantly includes in the shot a framed diploma behind her on the wall: her university degree. The diploma connotes Cheryl's training, her home office her professionalism, and her sessions with Mark her labour, knowledge, and skills.

Sex Surrogates: Enriching the Lives of People with Disabilities

The United Nations considers sexuality a basic human right and sex to be hugely beneficial, both physically and emotionally.[49] Yet, sexuality and disability have long been a taboo subject, even within the field of disability studies.[50] As Tom Shakespeare notes, the sexual rights of disabled people have come second to other struggles like securing affordable housing and access to public space.[51] Furthermore, ableism and lack of representation in popular culture have led many to believe that people with disabilities lack sexual desire and curiosity, or even that they do not have sex at all. Since the early 2000s, however, the intersections between disability and commercial sex work have emerged as a growing area of scholarly enquiry. As Kirsty Liddiard observes, the question of whether people with disabilities ought to have the right to buy services from commercial sex workers has become "a hot topic."[52] In one study, 75 per cent of people with disabilities responding to a survey believed that prostitution should be legalized.[53]

The Sessions validates sex surrogates by portraying the therapeutic and life-enriching effect Cheryl Cohen-Greene has on Mark O'Brien. In doing so, the film confirms what sociologists have argued for decades: that sex workers provide emotional support to their clients, some of whom live with disabilities,[54] and see clients that include "late in life virgins, the disabled, abuse or trauma victims, and those with erectile dysfunction, Asperger's syndrome, self-esteem issues, phobias, or crippling performance anxiety."[55] By showing Cheryl playing a pivotal role in supporting Mark achieve the self-regard and experiential pleasure he wanted, *The Sessions* confirms the contributions sex surrogates make to the lives of their clients.

The film dignifies Mark's struggles and desires while emphasizing the transformative impact of sex surrogacy on his life. When *The Sessions* opens, Mark spends up to twenty hours a day in an iron lung, a mechanical respirator that encases his body and stimulates the muscles paralyzed by polio, allowing him to breathe, but his disability does not define him. A Berkeley graduate, a poet and a journalist, and the founder of a small press dedicated to publishing the work of disabled authors, Mark is an intelligent and self-deprecatingly funny man who uses his wit to confront his disability head-on. "I was looking for an intelligent, literate woman for companionship and, perhaps, sexual play. I am, as you see, completely paralyzed, so there will be no walks on the beach," O'Brien later wrote.[56] Yet, underneath Mark's wit is a sense of loss stemming from unfulfilled sexual desires that are sometimes a source of embarrassment: "Sometimes I ejaculate during bed baths in front of my attendant," he tells his confidante in the film, a Catholic priest. "All I feel is shame and mortification, while other men apparently get pleasure." A poet who burnishes human experiences into crystal form, Mark is a sensuous man. He does not want to die without having had sex, an act he considers a pivotal human experience.

Scholars have noted that people with disabilities are often stereotyped as asexual and teenagers with disabilities are less likely to receive sex education.[57] The psychological impact of having this part of one's human experience denied and repressed is clear in the film as Mark describes the shroud of silence around sexuality that began in his childhood and only grew as he aged based on the assumption that sex was a moot issue for him. As an adult, he rues the lack of physical contact and intimate touch in his life, which has thus far been restricted to a doctor's clinical probing during an examination or the accidental graze of an attendant's hand. This is painful. In his poem "Being Washed" from his collection *Breathing* (1982), O'Brien describes how this lack of intimate physical touch has alienated him from himself and made him feel like a thing: "There's so much of it to wash / It being me, a former person."[58]

Mark is thirty-eight when the film opens and says that he is "getting close to my use-by date." He has exceeded his life expectancy and wants to experience intimacy while he still can. In his 1990 article in *The Sun*, O'Brien writes about his troubled relationship with his body and sex:

> As a man in my thirties, I still felt embarrassed by my sexuality. It seemed to be utterly without purpose in my life, except to mortify me when I became aroused during bed baths. I would not talk to my attendants about the orgasms I had then, or the profound shame I felt. I imagined they, too, hated me for becoming so excited. I wanted to be loved. I wanted to be held, caressed, and valued. But my self-hatred and fear were too intense.[59]

Interestingly, O'Brien learns about sex surrogacy through popular culture:

> About this time, a TV talk show featured two surrogates. I watched with suspicion: were surrogates the same as prostitutes? Although they might gussy it up with some psychology, weren't they doing similar work? The surrogates did not look

like my stereotypes of hookers: no heavy make-up, no spray-on jeans ... The surrogates emphasized that they deal mostly with a client's poor self-image and lack of self-esteem, not just the act of sex itself.[60]

The Sessions's portrayal of sex surrogacy being a supportive practice that is mutually enriching for both Mark and Cheryl challenges prohibitionist feminists who have argued that sex surrogacy is a way for men with disabilities to exploit women, only with a socially sanctioned rationale to do so.[61] In an article for *Feminist Current*, one writer excoriates sex surrogacy and argues that "the sexual appetites of disabled men should not take precedence over the advancement of women's equality."[62] She goes on to say that sex surrogacy is also redundant since "communication technology, mechanical technology, and public education" already meet the needs of people who seek help from sex surrogates.[63] The implication here is that people with disabilities should get their needs "met" by sex dolls, pornography, and robots. Yet, suggesting that automated, depersonalized sexual tools fulfil the same needs that sex surrogates do neglects to consider a host of other reasons why men buy sex – reasons that O'Brien compellingly articulates are rooted in the sensual experience of touch, taste, sound, and smell – that online or mechanical encounters cannot replicate. Furthermore, the assumption that men visit sex workers for carnal reasons alone is itself rooted in the persistent and the essentialist stereotype that all men are hypersexual.[64]

The Sessions suggests that, in addition to physical reasons, men with disabilities, like all buyers of sex, may seek out sexual services for emotional reasons, such as the wish for connection, conversation, warmth, validation, and to feel desirable.[65] Similarly, De Boer argues that men with disabilities who pay for sexual services seek "sexual inclusion" and to be seen as "sexual agents,"[66] and Liddiard found that "purchasing sex can be a fruitful means for disabled men to gain sexual experience."[67] Prohibitionist feminists have argued that learning with a sex worker is not possible, for the simulated nature of the situation nullifies any educational effects, yet the men in Liddiard's study described their encounters with the sex workers as "integral towards learning even the most 'rudimentary' of intimate experiences, such as sensuous and erotic touch."[68] *The Sessions* represents how Cheryl's guided exercises reduce Mark's shame and anxiety and increase his self-confidence. Furthermore, paying for sex divests the encounter of anxiety-provoking expectations that inevitably come with non-commercial sexual relations. Thus, the client is under no pressure to perform.

Furthermore, Mark's mobility limitations require Cheryl to lift, position, and move him as she teaches him how to use his body to give and receive pleasure in sexual encounters. No pornography or sex robot could play this dialogical, skill-building teaching role. *The Sessions* shows us that sex surrogates provide an important caring service and urge us to consider the healing role they play for people who have been unable to lead full sexual lives due to a variety of challenges including limited mobility; an isolated adolescence; not meeting socially constructed idealized notions of beauty; not conforming to standards of masculine and feminine sexuality; few opportunities to meet sexual partners; and little sexual experience and low self-esteem due to a culture that regularly constructs the sexuality of the disabled as deviant, strange, and wrong.[69] Nonetheless, as Liddiard rightly points out, conversations about people with disabilities buying sex run the risk of labelling "disabled sexualities with connotations of deviancy and ethical ambiguity" and framing them as "perverse"[70] and must therefore be conducted carefully.[71]

The Sessions represents Mark's work with Cheryl as a life-enriching process through which he starts to overcome his bodily shame, becomes more confident in his sexuality, and experiences physical intimacy. Of his decision to hire a sex surrogate, O'Brien wrote: "I wanted someone who would be sensitive to my unusual needs."[72] As an adult living with a disability, O'Brien longed to learn about sex from an expert – someone who would not judge him for his inexperience. *The Sessions* is a sex-positive film that affirms the sexual agency of people with disabilities and, by extension, the services sex surrogates offer. Further, by showing Mark seeking out Cheryl's services for intimacy, as much as for sex, the film rebuts the prohibitionist idea that men with disabilities who buy commercial sex are perpetuating the oppression of women.

In the film, Mark's self-actualization – a result of his relationship with Cheryl – also makes possible the beginning of his first ever romantic relationship. Once petrified of women, we now see Mark meet the woman who will become his partner until the end of his life. By ending the film as his new relationship begins, *The Sessions* offers powerful evidence of the social value of sex surrogacy. At Mark's funeral, which concludes the film, his friend, the priest, says, "He loved, and he was loved." With the story of the life-enriching impact Cheryl's care work has on Mark, *The Sessions* presents a new image of a sex worker as a care worker and body worker, a sexual healer who brings joy and dignity to the lives of her clients.

Relational Rewards: From the Sex Surrogate's Perspective

In addition to illustrating the positive and enriching impact working with a sex surrogate has on Mark, *The Sessions* depicts the self-actualization Cheryl experiences through her care work, which connects deeply to her value system. In 1972, Cheryl Cohen-Greene was a young wife and mother living in San Francisco when she happened upon a newly published memoir that would change her life: *Surrogate Wife: The True Confessions of a Sex-Therapist*. Never having heard the term, Cohen-Greene's curiosity was piqued. Like many women of her generation, she had grown up with a sense of shame and guilt about her sexuality, compounded by her Catholic background. Attracted to the idea of helping people find intimate satisfaction in their lives, she attended a surrogacy seminar sponsored by the San Francisco Sex Information (SFSI). A year later, she was working as a sex surrogate. By 2012, she had worked with over 900 clients.[73]

In *The Sessions*, Cheryl tells Mark that "the church didn't appreciate my attitude towards sex." Mark queries, "You had an attitude about sex?" Cheryl responds, "Yes, I liked it. They like to think they threw me out, but I threw them out." In her compelling memoir, *Intimate Life*, Cohen-Greene describes her transformation from repressed Catholic schoolgirl to professional sex surrogate as a metaphor for women's liberation:

> My young life straddled two eras. I was in my twenties in the 1960s. The shifting social winds of the time encouraged me to question and rethink nearly everything I had been taught. Held up to daylight, many of the beliefs about sexuality that I had been inculcated with as a child didn't survive. This process culminated in my career as a sex surrogate.[74]

The Sessions aligns Cheryl's work with sex-positive feminism and makes it into a calling that embodies her values and gives her the confidence to reject without guilt the conservative ideas about sexual docility she had grown up with. The film depicts sex surrogacy for Cheryl as an act of individualism that stretches her personal limits.

Cheryl also experiences the "relational rewards"[75] of care work. In a later interview with *The Sartogian*, Cohen-Greene described her work with O'Brien as a kind of mission: "He told me he felt like he was on the outside looking in at a banquet but he knew he would never be able to taste that food. As soon as I met him, I vowed that he would have a chance to taste the feast."[76] In *The Sessions*, when Cheryl's emotion management strategies fail, the film's tensions peak as she develops strong feelings for Mark, and he, in turn, falls in love with her. In the poem Mark writes for Cheryl in the film, "Love Poem for No One in Particular," he describes his body actively, in vivid language, revealing how Cheryl has reshaped his self-image and given him the confidence to regard himself as a sexual, sensual man:

> Let me touch you with my words
> For my hands lie limp as empty gloves
> Let my words stroke your hair
> Slide down your back
> And tickle your belly
> For my hands, light and free-flying as bricks,

Ignore my wishes and stubbornly refuse
To carry out my quietest desires
Let my words enter your mind
Bearing torches
Admit them willingly into your being
So they may caress you gently
Within.

Mark's sensual, corporeal, erotic language ("stroke," "slide," "tickle") shows how transformative the sessions have been. He imagines caring for Cheryl as she has cared for him. Cheryl is deeply moved and experiences his poem as a huge relational reward as she clutches the page to her face and cries. For her, working as a sex surrogate is a deeply personal vocation.

Indeed, as *The Sessions* shows, the more time Cheryl spends with Mark, the deeper her feelings for him grow. After their sessions, his words linger in her mind with a resonance that feels uplifting. When Mark telephones Cheryl one day to ask her out for coffee, Cheryl initially tries to decline, knowing she would be violating her professional code and personal boundaries. They do eventually meet at an intimate café, however, and when Mark asks if she would introduce him as her boyfriend should anyone ask, she leans into the playful "pretend" he is proposing and quips: "No, as my husband. Why not go all the way?" Mark is initially shocked, "You really can picture me as husband material?" Cheryl responds immediately: "As long as we're pretending, sure." Her tone is casual, but a close-up of her face shows her sadness and the difficulty of having to distance herself – to emotionally wrench herself away – from a man she finds so captivating. In her home office, she speaks into her tape recorder: "His deeper emotional needs are outside the scope of my potential involvement." Her words are clinical, but the camera focuses again on her face, which looks pained, and her voice trembles with unspoken emotion.

In what ends up being their final session, Mark asks Cheryl if she will try to have an orgasm with him. Forgoing her emotion management strategies and boundaries – her separation of self from role – she does, and when Mark whispers "I love you" in the moments immediately after, Cheryl whispers it back. But immediately Cheryl realizes that she has crossed a line and tells Mark they should end their sessions here because he no longer needs her and continuing would be dangerous for both of them. At this, their last session, she forgets to take the envelope of money – her payment – indicating that her professional relationship of care has ended. Cheryl began her relationship with Mark procedurally, maintaining boundaries, yet this climax reveals the delicateness of the sex surrogacy relationship that makes Cheryl vulnerable to experiencing dissonance between how she feels and how she must act. As Hochschild reminds us, inherent to emotional labour is "maintaining a difference between feeling and saying," which "over the long run leads to strain."[77] *The Sessions* portrays these strains without making Cheryl a victim of them; rather, the film portrays her as skilled care worker with strengths and vulnerabilities, shows us the value of her work, and humanizes her outside of rigid binaries, as a human.

Rare for a movie about a sex worker, *The Sessions* portrays Cheryl in her home life as a wife and a mother, and in sunlit and plant-filled domestic scenes of gardening, cooking, and eating meals with her family. Yet, the film is not naive to the challenges of maintaining a family as a sex worker and shows how even the most careful setting of boundaries is not a bulwark from the feelings of anxiety and responsibility that come with intensive care work that can leave providers feeling isolated. In fact, the very boundaries that protect her also lead to her bottling up feelings up she wants to share but can't. One example of such "emotion suppression"[78] occurs during her first session with Mark. Overcome by empathy for Mark's situation, Cheryl retreats to the bathroom where she stands at the mirror and takes several deep breaths to calm herself before returning to the bedroom. In this sequence, *The Sessions* shows that despite being a care worker who is paid to quell *other* people's anxieties, Cheryl is not immune to anxieties of her own and must work diligently to manage her own feelings, alone, which is sometimes a challenge, especially in her own relationships. After meeting Mark, Cheryl tells her husband that her new client is "trapped in a big metal box." Her husband, who lies beside her in bed reading, does not lift his eyes from the page, offering only an absentminded "you're a saint" before turning away and falling asleep.

It is unclear whether Cheryl's ignored bid for attention is rooted in her husband's own boundaries around hearing about her work, or even a pre-existing arrangement to keep these conversations hushed, but either way, confidentiality clauses make discussing work problematic. Cheryl sits awake looking pensive while her husband sleeps. Even when using emotion management strategies, the film suggests, it is not always possible to neatly compartmentalize care work, and care workers may struggle to get care for themselves. In *She's Lost Control*, another film about sex surrogacy, this is exactly what happens.

She's Lost Control: Chaos in Unregulated Care Work

She's Lost Control (2014), a less rosy film, tells the story of Ronah, a graduate student in behavioural psychology who lives and works in Manhattan. A committed sex surrogate in her early thirties, Ronah believes in sexual inclusion and takes pride in her work. But her track record of excellent clinical outcomes

Figure 6.4. *She's Lost Control* portrays the rewards and risks of being a sex surrogate through Ronah (Brooke Bloom), a thirty-something graduate student who finds her work gratifying but also terrifying due to its criminalization.

unravels dramatically when she begins work with a new client with "intimacy issues" named Johnny. When Ronah becomes personally involved, boundaries are breached with disturbing consequences. While *The Sessions* portrayed sex surrogacy as a safe job, *She's Lost Control* illuminates how the criminalization of sex work leaves practitioners vulnerable. The tonal difference between *The Sessions* and *She's Lost Control* is perceptible immediately through its production design, the buttery yellow California palette of *The Sessions*, which connoted safety, belonging, and warmth, replaced in *She's Lost Control* with dreary pewter and a spare, atonal soundtrack that suggests danger, insecurity, and loneliness.

Like *The Sessions*, *She's Lost Control* establishes sex surrogacy as a healing therapy with profoundly positive effects. The film's opening scene shows Ronah with a client who has chronic anxiety. In another vignette, she works with a client with severe burns all over his body who describes how ashamed he is of his scarred skin, the result of a horrific house fire. Like Cheryl, Ronah guides her client to take small steps towards body acceptance. Perhaps he would like to remove his shirt? Through this early montage, *She's Lost Control* establishes Ronah as an encouraging force for her emotionally fragile clients and sex surrogacy as a caring service in which emotion takes primacy over carnality.

She's Lost Control emphasizes the defining feature of the sex surrogacy relationship: the sex surrogate's control. A significant indicator of sex worker empowerment, as Ronald Weitzer has noted, is the degree to which the sex worker has decision-making power and controls her work environments.[79] At her first meeting with her new client Johnny, Ronah is in control: she produces a consent form stipulating that their relationship is "not for sexual gratification" and administers via saliva sample a rapid test for sexually transmitted diseases. She asks Johnny for payment up front. This opening is far from an erotic gambit and establishes Ronah as a care worker whose job isn't to gratify her client's sexual fantasies. The setting underscores this professional therapeutic relationship: a pallid hotel room with walls the colour of toothpaste and harsh, clinical lighting. As in *The Sessions*, Ronah is far from the stereotype sex worker who dresses to arouse. She wears brown pants and a brown blazer, and she keeps them on. "We're going to spend the session clothed," she says. "We're just going to talk. No sex."

She's Lost Control represents body work as a transformative experience as Ronah initiates Johnny into a deeper understanding of human intimacy through physical touch. At their second session, Ronah engages Johnny in an exercise called "passive versus active." She sets up two chairs facing one another and invites Johnny to select the passive or the active role. He chooses "passive," so Ronah becomes "active." She takes Johnny's hand and strokes it, turns it over, traces the lines on his palm, and touches his wrist in smooth, sensual motions, intimate and careful gestures of subtlety, which is exactly the point. Ronah is modelling the attentive small acts of kindness that constitute intimacy. A taciturn nurse anesthesiologist in his late thirties with a history of trauma, Johnny has been sent to Ronah by a referring therapist for his issues with "intimacy" and "connecting to people." Ronah then asks Johnny to take the "active" role. "Do you want to touch my hair?" she asks. He looks worried but gingerly does. "That's good, keep going," Ronah says. Deceptively simple, the "passive versus active" exercise is Ronah's tool for introducing Johnny to power sharing in a relationship, an intrinsic aspect of intimacy.

As it develops this relationship, the film draws our attention to the legitimization (or delegitimization) of care work depending on the setting in which it occurs. Ronah and Johnny are, in fact, both care workers. Johnny cares full-time for his disabled sister and professionally he is a nurse anesthesiologist. But while Ronah's work is about building relationships, working against the resistance of defences, Johnny's work of putting people to sleep with drugs precludes relationship building. "I'm not good at follow-ups," he says of his job, but it is an apt metaphor for his inability to connect intimately in his own personal life. While both work with people who are ailing, Johnny works in a legal setting, with a team that supports him, and treats pain with diagnostic tools and drugs; Ronah, in contrast, does work that is criminalized, works alone, and uses her training and intuition, and emotional labour, to diagnose and alleviate pain. "In order to make this work, to be effective, you need to trust that when I'm here, I'm completely here with you," she tells him. "Can we agree on that?" The film's subtle yet pointed comparison between their care work highlights the value of Ronah's work but also her vulnerability.

A turning point in the sex surrogate–client relationship occurs when the client drops his defences and begins to trust the surrogate and absorb her teachings. A breakthrough occurs when Ronah brings a portable music player to a session. The injection of melody sparks the deadlocked process, and Ronah and Johnny dance, twirling with abandon. The greyscale production design blooms into a palette of greens and blues, suggesting regeneration and growth, and progress follows. Soon, Ronah involves Johnny in "body awareness exercises." In one session, she uses her body to model what Rosenbaum, Aloni, and Heruti call "sexual comfort and confidence."[80] She undresses herself and then Johnny and places him before a mirror. Like Mark, Johnny doesn't want to look at first, but gradually he becomes more comfortable with his image as together he and Ronah face their naked selves in the mirror. "You have a nice body," she tells him. Johnny, taking the "active" role replies, "So do you." In facilitating this care and body work, *She's Lost Control* portrays Ronah as an expert practitioner who teaches in a therapeutic fashion to build her client's confidence.

But the film also stresses the firm line between Ronah's professional and private life: "You pay for my time, but you can't control how I feel," she says. Her periodic meetings with the referring therapist also underscores how the surrogacy relationship is triadic,[81] and while the therapist's involvement does not guarantee a smooth process, it does offer some support.

Sex Surrogates: Relational Rewards and the Costs of Emotional Labour

She's Lost Control further emphasizes the legitimacy of sex surrogacy through Ronah's commitment to developing a career as a sex surrogate. Ronah is pursuing a master's degree in behavioural psychology, training she believes will ground her practice theoretically and give her credibility. Her mentor, a more experienced sex surrogate, says, "It's good you're getting a master's degree. Protects you from a legal standpoint" (the comment obliquely foreshadows the utter lack of protection she has). Ronah is so serious about her career that she intends to buy an apartment out of which to practice full time. Clare Stacey notes that care workers may draw "a sense of dignity from constant, and often very intimate, social interaction,"[82] and in her sessions, Ronah frequently smiles. While the film's lighting is generally grey and dreary, the scenes with her clients are bright. On several occasions she tells the referring therapist, "I enjoy these challenges." Ronah likes her "tough cases" because they pose a professional challenge.

Yet, *She's Lost Control* is not an unbalanced film, and it shows the challenges Ronah faces in keeping her work and private life separate. Chapkis argues that in performing emotional labour, sex workers do not lose anything "essential" to themselves,[83] yet Masters and Johnson, in *Human Sexual Inadequacy*, raised concerns for the sex surrogate who would be "playing a role ... where her needs went unmet and no emotional bonds were formed."[84] *She's Lost Control* suggests that the intensity of Ronah's job leads to her sacrificing aspects of her personal life. Ronah's apartment is dark and drab, free of personal effects or mementoes. While New York student apartments are typically not known for their opulence, her home is also literally uncomfortable. A minor subplot revolves around her broken shower, which often runs only cold water that sprays uncontrollably; repair people storm her apartment constantly, yet the shower is never fixed. Cleanliness links to one's sense of dignity but is especially crucial for a sex surrogate, whose care and body work place her in close contact with other people's bodies. This out-of-control shower becomes a metaphor for "leakiness," suggesting that Ronah has less control than she imagines. In contrast to Cheryl's comfortable home in *The Sessions*, Ronah's drab and uncomfortable apartment in *She's Lost Control* implies that her work might be preventing her from having a balanced life.

She's Lost Control also suggests that the intensity of Ronah's care work impedes her ability to form meaningful relationships outside of her work. Her one social activity is an impromptu dinner with a neighbour: they eat at her bare table under a dim bulb. When the neighbour asks what Ronah's job is, she lies. "I'm seeing three clients now," she later tells her older sex surrogate mentor. "I don't know what I would do if I had a boyfriend." Throughout the film, she injects herself with fertility hormones as part of her undertaking to freeze her eggs for future use. While freezing one's eggs suggests the hopeful wish to have a child, it also implies a dearth of hope in meeting a life partner with whom to co-parent, which is a mark of Ronah's isolation. Furthermore, Ronah's family life is dysfunctional. Periodically, she Skypes with her angry brother who demands her care while giving nothing in return. Amid this bleakness, Ronah's work is her lodestar. Yet, it also leaves her craving care herself and vulnerable to crossing professional boundaries that result in disaster.

Can't Call 911: The Care Worker's Burden of Criminalization

In the first half of *She's Lost Control*, Ronah's cool professionalism allows her to maintain what Hochschild calls "a healthy estrangement" from her work. Yet, as she becomes increasingly preoccupied with healing her client Johnny, she begins to over-identify with her work – what Hochschild calls "wholehearted" identification, which places the worker at risk "for losing parts of herself" and forgoing the emotion management strategies that protect her.[85] Ronah develops romantic feelings for Johnny that erode her boundaries and blind her to his increasingly threatening behaviour. During one session, in a deadpan tone, he mutters, "I want to strangle you." When she catches him looking through her phone, she chastises him, but only briefly; letting this bald violation of her privacy slide signals her increasingly eroding boundaries.

One day she secretly visits his workplace, a local hospital, to watch him. Standing in his green scrubs at the nurse's station, Johnny appears confident as he talks with his colleagues. While the scene shows Ronah becoming inappropriately invested, it also juxtaposes Johnny's care work as a nurse – in a hospital, with regulations – with Ronah's care work, which has no fixed address, is solitary, unregulated, and lacks legitimacy and protection. *She's Lost Control* emphasizes this point when a security guard approaches Ronah and asks if he can help her find anything, implying she is unauthorized in the space. Flustered, Ronah leaves. "What do you do if you're falling in love with a client?" she asks a friend. The film suggests that Ronah's inappropriate feelings expand and distort in a context of isolation, which stems from the secrecy she must maintain about her job. Were the care work of sex surrogacy legal like Johnny's nursing work, the film insinuates, Ronah could access support from a professional organization or a union and guidance from friends and family. But as an isolated, marginalized, and stigmatized sex worker, she can't.

As a result, *She's Lost Control* shows how criminalization exacerbates existing relations of domination and subordination. Kristin M. De Griend and DeAnne K. Hilfinger Messias note that "women in highly gendered professions, such as nursing, teaching, domestic work, sex work, and other service professions, are frequently targets of workplace violence,"[86] and as one sex workers' rights activist recently noted, "efforts to criminalize the sex trade in recent years have made it more dangerous."[87] In my interview with Vera, a newly minted sex surrogate, she described the murky legal zone in which she operates: "As surrogates we technically live in a legal no man's land … there really is no legal support for us."

The climax of *She's Lost Control* is a sex worker's worst fear come true. During her eighth session with Johnny, Ronah breaks the cardinal rule of her work and spends the night with him at the hotel. They have passionate sex. Ronah forgoes all boundaries physically (she orgasms) and emotionally by waiving all emotion management strategies (believing she has cured Johnny's "intimacy issues"). Johnny confesses to Ronah that he "likes her." Ronah replies, "I like you, too, Johnny." When they fall asleep in an embrace, *She's Lost Control* seems poised to end on a hopeful note, but in the middle of the night, Johnny awakens and experiences what appears to be a psychotic episode and becomes violent. When Ronah rushes to comfort him, he redirects his anger at her and then insults her body: "Your hands are small. You're bony! I don't fucking like you!" Johnny has regressed to the angry man with "intimacy issues" and bitterly blames Ronah for his lack of progress: "I've done everything you asked me to! You didn't cure me!" It is this insult to her vocation that pierces her most and she retaliates by spitting in Johnny's face. He pushes Ronah onto the floor, pours leftover whiskey from his glass on her body, lights a match, and drops it on her. Miraculously, she suffers only superficial burns and manages to leave, going directly to a police station where she reports the crime.

It is through this police station encounter that *She's Lost Control* shows how criminalization places sex workers in an untenable position. In a questioning room, Ronah sits under a harsh neon light as though *she* is the criminal being questioned, though the sympathetic camera zooms in to show the raspberry-coloured contusions on her face. The two questioning officers, a man and a woman, begin by asking Ronah about the nature of her relationship with her attacker. Ronah's hesitation speaks to her dilemma: if she tells the truth, she implicates herself in prostitution, a felony. If she lies, she is committing perjury. Ronah prevaricates: "I just want to know what my options are," she says. Sensing her unease, the female police officer tells Ronah that the police "just want her to feel safe." Yet, given her two "options," Ronah cannot possibly feel safe, and so she creates a third option by excusing herself to the washroom. Once out of the officers' sights, she flees and returns to her apartment, whose starkness underscores the film's explicit conclusion: in Ronah's hour of need, she has nobody to care for her and is utterly alone.

Writing in the *Village Voice*, Alan Scherstuhl suggests that the film's violent climax seems to "reach the same simple conclusions about surrogacy – creepy! dangerous!"[88] This would be true if the entire film focused on a violent client, but Ronah's many other clients are peaceful and grateful, making Johnny the exception, not the rule. In light of this, the film's climax reads less as a condemnation of sex surrogacy or as an indictment of all men who buy sex and more as an appeal to recognize the powerlessness sex workers experience in the event they become the victims of violent crimes. Also, the injustice: if Ronah had assaulted Johnny at his workplace, she would have immediately been arrested. Ronah's journey from empowered sex surrogate to battered woman shows how the legitimization of certain types of care work creates an absurd and terrifying imbalance of power between Ronah, a benevolent care worker who is criminalized, and Johnny, an abusive care worker who is protected by the law. Ronah's powerlessness potently illustrates how criminalization grievously strips sex workers of rights and recourse if they are harmed while tacitly giving violent men the confidence to abuse sex workers, knowing how unlikely a sex worker is to report a crime. Johnny, we can assume, knew this when he violently assaulted Ronah. Her ordeal becomes exculpatory evidence for why criminalization imperils sex workers and places them in a double bind. Ronah enjoys and takes pride in her care work and sees it as a vocation. Yet, because her care work is criminalized, when she needs care herself, she is most powerless. *She's Lost Control* suggests that sex surrogacy – and by extension all sex work – must be decriminalized to protect women like Ronah.

Sex Workers and Sex Surrogates Unite

In the US, sex surrogacy is criminalized and synonymous with prostitution. Yet, sex surrogacy's history as a medical treatment has always given it an air of respectability, and for this reason it has often been defined against sex work. Indeed, in the media coverage of *The Sessions*, journalists emphasized the distinction between sex work and sex surrogacy. "Cohen Greene isn't a prostitute," noted a profile written for *Elle*, "She's a sexual surrogate."[89] *Fox News* likewise took pains to separate sex work and sex surrogacy: "These professionals are nothing like call girls or strippers. In most cases they're females – and attractive ones at that – who regard themselves as sexual priestesses of sorts. Far from dirty, seedy and perverted, their work involves honouring the body in a safe space marked by mutual respect."[90] In the *New York Post*, a sexologist wrote that "people tend to be ill informed about what a surrogate partner does … they think of it pejoratively, the same as a sex worker, but it's not … there is a huge difference between them."[91]

Both *The Sessions* and *She's Lost Control* portray sex surrogates as healing professionals who enrich their clients' lives. But they also draw our attention to how respectability politics still organize sex work in a "whorearchy,"[92] the top tier of which is occupied by sex surrogates, its origins in medical science having lent it respectability, as the reviews for *The Sessions* suggest. Yet, even with their relative privilege, sex surrogates remain at risk for stigmatization and social isolation, and they share with all other sex workers the battle for rights and safe working conditions.

In New South Wales, Australia, sex work is decriminalized, which means that there is no whorearchy, and sex surrogacy and sex work are not at odds. This is the message in *The Scarlet Road* (2011), a documentary film that follows thirty-four-year-old Rachel Wotton, a sex worker and the passionate co-founder of Touching Base, an organization devoted to building bridges between sex workers and people with disabilities. In *The Sessions* and *She's Lost Control*, hard lines were drawn between sex surrogacy and sex work, but Rachel publicly identifies as a sex worker and attends sex workers' rights rallies wearing a red T-shirt that reads "whore." Rachel's work is predominately emotional. Speaking to the assumption that because she's a sex worker, all she does is have sex, Rachel laughs: "I've never done one hour of penetration with a client. Ha!" *The Scarlet Road* locks horns with anti–sex work feminism and overtly critiques its ideologies that shame sex workers and deny them their right to be authorities on their own lives and work. Rachel, in fact, agreed to appear in the film because she wanted to rebut such representations. Says director Catherine Scott, "Rachel had to trust I wouldn't be like the mainstream and do what they typically do." Although the film allows Rachel to represent herself, she is also acutely aware of the stigma of her job. When she attends a conference about sex work in London, she passes a medical display showing pictures of "normal women's vaginas" and "sex workers' vaginas." She points to this sad example of the stigma sex workers still face, right down to the pathologizing of their genitals. "The stigma and discrimination against sex workers is still so great," she says. "It makes me feel like a second-class citizen and silenced." The film celebrates her work with people with disabilities as an alliance between two marginalized groups who enjoy a mutually beneficial relationship. "Sexual empowerment kind of drives me, I guess you could say. Because I think everyone has a right to sexual expression. I like that my job involves giving people pleasure. It's an honour to be part of their lives and a real joy. It's fun and interesting." Of her decision to be out as a sex worker, she says, "Life is too short. I am going to be open."

In *The Sessions* and *She's Lost Control*, the sex surrogate is a healing professional whose care work suggests the educative and healing role sex workers play and could play even more were they to be embraced rather than stigmatized. Together, the films reveal the care and body work skills sex surrogates possess, and the sophisticated emotion management techniques they use in the commission of their work, confronting the prohibitionist perspective that all sex workers are exploited women without skills. As well, they show how sex surrogates draw a sense of pride and accomplishment from their work. In Cheryl's case, based on the real-life Cheryl Cohen-Greene, the satisfaction of being a sex surrogate stems from her personal project rooted in empowerment feminist principles about free sexual expression. In Ronah's case, her professional pride is rooted in her training and her conviction that a good life includes sexual expression. By showing the contributions, skills, and subjectivities of two rounded, complex, smart, and agential sex surrogate characters, *The Sessions* and *She's Lost Control* compel us to think about how sex workers could safely operate in society were sex work – in all its forms – regarded as a legitimate job. Taken together, *The Sessions*, *She's Lost Control*, and *The Scarlet Road* offer evidence of a growing trend in popular culture towards destigmatizing sex surrogacy and treating all sex workers with greater empathy and dignity, regardless of the terms they use to describe their work.

7 Hardcore in the Big Apple: *The Deuce*'s Feminist Sex Work Epic

> *The sex industry is hardly a feminist utopia. It reflects the sexism that exists in the society as a whole. We need to analyse and oppose the manifestations of gender inequality specific to the sex industry. But this is not the same as attempting to wipe out commercial sex.*
>
> – Gayle Rubin[1]

> *I really believe that porn does matter, because it has a cultural impact on the society we live in. It's clear to me that porn has become sex education for a lot of people.*
>
> – Erika Lust, feminist porn-maker[2]

> *At my core I'm a political person, and I like challenges. I was the perfect person. I already had a scarlet letter on me. I had nothing left to lose.*
>
> – Candida Royalle, in *Candice* (2019)

The hit song known as "It's a Man's World" by James Brown could've been the theme for New York City's porn industry in the early 1970s. As men capitalized on newly slackened obscenity laws, cranked out 16 mm loops, and laid linoleum in peep show booths, the "Golden Age of Porn" was born. Adult theatres, once the stomping grounds of the sexual fringe, began screening porn blockbusters like *Deep Throat* (1972), what Camille Paglia called an "epochal shift,"[3] drawing in droves of ordinary people who lined up to see these films, spurred by curiosity and emboldened by sexual liberalization. But adult cinema was not growing without objection. While most feminists concurred that pornography glorified women's submission, they disagreed on what to do about it. Radical feminists set out to abolish porn. Andrea Dworkin famously claimed that women have a "visceral aversion to pornography,"[4] but in the early 1980s, a group of performers went on a mission of creative retrieval, their goal to create porn that made women's sexual agency and pleasure the chief visual and narrative goals.

The Deuce (2017–19), an HBO series, explores this stormy, salacious, risky, and transformative era through the often-buried stories of the women at the centre of it. Produced and created by David Simon and George Pelacanos of *The Wire* fame, *The Deuce* is Hollywood's most complex and labour-conscious historical epic about sex work, and a critique of capitalism's clash with feminist porn-making. *The Deuce*'s distinctively materialist approach takes porn seriously as a genre, an industry, and a job, and it draws its perspective from current sex worker activism and the self-advocacy of porn creators and performers. This was a priority for Simon and Pelacanos, who hired women and writers of colour to lead the series' development. As Pelacanos noted, "We needed a different kind of complexion [from *The Wire*], and so we went out to female novelists that we like a lot."[5] Indeed, women steered *The Deuce* – nine of its twelve directors are women – wrote many episodes, and produced it, and their influence is clear through the series' predominately female point of view, sex-positive feminist ethos, and diverse and complex sex worker characters, white and Black, LGBTQ and straight, old and young, veterans and newcomers. The narrative centres on Eileen "Candy" Merrell, a striving sex worker turned feminist porn auteur, her story a Künstlerroman as she builds a career making porn films about women's pleasure, sexual diversity, and equality.

Probing the invisible labour behind the "money shot," *The Deuce* recognizes the collective challenges sex workers face as well as their agency to make choices within admittedly constraining conditions. It examines how criminalization and stigmatization compelled some sex workers to move from street-based sex work into the porn industry in pursuit of a safer and more lucrative career. That said, the series is not a flaccid homage to a bygone era of porn, nor a tome of about porn as a pathway to "empowerment." Rather, *The Deuce* examines the uphill battle sex workers face in a voraciously profit-driven industry, exposes the misogyny and racism in porn, and intercedes into the feminist sex wars. The series treats porn as work, not as a symbol of women's oppression, and explores porn through an intersectional lens of gender, class, and race to relate the exploitation of sex workers to that of all women who toil under patriarchal capitalism. In contrast to popular culture where women in porn are assumed to be uniquely victimized or coerced, *The Deuce* tracks how a group of porn workers negotiate and try to benefit from challenging labour conditions with very different outcomes that reflect greater societal inequities and oppressions.

I begin this chapter by contextualizing porn historically (as a modern industry), politically (as a site of feminist debate), and popularly (as media products that tell and sell stories about porn). The remainder of the chapter examines how *The Deuce* represents a diversity of female experiences in this industry, interrogates feminist porn's opportunities and limits, and directly engages in and stages feminist theoretical-political debates about pornography – and about sex work itself.

Contexts: XXX Censorship, Politics, and Pop Culture

To fully grasp the originality of *The Deuce*, it's helpful to briefly look back at the history of pornography as a male-run and male-centred industry and genre. Pornography, broadly speaking, denotes any printed or visual work that is made to arouse, and it has existed since the earliest civilizations, from depictions on ancient Greek pottery, to the *Kama Sutra*, to nineteenth-century novels, to the turn of the twentieth century, when making, distributing, and selling erotic images became a lucrative American business. As bustling cities filled with people, entrepreneurs opened peep shows and Kinetoscope parlours,[6] and anonymous pornographers made short and primitive "stag films" featuring masturbation, oral sex, penetration, and voyeurism.[7] Until the sexual revolution when obscenity laws were dropped, these stag films screened in male-only spaces like barbershops, brothels, and in private residences, their allure coming, in part, from their outlawed status.

The US's first obscenity laws were enshrined in 1842 by postmaster Anthony Comstock and widened in the late nineteenth century to encompass any "obscene, lewd, or lascivious book, pamphlet, picture, [or] print … of a vulgar and indecent character."[8] For the next seventy years, the state censored thousands of "obscene" and "indecent" works of "pornography," including birth control information, but by the mid-twentieth century, erotica with artistic merit and social significance was tolerated (e.g., paintings by Pierre-Auguste Renoir and prose by James Joyce). While conservative anti-porn documentaries such as *Perversion for Profit* (1963) argued that porn caused moral decay, the anti-porn camp's battle was already lost as magazines like *Playboy* began to nettle the law and expose the arbitrary line dividing erotic art and obscene pornography. In 1963, the Supreme Court wrestled over whether Louis Malle's film *The Lovers* (1958) was pornographic, and in what would become the US's most famous obscenity case, Justice Potter Stewart, when asked to define pornography, replied: "I know it when I see it." In the end, the Malle film was screened, and the legal barrier to the production and consumption of pornography – obscene, artistic, or otherwise – dissolved. In 1968, the Supreme Court struck down obscenity laws, and, in 1973, *Miller v. California* gave local communities the right to define for themselves what was "vulgar." Meanwhile, the circulation of *Playboy* (first established in 1953) spiked, and other magazines sought to capitalize on the growing market for porn, including *Penthouse* (1965), *Screw* (1968), and *Hustler* (1974), which upped the ante by printing hardcore images. With these political and cultural conditions in place, the so-called Golden Age of Porn was born.

The "Golden Age of Porn" refers to the period from 1969 to 1984, when 35 mm porn features drew on the conventions of Hollywood film, screened to huge audiences, garnered critical acclaim, and were seen as aesthetic, even artistic. Following the release of *Deep Throat*, it was popularly dubbed the era of "porno chic."[9] Yet, porn remained contentious, seen by the public as conflicting things: a motion picture industry controlled by men (that made movies for men); a brave new world of sexual freedom and inhibition (especially because films depicted the taboo of women's sexual desire); a place (a seedy underworld); and a moral panic–inflected social problem ("solved" through censorship). As porn mainstreamed as a genre and industry, opposition for it peaked in what would become known as the feminist "sex wars." Anti-porn feminists argued that porn was eroticizing women's submission to and domination by men just as women were making economic and social inroads. Dworkin famously wrote that porn "documents … a rape first enacted when the women were set up and used; a rape repeated each time the viewer consumes the photographs,"[10] while Susan Brownmiller called for the rescue of its "dehumanized" performer-victims.[11] Larry Flynt, the publisher of *Hustler*, responded with his 1978 cover collage of a woman's naked body with a meat grinder, the headline "We will no longer hang women's bodies up like pieces of meat" announcing the mainstream pornography industry's contempt for feminism, and its own untouchability.[12] Around the same time, a group of disenchanted adult film actresses began drawing on sex-positive feminism to reconstitute porn into a feminist genre, though their stories were often hushed.

Movies, TV, and documentary have represented the porn industry since the 1970s, but, as Laura Kipnis has rightly noted, there was a dearth of "discussion of pornography as an expressive medium in the positive sense" and an excessive exegesis on its "misogyny or social decay."[13] Indeed, early popular culture – with some notable exceptions – largely replicated conservative and feminist binary thinking by producing porn stories of the super sad or super scary ilk. Brian McNair usefully divides popular culture about porn into two categories: "porno fear" and "porno chic."[14] Porno fear movies portrayed the dangers of the porn industry, emblematic being Paul Schrader's *Hardcore* (1979), a noir-ish thriller about a father's descent into Los Angeles' 8 mm porn industry in search of his putatively kidnapped teenage daughter. At their extreme, porno fear movies portrayed porn producers as predatory creeps, porn consumers as sick voyeurs, and porn performers as fallen angels (often blonde with double Ds), stoking the twin fires of sex and danger the box office loves. Distinct were "porno chic" films that explored the human side of the adult film industry, such as *The People vs. Larry Flynt* (1996), about first amendment rights, and *Boogie Nights* (1997), while more exploratory films, such as *Not a Love Story* (1981) and Bette Gordon's *Variety* (1983), engaged with feminism and the adult feature through female-driven stories.[15]

Popular culture about porn became more varied in the 2000s as comedies such as *The Girl Next Door* (2004), *The Moguls* (2005), and *Zack and Miri Make a Porno* (2008) portrayed average people making adult movies, while documentaries such as *After Porn Ends* (2012), *9 to 5: Days in Porn* (2008), *Mutantes: Punk Porn Feminism* (2009), *Pornocracy: The New Sex Multinationals* (2017), and *Candice* (2019) probed the business from women's points of view, covering issues from how tube sites (such as PornHub) have gutted salaries for porn workers to feminist porn-making. Historical films such as *Wonderland* (2003) and *Lovelace* (2013) probed porn scandals, while the inventive *Mrs. Fletcher* (2019) framed porn as sexual therapy for a depressed woman, and *Pleasure* (2021) tracked the seamier side of porn while allotting its workers agency. These sex-positive movies take up Clarissa Smith's call to portray porn performers as "multifaceted social beings capable of self-determination and agency."[16] Yet, popular culture still simplified the genre by equating anything that arouses a woman with feminism rather than encouraging more informed discussions of pornography and its political economy – that is, how the industry is still largely controlled by men and corporations whose interests are less in making feminist art or supporting female performers than they are in maximizing profit.

Today, public opinion on porn continues to be divided, stoking binary debates, though anti-porn sentiment has recently found "significant purchase in … populist spheres."[17] In his 2016 presidential campaign, Donald Trump pledged to crack down on porn (while it played in thousands of his hotel rooms). In 2019, four Republican members of Congress called on US Attorney General William Barr to make the prosecution of obscene pornography a criminal justice priority after blaming the adult industry for sex trafficking and other social problems. Clearly, public discourse about porn remains woefully stratified. On one side, conservatives and radical feminists speak about victimized women; on the other, neo-libertarians trumpet female agency and empowerment. This is an unhelpful binary that relies on cherry-picked examples of the impact porn has on the women in it, or on the men (and women) who view it. Undoubtedly, the porn industry has problems, from its ownership structures, to labour precarity, to racist and misogynist imagery, and women do experience harms in it,[18] but these are problems in larger patriarchal capitalist society and not the ones detractors fixate on. New popular stories that break with these binaries are needed, and HBO's *The Deuce* delivers this, dignifying porn workers without romanticizing the industry. While *The Deuce* is not the first popular story about the porn industry, it is probably the most complex one.

Times Square Time Capsule: *The Deuce*'s Sex Worker Community

"The Deuce" was the nickname for the New York City red-light district of peep shows, massage parlours, and adult cinemas that dotted 42nd Street between 7th and 8th Avenue until the mid-1980s, when Manhattan's massive gentrifying "rehabilitation project" paved it over into a tourist shopping paradise. Today, the area is rarely eulogized, and the women who lived and worked there are infrequently remembered and perhaps intentionally forgotten, but *The Deuce* (2017–19) masterfully recovers this history with a story about sex workers who come of age and try to make their way in the Golden Age of Porn. Setting is key on *The Deuce*, and the show's investments in its physical and temporal worlds are deep. Its CGI recreations of Times Square's peep shows, bars, cinemas, and neon signs glow with a thrilling realism that almost makes you squint, while its title sequences, changing every season, conjure up the evolving tensions of the era in fast-cut swirls of sequins, stilettos, cash, falling gavels, fishnets, heat, sex, and noise. The soundtrack, too, captures the tensions of the time and place, season one's mirthful soul combusting into season two's opiated dirges for stagflation and the Vietnam War, before capping off with skittery new wave, the geometric sounds marking Manhattan's makeover into a finance capital.

But it is the ordinary locales of work with which *The Deuce* is principally concerned: the greasy-spoon diners where sex workers trade tips on bad dates; the apartments with deceptively palatial names where sex workers pay out pimps; the porn studios where sex works star in loops; and the five and dimes where hustlers buy lipstick, condoms, and soap. These locales form the intimate backdrops for action over two decades. A triptych – set in 1971–2, 1977–8, and 1984–5 – each season of *The Deuce* traces the seismic social changes of its respective era, as corporations shifted from Fordist to service-oriented capitalism, neo-liberal policies restructured the economy, conservative politicians pledged to curb porn and radical feminists decried it, and movements for women's liberation and gay and civil rights put the rights of minorities on the public agenda. Drawing on these tensions, *The Deuce* examines the conditions that impel women into porn, the uphill battle sex workers face in a voraciously profit-driven industry, and issues of misogyny and racism. It also intercedes into the feminist sex wars. *The Deuce*'s memorable characters are Black and white, gay and straight, old and young, and as it probes their lives and labour, it recognizes the collective challenges they face as well as their agency within admittedly constraining conditions.

When *The Deuce* opens in 1971, it is a man's world, and men run peep shows, porn cinemas, and prostitution rings with feudal untouchability. Pimps, police, and businessmen control the area and commodify women's bodies while sex-shaming them, an irony *The Deuce* picks up on. "If she had as many pricks stickin' out of her as she had stuck in her, she'd be a fuckin'

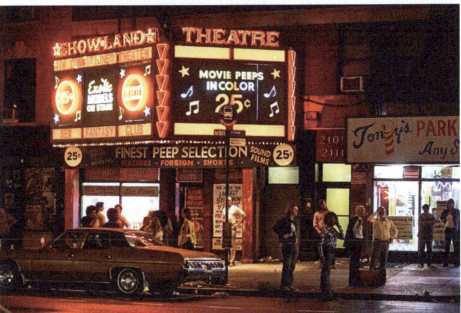

Figure 7.1. *The Deuce* portrays the lives of women sex workers in Times Square in the 1970s and 1980s, uncovering a forgotten history of hustling from their point of view.

porcupine," one pimp drawls, while men discuss sex workers with derogations like "thoroughbreds," "whores" and the "high-heeled army." Kingpin pimp C.C. wears monarchically golden three-piece suits, his gimmick to scout peach-faced girls at the Port Authority and whisk them to his Cadillac rigged with a clothesline of new dresses like a boutique. Take your pick, he tells them, be whoever you want to be. (But all the dresses, it turns out, turn them into his property.) More than simply portray sex work as uniquely exploitative, however, *The Deuce* shows how the commodification of women's sexuality runs insidiously throughout capitalist society. A bar owner forces his cocktail waitresses into spandex bodysuits and has them "bending all over the place, spilling stuff," while a journalist on the local beat has her story spiked after refusing to play by her editor's sexist rules. The series' frequent images of powerful men gorging on greasy food and palming wads of cash while stigmatized sex workers shiver on street corners, surviving on cigarettes, powerfully visualizes patriarchy's double standard: how the sexual commodification of women is normalized when it benefits men, while women's sexual self-commodification is stigmatized.

The Deuce's heroine, Eileen "Candy" Merrell (played by Maggie Gyllenhaal), is wise to this inequality, and her rich character arc gives a dignity to sex workers rarely seen in popular culture. A quick-witted thirty-something-year-old with soulful brown eyes and stacks of self-possession, Candy is a single mother, a movie lover, and a feminist whose story becomes a Künstlerroman as she shifts from street sex work to become one of the first female porn auteurs. We meet her in the pilot on 42nd Street doing the stroll in a white fur coat, a white pantsuit, and a vanilla blonde wig. Channelling the incandescent glamour of Marilyn Monroe and the street cat toughness of Lou Reed, she is a send-up of the lady in red, and the camera pans as she walks past a cinema, its marquee foreshadowing her future auteurism. In name, Candy evokes the feminist pornographer Candida Royalle and the rebel muse of Andy Warhol, Candy Darling, with whom she shares an outsider's ambition. Her name is also unthreateningly sweet to appeal to her customers. Indeed, Candy understands desire and capitalism. After a decade of hustling, she has metabolized the mercantile nature of her neon world, where "it's all about money, money, money." Her shrewd analysis of patriarchal capitalism's commodification of women's bodies has steeled her resolve to never work for a pimp. As she puts it, "Nobody makes money off my pussy except me." Candy likes her work, considers sex work a career, and sends money to her son who lives with her parents on Long Island. *The Deuce* dignifies Candy's work, lauding her grit, intelligence, and entrepreneurial spirit that propel her from street sex worker to porn auteur, and her lucid articulation of her labour is what sets her apart from popular culture's commonest sex worker tropes.[19]

Figure 7.2. In *The Deuce's* pilot, Eileen "Candy" Merrell (Maggie Gyllenhaal) in head-to-toe white attire challenges the stereotype of the lady in red. Smart and creative, she advocates for all sex workers.

We see this in the pilot when she leads a jittery virgin to a flyblown hotel off 42nd Street, having been hired by his friends to give him a "special" present for his eighteenth birthday. As Candy strokes his hand and whispers into his ear, she exudes the sugary femininity that her name promises and swells the young man's lust. But after they (quickly) finish, Candy becomes Eileen, the businesswoman, going to the vanity to fix her make-up, while the flushed rookie demands they "go again." She refuses: "Sorry, one ticket, one ride." When he protests – "You barely did any work" – Candy puts down her compact and asks her client what his father does for a living. He replies that he owns a car dealership. Candy meets his eyes in the mirror and quips:

> So imagine someone comes in, knows just the car he wants, doesn't dick around or need a test drive, doesn't argue about the colour. Does [your dad] give him the car for less? Does he pay less than the guy who comes in, needs six test drives, needs to talk about the radio? Does he pay less? No, he doesn't give the easy customer two cars for the price of one. This is my job, Stuart.

But *The Deuce* also shows Candy's stigmatization by family members who shame her for her work, her lovers who fetishize her as a sex object, and the police who regard her as a nuisance and criminalize her. *The Deuce* paints a vivid picture of how criminalization makes Candy's work unsustainable. Images of police shoving sex workers into vans bound for Rikers Island and contemptuously calling sex workers "whores" evince Candy's position as a second-class citizen. One police officer admits that he receives kickbacks to arrest sex workers and make "Times Square pussy free" for the massive redevelopment project that applied "rezoning laws" in the 1970s to exile public sexual culture and crack down on sex workers.[20] As the *Village Voice* reported, the mayor was being "pressured by real estate interests to get rid of the whores."[21]

As police sweep the streets and real estate developers imagine transforming grotty peep shows into luxe piano bars, Candy and her friends become more vulnerable to violence as they take clients to riskier locations to avoid arrest. Candy has been choked and had her arm broken, but she chooses not to report these crimes for fear of being arrested herself. To protect themselves, some sex workers have pimps. *The Deuce* establishes Candy's catch-22: work independently, as she does, and face daily threats, or work for a pimp who offers protection in exchange for her money and subservience. Candy's friends Darlene, Lori, and Dorothy, intelligent women, stay with their abusive pimps for fear of worse. Ruby "Thunder Thighs," a Black independent sex worker, is pushed to her death from a hotel window by a client who is never apprehended owing to police apathy for investigating sex worker murders. Sex workers brave enough to report crimes have their testimonies dismissed: "She was a known pro[stitute], so who's to say," one police officer says. In 1970s New York City, it was not uncommon for sex worker murders to be assigned an unofficial acronym: NHI, "no humans involved."[22] After a decade of facing down these threats, Candy looks to the pornography industry as "her ticket off the streets," as she puts it.

16 mm Exit Strategy: *The Deuce*'s Image of the Emerging Porn Industry

The Deuce takes viewers into porn's early days as an emerging cinematic genre to show how its profit-making imperative shaped content and form from the start. When Candy starts her career, it is still illegal to show sexual penetration in movie theatres. Porn-makers circumvent this restriction by producing films for the "loop machines," coin-operated viewing booths in adult magazine and sex toy shops – "brown paper bag stores" – which numbered 200 at their peak in the early 1970s.[23] According to Steven Ziplow's *The Film Makers Guide to Pornography* (1977), a how-to-guide that is now something of a historical repository for porn scholars, a successful loop included "seven money shots," ran from seven to twenty minutes, and was at least 85 per cent hardcore sex. No script was necessary. As the *Guide* notes, "A simple outline will do."[24] The loop machines shaped the genre in the sense that pornographers made films to keep viewers feeding quarters into the slots. Narrative was a liability, a chance for the viewer to leave the booth, and meteoric sexual action was the permanent pièce de résistance. Street-based sex workers, like Candy, looked to the loops for fast cash. But the real sex entrepreneurs were the men, who became overnight successes with loops, the jewel of the early porn industry. Marty Hodas, "King of the Peeps," owned 85 per cent of peep shows by the early 1970s[25] and was said to have earned "millions of dollars in quarters."[26] His machines drove demand for content, and the Deuce quickly became the country's porn-making epicentre.

One of the most prominent pornographers was Bob Wolfe, nicknamed "Four X" because he'd made about 4,000 loops.[27] His studio, in the basement of a building on 14th Street, served as both a set for porn films and an audition suite for hopefuls who posed for Polaroids, many of which survive today; they show men and women, mostly in their twenties, in front of makeshift living room sets. Linda Lovelace, former Ivory soap model turned hardcore star, made her first loop at Wolfe's. She likely saw his weekly ad in the *Village Voice*, which read:

GIRLS WANTED
$75–$100 per shooting
Figure Modelling & Films.
No experience necessary.

According to Josh Alan Friedman in *Tales of Times Square*, "loops were the tough, heartless training ground for the first generation of porn stars."[28] Wolfe shot up to six films a day in a studio so small it could hold only two actors and the crew. The ceilings were so low the lights had to be taped to the pipes running along it. It was hot and smelled funky.[29] There was only one bed, so props like "desks or sofas" were shoved into the corners of the tiny studio to create the illusion of multiple locations.[30] Hundreds of 8 mm loops were shot in Wolfe's studio, edited by Wolfe himself on a Moviola, and dropped off the next day to the peep shows.

The Deuce takes viewers into this underground world through Candy's eyes on her first shoot on a shabby set that looks like it was modelled after Wolfe's 14th Street grotto. Still naive to the loops' conventions, Candy asks about the script. Her co-star laughs: "Honey, there is no script. This ain't *Dr. Zhivago*. They don't even record the sound." Wearing a wig of flaxen braids, Candy is ravished by two Vikings in horned helmets, before the director pumps cold condensed chicken soup through a giant turkey baster onto her breasts while yelling, "Don't squint! Remember, you love Viking cum!" Candy finds the movie ridiculous, its "plot" a replication of the power relations she knows all too well from the street, but she enjoys the money, the subversive frisson of the form, but most of all, the safety of the porn set. "If the cops bust in, they say they're making art," she tells her friends later, the camera closing in on her smiling face, "This shit is genius!" Working against the assumption that women are coerced into porn, *The Deuce* makes Candy a hustler who chooses to break into a lucrative and legal business.

But as Candy becomes an in-demand performer, *The Deuce* makes her into an astute critic of loops, as she reads the genre as what Linda Williams calls "sexual action in, and as, narrative."[31] That "narrative," as Candy gradually learns, is that women are sex objects. On shoot after shoot, Candy observes how women are filmed from the male point of view, how sex acts privilege male pleasure only (fellatio is common while cunnilingus is not), and how women are assumed to be aroused by the same things men are. She is also critical of the ham-fisted dialogue ("I'm a plumber laying some pipe"; "Mmm, your pussy tastes like … pussy") and sees how the loops' restricted form wastes porn's subversive potential. She is also troubled by how women performers sit at the bottom of the profit chain. "Those machines," she laments, "you only get paid once! Every time a man puts a quarter into a machine, you don't get paid." So, she decides to learn how to make porn herself.

Her mentor, Harvey Wasserstein, an up-and-coming director, teaches her the mechanics of porn-making and becomes her creative partner. "I want to work at, like, Disney," Candy tells him at their first meeting, where they bond over corned beef sandwiches and their shared love of French New Wave films, blue skying a vision for porn that blends eros and intellect (later, they hang framed posters of auteur films at their office). This relationship is artistically pivotal for Candy. Dismissed by her family as a "whore," seen by clients as a body, and closeted about her work to everyone else, Candy's creative partnership with Harvey is an opportunity to be taken seriously as "Eileen," the intellectual and artist, by an equal who respects her and shares her passion for movies. Conscious of the class dynamics of creative production, *The Deuce* makes the porn set Candy's college, a place to learn a vocation that draws on, rather than conceals, her sexual expertise. Candy is a quick study after a decade of selling fantasies on 42nd Street, where every stroll was an audition, every client a casting agent, every hotel room a movie set, and every sex act a little film. She soon graduates from making loops to "three-day" wonders, 16 mm films with plot and character development, which signalled porn's graduation to a form with a more refined aesthetic sensibility.

The Deuce uniquely takes viewers into the heady early days of porn production without glamourizing it, showing instead how professional arousal is made. Under Harvey's mentorship, Candy learns camerawork, scriptwriting, production design, editing, and about the requisite money shots (seven per film are ideal) while picking up insider techniques, like how a daub of Vaseline on the lens creates a sexy dewy image and how to operate the rolling dollies that capture the action from below. It peels back the cinema magic to reveal the fluffers, the dollies, and the rubbers, the Taylorized labour behind the money shots, sanding off whatever illusions a casual porn viewer might have. For those without a union card in the 1970s, the porn set was, according to Gerard Damiano, director of *Deep Throat*, a popular school for film-making. "If you want to learn film, the only way to learn is as a member of an independent production," he said in 1977. "Any advice I would give to a young person … learn the mechanics of that art form."[32] Many scenes in *The Deuce* show Candy learning how to cut film, light scenes, mix sound, scout locations, and solve porn peccadillos from performer flaccidity (amyl nitrate) to taxes. In her pivotal 1989 text on adult films, *Hard Core*, Linda Williams argued that the embattled status of pornography has prevented a thorough exploration of it as a genre, but some thirty years later *The Deuce* does treat porn as a genre, gives its makers due expertise, and challenges prohibitionists who claim porn creators have no tangible skills. As it traces Candy's tenure, it also neutralizes porn's moral voltage and transforms the cliché of the industry as a grimy underworld of amoral fucking into what it is – a credible genre, a craft, and a job.

Yet, it also shows the limitations of a genre driven by male capital and desire. Women performers are referred to on set as "fresh meat," and one producer advises Candy to focus her creative efforts on "women getting filled up by dicks." Meanwhile, distributors develop a rating system whereby the coins from the loop machines are separately bagged and counted to determine which loops are hits. When a distributor shows Candy a workbook of "porn hits" and rattles off in an auctioneer's dispassionate voice the misogynistic images that sell ("the bigger the dick, the better" and "rough stuff"), Candy gets angry over how women are portrayed "as sex-crazed … [with] no inhibitions." She is also disturbed by porn's racism, especially how Black men are exoticized as ravishers of white women. Frustrated by images of female submission and white supremacy,[33] Candy tells two producers:

> Your scripts are shit! If you want me to keep banging out films for you, you've got to give me better material to work with and let me start banging out my own lines. The movies that make money, take more money. We need to get out of this shoebox. The best flicks … they give you story. The real money makers are good stories!

In 1972 it became legal to screen images of sexual penetration in cinemas, and feature porn films began supplanting "loops" and their rigid genre codes. Adult theatres, once the stomping grounds of the trench-coated set, began attracting ordinary people curious about porn and reassured by its resemblance to feature films. As strange as it is to imagine today, these films were made to be watched while munching popcorn, for two hours, in a public cinema – even chatted about over drinks. Adult features made once-taboo themes like fantasy, power, sex, and gender into broachable conversation. As Loren Glass writes, *Deep Throat* began "uninhibited public engagement with intimate issues previously suppressed by puritanism and prudery."[34] The Golden Age of Porn had dawned, and the porn feature, on 35 mm, exploded a genre and a public phenomenon. In 1960, there were twenty adult theatres in the US. By 1970, there were 750.[35] The huge success of *Deep Throat*, which cost $25,000 and grossed $25 million, ushered in a wave of feature porn with narrative aspirations, including *Behind the Green Door* (1972) and *The Devil in Miss Jones* (1973). With ensemble casts, multiple settings, and narrative arcs featuring assertive women who asked for what they wanted, and sometimes demanded it, the Golden Age of Porn coincided with women's liberation, and its female characters who kicked off their heels for kinky sex without consequences seemed a part of that zeitgeist.

Yet, some films were spuriously feminist and driven by male fantasies trumped up as women's empowerment.[36] In *Behind the Green Door*, for instance, a woman reaches sexual nirvana after being abducted and ravished by strangers, although the narrator assures us that while her "reactions may lead you to believe that she is being tortured … quite the contrary is true," massaging the rape into a fantasy of a woman who enjoys her violation. *Deep Throat* told the story of a frigid nurse who discovers that her clitoris is buried in her throat – "deep down in the bottom of your throat is better than having no clitoris at all!" says her therapist – sending her on a sexual liberation journey of fellating men for her own pleasure.

For porn scholar Linda Williams, pornography's visual iconography – its sequentially intensifying shots of bodies enlaced in sexual positions leading to the inevitable "money shot" – is what makes the genre recognizable, what defines it. But when this iconography is joined by narrative, the two "work together to intensify oppositions and contradictions that exist within a culture to seek imaginary forms of resolution."[37] Porn cinema can, she writes, "permit the resolution of deeper problems, not necessarily manifest on the surface."[38] For Candy, the "deeper problem" is the image of faux sexual empowerment that mainstream porn propped up. Porn's formula, as Williams sums up elsewhere, was "an abundance of interchangeable men – and their penises – in relation to a single woman."[39] For Candy, porn's surface problem is its claim that male pleasure *is* sexual pleasure, but its "deeper problem" is patriarchy's role restriction of all women. As Candy launches her career as a film-maker, *The Deuce* asks: Given that women's sexual expression tends to be commodified or shamed by men, how can a woman depict that expression without herself becoming complicit in that commodification?

More than Fuck Films: The Making of a Feminist Pornographer

The Deuce celebrates Candy's ascent as a feminist porn-maker as a dramatic transfer of power. Once a marginalized sex worker whose body and erotic capital was stigmatized, Candy becomes intent on using her creative power to make "more than fuck films" for an audience that, against all odds, existed.

Feminist porn emerged in the early 1980s to prioritize women's sexual pleasure and expression, to promote safe working conditions and ethical porn sets, and to challenge misogynistic aesthetics of mainstream porn. It appeared within a zeitgeist of what Lynn Commella describes as "a much wider cultural context ... of sex-positive feminist culture and commerce."[40] From the safely subversive *Mary Tyler Moore Show* to the underground lesbian magazine *On Our Backs*, popular culture was placing a magnifying glass on women's desires in all their valences to ask: How does sexual desire fit into women's liberation? Sex-positive feminism answered "a lot" and made its goal to widen the feminist conversation about sex from one focused on danger and oppression to one about sex as a site of pleasure and power. Pornography became the thorniest issue. While most feminists agreed that pornography objectified women, they disagreed on what to do about it.

Suck, published in London from 1969 to 1974, was possibly the first feminist porn magazine in the world. Since pornography wasn't going anywhere, its founders reasoned, women had an opportunity to reimagine the form into one that endorsed their power in their personal, sexual, and professional lives. A literary-minded potpourri of photographic spreads, feature articles, fiction, and poetry, sprinkled with celebrity interviews, horoscopes, and dispatches from the art world and united by the thematic of the erotic life, its mandate was to publish "avante-porn." According to Germaine Greer, it forged a "new kind of erotic art, away from the tits 'n' ass and the peep show syndrome."[41] The magazine's founders believed that with its wide appeal and scintillating imagery, porn could be much more than arousing – it could be what Chris Kraus calls a "locus of politics" and a way of "disrupting the social order."[42] *Suck* argued that pornography did not need to exploit women, which set it apart from the dominant discourse among feminists at the time, namely Women Against Pornography (WAP).[43] Loathe to admit that exploitation hardly began in or was confined to the porn industry, their declaration failed to consider women – like Candy – who chose to appear in porn and had bigger aspirations for the genre.

Yet, out of this crucible came change, and in the early 1980s, several performers from the Golden Age of Porn – including Annie Sprinkle, Veronica Vera, Candida Royalle, and Veronica Hart – tired of mainstream porn's limited roles for women and people of colour, formed a support group called Club 90 in New York City.[44] In 1984, they participated in a festival called Second Coming where they explored the question "Is there a feminist pornography?" While groups like WAP maintained that working to abolish porn was the only conscionable feminist course of action, Candida Royalle believed another path was preferable:

> So I began to think about making porn movies that were aimed at women.... I felt that adult entertainment could be very valid and life-enriching, but it wasn't being done with that in mind.... I wanted to show that it was possible to produce explicit porn that had integrity, I wanted to show that porn could be nonsexist, and I wanted to show that porn could be life-enriching.[45]

Candida Royalle (1950–2015) was an American porn performer, feminist porn-maker, activist, and writer. One of the most iconic film-makers in the history of feminist pornography, her sex-positive films and persona led her to be referenced as the spokeswoman for the genre. Her films widened the themes of pornography in the 1980s, 1990s, and post-2000 period to include discussions of gender, power, sex, violence, and pleasure. Royalle's career serves as the model for Candy's in *The Deuce*. Like Candy, Royalle began her career in the 1970s as a performer, transitioned into directing, and later founded the feminist porn company Femme Productions, whose imaginative, playful, and libidinous films were character- and narrative-driven and featured female characters who acted on their taboo desires for non-monogamous sex, casual sex, multiple partners, and lesbian sex without facing any social stigma.[46] Royalle's films were a response to mainstream porn's insipid image of women's sexuality and asserted that women were sexual subjects whose pleasure mattered.

Figure 7.3. From porn performer to feminist porn trailblazer, Candy challenges the restrictions women face in mainstream porn, both on- and off-screen, in content, form, and production. "I want to make more than fuck films," Candy says – and she does.

As Royalle said, "We were represented as having no sexuality, yet we were used to turn men on. There was no representation of women in our sexuality."[47]

Like Candy, Royalle began her porn career in low-budget loops directed and written by men. Young, broke, and driven by the idea of sexual revolution's imprint on cinema through porn, she enjoyed performing in porn at first. But after a few years in front of the camera, disenchantment with the storylines of these films set in. In *Candice* (2019), a documentary about her life, Royalle describes her turning point on the set of the porno flick *Easy Alice* (1976), in which she played a woman forced into sex by two strangers at a laundromat.

The climax played off with comic detachment as her character decides, halfway through her rape, that she actually wants it. Royalle, at that moment, decided that she could not go on acting in mainstream porn films, which she felt "contributed to women's sense of shame about themselves and their sexuality." As she later said, "It was the whole societal attitude that was harming, and the movies weren't helping." But it was also the stigma she faced as an ex-porn actress that emboldened her to start making porn herself. As she put it, "I already had a scarlet letter on me. I had nothing left to lose."[48] As head of Femme Productions, Royalle made nineteen films.

For feminist porn-makers, porn was a medium for activism. While working within the constraints of the corporate porn industry, they sought to make films that challenged the values of male-centred porn. Drawing on sex-positive feminism, they sought to use cinema to uncouple women's sexual desire from marriage and morality, release women from sexual standards to which men were not held, and endorse women's bodily autonomy in all areas. According to Tristan Taormino, feminist porn's goal was "to expand the ideas about desire, beauty, gratification, and power through unconventional representations, aesthetics, and film-making styles."[49] Like everything else "feminist," defining what feminist porn means then or today is challenging, and feminist pornographers themselves vocally resist the rigid demarcation of the genre's boundaries. But one thing remains true: feminist porn was invented to resist the fake, damaging, and violent imagery and messages propped up by mainstream porn and to call out the "education" it was providing to both men and women, such as that rape feels good and women have orgasms from fellating men.

Anger spurred feminist porn, but creators transfigured it into art, and *The Deuce* draws on this history as it narrates Candy's innovations in feminist porn, illuminating concretely how feminist porn *is* different. The show fascinatingly focuses on this difference in three areas: content, form, and production.

- **Content**: Films like *Deep Throat* and other porn hits painted women as first responders to men's lust. Candy's films, conversely, celebrate women who understand their desires, act on them without guilt, and get off on equality, not submission (and if submission *is* what gets them off, it's at their request). Steering away from the narrative centrepiece – male ejaculation – Candy's films activate what Betony Vernon describes as feminist porn's imperative: to "degenitalize."[50] She explores the psychological dimensions of arousal through dialogue, anticipation, active consent, and foreplay and, most uniquely, shows women assertively teaching men about what they enjoy – and men listening. Candy also subverts porn's racist tropes by casting people of colour in diverse roles. At the same time, she challenges mainstream porn's messages about which bodies deserve to experience sexual pleasure by hiring actresses with a range of body shapes and sizes, fulfilling feminist porn's mission to "expand the ideas about desire, beauty, [and] gratification ... through unconventional representations."[51] The stars of Candy's films celebrate and normalize, rather than fetishize, difference.

- **Form**: Feminist porn creates "alternative images and develops its own aesthetic and iconography to expand established sexual norms and discourses."[52] Candy activates a feminist aesthetic by directing the camera to follow the action from the female character's perspective so that the man (or other woman) becomes the desired object and she the desiring *subject*. She uses mis-en-scène (long shots from a point-of-view character) to emphasize the woman's *subjective* sexual experience encompassing a range of feeling states. She intercuts sex with still images that connote speed, power, and beauty – a bounding cheetah, an orange flower exploding into bloom, a starburst of fireworks, a hand squeezing the juice from an orange – to suggest orgasm. Not shying away from capturing disappointment in sex, she intercuts an image of a spinning ceiling fan into a scene of a woman with a selfish lover to signal the woman's frustration and boredom. These innovations privilege subjectivity, a strategy that *The Deuce*'s own camera adopted in the porn set scenes where we often see the clothed crew as Candy would, not the naked performers. As producer George Pelecanos notes, "We were not trying to turn anybody on in the audience ... that's not what this is."[53] These originalities challenge porn's visual preoccupation with the money shot and focus on women's *experiences*.
- **Production**: Candy also overhauls how porn is produced. Whereas on male-run sets (like her first Viking loop shoot), Candy was referred to as "fresh meat," was never shown her contracts, or scripts, and had almost no communication with directors, on Candy's own sets she prioritizes her workers' comfort and makes communication constant and consent explicit. Her productions embody feminist porn's commitment to labour conditions that are "safe, professional, political, empowering, and fun."[54] Not only does this approach align with Candy's values and ethics, but it is also good business: the more comfortable her performers feel, the more at ease they will appear on screen, and the more successful (and lifelike) the scene will be. Before shooting, Candy talks with performers to make sure they are comfortable, asks them questions about their preferences, and gives them the authority to write their own desires into the scene. Notably, *The Deuce* embodied feminist film-making principles in its own production. Its cameras seldom linger on the nude body, and action is often from the women performers' points of view to show what they see: the camera, and Candy behind it, offering support. The series also hired "intimacy coaches" to "protect the emotions and dignity of everybody who's involved."[55] In these ways, Candy and *The Deuce*'s own production innovate feminist porn as a subversive cinema synonymous with women feeling respected.

For Candy, feminist porn is an activist tool for teaching women how to imagine, seize, and enjoy the pleasure that patriarchal society has long claimed they don't need or want. Earning a living as a feminist porn-maker becomes the ultimate renunciation of a former life in which she was forced to internalize her desires as shameful.

The Feminist Pornographer as Auteur

The Deuce is a rare portrait of a sex worker who becomes an auteur. *Auteur*, the French word for "author," refers to movie directors whose works are considered artistically important and who innovated and disrupted the field. Auteur theory made three main arguments: first, it proclaimed that all stories – not just classic literary works – deserved consideration as art, and, second, it was the *treatment* of story, rather than the story itself, that determined its quality. As Richard Brody notes, "the way the story was told ... became the deciding factor of a film's importance."[56] This definition made it suddenly possible to consider genre films as art. Third, auteur theory held that film innovation occurred when the rules invented by the old masters were disrupted, typically by outsiders who brought to their work a uniquely personal vision. Peter Wollen writes that auteur theory was "the conviction that the masterpieces were made not by a small upper crust of directors ... but a whole range of authors whose work had been previously dismissed."[57] Candy is an auteur: as a former sex worker, she is the epitome of society's dismissed woman, and she disrupts the rules of the "old masters" (male pornographers) and of "how the story is told" (from a male perspective) to make porn from a woman's point of view. In these regards, *The Deuce* makes Candy into an auteur. Furthermore, her masterpiece isn't based on a literary classic, but a children's story she transforms into an ode to sex-positive feminism.

The Deuce makes Candy's 1975 feature film, *Red Hot*, a retelling of "Little Red Riding Hood," the apogee of her career as a feminist porn auteur. Just as she gave herself a confectionary street name to charm her customers, Candy uses the non-threatening form of the fairy tale to disarm viewers into engaging with a story that has long threatened patriarchy: women getting paid for sex, without being punished. While Candy originally hires a male writer to pen the script, the story he writes ultimately replicates the power relations that feminist porn sought to challenge. "All Little Red Riding Hood does is get chased and suck some dick," Candy complains. So, she writes the script herself to exploit porn's potential to draw out what Linda Williams, as mentioned earlier, calls

Figure 7.4. Candy's 1975 film *Red Hot*, the pinnacle of her feminist porn career, reimagines "Little Red Riding Hood," the traditional fairy tale of vanquished girls and heroic men, into a sex-positive ode to female solidarity, sexual pleasure, and erotic dissidence in *The Deuce*.

the "oppositions and contradictions that exist within a culture" – to intensify them and to seek ideal forms of resolution.

The fairy tale "Little Red Riding Hood," in brief, tells the story of a young woman who leaves the safety of her mother's home to visit her grandmother, a journey that requires her to cross a dark wood alone. On the way, she disregards her mother's advice to stay on the path and to ignore strangers and ends up being stalked by a wolf that almost kills her and her grandmother. She is saved at the last minute by a passing woodsman who slays the wolf with his axe. The moral of the story is twofold: (1) good girls stay on the path and follow instructions or risk death, having asked for it; and (2) men are rescuers of women.

Candy's revisionist fairy tale flips the script on every patriarchal element of the original tale. She moves the story from the woods into the neon Deuce and makes Little Red not a lost naïf but an inexperienced sex worker, who, fittingly, is played by Lori, a younger street sex worker also from 42nd Street, who, like Candy enters the porn industry. Little Red spends the first half of the film working for men who disregard her safety, dismiss her right to pleasure, and exploit her labour (much like Lori and other women were exploited by controlling men in the Deuce). Halfway through the film, however, Little Red meets an older woman, played by Candy, who embodies sex positivity and teaches the younger woman that she has the right to control her labour, keep the money she earns, and seek sexual pleasure. When the two women encounter the "wolf," rather than become his victims, as in the fairy tale, they turn him into their lover, dominating him and becoming his captors. Where the original fairy tale ends with Little Red Riding Hood returning to her mother's house, contrite at having broken the rules, Candy's film ends with Lori's climactic smile showing that *she now has the fangs*, having assumed her agency as a sensual woman, a lady wolf.

Candy's feminist porn film embodies sex-positive feminism by celebrating female pleasure, sexual agency, and solidarity between women. It rejects the essentialist idea perpetuated by radical feminism that only "male wolves" have sexual appetites.[58] In Candy's movie, women refuse to mute their desire or curtail their freedom in exchange for protection, the traditional bargain women struck with men to secure their safety. Instead, choice and expression, treasured sex-positive feminist values, become the movie's final message over compliance and inhibition. The film also challenges porn's white supremacy by casting Larry, a Black performer, as the wolf, but not before rewriting his role from a predator into a dynamic, anti-racist character, a lover who prizes pleasure and equality. While Dworkin wrote that male sexuality is "the stuff off murder, not love,"[59] Candy's male lead practises the ethics of feminist porn, sharing power and wanting to pleasure his partners.

The film also challenges the trope that sex workers are naive victims or fallen women as it transforms Little Red's crimson cloak – scarlet traditionally the colour of sin – into a flag of sexual agency, a precursor to the red umbrellas that symbolize the sex workers' rights movement. Ultimately, *The Deuce* makes the film a metaphor for Candy's own journey from the street to the editing suite. Having grown up in a conservative home where women's sexual self-expression was forbidden, Candy was called a "slut" for "breaking the rules" and was turned out of the family home when she became pregnant at seventeen. Like the character Little Red, she ventured into the "woods" – the streets of the Deuce – and despite challenges (criminalization, violence, stigmatization), built an independent life for herself. Whereas in the original fairy tale, the hero is the hunter who triumphantly brandishes the trophy (the wolf's dismembered head), in *The Deuce*, Candy is the hunter, her weapon the movie camera, and the trophy the powerful feature film she makes.

Auteur theory was revolutionary because it did not privilege one genre over another or dictate what kinds of stories deserved serious treatment. *Red Hot* becomes a critical hit within the narrative of *The Deuce*, with a review in *Variety* calling it "blunt and knowing" and "an instant art house tour de force." The review signals growing appreciation of feminist porn and Candy's auteurism, paralleling Royalle's career as a feminist creator. Candy is featured in magazines, invited to fetes, and booked on prime-time talk shows as "the feminist auteur who makes porn."[60] With this celebratory tone, *The Deuce* portrays how Candy's movies challenge mainstream porn's content, form, and production. By showing Candy disrupting the old rules of porn – the male point of view, the money shot, the unethical sets – and telling stories infused with her personal, aesthetic and political vision, *The Deuce* offers a rare portrayal of a sex worker who makes it as a successful artist.

Hidden Women behind the Money Shot: Exploitation, Racism, and Activism

The Deuce's two dozen or so sex worker characters are diverse in age, background, motivation, and outcome, but three in particular exemplify the tension between agency and structure that sex workers grapple with: Lori, a porn star with a meteoric rise and fall; Darlene, a Black performer from North Carolina who eventually leaves the industry; and Dorothy, an activist whose fate tragically echoes the very conditions she fought to end.

While Candy succeeds behind the camera, her shadow character, Lori Madison, becomes a star in front of it in early 1980s Los Angeles, an era when adult actresses gained fan bases and recognition beyond being "nameless bodies."[61] Lori's kittenish beauty and glass-shattering feigned orgasms attract producers who help skyrocket her to fame as porn's freshest face on VHS. Her early success highlights the opportunities in porn to earn money, adulation, and status typically unknown to most twenty-two-year-olds. For a time, Lori takes pride in her work and revels in the financial and personal freedom it gives her, believing that she has finally left her abusive barnacle of a pimp in New York for good. However, as the industry's competitive pressure mounts, the demands it places on women's bodies – from aesthetic labour, such as getting breast implants, tanning, and waxing away body hair, to physically and emotionally uncomfortable work – takes a toll. She wants to leave porn, but having spent her adult life in it, she views herself as a commodity, loses touch with her innermost needs, and falls into relationships with abusive men. While she can technically walk away from the porn industry, her attempts to do so are unsuccessful, and her "choices" and the conditions of her work are shaped by industry intermediaries and producers who call the shots – and for increasingly extreme sex acts.

The series doesn't soft-pedal the brutal conditions passed off as "business as usual" on some porn sets. In one instance, Lori's male co-star is directed to shove an ear of corn into her anus and gag her with a handkerchief. When Lori objects and calls her agent in tears, she is told to "grin and bear it" because "other girls are lining up for this job." The more Lori tries to establish boundaries, the more she is labelled as "difficult," but eventually, the jobs dry up anyway, and in her late twenties Lori finds that her erotic capital is spent in an industry that worships, above all else, fresh faces, flexible bodies, and compliance. In this way, *The Deuce* portrays unethical, even abusive porn productions, and shows a wide world of porn sets outside of Candy's ethical one. Furthermore, while Lori gets paid for lucrative shoots, in the end, she possesses no ownership over the copyrighted content she appears in and earns no royalties. Having begun her career as a teenage sex worker controlled by a pimp, Lori has been taught to measure her self-worth according to the lust she can create, and she matures into a woman who equates her desirability with having value as a person and an identity. As an ageing Lori faces stiff competition from younger porn wannabees from all walks of life – "college girls … it's like they sat down with their guidance counsellors and made a plan," as she says – she struggles to imagine life after porn, a second act.

What conditions allow a porn performer to quit when she wants to? It is rare in popular culture to see a sex worker transitioning into a new career, a strange elision considering that sex work has a high attrition rate owing to burnout, aging, health concerns, or simply a desire for new pursuits. The interesting and smart documentary *After Porn Ends* (2012) – and its two sequels, in 2017 and 2018 – offer a dynamic, non-judgemental look into the lives of adult film stars after they leave the industry.[62] But in fictional popular culture it's rare to see a sex worker transitioning into a new career, as Lori does when she attempts to launch herself as a mainstream film actress. Connecting the misogyny of porn to that of the broader movie industry, *The Deuce* masterfully shows how the stereotypical roles Lori played in porn are also endemic to Hollywood through the typecasting of young women as sex objects or victims. At an audition for what she thinks is a small but serious role in a drama, she learns that she is actually reading for a non-speaking part in a film about a serial killer whose murderous spree is triggered by learning that his mother was a sex worker. Lori's role, blending virgin and whore, is an innocent department store clerk who the killer sees as a proxy for his mother and strangles. The film's breezy association of sex worker mothers with degeneracy reminds us of the heavy whore stigma Lori faces as she transitions out of porn. Demoralized, and drug-addicted, Lori takes dispiriting jobs adjacent to the sex industry, including an "appearance" gig at a seedy erotic dance club where an obsessed fan pounds on her motel room door, demanding she let him in because he's seen her movies and "knows her," underscoring how Lori's screen image and personal life have become indistinguishable. As the angry man pounds on the door, Lori shrinks into a corner, the image crystallizing her total marginalization.

One of the series' most moving scenes takes place in Candy's apartment around this time and lays bare the dichotomy between the two women's lives rooted in whore stigma. Still reeling from the scary motel encounter, Lori tells Candy that she feels exiled from both the adult industry, which considers her washed-up, and from broader whorephobic society, which regards her as a tainted woman. Candy leads a full life and embraces her many facets – mother, daughter, performer, and auteur – and encourages Lori to see herself multidimensionally too: "You gotta save something for yourself. You can't be just her," she tells Lori, referring to the fantasy of Lori Madison. "We live two lives, that's how we do it," Candy says. Lori, however, has "saved nothing" for herself and fallen victim to what Diane Negra calls "confusion between empowerment and role restriction."[63] She makes this clear to Candy: "I don't have a kid, I don't have a lover. I drove past my old house in Minnesota and it was boarded up. This [a porn star] is all I am." In a desperate bid to transcend the porn persona that has now totalized her, Lori tells Candy her real name: "Sarah." Tragically, she is unable to recover "Sarah." After leaving Candy's apartment, she goes to 42nd Street, to a dive hotel where she first felt significant, and dies by self-inflicted gunshot wound to the head.

In an October 2019 *Rolling Stone* interview, one of *The Deuce*'s creators, David Simon, remarked that Lori's story was inspired by "an adult actress in the Eighties ... Shauna Grant, who killed herself with a gun."[64] Like Lori, Shauna Grant (1963–84) – born Colleen Marie Applegate – hailed from Minnesota. In 1983, she moved to Los Angeles to work in the burgeoning VHS porn scene. Her wholesome blonde looks made her a darling of the adult film world. In an interview in the first months of her career, she described enjoying her work in the industry, but later accounts suggest she never felt comfortable in front of the camera. She fought addictions. Sensitive to rejection, the industry's flashbulb attentiveness skyrocketed her self-confidence, until self-doubt about the exposure and the stigma that came with being in adult films crept in. She retired from films in 1984. For a time, she thought of returning home to Minnesota to enrol in college but decided she was too stigmatized to resume a normal life there; on one trip home, an old friend had asked her not to attend her wedding because of her work in porn. Like Lori, Grant felt caught between two worlds yet shut out of both. In 1984, several days before she was set to shoot a new film, she took her own life. She was twenty-one.

Grant's short life has inspired a number of films, including *Shauna: Every Man's Fantasy* (1985), *Shattered Innocence* (1988), and the PBS *Frontline* documentary episode "Death of a Porn Queen" (1987). Alas, except for *Frontline*, they are evangelical and take a morally superior tone to the woman from whom they profit. They portray a scummy porn industry and a lost young woman, doll-like in her passivity, and follow the predictable arc of "naive woman becomes a sex worker and dies for it," stripping away all semblance of Grant's individuality, unique pain and struggle, and agency to furnish a cautionary tale.[65] *The Deuce*, fortunately, does not. Much more than a cautionary tale, it makes Lori into an endlessly layered character whose story arc exemplifies the lures and perils of a career in porn at that time and how factors such as addiction, isolation, and stigmatization contributed to her despair and end. While Lori's story, like Grant's, is haunting and tragic, *The Deuce* gives Lori what most popular culture has not given sex workers characters, ever: a rich life story.

The storyline of Darlene spotlights a taboo topic: the opportunities Black women found during the Golden Age of Porn. The history of Black women's performance in pornography during the 1970s has largely gone unexplored due to the patriarchal racist sexualization of Black women, a tactic for rationalizing rape, stigma, and abuse,[66] as well as a concern that exploring those images would reproduce their harms. According to Mireille Miller-Young, in the fascinating *A Taste for Brown Sugar* (2014), Black women in porn were constrained by structural forces, and the films they appeared in did draw on racist tropes. Nevertheless, she champions the importance of exploring how Black women negotiated their erotic labour and "thought about their own work as image-makers."[67] *The Deuce* takes up this challenge with Darlene, whose transformation reveals the Golden Age of Porn's patriarchal racism, but also the ways in which Black women expressed their agency.

Like Lori and Candy, Darlene starts her career on 42nd Street. A bibliophile who beelines to the library between tricks to check out paperback classics, Darlene dreams of going to college. Yet, as a Black woman who relocates to New York City from North Carolina in the late 1960s, structural racism bears down on her prospects, and she resorts to sex work with stoic determination. In sex work, predictably, she finds herself being paid to play out the white supremacy that has limited her life options. In one scene, a white client pays Darlene to perform as his rape victim, leaving her with a bruised and swollen jaw, for which he pays her "an extra $20." In another scene of exploitation, Darlene's client secretly films their encounter and sells the footage to a brown paper bag store where it's screened in loop machines. After learning of this theft, Darlene demands payment for her images. *The Deuce* turns these stolen images into a potent symbol for the disempowerment Black women experienced in the Golden Age of Porn. Sex work is Darlene's choice, but the constraints she is under are extreme, as are the consequences. As a Black woman, Darlene is more likely to be charged with prostitution and to become a target of violence. Furthermore, she has little negotiating power with her clients or pimps. When asked by a middle-class university student why she works at such a "demeaning job," Darlene replies, "Daddy doesn't pay for my college." Like Candy, Darlene enters the adult industry to escape street sex work and stays to build a career.

The Deuce possibly modelled Darlene on Desiree West, one of the few women of colour porn actresses to gain mainstream recognition in the Golden Age and an icon of Black women's erotic performance. She worked consistently through the 1970s, paving the way for other Black adult actresses of the era including Shauna Evans, Flower, Kelly Stewart, Nancy Edwards, and Trinket Fowler.[68] Black women starred in stag films starting in the 1920s, but it was only in the 1960s that they became more visible in 8 mm and 16 mm films loops, with interracial porn produced at a rate far exceeding that of the stag era. Loops were keen on "exposing and exploring sexual taboos ... [and the] crossing of racial borders through new intimacies."[69] This "crossing" denoted the fetishization of Black women by white audiences, but also Black women's sexual self-definition in the public sphere, within the confines of patriarchal capitalism. As Miller-Young writes, Black women performers during the Golden Age "still lacked the power to decisively shape the marketing of their sexuality."[70] Power was held by white male pornographers whose interest was getting quarters into the loop machines, which they did by recycling racist tropes.

The Deuce is a rare show that explicitly critiques the racism in the Golden Age of Porn – and all porn, by extension. It shows Darlene being typecast as hyper-sexual characters, or as near-silent sex objects with few or vapid lines. When she learns that she is paid half of what her white co-star is and asks the director why, she is told that she is "the wrong part of the Oreo." Ultimately, as a non-unionized worker, Darlene's only recourse is to accept racist roles and demeaning labour practices, or to decline the work, an individualistic response to a structural problem, which she can't afford to do. It is a catch-22. Darlene chooses to keep working in porn, yet she suffers from stage fright and worries about limiting her future career options, resorting to wearing wigs to disguise herself.

But *The Deuce* also portrays Darlene's agency. Specifically, as she expands her career, she develops the confidence to negotiate the terms of her labour, distances herself from her pimp, and starts setting boundaries with her clients. One john has seen her in films and wants to have sex while they watch one of the videos. Darlene is not pleased. "Lemme tell you how this is going to go. I am going to ride you on this bed with my back to the TV. And it's going to cost you double." Her career in porn sets in motion a chain of other bold acts: she secretly begins attending night school, earns her GED, and saves enough money to leave her pimp and, later, sex work altogether. Her exit is not that of a defeated victim but of a seasoned woman who knows what she wants.

Darlene's self-actualization after porn is hard won, with support coming from other sex workers, not paternalism or white women who try to "save her." And unlike Lori's arc, which put the virulence of whore stigma on display with tragic effect, Darlene's story is one of renewal, transformation, and growth as she integrates her past in sex work into her self-identity. After quitting the adult industry, she develops an intense relationship with a man in her literature class. This part of Darlene's narrative is unique in several ways. First, popular culture rarely portrays sex workers in romantic relationships except those of the *Pretty Woman* princess-rescuer type, and if Black sex workers do have relationships on screen, it's usually with white men for whom they play hyper-sexualized roles. Darlene's bond with an exchange student from Nigeria is intellectual, and they remain platonic for some time as Darlene struggles over whether to disclose her past in sex work. Finally, she does: "So now you know. It's a job, and I did it," she says. He answers by extending his hand: "Come to class." His response is not a rescue but an offering of respect and support. Eventually, Darlene will become a nurse and petition to have her criminal record – made up of prostitution charges, exclusively – expunged.

Darlene's story critiques the adult industry while dignifying her work and use of erotic capital. It does so against the taboo of exploring the stories of Black women in pornography and with recognition of the injurious history of sexualized racism. The risk of replicating stereotypes was at top of mind for Dominique Fishback, who plays Darlene: "I didn't want to play her as a stereotypical prostitute," she said in an HBO interview, "[but to] *be someone* ... and in the end, when she walks away, she got what she wanted."[71] Darlene embodies erotic self-determination within the constraints of capitalism and racist disenfranchisement, and her story of self-actualizing without capitulating to the dogmatism of radical feminism is one of the great transformations on the series – and a rare portrayal of a sex worker who gets a range of life experiences. And in the end, she gets paid for that stolen image.

Sex worker activist characters rarely appear on TV because they are sex workers who challenge the status quo rather than fold themselves into it, which is what makes *The Deuce*'s Dorothy Spina such an original character. Dorothy represents the activist movement for visibility and rights driven by minority groups beginning in the 1960s. From the civil rights movements to gay and lesbian liberation struggles to the second-wave of feminism, marginalized people confronted racist, homophobic, and patriarchal institutions powered by a new awareness that they "could make a difference in their own lives, on their own terms."[72] This activism was personal and, in the 1960s, included women whose sexual behaviour – real or imagined – was stigmatized and policed, literally, by whorephobic campaigns. This is how Margo St. James unwittingly came to lead the sex workers' rights movement.

The story is now apocryphal. In 1962, St. James was a part-time cocktail waitress in San Francisco who was thinking about going to law school. In her early twenties, she was bright and popular, and she liked having parties. Because she was a single woman, however, the many people who came and went from her house raised police suspicion about her work, so they began doing surveillance on her. One day a stranger rang her doorbell. When St. James answered, the stranger asked if she would accept his cash in exchange for sex. She refused, but he arrested her anyway for solicitation of prostitution. Later, the judge put weight on the fact that St. James understood the term used by the undercover cop – "turn a trick" – and deemed it a signification of her guilt.[73] The prostitution charge prevented St. James from finding employment, and the miscarriage of justice it denoted extinguished her aspirations for law school.[74] Meanwhile, she found no support from feminists, who rejected anyone linked to sex work unless they were ready to denounce it. This alienation galvanized St. James. In 1973, she founded COYOTE (Call Off Your Old Tired Ethics), the first union for sex workers. As Gail Pheterson has noted, prior to COYOTE, it was "rarely acknowledged that sex workers were capable of speaking for themselves."[75] The media blitz that followed COYOTE's founding not only exposed that myth but elevated St. James – who was exquisitely quotable – as the movement's public face. "Coyote will give whores a voice in what happens in public policies and laws that affect their profession," she promised.[76] COYOTE's goal was fourfold: to advocate for the decriminalization of prostitution; to empower sex workers to represent their own interests; to disrupt second-wave feminism's exploitation narrative and its social influence; and to broadcast the idea that "most women who do sex work choose to do so."[77]

When St. James later decided to become a sex worker, seeing as she had already been classified as a "prostitute" by the court, she identified as a politicized "whore," seeking to reclaim the slur as a badge of dissent. St. James framed sex work as a labour issue ("A blow job is better than no job," she once quipped[78]) and built a stage from which sex workers could speak. In the next decades, she became a trailblazer in sex workers' rights, organized huge fundraiser balls for COYOTE, published a sex worker magazine (*Coyote Howls*), built connections between American and global sex workers' rights organizations, lectured at Harvard, and co-founded the St. James Infirmary Clinic in San Francisco to provide peer-led health care to people in the sex industry. When she died in 2021, her obituary in the *New York Times* described her as an activist who "devoted to her life to decriminalizing prostitution."[79]

Sex worker activists like St. James challenge the status quo by combining lucid arguments for sexual autonomy with female anger, which together continue to be one of the last TV taboos. This is what makes Dorothy, aspects of whose activism is likely modelled in part on St. James, such an important character. Introduced during a rainstorm after being ordered to work by her pimp, Dorothy is one of the series' most immiserated sex worker characters. After breaking away from her pimp, she decides to channel her energy into activism. Margo St. James described COYOTE as an organization for "the invisible constituency."[80] Serving this constituency is Dorothy's goal as well when she joins a grass-roots organization for sex workers' rights. Operating out of a van that loops the area, she and her organization provide sex workers with health care, non-judgmental counselling, self-defence training, as well as hot coffee, contraceptives, and access to social workers and other supportive services. While Dorothy's feminist peers are busy picketing porn theatres and theorizing the symbolic prostitute, Dorothy supports real sex workers, her goal to "make relationships" by meeting women "where they are," whether through buying a sex worker a bus ticket home, offering strategies for practising safer sex, or providing advice on self-advocacy in the criminal justice system.

The impact of sex work's criminalization on sex workers is a theme at the heart of *The Deuce,* and over three seasons the show argues that prostitution laws push sex workers to the margins and deny them civil rights. During the decade Dorothy works in outreach, she is deeply troubled by the number of sex workers who die violent, lonely deaths. When a local sex worker perishes in a massage parlour fire and her body at the morgue is never claimed, Dorothy tracks her family down and delivers the tragic news. They are indifferent, having disowned her when she became a sex worker, and the image of Dorothy and her two activist colleagues in a cemetery as the woman's coffin is lowered into the ground speaks volumes about the stigmatization sex workers face from family. Dorothy also witnesses how violent crimes against sex workers are unlikely to be prosecuted. A predator who rapes sex workers is referred to by police by his day job, "an upstanding biology teacher." A police officer who beats his sex worker girlfriend to death later dies by suicide, and his colleagues cover up the murder so his widow can collect his pension. Six sex workers are murdered over the course of the show's three seasons, and none of these homicides are prosecuted, as police view these women as guilty victims. Dorothy's lived experience gives her insight into the constrained options in which sex workers sometimes choose this work, but chooses to meet sex workers where they are, and to reject radical feminist orthodoxy's sole strategy of rescue. "If they keep targeting [sex workers], they make women feel even more stigmatized," Dorothy says, understanding that "most women who do sex work choose to do so."[81]

Dorothy embodies the activist movement's focus on self-representation and peer support and gives her practical insight into why women choose to sell sex.

"Church bus ain't gonna help me make my day to day," says one sex worker, referring to the rescue mission of radical feminists who demand that sex workers quit their jobs without offering solutions to their daily struggle of living. Tragically, Dorothy is murdered, and that crime remains unsolved, becoming a final catastrophic indictment of the criminalization and marginalization she was fighting to end.

With Lori, Darlene, and Dorothy, *The Deuce* challenges the idea that sex work can be summed up with labels like "exploited" or "empowered." Lori, who lacks a stable sense of self and a plan for life after porn, contrasts with Candy, who is independent and leads a rich life. Darlene attends college, leaving the racism of mainstream porn behind. Dorothy becomes a victim of the whorephobia she fought tirelessly against.

The Money Makes the Money Shot: Can a Feminist Pornographer Succeed?

The Deuce's last season is set during the accelerating neo-liberal capitalism of the 1980s. During this time, Candy's feminist porn-making increasingly comes to rely on financing from institutions that replicate the systems of oppression she critiques. When the bank rejects her loan application, a producer offers her cash for sex. The irony of Candy financing her feminist film on her knees is just one of the many ways *The Deuce* troubles the notion of "empowerment" against porn's fundamentally capitalistic (and patriarchal) structure, reminding viewers that abuses of power occur at all levels and are perpetrated by whomever has the money to – literally and figuratively – call the shots.

Like dominoes, Candy's ideals for feminist porn-making start toppling as the industry grows. Porn companies begin to co-opt the rhetoric of feminism while privately eroding it. Candy's financiers agree that "a fuck film made by a broad ... is good for the feminism part," yet they ask her to leave the room so "the men [can] talk about business." Corporate porn entities also distort feminist porn's ideals with male fantasy–driven marketing. *Red Hot*'s poster erases the film's feminist storyline by blowing up Lori's breasts and deleting the Black performer Larry because, as one producer says, "the audience [i.e., white men] will find him too provocative." Outside the industry, Candy likewise finds her voice being dismissed. When she appears on a late-night talk show, the host asks her what it's like to watch people have sex for a living, and as she begins to describe the professionalism of her feminist porn set, he interrupts her and accuses her of speaking like she's made "an Oscar-winning film." With the mocking dismissal she is reduced from a feminist porn auteur to a "broad who makes fuck films."

The debut film-maker's reward for critical success is financial security and more resources to make a sophomore film. But after *Red Hot*, Candy learns that the producers have exclusive ownership rights and she owns nothing of her film, will collect no royalties, and has no claims to her own art. Furthermore, a new form is booming, the VHS cassette, and just as the loop machines dictated the form and content a decade earlier, VHS demands less story-driven segments, and stiff competition pushes makers to depict extreme sex acts. The hottest blockbuster, *New Wave Hookers*, a real film released in 1985, is about naive women whose "new wave music" triggers them into wanting sex – with anyone. As the audience roars with appreciation for the film's empowered nymphomaniac heroine, Candy walks out. Later, she describes her ambition of making feminist porn as increasingly impossible – "like pushing string."

VHS porn began shuttering porn cinemas in the mid-1980s, making the 35 mm porn feature of the Golden Age of Porn all but obsolete. In response, Harvey confronts her about changing their content. "What part of profit do you not understand?" he asks, dejectedly. Candy responds: "You want to go backwards? If I had to make that trash, I would get the fuck out of porn." Harvey tells Candy that she needs to compromise to make a product that sells:

> This new stuff is what men want. And the people who are watching are mostly men. Degenerate, reptilian, that makes my dick jump kind of men. You are a good film-maker. But the feminist porn shit is a niche product that I can no longer invest in. It is negatively impacting our balance sheet.

The turning point in Candy's career occurs when market demands clash with the goals of feminist porn-making. To stay in the industry, she will need to sacrifice her vision and make films that stage backlashes against feminism by portraying misogyny as empowerment.[82] Thus, the revolution she tried to spark is ultimately unrealized against a backdrop of corporate power that needed a woman director to legitimize its enterprise, fend off radical feminists, and prove its "authenticity" and links to women's liberation. Candida Royalle's story is different from Candy's as she made films a few years later and was able to exploit the VHS format. Candy, a pioneer, made feminist porn at a time when few women spoke of porn, much less got behind the camera.

Walking into the Feminist Sex Wars: A Price Tag Hanging Off

Candy's disenchantment catalyzes her return to the Deuce and a period of artistic confusion where she turns to other sex workers for support. In a diner over coffee and scrambled eggs, she asks questions and listens to sex workers tell stories that would never make it into the *New Wave Hookers* porn script: tales about leaving home, turning tricks, losing family, finding love, and chasing elusive security, and she identifies with all of them.[83] Candy's collecting of personal narratives is important work, part of how sex workers began using testimony in the 1980s to challenge the hegemony of radical feminism and its claim that sex workers were not authorities on their lives or work. One sex worker asks Candy: "Are you, like, making a film about our lives?" Candy knows she is, but what story does she want to tell? Surprisingly, she finds her answer at a Women Against Pornography meeting at the height of the sex wars over the meaning and effects of pornography.

Popular culture usually stays clear of the sex wars – for fear of too many angry feminists on screen at once! – but *The Deuce* walks straight into them, bringing the two factions together in a climactic scene that crib notes from feminist theory with loyalties to Candy's labour perspective.[84] Candy considers WAP activists "sad housewives and pissed off lesbians" who are in a privileged position to judge her,[85] but she goes to the meeting at the behest of a friend who thinks that Candy's story will move the deadlocked conversation: "They are feminists and so are you." *The Deuce* personifies the sex wars through a meeting in a windowless basement that begins with Candy screening clips of her feminist films and talking about her artistic process. Chilly is too balmy a word to describe the reception as a member of WAP accuses her of being anti-feminist. Candy rejects this allegation:

> Well I've done what I've done. I make sense to me. Maybe not to you. And this (*gesturing to the porn on the TV*) makes sense to me. Maybe not to you. Okay. But if we're going to stand together on this as women, I mean, look, you're not going to want to tell me who to fuck, right?

But WAP does not accept Candy's appeal to freedom of speech or alternative sexual truth and calls her privileged. They criticize her for being complicit in a "multimillion-dollar industry that feeds off and fuels American sexual oppression ... of women." While most sex workers will not become feminist auteurs, their criticism rests upon the notion that Candy has not struggled and should, somehow, represent all sex workers. "Do you think I was born with a camera in my hand? You know where I've been? You know how hard it was for me to get here?" she asks. We do, so we feel indignant when a WAP member silences Candy, dismissing her as the Cinderella of porn:

> For every prostitute that thinks that she can manage her own commodification, there are two dozen who can't. Okay? They are brutalized by the process. For every porn actress who thinks she can stand in the light, there are two dozen who are used up and tossed aside. You are the strong one. That's very good for you. Candy

or Arlene or whatever your name is. But how many women do you know whose outcome is as good as yours? Where are they now?

The Deuce critiques radical feminism's polemical analysis of sex work, particularly its imposition of a narrative on Candy and its declaration that sex workers have no agency. It probes how WAP's insistence on sex worker victimization produces two ways for them to relate to sex workers: as saviours or moral superiors. That said, *The Deuce* doesn't caricaturize WAP. It recognizes the importance of WAP's structural analysis – particularly of sex work's relationship to and within patriarchal capitalism. "Maybe I needed to hear some of that shit," Candy says after the meeting.

The Deuce takes seriously the inequalities that bear upon Candy's – and other sex workers' – labour and asks us to consider the stories of the "used up and tossed aside," like those of Lori and Dorothy, and the limits of the rhetoric of agency Candy has espoused. Was she as empowered as she thought? Candy's ambivalence is palpable as she fixatedly rewatches a sequence of *Red Hot*, zooming in on Lori's face again and again as if searching for the answer to the question of what their careers in feminist porn meant and who actually had the power. We recall how, during the *Red Hot* shoot, Candy helped Lori find her motivation in one scene by asking her to remember herself as that gutsy seventeen-year-old woman arriving at Port Authority bus station. "You ever think about that day you stepped off that bus from Hicksville? Wanted so badly to take a bite out of the Big Apple? And how it felt? Ready to conquer?" Lori answers, "I never felt that way," exposing her tough-girl act as a front for so much insecurity. As Candy's screen fills with the image of she and Lori in low-cut tops tying up the wolf, we reflect on how marginally burdensome this image was for the audience, however subversive it looked. With Candy, we wonder if Lori's purportedly empowering transfiguration was merely exchanging one type of sex object for another.[86]

Candy's critical re-evaluation of her opus is not a disavowal of her career but a crucial complication to her vision for feminist porn. Candy recognizes that the sex industry reflects – and sometimes magnifies – gender inequality, though it is not a uniquely oppressive force.[87] Her questioning leads to a nuanced perspective that considers women's agency *and* the structures that bear on it. She decides that for her next film she will collect such stories from the sex workers she knew on 42nd Street and "make them into one character … a composite" that shows their agency and determination, but also the despair and disempowerment. But who will this composite be?

Her answer comes one night in a diner as she watches a waitress being harassed by a table of construction workers. The men begin by complimenting her, but when rebuffed, become aggressive. The camera zooms in on Candy's face, her eyes wet with tears as she identifies with the waitress. While the waitress wears an apron, *The Deuce* likens her experience to Candy's as a street sex worker on 42nd Street where she frequently suffered harassment from police and pimps who threatened her with "Drano cocktails." Like the waitress, she was an emotional labourer and actress, a master of pretending happiness when feeling angry or scared, and like the waitress, was underpaid, precarious, disrespected, alone, underestimated, and fundamentally without rights as a worker. After the men leave, Candy approaches the waitress and asks her how she puts up with it. The woman's answer is perfect: "I work for tips. What world do you live in?" While *The Deuce* began as a show about the porn industry, it closes as one about all women's work under patriarchal capitalism. For this reason, Candy chooses to make her film's protagonist a waitress, the worker most symbolic of women's reproductive labour.

Candy's film, *A Pawn in Her Game*, is about how every woman, especially the working-class woman, has a "price tag hanging off her," as Candy says. Based on the stories she collected from other sex workers and her own experiences, the film tells the story of a waitress and the challenges she faces in her everyday life, from harassment to struggling to pay rent. *The Deuce* suggests that the labour of sex workers shares much with all women under patriarchal capitalism. As Brooke Meredith Beloso notes, "We stand to realize that the exploitation endemic to some sex workers is not just something that happens to prostitutes; rather, it is part and parcel of everything that happens under the sign of capitalism."[88] As Candy's explains it,

> It's not *my* truth. It's the *whole fucking world*. This is how we learn to live. What we trade, what we give away, what the fucking price of everything is. Okay, I used to fuck guys for thirty dollars. I was selling myself short. But every woman in this world is selling shit, even if she doesn't want to be. She's still got a price tag on her somewhere. Every woman, every one of us. No, this movie is just going to be about a woman in this world. She can be a waitress, a secretary. It doesn't fucking matter.

With her film, Candy takes her experience of marginality as a sex worker and globalizes it, achieving her potential as an auteur. Her obituary, some thirty years later, is a vindication of her struggles and an ode to her multidimensionality:

Feminist Director/Porn Star Dead at 73 – Candy Renee made 89 adult films and one celebrated cinematic classic, *A Pawn in Her Game*, regarded as an art house classic. It is now being re-issued by the Criterion Collection. At the time, the film did not receive wide release or public notice.

While popular culture has long stereotyped the porn industry as a seedy underworld, *The Deuce* flips on the lights to tell another story that, while not denying the existence of seediness, tells a story that is much more original: the porn industry as a microcosm of capitalism, where the slick porn producer or the entitled client who demands he and Candy "go again … because you didn't do any work" is like the restaurant owner who hustles his workers to work harder for less, where the street pimp uses the same tactics of buy low, sell high as the Wall Street banker. While some characters on *The Deuce* succeed, many do not, and it is this ambivalent picture that makes the series rich and humane. Candy becomes a feminist film-maker; Lori dies by suicide; Darlene leaves the industry; Dorothy is murdered; and Shawna, another porn star, marries a wealthy businessman and lives out her days in "a twelve-bedroom mansion in Tuxedo Park … just another woman in a gilded cage." What began as a show about the women of the Golden Age of Porn closes as one about the inequality of women's work under patriarchal capitalism.

New Product, Same Producer? From Porno Palaces to Forever 21

The Deuce winds down in 1984 as Times Square's rehabilitation project is well underway and the porn theatres are being torn down. The final elegiac scene, a brief five-minute coda, is set in 2019, and it unveils a dramatically changed 42nd Street, with its Disney entertainers and fast fashion outlets. While the old neighbourhood was transactional in the extreme, it was a community. The present-day Times Square is not, *The Deuce* suggests, as the camera pans the crowds glued to iPhones in the labyrinth of LED advertising signage. This final scene asks the audience to reflect on exploitation and visibility. In 1972, exploitation was visible in the figuration of the precarious sex workers on 42nd Street, the area a man's world in every respect. Today, women work still at that same corner in similarly precarious jobs: the shirt folders at Forever 21, the door greeters at the Disney Store, the hostesses at Ruby Tuesday – the twenty-first-century's new hustlers. As Candy says, "Every woman in this world is selling shit, even if she doesn't want to be." Co-creator David Simon echoed this idea: "The show is set in the most mercantile environment. It's all transactional."[89] And so, these parting images reinforce Candy's – and the show's – labour perspective and whisper "plus ça change" as they layer the selling of sex in 1972 with the selling of T-shirts in the 2020s. With this ambivalent send-up, *The Deuce* goes against popular culture's neo-liberal grain by refusing to make its female characters into Horatio Alger stories of extraordinary individuals who win through grit and bootstrapping. It does not trumpet the porn industry as the exculpatory evidence of the attainability of the American Dream. Rather, it exposes how pornography – like all commodities – is largely controlled by corporations whose interest is not worker safety or art but maximizing profit. It goes against popular culture's neo-liberal grain of happily ever after – the protagonist experiencing growth and catharsis and healing. As such, *The Deuce* exposes the wires under the board and how they all connect to the persistence of capitalism.

The Deuce's labour perspective, and its unusual decision to end with a time jump to the present, also impels us to reflect on how Candy and her peers would fare today in our so-called pornified twenty-first century. When Candy rose, she worked alone in a male-dominated industry, and feminist porn was a barely established genre. Today, Candy would be part of a community of feminist porn creators that include Stoya, Casey Calvert, Erika Lust, Madison Young, and Jacky St. James and enjoy collaboration and an established audience. Film-making is also much more accessible today than it was in Candy's 16 mm days when making a movie was both expensive and technically demanding. Today, Candy might've funded her feminist porn-making through crowdsourcing or cut costs by shooting on her iPhone. She would also have more options after leaving porn, and would have perhaps transitioned into making smart erotic feminist cinema, like French directors Virginie Despentes and Coralie Trinh Thi, who mixed porn and drama in their electrifying *Baise-moi* (2000), or become a public figure like Stormy Daniels, who sparked a political scandal and showed the world that porn performers are multidimensional women. Yet, she would also face fierce competition by way of the hegemony of tube sites and the binary between mainstream and feminist porn that continues to persist.[90] As feminist porn-maker Tristan Taormino writes,

> I basically had two different ways to go. I could try the feminist way, which is that you beg, borrow, and steal, and you do it on a shoestring, you ask all your friends to do stuff for free, you try to distribute it yourself. Or, I could go directly to the man and sell out, and go to a mainstream adult company, where I would have to compromise some of my, like, artistic integrity.[91]

Had Lori Madison worked today, she would no doubt join the pantheon of adult film actresses who create their own content, represent themselves on social media, and transition into mainstream movies, as Lori hoped she would. The globally famous porn star Sasha Grey, the lead in Steven Soderbergh's *The Girlfriend Experience*, is a proud sexual entrepreneur. (As she told *Rolling Stone*, "I am determined and ready to be a commodity that fulfills everyone's fantasies."[92]) While Lori's opportunities for reinvention shrunk as she was stigmatized as an "ex-porn performer," Grey has a well-established identity beyond porn: she's written a novel, advocates for children's literacy programs, and cites Godard and Nietzsche as influences.[93] In any event, Lori would've benefited from far more support during and after her career, and she could have drawn strength from initiatives like the Pineapple Project (providing mental health support for porn performers) and the STD Clinic (run by former porn star Sharon Mitchell). With the industry more solidified, she might've had an excellent manager protecting her interests, not to mention peers. Had Darlene worked in porn today, she would have joined an engaged group of Black porn performers and found roles in productions that refused to fetishize her. (Yet, she would still face challenges in an industry where racism in storylines and unequal pay remains widespread.) Dorothy Spina might've led a thriving community of activists across North America and the world similar to the Red Umbrella Project or the Sex Workers Alliance of Toronto (SWAT).

With its labour focus and regard for *both* the opportunity *and* the exploitation in the porn industry, *The Deuce* laid the groundwork for *Pleasure* (2021), Ninja Thyberg's harrowing film that situates us in Los Angeles' contemporary porn industry. With documentary detail it tells the story of "Bella Cherry," a nineteen-year-old woman who moves from Sweden to try her luck at a career as a porn performer. While Bella feels empowered to monetize her sexuality, she quickly learns that pushing her limits and catering to the men who control the industry is her only way to get ahead. The utterly unsentimental film reveals porn's twenty-first-century character, at once a streamlined business where producers use words like "consent" earnestly while trading in images and practices of misogyny. But the film never comes down on either side of the deadlocked porn debate, nor does it trowel at arguments about porn being "good" or "bad" for women. Instead, it follows Bella through her first few months in Los Angeles, in vérité, as she meets other porn workers and tries to get a foothold in the super competitive industry. The film's sex workers are all individuals, not types, whom Thyberg portrays without stigmatizing them.

Like *The Deuce*, *Pleasure* is all about juxtaposition. On some sets, porn is a well-oiled machine. At Bella's first shoot the director walks her through the paperwork, making clear that she's in control and may withdraw her consent at any time. It's the porn industry 2.0, where women are empowered, get their choice of lubes and enema kits, and have frequent checks-ins to make sure they're comfortable. On other sets, however, control masks violence. One harrowing scene on a low-budget shoot with just Bella and three men, two actors and a director with a handheld camera, is a brutal, unending spiral of hitting, spitting, choking, and abuse that is so terrifying it's hard to watch. As one man throttles her, the other grabs her neck and pulls her up by her eyelids and calls her a whore. From here, the scene is shot entirely from Bella's point of view, blurry bodies intercut with a black screen soundtracked to panting, gasping, hitting, and slapping that intensifies as the camera frames the men's faces leering down at her, a terrifying image of the violence that porn can exalt. Ironically, after Bella bellows "*Stop!*" her co-stars do and kneel to stroke her back: "It's okay, it's okay," they coo. One tells her, without any irony, "You're a very strong woman." The scene cracks open and awakens Bella to porn's dichotomy: that she can make it big in this business precisely by playing crushed women.

If *Pleasure* and *The Deuce* teach us one thing, it's that porn is multifaceted: it can be challenging, fun, edgy, playful, feminist, and cutting-edge, or it can be violent, artless, derogatory, racist, misogynistic, and gross. And where one person may think a film is the former, another will deem it (and defend it as) the latter, the images on screen telling us very little about the actual conditions of their making. Porn can be made respectfully and ethically, or without any respect for worker safety or rights. In this regard, *The Deuce*'s multidimensional story reflects this complexity as it destroys binary thinking about sex work and porn. Its rich ensemble of characters demonstrates the opportunities and risks of sex work, and each of their arcs shows us how porn performers can't be understood through simplistic notions of harm or liberation. As co-creator David Simon said,

> A lot of what I might've believed about sex work and pornography [before making the show] would have been stereotypical. I would have been much more inclined to categorize people in very general ways. But I learned nothing comports to stereotype. When it came to the characters, the more people we met and talked to, the better the writing got.[94]

While David Simon was preparing to start shooting *The Deuce*, the porn auteur Candida Royalle died. He attended her funeral. Later, Simon told *Rolling Stone* that as he was leaving, he ran into porn performer Veronica Hart, who had been a good friend and colleague of Royalle's during the Golden Age of Porn. They talked about his new show. Then, she gave him this advice about his characters:

> Do not make it so that everyone is a victim. For some of us, this defined us in ways that worked. Some people could handle it, some couldn't. Some seized on moments that they're glad they had, and some wish that they'd never walked in the door. If you don't include the other ones, then you're lying.[95]

The Deuce shows the shadows among the bright lights and denies us a happy ending, for it understands that the story is ongoing. Its choice to tell the story of porn from sex workers' points of view challenges the orthodoxy of anti-porn feminism and treats porn as a labour issue, a genre, and a practice. Once the pariahs of the feminist movement, sex workers become the feminist heroines of *The Deuce* and, just as importantly, workers who demand respect, rights, and dignity.

In the late 1980s, President Reagan introduced the Meese Commission prohibiting the transmission of porn on cable TV. Reagan said, "If this nation can send men to the moon, we can certainly do some cleaning up at home." Candida Royalle made these remarks in response:

> I've always maintained that the answer to bad porn was not censorship. That only made it more enticing forbidden fruit. To blame pornography for society's ills is no longer a popular line of thought for the overall feminist community. If you really want to be helping women I would suggest that you sponsor legislation that would improve women's social and economic lot in life.[96]

The Golden Age of Porn was far from glittery for women on set and on screen, but with its epic story of labour, sex, and power, *The Deuce* recovers a lost history of sex workers who defy all stereotypes. And we root for them.

Curtains: From Victimhood and Vice to Sex Workers' Rights

According to the mainstream media and popular prejudice, the marginal sex worlds are bleak and dangerous. They are portrayed as impoverished, ugly, and inhabited by psychopaths and criminals.

– Gayle Rubin, 1984[1]

Shows about gigolos, high-class escorts and porn stars hint at a new wave of small-screen attempts to offer an introspective look at the sex industry.... Becoming a sex worker is now seen, by an ever-increasing number of people, as a viable, non-judgment-inducing career choice, as benign as working in an office or at any other "straight" job.

– Megan Koester, 2016[2]

I think the film industry has a responsibility to help normalize [sex work]. They're quick to take a story and tell [it] for entertainment, but they don't really understand the depths of what these people really go through. [Hollywood] knows how the industry itself plays a huge part in how normal something is or how shameful something is. So, I think showing more of it the way that it actually happens is necessary.

– A'Ziah (Zola) King, 2021[3]

Once upon a time, popular culture's sex workers were cautionary tales about the fate of a woman who "goes wrong." Sex workers threatened patriarchy with their sexual independence, financial autonomy, and disinterest in serving one man through marriage, so the screen restricted them to predictable typologies and storylines leading to death or marriage, these endings reinforcing restrictions around women's sexual expression and bodily autonomy, access to power and money, and independence. Even at their most sympathetic and compelling, sex worker characters were often vehicles for the male hero to flex his rescuing muscles. Sometimes, sex workers challenged conventional gender roles by flouting monogamy guilt-free and leading unrepentant lives, but often they succumbed to early death. What's more, popular culture rarely portrayed the sex worker's life outside of her work, judgement-free, through her own eyes. Rather, she was written and shot from a male perspective that reduced her to a charity case or a fantasy figure, perky and eager to please.

In the twentieth century, 95 per cent of Hollywood movies with sex worker leads were made by men. Today, women direct, write, and produce much more of this popular culture, and their feminist imprint is visible in the new sex worker's characterization and imagery, and in the shift of focus from her body to her work and inner struggles and subjectivity. With understanding of the huge role that popular culture plays in shaping beliefs, these creators have thrown out moral narratives for clear-eyed stories of hustlers in hard economic times. Gone are the endings of nuptials or caskets. Instead, sex workers can be found at local cafés updating their websites, picking their kids up from school, or consulting with referring therapists. An entrepreneur and a care worker, the new sex worker treats sex as a business and experiences its benefits and its drawbacks. She also coincides with a period of transformation around the politics of sex work that is raising new questions where certainty used to be.[4] The new sex worker in popular culture is a product of her time and an expression of how sex workers in real life, whose unmet needs are an issue of human rights, are finally getting a hearing.

Powerful organizations are lobbying for decriminalization, mainstream media increasingly supports the sex workers' cause, and feminist conversations are finally welcoming the perspectives of sex workers who voice how their demands and needs are not isolated from but deeply connect to the needs of all women. As Victoria Bateman writes, "No one who honestly believes in the feminist phrase 'my body, my choice' should be ignoring the most marginalized and stigmatized group of working women in our society."[5] At the same time, social and economic shifts under neo-liberal capitalism have normalized intimate transactions and how people bring "feelings" into their precarious jobs. These changes have begun to redefine sex work as just another type of hustle in a gig-based economy, shifting away from the long-held criminal definition of sex work. With these shifts, popular culture has registered, at last, that sex workers don't want to be saved but listened to and legitimized as workers.

Consequently, popular culture's new sex worker defies typologies with her agency, sass, and dynamism. She's a mother, a wife, a daughter, an entrepreneur, a student, a healer, and an artist. She's racially diverse and broad in age and class. She is articulate about her reasons for choosing sex work, which include the potential to earn a great deal of money in a short time, scheduling flexibility conducive to single mothering, disenchantment with low-paying service gigs, rising tuition costs, the empowering feeling of being paid for sexual services, and enjoying it, seeing it both as a chance to control the means of production and be independent. Some describe taking pride in their work, like Georgia on

The Client List who retires with a plump savings account, while others are more reserved, like Gigi in *P.O.P.* who "does it all for her daughter." Some sex workers see their jobs as a subversive confrontation between sexism and the repression of women's sexuality.[6] And while comparatively privileged by indoor work, they are part of a stratum of the sex industry once ignored or treated superficially by popular culture, which assumed that all sex workers came from traumatized backgrounds and didn't choose their jobs.

What makes new popular culture most original, however, is its focus on the *work* of sex work, from the emotional labour of performing "feelings" and "authenticity," to the aesthetic labour of conspicuous consumption, to the display work of mounting scintillating stage shows, to the care work of facilitating healing experiences. With respect for her skills and talents, popular culture challenges prohibitionist denials of her talents and reveals the sex worker's labour process through her own eyes. Yet far from sugar-coated, it also portrays the hazards she faces from the potential self-alienation brought on by her intense emotional work, and the agony of leading a double life in fear of exposure and its consequences, including the potential of violence and arrest under current laws.

Furthermore, it draws our attention to how criminalization imperils sex workers by compelling them to conduct their business in clandestine locations, where they become more vulnerable to violence, and blocks access to labour rights and escalates their stigmatization. *She's Lost Control*, for example, portrays Ronah choosing not to report a violent assault for fear of incriminating herself and facing devastating criminal consequences that could endanger her future career prospects. As sex workers' own writings have shown, women who have worked in the sex industry face potentially devastating social and economic reprisals, particularly around employment.[7] In 2012, US journalist Sarah Tressler was fired from her job at the *Houston Chronicle* after it came to light that she had once worked as an erotic dancer.[8] Writer Melissa Petro was sacked from her school teaching job in 2011 after publishing a piece in the *Huffington Post* about doing sex work, her dismissal sending, as Petro writes, "a chilling message to any sex worker out there looking to leave the life."[9] New popular culture recognizes and challenges whorephobia at work in stories such as Christine's in *The Girlfriend Experience*, rallying for the labour paradigm and proclaiming that sex workers deserve the legal and labour rights of other workers. Yet, there remains much work to do, as activist Savannah Sly notes, to "expand discrimination protections to include people who have traded sex."[10] The new sex worker in popular culture is playing an important destigmatizing role in this work at a time of social change around the meaning of sex work. But what does this new sex worker leave out?

Post-Feminist Sensibilities: The Limits of the New Sex Worker in Popular Culture

While marking a positive break with stereotypes, the new sex worker in popular culture sometimes links with what Rosalind Gill calls a "post-feminist sensibility," an ethos emphasizing one's sexy body, sexual expression, freedom, choice, and entrepreneurship as feminist empowerment and stressing that social problems find solutions exclusively in the marketplace.[11] At its most extreme, she reveals the bargain sex workers on screen sometimes strike: that to secure a friendly reception she must embody a celebrated feminine ideal of late capitalism – to be hot and entrepreneurial, and not too political. Hardly confined to sex workers, Andi Zeisler captures this phenomenon well:

> The aspects of feminism currently given voice in popular culture are the most media friendly ones, the ones that centre on heterosexual relationships and marriage, on economic success that doesn't challenge existing capitalistic structures, on the right to be desirable yet have bodily autonomy.[12]

And while the new sex worker is far from the glib adventuress we saw often in movies a few decades ago – what Sherene Razack termed "tourist tales,"[13] in which middle-class women "transgress" bourgeois sexuality for kicks before returning to the safety of their class positions – she is still relatively privileged, works indoors, and is generally a young and attractive businesswoman who pulls herself up by her bootstraps and makes it outside of collective feminist action, without challenging capitalism or any of its supporting structures.

As well, popular culture mostly elides the issue of racism within the sex industry, particularly white supremacy and its impact on erotic labour. While several characters in films and TV shows, such as Georgia on *The Client List* and Darlene on *The Deuce*, challenge the stereotypical depiction of Black women as exotic sex objects or mere sidekicks, most of these portrayals stop short of deeply exploring the intersections of race and sex work. *The Deuce* stands out, in fact, because of its historically and politically informed storylines, particularly those examining how sex workers of colour in the US are exponentially more likely to be arrested and charged with prostitution. As Suraj Patel notes, in 2018, 70 per cent of defendants facing prostitution charges in Brooklyn were Black women; in fact, the discrimination against women of colour is so pervasive that the Legal Aid Society of New York mounted a challenge to the "constitutionality" of anti-loitering laws that are disproportionately invoked against Black and Hispanic women.[14] While drawing on the rhetoric of empowerment, some popular culture portrays Black women characters as having the identical experience as white sex workers, and this problematically disavows the significant ways that race structures sex work within the criminal justice system and US society at large. Popular culture must do more to show how prostitution laws target poor Black women and transgender women, who pay the highest price for society's misogyny, and to connect this reality to historical white supremacy and its endurance today in the criminal justice system and policing.

It's also worrying that certain portrayals stress women's bodies as the mantles of their empowerment. To be clear, Catherine Hakim's theory of "erotic capital" gives shape to and validates a practice that patriarchy has long shamed, while demanding it, but erotic capitalism is not a collective feminist strategy, and looking like "the heterosexual male fantasy found in pornography" isn't subversive, although it might feel personally rewarding.[15] *Pleasure* (2021), in fact, vividly makes this critique when aspiring porn performer Joy, who is in her early twenties, remarks that her shelf life in porn is short compared to the fifty-something executives who own her movies and tell her what to do, and she riffs out a subversive fantasy of levelling the playing field: "You know, fuck these guys! I wish that we could all start our own company … and just … get really fat and ugly … and if guys want to work, they have to eat our pussies!" Another porn performer interjects: "She's just saying that women should have more power about what happens to them at work." In the end, Joy's idea gets a few laughs, but that's that, and the women go back to work for the men who own the companies and demand their aesthetic perfection and docility. The limits of erotic capital is an important topic for further enquiry.

It's noticeable, too, how popular culture suggests that there are acceptable vs. unacceptable emotions that women – but especially sex workers – may express. Save for the women in *The Deuce*, *Pleasure*, and *Hustlers*, we saw very few of the sex worker characters explored here express anger. In *The Client List*, Riley mostly displays the more socially acceptable female sadness in the form of crying spells (often to soft saxophone music), and even in the nuanced *The Girlfriend Experience*, call girl Christine exhibits a kind of emotional aphasia in the face of significant personal challenges. This absence of anger may suggest self-control and evolved poise, but to me it reflects how women's feelings – especially anger – are rarely taken seriously, and how an angry woman is still one of the most uncommon sights on screen, women's rage long considered box office poison, while men's rage fills theatres and stacks up awards. We can explain this disparity by way of Arlie Hochschild, who argues that patriarchy discounts women's feelings in two ways: by deeming women's "rational" feelings – acceptable feelings, like longing and sorrow – "unimportant," and by portraying women's "irrational" feelings" – like anger – as "dismissible."[16] And the weaker the economic position a woman holds – the lower her "status shield" – the more likely it becomes that her feelings will be dismissed, and women who do express anger may find that their amplification activates an angry response and gets her the label of "emotional," "irrational," or simply "crazy."[17] In popular

Figure 8.1. In *Pleasure,* a young porn actress imagines a future where she and other performers have more control over their work.

culture, alas, few sex workers become "emotional" – angry – because to show an "emotional" sex worker would risk torpedoing her sympathetic appeal and bring her dangerously close to the image of "angry feminist," to which our culture is allergic. Mind you, this is not a phenomenon exclusive to sex workers. Today, as Stassa Edwards writes, anger as a form of agitation "seems banished from contemporary conversations on feminism – replaced, instead, with a kind of cathartic baring of wounds."[18] Compliance, it would then seem, makes for a likeable sex worker character. Yet, compliance on the screen is what prevents representations from making stronger political statements, and compliance in reality is what stalls change and progress.

It is appreciable, too, that anger is even more of a taboo among sex workers of colour on screen, an elision that mirrors the silencing of activism by Black women. Even during the second-wave feminist movement, when anger was the emotion *du jour* for public intellectual feminists, it was still largely the privilege of white feminists. Writing in the *New York Times,* Roxane Gay explains: "I am often accused of being angry. This accusation is made because a woman, a Black woman who is angry, is making trouble.... Race complicates anger. Black women are often characterized as angry simply for existing."[19] Were popular culture to start portraying strident sex workers who boldly and freely express their anger about the criminalization of their work, their status as second-class citizens, in tactical ways, it would go even greater distances in articulating the long-denied rights and privileges that sex workers need. For this reason, it would be key to showing anger in sex worker popular culture. Gay puts it well: "Anger allows us to express dissatisfaction. It allows us to say something is wrong."[20]

In the absence of showing sex worker anger, popular culture sometimes lacks the political bite to assert what's wrong and what needs to change to make it right, and in place of demands for change is the tactic of fitting the status quo, of sex workers who conform to neo-liberalism's ideal subjects: "entrepreneurs" and flexible precarious service workers who are young, conventionally attractive, individualistic, and apolitical. These popular culture sex workers certainly bare wounds and have struggles, but rather than use anger to agitate for change, they work on changing themselves through self-improvement and entrepreneurial activities, two arenas in which women's anger finds no place. An angry woman is indeed incongruent with capitalist logic, and for this reason, the angry sex worker is still one of the rarest sights on screen. So, while new popular culture brings sex workers from the margins to the centre, that centre is often the centre of the marketplace, which is key for visibility, but not where change happens. As Jane Arthurs notes, popular culture's individualistic sex worker stories "cannot substitute for meticulous research that ... [goes] beyond the personal."[21] Similarly, Sara Suleri argues that as important as personal narratives are, they "cannot function as a sufficient alternative" to rigorous examinations of power relations lest they be accorded "an iconicity that is altogether too good to be true."[22] The new sex worker in popular culture superbly illuminates personal experiences, and deeper portrayals of the politics of sex work are gradually emerging, as in *Cam*, *The Deuce*, *Tangerine*, and *Pleasure*, which focus on agency *and* structure by locating sex worker power within and outside the personal.

The Stakes, Revisited

Despite these limits, popular culture about sex work matters now more than ever as sex workers in the US face huge new challenges, from the street to the legislative level. In 2016, sex workers faced a pervasive threat to their livelihoods and safety when federal legislation shut down Backpage, a website on which sex workers advertised their services and communicated with clients. For years, Backpage had helped sex workers stay safe by giving them a platform to advertise their services – allowing some to move from more dangerous street sex work to indoor sex work – and communicate with clients before meeting, thereby creating a digital trail and accountability. The 2018 passing of two pieces of legislation – the bills Allow States and Victims to Fight Online Sex Trafficking Act (FOSTA) and the Stop Enabling Sex Traffickers Act (SESTA), known as FOSTA-SESTA, legislated by Donald Trump in April 2018 – effected great change. The new legislation amended a loophole in legislation that had absolved platforms of responsibility for the content users posted or the results of services offered. With FOSTA-SESTA, any website hosting advertisements for sex workers is considered a participant in sex trafficking and its operators can face up to ten years in prison.[23] Supporters of FOSTA-SESTA, including anti-trafficking groups, argue that the shutdown of online advertising platforms will protect women from being trafficked. But critics of the bill argue that FOSTA-SESTA is rolling back internet freedoms, removing consensual sex workers' only way of safely advertising and vetting clients, and exposing an already marginalized community to violence.

The closure of Backpage is the latest in a crackdown on internet sex work platforms, which began in 2015 with the closure of MyRedBook.com and the shuttering of the "erotic services" section on Craigslist in 2018. Furthermore, while FOSTA-SESTA erroneously conflates sex trafficking and sex work, it may not even succeed at its intended purpose of preventing sex trafficking. The largest anti-trafficking organization in the US, Freedom Network USA, says the bill "will not provide a meaningful improvement in anti-trafficking efforts, and may cause severe consequences for sex workers and trafficking victims alike."[24] The American Civil Liberties Union (ACLU) also rejects the bill, calling it "a risk to freedom of speech."[25] Even the Department of Justice admitted that the bill would make it harder to prosecute traffickers and could have "unintended consequences" on sex workers.[26] As Rick Paulas writes, "With each site's closure in this latest generation of communication crackdown, sex workers, already unprotected as a workforce, will be left further vulnerable to dangerous clients."[27] SESTA-FOSTA, in sum, is just the latest example of the still widely held assumption that all sex workers are victims.

In an environment in which sex workers' civil liberties and self-determination are imperiled, popular culture can be a path to increasing knowledge and instigating more nuanced conversations. Treating sex work as *work*, as new popular culture does, allows us to set aside moral judgements, and assumptions, and orations about empowerment to focus on the heart of the matter when talking about why women sell sex: as a job for money. One writer and former erotic dancer describes her economic motivation thus:

The unglamorous truth about my experience as an adult entertainer is that I felt empowered – as a woman, as a feminist, and as a human being – by the money I made, not by the work I did. The performances I gave didn't change anyone's ideas about women ... I wasn't "owning" or "subverting" anything other than my own working-class status ... [and the work] didn't make me a better feminist. It just made me a feminist who could afford her own rent.[28]

In the past few years, sex workers have also been making movies and collaborating with other creators with greater frequency. Sex worker involvement in the making of popular culture both behind and in front of the camera has made productions more ethical and increased their authenticity. From *The Deuce*, which sought input from porn stars from the Golden Age of Porn, to *The Girlfriend Experience*, which consulted with call girls, movies and TV shows of late embody how collaboration with sex workers can give popular culture the dignity and nuance that comes only from lived experience. As Isa Mazzei, the writer of *Cam* and a former webcam model herself, puts it: "There is a huge power in telling your own story and reclaiming your narrative."[29] Sex worker creators screen their films on YouTube, Sexworkerfest.com, and at the bi-annual San Francisco Sex Worker Film and Arts Festival. Movies written by sex workers, including *Cam*, are winning acclaim for their artistry and attention to the intersectional dynamics of race, class, and power that shape sex work, and which once got left out of popular culture. A'Ziah (Zola) King, whose 2015 viral Twitter story about being a road-tripping erotic dancer became the 2020 movie *Zola*, agrees that sex worker–led popular culture is the future. "I think that sex work stories need to be told by sex workers, just like I think Black stories need to be told by Black creatives," King said. "I don't think anyone who has not had this experience could tell this experience."[30]

One of the finest examples of this much-needed authenticity and activism is Sean Baker's *Tangerine* (2015), a film with a commitment to doing the sex worker movie differently. Novel in both content and form, it starred former sex workers and was shot on an iPhone 5S. Infused with equal parts dignity, elegance, and irreverence, it is to my knowledge the first feature film about transgender sex workers, and it immediately garnered praise when it premiered at the Sundance Film Festival. Until *Tangerine*, Hollywood's transgender sex workers were stock characters, objectified novelties inserted into gaudy plots. That transgender sex workers, and Black transgender sex workers, particularly, are more likely to be arrested and victimized than any other sex worker made these representations doubly disturbing, as they contributed to their continued stigmatization and the violence perpetuated against them. *Tangerine*, however, is a rare film that uses its awareness of transphobia to challenge it. With style, seriousness, and comedic sass, it invites the viewer into the world of sex workers in difficult circumstances while never reducing these women to types nor

Figure 8.2. Sean Baker's award-winning film *Tangerine* put Black transgender sex workers in the spotlight with a story that was respectful, dynamic, and sex worker led.

defining them exclusively through sex, but exploring their complex lives, work, dreams, and friendships. *Tangerine* signalled a sea change in the representation of Black and transgender sex workers, and its authenticity came in large part from its performances that drew on the lived experiences of its two stars, Kitana Kiki Rodriguez and Mya Taylor, former sex workers. Speaking to the characters' multidimensionality, Taylor said: "The film is not about people in sex work. The film is about friendship. The people just happen to be sex workers. It's just like a real-life story, you know?"[31]

The wide audience and critical acclaim *Tangerine* received (Taylor won the Independent Spirit Award for Best Supporting Female, the first transgender woman to do so, and the San Francisco Bay Area Film Critics Circle Award for Best Supporting Actress) will surely encourage more studios to support such projects that do the sex worker movie differently in both form and content. As Melissa Ditmore writes, "the way forward is to listen to sex workers and ask what would truly be of use to them – whether in law reform, research, or any other area – to offer suggestions, and to support the needs of sex workers without imposing another agenda."[32] While this book was limited to wide release works, there is much more to explore of smaller budget films made by sex workers as they impart an important message: that when a marginalized group is given the chance to make their own media, better stories get told.

Sex Work Popular Culture: Directions for Research

In this book, I focused on popular culture's new sex worker, but this is not to suggest that cliché, harmful, and denigrating portrayals have been swept from the screens, nor have those that claim to dignify sex workers while painting them as victims without agency. Representations of sex trafficking and violence against sex workers are vital, yet these often conflate such crimes with sex work and, at their worst, are produced at the expense of sex workers, epitomized recently by the reality television show *8 Minutes* (2015), which aired on A&E. The series follows a pastor and former police officer, Kevin Brown, who poses as a client and arranges to meet sex workers in hotel rooms, casting himself in the role of moral rescuer. Unbeknownst to each sex worker, she is being secretly filmed, and Brown has given himself eight minutes to evangelize on why sex work is degrading and persuade her to leave the industry by offering financial help, drug treatment, and emotional support in exchange for her signing a waiver agreeing to appear on the show (she is promised her face will be blurred).

Often, Brown entreats sex workers to tell sad stories about their childhoods that centre on themes like abuse, neglect, and despair, effectively compelling sex workers to become what Melissa Gira Grant calls "objects of social control ... and charitable concerns ... there for the sake of unseen owner's profits,"[33] in this case, the TV network. Once finished, Brown brings in two women, purportedly ex-escorts, who continue to try and convince the women to leave the sex industry. Most of the women featured on the show *do* agree to leave sex work provided they receive the help promised (and no doubt because of being entrapped in a hotel room by a pastor). Yet, importantly, none are asked how they will support themselves, and most look scared. No wonder. The series sprung from the condescending premise that sex workers have never contemplated leaving the industry or considered alternatives, having stumbled into this work illogically because of their broken moral compasses. In typical rescuer fashion, the show prescribes a course of action without consideration for the economic conditions motivating women into sex work in the first place, nor does it offer a cogent exit plan. Alana Massey, writing in the *New Republic*, put it well: "Any attempt to coerce them out of sex work in the absence of viable alternatives is an invitation to starve."[34]

After *8 Minutes* premiered, sex workers began coming forward to say they never received the housing, medical, or job searching help they were promised; some were given a hotline phone number or a few hundred dollars, one was offered "prayers" from the pastor, while others received no help at all.[35] One reported that the so-called rescue van that was shown ferrying her away to "safety" dropped her off around the corner. In the end, the show humiliated sex workers, placed them in legal jeopardy, and left them financially worse off and emotionally scarred. "This show, these people, it's a disaster in my life," said one woman who appeared on the show.[36] She describes the producers giving her a $200 flat fee and never returning her telephone calls. While she waited for the help she was promised, her savings dwindled and eventually she returned to sex work. On her first day back on the job, she was arrested.[37] Writing in *Reason*, Elizabeth Nolan Brown points out that not only did these sex workers not ask for help, but their lives were made worse for the intervention.[38] In the wake of the scandal, A&E cancelled the show after just five episodes. Similar to the mug shots of women arrested for prostitution that sheriffs' departments across the US publish on their websites, *8 Minutes* capitalized on sex workers' vulnerability, reinforced their stigmatized status, and put them at risk for the possible loss of other jobs and custody of their children while creating a permanent record of their so-called criminality.

Media campaigns about sex workers from a prohibitionist perspective are also becoming more sophisticated. One day in early 2016, men who conducted online searches for "call girls" reached a site called Girls of Paradise. It looked like a typical call girl website with a grid of photographs of attractive women in revealing clothes. When the prospective customer clicked on a photograph, a chat window popped up and a message invited would-be clients to communicate live with the pictured call girl. After a perfunctory conversation, the call girl would ask the prospective customer if he wanted to see more photos. Regardless of his response, photographs would then begin appearing in the chat window: first a bikini shot, then a slew of disturbing photographs. One set showed a woman with a bloody and bruised face, with the accompanying text: "I was found dead in my apartment, stabbed 53 times." Other sets showed sex workers with ligature marks on their necks and text explaining that they had killed themselves or been murdered by violent men.

Girls of Paradise was not a call girl website but rather a media campaign collaboration between a French sex work prohibitionist organization, Le Mouvement du Nid, and McCann Paris, the multinational advertising agency, and its goal was to spread awareness of how "to be a prostitute today means to be a victim of extreme violence. By putting money in the system, clients are accomplices of this violence. We wanted them to realize the consequences of their actions."[39] The Gold Clio Award–winning campaign had a noble intention – to raise public awareness about the violence sex workers disproportionately face – yet it was limited in two ways. First, call girls – like other indoor sex workers – are exponentially less likely to face violence than outdoor sex workers.[40] If Girls of Paradise wanted to factually represent the sex workers who are most at risk, it would portray street-based sex workers, especially sex workers of colour and transgender women who are at most risk for violence and criminalization. Second, Girls of Paradise elided how decriminalization – not prohibition – could make sex workers' lives safer by allowing them to conduct their business out of the shadows and gain vital legal and labour rights that would destigmatize sex workers and send the message to would-be perpetrators of violence that they would be held accountable. As Ann Lucas notes, "criminalization makes [sex] work more insecure, dangerous, isolating, and socially disreputable."[41] Campaigns such as these are worthy of further examination from a feminist media studies perspective.

Video and computer games portrayals of sex workers also merit further inquiry, and while beyond the scope of this book, one example stands out as so egregious that it must be shared. *HunieCam Studio*, a video game released in 2016, invites players to "Invest in growing your filthy business!" as the owner and manager of "a sleazy cam-girl operation!"[42] While managing up to a dozen models, the player's goal is to attract as many fans as possible in twenty-one days. *HunieCam Studio* revolves around players controlling every aspect of its webcam models' lives. For example, players are empowered to customize the bodies of their webcam models based on market research and consumer demand ("See what fans are smackin' it to!"), force models to eat and drink to perform fetish shows (drink a jug of water to perform a pee fetish; eat cake to get gassy to do a show for fart fetishists), and control models' minds by forcing them to smoke marijuana (to calm them) or take cocaine (to make them work faster). *HunieCam Studio* jubilantly gamifies the exploitation and abuse of sex workers. A frenzied celebration of the "male sex right" as the player hero's source of power, the game is won by extinguishing the kind of self-determination described by webcam models in *Cam Girlz* who could choose their own hours, which sex acts to perform, how much to charge, who to interact with, and how to present themselves on screen, including the right to perform subversive shows that challenge the codes of pornography (by dressing as a Pierrot or wearing a dinosaur head, for example). *HunieCam* gives all this power to the player/manager/owner in a patriarchal capitalist fantasy of women's total subordination to men. But be careful, the game warns: don't make your model take too many drugs or else her productivity could dip. The player can also take any of his webcam models to a "sleazy motel" for sex, similar to *Grand Theft Auto*'s workaround for manipulating strippers into sex. Yet, unlike that video game, where there was no mention of stripper salaries, webcam models in *HunieCam Studio* are paid: $4 per hour. Like *8 Minutes* but more debased, *HunieCam Studio* gamifies the exploitation of sex workers by turning them into objects for men to watch, exploit, and profit from.

A further area of enquiry are websites like The Erotic Review, which aggregate reviews of erotic service providers. For newer sex workers, excellent reviews can boost business and credibility and translate into more bookings and higher income. Yet, the huge power wielded by these sites also make them threats, as we see in *The Girlfriend Experience* film. In response to this centralization of power, sex workers have fostered collective action by starting their own review websites or by adding review sections to their personal web pages. Relatedly, more enquiry is needed into how sex workers self-represent on platforms such as Reddit, Instagram, and X (formerly Twitter). As Valerie Feldman notes, "in the face of very real and sometimes violent legal and social sanctions faced by sex workers, the Internet's anonymity allows sex workers to 'come out' online and speak as sex workers on issues of interest to them."[43] Popular culture about sex workers produced outside the US,[44] while beyond the scope of this book, is also worthy of further exploration.[45]

Finally, popular culture about male sex workers is increasing and deserves more enquiry. A standout in this group is the film *Good Luck to You, Leo Grande* (2022), which daringly breaks the taboo of women paying men for sex. Directed by Sophie Hyde, the film introduces us to Nancy (played by Emma Thompson), a retired schoolteacher who hires an impishly handsome twenty-something sex worker, Leo Grande, to teach her how to experience pleasure after a lifetime of sexual lockdown. While tender and light-hearted, the film is serious about challenging stigma, and Leo and Nancy's relationship becomes a stage for undoing assumptions. Nancy admits that she once assigned her students the essay topic of "why sex work is wrong." She assumes that Leo's reasons for doing sex work are sad. "You're probably a very vulnerable young man," she says. But Leo is adamant: "I don't feel degraded," he tells Nancy, "I like my job." As Leo guides Nancy in the bedroom, Nancy begins to shed her assumptions about sex workers and to accept that for Leo, sex work is a job. Moreover, she connects the sexual repression of women like herself to the repression sex workers have always faced. In the end, Nancy's journey of self-discovery becomes an argument for sexual fulfilment as a key part of human life and an appeal to destigmatize sex work and recognize it as real work. As Leo puts it,

> Think how civilized it can be if it was available without shame or judgement attached. You want sex and you're frustrated you can't get it. You're shy, you're unwell, you're physically struggling, so you just hire someone like me. It's all regulated and safe for you, for me, better for everyone.

Other movies, such as *Magic Mike* (2012) and *American Gigolo* (1980), have portrayed male sex workers before in a positive way. But the trope of the gigolo is almost always presented comedically, as if to suggest the absurdity of a woman paying a man for sex, reinforcing puritanical ideas about women's asexuality. *Good Luck to You, Leo Grande* challenges such ideas and shows how sex can be healing, and sex workers a part of that healing process. As Emma Thompson said in an interview, "Leo is a sex worker, but he's also a care worker."[46] As Leo

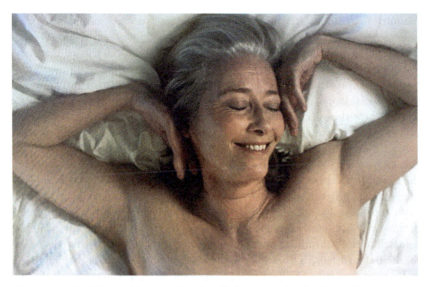

Figure 8.3. *Good Luck to You, Leo Grande* calls for sex workers' rights with a story about a woman's sexual repression cured by a male sex worker.

guides Nancy on a physical and emotional journey that leads her to experiencing sexual pleasure for the first time in her life, that care is transformative. For Leo, who the film dignifies as a smart and kind professional, it is just another job, and that is exactly the point. As he says, tucking his fee into his wallet, "there's nothing crass about getting paid for your work, Nancy," the film boldly validating sex work as *real* work.

A Thousand Years of Sex Worker Representation: Twenty-First-Century Transitions

When I first became interested in this topic as a graduate student, I took a trip to the Toronto Reference Library, the largest public reference library in Canada. Soaring, clad in glass, and pyramidal, the building's distinctively 1970s look stands in contrast to its somewhat hidden sixth-floor Picture Collection – a relic of the analogue age – with its dozens of filing cabinets containing magazine- and newspaper-clipped pictures of almost every earthly phenomenon, organized alphabetically according to subject area, from "animals" to "countries" to "foods" to, most interesting to me, "occupations" and "social issues." At the time of my visit in 2013, Canada had just (very temporarily, it turned out) suspended its prostitution laws after the judiciary ruled that they put sex workers at risk, and sex work was very much in the headlines. After locating the "prostitution" folder – so voluminous it was actually *two* folders – in the "social issues" section, I brought it over to a librarian. I was curious to learn of how the social transformations around sex work were trickling into everyday life, into language, one of the surest ways of measuring social progress. I decided on a direct approach: "Are you thinking about moving the prostitution folder to the 'occupations' drawer?" The librarian immediately understood the larger debate I was referring to. "We know that this is important – and it is happening, it is in the works," they said. A year later, I followed up and learned that the process was underway, but the immensity of the collection – hundreds of files and thousands of images – made the task of evaluating the contents colossally time consuming. But it had begun. "This collection was started in the 1950s and 1960s," a librarian told me. "We inherited a lot of that language and now we are trying to change that." In 2024, when I reconnected with the Library, it seemed this transition was starting, though "prostitution" was still being used over "sex work" in most of the catalogue. There was, however, significant interest in updating this language, and I was invited to provide input – an invitation I'll accept and share with local sex worker advocacy groups. The old-fashioned Picture Collection contained thousands of sex work images from throughout the twentieth and twenty-first centuries and, as I saw it, was a metaphor for our social imaginary about sex work. That the move was taking time made sense, and the word "change" seemed to fittingly sum up the larger renegotiating of sex work in wider society today, and in popular culture.

Today, we are changing how we think about sex workers, and popular culture, in turn, is challenging offensive and damaging stereotypes. As we become more critical about the stories popular culture tells us about sex workers – as we have done with other marginalized groups – we can also begin to question our most deeply held biases and morally driven assumptions that often guide this subject. Regardless of our personal feelings about sex work, the reality of it is more complicated than the screen would have once had us think, and popular culture of late recognizes this and is providing us with a more nuanced image, free of the characterizations of victimhood, which is rooted in the virgin–whore binary, as well as blithe pronouncements about empowerment that are characteristic of post-feminist media. At her most sophisticated, canny, intrepid, sensitive, and fascinating, the new sex worker in popular culture explores both the benefits and drawbacks of sex work and voices what sex workers have said all along, summed up well by the writer and sex worker Maggie McNeill:

> Real life is not like a silent melodrama; the baddies do not all wear black hats and sport waxed moustaches, and many of the women who are tied to the railroad

tracks are there because they consented to be and will not appreciate ham-fisted attempts at "rescue." There is a whole spectrum between the party girl whoring herself for thrills and the chained sex slave, and the number of prostitutes at the one end is no higher than that at the other. The vast majority of us, like the vast majority of the human race, exist in the murky grey area between absolute freedom and abject slavery, trying our best to balance the pursuit of happiness with the toil necessary for survival.[47]

Popular culture's new sex worker, at her most incisive, shows us the complex lives of women who make choices and can't be reduced to a stereotype. As the activist Silva Leite says, "It's dangerous to start from a perspective that people have no choices in life, because if we do that we start looking at them as victims and victims have no choice, and no voice."[48] While popular culture in itself doesn't change the legal system, it does change hearts and minds. Today, as sex work is increasingly recognized as an issue of human rights, popular culture's new sex worker, while imperfect, embodies that hope – and battle – for the rights, safety, and dignity that all sex workers deserve, and is one important step forward in that achievement.

The iconic opening scene of *Hustlers* is all about this dynamism and visibility. Erotic dancer Ramona acrobatically spins, whirls, and drops on the brass pole, a spangled masterpiece in motion who's also an ordinary woman, her razzle-dazzle on stage her way of making ends meet. In the original script, this sequence didn't exist, and the first scene was perfunctory, the direction simply reading: "Ramona ends her dance with a flourish." But Jennifer Lopez, who took her role so seriously that she spent months learning how to pole dance, convinced the director that the film should open with an extended show – to set off on the right note and underscore and dignify Ramona's *work*, her talents and artistry as an erotic dancer. As Lopez later said, "We designed the dance to not just be kind of a gratuitous, you know, strip pole scene, but actually to really inform who she was as a person."[49] As Ramona dances to the song "Criminal," its lyrics an ironic *mea culpa* sung by a swaggering woman, she struts over carpets of cash, leonine in the spotlight, savouring it. The new sex worker in popular culture is a similarly unrepentant figure. Having lived in the shadows, having endured stigmatization, criminalization, silencing, and judgement for her work, today she demands to be seen and recognized for who she really is – and always was: a worker, a mother, a daughter, a sister, a friend, and an entrepreneur. She is an individual with her own unique struggles, motivations, desires, talents, secrets, longings, drives, and despairs, but she also wants what all women workers do: fair pay, respect, bodily autonomy, safety, and basic human rights.

Acknowledgments

It's a long journey for a book to reach publication, and it gives me great pleasure to thank all the people who helped me get here.

First, I'd like to thank the sex workers whose epigraphs launch almost all the chapters in this book. Their insights and candour about sex work in popular culture were among the most valuable research I sought out for this book, and I learned much from and immensely enjoyed our conversations. While names are anonymized, I'm grateful to each of you. I also want to thank the sex workers who spoke to me off the record, whose stories I will always cherish. Academics have a long history of utilizing sex workers' stories to bolster their own (usually prohibitionist) arguments. Aware of this history, I consulted many sex worker–led resources before embarking on this project. Maggie's Toronto Sex Worker's Action Project, known for its peerless advocacy, was an invaluable resource, and I am deeply appreciative of their insights and the unparalleled work that they do.

A number of sex work scholars have influenced me, and the beacon among them is Emily van der Meulen, whose research and activism is incomparable. Emily, thank you for your generosity of ideas and encouragement. I'd also like to thank Chris Bruckert, whose research on erotic labour paved the way for so much scholarship that followed, including my own approach. I had the pleasure of interviewing Chris, along with Emily van der Meulen and Elya Durisin, for a piece later published in *Shameless*, at a key point in my research process, and their ideas helped light my path.

The writings of numerous sex worker activists and scholars have inspired me, but Melissa Gira Grant, Carol Queen, Gayle Rubin, Carole Vance, Jill Nagle, Priscilla Alexander, Nickie Roberts, and Ronald Weitzer were particularly foundational. Carol Leigh (aka Scarlot Harlot), Candida Royalle, and Margo St. James were also hugely influential, and it was during the writing of this book that these three trailblazing sex worker activist visionaries and writers passed away. Though sorrowful occasions, it was heartening to see their legacies celebrated in media worldwide, a testament to their history-changing advocacy for the rights of sex workers.

My publisher, University of Toronto Press, has been a steadfast supporter of this book. In particular, I thank Mark Thompson, my editor, for his unwavering commitment to and care for this project. Thanks to Janice Evans who kept this book on schedule and went above and beyond to make it look great. I'd also like to thank Anna Del Col, Stephanie Mazza, and Ashley Bernicky. My copy editor, Samantha Rohrig, was delightful to work with and superbly professional, and I deeply appreciate her thoughtfulness and attention to detail.

I designed sixteen of the nineteen dingbats seen throughout this book using Creative Commons images. The remaining three – which appear in chapter 2 – are from the saucy "BeautyMarks" collection created by bobistheeowl. Each dingbat seeks to reflect the content of the chapters in which it appears.

Research for this book was supported by the Social Sciences and Humanities Research Council of Canada and Toronto Metropolitan University's Faculty of Arts.

I'd also like to thank my wonderful colleagues in the Department of English at Toronto Metropolitan University. I can't imagine a better place to write and teach. A special thank you goes to my department chairs, Andrew O'Malley, Anne-Marie Lee-Loy, and Colleen Derkatch, for their steadfast guidance and warm support. I'm especially grateful to Pamela Sugiman, whose support has been incredibly encouraging. Thank you to Elizabeth Podnieks, whose scholarship on motherhood influenced my massage parlour chapter. Nima Naghibi, thank you for your enduring insights and wise advice on writing and things beyond for the last decade plus. Your friendship is a gift. Ruth Panofsky: there are no words to fully express my gratitude for your support and care over the years. Thank you for inspiring me, for believing in me, and for being an all-around remarkable person.

In addition, I want to thank the following caring people who supported this book – and me – through the years: Ian McLatchie, Elah Feder, Teela Johnson, Dale Smith, Brooke Lockyer, Marina Hess, Joe Kispal Kovacs, Gail Vanstone, Catherine Mirrlees, the Ezrins, Sandi and Bill Coyle, Kevin Sartorio, Katherine McLeod, Eva-Lynn Jagoe, Jonathan Garfinkel, and Rosemary Sullivan.

My family has been a constant source of strength. Mia, thanks for your love and warm support. Dad and Mom, I am so grateful for your cheer, advice, and love through the entire book-writing process. Thank you for your bottomless patience and devotion to me.

Thank you to my sweetie, the one and only Scarfie, for inspiring joy.

The final ovation goes to Tanner Mirrlees for, well, everything he knows and has shared with me. Thank you for a sky's worth of love and support – through delicious meals and long conversations, warm feedback, and enthusiastic encouragement – and for being my confidante, best friend, and partner in life, always.

Filmography

Akerman, Chantal, dir. *Jeanne Dielman, 23 quai du commerce, 1080 Bruxelles*. Belgium: Paradise Films, 1975.
Anderson, Paul Thomas, dir. *Boogie Nights*. United States: New Line Cinema, 1997.
–, dir. *Inherent Vice*. United States: Warner Bros., 2014.
Armitage, Frederick S., dir. *Birth of the Pearl*. United States: American Mutoscope & Biograph Company, 1901.
Aronofsky, Darren, dir. *The Wrestler*. United States: Wild Bunch, 2008.
[A Wise Guy], dir. *A Free Ride* [*A Grass Sandwich*]. United States: [Gay Paree Picture Co.], 1915.
Ayouch, Nabil, dir. *Much Loved*. Morocco: Celluloid Dreams, 2015.
Baker, Sean, dir. *Tangerine*. United States: Magnolia Pictures, 2015.
Baldini, Marcus, dir. *Confessions of a Brazilian Call Girl* [*Bruna Surfistinha*]. Brazil: Damasco Filmes, 2011.
Bell, Martin, dir. *Streetwise*. United States: Bear Creek, 1984.
Borden, Lizzie, dir. *Working Girls*. United States: Alternate Current, 1986.
Bravo, Janicza, dir. *Zola*. United States: Killer Films, 2020.
Brickman, Paul, dir. *Risky Business*. United States: Geffen Film Company, 1983.
Buñuel, Luis, dir. *Belle de Jour*. France: Valoria, 1967.
Carchietta, John, dir. *Teenage Cocktail*. United States: Backup Media, 2016.
Chase, Brandon, dir. *Girl in Trouble*. United States: Federate Arts Studios, 1963.
Collins, Robert L., dir. *Money on the Side*. United States: Columbia Pictures Television, 1982.
Conn, Nicole, dir. *A Perfect Ending*. United States: Soul Kiss Films, 2012.
Connell, W. Merle, dir. *A Night at the Follies*. United States: Excelsior Pictures, 1947.
Cox, James, dir. *Wonderland*. United States: Lions Gate Films, 2003.
Cromwell, John, dir. *Of Human Bondage*. United States: RKO Radio Pictures, 1934.
Curtiz, Michael, dir. *Mildred Pierce*. United States: Warner Bros., 1945.
Damiano, Gerard, dir. *Deep Throat*. United States: Gerard Damiano Film Productions, 1972.

–, dir. *The Devil in Miss Jones*. United States: Pierre Productions, 1973.
Dark, Gregory, dir. *New Wave Hookers*. United States: VCA Pictures, 1985
Demaizière, Thierry, and Alban Teurlai, dirs. *Rocco*. France: Program 33, 2016.
De Palma, Brian, dir. *Dressed to Kill*. United States: Filmways Pictures, 1980.
Despentes, Virginie, dir. *Mutantes: Punk Porn Feminism*. France: Pink TV, 2009.
Despentes, Virginie, and Coralie Trinh Thi, dirs. *Baise-moi*. France: Toute Premiere Fois, 2000.
Dick, Kirby, dir. *Private Practices: The Story of a Sex Surrogate*. United States: Kirby Dick, 1985.
Dunne, Sean, dir. *Cam Girlz*. United States: Film Emporium, 2015.
Edwards, Blake, dir. *Breakfast at Tiffany's*. United States: Jurow-Shepherd Production, 1961.
Epstein, Rob, and Jeffrey Friedman, dirs. *Lovelace*. United States: Millennium Films, 2013.
Figgis, Mike, dir. *Leaving Las Vegas*. United States: Lumiére Pictures, 1995.
Findlay, Roberta, dir. *Shauna: Every Man's Fantasy*. United States: Sendy Film Corporation, 1985.
Forman, Milos, dir. *The People vs. Larry Flynt*. United States: Columbia Pictures, 1996.
Fosse, Bob, dir. *Star 80*. United States: The Ladd Company, 1983.
Fox, Chester, and Alex Stevens, dirs. *Massage Parlor Murders!* United States: Cinemid Films, 1973.
Funari, Vicky, and Julia Query, dirs. *Live Nude Girls Unite!* United States: Constant Communication, 2000.
Garbarski, Sam, dir. *Irina Palm*. Belgium: Entre Chien de Loup, 2007.
Garbus, Liz, dir. *Lost Girls*. United States: Archer Gray, 2020.
Godard, Jean-Luc, dir. *Vivre sa vie: Film en douze tableaux*. France: Les Films de la Pléiade, 1962.
Goldhaber, Daniel, dir. *Cam*. United States: Blumhouse Productions, 2018.
Gordon, Bette, dir. *Variety*. United States: Variety Motion Pictures, 1983.
Green, Alfred E., dir. *Baby Face*. United States: Warner Bros., 1933.
Greenfield, Lauren, dir. *Magic City*. United States: Evergreen Pictures, 2015.
–, dir. *The Queen of Versailles*. United States: Magnolia Pictures, 2012.
Greenfield, Luke, dir. *The Girl Next Door*. United States: New Regency Productions, 2004.
Higgins, Colin, dir. *The Best Little Whorehouse in Texas*. United States: Universal Pictures, 1982.
Hoffmann, Jens, dir. *9 to 5: Days in Porn*. Germany: Casa Bonita, 2008.
Howard, Ron, dir. *Night Shift*. United States: The Ladd Company, 1982.
Hurley, Tara, dir. *Happy Endings?* United States: It's Not Easy Productions, 2009.
Hyde, Sophie, dir. *Good Luck to You, Leo Grande*. United States: Align, 2022.
Ice Cube, dir. *The Players Club*. United States: New Line Cinema, 1998.
Jenkins, Artemus, dir. *Power of Pussy (P.O.P.)*. United States: christmasinjuly1982, 2012. https://youtube.com/playlist?list=PLkIQzk2RR6WwiA86RGJsz9ucA6kXgPTll.

Jenkins, Patty, dir. *Monster*. United States: Media 8 Entertainment, 2003.
Jhally, Sut, dir. *Killing Us Softly 3: Advertising's Image of Women*. United States: Media Education Foundation, 1999.
Kaplan, Patti, dir. *Cathouse*. United States: HBO, 2002.
Kazan, Elia, dir. *East of Eden*. United States: Warner Bros., 1955.
Kirchner, Albert, dir. *Le Coucher de la Mariée*. France: Pathé Frères, 1896.
Klein, Bonnie Sherr, dir. *Not a Love Story: A Film about Pornography*. Canada: Studio D, 1981.
Kleiser, Randal, dir. *Dawn: Portrait of a Teenage Runaway*. United States: Douglas S. Cramer Company, 1976.
Kubrick, Stanley, dir. *Eyes Wide Shut*. United States: Warner Bros., 1999.
–, dir. *Full Metal Jacket*. United States: Warner Bros., 1987.
Laneuville, Eric, dir. *The Client List*. United States: Sony Pictures Television, 2010.
Lanthimos, Yorgos, dir. *Poor Things*. Ireland: Element Pictures, 2023.
Legon, Gary, and Al Rossi, dirs. *My Therapist*. United States: TPL Productions, 1983.
Lewin, Ben, dir. *The Sessions*. United States: Searchlight Pictures, 2012.
Loach, Ken. *I, Daniel Blake*. United Kingdom: Wild Bunch, 2016.
Luhrmann, Baz, dir. *Moulin Rouge!* United States: 20th Century Fox, 2001.
Lyne, Adrian, dir. *Flashdance*. United States: Paramount Pictures, 1983.
Mahurin, Matt, dir. *Feel*. United States: Vox3 Films, 2006.
Malle, Louis, dir. *The Lovers* [*Les amants*]. France: Nouvelles Éditions de Film, 1958.
–. *Pretty Baby*. United States: Paramount Pictures, 1978.
Manganiello, Joe, dir. *La Bare*. United States: 3:59, 2014.
Mann, Daniel, dir. *BUtterfield 8*. United States: Afton-Linebrook, 1960.
Marshall, Gary, dir. *Pretty Woman*. United States: Touchstone Pictures, 1990.
Marquardt, Anja, dir. *She's Lost Control*. United States: SLC Film, 2014.
Marvin, Arthur, dir. *The Downward Path*. United States: American Mutoscope & Biograph Company, 1900.
Mawra, Joseph P., dir. *Mme. Olga's Massage Parlor*. United States: American Film Distributing Corporation, 1965.
McDonald, Sheona, dir. *Candice*. United States: Dimestore Productions, 2019.
Milestone, Lewis, dir. *Rain*. United States: United Artists, 1932.
Mitchell, Artie, and Jim Mitchell, dirs. *Behind the Green Door*. United States: Jartech, 1972.
Mitchell, John Cameron, dir. *Shortbus*. Canada: THINKFilm, 2006.
Morel, Pierre, dir. *Taken*. France: EurpoaCorp, 2008.
O'Neil, Robert Vincent, dir. *Avenging Angel*. New World Pictures, 1985.
Ovidie, dir. *Pornocracy: The New Sex Multinationals* [*Pornocratie: Les nouvelles multinationales du sexe*]. France: Magneto Presse, 2017.
Pakula, Alan J., dir. *Klute*. United States: Warner Bros., 1971.
Parrish, Robert, dir. *Fire Down Below*. United States: Warwick Film Productions, 1957.
Putnam, George, narrator. *Perversion for Profit*. United States: Citizens for Decent Literature, 1963.

Rau, Rama, dir. *League of Exotique Dancers*. United States: Storyline Entertainment, 2015.
Ritt, Martin, dir. *Nuts*. United States: Warner Bros., 1987.
Rosenberg, Stuart, dir. *WUSA*. United States: Paramount Pictures, 1970.
Rotsler, William, dir. *Agony of Love*. United States: Boxoffice International Pictures, 1966.
Royalle, Candida, dir. *My Surrender*. United States: Femme Productions, 1996.
Royalle, Candida, and R. Lauren Niemi, dirs. *Femme*. United States: Femme Productions, 1984.
Russell, Ken, dir. *Crimes of Passion*. United States: New World Pictures, 1984.
Saks, Gene, dir. *Cactus Flower*. United States: Frankovich Productions, 1969.
Scafaria, Lorene, dir. *Hustlers*. United States: STXfilms, 2019.
Schrader, Paul, dir. *American Gigolo*. United States: Paramount Pictures, 1980.
–, dir. *Hardcore*. United States: Columbia Pictures, 1979.
Scott, Catherine, dir. *The Scarlet Road*. Australia: Paradigm Pictures, 2011.
Scorsese, Martin, dir. *Taxi Driver*. United States: Columbia Pictures, 1976.
Seligman, Emma, dir. *Shiva Baby*. United States: Dimbo Pictures, 2021.
Sgarro, Nicholas, dir. *The Happy Hooker*. United States: Cannon Films, 1975.
Shea, Katt, dir. *Streets*. United States: Concorde Pictures, 1990.
Sherin, Edwin, dir. *Daughter of the Streets*. United States: 20th Century Fox Television, 1990.
Silvera, Joey, dir. *Easy Alice*. United States: California Continental Cinema, 1976.
Slocombe, Will, dir. *The Escort*. United States: Cloverhill Pictures, 2015.
Smith, Kevin, dir. *Zack and Miri Make a Porno*. United States: The Weinstein Company, 2008.
Soderbergh, Steven, dir. *The Girlfriend Experience*. United States: Magnolia Pictures, 2009.
–, dir. *Magic Mike*. United States: Iron Horse Entertainment, 2012.
Soloway, Joey, dir. *Afternoon Delight*. United States: 72 Productions, 2013.
Sonney, Dan, producer. *Striptease Girl*. United States: Sonney Amusement Enterprises, 1952.
Spinello, Barry J., dir. *Massage Parlor Wife*. United States: Global Pictures, 1975.
Stern, Sandor, dir. *Shattered Innocence*. United States: Green/Epstein Productions, 1988.
Thurber, Rawson Marshall, dir. *We're the Millers*. United States: New Line Cinema, 2013.
Thyberg, Ninja, dir. *Pleasure*. Sweden: Film i Väst, 2021.
Traeger, Michael, dir. *The Moguls*. United States: First Look International, 2005.
Tucker, George Loane, dir. *Traffic in Souls*. United States: Independent Moving Pictures Co. of America, 1913.
Verhoeven, Paul, dir. *Showgirls*. United Kingdom: United Artists, 1995.
VICE (@VICE). "Life as a Truck-Stop Stripper." YouTube video, 27:24. 12 February 2014. https://www.youtube.com/watch?v=eHlDo3Zj_58.

von Sternberg, Josef, dir. *The Blue Angel* [*Der Blaue Engel*]. Germany: Universum Film, 1930.
–, dir. *Shanghai Express*. United States: Paramount Pictures, 1932.
Wagoner, Bryce, dir. *After Porn Ends*. United States: Oxymoron Entertainment, 2012.
Walsh, Raoul, dir. *Sadie Thompson*. United States: Glora Swanson Productions, 1928.
Whale, James, dir. *Waterloo Bridge*. United States: Universal Pictures, 1931.
What the Butler Saw. United States: Mutoscope Company, early 1900s.
White, James H., dir. *Fatima's Coochee-Coochee Dance*. United States: Edison Manufacturing Company, 1896.
Wilcox, Lucy, dir. *Strippers*. Scotland: Firecracker Films, 2014.
Wilder, Billy, dir. *Irma La Douce*. United States: The Mirisch Corporation, 1963.
Wolmark, Gilbert, dir. *Little Girls*. United States: Olympic International Films, 1966.
Yu, Jessica, dir. *Breathing Lessons: The Life and Work of Mark O'Brien*. United States: Inscrutable Films, 1996.

List of TV Series

Ashford, Michelle, creator. *Masters of Sex*. United States: Showtime, 2013–16.
Austin, Alan, writer. *Frontline*. Season 5, episode 13, "Death of a Porn Queen." Aired 8 June 1987. PBS.
Blumenfield, Jay, and Anthony Marsh, dirs. *Family Business*. United States: Showtime, 2003–6.
Brooks, James L., and Allan Burns, creators. *The Mary Tyler Moore Show*. United States: CBS, 1970–7.
Brown, Kevin, presenter. *8 Minutes*. United States: A&E, 2015.
Calvert, Misha, creator. *Strut*. United States: Revry, 2021–.
Chase, David, creator. *The Sopranos*. United States: HBO, 1999–2007.
Hall, Katori, creator. *P-Valley*. United States: Starz, 2020–.
Hollander, David, creator. *American Gigolo*. United States: Showtime, 2022.
Kaplan, Patti, dir. *G String Divas*. United States: HBO, 2000.
Kerrigan, Lodge, and Amy Seimetz, creators. *The Girlfriend Experience*. United States: Starz, 2016–21.
Ling, Lisa, presenter. *This Is Life with Lisa Ling*. Season 1, episode 6, "Road Strip." Aired 2 November 2014. CNN.
Martin, Suzanne, creator. *The Client List*. United States: Lifetime, 2012–13.
Paige, Shante, producer. *Beyond the Pole*. United States: Urban Movie Channel, 2018–21.
Pelecanos, George, and David Simon, creators. *The Deuce*. United States: HBO, 2017–19.
Perrotta, Tom, creator. *Mrs. Fletcher*. United States: HBO, 2019.
Rhimes, Shonda, creator. *Grey's Anatomy*. United States: ABC, 2005–.
Springer, Jerry, presenter. *The Jerry Springer Show*. United States: NBC Universal Television Distribution, 1991–2018.
Sud, Veena, creator. *The Killing*. United States: AMC, 2011–14.
Vile, Jesse, and Ellena Wood, dirs. *The Ripper*. United States: Netflix, 2020.
White, Mike, creator. *The White Lotus*. United States: HBO, 2021–.
Willimon, Beau, creator. *House of Cards*. United States: Netflix, 2013–18.
Wolf, Dick, creator. *Law & Order*. United States: NBC Universal Television, 1990–.
Zuiker, Anthony E., creator. *CSI: Crime Scene Investigation*. United States: CBS, 2000–15.

Notes

Introduction: A New Sex Worker in Popular Culture

1 Full details for all films and TV series discussed throughout can be found, respectively, in the filmography and list of TV series at the end of the book.
2 Émile Zola, *Nana*, trans. Douglas Parmée (Oxford: Oxford University Press, 1992).
3 Russell Campbell, *Marked Women: Prostitutes and Prostitution in the Cinema* (Madison: University of Wisconsin Press, 2006).
4 James Robert Parish, *Prostitution in Hollywood Films: Plots, Critiques, Casts, and Credits for 389 Theatrical and Made-for-Television Releases* (Jefferson, NC: McFarland, 1992). Janet Gaynor won two Oscars for playing sex workers in *7th Heaven* (1927) and *Sunrise: A Song of Two Humans* (1927); Helen Hayes won for *The Sin of Madelon Claudet* (1931); Anne Baxter for *The Razor's Edge* (1946); Donna Reed for *From Here to Eternity* (1953); Jo Van Fleet for *East of Eden* (1955); Susan Hayward for *I Want to Live!* (1958); Elizabeth Taylor for *BUtterfield 8* (1960); Shirley Jones for *Elmer Gantry* (1960); and Jane Fonda for *Klute* (1971).
5 Today prostitution continues to be criminalized in every US state except Nevada, which allows brothels to operate in six of its seventeen counties. As of September 2023, there were nineteen legal brothels operating in Nevada. Different states have various prostitution laws, but broadly speaking, the buying, selling, offering, soliciting, or agreeing to engage in sexual acts for money is illegal. For a map of the US outlining prostitution-related crimes, see https://decriminalizesex.work/advocacy/prostitution-laws-by-state.
6 Helga Hallgrimsdottir, Rachel Phillips, and Cecilia Benoit, "Fallen Women and Rescued Girls: Social Stigma and Media Narratives of Sex Industry in Victoria, B.C, from 1980–2005," *Canadian Review of Sociology/Revue Canadienne de Sociologie* 43, no. 3 (August 2006): 276, https://doi.org/10.1111/j.1755-618X.2006.tb02224.x.

7. Andrea Dworkin and Catharine A. MacKinnon, *Pornography and Civil Rights: A New Day for Women's Equality* (Minneapolis: Organizing Against Pornography, 1988); Andrea Dworkin, *Right-Wing Women: The Politics of Domesticated Females* (New York: Putnam, 1983).
8. Rochelle L. Dalla, "Exposing the *Pretty Woman* Myth: A Qualitative Examination of the Lives of Female Streetwalking Prostitutes," *Journal of Sex Research* 37, no. 4 (2000): 344–53, https://doi.org/10.1080/00224490009552057.
9. Molly Haskell, *From Reverence to Rape: The Treatment of Women in the Movies* (New York: Holt, Rhinehart and Winston, 1973), 298.
10. Arlie Russell Hochschild, *The Managed Heart: Commercialization of Human Feeling* (Berkeley: University of California Press, 1983), 163–7.
11. Angela Jones, "'I Get Paid to Have Orgasms': Adult Webcam Models' Negotiation of Pleasure and Danger," *Signs: Journal of Women in Culture and Society* 42, no. 1 (Autumn 2016): 251, https://doi.org/10.1086/686758.
12. Kimberle Crenshaw, "Mapping the Margins: Intersectionality, Identity Politics, and Violence against Women of Color," *Stanford Law Review* 43, no. 6 (July 1991): 1241–99, https://doi.org/10.2307/1229039.
13. Lisa Duggan, *The Twilight of Equality: Neoliberalism, Cultural Politics, and the Attack on Democracy* (Boston: Beacon Books, 2004); Nina Power, *One-Dimensional Woman* (Winchester: Zero Books, 2009).
14. Jessica Spector, ed., *Prostitution and Pornography: Philosophical Debate about the Sex Industry* (Stanford, CA: Stanford University Press, 2006).
15. Jennifer Heineman, Rachel T. MacFarlane, and Barbara G. Brents, "Sex Industry and Sex Workers in Nevada," The Social Health of Nevada: Leading Indicators and Quality of Life in the Silver State (Las Vegas: UNLV Center for Democratic Culture, 2012), http://cdclv.unlv.edu/mission/index.html; Ronald Weitzer, *Legalizing Prostitution: From Illicit Vice to Lawful Business* (New York: New York University Press, 2012); Victoria's Friends, "Statistics," accessed 18 May 2022, http://www.victoriasfriends.com/statistics (site discontinued).
16. Tamarra Kemsley and Brad Hamilton, "Inside the $1 Billion Business of Erotic Massage Parlors," *New York Post*, 5 April 2015, http://nypost.com/2015/04/05/inside-the-1-billion-business-of-erotic-massage-parlors; Annie Lowrey, "In-Depth Report Details Economics of Sex Trade," *New York Times*, 12 March 2014, https://www.nytimes.com/2014/03/12/us/in-depth-report-details-economics-of-sex-trade.html.
17. "Global Sex Toys Market Size Share Report, 2021–2028," Grand View Research, accessed 7 December 2021, https://www.grandviewresearch.com/industry-analysis/sex-toys-market.
18. "Webcam Market Size and Trends Analysis Report, 2021–2028," Grand View Research, accessed 1 August 2021, https://www.grandviewresearch.com/industry-analysis/webcams-market. Market researchers have forecasted that until at least 2028 the industry will continue to grow at a rate of 12.9 per cent annually.

19 Derek Thompson, "8 Facts about the U.S. Sex Economy," *The Atlantic*, 12 March 2014, https://www.theatlantic.com/business/archive/2014/03/8-facts-about-the-us-sex-economy/284376.

20 Alexis Kleinman, "Porn Sites Get More Visitors than Netflix, Amazon and Twitter Combined," *HuffPost*, 4 May 2013, http://www.huffingtonpost.com/2013/05/03/internet-porn-stats_n_3187682.html.

21 Catherine Hakim, "Erotic Capital," *European Sociological Review* 26, no. 5 (October 2010): 499–518, https://doi.org/10.1093/esr/jcq014.

22 Charlie Cooper, "'Decriminalise Prostitution': Top Medical Journal *Lancet* Calls for Global Action to Protect Sex Workers from HIV," *The Independent*, 22 July 2014, http://www.independent.co.uk/life-style/health-and-families/decriminalise-prostitution-top-medical-journal-lancet-calls-for-global-action-to-protect-sex-workers-9620273.html; Laurie K. Burtram and Megan Ross, curators, *Canada's Oldest Profession: Sex Work and Bawdy House Legislation*, organized and presented by the University of Toronto Libraries, 2 March–1 June 2016, https://exhibits.library.utoronto.ca/exhibits/show/bawdy.

23 Quoted in Juno Mac and Molly Smith, *Revolting Prostitutes: The Fight for Sex Workers' Rights* (London: Verso, 2018), 16.

24 Tawandah Mustafah, quoted in Caroline Mortimer, "Amnesty International Officially Calls for Complete Decriminalization of Sex Work," *The Independent*, 27 May 2016, https://www.independent.co.uk/life-style/health-and-families/health-news/amnesty-international-officially-calls-for-complete-decriminalisation-of-sex-work-a7050021.html.

25 Jonah E. Bromwich, "Manhattan to Stop Prosecuting Prostitution, Part of Nationwide Shift," *New York Times*, 21 April 2021, https://www.nytimes.com/2021/04/21/nyregion/manhattan-to-stop-prosecuting-prostitution.html.

26 Helga Hallgrimsdottir et al., "Sporting Girls, Streetwalkers, Inmates of Houses of Ill Repute: Media Narratives and the Historical Mutability of Prostitution Stigmas," *Sociological Perspectives* 51, no. 1 (March 2008): 119–38, https://doi.org/10.1525/sop.2008.51.1.119; John Lowman, "Violence and the Outlaw Status of (Street) Prostitution in Canada," *Violence Against Women* 6, no. 9 (September 2000): 987–1011, https://doi.org/10.1177/10778010022182245; Susan Strega et al., "Never Innocent Victims: Street Sex Workers in Canadian Print Media," *Violence Against Women* 20, no. 1 (January 2014): 6–25, https://doi.org/10.1177/1077801213520576.

27 Mary Emily O'Hara, "How Sex Workers Dominated the News in 2015," *Daily Dot*, 31 December 2015, https://www.dailydot.com/irl/2015-sex-work.

28 Mac McClelland, "Is Prostitution Just Another Job?," *The Cut*, 21 March 2016, https://www.thecut.com/2016/03/sex-workers-legalization-c-v-r.html.

29 Emily Bazelon, "Should Prostitution Be a Crime?," *New York Times Magazine*, 5 May 2016, https://www.nytimes.com/2016/05/08/magazine/should-prostitution-be-a-crime.html.

30 Iris Pase, "Tips for Reporting on Sex Work," *International Journalists' Network*, 19 February 2021, https://ijnet.org/en/story/tips-reporting-about-sex-work.
31 Pamela Paul, "What It Means to Call Prostitution 'Sex Work,'" *New York Times*, 17 August 2023, https://www.nytimes.com/2023/08/17/opinion/prostitution-sex-work.html.
32 Margaret Cho, quoted in Lily Burana, "Margaret Cho Wants to Talk about Sex Work," *New York Times*, 4 November 2015, https://www.nytimes.com/2015/11/03/fashion/margaret-cho-sex-work.html.
33 Janet Mock, quoted in Catie L'Heureux, "Read Janet Mock's Empowering Speech on Trans Women of Color and Sex Workers," *The Cut*, 21 January 2017, http://nymag.com/thecut/2017/01/read-janet-mocks-speech-at-the-womens-march-on-washington-trans-women-of-color-sex-workers.html.
34 Melissa Gira Grant, "Organized Labor's Newest Heroes: Strippers," *The Atlantic*, 9 November 2012, https://www.theatlantic.com/sexes/archive/2012/11/organized-labors-newest-heroes-strippers/265376.
35 Rachel Abrams, "Sex Shop Workers Welcome the Protection of Retail Union," *New York Times*, 23 May 2016, https://www.nytimes.com/2016/05/24/business/sex-shop-workers-welcome-the-protections-of-a-retail-union.html; CUPE Organizing (@joincupe), "Today we are very excited to welcome the sex workers at Maggie's Toronto Sex Worker's Action Project, who voted unanimously to join CUPE!," X (formerly Twitter), 8 September 2021, https://twitter.com/joincupe/status/1435737564837728260.
36 NPR, "Strippers in the U.S. Want Better Work Conditions. Some Are Trying to Unionize," *Consider This*, 16 September 2022, https://www.npr.org/2022/09/14/1122937491/strippers-in-the-u-s-want-better-work-conditions-some-are-trying-to-unionize.
37 Ronald Weitzer, "Sociology of Sex Work," *Annual Review of Sociology* 35 (August 2009): 213–34, https://doi.org/10.1146/annurev-soc-070308-120025.
38 McClelland, "Is Prostitution"; Zack Budryk, "Poll: Majority Supports Decriminalizing Sex Work," *The Hill*, 30 January 2020, https://thehill.com/regulation/other/480725-poll-majority-supports-decriminalizing-sex-work.
39 Gayle Rubin, "Thinking Sex: Notes for a Radical Theory of the Politics of Sexuality," in *Pleasure and Danger: Exploring Female Sexuality*, ed. Carole Vance (New York: Routledge, 1984), 267.
40 Campbell, *Marked Women*, 8.
41 Lisa McLaughlin, "Discourses of Prostitution/Discourses of Sexuality," *Critical Studies in Mass Communication* 8, no. 3 (1991): 249–72, https://doi.org/10.1080/15295039109366797.
42 Juana Gallego, "Cinema and Prostitution: How Prostitution Is Interpreted in Cinematographic Fiction," *Quaderns Del CAC* 8, no. 2 (2010): 63–71.
43 Nickie Roberts, *Whores in History: Prostitution in Western Society* (London: HarperCollins, 1992), xi.

44 Shulamith Firestone, *The Dialectic of Sex: The Case for Feminist Revolution* (New York: William Morrow and Company, 1970); David Henry Sterry and R.J. Martin Jr., eds., *Hos, Hookers, Call Girls, and Rent Boys: Professionals Writing on Life, Love, Money, and Sex* (Brooklyn: Soft Skull Press, 2009).

45 In *The Second Sex*, Simone de Beauvoir argues that women in patriarchal society are "defined and differentiated with reference to man ... he is the Absolute – she is the Other." Simone de Beauvoir, *The Second Sex*, trans. Constance Borde and Sheila Malovany-Chevallier (New York: Vintage, 2011), 16. Sex workers exemplify an accentuation of this "Other" status, according to Beauvoir, who was a defender of sex workers.

46 Gerda Lerner, *The Creation of Patriarchy* (New York: Oxford University Press, 1986).

47 Elizabeth C. Hirschman and Barbara B. Stern, "Consuming Beings: A Feminist Perspective on Prostitution in American Film," *The American Journal of Semiotics* 11, no. 3–4 (1994): 267.

48 Campbell, *Marked Women*, 243.

49 Campbell, *Marked Women*, 361. Campbell elaborates: "The figure of the prostitute who engages in the trade willingly and enthusiastically can arouse great anxieties in the patriarchal mind, both as a woman who initiates sex independently of her male partner and as a woman, who, teeming with sexuality to her advantage, steps out of male control and achieves individual autonomy."

50 Andrew Collins, "Turning a Trick with Oldest Profession in Film," *The Guardian*, 30 April 2000, https://www.theguardian.com/film/2000/apr/30/2; Haskell, *From Reverence to Rape*; Eithne Johnson, "The Business of Sex: Prostitution and Capitalism in Four Recent Films," *Journal of Popular Film and Television* 12, no. 4 (1984): 148–55, https://doi.org/10.1080/01956051.1985.10661981.

51 McLaughlin, "Discourses," 257.

52 Haskell, *From Reverence to Rape*; Mick LaSalle, *Complicated Women: Sex and Power in Pre-Code Hollywood* (New York: St. Martin's Press, 2000).

53 Parish, *Prostitution in Hollywood Films*.

54 "Excerpts from the *Motion Picture Herald*, 11 August 1934," Margaret Herrick Library Digital Collections, accessed 13 November 2023, https://digitalcollections.oscars.org/digital/collection/p15759coll11/id/11871.

55 Meryl Streep, quoted in Collins, "Turning a Trick."

56 Rosalind Gill, "Postfeminist Media Culture: Elements of a Sensibility," *Cultural Studies* 10, no. 2 (May 2007): 147–66, https://doi.org/10.1177/1367549407075898.

57 Gail Dines, *Pornland: How Porn Has Hijacked Our Sexuality* (Boston: Beacon Press, 2011).

58 Brian McNair, *Striptease Culture: Sex, Media and the Democratisation of Culture* (London: Routledge, 2002).

59 Ariel Levy, *Female Chauvinist Pigs: Women and the Rise of Raunch Culture* (New York: Free Press, 2005).

60 Maddy Coy, Josephine Wakeling, and Maria Garner, "Selling Sex Sells: Representations of Prostitution and the Sex Industry in Sexualized Popular Culture as Symbolic Violence," *Women's Studies International Forum* 34, no. 5 (September–October 2011): 441–8, https://doi.org/10.1016/j.wsif.2011.05.008.

61 Marina Della Giusta and Laura Scuriatti, "The Show Must Go On: Making Money Glamourizing Oppression," *European Journal of Women's Studies* 12, no. 1 (February 2005): 31–44, https://doi.org/10.1177/1350506805048854; Feona Attwood, "No Money Shot? Commerce, Pornography and New Sex Taste Cultures," *Sexualities* 10, no. 4 (October 2007): 441–56, https://doi.org/10.1177/1363460707080982. In "Selling Sex Sells," Maddy Coy, Josephine Wakeling, and Maria Garner have described this mainstreaming of sex work aesthetics as "ho chic," a trend in which sex work is connected positively to everyday objects and activities, fashion, and language through the lens of empowerment. Marina Della Giusta and Laura Scuriatti similarly found that the pretend act of prostitution has been an effective marketing gambit to sell clothing and, in their content analyses, found that luxury designers Gucci and Louis Vuitton both presented advertising campaigns in which models were made to look like stereotypes of sex workers. Feona Attwood examined contemporary advertising and found that images associated with sex work and pornography are being used to market consumer products to women.

62 Rosalind Gill and Akane Kanai, "Mediating Neoliberal Capitalism: Affect, Subjectivity and Inequality," *Journal of Communication* 68, no. 2 (April 2018): 323, https://doi.org/10.1093/joc/jqy002.

63 Catherine Roach, *Stripping, Sex, and Popular Culture* (Oxford: Berg, 2007).

64 Della Giusta and Scuriatti, "Show Must Go On," 38.

65 According to Jane Arthurs, docu-porn is a double-edged sword. As she writes, "not all documentaries about the sex industry are inevitably exploitative, but some certainly are," while others have led to a "better understanding of and empathy with the women involved, which destabilizes the rigid boundary between 'us' and 'them.'" Jane Arthurs, *Television and Sexuality: Regulations and the Politics of Taste* (Maidenhead: Open University Press, 2004), 109.

66 Karen Boyle, "Courting Consumers and Legitimizing Exploitation: The Representation of Commercial Sex in Television Documentaries," *Feminist Media Studies* 8, no. 1 (2008): 36–50, https://doi.org/10.1080/14680770701824894.

67 Mac and Smith, *Revolting Prostitutes*, 4.

68 Stuart Hall, "The Rediscovery of 'Ideology': Return of the Repressed in Media," in *Culture, Society and the Media*, ed. Michael Gurevitch et al. (London: Routledge, 1982), 77, https://doi.org/10.4324/9780203978092.

69 Hakim, "Erotic Capital," 88.

70 Erving Goffman, *Stigma: Notes on the Management of Spoiled Identity* (New York: Simon and Schuster, 1963), 1.

71 Goffman, *Stigma*, 5.

72 Haskell, *From Reverence to Rape*, 9.
73 Sex workers have historically faced – and continue to face – huge barriers to self-representation due to the hegemony of anti–sex work feminism, limited outlets in media for sex workers to tell their stories, and the social stigma that sex work continues to carry in society at large. Canadian writer Amber Dawn powerfully articulates this in her memoir: "It takes an abundance of strength and inspiration to write and publish a book about sex work. It continues to perplex me that, in most large cities, like my own hometown of Vancouver, there are an estimated 10,000 people, mainly women, working as prostitution-based sex workers – this statistic includes only those who've been counted – and yet we rarely hear from them. Why do we so seldom hear from the voice of those whose experience is so widespread?" Amber Dawn, *How Poetry Saved My Life: A Hustler's Memoir* (Vancouver: Arsenal Pulp Press, 2013), 12.
74 Hallgrimsdottir, Phillips, and Benoit, "Fallen Women," 267.
75 Danielle A. Sawicki et al., "Culturally Competent Health Care for Sex Workers: An Examination of Myths That Stigmatize Sex Work and Hinder Access to Care," *Sexual and Relationship Therapy* 34, no. 3 (February 2019): 355–71, https://doi.org/10.1080/14681994.2019.1574970.
76 Madison Miller, "Mug Shots Released of Nine Women Arrested in Prostitution Sting in Beaumont," *Fox4Beaumont.com*, 7 October 2016, http://fox4beaumont.com/news/local/mug-shots-released-of-nine-women-arrested-in-prostitution-sting-in-beaumont; "Mugshots (Orange County Jail Booking Blotter)," *Orlando Sentinel*, accessed 30 June 2017, http://mugshots.orlandosentinel.com/mobile.php (site discontinued).
77 Canadian Press, "Olympian Suzy Favor Hamilton, Who Secretly Worked as a Las Vegas Escort, Reclaims Her Life after Bipolar Diagnosis," *National Post*, 17 September 2015, http://nationalpost.com/sports/olympics/olympian-suzy-favor-hamilton-who-secretly-worked-as-a-las-vegas-escort-reclaims-her-life-after-bipolar-diagnosis.
78 E.J. Dickson, "Fired for Doing Porn: The New Employment Discrimination," *Salon*, 30 September 2013, https://www.salon.com/2013/09/30/fired_for_doing_porn_the_new_employment_discrimination; Roy Greenslade, "Journalist Fired for Being a Stripper Wants Her Newspaper Job Back," *The Guardian*, 27 June 27, 2012, https://www.theguardian.com/media/greenslade/2012/jun/27/usa-women.
79 Margaret A. Baldwin, "Split at the Root: Prostitution and Feminist Discourses of Law Reform," in *Prostitution and Pornography: Philosophical Debate about the Sex Industry*, ed. Jessica Spector (Stanford, CA: Stanford University Press, 2006), 106–47; Sarah Mirk, "More Sex Workers Are Killed in the US than Any Other Country," *Bitch Media*, 14 December 2014, https://www.bitchmedia.org/post/more-sex-workers-are-killed-in-the-us-than-any-other-country (site discontinued); Christine Pelisek, *Grim Sleeper: The Lost Women of South Central* (Berkley, CA: Counterpoint, 2016).

80 Adam Janos, "Why Are Sex Workers Often a Killer's Victim of Choice?," *AETV.com*, last modified 30 June 2022, https://www.aetv.com/real-crime/why-do-serial-killers-target-sex-workers.
81 Michael Havers, quoted in Alexandra Topping and Helen Pidd, "Police Offer Heartfelt Apology to Families of Peter Sutcliffe Victims," *The Guardian*, 13 November 2020, https://www.theguardian.com/uk-news/2020/nov/13/police-offer-heartfelt-apology-to-families-of-yorkshire-ripper-peter-sutcliffe-victims.
82 Mahita Gajanan, "The True Story behind the Netflix Movie *Lost Girls*," *Time*, 13 March 2020, https://time.com/5801794/lost-girls-netflix-true-story.
83 Robert Kolker, "The Botched Hunt for the Gilgo Beach Killer," *New York Times*, last modified 3 November 2023, https://www.nytimes.com/2023/10/19/magazine/gilgo-beach-killer-suffolk-police.html.
84 Horace M. Newcomb and Paul M. Hirsch, "Television as a Cultural Forum: Implications of Research," *Quarterly Review of Film Studies* 8, no. 3 (1983): 45, https://doi.org/10.1080/10509208309361170.
85 John Fiske, quoted in Imre Szeman and Susie O'Brien, *Popular Culture: A User's Guide*, 3rd ed. (Toronto: Nelson Education, 2014), 11.
86 Pseudonyms have been used for the privacy of the interviewees.
87 Cecilia Benoit et al., "Prostitution Stigma and Its Effect on the Working Conditions, Personal Lives, and Health of Sex Workers," *Journal of Sex Research* 55, no. 4–5 (2017): 457–71, https://doi.org/10.1080/00224499.2017.1393652; Emily van der Meulen, Elya M. Durisin, and Victoria Love, *Selling Sex: Experience, Advocacy and Research on Sex Work in Canada* (Vancouver: UBC Press, 2013).
88 Carol Leigh, quoted in "Notable People," Decriminalize Sex Work, accessed 15 January 2024, https://decriminalizesex.work/why-decriminalization/notable-people.
89 Melissa Petro, "The H-Word: She Works Hard for the Money (So You Better Treat Her Right," *Bitch Media*, 28 October 2011, https://www.bitchmedia.org/post/the-h-word-she-works-hard-for-the-money (site discontinued).
90 On sex trafficking – the unlawful transportation, confinement, indenture, and exploitation of women and children for the purpose of sexual enslavement – see especially Kathryn Farr, *Sex Trafficking: The Global Market in Women and Children* (New York: Worth Publishers, 2005); Janet E. Halley et al., "From the International to the Local in Feminist Legal Responses to Rape, Prostitution/Sex Work and Sex Trafficking: Four Studies in Contemporary Governance Feminism," *Harvard Journal of Law & Gender* 29, no. 2 (2006): 335–423; Sheila Jeffreys, *The Industrial Vagina: The Political Economy of the Global Sex Trade* (London: Routledge, 2008), https://doi.org/10.4324/9780203698303.
91 Teela Sanders, *Paying for Pleasure: Men Who Buy Sex* (Cullompton, UK: Willan Publishing, 2008), 439; my emphasis.
92 Weitzer, *Legalizing Prostitution*, 12.

93 Elizabeth Bernstein, *Temporarily Yours: Intimacy, Authenticity, and the Commerce of Sex* (Chicago: University of Chicago Press, 2007); "Sex Work for the Middle Classes," *Sexualities* 10, no. 4 (October 2007): 473–88, https://doi.org/10.1177/1363460707080984.

94 I exclude from my study popular culture representations of street-based sex workers (which tend to advance a prohibitionist feminist perspective), women in euphemized forms of sex work (such as sugar babies), male sex workers, and phone sex operators, though these subjects all merit further exploration.

95 Raymond Williams, *Marxism and Literature* (Oxford: Oxford University Press, 1977), 198.

96 bell hooks, quoted in Sut Jhally, dir., *bell hooks: Cultural Criticism and Transformation*, film transcript (Northampton, MA: Media Education Foundation, 2005), 2, http://www.mediaed.org/transcripts/Bell-Hooks-Transcript.pdf.

97 Haskell, *From Reverence to Rape*, 45.

98 Deborah R. Brock, *Making Trouble, Making Work: Prostitution as a Social Problem* (Toronto: University of Toronto Press, 1998), https://doi.org/10.3138/9781442676930.

99 Joanna Brewis and Stephen Linstead, *Sex, Work, and Sex Work: Eroticizing Organization* (London: Routledge, 2000), https://doi.org/10.4324/9780203360965.

100 Sharon Hays, *The Cultural Contradiction of Motherhood* (New Haven, CT: Yale University Press, 1996).

101 Rebecca Bromwich and Monique Marie DeJong, eds., *Mothers, Mothering and Sex Work* (Bradford, ON: Demeter Press, 2015).

102 Juno Mac and Molly Smith point out that prohibitionist feminists have used the *idea* of the sex worker as a metaphor for the universal exploited woman in patriarchal capitalism without offering "much practical support for sex workers' efforts to tackle criminalization." Early sex worker activists picked up on this, like in 1977, when a sex worker collective in the feminist magazine *Spare Rib* entreated the women's liberation movement to "think about the whole thing [prostitution] and discuss it, but not just use it," calling out how the very "word prostitute [had been used] in a really nasty way ... to sum up their idea of the exploited situation of women." Mac and Smith, *Revolting Prostitutes*, 2. Anne McClintock echoes this idea: "In the arguments of the anti–sex work lobby, the prostitute becomes the other's other, a mute, cutout paper doll.... The slave-doll image serves as a ventriloquist's dummy, through which (generally white, middle-class) women voice their interests, at the expense of the sex workers' needs." Anne McClintock, "Sex Workers and Sex Work: Introduction," *Social Text* 37 (Winter 1993): 8–9, https://www.jstor.org/stable/466255.

1. Working It: Popular Culture, Feminism, and Sex Work

1 Lizzie Borden, quoted in Lynne Jackson, "Labor Relations: An Interview with Lizzie Borden," *Cinéaste* 15, no. 3 (1987): 4, quoted in Campbell, *Marked Women*, 311.

2 Carol Leigh, quoted in Cheryl Yanek, "The Real New York City: Friendship, Sex Work and Beyond," self-published zine, 2001. See also Carol Leigh, "Inventing Sex Work," in *Whores and Other Feminists*, ed. Jill Nagle (New York: Routledge, 1997), 223–31.
3 Valerie Jenness, "From Sex as Sin to Sex as Work: COYOTE and the Reorganization of Prostitution as a Social Problem," *Social Problems* 37, no. 3 (August 1990): 403–20, https://doi.org/10.2307/800751; Lacey Sloan and Stephanie Wahab, "Feminist Voices on Sex Work: Implications for Social Work," *Affilia* 15, no. 4 (Winter 2000): 457–79, https://doi.org/10.1177/088610990001500402.

The sex workers' rights movement in the 1970s played a crucial role in introducing the labour paradigm to a wider audience. The mandate of COYOTE was to improve working conditions for sex workers, reduce hostility and violence, and rally for the decriminalization of sex work. While sex workers have organized themselves since the 1600s, the reach of COYOYE was new. With gravitas and style, the leadership of COYOTE established a safe community for diverse sex workers to discuss their experiences of labour, including its racial, sexual, class, and personal dimensions. Its advocacy and fundraising initiatives, including St. James's pioneering "Hooker's Ball," enhanced public opinion about sex workers, associating them with positive qualities.
4 Margo St. James, quoted in David Templeton, "Bedside Manner: Margo St. James on the Power of Sex and *Dangerous Beauty*," *Sonoma County Independent*, 5 March 1998, http://www.metroactive.com/papers/sonoma/03.05.98/talk-pix-9809.html.
5 Dworkin, *Right-Wing Women*, 61.
6 Kate Millett, *Sexual Politics* (New York: Doubleday, 1971), 98.
7 Margo St. James, quoted in Robert Andrews, *The Columbia Dictionary of Quotations* (New York: Columbia University Press, 1993), 743.
8 Matthew Monagle, "The Oldest Profession: Looking Back at Alan J. Pakula's Klute," *Film School Rejects*, 28 August 2015, https://filmschoolrejects.com/jane-fonda-klute/.
9 Jane Fonda, "44th Academy Awards Acceptance Speech," transcript of speech delivered at Dorothy Chandler Pavilion, Los Angeles, CA, 10 April 1972, Academy Awards Acceptance Speech Database, http://aaspeechesdb.oscars.org/link/044-3.
10 Roger Ebert, "Klute," *RogerEbert.com*, 1 January 1971, https://www.rogerebert.com/reviews/klute-1971.
11 Kat Banyard, *The Equality Illusion: The Truth about Women and Men Today* (London: Faber and Faber, 2010); Andrea Dworkin, "Prostitution and Male Supremacy," *Michigan Journal of Gender and Law* 1, no. 1 (1993): 1–12; Catharine A. MacKinnon, *Women's Lives, Men's Laws* (Cambridge, MA: Belknap Press of Harvard University Press, 2005); Millett, *Sexual Politics*.
12 Jill Nagle, "Introduction," in *Whores and Other Feminists*, ed. Jill Nagle (New York: Routledge, 1997), 1–15; Carol Queen, "Sex Radical Politics, Sex-Positive Feminist Thought, and Whore Stigma," in *Whores and Other Feminists*, ed. Jill Nagle (New York: Routledge, 1997), 125–35; Patrick Califia, *Public Sex: The Culture of Radical Sex* (Pittsburgh, PA: Cleis Press, 1994).
13 Spector, *Prostitution and Pornography*.

14 Queen, "Sex Radical Politics"; Ronald Weitzer, "Prostitution as a Form of Work," *Sociology Compass* 1, no. 1 (September 2007): 143–55, https://doi.org/10.1111/j.1751-9020.2007.00010.x.
15 Meulen, Durisin, and Love, *Selling Sex*, 1.
16 Hilary Evans, *Harlots, Whores and Hookers: A History of Prostitution* (New York: Taplinger, 1979), 57.
17 Zola, *Nana*, 190.
18 In English translation, see Cesare Lombroso and William Ferrero, *The Female Offender* (New York: D. Appleton and Company, 1898), 57.
19 Marilynn Wood Hill, *Their Sisters' Keepers: Prostitution in New York City: 1830–1870* (Berkeley: University of California Press, 1993), 62.
20 Carole Pateman, *The Sexual Contract* (Stanford, CA: Stanford University Press, 1988), 196.
21 Havelock Ellis, quoted in Evans, *Harlots, Whores and Hookers*, 115.
22 William Acton, quoted in Khalid Kishtainy, *The Prostitute in Progressive Literature* (London: Allison and Busby, 1982), 42.
23 William Sanger, *The History of Prostitution: Its Extent, Causes, and Effects throughout the World* (New York: Harper & Brothers, 1858), 18.
24 Sanger, *History of Prostitution*, 19.
25 Scholarship on sex work has crossed disciplines in the past several decades. Today, "sex work studies" cover a range of areas, including sex work and public health: Cathy Spatz Widom and Joseph B. Kuhns, "Childhood Victimization and Subsequent Risk for Promiscuity, Prostitution, and Teenage Pregnancy: A Prospective Study," *American Journal of Public Health* 86, no. 11 (November 1996): 1607–12, https://psycnet.apa.org/doi/10.2105/AJPH.86.11.1607; indoor sex work: Vicky Bungay et al., "Structure and Agency: Reflections from an Exploratory Study of Vancouver Indoor Sex Workers," *Culture, Health & Sexuality* 13, no. 1 (January 2011): 15–29, https://doi.org/10.1080/13691058.2010.517324; Eva Büschi, "Sex Work and Violence: Focusing on Managers in the Indoor Sex Industry," *Sexualities* 17, no. 5–6 (September 2014): 724–41, https://doi.org/10.1177/1363460714531271; Weitzer, *Legalizing Prostitution*; outdoor sex work: Bernard Cohen, *Deviant Street Networks: Prostitution in New York City* (Lexington, MA: Lexington Books, 1980); Lowman, "Violence"; feminist theories of sex work: Karni Kissil and Maureen Davey, "Prostitution Debate in Feminism: Current Policy and Clinical Issues Facing an Invisible Population," *Journal of Feminist Family Therapy* 22, no. 1 (2010): 1–21, https://doi.org/10.1080/08952830903453604; Rubin, "Thinking Sex"; sex worker activism: Leslie Ann Jeffrey and Gayle MacDonald, *Sex Workers in the Maritimes Talk Back* (Vancouver: UBC Press, 2006); postcolonial sex work: Kamala Kempadoo and Jo Doezema, *Global Sex Workers: Rights, Resistance, and Redefinition* (New York: Routledge, 1998), https://doi.org/10.4324/9781315865768; sex work and the military: Cynthia Enloe, *Maneuvers: The International Politics of Militarizing Women's Lives* (Berkeley: University of California Press, 2000); sex tourism:

Denise Brennan, *What's Love Got to Do with It? Transnational Desires and Sex Tourism in the Dominican Republic* (Durham, NC: Duke University Press, 2004), https://doi.org/10.1215/9780822385400; Amalia L. Cabezas, "Between Love and Money: Sex, Tourism, and Citizenship in Cuba and the Dominican Republic," *Signs: Journal of Women in Culture and Society* 29, no. 4 (Summer 2014): 987–1015, https://doi.org/10.1086/382627; grounded sex worker research: Frances M. Shaver, "Sex Worker Research: Methodological and Ethical Challenges," *Journal of Interpersonal Violence* 20, no. 3 (2005): 296–319, https://doi.org/10.1177/0886260504274340; Emily van der Meulen, "Action Research with Sex Workers: Dismantling Barriers and Building Bridges," *Action Research* 9, no. 4 (December 2011): 370–84, https://doi.org/10.1177/1476750311409767; sex work and stigma: Juline A. Koken, "Independent Female Escort's Strategies for Coping with Sex Work Related Stigma," *Sexuality and Culture* 16 (2012): 209–29, https://doi.org/10.1007/s12119-011-9120-3; Ronald Weitzer, "Resistance to Sex Worker Stigma," *Sexualities* 21, no. 5–6 (2018): 717–29; digital sex work: Scott Cunningham and Todd D. Kendall, "Prostitution 2.0: The Changing Face of Sex Work," *Journal of Urban Economics* 69, no. 3 (May 2011): 273–87, https://doi.org/10.1016/j.jue.2010.12.001; Nicola M. Döring, "The Internet's Impact on Sexuality: A Critical Review of 15 Years of Research," *Computers in Human Behavior* 25, no. 5 (September 2009): 1089–101, https://doi.org/10.1016/j.chb.2009.04.003; Angela Jones, "Sex Work in the Digital Era," *Sociology Compass* 9, no. 7 (July 2015): 558–70, https://doi.org/10.1111/soc4.12282; Teela Sanders, "Researching the Online Sex Work Community," in *Virtual Methods: Issues in Social Research on the Internet*, ed. Christine Hine (Oxford: Berg, 2005), 67–79; Theresa Senft, *Camgirls: Celebrity and Community in the Age of Social Networks* (New York: Peter Lang, 2008); sex workers in news media: Hallgrimsdottir, Phillips, and Benoit, "Fallen Women"; Erin Gibbs Van Brunschot, Rosalind A. Sydie, and Catherine Knull, "Images of Prostitution: The Prostitute and Print Media," *Women & Criminal Justice* 10, no. 4 (1999): 56–78, https://doi.org/10.1300/J012v10n04_03; and most germane to my work, sex workers in popular culture: Campbell, *Marked Women*; Karen Boyle, "Selling the Selling of Sex: The Secret Diary of a Call-Girl on Screen," *Feminist Media Studies*, 10, no. 1 (January 2010): 113–16; Jennifer C. Dunn, "'It's Not Just Sex, It's a Profession': Reframing Prostitution through Text and Context," *Communication Studies* 63, no. 3 (2012): 345–63, https://doi.org/10.1080/10510974.2012.678924; Kaitlynn Mendes et al., "Commentary and Criticism: Representations of Sex Workers," *Feminist Media Studies* 10, no. 1 (January 2010): 99–116, https://doi.org/10.1080/14680770903457469.

26 Laura María Agustín, *Sex at the Margins: Migration, Labour Markets and the Rescue Industry* (London: Zed Books, 2007). See also Paula Bartley, "Preventing Prostitution: The Ladies' Association for the Care and Protection of Young Girls in Birmingham, 1887–1914," *Women's History Review* 7, no. 1 (March 1998): 37–60, https://doi.org/10.1080/09612029800200160.

27 Quoted in Laura María Agustín, "Fallen Women, Including the One Charles Dickens Didn't Save," *Naked Anthropologist* (blog), 11 February 2012, https://www.lauraagustin.com/fallen-women-including-the-one-who-refused-to-be-saved-by-charles-dickens.
28 Mary Wollstonecraft, quoted in Pateman, *Sexual Contract*, 51.
29 Friedrich Engels, quoted in Kishtainy, *Prostitute in Progressive Literature*, 47.
30 Friedrich Engels, quoted in Hirschman and Stern, "Consuming Beings," 230.
31 Emma Goldman, *Anarchism and Other Essays* (New York: Mother Earth Publishing Association, 1911), 200.
32 Goldman, *Anarchism*, 186.
33 Goldman, *Anarchism*, 188.
34 Gill, "Postfeminist Media Culture," 161.
35 Weitzer, *Legalizing Prostitution*, 12.
36 Kathleen Barry, *The Prostitution of Sexuality: The Global Exploitation of Women* (New York: New York University Press, 1995); MacKinnon, *Women's Lives, Men's Laws*; Millett, *Sexual Politics*; Maggie O'Neill, *Prostitution and Feminism: Towards a Politics of Feeling* (Malden, MA: Polity Press, 2000); Janice G. Raymond, *Not a Choice, Not a Job: Exposing the Myths about Prostitution and the Global Sex Trade* (Washington, DC: Potomac Books, 2013).
37 Kathleen Barry, *Female Sexual Slavery* (New York: New York University Press, 1984), 1.
38 Pateman, *Sexual Contract*.
39 Carter Vednita and Evelina Giobbe, "Duet: Prostitution, Racism, and Feminist Discourse," in *Prostitution and Pornography: Philosophical Debate about the Sex Industry*, ed. Jessica Spector (Stanford, CA: Stanford University Press, 2006), 28.
40 Sheila Jeffreys argues that in the 1980s the mainstreaming of pornography created a system in which the "commercialization of women's subordination" became part of the "corporate sphere." She calls this a "public relations victory for the international sex industry." Jeffreys, *Industrial Vagina*, 1, 3, 15.
41 Dworkin, *Right-Wing Women*; Melissa Farley, "Bad for the Body, Bad for the Heart: Prostitution Harms Women Even If Legalized or Decriminalized," *Violence Against Women* 10, no. 10 (October 2004): 1087–125, https://doi.org/10.1177/107780120426860.
42 Dworkin, *Right-Wing Women*.
43 Janice G. Raymond, "Prostitution Is Rape That Is Paid For," *Los Angeles Times*, 11 December 1995, B6.
44 Jeffreys, *Industrial Vagina*; Raymond, *Not a Choice*.
45 Barry, *Prostitution of Sexuality*.
46 Baldwin, "Split at the Root," 137.
47 Dworkin, "Prostitution and Male Supremacy," 1.
48 Jacqueline Comte, "Decriminalization of Sex Work: Feminist Discourses in Light of New Research," *Sexuality and Culture* 18 (2013): 196–217, https://doi.org/10.1007/s12119-013-9174-5.

49 Campbell, *Marked Women*, 10.
50 Parish, *Prostitution in Hollywood Films*, xiii.
51 Baldwin, "Split at the Root"; Barry, *Female Sexual Slavery*.
52 Barry, *Prostitution of Sexuality*, 34. Barry proposes that even everyday acts performed by sex workers, including the donning of costumes and stage names, makes disassociation a job requirement.
53 *Monster* elicits a range of emotions, from empathy to compassion to despair, by focusing on Wuornos's life beyond sex work, particularly on her relationship with her girlfriend in the film, Shelby Wall (played by Christina Ricci). Yet, the film doesn't shy from depicting the gritty reality of her life. One poignant moment shows her giving herself a sponge bath in a gas station bathroom after being violently assaulted. The haunting and awe-striking image captures Wuornos's resilience and anguish as she futilely tries to wash away the sensation of violation seeping from every pore of her skin. But what truly sets *Monster* apart is its depiction of Wuornos as a self-possessed woman who never yearns for rescue from her profession nor redemption through "respectable" work. She defiantly scoffs at the idea of upward mobility through a hypothetical career change, asking us to reconsider societal norms: "Fuckin' office job! Who the fuck wants a job like that? You fuckin' sit at a little desk, you got your little phone, you got your little fuckin' piece of paper, your little pen, you write shit down, blah blah blah. Fuck, a monkey could do that shit, man!" Wuornos doesn't kowtow to the stereotype of the lost, gullible girl that prohibitionist and mainstream media often portrays. Despite her background, Wuornos is portrayed as the master of her own fate, and it is her ownership of that fate that dignifies her, even if it often causes her life to take turns for the worse. The very title of the film – *Monster* – subverts expectations of Wuornos being a victim of monstrous men or being a monster herself as a killer. The title actually refers to a sweet childhood memory she shares with her Shelby: "Life is funny … it's hard. But it's also strange how things can be so different than you think. I remember I was just a kid. [There was] this beautiful gigantic red and yellow Ferris wheel. It lit up the night sky. They called it … the Monster."
54 For prohibitionists, murdered sex workers are the expression of men's hatred of women writ large. Kathleen Barry refers to Jane Caputi's assertion that Jack the Ripper's well-documented targeting of sex workers "cannot be viewed as the inexplicable work of a rogue psychopath, but as an eminently logical step in the procession of patriarchal roles, values, needs and rule of force." Barry, *Prostitution of Sexuality*, 47.
55 Jeffreys argues that sex work doesn't require specific skills or abilities from the women involved, as the sex industry values "youth and inexperience" the most (Jeffreys, *Industrial Vagina*, 19). Ronald Weitzer critiques such oppression paradigm premises for how they "deny that there can be anything positive about sex work, but also reject the idea that it can be neutral – revolving around everyday routine work practices. To concede to the latter would be to acknowledge 'the work dimension,' which they flatly deny." Weitzer, *Legalizing Prostitution*, 12.

56 Baldwin, "Split at the Root," 138.
57 Anne McClintock, by way of Carol Jacobsen, recounts how "[Kathleen] Barry refuses to appear publicly with sex workers or let them speak for themselves, on the grounds that they are too poor, too victimized, and too prone to false consciousness to be able to represent themselves objectively." McClintock, "Sex Workers and Sex Work," 7.
58 Melissa Farley, *Prostitution, Trafficking, and Traumatic Stress* (New York: Routledge, 2003), https://doi.org/10.4324/9780203822463.
59 Barry, *Prostitution of Sexuality*; Dworkin and MacKinnon, *Pornography and Civil Rights*.
60 Robyn Urback, "Peter McKay Still Hopes Bill C-36 Will Eliminate Prostitution in Canada. Good Luck with That," *National Post*, 8 July 2014, https://nationalpost.com/opinion/robyn-urback-peter-mackay-hopes-bill-c-36-will-eliminate-prostitution-in-canada-good-luck-with-that.
61 Melanie Simmons, "Theorizing Prostitution: The Question of Agency," in *Sex Work and Sex Workers*, ed. Barry M. Dank and Roberto Refinetti (New Brunswick, NJ: Transaction Publishers, 1999), 125–49, https://doi.org/10.4324/9781351306683.
62 Baldwin, "Split at the Root," 144.
63 Nagle, "Introduction"; Queen, "Sex Radical Politics"; Califia, *Public Sex*.
64 Xaviera Hollander, *The Happy Hooker: My Own Story* (New York: Dell, 1972); Ellen Willis, *Beginning to See the Light: Sex, Hope and Rock-and-Roll* (Minneapolis: University of Minnesota Press, 1992), 219–27.
65 Carol Queen and Lynn Comella, "The Necessary Revolution: Sex-Positive Feminism in the Post-Barnard Era," *Communication Review* 11, no. 3 (2008): 278, https://doi.org/10.1080/10714420802306783.
66 Quoted in Baldwin, "Split at the Root," 131.
67 Ellen Willis, "Lust Horizons: Is the Women's Movement Pro-Sex?," *Village Voice*, 17 June 1981.
68 Wendy Chapkis, *Live Sex Acts: Women Performing Erotic Labor* (New York: Routledge, 1997), https://doi.org/10.4324/9781315811512.
69 Eva Pendleton, "Love for Sale: Queering Heterosexuality," in *Whores and Other Feminists*, ed. Jill Nagle (New York: Routledge, 1997), 79.
70 Beauvoir, *Second Sex*, 541
71 Nagle, "Introduction"; Frédérique Delacoste and Priscilla Alexander, eds., *Sex Work: Writings by Women in the Sex Industry* (London: Virago, 1988).
72 Hakim, "Erotic Capital," 510.
73 Belle Knox, quoted in Charlotte Alter, "The Duke Porn Star Is Right: Kink Can Be a Feminist Choice," *Time*, 20 March 2014, https://time.com/30397/duke-porn-star-is-right-kink-can-be-a-feminist-choice.
74 Intelligence Squared (@Intelligence-Squared), "Pornography Is Good For Us," YouTube video, 1:25:23, 1 May 2013, https://www.youtube.com/watch?v=AASzf68w1JU.

75 Melissa Hope Ditmore, "Transactional Sex," in *Encyclopedia of Prostitution and Sex Work*, ed. Melissa Hope Ditmore (Westport, CT: Greenwood Press, 2006), 498–9; Elya M. Durisin, Emily van der Meulen, and Chris Bruckert, eds., *Red Light Labour: Sex Work, Regulation, Agency, and Resistance* (Vancouver: UBC Press, 2018); Queen, "Sex Radical Politics"; Willis, *Beginning*, 219–27; Melissa Gira Grant, *Playing the Whore: The Work of Sex Work* (London: Verso, 2014); Mac and Smith, *Revolting Prostitutes*.

76 Ryan Cole, "Sex Workers: We Know What We Want," *Right Now Inc.*, 13 November 2012, http://rightnow.org.au/writing-cat/opinion/sex-workers-we-know-what-we-want; Paul J. Goldstein, "Occupational Mobility in the World of Prostitution: Becoming a Madam," *Deviant Behavior* 4, no. 3–4 (1983): 267–79, https://doi.org/10.1080/01639625.1983.9967617; Melissa Petro, "I Did It ... for the Money: Sex Work as a Means to Socio-economic Opportunity," *Research for Sex Work* 9 (2006): 25–8; Joanna Phoenix, *Making Sense of Prostitution* (New York: St. Martin's Press, 1999); Ravishly, "Is Sex Work Empowering or Enslaving? 12 Experts Weigh In," *HuffPost*, last modified 6 December 2017, https://www.huffpost.com/entry/is-sex-work-empowering-or-enslaving_b_5825882.

77 Grant, *Playing the Whore*; Alana Massey, "Keeping Sex Workers Quiet," *Jacobin*, 2 November 2014, https://www.jacobinmag.com/2014/11/keeping-workers-quiet.

78 Crystal A. Jackson, "Framing Sex Worker Rights: How U.S. Sex Worker Activists Perceive and Respond to Mainstream Anti–Sex Work Trafficking Advocacy," *Sociological Perspectives* 59, no. 1 (March 2016): 27, https://doi.org/10.1177/0731121416628553.

79 Lizzie Borden, quoted in Campbell, *Marked Women*, 311.

80 Comte, "Decriminalization"; Megan Rivers-Moore, "But the Kids Are Okay: Motherhood, Consumption, and Sex Work in Neo-Liberal Latin America," *The British Journal of Sociology* 61, no. 4 (December 2010): 716–36, https://doi.org/10.1111/j.1468-4446.2010.01338.x.

81 Rachel West, quoted in Baldwin, "Split at the Root," 134.

82 Lily Burana, "The Old Bump and Grind: Can Stripping Support the Arts?," *Village Voice*, 5 May 1998, 138–40; Grant, *Playing the Whore*; Hollander, *Happy Hooker*; Sidney Katz, "Body Rub Girl 'a Social Worker' at $300 a Week," *Toronto Star*, 11 December 1973; Ann M. Lucas, "The Work of Sex Work: Elite Prostitutes' Vocational Orientations and Experiences," *Deviant Behaviour* 26, no. 6 (2005): 513–46, https://doi.org/10.1080/01639620500218252; Martha L. Stein, *Lovers, Friends, Slaves ... The Nine Male Sexual Types: Their Psycho-Sexual Transactions with Call-Girls* (New York: Putnam, 1974); Sudhir Venkatesh, *Floating City* (London: Allen Lane, 2009).

83 The legalization of sex work, not to be confused with decriminalization, regulates the sex industry through zoning by-laws and mandatory testing for sexually transmitted diseases. This model is in place in certain jurisdictions of Nevada.

84 "The Harmful Consequences of Sex Work Criminalization on Health and Rights," Sex Workers and Allies Network, June 2020, https://law.yale.edu/sites/default

/files/area/center/ghjp/documents/consequences_of_criminalization_v2.pdf; "Why Decriminalization of Sex Work?," Decriminalize Sex Work, accessed 15 January 2024, https://decriminalizesex.work/why-decriminalization.

85 Jasmine Sanofka, "From Margin to Centre: Sex Work Decriminalization Is a Racial Justice Issue," Amnesty International, accessed 15 January 2024, https://www.amnestyusa.org/updates/from-margin-to-center-sex-work-decriminalization-is-a-racial-justice-issue.
86 Norma Jean Almodóvar, a former Los Angeles police officer and sex worker, points out this hypocrisy in Virginie Despentes, dir., *Mutantes: Punk Porn Feminism* (France: Pink TV, 2009).
87 Comte, "Decriminalization," 205.
88 Lola Davina, *Thriving in Sex Work: Sex Work and Money* (Oakland, CA: Erotic as Power Press, 2020), xxvi.
89 See, for example, Pateman, *Sexual Contract*.
90 Kathleen Hanna, "Getting in on the Action," *Kathleenhanna.com*, 14 August 2013, http://www.kathleenhanna.com/getting-in-on-the-action (site discontinued).
91 Grant, *Playing the Whore*, 80.
92 Lily Burana, *Strip City: A Stripper's Farewell Journey across America* (New York: Miramax Books, 2001), quoted in Karen D., "A Survey of the Stripper Memoir," *The Rumpus*, 20 July 2009, http://therumpus.net/2009/07/a-survey-of-the-stripper-memoir.
93 Bernstein, *Temporarily Yours*, 16.
94 Weitzer, *Legalizing Prostitution*, 32. Weitzer's paradigm captures how the experience of sex work is shaped by variables such as location, class, gender, reasons for entry, public visibility, vulnerability to arrest, support networks, number of clients, and impact on the community.
95 Benoit et al., "Prostitution Stigma," 2.
96 Power, *One-Dimensional Woman*, 17.
97 Lucas, "Work of Sex Work"; Stein, *Lovers, Friends, Slaves*.
98 Tawnya Dudash, "Peepshow Feminism," in *Whores and Other Feminists*, ed. Jill Nagle (New York: Routledge, 1997), 98–119.
99 Paul Bleakley, "500 Tokens to Go Private: Camgirls, Cybersex, and Feminist Entrepreneurship," *Sexuality and Culture* 18, no. 4 (2014): 892–910, https://doi.org/10.1007/s12119-014-9228-3; Jones, "Sex Work"; "For Black Models Scroll Down: Webcam Modeling and the Racialization of Erotic Labor," *Sexuality and Culture* 19, no. 4 (December 2015): 776–99, https://doi.org/10.1007/s12119-015-9291-4.
100 Carol Wolkowitz, "The Social Relations of Body Work," *Work, Employment and Society* 16, no. 3 (September 2002): 497–510, https://doi.org/10.1177/095001702762217452.
101 Lisa McLaughlin, "Looking for Labor in Feminist Media Studies," *Television & New Media* 10, no. 1 (January 2009): 112, https://doi.org/10.1177/1527476408325363.

102 Eileen Boris, Stephanie Gilmore, and Rhacel Parreñas, "Sexual Labors: Interdisciplinary Perspectives toward Sex Work as Work," *Sexualities* 13, no. 2 (April 2010): 132, https://doi.org/10.1177/1363460709359228.

103 Patricia Alexander, "Prostitution: A Difficult Issue for Feminists," in *Sex Work: Writings by Women in the Sex Industry*, ed. Frédérique Delacoste and Priscilla Alexander (London: Virago, 1988), 184–214.

104 Ava Carrarra, quoted in Lauren Levitt, "Sex Work/Gig Work: A Feminist Analysis of Precarious Domina Labor in the Gig Economy," in *The Gig Economy: Workers and Media in the Age of Convergence*, ed. Brian Dollber et al. (New York: Routledge, 2021), 59, https://doi.org/10.4324/9781003140054.

105 David Harvey, *A Brief History of Neoliberalism* (Oxford: Oxford University Press, 2005), 22, https://doi.org/10.1093/oso/9780199283262.001.0001. While debate about the definition of neo-liberalism is ongoing, scholars agree that since the 1990s we have been living in a neo-liberal society. Harvey suggests that neo-liberal ideologies are so deeply imbedded within society that they are "taken for granted without question" (24). See also Eva Illouz, *Consuming the Romantic Utopia: Love and Cultural Contradictions of Capitalism* (Berkeley: University of California Press, 1997); George Monbiot, "Neoliberalism: The Ideology at the Root of All of Our Problems," *The Guardian*, 15 April 2016, https://www.theguardian.com/books/2016/apr/15/neoliberalism-ideology-problem-george-monbiot; Catherine Rottenberg, "The Neoliberal Feminist Subject," *Los Angeles Review of Books*, 7 January 2018, https://lareviewofbooks.org/article/the-neoliberal-feminist-subject.

106 Monbiot, "Neoliberalism."

107 Neo-liberalism emerged in the mid-1970s in response to an economic slump that brought widespread unemployment and skyrocketing inflation. According to Harvey, "discontent was widespread." Harvey, *Brief History*, 27. Neo-liberal policymakers, buoyed by the banking industry, promoted a regime that quickly grew under the Carter administration, and especially under the Reagan administration.

108 Stephen Edgell, *The Sociology of Work: Continuity and Change in Paid and Unpaid Work*, 2nd ed. (London: SAGE Publications, 2012).

109 In the early 1950s, the radical sociologist C. Wright Mills wrote that in the service-based American economy, "fewer individuals manipulate things, more handle people and symbols." C. Wright Mills, *White Collar* (New York: Oxford University Press, 1951), 65. Mills was referring to how the American economic base was transitioning from a manufacturing-dominated past to a future of new service jobs where workers would handle not things but people. Accordingly, workers would move from the factory to the call centre, he wrote, and their work would change from the manufacturing of tangible goods to the selling of intangible services. By the 1970s, this proved true as manufacturing jobs at large were replaced by service jobs that relied on workers' intellectual, interpersonal, emotional, and communicative skills, qualities that were amenable to the new

service jobs. This process involved transferring emotion from the personal sphere into the market, which Mills suggested would result in the commodification of workers' feelings: "For in the great shift from manual skills to the art of 'handling,' selling, and servicing people, personal or even intimate traits of the employee are drawn into the sphere of exchange and become of commercial relevance, become commodities in the labour market" (182). Mills wasn't referring to sexual labour, of course, but the feelings and performances that he predicted would become part and parcel of every service worker's professional skill set now drive the service economy of which sex work is a part.

110 Nicole S. Cohen, *Writers' Rights: Freelance Journalism in a Digital Age* (Montreal: McGill-Queen's University Press, 2016), 29.
111 Robert J. Samuelson, "The Rise of Downward Mobility," *Washington Post*, 5 August 2018, https://www.washingtonpost.com/opinions/upward-mobility-is-a-myth/2018/08/05/bb960ce4-972c-11e8-80e1-00e80e1fdf43_story.
112 Power, *One-Dimensional Woman*, 43. Neo-liberal discourse celebrates entrepreneurs who are said to have found particularly fulfilling opportunities in entrepreneurship by becoming "empowered," "flexible," and "creative" workers, but as Nina Powers notes, under neo-liberalism women work longer hours with less security and for lower pay. She adds that this is normalized through the rhetoric of "choice" aimed at the "flex worker women" who are still holding the lion's share of temporary work (19).
113 Alex Tanzi, "Side Hustle Nation: The Number of Americans Working Multiple Gigs to Just Pay the Bills Is Nearly Double What We Thought," *Fortune*, 6 February 2023, https://fortune.com/2023/02/06/side-hustle-americans-working-multiple-gigs-double-previous-estimates; Economic Policy Paper (EPI), "6.4 Million Americans Are Working Involuntarily Part Time," news release, 5 December 2016, https://www.epi.org/press/6-4-million-americans-are-working-involuntarily-part-time-employers-are-shifting-toward-part-time-work-as-a-new-normal.
114 Patrick Gillespie, "America's Part-Time Workforce Is Huge," *CNN*, 25 April 2016, https://money.cnn.com/2016/04/25/news/economy/part-time-jobs/index.html.
115 Bernstein, *Temporarily Yours*, 7.
116 Gillian Friedman, "Jobless, Selling Nudes Online and Still Struggling," *New York Times*, 21 October 2021, https://www.nytimes.com/2021/01/13/business/onlyfans-pandemic-users.html.
117 Michael Aaron, "Sex Work and Higher Education: A Mix of Disparate Identities," *Standard Deviation* (blog), Psychology Today, 5 May 2017, https://www.psychologytoday.com/ca/blog/standard-deviations/201705/sex-work-and-higher-education-a-mix-of-disparate-identities; Noah Berlatsky, "Students Who Do Sex Work," *The Atlantic*, 19 March 2014, https://www.theatlantic.com/education/archive/2014/03/students-who-do-sex-work/284505; Ron Roberts et al., "Participation in Sex Work: Students' Views," *Sex Education* 10, no. 2 (May 2010): 145–56, https://doi.org/10.1080/14681811003666507; Aurora Snow, "Naughty

Nerds: College Grads Do Porn," *Daily Beast*, 1 January 2015, http://www.thedailybeast.com/articles/2015/01/31/naughty-nerds-college-grads-do-porn.
118 Alexis Okeowo, "The Fragile Existence of Sex Workers during the Pandemic," *New Yorker*, 21 May 2020, https://www.newyorker.com/news/news-desk/the-fragile-existence-of-sex-workers-during-the-pandemic.
119 Caitlin Hu, "Can the World's Oldest Profession Survive the Age of Social Distancing?," *CNN*, 25 May 2020, https://www.cnn.com/2020/05/24/us/sex-workers-coronavirus-intl/index.html.
120 Gill and Kanai, "Mediating," 320.
121 Betty Friedan, *The Feminine Mystique* (New York: W.W. Norton, 1963); Marjorie Rosen, *Popcorn Venus* (New York: Coward, McCann & Geoghegan, 1973); Susan J. Douglas, *Where the Girls Are: Growing up Female with the Mass Media* (New York: Three Rivers Press, 1995); Sut Jhally, dir., *Killing Us Softly 3: Advertising's Image of Women* (United States: Media Education Foundation, 1999).
122 The noir classic *Mildred Pierce* (1945), for example, is a study of a woman entrepreneur that tracks its lead restaurateur's professional journey, right down to the particulars of pie making; *Jeanne Dielman, 23 quai du commerce, 1080 Bruxelles* (1975) contains an unforgettable scene of a woman – who moonlights as a sex worker, it is suggested – preparing veal cutlets for four minutes in real-time.
123 Pauline Kael, quoted in Studs Terkel, *Working* (New York: New Press, 1974), 155.
124 Martha M. Lauzen and David M. Dozier, "Maintaining the Double Standard: Portrayals of Age and Gender in Popular Films," *Sex Roles* 52 (2005): 437–46, https://doi.org/10.1007/s11199-005-3710-1.
125 Lucas, "Work of Sex Work," 514.
126 Nicole Constable, "The Commodification of Intimacy: Marriage, Sex, and Reproductive Labor," *Annual Review of Anthropology* 38 (2009): 50, https://doi.org/10.1146/annurev.anthro.37.081407.085133.
127 What Richard Florida calls "the driving force of wealth and growth across the country." Richard L. Florida, *The Rise of the Creative Class: Revisited* (New York: Basic Books, 2002), 22.
128 Pierre Bourdieu, *Distinction: A Social Critique of the Judgement of Taste* (Cambridge, MA: Harvard University Press, 1987).
129 Hakim, "Erotic Capital," 510.
130 Hakim, "Erotic Capital," 510.
131 Hochschild, *Managed Heart*, 5.
132 Hochschild, *Managed Heart*, 190.
133 Hochschild, *Managed Heart*, 85, 190.
134 Hochschild, *Managed Heart*, 187–88.
135 Hochschild, *Managed Heart*, 183.
136 Edgell, *Sociology of Work*, 121.
137 Ashley Mears and Catherine Connell, "The Paradoxical Value of Deviant Cases: Toward a Gendered Theory of Display Work," *Signs: Journal of Women in Culture and Society* 41, no. 2 (Winter 2016): 333, https://doi.org/10.1086/682922.

138 Wolkowitz, "Social Relations," 497.
139 Julia Twigg et al., "Conceptualising Body Work in Health and Social Care," *Sociology of Health & Illness* 33, no. 2 (February 2011): 171–88, https://doi.org/10.1111/j.1467-9566.2010.01323.x.
140 This shifts attention from the moral status of sex workers to the physical labour they perform and unites them with other body workers, such as massage therapists and occupational therapists. As Carol Wolkowitz points out, body workers are divided into two groups: those who work with the body to control and discipline it, like doctors and nurses, who accrue high social status, and those who work the body to give pleasure and adorn it, like tattoo artists and massage therapists, who accrue lower social status (Wolkowitz, "Social Relations"). Those who control bodies tend to be from higher classes and garner more respect in society. This popular culture dignifies the latter, more un-sung group.
141 Emma Dowling, "Dilemmas of Care," in *Take Care* (Mississauga, ON: Blackwood Gallery, 2017), 18.
142 Evans, *Harlots, Whores and Hookers*, 245.
143 Boris, Gilmore, and Parreñas, "Sexual Labors," 132.
144 Viviana A. Zelizer, *The Purchase of Intimacy* (Princeton, NJ: Princeton University Press, 2005).
145 Douglas William Haines, "Left Out/Left Behind: On Care Theory's Other," *Hypatia* 32, no. 3 (Summer 2017): 525, https://doi.org/10.1111/hypa.12336.
146 See Weitzer, *Legalizing Prostitution*.
147 Christine Harcourt and Basil Donovan, "The Many Faces of Sex Work," *Sexually Transmitted Infections* 81, no. 3 (June 2005): 201–6, http://dx.doi.org/10.1136/sti.2004.012468.
148 Lucas, "Work of Sex Work," 515.
149 David Thomson, "Francois Ozon's New Movie Makes Prostitution Look like an Yves San Laurent Ad," *New Republic*, 18 May 2014, https://newrepublic.com/article/117780/francois-ozons-jeune-belle-review.

2. Dancing to an American Dream: Dignifying Erotic Dancers' Labour in "Road Strip," *P.O.P., Magic City, Afternoon Delight*, and *Hustlers*

1 Debi Sundahl, "Stripper," in *Sex Work: Writings by Women in the Sex Industry*, ed. Frédérique Delcasote and Priscilla Alexander (London: Virago, 1988), 177.
2 Zac Johnson, "Unveiling Figures: How Much Money Do Strippers Make in the US?," ZacJohnson.com, accessed 6 January 2024, https://zacjohnson.com/how-much-money-do-strippers-make; Adrienne Green, "What It's Like to Work as an Exotic Dancer," *The Atlantic*, 19 October 2016, https://www.theatlantic.com/business/archive/2016/10/exotic-dancer/504680.
3 Burana, "Old Bump and Grind," 138.
4 Tom Pollard, *Sex and Violence: The Hollywood Censorship Wars* (New York: Routledge, 2015), https://doi.org/10.4324/9781315632162.

5. McNair, *Striptease Culture*.
6. Alexandra M., "Why Stripping Isn't Empowering for Anyone," *Ravishly*, 8 September 2014, https://ravishly.com/2014/10/18/why-stripping-isnt-empowering-anyone.
7. Rachel Shteir, *Striptease: The Untold History of the Girlie Show* (Oxford: Oxford University Press, 2004).
8. Shteir, *Striptease*, 63.
9. Quoted in Shteir, *Striptease*, 63.
10. Shteir, *Striptease*, 76.
11. Shteir, *Striptease*, 6, 235.
12. Shteir, *Striptease*, 339.
13. Hakim, "Erotic Capital," 510.
14. Shteir, *Striptease*, 242.
15. Gypsy Rose Lee, quoted in Shteir, *Striptease*, 339.
16. Belinda Smaill, "Documentary Investigations and the Female Porn Star," *Jump Cut: A Review of Contemporary Media*, 2009, https://www.ejumpcut.org/archive/jc51.2009/femalePornstars/index.html.
17. Shteir, *Striptease*, 287.
18. Shteir, *Striptease*, 296.
19. Peter Lee-Wright, *The Documentary Handbook* (London: Routledge, 2009), https://doi.org/10.4324/9780203867198.
20. Laurie Oullette and James Hay, *Better Living through Reality TV: Television and Post-Welfare Citizenship* (Malden, MA: Blackwell, 2008), 63.
21. In the first-person sandbox game, the player moves freely around Sin City – a simulated metropolis that resembles Los Angeles – where daylight is replaced by every carnal amusement. In one sequence, the player enters a strip club. The corporeal sameness of the strippers – all young, white, and thin, with globular breasts barely contained by string bikini tops – suggests their interchangeability and utility to be watched. After downing a drink, the player follows two strippers into the backroom – the champagne room; remember, for the stripper, this is her only opportunity to earn tips. Here, still from the male point-of-view, the player watches the two strippers kiss and fondle each other. By pressing certain button combinations on the controller, the player can extend his arm to fondle the strippers' breasts and buttocks as they utter encouragement that makes it sound like they're having fun: "She's feels so soft"; "What would you like to do to us?"; "I love touching another girl." But even this palaver is too much for the player: "Don't tell me your life story," he tells them, silencing them to resume the lesbian act. While *Grand Theft Auto* shows the strip club in pointillist detail, it denies that stripping is a job. The ultimate coup of this sequence is to manipulate one of the strippers to come home to have sex for free (a YouTube tutorial viewed by 4 million people shows how this can be achieved). Ultimately, *Grand Theft Auto* devalues the labour of stripping and makes it seem as though strippers work because they like being fantasy objects for men and, at a moment's notice, will gladly go home with anyone who asks.

22 High Voltage Software, *Leisure Suit Larry: Magna Cum Laude* (Vivendi Universal Games and Sierra Entertainment, 2004).
23 Roach, *Stripping*, 173–5. These figures come from the University of Alabama's Capstone Poll. The survey included 484 respondents.
24 Bill Nichols, *Introduction to Documentary* (Bloomington: Indiana University Press, 2001), 82.
25 Nichols, *Introduction to Documentary*, 167.
26 Arthurs, *Television and Sexuality*, 94.
27 Nicholas de Villiers, *Sexography: Sex Work in Documentary* (Minneapolis: University of Minnesota Press, 2017); Smaill, "Documentary Investigations."
28 Arthurs, *Television and Sexuality*, 98.
29 Arthurs, *Television and Sexuality*, 97.
30 Arthurs, *Television and Sexuality*, 98.
31 Nichols, *Introduction to Documentary*, 157.
32 A. Green, "What It's Like."
33 writermaia, "*This Is Life with Lisa Ling*: Storyline," IMDb, accessed 11 June 11, 2022, https://www.imdb.com/title/tt4071576/plotsummary?ref_=tt_stry_pl.
34 In 2017, *This Is Life with Lisa Ling* drew an average weekly audience of 321,000, making it the most watched non-fiction television series among the twenty-five to fifty-four age demographic for the 10:00 p.m. slot across all networks, and the series remained hugely popular through to its final season in 2022 (A.J. Katz, "2017 Ratings: CNN Has Its Largest Audience Ever, but Sees Prime Time Losses," *TVNewster*, 27 December 2017, https://adweek.it/2w67LOW).
35 Boyle, "Courting Consumers."
36 Nichols, *Introduction to Documentary*, 157.
37 Nichols, *Introduction to Documentary*, 158.
38 Rottenberg, "Neoliberal Feminist Subject."
39 Greg Larkin, "The Smartest Entrepreneur I Know Is a Stripper," LinkedIn, 5 October 2016, https://www.linkedin.com/pulse/smartest-entrepreneur-i-know-stripper-greg-larkin.
40 "Meet the Team: 'Road Strip' Producer/Director Heidi Burke," Part2 Pictures, 30 October 2014, https://web.archive.org/web/20160427123704/https://www.part2pictures.com/news/meet-the-team-road-strip-producer-heidi-burke.
41 Antonia Crane, *Spent: A Memoir* (Los Angeles: Rare Bird Books, 2014).
42 Chris Bruckert, "The World of the Professional Stripper," in *Feminisms and Womanisms: A Women's Studies Reader*, ed. Althea Prince and Susan Silva-Wayne (Toronto: Women's Press, 2004), 321–34.
43 Edgell, *Sociology of Work*, 121.
44 Dahlia Schweitzer, "Striptease: The Art of Spectacle and Transgression," *Journal of Popular Culture* 34, no. 1 (Summer 2000): 68, https://doi.org/10.1111/j.0022-3840.2000.3401_65.x.
45 Bruckert, "World," 325.

46 Lili St. Cyr, quoted in Shteir, *Striptease*, 260.
47 Sundahl, "Stripper," 177.
48 John Berger, *Ways of Seeing* (New York: British Broadcasting Corporation and Penguin Books, 1972).
49 Boyle, "Selling the Selling of Sex."
50 Heidi Mattison, quoted in Schweitzer, "Striptease," 66.
51 Barry, *Prostitution of Sexuality*.
52 Elissa Wald, "Notes from the Catwalk," *Creative Nonfiction*, 2000, https://www.creativenonfiction.org/online-reading/notes-catwalk.
53 Muriel Dimen, "Politically Correct? Politically Incorrect?," in *Pleasure and Danger: Exploring Female Sexuality*, ed. Carole Vance (New York: Routledge, 1984), 140.
54 Pendleton, "Love for Sale," 79.
55 Shteir, *Striptease*, 322.
56 Bruckert, "World."
57 Antonia Crane, "Stop Stealing from Strippers," *New York Times*, 13 August 2015, https://www.nytimes.com/2015/08/13/opinion/stop-stealing-from-strippers.html.
58 Crane, *Spent*, 32.
59 Camille Paglia, *Vamps and Tramps: New Essays* (New York: Vintage Books, 1994), 57.
60 Carol Rambo Ronai and Carolyn Ellis, "Turn-Ons for Money: Interactional Strategies of the Table Dancer," *Journal of Contemporary Ethnography* 18, no. 3 (October 1989): 271–98, https://doi.org/10.1177/089124189018003002; Crane, *Spent*; Dudash, "Peepshow Feminism"; Roach, *Stripping*.
61 Hochschild, *Managed Heart*, 67.
62 Hochschild, *Managed Heart*, 2.
63 Katherine Frank, "Stripping," in *Encyclopedia of Prostitution and Sex Work*, ed. Melissa Hope Ditmore (Westport, CT: Greenwood Press, 2006), 466–7.
64 Ronai and Ellis, "Turn-Ons for Money," 285.
65 Ronai and Ellis, "Turn-Ons for Money," 286.
66 Hochschild, *Managed Heart*, 190.
67 Nichols, *Introduction to Documentary*, 164.
68 Hochschild, *Managed Heart*, 183.
69 Hochschild, *Managed Heart*, 98.
70 "I Wasn't Really Naked. I Simply Didn't Have Any Clothes On," *Dance History Blog*, 11 July 2013, https://dancehistoryblog.wordpress.com/2013/07/11/i-wasnt-really-naked-i-simply-didnt-have-any-clothes-on.
71 Ivy Downer, "Why We Need to Talk about Stripping as Labour," *BGD*, 26 April 2016, https://www.bgdblog.org/2016/04/why-we-need-to-talk-about-stripping-as-labor.
72 Mears and Connell, "Paradoxical Value."
73 Downer, "Why We Need."
74 Nichols, *Introduction to Documentary*, 166.

75 Kimberly Foster, "On bell hooks and Feminist Blind Spots: Why Theory Will Not Set Us Free," *For Harriet* (blog), 12 May 2014, https://www.forharriet.com/2014/05/on-bell-hooks-and-feminist-blind-spots.html.
76 Amberly McAteer, "'Repeat after me: Do not pay women for sex': Why I Advise Readers to Avoid Prostitutes," *Globe and Mail*, 18 June 2014, http://www.theglobeandmail.com/life/relationships/repeat-after-me-do-not-pay-women-for-sex-why-i-advise-readers-to-avoid-prostitutes/article12634086.
77 Jessica Pressler, "The Hustlers at Scores: A Modern Robin Hood Story: The Strippers Who Stole from (Mostly) Rich, (Usually) Disgusting Men and Gave to, Well, Themselves," *The Cut*, 27 December 2015, https://www.thecut.com/2015/12/hustlers-the-real-story-behind-the-movie.html.
78 Pateman, *Sexual Contract*, 194.
79 In *Evicted*, Matthew Desmond writes that during the 2007 financial crisis, racialized neighbourhoods were targeted by the subprime lending industry. When spiking interest rates raised monthly mortgage bills exponentially, sending the homes of huge numbers of Americans into foreclosure, it was actually people of colour who spiralled into debt more so than any other group. Between 2007 and 2010, as Desmond reports, "the average white family experienced an 11 percent reduction in wealth, but the average black family lost 31 percent of its wealth. The average Hispanic family lost 44 percent." Matthew Desmond, *Evicted: Poverty and Profit in the American City* (New York: Crown Publishing, 2016), 125.
80 Harriet Goldhor Lerner, *The Dance of Anger: A Woman's Guide to Changing the Patterns of Intimate Relationships* (New York: Harper & Row, 1985), 7–8.
81 Susan J. Douglas, *The Rise of Enlightened Sexism: How Pop Culture Took Us from Girl Power to Girls Gone Wild* (New York: St. Martin's Griffin, 2010); Levy, *Female Chauvinist Pigs*; Angela McRobbie, *The Aftermath of Feminism: Gender, Culture and Social Change* (Thousand Oaks, CA: SAGE Publications, 2009).
82 Adam Isaiah Green, "'Erotic Capital' and the Power of Desirability: Why 'Honey Money' Is a Bad Collective Strategy for Remediating Gender Inequality," *Sexualities* 16, no. 1–2 (2012): 137–58, https://doi.org/10.1177/1363460712471109.
83 Jonathan Edwards, "Ex-Stripper's Lawsuit Says Clubs Blocked Her from Working Because They Didn't Want 'Too Many Black Girls,'" *Washington Post*, 19 August 2021, https://www.washingtonpost.com/nation/2021/08/19/houston-former-stripper-sues-strip-clubs-racial-discrimination.
84 Susan Shepard, "Taking the Boom out of the Boom-Boom Room: Why Are Strip Clubs Banning Rap?," *Complex*, 4 December 2013, http://ca.complex.com/music/2013/12/strip-clubs-ban-on-rap.
85 Downer, "Why We Need."
86 In 2014, one erotic dancer writing in *The Guardian* described how her day job as a cafeteria worker in the US Senate did not pay enough to support herself and her son: "While my customers give speeches … promising to deliver the American Dream to hard-working people, they aren't lifting a finger to help the workers

like me who serve them every day; not everyone has another job, but it's almost impossible to support a family without one." Kim, "I Work at the US Senate. I Shouldn't Have to Dance at Strip Clubs to Feed My Son," *The Guardian*, 5 August 2015, https://www.theguardian.com/commentisfree/2015/aug/05/us-senate-worker-shouldnt-have-dance-strip-clubs.
87 Barbara Cruikshank, quoted in Oullette and Hay, *Better Living*, 75.
88 Ashley Mears, "Aesthetic Labor for the Sociologies of Work, Gender, and Beauty," *Sociology Compass* 8, no. 12 (December 2014): 1334, https://doi.org/10.1111/soc4.12211.
89 A.I. Green, "'Erotic Capital,'" 138.
90 NPR, "Strippers in the U.S."

3. Massage Parlour Mothers on Prime Time: How the Fallen Woman Became a Mompreneur on *The Client List*

1 Bromwich and DeJong, *Mothers*, 31–2.
2 Rottenberg, "Neoliberal Feminist Subject."
3 Internet Movie Database (IMDb), "The Client List," IMDb, accessed 26 June 2022, https://www.imdb.com/title/tt2022170/?ref_=fn_al_tt_1.
4 Brian Lowry, "The Client List," *Variety*, 5 April 2012, http://variety.com/2012/tv/reviews/the-client-list-2-1117947354.
5 Troy Patterson, "Ultra-Soft Porn," *Slate*, 6 April 2012, http://www.slate.com/articles/arts/television/2012/04/client_list_jennifer_love_hewitt_s_call_girl_drama_reviewed_.html.
6 David Hinckley, "TV Review: *The Client List*," *New York Daily News*, 6 April 2012, http://www.nydailynews.com/entertainment/tv-movies/tv-review-client-list-article-1.1056533.
7 Hena John-Fisk, "Uncovering the Realities of Prostitutes and Their Children in a Cross National Comparative Study between India and the U.S." (PhD diss., University of Utah, 2013), https://collections.lib.utah.edu/details?id=196123.
8 Georgia Aspinall, "Why Can't We Reconcile Motherhood With Sexual Agency? The Reaction to Lana Rhoades' Pregnancy Proves We Still Have Work to Do," *Grazia*, 6 July 2021, https://graziadaily.co.uk/life/in-the-news/who-is-father-lana-rhoades-baby-pregnant.
9 Hays, *Cultural Contradiction*.
10 Steve Hargreaves, "Deadbeat Parents Cost Taxpayers $53 Billion," *CNN*, 5 November 2012, https://money.cnn.com/2012/11/05/news/economy/unpaid-child-support; Glenn Kessler, "Do Nine out of 10 New Businesses Fail, as Rand Paul Claims?," *Washington Post*, 27 January 2014, https://www.washingtonpost.com/news/fact-checker/wp/2014/01/27/do-9-out-of-10-new-businesses-fail-as-rand-paul-claims.
11 The term "massage parlour" has served as a front for sexual service establishments for over a century (Edward G. Armstrong, "Massage Parlors and Their

Customers," *Archives of Sexual Behavior* 7, no. 2 (1978): 117–25, https://doi.org/10.1007/BF01542061). In 1894, the *British Medical Journal* published an editorial calling for a stop to "amoral prostitutes" tarnishing the reputation of therapeutic massage by passing their establishments off as hospitals (David A. Nicholls and Julianne Cheek, "Physiotherapy and the Shadow of Prostitution: The Society of Trained Masseuses and the Massage Scandals of 1894," *Social Science & Medicine* 62, no. 9 (2006): 2336, https://doi.org/10.1016/j.socscimed.2005.09.010).

12 Albert J. Velarde, "Becoming Prostituted: The Decline of the Massage Parlor Profession and the Masseuse," *British Journal of Criminology* 3, no. 15 (1975): 251–63.

13 Joanna Mermey, "New York's 100 Kneadiest Cases," *Village Voice*, 14 December 1972, http://www.villagevoice.com/news/chasing-massage-parlors-out-of-times-square-also-a-fateful-kiss-ad-6708700.

14 Brock, *Making Trouble*, 31; Josh Alan Friedman, *Tales of Times Square* (New York: Delacorte Press, 1986), 117.

15 P. Hodge, "Massage Parlour Boom: Sex Spots Proliferating in the Capital," *Washington Post*, 30 May 1975; "Clergy Calls Times Square an 'Open Sewer of Sex,'" *Variety*, 3 November 1971; Daniel Ross, "Sex on Yonge: Examining the Decade When Yonge Street Was the City's Sin Strip," *Spacing*, 9 March 2017, https://spacing.ca/toronto/2017/03/09/sex-yonge-examining-decade-yonge-street-citys-sin-strip.

16 Quoted in Brock, *Making Trouble*, 40. The public-facing rationale for ousting the parlours centred on public safety – of making Times Square a safer, more respectable area – but financial motivations also spurred the city's "clean-up" campaign and its focus on sex establishments. In the *Village Voice*, Joanna Mermey noted that powerful landlords were placing pressure on the city to pass by-laws that would empower them to evict massage parlours in order to bring in new, higher-paying tenants, thereby increasing their revenue while building Times Square into a tourist shopper's paradise (Mermey, "New York's"). At the same time, other North American cities, notably Toronto, rolled out similar "clean-up" campaigns (D. Ross, "Sex on Yonge").

17 Brock, *Making Trouble*, 37.

18 While sexual liberation and the suspension of the Hays Code in the 1960s brought more explicit depictions of women's sexuality to the screen, women of colour – especially sex workers – continued to be sexualized as submissive, morally tempting, uninhibited seductresses (and compliant lovers for Western men). In Richard Mason's novel *The World of Suzie Wong* (1957) – made into a film in 1960 – a Chinese brothel worker leaves Hong Kong for Western society in London. For all the novel attempted to accomplish by making a sex worker the main character of the story, it reinforced in east–west stereotypes and essentialist ideas of the exotic "Other" by portraying Suzie as an irrational, innately sexual creature without self-knowledge – a libidinous sex object ruled by impulse. In chapter 6, reflecting on Suzie's decision to become a sex worker, economic factors are cast aside as Robert Lomax, the book's narrator, says, "I wondered vaguely why she had done it; I suppose it was just a reversion to type."

19 Indeed, ethnographies of this era tell complex stories about workers from a range of backgrounds that included mothers, daughters, students, and career sex workers; many of those interviewed emphasized their skills and how they spent most of their time with clients talking and providing emotional support. Some felt empowered by their jobs. As researchers noted in 1973, "These women have met the male chauvinist on his home ground, making the massage parlor a creative environment – a place for self-realization rather than sexual exploitation." Albert J. Velarde and Mark Warlick, "Massage Parlors: The Sensuality Business," *Society* 11 (November 1973): 63–74, https://doi.org/10.1007/BF03181022. See also Velarde, "Becoming Prostituted"; Clifton D. Bryant and C. Eddie Palmer, "Massage Parlors and 'Hand Whores': Some Sociological Observations," *Journal of Sex Research* 11, no. 3 (1975): 227–41, https://doi.org/10.1080/00224497509550898.
20 Bromwich and DeJong, *Mothers*, 1.
21 E. Ann Kaplan, *Motherhood and Representation: The Mother in Popular Culture and Melodrama* (London: Routledge, 1992), https://doi.org/10.4324/9781315001999.
22 Comte, "Decriminalization," 212.
23 Lucy Bland, *Banishing the Beast: Feminism, Sex and Morality* (London: Tauris Parke, 2001), 58.
24 Brewis and Linstead, *Sex*, 192. See also Nils Johan Ringdal, *Love for Sale: A World History of Prostitution* (New York: Grove Press, 2004).
25 Carole Vance, "Pleasure and Danger: Toward a Politics of Sexuality," in *Pleasure and Danger: Exploring Female Sexuality*, ed. Carole Vance (New York: Routledge, 1984), 2.
26 Firestone, *Dialectic of Sex*, 59.
27 See, for example, Lynda Nead, curator, *The Fallen Woman*, organized and presented by the Foundling Museum, 25 September 2015–3 January 2016, https://foundlingmuseum.org.uk/event/the-fallen-woman.
28 Brewis and Linstead, *Sex*, 192.
29 Lynda R. Ross, *Interrogating Motherhood* (Edmonton: Athabasca University Press, 2016).
30 Bromwich and DeJong, *Mothers*, 31–2.
31 Grant, *Playing the Whore*; Kissil and Davey, "Prostitution."
32 John-Fisk, "Uncovering," 60.
33 Juniper Fitzgerald, "What It's Like Being a Mom and a Sex Worker," *Vice*, 11 May 2018, https://broadly.vice.com/en_us/article/bj388w/what-its-like-being-a-mom-and-a-sex-worker.
34 Elizabeth Podnieks, *Mediating Moms: Mothers in Popular Culture* (Montreal: McGill-Queen's University Press, 2012), 12.
35 Suzanna Danuta Walters and Laura Harrison, "Not Ready to Make Nice: Aberrant Mothers in Contemporary Culture," *Feminist Media Studies* 14, no. 1 (2014): 38–55, https://doi.org/10.1080/14680777.2012.742919.
36 Hu, "Can the World's Oldest Profession."

37 Katy Vine, "She Had Brains, a Body, and the Ability to Make Men Love Her," *Texas Monthly*, January 2005, http://www.texasmonthly.com/articles/she-had-brains-a-body-and-the-ability-to-make-men-love-her.
38 Velarde, "Becoming Prostituted," 258.
39 Campbell, *Marked Women*, 133–4.
40 Campbell, *Marked Women*, 127.
41 G. Lerner, *Creation of Patriarchy*.
42 Roberts, *Whores in History*, 328.
43 Nancy Dubuc, quoted in Nellie Andreeva, "Lifetime Greenlights *The Client List* Series Starring and Produced by Jennifer Love Hewitt," *Deadline*, 10 August 2011, http://deadline.com/2011/08/lifetime-greenlights-the-client-list-series-starring-produced-by-jennifer-love-hewitt-155920.
44 Christopher J. Goodman and Steven M. Mance, "Employment Loss and the 2007–09 Recession: An Overview," *Monthly Labour Review* (April 2011): 3–12, http://www.bls.gov/opub/mlr/2011/04/art1full.pdf.
45 Cari Mitchell, "Sex Work Should Not Be a Crime," *The Guardian*, 7 April 2010, https://www.theguardian.com/commentisfree/2010/apr/07/sex-work-crime-legislation; "Sex Workers in the Recession," *The Economist*, 6 February 2009, https://www.economist.com/free-exchange/2009/02/06/sex-workers-in-the-recession; Stephen Fineman, *Work: A Very Short Introduction* (Oxford: Oxford University Press, 2012).
46 ClaLoveHewitt (@ClaLoveHewitt), "The Client List ~ ET Interview Feb4th ~ Jennifer Love Hewitt," YouTube video, 3:41, 4 February 2013, https://www.youtube.com/watch?v=TmcLtIOBGMM.
47 Goldstein, "Occupational Mobility"; Liz Hoggard, "Melissa Gira Grant: 'I Got into Sex Work to Afford to Be a Writer,'" *The Guardian*, 15 March 2014, http://www.theguardian.com/society/2014/mar/15/melissgira-grant-sex-work-afford-be-writer; Hollander, *Happy Hooker*; Rivers-Moore, "But the Kids"; Petro, "I Did It"; Phoenix, *Making Sense*.
48 Hakim, "Erotic Capital."
49 Patricia Hill Collins, quoted in Chapkis, *Live Sex Acts*, 44.
50 HappyCool (@HappyCoolOfficial), "Loretta Devine (The Client List) Interview," YouTube video, 8:21, 5 April 2012, https://www.youtube.com/watch?v=aiLSfwE3E1c.
51 *Oxford English Dictionary*, s.v. "mompreneur," accessed 18 May 2022, https://en.oxforddictionaries.com/definition/us/mompreneur.
52 P. Nel, Alex Martin, and Onnida Thongprovati, "Motherhood and Entrepreneurship: The Mumpreneur Phenomenon," *International Journal of Organizational Innovation* 3, no. 1 (2010): 6–34.
53 John-Fisk, "Uncovering," 24.
54 Jodyanne Kirkwood, "Motivational Factors in a Push-Pull Theory of Entrepreneurship," *Gender in Management* 24, no. 5 (2009): 346–64, https://doi.org/10.1108/17542410910968805.

55 Melissa Jean and Caroline S. Forbes, "An Exploration of the Motivations and Expectation Gaps of Mompreneurs," *Journal of Business Diversity* 12, no. 2 (2012): 118.
56 Tim Worstall, "Services, the Only Important Part of the U.S. Economy, Growing Nicely – PMI to 57.1%," *Forbes*, 5 October 2016, https://www.forbes.com/sites/timworstall/2016/10/05/services-the-only-important-part-of-the-us-economy-growing-nicely-pmi-to-57-1/#37d5946f1d1c.
57 Hochschild, *Managed Heart*; Bernstein, *Temporarily Yours*.
58 Eva Illouz, quoted in Brewis and Linstead, *Sex*, 195.
59 Eva Illouz, quoted in Brewis and Linstead, *Sex*, 195.
60 Jeffreys, *Industrial Vagina*, 19.
61 Twigg et al., "Conceptualising Body Work," 171.
62 Twigg et al., "Conceptualising Body Work," 178.
63 Hochschild, *Managed Heart*, 170.
64 Evans, *Harlots, Whores and Hookers*; S. Katz, "Body Rub Girl"; Velarde and Warlick, "Massage Parlors."
65 Andrea Dworkin, quoted in Alice Echols, "The Taming of the Id: Feminist Sexual Politics, 1968–83," in *Pleasure and Danger: Exploring Female Sexuality*, ed. Carole Vance (New York: Routledge, 1984), 59.
66 Hochschild, *Managed Heart*.
67 Clare L. Stacey, "Finding Dignity in Dirty Work: The Constraints and Rewards of Low-Wage Home Care Labour," *Sociology of Health and Illness* 27, no. 6 (September 2005): 831–54, https://doi.org/10.1111/j.1467-9566.2005.00476.x.
68 Lucas, "Work of Sex Work"; Mears, "Aesthetic Labor."
69 George Reynolds, *Matilda*, quoted in Campbell, *Marked Women*, 126.
70 Donald Winnicott, *The Child, the Family, and the Outside World* (New York: Penguin, 1964).
71 Hays, *Cultural Contradiction*, xi.
72 Hays, *Cultural Contradiction*, xi.
73 Hays, *Cultural Contradiction*, xi.
74 Hays, *Cultural Contradiction*, 132.
75 Hays, *Cultural Contradiction*, 149.
76 Benoit et al., "Prostitution Stigma," 465.
77 Gail Pheterson, quoted in Shawna Ferris, *Street Sex Work and Canadian Cities: Resisting a Dangerous Order* (Edmonton: University of Alberta Press, 2015), 26. See also Gail Pheterson, "The Whore Stigma: Female Dishonor and Male Unworthiness," *Social Text* 37 (Winter 1993): 39–64, https://doi.org/10.2307/466259.
78 Chris Bruckert and Colette Parent, "The Work of Sex Work," in *Sex Work: Rethinking the Job, Respecting the Workers*, ed. Colette Parent et al. (Vancouver: UBC Press, 2013), 75.
79 Comte, "Decriminalization of Sex Work."

80 Early researchers of massage parlours found that stigmatization was a primary concern for parlour workers, who accordingly kept their work secret from family and friends (Velarde and Warlick, "Massage Parlors"). According to Clifton D. Bryant and C. Eddie Palmer, many were disturbed by the media's negative portrayal of their work and felt umbrage at being labelled "deviants, sluts, and whores." To contest this negative portrayal, some had taken to writing letters to local newspapers and defending themselves on the grounds that they were simply participating in the "open marketplace," reminding readers to "judge not" since customers came of their own volition (Bryant and Palmer, "Massage Parlors").

81 See, for example, anonomaxtacular, "Would You Seriously/Exclusively Date a Sex Worker?," Reddit, 21 March 2018, www.reddit.com/r/AskMenOver30/comments/85ze22/would_you_seriouslyexclusively_date_a_sex_worker; Vertueux, "Would You and/or Have You Ever Dated a Sex Worker?," Reddit, 19 January 2015, https://www.reddit.com/r/AskMen/comments/2t05p1/would_you_andor_have_you_ever_dated_a_sex_worker. The socially marginal status of sex workers continues to be an accepted fact. As one TED Talk speaker put it in 2013 (in a video that has, to date, garnered more than 21 million views on YouTube), "If you are a prostitute … you are in the situation that we can refer to as social death." TEDx Talks (@TEDx), "Why I Stopped Watching Porn | Ran Gavrieli | TEDxJaffa," YouTube video, 15:57, 26 October 2013, https://www.youtube.com/watch?v=gRJ_QfP2mhU.

82 Bruckert and Parent, "Work of Sex Work," 71.

83 Grant, *Playing the Whore*, 54. Noting the inequality between how sex workers and johns are treated by police, the poet Adrienne Rich remarked that "women have always been outside the (manmade) law … [and] have been much more stringently punished than men for breaking the law, as in the case of prostitution." Quoted in Ruth Panofsky, "'This Was Her Punishment': Jew, Whore, Mother in the Fiction of Adele Wiseman and Lilian Nattel," in *Textual Mothers/Maternal Texts: Motherhood in Contemporary Women's Literatures*, ed. Elizabeth Podnieks and Andrea O'Reilly (Waterloo, ON: Wilfrid Laurier University Press, 2010), 101.

84 Harvey, *Brief History*, 22.

85 Power, *One-Dimensional Woman*, 43.

86 Statista, "Unemployment Rate in the United States from 1990 to 2022," accessed 2 May 2022, https://www.statista.com/statistics/193290/unemployment-rate-in-the-usa-since-1990.

87 Hargreaves, "Deadbeat Parents"; Kessler, "Do Nine." The Stanford Center on Poverty and Inequality calculated the gendered pay gap by measuring the ratio of income for "upper tail" earners – women who earn average salaries (in the fiftieth percentile) up to women who earn high salaries (the ninetieth percentile) – and "lower tail" earners who earn average and low salaries (in the tenth percentile). While "upper tail" earners have seen a slight increase in their wages since the 1980s, "lower tail" workers – women like Riley – have seen their incomes

plummet. At the same time, the average CEO earns twenty-four times what they did in 1964. In 2007, just before the financial collapse, CEOs were earning 277.3 times that of their workers. By 2010, that number had fallen slightly to 185.3. Despite recent gains made by women entering the white-collar professions, women in the workforce at large continue to be disproportionately represented in low-wage jobs (Stanford Center on Poverty and Inequality, "20 Facts about U.S. Inequality That Everyone Should Know," accessed 8 November 2023, https://web.stanford.edu/group/scspi/cgi-bin/facts.php).

As Alanna Petroff reports for *CNN Money*, at the current rates, it would take 217 years to close the gender pay gap (Alanna Petroff, "It's Getting Even Harder to Be a Woman," *CNN Money*, 2 November, 2017, http://money.cnn.com/2017/11/02/news/gender-gap-inequality/index.html). Further, the Stanford Center on Poverty and Inequality found that the number of what the authors termed "bad jobs" – jobs that are precarious and offer no benefits or health insurance – is rising. Additionally, as Debra Satz notes, the "roles which women disproportionately occupy – secretaries, housecleaners, babysitters, waitresses, and saleswomen – will be far more significant in reinforcing (as well as constituting) a gender-segregated division of labour." Debra Satz, "Markets in Women's Sexual Labour," *Ethics* 106, no. 1 (1995): 77.

88 Nora Caplan-Bricker, "The Best and Worst Parts of Calling Yourself 'Mompreneur,'" *Slate*, 16 May 2016, http://www.slate.com/blogs/xx_factor/2016/05/16/is_mompreneur_sexist_or_a_revolutionary_term.html.
89 Susan J. Douglas and Meredith W. Michaels, *The Mommy Myth: The Idealization of Motherhood and How It Has Undermined All Women* (New York: Free Press, 2004); L. Ross, *Interrogating Motherhood*.
90 L. Ross, *Interrogating Motherhood*, 25.
91 Douglas and Michaels, *Mommy Myth*, 4.
92 Julie Wilson and Emily Chivers Yochim, *Mothering through Precarity: Women's Work and Digital Media* (Durham, NC: Duke University Press, 2017), 17, https://doi.org/10.1215/9780822373193.
93 Fien Adriaens and Sofie Van Bauwen, "*Sex and the City*: A Postfeminist Point of View? Or How Popular Culture Functions as a Channel for Feminist Discourse," *Journal of Popular Culture* 47, no. 1 (February 2014): 174–95, https://doi.org/10.1111/j.1540-5931.2011.00869.x; Douglas, *Rise of Enlightened Sexism*; Gill, "Postfeminist Media Culture."
94 Liz Fraser, *The Yummy Mummy's Survival Guide* (London: HarperCollins, 2006).
95 L. Ross, *Interrogating Motherhood*, 26.
96 While North American advertising has long stoked women's preoccupations with their weight and shape, incidences of eating disorders among women in their thirties, forties, and fifties has risen at an alarming rate in the last fifteen years. Motivating this uptick may be a sense of rootlessness accelerated by late capitalism that prompts some to "grab for the mythical chimera of our culture's

narrow standards of beauty as the way to acculturate ourselves and organize our lives." Margo Maine and Joe Kelly, *The Body Myth: Adult Women and the Pressure to Be Perfect* (New York: John Wiley & Sons, 2005), 15. A new term for these mid-life eating disorders is plucked right out of the popular culture playbook: the "Desperate Housewives effect," referring to the popular TV series in which "improbably thin women in their 40s prance around in short shorts." Adriana Barton, "Are Middle-Aged Women Succumbing to 'Desperate Housewives Syndrome'?," *Globe and Mail*, 1 May 2011, https://www.theglobeandmail.com/life/health-and-fitness/are-middle-aged-women-succumbing-to-desperate-housewives-syndrome/article578178. While eating disorders are usually associated with teenage girls, according to the National Eating Disorders Association, "a growing number" of middle-aged women are developing anorexia and bulimia (quoted in Barton, "Are Middle-Aged Women").

97 McLaughlin, "Discourses," 258.
98 Gill and Kanai, "Mediating," 320.
99 Elin Diamond, Denise Varney, and Candice Amich, eds., *Performance Feminism and Affect in Neoliberal Times* (London: Palgrave Macmillan, 2017), 3.

4. Twenty-First-Century Peep Show: Feminist Entanglements in *Cam Girlz, Cam,* and *Teenage Cocktail*

1 Tristin Hopper, "Public Libraries a New Hot Spot Risqué – and Risky – Erotic Webcam Performances," *National Post*, 4 March 2015, https://nationalpost.com/news/canada/public-libraries-a-new-hot-spot-for-risque-and-risky-erotic-webcam-performances.
2 "Webcam Model Streaming Sex Show at Library Caught in Act," *CBC News*, 4 March 2015, http://www.cbc.ca/news/canada/windsor/webcam-model-streaming-sex-show-at-library-caught-in-act-1.2981531.
3 Carolyn Thompson, "Windsor Has Been Canada's Most Unemployed City for More than Five Years," *Windsor Star*, 10 July 2015, https://windsorstar.com/business/windsor-unemployment-rate-falls-to-8-9-per-cent.
4 Lynn Commella, "Webcam Girls" (presentation at the International Communication Association Conference, Portland, OR, 14 April 2016).
5 Alexander Eser, "Essential Webcam Industry Statistics in 2024, " Zipdo, last modified 16 July 2023, https://zipdo.co/statistics/webcam-industry.
6 Meghan Murphy, "*Cam Girlz* Director Believes Male Fantasies about Women Challenge Social Norms," *Feminist Current*, 6 March 2015, http://www.feministcurrent.com/2015/03/06/cam-girlz-director-believes-male-fantasies-about-women-challenge-social-norms.
7 Gill, "Postfeminist Media Culture."
8 "New Subjects in Sprocket Films and Mutoscopes," *Film Historiography* (blog), 15 March 2007, https://wp.nyu.edu/filmhist/tag/peep-shows; "Mutoscope,"

Wikipedia, last modified 16 August 2023, https://en.wikipedia.org/wiki/Mutoscope.
9 Quoted in "Mutoscope."
10 J.A. Friedman, *Tales of Times Square*, 64.
11 Cunningham and Kendall, "Prostitution 2.0"; Sanders, "Researching."
12 Bernstein, "Sex Work," 474.
13 Senft, *Camgirls*, 11.
14 Amy Shields Dobson, "Femininities as Commodities: Cam Girl Culture," in *Next Wave Cultures: Feminism, Subcultures, Activism*, ed. Anita Harris (New York: Routledge, 2007), 127, https://doi.org/10.4324/9780203940013.
15 Senft, *Camgirls*, 24.
16 Michele White, "Too Close to See: Men, Women, and Webcams," *New Media and Society* 5, no. 1 (March 2003): 7–28, https://doi.org/10.1177/1461444803005001901.
17 Senft, *Camgirls*, 21.
18 Jennifer Ringley, quoted in Senft, *Camgirls*, 17.
19 Senft, *Camgirls*, 43.
20 Senft, *Camgirls*, 17.
21 Dobson, "Femininities."
22 Laura Mulvey, "Visual Pleasure and Narrative Cinema," *Screen* 16, no. 3 (Autumn 1975): 6–18, https://doi.org/10.1093/screen/16.3.6.
23 John Dvorak, quoted in White, "Too Close to See," 10.
24 White, "Too Close to See," 18.
25 Dobson, "Femininities."
26 Bleakley, "500 Tokens"; Jones, "Sex Work."
27 Bleakley, "500 Tokens," 893.
28 Jones, "'I Get Paid,'" 782.
29 Sean Dunne, quoted in Murphy, "*Cam Girlz* Director."
30 "Director's Statement," *Cam Girlz* Press Kit, March 2015, 3, http://www.camgirlzdoc.com/images/camgirlz_presskit_march2015.pdf.
31 "Director's Statement," 3.
32 Bleakley, "500 Tokens"; Tim Rogers, "Can Camgirls Be Feminists?," *Splinter*, 16 July 2015, https://splinternews.com/can-camgirls-be-feminists-1793849204.
33 Hochschild, *Managed Heart*, 190.
34 Jones, "For Black Models," 784.
35 Mears and Connell, "Paradoxical Value," 333.
36 *Cam Girlz* also suggests that webcam models use sartorial strategies to augment their auras of authenticity. While some models wear clothing that is tight, short, and low-cut, many adopt less overtly sexualized styles by wearing ordinary clothes, such as jogging pants and plain T-shirts. In her ethnography of webcam models, Angela Jones explains that by wearing clothes that they potentially "would go to the grocery store in," webcam models accentuate their authenticity and produce a fantasy of being a woman the viewer could potentially meet and get to know in real life (Jones, "For Black Models," 787).

37 Hochschild, *Managed Heart*, 190.
38 Martha C. Nussbaum, "Objectification," *Philosophy and Public Affairs* 24, no. 4 (1995): 249–91, https://doi.org/10.1111/j.1088-4963.1995.tb00032.x.
39 Martha Nussbaum defines "objectification" with respect to seven characteristics: instrumentality, denial of autonomy, inertness, fungibility, violability, ownership, and denial of subjectivity wherein "the objectifier treats the object as something whose experience and feelings (if any) need not be taken into account." Nussbaum, "Objectification," 257.
40 Jones, "'I Get Paid.'"
41 Dorothy Allison, "Public Silence, Private Terror," in *Pleasure and Danger: Exploring Female Sexuality*, ed. Carole Vance (New York: Routledge, 1984), 113.
42 Lauzen and Dozier, "Maintaining the Double Standard."
43 Gill, "Postfeminist Media Culture," 163.
44 Kalpana Wilson, quoted in Andrea Cornwall, Jasmine Gideon, and Kalpana Wilson, "Introduction: Reclaiming Feminism: Gender and Neoliberalism," *IDS Bulletin* 39, no. 6 (2008): 3, https://doi.org/10.1111/j.1759-5436.2008.tb00505.x.
45 Jones, "'I Get Paid,'" 249.
46 Shirely Lara, quoted in Rogers, "Can Camgirls Be Feminists?"
47 An article appearing in the *New York Times* in 2013 explored the benefits and challenges of this occupation and included stories from several models who reported being doxxed – that is, having their real names and other personal information published on the internet without their consent (Matt Richtel, "Intimacy on the Web, With a Crowd," *New York Times*, 21 September 2013, https://www.nytimes.com/2013/09/22/technology/intimacy-on-the-web-with-a-crowd.html). In his book *The Dark Net: Inside the Digital Underworld* (2014), Jamie Bartlett explores doxxing on a wider scale. One incident described in his book involves online "trolls" pressuring a webcam model to write her name on her body and post photographs of herself with her prescription medication bottle to the misogynistic website 4chan. The information provided was enough to identify her, set up a Facebook page with her real name, post naked photos of her, and forward the account to her friends and family with the message: "Hey, do you know Sarah? The poor little sweetie has done some really bad things. So you know, here are the pictures she's posted on the internet for everyone to see." Quoted in Natasha Bertrand, "How Webcam Models Make Money," *Business Insider*, 18 November 2014, http://www.businessinsider.com/heres-how-webcam-models-make-money-2014-11. Millie Martins, a popular webcam model from Colombia, has even received a series of death threats (Rogers, "Can Camgirls Be Feminists?").
48 Nichols, *Introduction to Documentary*, 164.
49 Gill, "Postfeminist Media," 147.
50 Levy, *Female Chauvinist Pigs*.
51 Hochschild argued that women's "weak social shield" – their historical inability to earn money to support themselves – compelled them to make "defensive use of sexual beauty, charm, relational skills." As we saw in chapter 1, Hochschild

further postulated that in order to guard against the hazards of emotional labour, sex workers drew on one of three emotion management strategies to manage the demands of their jobs (and their own feelings about their jobs): identifying "wholeheartedly" with their work; identifying "cynically" with their work; or developing a "healthy estrangement of self from role," while taking pride in one's skills as "an illusion maker" (Hochschild, *Managed Heart*, 187–88).
52 Hochschild, *Managed Heart*, 188.
53 Hochschild, *Managed Heart*, 188.
54 Hochschild, *Managed Heart*, 197.
55 Grant, *Playing the Whore*, 90.
56 Hochschild, *Managed Heart*, 197.
57 Isa Mazzei, quoted in "Camgirl: Isa Mazzei Unveils the Enigma," *Subvrt*, 31 October 2019, https://www.subvrtmag.com/camgirl-isa-mazzei-unveils-the-enigma.
58 Frederick Blichert, "This Horror Screenwriter Subverted Every Shitty Sex Worker Trope," *Vice*, 13 November 2018, https://www.vice.com/en_us/article/j5z8p3/screenwriter-isa-mazzei-subverted-every-shitty-sex-work-trope-for-cam.
59 Isa Mazzei, quoted in "Camgirl: Isa Mazzei."
60 The pattern followed with TV's first portrayal of a teen sex worker in *Dawn: Portrait of a Teenage Runaway* (1976), starring Eve Plumb (who played wholesome Jan on the Brady Bunch), and the film *Pretty Baby* (1978), which focused on child prostitution. *Taxi Driver* (1976) launched Jodi Foster in the role of a teenage girl who becomes crazed Travis Bickle's path to heroism. *Hardcore* (1979) riffed on the same theme. A suite of variations followed with *Avenging Angel* (1985), *Daughter of the Streets* (1990), and *Streets* (1990). These films used the figure of the teen sex worker to embody sex and danger at the same time.
61 Bernstein, *Temporarily Yours*, 16.
62 John Carchietta, quoted in Sophia Cowley, "Queer Romance Meets Classical Thriller: An Interview with John Carchietta, Director of *Teenage Cocktail*," *Film Inquiry*, 10 August 2016, https://www.filminquiry.com/interview-carchietta-teenage-cocktail.
63 John Carchietta, quoted in Cowley, "Queer Romance."
64 Jones, "For Black Models," 792.
65 See Jia Tolentino, "How 'Empowerment' Became Something for Women to Buy," *New York Times*, 12 April 2016, https://www.nytimes.com/2016/04/17/magazine/how-empowerment-became-something-for-women-to-buy.html.

5. Sex and Entrepreneurship in the City: Building Intimate Business in *The Girlfriend Experience*

1 Roberta Victor, quoted in Terkel, *Working*, 64.
2 Riley Keough, quoted in Katie Van Syckle, "Riley Keough on Her Sexy, Disturbing New Show *The Girlfriend* Experience," *Cosmopolitan*, 8 April 2016, https://www

.cosmopolitan.com/entertainment/tv/q-and-a/a56560/riley-keough-the-girlfriend-experience-interview.
3   Bernstein, *Temporarily Yours*, 7.
4   Ringdal, *Love for Sale*, 58.
5   Evans, *Harlots, Whores and Hookers*, 37.
6   Roberts, *Whores in History*, 20.
7   Luc Sante, *The Other Paris* (New York: Farrar, Straus and Giroux, 2015), 122.
8   Karen Abbott, *Sin in the Second City: Madams, Ministers, Playboys, and the Battle for America's Soul* (New York: Random House, 2007), 3.
9   Abbott, *Sin in the Second City*, 3.
10 Quoted in Edward J. Zulkey, "The Ladies Everleigh," *Chicago Tribune*, 21 January 1979.
11 Abbott, *Sin in the Second City*, 17.
12 Stein, *Lovers, Friends, Slaves*; Venkatesh, *Floating City*.
13 Lucas, "Work of Sex Work."
14 Quoted in Lucas, "Work of Sex Work," 530.
15 Pendleton, "Love for Sale," 76.
16 Janet Lever and Deanne Dolnick, "Clients and Call Girls: Seeking Sex and Intimacy," in *Sex for Sale: Prostitution, Pornography and the Sex Industry*, ed. Ronald Weitzer (New York: Routledge, 2000), 97; Hollander, *Happy Hooker*, 178–9.
17 Stein, *Lovers, Friends, Slaves*, 19.
18 Maggie McNeill, "Quicker Than the Eye," *Honest Courtesan* (blog), 19 June 2013, https://maggiemcneill.com/2013/06/19/quicker-than-the-eye.
19 Harold Greenwald, *The Call Girl: A Social and Psychoanalytic Study* (New York: Ballantine Books, 1958), 4.
20 Terkel, *Working*, 60.
21 Thorstein Veblen, *The Theory of the Leisure Class* (New York: Macmillan, 1899).
22 Bourdieu, *Distinction*, 57.
23 Ringdal, *Love for Sale*, 345.
24 William Stadiem, "Behind Claude's Doors," *Vanity Fair*, 22 August 2014, http://www.vanityfair.com/style/society/2014/09/madame-claude-paris-prostitution.
25 Bernstein, "Sex Work," 481.
26 Stein, *Lovers, Friends, Slaves*, 13.
27 Bernstein, *Temporarily Yours*, 7.
28 Weitzer, *Legalizing Prostitution*, 33.
29 James H. Bryan, "Occupational Ideologies and Individual Attitudes of Call Girls," *Social Problems* 13, no. 4 (Spring 1966): 441–50, https://doi.org/10.2307/798593; Roger Ebert, "Chelsea, from Five to Nine," *RogerEbert.com*, 20 May 2009, https://www.rogerebert.com/reviews/the-girlfriend-experience-2009; Hollander, *Happy Hooker*; Lucas, "Work of Sex Work."
30 Lever and Dolnick, "Clients and Call Girls," 92.
31 Bernstein, *Temporarily Yours*.

32　Lever and Dolnick, "Clients and Call Girls," 86.
33　Hochschild, *Managed Heart*, 167.
34　Haskell, *From Reverence to Rape*, 91.
35　LaSalle, *Complicated Women*.
36　Quoted in Anne Helen Petersen, "Scandals of Classic Hollywood: The Many Faces of Barbara Stanwyck," *The Hairpin*, 13 March 2013, https://thehairpin.com/scandals-of-classic-hollywood-the-many-faces-of-barbara-stanwyck-a1dbaf8648a2.
37　Truman Capote, quoted in Macy Halford, "Was Holly Golightly Really a Prostitute?," *New Yorker*, 7 September 2009, https://www.newyorker.com/books/page-turner/was-holly-golightly-really-a-prostitute.
38　Lauren Valenti, "In Honor of Audrey Hepburn's Birthday, We Got Holly Golightly Highlights," *Marie Claire*, 2 May 2014, https://www.marieclaire.com/beauty/a9490/holly-golightly-costume-audrey-hepburn-style.
39　Xaviera Hollander's memoir *The Happy Hooker* opens with her and a group of other sex workers heading to prison on Rikers Island after being arrested.
40　Hollander's memoir is a primer on call girl entrepreneurship, drawing on wisdom she gleaned as a sole proprietor and later successful Manhattan madam. From the necessity of having multiple phone lines to keeping meticulous records to avoiding police scrutiny, Hollander writes candidly and vividly, with humorous detail.
41　Reading the films *Risky Business* and *Night Shift*, Eithne Johnson found that the sex worker character in each functions to affirm the supremacy of white, upper-middle-class men. Johnson found that the films attempted to set up an equivalency between prostitution and business. In both films, aspiring young businessmen hire sex workers and involve them in their business deals. The sex workers are smart but have but no social capital, while the men have social capital but limited life experience. According to Johnson, the films draw a glib equivalence between sex workers and businesspeople, without acknowledging the criminalization and stigmatization of sex workers. Furthermore, the sex workers are simply devices, as Johnson's analysis of the endings of these two films shows. When both young men become successful with the help of their sex worker friends, they go on to Ivy League universities, leaving the sex workers behind with their economic situations unchanged. For Johnson, these films emblematize the patriarchal view that sex workers – and by extension all women – are tolerable only if they serve white males' interests and the next "business opportunity" without advancing their own prospects. Ultimately, Johnson argues that the sex worker in these films is a one-dimensional "sex machine available to men." E. Johnson, "Business of Sex," 155.
42　Lizzie Borden's *Working Girls* is the finest example of a moral-free film about call girls in its unqualified refusal to pathologize, demonize, romanticize, or reduce these workers to a "type." It depicts three women who work at a Manhattan in-call agency, exploring their aspirations, friendships, romantic relationships, and goals. The vérité camerawork gives the viewer the impression of watching an average workday, as when Molly and her two colleagues sit on low velvet couches in a beige living room

talking about customers, complaining about their boss, and eating. Watching Molly squeeze salad dressing onto lettuce in real time provocatively challenges the stereotype of the call girl spending her day having ostentatious sex, squaring the fantasy of sex work with the reality of its often banal labour processes. These processes include aesthetic labour (Molly bathing in a marine-blue tub), financial management (Molly recording her dates in a small black booklet and adding up figures, reminding us this is a business), and shopping. In one scene Molly visits the pharmacy to buy "supplies," a scene played so banally she could be purchasing photocopy paper: "Yeah, I need three boxes of a dozen Trojans, one regular, one ribbed, and one lubricated. A sanitary sponge, one K-Y Jelly, one Caramex contraceptive cream, and an herbal douche. Oh, and can you fill this prescription for Loestrin 21?"

Molly is not damaged by her work nor defined by her job – she is an artist, a partner to her girlfriend, and a mother to her stepdaughter. But *Working Girls* does show the risks of internalizing stigma, which Molly manages through language ("I prefer working girl"). She is also ambivalent: "Sometimes I can't believe I'm still doing this ... I keep saying I'll quit," she says. *Working Girls* shows both the benefits and the pitfalls of Molly's work.

43 As *Strut*'s creator Misha Calvert said, "I just thought, well, the natural conclusion to this narrative of technology and intimacy and transaction is to just put a price on sex." Quoted Kylie Cheung, "New Series *Strut* Normalizes Sex Work with a Group of Friends Who Start an Escorting Agency," *Salon*, 18 June 2021, https://www.salon.com/2021/06/18/strut-tv-escorting-revry-misha-calvert.
44 Hochschild, *Managed Heart*, 188.
45 According to Hochschild, "surface acting" includes feigned expressions one is aware of putting on, as when raising an eyebrow to express incredulity without actually feeling any such emotion.
46 Charles Guignon, "Authenticity," *Philosophy Compass* 3, no. 2 (March 2008): 277–90, https://doi.org/10.1111/j.1747-9991.2008.00131.x.
47 Hochschild, *Managed Heart*, 187–8.
48 Hochschild, *Managed Heart*, 36.
49 Lever and Dolnick, "Clients and Call Girls."
50 Beauvoir, *Second Sex*, 536.
51 Ziyad Marar, *Intimacy* (London: Acumen, 2012).
52 Constable, "Commodification of Intimacy."
53 Hochschild, *Managed Heart*, 8.
54 Lynne Pettinger, "'Knows How to Please a Man': Studying Customers to Understand Service Work," *Sociological Review* 59, no. 2 (May 2011): 233, https://doi.org/10.1111/j.1467-954X.2011.02005.x.
55 Lucas, "Work of Sex Work."
56 Steven Soderbergh, quoted in Shani Harris (@binsidetv), "The Girlfriend Experience Steven Soderbergh Interview," YouTube video, 7:47, 23 May 2009, https://www.youtube.com/watch?v=07QqpkQAhZ8.

57 Cunningham and Kendall, "Prostitution 2.0."
58 Anka Radakovich, "The Real-Life Girlfriend Experience," *British GQ*, 29 March 2012, http://www.gq-magazine.co.uk/article/gq-girls-anka-radakovich-on-the-girlfriend-escort-experience.
59 Abbe Horswill and Ronald Weitzer, "Becoming a Client: The Socialization of Novice Buyers of Sexual Services," *Deviant Behavior* 39, no. 2 (2018): 148–58, https://doi.org/10.1080/01639625.2016.1263083; Kim Davies and Lorraine Evans, "A Virtual View of Managing Violence among British Escorts," *Deviant Behavior* 28 (2007): 525–51, https://doi.org/10.1080/01639620701316830.
60 Beauvoir, *Second Sex*, 504.
61 Gill, "Postfeminist Media Culture," 148.
62 Mears, "Aesthetic Labor," 1336.
63 Hochschild, *Managed Heart*, 188.
64 Hochschild, *Managed Heart*, 90.
65 Harvey, *Brief History*.
66 The promise of economic freedom as an entrepreneurial call girl is tempered by the financial risk, as suggested by sex workers' accounts and ethnographies. As Lola Davina writes, "Sex workers, like other independent contractors, earn money inconsistently, so require a high level of financial planning." Davina, *Thriving in Sex Work*, 138. Ann Lucas likens being a call girl to being a fruit picker: "There are times, some foreseeable (Christmas) and some not (September 11, 2001), when there will be few or no fruit to harvest, even if [she] has done everything right." Lucas, "Work of Sex Work," 524.
67 Riley Keough, quoted in Van Syckle, "Riley Keough."
68 Gill, "Postfeminist Media Culture," 151.
69 Canadian Press, "Olympian." Right-wing pundit, frequent right-wing television news guest, and self-styled "expert on radical Islam," Debbie Schlussel wrote an article on her personal blog titled "Suzy Favour Hamilton: Former Olympian Uses Bipolarity as BS Excuse for Being Hooker, Slut." Schlussel went on to characterize Hamilton as a "lowlife," "sleazebag," and "hooker" who – as sources told her – was also a "slut" in university who "did some pretty nasty things." Debbie Schlussel, "Suzy Favour Hamilton: Former Olympian Uses Bipolarity as BS Excuse for Being Hooker, Slut," *Debbie Schlussel* (blog), 11 September 2015, http://www.debbieschlussel.com/79722/suzy-favor-hamilton-former-olympian-i.
70 Dorothy Pomerantz, "Hollywood's Highest Paid Actors," *Forbes*, 11 October 2011, https://www.forbes.com/sites/dorothypomerantz/2011/10/11/hollywoods-highest-paid-tv-actors/#741460634d5b; Shawn Hubler, "Actor Says He Got Call Girls from Fleiss on at Least 27 Occasions: Trial: Jury Views Videotape of Testimony by Fidgeting Charlie Sheen. Checks Totaled More Than $50,000," *Los Angeles Times*, 21 July 1995, https://www.latimes.com/archives/la-xpm-1995-07-21-me-26278-story.html.
71 Annabel Rackham, "Stephen Bear: Revenge Porn Prison Sentence 'Sends Clear Message,'" *BBC*, 3 March 2023, https://www.bbc.com/news/entertainment

-arts-64799815; Wilfred Chan, "What Legal Protections Do Revenge Porn Victims Have at Work in the US?," *The Guardian*, 29 September 2022, https://www.theguardian.com/law/2022/sep/29/legal-protections-revenge-porn-victims-work-erick-adame.
72 Hochschild, *Managed Heart*, 172.
73 Grant, *Playing the Whore*, 65.

6. Sexual Healing: Sex Surrogate Care Workers in *The Sessions* and *She's Lost Control*

1 Helen Hunt, quoted in Kyle Buchanan, "Helen Hunt on Sex, *The Sessions*, and the Choice She Had to Fight For," *Vulture*, 17 October 2012, https://www.vulture.com/2012/10/helen-hunt-on-sex-and-the-sessions.html.
2 Tracy De Boer, "Disability and Sexual Inclusion," *Hypatia* 30, no. 1 (Winter 2015): 66, https://doi.org/10.1111/hypa.12118.
3 Marion Jacobs, Linda A. Thompson, and Patsy Truxaw, "The Use of Sexual Surrogates in Counseling," *The Counseling Psychologist* 5, no. 1 (Spring 1975): 73–7, https://doi.org/10.1177/001100007500500118.
4 Yitzchak M. Binik and Marta Meana, "The Future of Sex Therapy: Specialization or Marginalization?," *Archives of Sexual Behaviour* 38, no. 6 (2009): 1016–27, https://doi.org/10.1007/s10508-009-9475-9.
5 Rafer Guzman, "*The Sessions* Review: Physical, Emotional Triumphs," *Newsday*, 8 November 2012, https://www.newsday.com/entertainment/movies/the-sessions-review-physical-emotional-triumphs-u63781.
6 Stephen Holden, "Review: In *She's Lost Control*, Crossing Boundaries in Pursuit of Intimacy," *New York Times*, 20 March 2015, https://www.nytimes.com/2015/03/20/movies/review-in-shes-lost-control-crossing-boundaries-in-pursuit-of-intimacy.html.
7 Katie Walsh, "Review: *Control* Is a Quiet Triumph with a Distinctive Voice," *Los Angeles Times*, 30 March 2015, https://www.latimes.com/entertainment/movies/la-et-mn-shes-lost-control-review-20150327-story.html.
8 Cheryl Cohen-Greene and Lorna Garano, *An Intimate Life: Sex, Love, and My Journey as a Surrogate Partner* (Berkley, CA: Soft Skull Press, 2012), 5.
9 Roberts, *Whores in History*, 2.
10 Evans, *Harlots, Whores and Hookers*, 29.
11 William J. Robinson, quoted in Evans, *Harlots, Whores and Hookers*, 245.
12 Stein, *Lovers, Friends, Slaves*, 6–7.
13 See Alan F. Guttmacher, "Human Sexual Inadequacy for the Non-layman," *New York Times*, 12 July 1970, http://www.nytimes.com/books/97/03/23/reviews/bright-inadequacy.html; NPR, "Pioneering *Masters of Sex* Brought Science to the Bedroom," *Fresh Air*, 30 July 2013, https://www.npr.org/2013/07/30/206704520/pioneering-masters-of-sex-brought-science-to-the-bedroom.
14 NPR, "Pioneering."

15 William H. Masters and Virginia E. Johnson, *Human Sexual Inadequacy* (Boston: Little, Brown and company, 1970), 5.
16 Masters and Johnson, *Human Sexual Inadequacy*, 148.
17 Talli Rosenbaum, Ronit Aloni, and Rafi Heruti, "Surrogate Partner Therapy: Ethical Considerations in Sexual Medicine," *Journal of Sexual Medicine* 11, no. 2 (February 2014): 321–9, https://doi.org/10.1111/jsm.12402.
18 Binik and Meana, "Future of Sex Therapy"; Jane Ridley, "Secrets of Sex Surrogates," *New York Post*, 25 October 2012, http://nypost.com/2012/10/25/secrets-of-the-sex-surrogates. See also the website of the International Professional Surrogates Association: https://www.surrogatetherapy.org.
19 Teela Sanders, "The Politics of Sexual Citizenship: Commercial Sex and Disability," *Disability & Society* 22, no. 5 (2007): 440, https://doi.org/10.1080/09687590701427479.
20 Binik and Meana, "Future of Sex Therapy," 1017.
21 Thomas Szasz, *Sex by Prescription* (Garden City, NY: Anchor Press/Doubleday, 1980), 50.
22 Szasz, *Sex by Prescription*; NPR, "Pioneering."
23 William H. Masters and Virginia E. Johnson, *Human Sexual Response* (Boston: Little, Brown and Company, 1966), 11.
24 Masters and Johnson, *Human Sexual Inadequacy*, 148.
25 Masters and Johnson more or less limited their treatment to married couples, but from 1959 to 1970 the fifty-four single men referred to them for treatment posed one of their greatest clinical challenges. Rather than turn these men away, Masters and Johnson conceptualized two solution "partner" types: the replacement partner and the partner surrogate. The replacement partner was selected and brought by the man being treated, usually a woman he was presently or in the past had dated, or even been married to. A partner surrogate was a single woman volunteer. "The specific function of the partner surrogate is to approximate insofar as possible the role of a supportive, interested, cooperative wife. Her contributions are infinitely more valuable as a means of psychological support than a measure of physiological initiation, although obviously both roles are vitally necessary if a male's inadequacies are to be reversed successfully." Masters and Johnson, *Human Sexual Inadequacy*, 150.
26 Satz, "Markets," 66.
27 Sanders, "Politics of Sexual Citizenship," 441.
28 Rosenbaum, Aloni, and Heruti, "Surrogate Partner Therapy," 322.
29 David R. Reuben, *Everything You Always Wanted to Know about Sex (But Were Afraid to Ask)* (New York: D. McKay, 1969); Joan Terry Garrity, *How to Become the Sensuous Woman* (London: Mayflower, 1971); Bernie Zilbergeld and John Ullman, *Male Sexuality: A Guide to Sexual Fulfillment* (New York: Bantam Books, 1978); Julia Heiman, Leslie LoPiccolo, and Joseph LoPiccolo, *Becoming Orgasmic: A Sexual Growth Program for Women* (Englewood Cliffs, NJ: Prentice-Hall, 1976).

30 Dowling, "Dilemmas of Care"; Haines, "Left Out/Left Behind."
31 Boris, Gilmore, and Parreñas, "Sexual Labors."
32 Zelizer, *Purchase of Intimacy*.
33 Dowling, "Dilemmas of Care," 10.
34 Haines, "Left Out/Left Behind," 525.
35 Nathaniel B. Burke, "Intimate Commodities: Intimate Labor and the Production and Circulation of Inequality," *Sexualities* 19, no. 7 (October 2016): 781, https://doi.org/10.1177/1363460715616948.
36 Haines, "Left Out/Left Behind," 525.
37 Mark O'Brien, quoted in Walter Goodman, "He Rejects Myths, Not Miracles," *New York Times*, 22 May 1997, https://www.nytimes.com/1997/05/22/arts/he-rejects-myths-not-miracles.html.
38 Cohen-Greene and Garano, *Intimate Life*, 3.
39 Jeffreys, *Industrial Vagina*, 19.
40 International Professional Surrogates Association (IPSA), "What Is Surrogate Partner Therapy?," accessed 3 June 2022, https://www.surrogatetherapy.org/what-is-surrogate-partner-therapy.
41 Hochschild, *Managed Heart*, 188.
42 Guttmacher, "Human Sexual Inadequacy"; Jacobs, Thompson, and Truxaw, "Use of Sexual Surrogates"; "Sex Surrogates Seem like Prostitutes but Are Helping Hands," *ABC News*, 1 August 2011, http://abcnews.go.com/Health/sex-surrogates-prostitutes-helping-hands-therapists/story?id=14207647; Ridley, "Secrets of Sex Surrogates."
43 Rosenbaum, Aloni, and Heruti, "Surrogate Partner Therapy," 323.
44 Twigg et al., "Conceptualising Body Work," 171.
45 Masters and Johnson, *Human Sexual Inadequacy*, 72.
46 "Mark O'Brien: The Real Person behind *The Sessions*," *The Sartogian*, 4 October 2012, https://www.saratogian.com/2012/10/24/mark-obrien-the-real-person-behind-hollywoods-the-sessions.
47 Campbell, *Marked Women*, 167.
48 Chapkis, *Live Sex Acts*, 75.
49 De Boer, "Disability and Sexual Inclusion."
50 Sanders, "Politics of Sexual Citizenship."
51 Tom Shakespeare, "Disabled Sexuality: Toward Rights and Recognition," *Sexuality and Disability* 18, no. 3 (2000): 159–66, https://doi.org/10.1023/A:1026409613684.
52 Kirsty Liddiard, "'I Never Felt like She Was Just Doing It for the Money': Disabled Men's Intimate (Gendered) Realities of Purchasing Sexual Pleasure and Intimacy," *Sexualities* 17, no. 7 (October 2014): 837, https://doi.org/10.1177/1363460714531272.
53 M. Griffiths, "Sex: Should We All Be at It?" (PhD diss., University of Leeds, 2006), 107.
54 Lucas, "Work of Sex Work"; Sanders, *Paying for Pleasure*; Rosenbaum, Aloni, and Heruti, "Surrogate Partner Therapy."

55. Marisa Fox, "Patients with Benefits," *Elle*, 4 January 2013, https://www.elle.com/life-love/sex-relationships/advice/a12548/sex-surrogacy.
56. Mark O'Brien, quoted in "Mark O'Brien: The Real Person."
57. Shakespeare, "Disabled Sexuality."
58. Mark O'Brien, quoted in Jessica Yu, dir., *Breathing Lessons: The Life and Work of Mark O'Brien* (United States: Inscrutable Films, 1996).
59. Mark O'Brien, "On Seeing a Sex Surrogate," *The Sun*, May 1990, https://www.thesunmagazine.org/issues/174/on-seeing-a-sex-surrogate-issue-174.
60. O'Brien, "On Seeing."
61. Sheila Jeffreys, "Disability and the Male Sex Right," *Women's Studies International Forum* 31, no. 5 (September–October 2008): 327–35, https://doi.org/10.1016/j.wsif.2008.08.001.
62. Jess Martin, "The Notion That It's Ok for Disabled Men to Pay for Sex Is Rooted in Misogyny and Ableism," *Feminist Current*, 11 November 2014, http://www.feministcurrent.com/2014/11/11/the-notion-that-its-ok-for-disabled-men-to-pay-for-sex-is-rooted-in-misogyny-and-ableism.
63. Martin. "Notion."
64. Liddiard, "'I Never Felt.'"
65. Sanders, "Politics of Sexual Citizenship"; Shakespeare, "Disabled Sexuality."
66. De Boer, "Disability and Sexual Inclusion," 73.
67. Liddiard, "'I Never Felt,'" 839.
68. Liddiard, "'I Never Felt,'" 842.
69. Sanders, *Paying for Pleasure*; Shakespeare, "Disabled Sexuality."
70. Liddiard, "'I Never Felt,'" 837.
71. Some scholars have argued that designating a group of sex workers for people with disabilities problematically implies that sex workers need special training to work with disabled people. De Boer rightly points out that the medicalization of sex that is part and parcel of sex surrogacy is problematic, for it runs the risk of re-stigmatizing people with disabilities (De Boer, "Disability and Sexual Inclusion"). By involving a therapist, clinician, and even a physician, as well as clinical check-ins, appointments, feedback forms, and interviews, the sex surrogacy process can be invasive and run the risk of making a client feel like an object of scrutiny. For persons who may have been objectified and medicalized for much of their lives, turning the sex experience into a medical experience may therefore carry unwanted negative consequences.
72. O'Brien, "On Seeing."
73. Fox, "Patients with Benefits."
74. Cohen-Greene and Garano, *Intimate Life*, 4.
75. Stacey, "Finding Dignity."
76. Cheryl Cohen-Greene, quoted in "Mark O'Brien: The Real Person."
77. Hochschild, *Managed Heart*, 90.
78. Stacey, "Finding Dignity."

79 Weitzer, *Legalizing Prostitution*, 12.
80 Rosenbaum, Aloni, and Heruti, "Surrogate Partner Therapy," 323.
81 Sanders, "Politics of Sexual Citizenship."
82 Stacey, "Finding Dignity," 850.
83 Chapkis, *Live Sex Acts*.
84 Masters and Johnson, *Human Sexual Inadequacy*, 6.
85 Hochschild, *Managed Heart*, 188.
86 Kristin M. Van De Griend and DeAnne K. Hilfinger Messias, "Expanding the Conceptualization of Workplace Violence: Implications for Research, Policy, and Practice," *Sex Roles* 71, no. 1 (July 2014): 33, https://doi.org/10.1007/s11199-014-0353-0.
87 Quoted in Justin Ling and Tu Thanh Ha, "Killings in Toronto's Gay Community Highlight Dangers Faced by Sex Workers," *Globe and Mail*, 30 January 2018, https://www.theglobeandmail.com/news/toronto/killings-in-torontos-gay-community-highlight-dangers-faced-by-sex-workers/article37800442.
88 Alan Scherstuhl, "Sex Surrogate Therapy Drama *She's Lost Control* Is Shot with a Vigorous Chilliness," *Village Voice*, 18 March 2015, https://www.villagevoice.com/2015/03/18/sex-surrogate-therapy-drama-shes-lost-control-is-shot-with-a-vigorous-chilliness.
89 Fox, "Patients with Benefits."
90 "FOXSexpert: Sex Surrogacy – Prostitution or Therapy?," *Fox News*, 14 January 2015, https://www.foxnews.com/story/foxsexpert-sex-surrogacy-prostitution-or-therapy.
91 Quoted in Ridley, "Secrets of Sex Surrogates."
92 Belle Knox, "Tearing Down the Whorearchy from the Inside," *Jezebel*, 2 July 2014, https://jezebel.com/tearing-down-the-whorearchy-from-the-inside-1596459558.

7. Hardcore in the Big Apple: *The Deuce*'s Feminist Sex Work Epic

1 Rubin, "Thinking Sex," 166.
2 Erika Lust, quoted in Kate Fane, "The Frontier of Feminist Porn: An Interview with Erika Lust," *Maisonneuve*, 26 May 2015, https://maisonneuve.org/post/2015/05/26/frontier-feminist-porn-interview-erika-lust.
3 Camille Paglia, quoted in Mireille Miller-Young, *A Taste for Brown Sugar: Black Women in Pornography* (Durham, NC: Duke University Press 2014), 72, https://doi.org/10.1215/9780822375913.
4 Andrea Dworkin, *Pornography: Men Possessing Women* (New York: Putnam, 1981), 28.
5 George Pelacanos, quoted in Andy Greenwald and Chris Ryan, "*The Deuce* Is about Porn, but It Isn't Pornographic," *The Ringer*, 8 September 2017, https://www.theringer.com/tv/2017/9/8/16271260/the-deuce-james-franco-nudity.

6 In the late nineteenth century, Thomas Edison invented the Kinetoscope, a coin-operated peephole viewing cabinet that exhibited short motion pictures; a similar device, the Mutoscope, appeared a few years later. In the twentieth century, "peep shows" referred to the exhibition of any sexually explicit material viewed through a peephole.

7 The earliest known stag film, *A Free Ride* (1915), also known as *A Grass Sandwich*, combines the novelty of motor cars with casual sex in a story about a male motorist who picks up two female hitchhikers for a ménage à trois. Recognized as the oldest surviving American hardcore film, it was also the first made for commercial purposes. In content and form it emblematized the genre codes that endured for decades, with sex prioritized over story and formal simplicity, the film being silent with very little editing. See Linda Williams, *Hard Core: Power, Pleasure, and the "Frenzy of the Visible"* (Berkeley: University of California Press, 1989).

8 Marjorie Heins, "Sex and the Law: A Tale of Shifting Boundaries," in *Pornography: Film and Culture*, ed. Peter Lehman (New Brunswick, NJ: Rutgers University Press, 2006), 169.

9 Richard Corliss, "That Old Feeling: When Porno Was Chic," *Time*, 29 March 2005, http://content.time.com/time/arts/article/0,8599,1043267,00.html.

10 Dworkin, *Pornography*, 137.

11 "Pornography, like rape, is a male invention, designed to dehumanize women, to reduce the female to an object of sexual access, not to free sensuality from moralistic or parental inhibition." Susan Brownmiller, *Against Our Will: Men, Women, and Rape* (New York: Fawcett Books, 1993), 38.

12 Alison M. Gingeras, "Revisiting *Suck* Magazine's Experiment in Radical Feminist Pornography," *Document Journal*, 28 November 2018, https://www.documentjournal.com/2018/11/revisiting-suck-magazines-experiment-in-radical-feminist-pornography.

13 Laura Kipnis, "How to Look at Pornography," in *Pornography: Film and Culture*, ed. Peter Lehman (New Brunswick, NJ: Rutgers University Press, 2006), 119.

14 Brian McNair, "Pornography in the Multiplex," in *Hard to Swallow: Hard-Core Pornography on Screen*, ed. Claire Hines and Darren Kerr (New York: Wallflower Press, 2012).

15 The inventive and controversial documentary *Not a Love Story: A Film about Pornography* (1981) pairs a radical feminist film-maker with a sex-positive erotic dancer and sends them on a journey into the sex industry, the goal being to "learn" from each other. The documentary unfolds with the prohibitionist trying to "persuade" or "re-educate" the erotic dancer into understanding that her job is dehumanizing and her "choice" complicit with misogyny, an exercise that becomes increasingly uncomfortable as the film draws to a close and one realizes that while the film-maker will return to her middle-class lifestyle, the newly "reformed" erotic dancer will be unemployed.

16 Clarissa Smith, "Reel Intercourse: Doing Sex on Camera," in *Hard to Swallow: Hard-Core Pornography on Screen*, ed. Claire Hines and Darren Kerr (New York: Wallflower Press, 2012), 212.
17 Clarissa Smith and Feona Attwood, "Emotional Truths and Thrilling Slide Shows," in *The Feminist Porn Book: The Politics of Producing Pleasure*, ed. Tristan Taormino et al. (New York: The Feminist Press at the City University of New York, 2012), 47.
18 For example, the 2019 GirlsDoPorn scandal, now documented extensively by the popular press, involved a porn production company deceiving scores of young women to persuade them into performing in "amateur videos." The women were led to believe the videos would be available for sale and viewing outside the US only, but they were subsequently released online, resulting in significant duress and psychological damage for the women (for many, this was their first and last porn gig). *Jane Does v. GirlsDoPorn* resulted in a $20-million settlement for the twenty-two anonymous women who were manipulated and defrauded by the GirlsDoPorn production company. See Michael Levenson, "Judge Awards Nearly $13 Million to Women Who Say They Were Exploited by Porn Producers," *New York Times*, 3 January 2020, https://www.nytimes.com/2020/01/02/us/girls-do-porn-lawsuit-award.html.
19 Misogynistic explanations for why women sell sex often overlook economic motivations in favour of describing sex workers' amorality or mental defectiveness. Some radical feminists extended this line of thinking. In *The Prostitution Papers* (1975), Kate Millett described a sex worker whose "grandiose neuroticism, however paradigmatic of the personal disorientation of the Uptown call girl, rendered her completely impervious to logic of any kind." Kate Millett, quoted in Roberts, *Whores in History*, 341.
20 Benjamin Shepard, "From Emma Goldman to Riot Grrrl: Sex Work, Public Space and the Transformation of Streets," *New Political Science* 37, no. 3 (2015): 424–8, https://doi.org/10.1080/07393148.2015.1056626.
21 Mermey, "New York's."
22 Gina Tron, "In Netflix's *Crime Scene: The Times Square Killer*, Who Was 'Porno King Of NYC' Marty Hodas?," *Oxygen*, 23 December 2021, https://www.oxygen.com/true-crime-buzz/in-crime-scene-the-times-square-killer-who-was-marty-hodas. The convicted mass murderer Richard Cottingham targeted sex workers in the area from 1968 to 1980.
23 J.A. Friedman, *Tales of Times Square*.
24 Steven Ziplow, *The Film Maker's Guide to Pornography* (New York: Drake, 1977), 8.
25 While the peep show was initially invented to manipulate the object of illusion (to enlarge or shrink it), it later became a way to exhibit clandestine material such as pornography. Peep shows came to Times Square in the 1960s. There were two types. Live peep shows, popularized in the 1960s, consisted of private booths surrounding a rotating centre stage where naked female performers danced and

performed sexually explicit acts. Viewers could watch the performers by feeding quarters into a slot, which activated a shade to rise or a window to open. Film or movie peep shows were presentations of pornographic film viewed through a peephole or viewing slot operated by coin that could be purchased at a counter. They were usually in adult bookstores or sex shops, at the back, and operated under the pretence that customers were "sampling" films they might later buy. An adult video arcade was typically set up as a dozen booths, each containing a screen or video monitor, projector, a control panel, and a seat. The lighting was dim, and often red or green lights were affixed to the outside of the booth to indicate whether the booth was occupied (J.A. Friedman, *Tales of Times Square*, 67).

26 "Marty Hodas: King of the Peeps," *Rialto Report*, 29 June 2014, https://www.therialtoreport.com/2014/06/29/marty-hodas.
27 "Ghosts of New York Adult Film: Bob Wolfe's 14th St. Studio," *Rialto Report*, 17 August 2014, https://www.therialtoreport.com/2014/08/17/ghosts-of-new-york-adult-lm-bob-wolfes-14th-st-studio.
28 J.A. Friedman, *Tales of Times Square*, 133.
29 "Ghosts of New York Adult Film."
30 "Ghosts of New York Adult Film."
31 Linda Williams, "Generic Pleasures: Number and Narrative," in *Pornography: Film and Culture*, ed. Peter Lehman (New Brunswick, NJ: Rutgers University Press, 2006), 60.
32 Gerard Damiano, quoted in Ziplow, *Film Maker's Guide*, 160.
33 Shira Tarrant, by way of Jaclyn Friedman, describes the overarching theme of mainstream porn well: "Female pleasure is portrayed as existing in service of male sexuality. Porn that doesn't feature putatively straight women, white people, cisgendered performers, and heterosexual coupling is marginalized as taboo or fetish. This gives viewers the repeated impression, says Friedman, that male ejaculation is the purpose of sex." Shira Tarrant, *The Pornography Industry: What Everyone Needs to Know* (New York: Oxford University Press, 2016), 31.
34 Loren Glass, "Second Wave: Feminism and Porn's Golden Age," *Radical Society* 29, no. 3 (October 2002): 55.
35 J.A. Friedman, *Tales of Times Square*, 67.
36 "The most watched films," writes Natalie Purcell, were "a glorification of misogynistic violence." Natalie Purcell, *Violence and the Pornographic Imaginary: The Politics of Sex, Gender, and Aggression in Hardcore Pornography* (New York: Routledge, 2012), 42–3.
37 L. Williams, "Generic Pleasures," 67.
38 L. Williams, "Generic Pleasures," 67.
39 L. Williams, *Hard Core*, 159.
40 Lynn Commella, "From Text to Context: Feminist Porn and the Making of a Market," in *The Feminist Porn Book: The Politics of Producing Pleasure*, ed. Tristan Taormino et al. (New York: The Feminist Press at the City University of New York, 2012), 91.

Notes to pages 228–31

41 Germaine Greer, quoted in Gingeras, "Revisiting *Suck*."
42 Chris Kraus, quoted in Gingeras, "Revisiting *Suck*."
43 Barry, *Prostitution of Sexuality*; Dworkin, "Prostitution and Male Supremacy"; Robin Morgan, *Going Too Far: The Personal Chronicle of a Feminist* (New York: Random House, 1977).
44 Maggie Ann Labinski, "The Social/Political Potential of Illusions: Enthusiasm and Feminist Porn," *Porn Studies* 6, no. 1 (2019): 100–13, https://doi.org/10.1080/23268743.2018.1559082.
45 Candida Royalle, quoted in Labinski, "Social/Political Potential," 107.
46 In Royalle's debut film *Femme* (1984), the female lead experiences a range of wish fulfilments as her beloved TV idol appears in her living room ready to pleasure her; a woman flirts with two photographers at an art gallery and lets her mind run wild with fantasy; a woman dealing with an arrogant photographer gets even by inducing him to pleasure her. Her films winkingly reversed the power dynamics in mainstream porn, such as in *My Surrender* (1996), in which a female studio executive reverses the infamous "casting couch" when she asks, "So what makes you think *you* can be in the movies?" and implores her (very willing) male starlet to offer her sexual favours. Royalle's films were also educational, geared towards correcting misinformation propagated by mainstream porn. As she said on *The Dr. Ruth Show*, "I purposefully instructed my actor to, after having intercourse with her for a while, to pull out and perform oral sex on her. I wanted to show husbands of the world that women needed special attention." Candida Royalle, quoted in Sheona McDonald, dir., *Candice* (United States: Dimestore Productions, 2019).
47 Candida Royalle, quoted in McDonald, *Candice*.
48 Candida Royalle, quoted in McDonald, *Candice*.
49 Tristan Taormino, quoted in "What Is Feminist Porn?," Feminist Porn Awards, accessed 19 July 2022, https://www.feministpornawards.com/what-is-feminist-porn-2.
50 Betony Vernon, quoted in Despentes, *Mutantes*.
51 Tristan Taormino, quoted in "What Is Feminist Porn?"
52 Constance Penley et al., "Introduction: The Politics of Producing Pleasure," in *The Feminist Porn Book: The Politics of Producing Pleasure*, ed. Tristan Taormino et al. (New York: The Feminist Press at the City University of New York, 2012), 10.
53 George Pelecanos, quoted in Greenwald and Ryan, "*The Deuce*."
54 Tristan Taormino, quoted in Rebecca Whisnant, "'But What about Feminist Porn?' Examining the Work of Tristan Taormino," *Sexualization, Media, & Society* 2, no. 2 (2016): para. 12, https://doi.org/10.1177/2374623816631727.
55 David Simon, quoted in Sean Woods, "The Last Word: David Simon on Twitter Trolls, Trump and Making *The Deuce* in the #MeToo Era," *Rolling Stone*, 8 September 2018, https://www.rollingstone.com/tv-movies/tv-movie-features/david-simon-interview-deuce-hbo-719397. Producers David Simon and George Pelacanos

prioritized constant communication with performers. Pelecanos notes: "Nina Noble [executive producer] had meetings with all the women before we shot each episode. If we were asking them to do something, Nina would have a nudity meeting with them and tell them." George Pelacanos, quoted in Greenwald and Ryan, "*The Deuce*." Emily Meade, who plays Lori Madison, requested a further level of protection, which resulted in the hiring of an "intimacy coach" to facilitate the filming of sex scenes and to ensure communication between director and performers and to prevent any "surprises." Meade describes the intimacy coach as a "guide" who provides "emotional and psychological protection." Emily Meade, quoted in Michelle Darrisaw, "Despite Allegations against Co-Star James Franco, *The Deuce*'s Emily Meade Is Fighting for Women," *Oprah Daily*, 15 October 2018, https://www.oprahdaily.com/entertainment/tv-movies/a23643803/emily-meade-the-deuce-season-2.

56 Richard Brody, "An Auteur Is Not a Brand," *New Yorker*, 10 July 2014, https://www.newyorker.com/culture/richard-brody/an-auteur-is-not-a-brand.
57 Peter Wollen, *Signs and Meaning in the Cinema* (Bloomington: Indiana University Press, 1973), 16.
58 As Ethel Person wrote, "women have the ability to abstain from sex without any negative psychological consequences." Ethel Person, quoted in Echols, "Taming of the Id," 60.
59 Andrea Dworkin, quoted in Echols, "Taming of the Id," 59.
60 Royalle was likewise a *cause celebre* in the 1980s. Her wit and succinct ability to articulate how sex fit into feminism earned the respect of intellectuals and popular media, and when she appeared on *The Phil Donahue Show* she was introduced as a former porn star who got "smart and figured out that the real money was in producing." See McDonald, *Candice*.
61 Miller-Young, *Taste for Brown Sugar*, 69.
62 Departing from romantic notions of lifelong careers or riches, *After Porn Ends* and its sequels profile hard-working ex-performers, some of whom, like Candy, move behind the camera and use their knowledge of the adult industry to challenge porn tropes and innovate new ways of imagining the porn genre.
63 Diane Negra, *What a Girl Wants? Fantasizing the Reclamation of Self in Postfeminism* (London: Routledge, 2008), 100, https://doi.org/10.4324/9780203869000.
64 Alan Sepinwall, "David Simon and Emily Meade on What Lori Means to *The Deuce*," *Rolling Stone*, 22 October 2019, https://www.rollingstone.com/tv/tv-features/deuce-lori-season-3-episode-7-david-simon-emily-meade-interview-900235.
65 A 1980 radical feminist advertisement shows a still from the film *Star 80* (1983) – based on the life and death of Playboy Bunny Dorothy Stratton – of a blood covered naked woman's body with the caption "What sort of man reads *Playboy*?" suggesting that men who like looking at centrefolds are homicidal. The hyper-sexualized woman who dies young is a common trope that has become an ideological argument, her death being "used" for anti-porn cause. Indeed, popular culture is eerily fascinated by the deaths of porn stars: the morbid "dead pornstar

list" (https://www.iafd.com/deadporn) has hundreds of entries documenting porn stars' known birth and death dates as well as what calamity – drug overdose, HIV/AIDS, suicide, murder – felled them.

66 Miller-Young, *Taste for Brown Sugar*, 6.
67 Miller-Young, *Taste for Brown Sugar*, xii.
68 Miller-Young, *Taste for Brown Sugar*, 75.
69 Miller-Young, *Taste for Brown Sugar*, 67.
70 Miller-Young, *Taste for Brown Sugar*, 69.
71 Dominique Fishback, quoted in HBO, "Meet Darlene | The Deuce (HBO)," Facebook video, 24 September 2017, https://www.facebook.com/HBO/videos/meet-darlene-the-deuce-hbo/10155917978243933.
72 Roberts, *Whores in History*, 340.
73 Ringdal, *Love for Sale*, 369.
74 St. James describes her "politicization" as a "whore" and a sex workers' rights activist: "'What's a nice girl like you …' was the usual reaction of men to my becoming a feminist as well as to my becoming a prostitute. The difference for me was that I *chose* to be a feminist, but I *decided* to work as a prostitute after being labelled officially by a misogynist judge in San Francisco at age twenty-five. It was 1962. I said in court, 'Your Honor, I've never turned a trick in my life!' He responded, 'Anyone who knows the language is obviously a professional.' My crime? I knew too much to be a nice girl." Margo St. James, quoted in Gail Pheterson, ed., *A Vindication of the Rights of Whores* (Seattle: Seal Press, 1989), xvii.
75 Gail Pheterson, quoted in Sloan and Wahab, "Feminist Voices," 11.
76 Margo St. James, quoted in Susan Margolis, "Taking the Bull by the Horns," *City Magazine*, 1 January 1973, https://iiif.lib.harvard.edu/manifests/view/drs:496223627$34i.
77 Jenness, "From Sex as Sin," 406.
78 Margo St. James, quoted in Alexandra Lutnick, "Beyond Prescientific Reasoning: The Sex Worker Environment Assessment Team Study," in *Negotiating Sex Work: Unintended Consequences of Policy and Activism*, ed. Carisa R. Showden and Samantha Majic (Minneapolis: University of Minnesota Press, 2014), 47.
79 Katharine Q. Seelye, "Margo St. James, Advocate for Sex Workers, Dies at 83," *New York Times*, 20 January 2021, https://www.nytimes.com/2021/01/20/us/margo-st-james-dead.html.
80 Roberts, *Whores in History*, 344.
81 Jenness, "From Sex as Sin," 406.
82 Susan Buck-Morss has aptly described this as post-feminism's "nightmarish effect of 'freeing' all women to be sexual objects." Susan Buck-Morss, "The Flaneur, the Sandwichman and the Whore: The Politics of Loitering," *New German Critique* 39 (Autumn 1986): 132, https://doi.org/10.2307/488122.
83 Candy recalls her own first trick: "Then he tells me to suck his dick. And I'm not kidding you, he hadn't washed it in years. I was gagging. I was like, 'I should jump out the window right now.' But it got easier from there."

84 In the 1980s, anti-porn sentiment from right-wing evangelical conservatives believed porn was sinful because it portrayed sex outside of the family unit and glorified sex acts that were non-procreative. The conservative movement against pornography and the radical feminist contingent dovetailed in the mid-1980s, strange bedfellows forming a powerful bloc with public support that sought and sometimes secured legislative changes, including the Minneapolis ordinance of 1983 that sought to criminalize pornography. It never passed, and porn was subsequently protected under first amendment rights (free expression), but WAP remained a formidable force in feminism with wide ranging influence.

85 On one side, radical feminists argued that pornography reduced women to sex objects, instigated violence, and perpetuated their continued oppression (Dworkin and MacKinnon, *Pornography and Civil Rights*; Pateman, *Sexual Contract*; Jeffreys, *Industrial Vagina*; Dworkin, *Pornography*). Sex-positive feminists, on the other side, sought to reframe sex as a site of pleasure and exploration wherein women could subversively unshackle themselves from compulsory female submissiveness.

86 Ariel Levy argues that women's complicity in their own sexual objectification is one of neo-liberal feminism's greatest coups (Levy, *Female Chauvinist Pigs*). In her extensive study of the global sex industry, Sheila Jeffreys traces this development to the 1980s, when mainstreaming of pornography created a system in which the "commercialization of women's subordination" became part of the "corporate sphere" (Jeffreys, *Industrial Vagina*, 1, 3). These scholars are especially critical of neo-liberal discourses that link sex work with terms like "freedom" and "equality," which they hold responsible for sanitizing and erasing the harms perpetrated on sex workers by the sex industry and duping young women into believing that selling sex is empowering. In this vein, Sheila Jeffreys echoes Betty Friedan, who described what she saw as a growing cultural obsession with a "hollowed out sexuality" that tricked young women into believing that sexual inhibition was a primary pathway to selfhood (Friedan, *Feminine Mystique*, 250).

87 Gayle Rubin writes: "Anti-porn propaganda often implies that sexism originates within the commercial sex industry and subsequently infects the rest of society. This is sociologically non-sensical. The sex industry is hardly a feminist utopia. It reflects the sexism that exists in the society as a whole. We need to analyse and oppose the manifestations of gender inequality specific to the sex industry. But this not the same as trying to wipe out commercial sex." Rubin, "Thinking Sex," 302.

88 Brooke Meredith Beloso, "Sex, Work, and the Feminist Erasure of Class," *Signs: Journal of Women in Culture and Society* 38, no. 1 (Autumn 2012): 65–6, https://doi.org/10.1086/665808.

89 David Simon, quoted in Woods, "Last Word."

90 The well-researched documentary *Pornocracy: The New Sex Multinationals* (2017) examines how the rise of tube sites permanently changed the porn industry. Beginning in 2016, YouPorn started offering free unlimited pirated clips, and the

site quickly became hugely popular. When porn producers realized they could not compete against the glut of free porn, they accepted invitations to "partner" with the tube sites, which meant giving content for free in hope that viewers would subscribe to their sites later for a fee. This rarely happens. The subsequent lost revenues for porn production companies changed production conditions, as makers were compelled to churn out movies faster, and performers were forced to work longer hours for less pay. Stoya, a performer whose career spanned the transition to tube sites, described the new landscape functioning to "the detriment of humans." Today, only a few porn performers become household names, and people watch porn less to see their favourite performer than to witness a new sex act. Ovidie compares the porn performers today to "cannon fodder ... one gaping hole among many." Ovidie, dir., *Pornocracy: The New Sex Multinationals* (France: Magneto Presse, 2017).

91 Tristan Taormino, quoted in Whisnant, "'But What,'" 2.
92 Sasha Grey, quoted in "Sasha Grey, the Dirtiest Girl in the World: The Story behind the Story," *Rolling Stone*, 29 April 2009, https://www.rollingstone.com/tv-movies/tv-movie-news/sasha-grey-the-dirtiest-girl-in-the-world-the-story-behind-the-story-63211.
93 "Sasha Grey."
94 David Simon, quoted in Woods, "Last Word."
95 Quoted in Woods, "Last Word."
96 Candida Royalle, quoted in McDonald, *Candice*.

Curtains: From Victimhood and Vice to Sex Workers' Rights

1 Rubin, "Thinking Sex," 295.
2 Megan Koester, "The New Normal: Why Television Has Chosen to Humanize Sex Workers," *The Guardian*, 14 November 2016, https://www.theguardian.com/tv-and-radio/2016/nov/14/television-sex-workers-porn-the-girlfriend-experience.
3 A'Ziah (Zola) King, quoted in Rachel Ho, "A'Ziah King Hopes *Zola* Will Inspire More Authentic Sex Work Stories in Hollywood," *Exclaim!*, 30 June 2021, https://exclaim.ca/film/article/aziah_king_hopes_zola_will_inspire_more_authentic_sex_work_stories_in_hollywood.
4 As Chris Bruckert has noted, the contours of the conversation about sex work have shifted over the last decade or so: "We have moved away from explicitly moral arguments (even if morality still clearly infuses the perspectives)." Quoted in Lauren Kirshner, "Shining a Light on the Labour of Sex Work," *Room*, 19 August 2019, https://roommagazine.com/shining-a-light-on-the-labour-of-sex-work-2.
5 Victoria Bateman, "Feminists Should Support a Woman's Right to Sell Sex," *UnHerd*, 11 October 2018, https://unherd.com/2018/10/feminists-support-womans-right-sell-sex.

6 Concerns related to identity formation also drive sex workers through what Elizabeth Bernstein calls the pursuit of "class specific cultural distinctions." In light of the end of standard employment relations and a rise of downward mobility, young people increasingly distance themselves from significations of middle-class status, such as home ownership, and pursue an ethos of self-actualization (Bernstein, "Sex Work," 476).
7 Bruckert and Parent, "Work of Sex Work"; Abigail Pesta, "Exclusive: Diary of a Call Girl Turned Teacher, Part 1," *Marie Claire*, 6 December 2010, https://www.marieclaire.com/culture/a5670/melissa-petro-exclusive-interview; Petro, "H-Word."
8 Greenslade, "Journalist Fired."
9 Melissa Petro, "Life after Sex Work," *Daily Beast*, 14 July 2017, https://www.thedailybeast.com/life-after-sex-work.
10 Savannah Sly, "Good Work (If You Can Get It): Job Discrimination against Sex Workers," Woodhull Freedom Foundation, August 2022, https://www.woodhullfoundation.org/wp-content/uploads/2022/08/Savannah-Sly-Good-Work-If-You-Can-Get-It.pdf.
11 Gill, "Postfeminist Media Culture."
12 Andi Zeisler, *Feminism and Pop Culture* (Berkeley, CA: Seal Press, 2008), xv.
13 Sherene, Razack, "Race, Space, and Prostitution: The Making of the Bourgeois Subject," *Canadian Journal of Women and the Law* 10, no. 2 (1998): 338–76.
14 Suraj Patel, "We Must Repeal SESTA, a Deadly Law That Does Nothing to Help Trafficking Victims," *Vice*, 21 May 2018, https://broadly.vice.com/en_us/article/xwmdkk/repeal-sesta-fosta-sex-work-suraj-patel.
15 Gill, "Postfeminist Media Culture," 152.
16 Hochschild, *Managed Heart*, 173.
17 Hochschild, *Managed Heart*, 173.
18 Stassa Edwards, "The History of Female Anger," *Vice*, 21 September 2015, https://broadly.vice.com/en_us/article/4xke4b/the-history-of-female-anger.
19 Roxane Gay, "Who Gets to Be Angry?," *New York Times*, 12 June 2016, https://www.nytimes.com/2016/06/12/opinion/sunday/who-gets-to-be-angry.html.
20 Gay, "Who Gets to Be Angry?"
21 Arthurs, *Television and Sexuality*, 102.
22 Sara Suleri, quoted in Gail Vanstone, *D Is for Daring: The Women behind Studio D* (Toronto: Sumach Press, 2007), 20.
23 Emily Witt, "After the Closure of Backpage, Increasingly Vulnerable Sex Workers Are Demanding Their Rights," *New Yorker*, 8 June 2018, https://www.newyorker.com/news/dispatch/after-the-closure-of-backpage-increasingly-vulnerable-sex-workers-are-demanding-their-rights.
24 Patel, "We Must Repeal SESTA."
25 Patel, "We Must Repeal SESTA."
26 Patel, "We Must Repeal SESTA."
27 Rick Paulas, "Sex Workers vs. the Internet," *Longreads*, 14 June 2018, https://longreads.com/2018/06/14/sex-workers-vs-the-internet.

28 Quoted in Zeisler, *Feminism and Pop Culture*, 137.
29 Isa Mazzei, quoted in "Camgirl: Isa Mazzei."
30 Ho, "A'Ziah King."
31 Mya Taylor, quoted in Zack Ford, "Transgender Actress Mya Taylor's Journey from Impoverished Sex Worker to Oscar Contender," *Think Progress*, 4 December 2015, https://archive.thinkprogress.org/transgender-actress-mya-taylors-journey-from-impoverished-sex-worker-to-oscar-contender-4893ef247092.
32 Melissa Ditmore, quoted in Villiers, *Sexography*, 181.
33 Grant, *Playing the Whore*, 25.
34 Alana Massey, "A&E Completely Misunderstands the Reality of Sex Workers," *New Republic*, 2 April 2015, https://newrepublic.com/article/121445/aes-show-8-minutes-damaging-sex-workers.
35 Katie Sola, "This A&E Reality Show Promised to Help Sex Workers. It Just Made Their Lives Worse," *HuffPost*, 5 May 2015, https://www.huffpost.com/entry/sex-workers-8-minutes_n_7213182.
36 Quoted in Debbie Emery, "Sex Workers Claim A&E Show *8 Minutes* Lied to Them," *The Wrap*, 4 May 2015, http://www.thewrap.com/sex-workers-claim-ae-show-8-minutes-lied-to-them.
37 Emery, "Sex Workers."
38 Elizabeth Nolan Brown, "A&E Cancels Prostitution 'Reality' Series *8 Minutes*," *Reason*, 6 May 2015, https://reason.com/2015/05/06/ae-pulls-8-minutes-sex-work-show.
39 "Men Who Visit This Website Get a Grim Reminder and Eye-Opening Surprise," Women in the World, 29 June 2016, https://womenintheworld.com/2016/09/29/men-who-tried-contacting-the-escorts-advertised-on-this-site-got-an-unsettling-surprise (site discontinued).
40 Lever and Dolnick, "Clients and Call Girls"; Weitzer, *Legalizing Prostitution*.
41 Lucas, "Work of Sex Work," 540.
42 HuniePot (@HunieKyu), "HunieCam Studio Release Trailer," YouTube video, 2:06, 26 March 2016, https://www.youtube.com/watch?v=g48fRvaxaiM; "Hunie-Cam Studio," TVTropes.com, accessed 30 June 2017, https://tvtropes.org/pmwiki/pmwiki.php/VideoGame/HuniecamStudio.
43 Valerie Feldman, "Sex Work Politics and the Internet: Carving Out Political Space in the Blogosphere," in *Negotiating Sex Work: Unintended Consequences of Policy and Activism*, ed. Carisa R. Showden and Samantha Majic (Minneapolis: University of Minnesota Press, 2014), 248.
44 Recent popular culture from outside the US includes the Brazilian series *Confessions of a Brazilian Call Girl* (2011), the Scottish documentary *Strippers* (2014), and the Moroccan documentary *Much Loved* (2015). The European film *Irina Palm* (2007) stars Marianne Faithfull as a grandmother who becomes a massage parlour worker to pay for her grandson's life-saving medical treatment. In the Ken Loach film *I, Daniel Blake* (2016), a single mother is denied benefits due to

bureaucratic red tape; after nearly collapsing and eating a tin of cold beans in a food bank, she becomes a sex worker, after which her life improves dramatically. European popular culture about sex workers – in comparison to that from the US – is a further area that warrants enquiry.

45 Popular culture is also portraying male sex workers with greater frequency. A miniseries based on the 1980 blockbuster *American Gigolo* starring Jon Bernthal premiered on Showtime in 2022. *La Bare* (2014) is a documentary about the male erotic dancing industry. *Rocco* (2016), another documentary, is the story of Italian porn star Rocco Siffredi's last year as a performer. More research is needed on popular culture representations of street sex work, trafficking, male sex workers, and trans sex workers. Projects similar to this one could be undertaken to understand how popular culture represents sex workers whose lives and work are studied even less than women sex workers.

46 Emma Thompson, quoted in Late Show with Stephen Colbert (@ColbertLateShow), "The Strange Intimacy of Emma Thompson's New Film, 'Good Luck to You, Leo Grande,'" YouTube video, 5:16, 16 June 2022, https://www.youtube.com/watch?app=desktop&v=fB6nsEKIYmQ.

47 Maggie McNeill, "A False Dichotomy," *Honest Courtesan* (blog), 22 June 2011, https://maggiemcneill.wordpress.com/2011/06/22/a-false-dichotomy.

48 Silva Leite, quoted in Theresa Anasti, "From Sex Worker as Character to Sex Worker as Producer: A Review of Nicholas de Villier's *Sexography: Sex Work in Documentary*," *Los Angeles Review of Books*, 6 July 2017, https://lareviewofbooks.org/article/sex-worker-character-sex-worker-producer-review-nicholas-de-villiers-sexography-sex-work-documentary.

49 Jennifer Lopez, quoted in Tonight Show Starring Jimmy Fallon (@fallontonight), "Jennifer Lopez Teases Super Bowl Halftime Show, Reacts to Changing Google with THAT Dress," YouTube video, 6:35, 6 December 2019, https://www.youtube.com/watch?v=YguJqGu52V0.

Bibliography

Aaron, Michael. "Sex Work and Higher Education: A Mix of Disparate Identities." *Standard Deviation* (blog). Psychology Today, 5 May 2017. https://www.psychologytoday.com/ca/blog/standard-deviations/201705/sex-work-and-higher-education-a-mix-of-disparate-identities.

Abbott, Karen. *Sin in the Second City: Madams, Ministers, Playboys, and the Battle for America's Soul*. New York: Random House, 2007.

Abrams, Rachel. "Sex Shop Workers Welcome the Protection of Retail Union." *New York Times*, 23 May 2016. https://www.nytimes.com/2016/05/24/business/sex-shop-workers-welcome-the-protections-of-a-retail-union.html.

Adriaens, Fien, and Sofie Van Bauwen. "*Sex and the City*: A Postfeminist Point of View? Or How Popular Culture Functions as a Channel for Feminist Discourse." *Journal of Popular Culture* 47, no. 1 (February 2014): 174–95. https://doi.org/10.1111/j.1540-5931.2011.00869.x.

Agustin, Laura María. "Fallen Women, Including the One Charles Dickens Didn't Save." *Naked Anthropologist* (blog), 11 February 2012. https://www.lauraagustin.com/fallen-women-including-the-one-who-refused-to-be-saved-by-charles-dickens.

– *Sex at the Margins: Migration, Labour Markets and the Rescue Industry*. London: Zed Books, 2007.

Alexander, Patricia. "Prostitution: A Difficult Issue for Feminists." In *Sex Work: Writings by Women in the Sex Industry*, edited by Frédérique Delacoste and Priscilla Alexander, 184–214. London: Virago, 1988.

Allison, Dorothy. "Public Silence, Private Terror." In *Pleasure and Danger: Exploring Female Sexuality*, edited by Carole Vance, 103–15. New York: Routledge, 1984.

Alter, Charlotte. "The Duke Porn Star Is Right: Kink Can Be a Feminist Choice." *Time*, 20 March 2014. https://time.com/30397/duke-porn-star-is-right-kink-can-be-a-feminist-choice.

Anasti, Theresa. "From Sex Worker as Character to Sex Worker as Producer: A Review of Nicholas de Villier's *Sexography: Sex Work in Documentary*." *Los Angeles Review of Books*, 6 July 2017. https://lareviewofbooks.org/article/sex-worker-character-sex-worker-producer-review-nicholas-de-villiers-sexography-sex-work-documentary.

Andreeva, Nellie. "Lifetime Greenlights *The Client List* Series Starring and Produced by Jennifer Love Hewitt." *Deadline*, 10 August 2011. http://deadline.com/2011/08/lifetime-greenlights-the-client-list-series-starring-produced-by-jennifer-love-hewitt-155920.

Andrews, Robert. *The Columbia Dictionary of Quotations*. New York: Columbia University Press, 1993.

anonomaxtacular. "Would You Seriously/Exclusively Date a Sex Worker?" Reddit, 21 March 2018. https://www.reddit.com/r/AskMenOver30/comments/85ze22/would_you_seriouslyexclusively_date_a_sex_worker.

Armstrong, Edward G. "Massage Parlors and Their Customers." *Archives of Sexual Behavior* 7, no. 2 (1978): 117–25. https://doi.org/10.1007/BF01542061.

Arthurs, Jane. *Television and Sexuality: Regulation and the Politics of Taste*. Maidenhead: Open University Press, 2004.

Aspinall, Georgia. "Why Can't We Reconcile Motherhood With Sexual Agency? The Reaction to Lana Rhoades' Pregnancy Proves We Still Have Work to Do." *Grazia*, 6 July 2021. https://graziadaily.co.uk/life/in-the-news/who-is-father-lana-rhoades-baby-pregnant.

Attwood, Feona. "No Money Shot? Commerce, Pornography and New Sex Taste Cultures." *Sexualities* 10, no. 4 (October 2007): 441–56. https://doi.org/10.1177/1363460707080982.

Baldwin, Margaret A. "Split at the Root: Prostitution and Feminist Discourses of Law Reform." In *Prostitution and Pornography: Philosophical Debate about the Sex Industry*, edited by Jessica Spector, 106–47. Stanford, CA: Stanford University Press, 2006.

Banyard, Kat. *The Equality Illusion: The Truth about Women and Men Today*. London: Faber and Faber, 2010.

Barry, Kathleen. *Female Sexual Slavery*. New York: New York University Press, 1984.

– *The Prostitution of Sexuality: The Global Exploitation of Women*. New York: New York University Press, 1995.

Bartley, Paula. "Preventing Prostitution: The Ladies' Association for the Care and Protection of Young Girls in Birmingham, 1887–1914." *Women's History Review* 7, no. 1 (March 1998): 37–60. https://doi.org/10.1080/09612029800200160.

Barton, Adriana. "Are Middle-Aged Women Succumbing to 'Desperate Housewives Syndrome'?" *Globe and Mail*, 1 May 2011. https://www.theglobeandmail.com/life/health-and-fitness/are-middle-aged-women-succumbing-to-desperate-housewives-syndrome/article578178.

Bateman, Victoria. "Feminists Should Support a Woman's Right to Sell Sex." *UnHerd*, 11 October 2018. https://unherd.com/2018/10/feminists-support-womans-right-sell-sex.

Bazelon, Emily. "Should Prostitution Be a Crime?" *New York Times Magazine*, 5 May 2016. https://www.nytimes.com/2016/05/08/magazine/should-prostitution-be-a-crime.html.

Beauvoir, Simone de. *The Second Sex*. Translated by Constance Borde and Sheila Malovany-Chevallier. New York: Vintage Books, 2011.
Beloso, Brooke Meredith. "Sex, Work, and the Feminist Erasure of Class." *Signs: Journal of Women in Culture and Society* 38, no. 1 (Autumn 2012): 47–70. https://doi.org/10.1086/665808.
Benoit, Cecilia, S. Mikael Jansson, Michaela Smith, and Jackson Flagg. "Prostitution Stigma and Its Effect on the Working Conditions, Personal Lives, and Health of Sex Workers." *The Journal of Sex Research* 55, no. 4–5 (2017): 457–71. https://doi.org/10.1080/00224499.2017.1393652.
Berger, John. *Ways of Seeing*. New York: British Broadcasting Corporation and Penguin Books, 1972.
Berlatsky, Noah. "Students Who Do Sex Work." *The Atlantic*, 19 March 2014. https://www.theatlantic.com/education/archive/2014/03/students-who-do-sex-work/284505.
Bernstein, Elizabeth. "Sex Work for the Middle Classes." *Sexualities* 10, no. 4 (October 2007): 473–88. https://doi.org/10.1177/1363460707080984.
– *Temporarily Yours: Intimacy, Authenticity, and the Commerce of Sex*. Chicago: University of Chicago Press, 2007.
Bertrand, Natasha. "How Webcam Models Make Money." *Business Insider*, 18 November 2014. http://www.businessinsider.com/heres-how-webcam-models-make-money-2014-11.
Binik, Yitzchak M., and Marta Meana. "The Future of Sex Therapy: Specialization or Marginalization?" *Archives of Sexual Behaviour* 38, no. 6 (2009): 1016–27. https://doi.org/10.1007/s10508-009-9475-9.
Bland, Lucy. *Banishing the Beast: Feminism, Sex and Morality*. London: Tauris Parke, 2001.
Bleakley, Paul. "500 Tokens to Go Private: Camgirls, Cybersex, and Feminist Entrepreneurship." *Sexuality and Culture* 18, no. 4 (2014): 892–910. https://doi.org/10.1007/s12119-014-9228-3.
Blichert, Frederick. "This Horror Screenwriter Subverted Every Shitty Sex Worker Trope." *Vice*, 13 November 2018. https://www.vice.com/en_us/article/j5z8p3/screenwriter-isa-mazzei-subverted-every-shitty-sex-work-trope-for-cam.
Boris, Eileen, Stephanie Gilmore, and Rhacel Parreñas. "Sexual Labors: Interdisciplinary Perspectives toward Sex Work as Work." *Sexualities* 13, no. 2 (April 2010): 131–7. https://doi.org/10.1177/1363460709359228.
Bourdieu, Pierre. *Distinction: A Social Critique of the Judgement of Taste*. Cambridge, MA: Harvard University Press, 1987.
Boyle, Karen. "Courting Consumers and Legitimizing Exploitation: The Representation of Commercial Sex in Television Documentaries." *Feminist Media Studies* 8, no. 1 (2008): 36–50. https://doi.org/10.1080/14680770701824894.
– "Selling the Selling of Sex: The Secret Diary of a Call-Girl on Screen." *Feminist Media Studies* 10, no. 1 (2010): 113–16.
Brennan, Denise. *What's Love Got to Do with It? Transnational Desires and Sex Tourism in the Dominican Republic*. Durham, NC: Duke University Press, 2004. https://doi.org/10.1215/9780822385400.

Brewis, Joanna, and Stephen Linstead. *Sex, Work and Sex Work: Eroticizing Organization*. London: Routledge, 2000. https://doi.org/10.4324/9780203360965.

Brock, Deborah R. *Making Trouble, Making Work: Prostitution as a Social Problem*. Toronto: University of Toronto Press, 1998. https://doi.org/10.3138/9781442676930.

Brody, Richard. "An Auteur Is Not a Brand." *New Yorker*, 10 July 2014. https://www.newyorker.com/culture/richard-brody/an-auteur-is-not-a-brand.

Bromwich, Jonah E. "Manhattan to Stop Prosecuting Prostitution, Part of Nationwide Shift." *New York Times*, 21 April 2021. https://www.nytimes.com/2021/04/21/nyregion/manhattan-to-stop-prosecuting-prostitution.html.

Bromwich, Rebecca, and Monique Marie DeJong, eds. *Mothers, Mothering and Sex Work*. Bradford, ON: Demeter Press, 2015.

Brown, Elizabeth Nolan. "A&E Cancels Prostitution 'Reality' Series *8 Minutes*." *Reason*, 6 May 2015. https://reason.com/2015/05/06/ae-pulls-8-minutes-sex-work-show.

Brownmiller, Susan. *Against Our Will: Men, Women, and Rape*. New York: Fawcett Books, 1993.

Bruckert, Chris. "The World of the Professional Stripper." In *Feminisms and Womanisms: A Women's Studies Reader*, edited by Althea Prince and Susan Silva-Wayne, 321–34. Toronto: Women's Press, 2004.

Bruckert, Chris, and Colette Parent. "The Work of Sex Work." In *Sex Work: Rethinking the Job, Respecting the Workers*, edited by Colette Parent, Chris Bruckert, Patrice Corriveau, Maria Nengeh Mensah, and Louise Toupin, 57–81. Vancouver: UBC Press, 2013.

Bryan, James H. "Occupational Ideologies and Individual Attitudes of Call Girls." *Social Problems* 13, no. 4 (Spring 1966): 441–50. https://doi.org/10.2307/798593.

Bryant, Clifton D., and C. Eddie Palmer. "Massage Parlors and 'Hand Whores': Some Sociological Observations." *Journal of Sex Research* 11, no. 3 (1975): 227–41. https://doi.org/10.1080/00224497509550898.

Buchanan, Kyle. "Helen Hunt on Sex, *The Sessions*, and the Choice She Had to Fight For." *Vulture*, 17 October 2012. https://www.vulture.com/2012/10/helen-hunt-on-sex-and-the-sessions.html.

Buck-Morss, Susan. "The Flaneur, the Sandwichman and the Whore: The Politics of Loitering." *New German Critique* 39 (Autumn 1986): 99–140. https://doi.org/10.2307/488122.

Budryk, Zack. "Poll: Majority Supports Decriminalizing Sex Work." *The Hill*, 30 January 2020. https://thehill.com/regulation/other/480725-poll-majority-supports-decriminalizing-sex-work.

Bungay, Vicky, Michael Halpin, Christ Atchison, and Caitlin Johnston. "Structure and Agency: Reflections from an Exploratory Study of Vancouver Indoor Sex Workers." *Culture, Health & Sexuality* 13, no. 1 (January 2011): 15–29. https://doi.org/10.1080/13691058.2010.517324.

Burana, Lily. "Margaret Cho Wants to Talk about Sex Work." *New York Times*, 4 November 2015. https://www.nytimes.com/2015/11/03/fashion/margaret-cho-sex-work.html.

- "The Old Bump and Grind: Can Stripping Support the Arts?" *Village Voice*, 5 May 1998, 138–40.
- *Strip City: A Stripper's Farewell Journey across America*. New York: Miramax Books, 2001.

Burke, Nathaniel B. "Intimate Commodities: Intimate Labor and the Production and Circulation of Inequality." *Sexualities* 19, no. 7 (October 2016): 780–801. https://doi.org/10.1177/1363460715616948.

Burtram, Laurie K., and Megan Ross, curators. *Canada's Oldest Profession: Sex Work and Bawdy House Legislation*. Organized and presented by the University of Toronto Libraries, 2 March–1 June 2016. https://exhibits.library.utoronto.ca/exhibits/show/bawdy.

Büschi, Eva. "Sex Work and Violence: Focusing on Managers in the Indoor Sex Industry." *Sexualities* 17, no. 5–6 (September 2014): 724–41. https://doi.org/10.1177/1363460714531271.

Cabezas, Amalia L. "Between Love and Money: Sex, Tourism, and Citizenship in Cuba and the Dominican Republic." *Signs: Journal of Women in Culture and Society* 29, no. 4 (Summer 2014): 987–1015. https://doi.org/10.1086/382627.

Califia, Patrick. *Public Sex: The Culture of Radical Sex*. Pittsburgh, PA: Cleis Press, 1994.

"Camgirl: Isa Mazzei Unveils the Enigma." *Subvrt*, 31 October 2019. https://www.subvrtmag.com/camgirl-isa-mazzei-unveils-the-enigma.

Campbell, Russell. *Marked Women: Prostitutes and Prostitution in the Cinema*. Madison: University of Wisconsin Press, 2006.

Canadian Press. "Olympian Suzy Favor Hamilton, Who Secretly Worked as a Las Vegas Escort, Reclaims Her Life after Bipolar Diagnosis." *National Post*, 17 September 2015. https://nationalpost.com/sports/olympics/olympian-suzy-favor-hamilton-who-secretly-worked-as-a-las-vegas-escort-reclaims-her-life-after-bipolar-diagnosis.

Caplan-Bricker, Nora. "The Best and Worst Parts of Calling Yourself a 'Mompreneur.'" *Slate*, 16 May 2016. http://www.slate.com/blogs/xx_factor/2016/05/16/is_mompreneur_sexist_or_a_revolutionary_term.html.

Chan, Wilfred. "What Legal Protections Do Revenge Porn Victims Have at Work in the US?" *The Guardian*, 29 September 2022. https://www.theguardian.com/law/2022/sep/29/legal-protections-revenge-porn-victims-work-erick-adame.

Chapkis, Wendy. *Live Sex Acts: Women Performing Erotic Labor*. New York: Routledge, 1997. https://doi.org/10.4324/9781315811512.

Cheung, Kylie. "New Series *Strut* Normalizes Sex Work with a Group of Friends Who Start an Escorting Agency." *Salon*, 18 June 2021. https://www.salon.com/2021/06/18/strut-tv-escorting-revry-misha-calvert.

ClaLoveHewitt (@ClaLoveHewitt). "The Client List ~ ET Interview Feb4th ~ Jennifer Love Hewitt." YouTube video, 3:41. 4 February 2013. https://www.youtube.com/watch?v=TmcLtIOBGMM.

"Clergy Calls Times Square an 'Open Sewer of Sex.'" *Variety*, 3 November 1971.

Cohen, Bernard. *Deviant Street Networks: Prostitution in New York City*. Lexington, MA: Lexington Books, 1980.

Cohen, Nicole S. *Writers' Rights: Freelance Journalism in a Digital Age*. Montreal: McGill-Queen's University Press, 2016.

Cohen-Greene, Cheryl, and Lorna Garano. *An Intimate Life: Sex, Love, and My Journey as a Surrogate Partner*. Berkley, CA: Soft Skull Press, 2012.

Cole, Ryan. "Sex Workers: We Know What We Want." *Right Now Inc.*, 13 November 2012. http://rightnow.org.au/writing-cat/opinion/sex-workers-we-know-what-we-want.

Collins, Andrew. "Turning a Trick with the Oldest Profession in Film." *The Guardian*, 30 April 2000. https://www.theguardian.com/film/2000/apr/30/2.

Commella, Lynn. "From Text to Context: Feminist Porn and the Making of a Market." In *The Feminist Porn Book: The Politics of Producing Pleasure*, edited by Tristan Taormino, Celine Parreñas Shimizu, Constance Penley, and Mireille Miller-Young, 79–93. New York: The Feminist Press at the City University of New York, 2012.

– "Webcam Girls." Presentation at the International Communication Association Conference, Portland, OR, 14 April 2016.

Comte, Jacqueline. "Decriminalization of Sex Work: Feminist Discourses in Light of New Research." *Sexuality and Culture* 18 (2013): 196–217. https://doi.org/10.1007/s12119-013-9174-5.

Constable, Nicole. "The Commodification of Intimacy: Marriage, Sex, and Reproductive Labor." *Annual Review of Anthropology* 38 (2009): 49–64. https://doi.org/10.1146/annurev.anthro.37.081407.085133.

Cooper, Charlie. "'Decriminalise Prostitution': Top Medical Journal *Lancet* Calls for Global Action to Protect Sex Workers from HIV." *The Independent*, 22 July 2014. http://www.independent.co.uk/life-style/health-and-families/decriminalise-prostitution-top-medical-journal-lancet-calls-for-global-action-to-protect-sex-workers-9620273.html.

Corliss, Richard. "That Old Feeling: When Porno Was Chic." *Time*, 29 March 2005. http://content.time.com/time/arts/article/0,8599,1043267,00.html.

Cornwall, Andrea, Jasmine Gideon, and Kalpana Wilson. "Introduction: Reclaiming Feminism: Gender and Neoliberalism." *IDS Bulletin* 39, no. 6 (2008): 1–9. https://doi.org/10.1111/j.1759-5436.2008.tb00505.x.

Cowley, Sophia. "Queer Romance Meets Classical Thriller: An Interview with John Carchietta, Director of *Teenage Cockt*ail." *Film Inquiry*, 10 August 2016. https://www.filminquiry.com/interview-carchietta-teenage-cocktail.

Coy, Maddy, Josephine Wakeling, and Maria Garner. "Selling Sex Sells: Representations of Prostitution and the Sex Industry in Sexualized Popular Culture as Symbolic Violence." *Women's Studies International Forum* 34, no. 5 (September–October 2011): 441–8. https://doi.org/10.1016/j.wsif.2011.05.008.

Crane, Antonia. *Spent: A Memoir*. Los Angeles: Rare Bird Books, 2014.

– "Stop Stealing from Strippers." *New York Times*, 13 August 2015. https://www.nytimes.com/2015/08/13/opinion/stop-stealing-from-strippers.html.

Crenshaw, Kimberle. "Mapping the Margins: Intersectionality, Identity Politics, and Violence against Women of Color." *Stanford Law Review* 43, no. 6 (July 1991): 1241–99. https://doi.org/10.2307/1229039.

Cunningham, Scott, and Todd D. Kendall. "Prostitution 2.0: The Changing Face of Sex Work." *Journal of Urban Economics* 69, no. 3 (May 2011): 273–87. https://doi.org/10.1016/j.jue.2010.12.001.

CUPE Organizing (@joincupe). "Today we are very excited to welcome the sex workers at Maggie's Toronto Sex Worker's Action Project, who voted unanimously to join CUPE!" X (formerly Twitter), 8 September 2021. https://twitter.com/joincupe/status/1435737564837728260.

Dalla, Rochelle L. "Exposing the *Pretty Woman* Myth: A Qualitative Examination of the Lives of Female Streetwalking Prostitutes." *The Journal of Sex Research* 37, no. 4 (2000): 344–53. https://doi.org/10.1080/00224490009552057.

Darrisaw, Michelle. "Despite Allegations against Co-Star James Franco, *The Deuce*'s Emily Meade Is Fighting for Women." *Oprah Daily*, 15 October 2018. https://www.oprahdaily.com/entertainment/tv-movies/a23643803/emily-meade-the-deuce-season-2.

Davies, Kim, and Lorraine Evans. "A Virtual View of Managing Violence among British Escorts." *Deviant Behavior* 28 (2007): 525–51. https://doi.org/10.1080/01639620701316830.

Davina, Lola. *Thriving in Sex Work: Sex Work and Money*. Oakland, CA: Erotic as Power Press, 2020.

Dawn, Amber. *How Poetry Saved My Life: A Hustler's Memoir*. Vancouver: Arsenal Pulp Press, 2013.

De Boer, Tracy. "Disability and Sexual Inclusion." *Hypatia* 30, no. 1 (Winter 2015): 66–81. https://doi.org/10.1111/hypa.12118.

Delacoste, Frédérique, and Priscilla Alexander, eds. *Sex Work: Writings by Women in the Sex Industry*. London: Virago, 1988.

Della Giusta, Marina, and Laura Scuriatti. "The Show Must Go On: Making Money Glamourizing Oppression." *European Journal of Women's Studies* 12, no. 1 (February 2005): 31–44. https://doi.org/10.1177/1350506805048854.

Desmond, Matthew. *Evicted: Poverty and Profit in the American City*. New York: Crown Publishings, 2016.

Diamond, Elin, Denise Varney, and Candice Amich, eds. *Performance Feminism and Affect in Neoliberal Times*. London: Palgrave Macmillan, 2017.

Dickson, E.J. "Fired for Doing Porn: The New Employment Discrimination." *Salon*, 30 September 2013. https://www.salon.com/2013/09/30/fired_for_doing_porn_the_new_employment_discrimination.

Dimen, Muriel. "Politically Correct? Politically Incorrect?" In *Pleasure and Danger: Exploring Female Sexuality*, edited by Carole Vance, 138–49. New York: Routledge, 1984.

Dines, Gail. *Pornland: How Porn Has Hijacked Our Sexuality*. Boston: Beacon Press, 2011.

"Director's Statement." *Cam Girlz* Press Kit, March 2015. http://www.camgirlzdoc.com/images/camgirlz_presskit_march2015.pdf.

Ditmore, Melissa Hope. "Transactional Sex." In *Encyclopedia of Prostitution and Sex Work*, edited by Melissa Hope Ditmore, 498–9. Westport, CT: Greenwood Press, 2006.

Dobson, Amy Shields. "Femininities as Commodities: Cam Girl Culture." In *Next Wave Cultures: Feminism, Subcultures, Activism*, edited by Anita Harris, 123–48. New York: Routledge, 2007. https://doi.org/10.4324/9780203940013.

Döring, Nicola M. "The Internet's Impact on Sexuality: A Critical Review of 15 Years of Research." *Computers in Human Behavior* 25, no. 5 (September 2009): 1089–101. https://doi.org/10.1016/j.chb.2009.04.003.

Douglas, Susan J. *The Rise of Enlightened Sexism: How Pop Culture Took Us from Girl Power to Girls Gone Wild*. New York: St. Martin's Griffin, 2010.

– *Where the Girls Are: Growing up Female with the Mass Media*. New York: Three Rivers Press, 1995.

Douglas, Susan J., and Meredith W. Michaels. *The Mommy Myth: The Idealization of Motherhood and How It Has Undermined All Women*. New York: Free Press, 2004.

Dowling, Emma. "Dilemmas of Care." In *Take Care*. Mississauga, ON: Blackwood Gallery, 2017.

Downer, Ivy. "Why We Need to Talk about Stripping as Labour." *BGD*, 26 April 2016. https://www.bgdblog.org/2016/04/why-we-need-to-talk-about-stripping-as-labor.

Dudash, Tawnya. "Peepshow Feminism." In *Whores and Other Feminists*, edited by Jill Nagle, 98–119. New York: Routledge, 1997.

Duggan, Lisa. *The Twilight of Equality: Neoliberalism, Cultural Politics, and the Attack on Democracy*. Boston: Beacon Press, 2004.

Dunn, Jennifer C. "'It's Not Just Sex, It's a Profession': Reframing Prostitution through Text and Context." *Communication Studies* 63, no. 3 (2012): 345–63. https://doi.org/10.1080/10510974.2012.678924.

Durisin, Elya M., Emily van der Meulen, and Chris Bruckert, eds. *Red Light Labour: Sex Work, Regulation, Agency, and Resistance*. Vancouver: UBC Press, 2018.

Dworkin, Andrea. *Pornography: Men Possessing Women*. New York: Putnam, 1981.

– "Prostitution and Male Supremacy." *Michigan Journal of Gender and Law* 1, no. 1 (1993): 1–12.

– *Right-Wing Women: The Politics of Domesticated Females*. New York: Putnam, 1983.

Dworkin, Andrea, and Catharine A. MacKinnon. *Pornography and Civil Rights: A New Day for Women's Equality*. Minneapolis: Organizing Against Pornography, 1988.

Ebert, Roger. "Chelsea, from Five to Nine." *RogerEbert.com*, 20 May 2009. https://www.rogerebert.com/reviews/the-girlfriend-experience-2009.

– "Klute." *RogerEbert.com*, 1 January 1971, https://www.rogerebert.com/reviews/klute-1971.

Echols, Alice. "The Taming of the Id: Feminist Sexual Politics, 1968–83." In *Pleasure and Danger: Exploring Female Sexuality*, edited by Carole Vance, 50–72. New York: Routledge, 1984.

Edgell, Stephen. *The Sociology of Work: Continuity and Change in Paid and Unpaid Work*. 2nd ed. London: SAGE Publications, 2012.

Edwards, Jonathan. "Ex-Stripper's Lawsuit Says Clubs Blocked Her from Working Because They Didn't Want 'Too Many Black Girls.'" *Washington Post*, 19 August

2021. https://www.washingtonpost.com/nation/2021/08/19/houston-former-stripper-sues-strip-clubs-racial-discrimination.

Edwards, Stassa. "The History of Female Anger." *Vice*, 21 September 2015. https://broadly.vice.com/en_us/article/4xke4b/the-history-of-female-anger.

Emery, Debbie. "Sex Workers Claim A&E Show *8 Minutes* Lied to Them." *The Wrap*, 4 May 2015. http://www.thewrap.com/sex-workers-claim-ae-show-8-minutes-lied-to-them.

Enloe, Cynthia. *Maneuvers: The International Politics of Militarizing Women's Lives*. Berkeley: University of California Press, 2000.

Economic Policy Paper (EPI). "6.4 Million Americans Are Working Involuntarily Part Time." News release, 5 December 2016. https://www.epi.org/press/6-4-million-americans-are-working-involuntarily-part-time-employers-are-shifting-toward-part-time-work-as-a-new-normal.

Eser, Alexander. "Essential Webcam Industry Statistics in 2024." Zipdo, last modified 16 July 2023. https://zipdo.co/statistics/webcam-industry.

Evans, Hilary. *Harlots, Whores and Hookers: A History of Prostitution*. New York: Taplinger, 1979.

"Excerpts from the *Motion Picture Herald*, 11 August 1934," Margaret Herrick Library Digital Collections, accessed 13 November 2023, https://digitalcollections.oscars.org/digital/collection/p15759coll11/id/11871.

Fane, Kate. "The Frontier of Feminist Porn: An Interview with Erika Lust." *Maisonneuve*, 26 May 2015. https://maisonneuve.org/post/2015/05/26/frontier-feminist-porn-interview-erika-lust.

Farley, Melissa. "'Bad for the Body, Bad for the Heart': Prostitution Harms Women Even If Legalized or Decriminalized." *Violence Against Women* 10, no. 10 (October 2004): 1087–125. https://doi.org/10.1177/1077801204268607.

– *Prostitution, Trafficking, and Traumatic Stress*. New York: Routledge, 2003. https://doi.org/10.4324/9780203822463.

Farr, Kathryn. *Sex Trafficking: The Global Market in Women and Children*. New York: Worth Publishers, 2005.

Feldman, Valerie. "Sex Work Politics and the Internet: Carving Out Political Space in the Blogosphere." In *Negotiating Sex Work: Unintended Consequences of Policy and Activism*, edited by Carisa R. Showden and Samantha Majic, 243–66. Minneapolis: University of Minnesota Press, 2014.

Ferris, Shawna. *Street Sex Work and Canadian Cities: Resisting a Dangerous Order*. Edmonton: University of Alberta Press, 2015.

Fineman, Stephen. *Work: A Very Short Introduction*. Oxford: Oxford University Press, 2012.

Firestone, Shulamith. *The Dialectic of Sex: The Case for Feminist Revolution*. New York: William Morrow and Company, 1970.

Fitzgerald, Juniper. "What It's Like Being a Mom and a Sex Worker." *Vice*, 11 May 2018. https://broadly.vice.com/en_us/article/bj388w/what-its-like-being-a-mom-and-a-sex-worker.

Florida, Richard L. *The Rise of the Creative Class: Revisited*. New York: Basic Books, 2002.
Fonda, Jane. "44th Academy Awards Acceptance Speech." Transcript of speech delivered at Dorothy Chandler Pavilion, Los Angeles, CA, 10 April 1972. Academy Awards Acceptance Speech Database. http://aaspeechesdb.oscars.org/link/044-3.
Ford, Zack. "Transgender Actress Mya Taylor's Journey from Impoverished Sex Worker to Oscar Contender." *Think Progress*, 4 December 2015. https://archive.thinkprogress.org/transgender-actress-mya-taylors-journey-from-impoverished-sex-worker-to-oscar-contender-4893ef247092.
Foster, Kimberly. "On bell hooks and Feminist Blind Spots: Why Theory Will Not Set Us Free." *For Harriet* (blog), 12 May 2014. https://www.forharriet.com/2014/05/on-bell-hooks-and-feminist-blind-spots.html.
Fox, Marisa. "Patients with Benefits." *Elle*, 4 January 2013. https://www.elle.com/life-love/sex-relationships/advice/a12548/sex-surrogacy.
"FOXSexpert: Sex Surrogacy – Prostitution or Therapy?" *Fox News*, 14 January 2015. https://www.foxnews.com/story/foxsexpert-sex-surrogacy-prostitution-or-therapy.
Frank, Katherine. "Stripping." In *Encyclopedia of Prostitution and Sex Work*, edited by Melissa Hope Ditmore, 466–7. Westport, CT: Greenwood Press, 2006.
Fraser, Liz. *The Yummy Mummy's Survival Guide*. London: HarperCollins, 2006.
Friedan, Betty. *The Feminine Mystique*. New York: W.W. Norton, 1963.
Friedman, Gillian. "Jobless, Selling Nudes Online and Still Struggling." *New York Times*, 21 October 2021. https://www.nytimes.com/2021/01/13/business/onlyfans-pandemic-users.html.
Friedman, Josh Alan. *Tales of Times Square*. New York: Delacorte Press, 1986.
Gajanan, Mahita. "The True Story behind the Netflix Movie *Lost Girls*." *Time*, 13 March 2020. https://time.com/5801794/lost-girls-netflix-true-story.
Gallego, Juana. "Cinema and Prostitution: How Prostitution Is Interpreted in Cinematographic Fiction." *Quaderns Del CAC* 8, no. 2 (2010): 63–71.
Garrity, Joan Terry. *How to Become the Sensuous Woman*. London: Mayflower, 1971.
Gay, Roxane. "Who Gets to Be Angry?" *New York Times*, 12 June 2016. https://www.nytimes.com/2016/06/12/opinion/sunday/who-gets-to-be-angry.html.
"Ghosts of New York Adult Film: Bob Wolfe's 14th St. Studio." *Rialto Report*, 17 August 2014. https://www.therialtoreport.com/2014/08/17/ghosts-of-new-york-adult-film-bob-wolfes-14th-st-studio.
Gill, Rosalind. "Postfeminist Media Culture: Elements of a Sensibility." *Cultural Studies* 10, no. 2 (May 2007): 147–66. https://doi.org/10.1177/1367549407075898.
Gill, Rosalind, and Akane Kanai. "Mediating Neoliberal Capitalism: Affect, Subjectivity and Inequality." *Journal of Communication* 68, no. 2 (April 2018): 318–26. https://doi.org/10.1093/joc/jqy002.
Gillespie, Patrick. "America's Part-Time Workforce Is Huge." *CNN*, 25 April 2016. https://money.cnn.com/2016/04/25/news/economy/part-time-jobs/index.html.

Gingeras, Alison M. "Revisiting *Suck* Magazine's Experiment in Radical Feminist Pornography." *Document Journal*, 28 November 2018. https://www.documentjournal.com/2018/11/revisiting-suck-magazines-experiment-in-radical-feminist-pornography.

Glass, Loren. "Second Wave: Feminism and Porn's Golden Age." *Radical Society* 29, no. 3 (October 2002): 55–65.

"Global Sex Toys Market Size Share Report, 2021–2028." Grand View Research. Accessed 7 December 2021. https://www.grandviewresearch.com/industry-analysis/sex-toys-market.

Goffman, Erving. *Stigma: Notes on the Management of Spoiled Identity*. New York: Simon and Schuster, 1963.

Goldman, Emma. *Anarchism and Other Essays*. New York: Mother Earth Publishing Association, 1911.

Goldstein, Paul J. "Occupational Mobility in the World of Prostitution: Becoming a Madam." *Deviant Behavior* 4, no. 3–4 (1983): 267–79. https://doi.org/10.1080/01639625.1983.9967617.

Goodman, Christopher J., and Steven M. Mance. "Employment Loss and the 2007–09 Recession: An Overview." *Monthly Labour Review* (April 2011): 3–12. http://www.bls.gov/opub/mlr/2011/04/art1full.pdf.

Goodman, Walter. "He Rejects Myths, Not Miracles." *New York Times*, 22 May 1997. https://www.nytimes.com/1997/05/22/arts/he-rejects-myths-not-miracles.html.

Grant, Melissa Gira. "Organized Labor's Newest Heroes: Strippers." *The Atlantic*, 9 November 2012. https://www.theatlantic.com/sexes/archive/2012/11/organized-labors-newest-heroes-strippers/265376.

– *Playing the Whore: The Work of Sex Work*. London: Verso, 2014.

Green, Adam Isaiah. "'Erotic Capital' and the Power of Desirability: Why 'Honey Money' Is a Bad Collective Strategy for Remediating Gender Inequality." *Sexualities* 16, no. 1–2 (2012): 137–58. https://doi.org/10.1177/1363460712471109.

Green, Adrienne. "What It's Like to Work as an Exotic Dancer." *The Atlantic*, 19 October 2016. https://www.theatlantic.com/business/archive/2016/10/exotic-dancer/504680.

Greenslade, Roy. "Journalist Fired for Being a Stripper Wants Her Newspaper Job Back." *The Guardian*, 27 June 2012. https://www.theguardian.com/media/greenslade/2012/jun/27/usa-women.

Greenwald, Andy, and Chris Ryan. "*The Deuce* Is about Porn, but It Isn't Pornographic." *The Ringer*, 8 September 2017. https://www.theringer.com/tv/2017/9/8/16271260/the-deuce-james-franco-nudity.

Greenwald, Harold. *The Call Girl: A Social and Psychoanalytic Study*. New York: Ballantine Books, 1958.

Griffiths, M. "Sex: Should We All Be at It?" PhD diss., University of Leeds, 2006.

Guignon, Charles. "Authenticity." *Philosophy Compass* 3, no. 2 (March 2008): 277–90. https://doi.org/10.1111/j.1747-9991.2008.00131.x.

Guttmacher, Alan F. "Human Sexual Inadequacy for the Non-layman." *New York Times*, 12 July 1970. http://www.nytimes.com/books/97/03/23/reviews/bright-inadequacy.html.

Guzman, Rafer. "*The Sessions* Review: Physical, Emotional Triumphs." *Newsday*, 8 November 2012. https://www.newsday.com/entertainment/movies/the-sessions-review-physical-emotional-triumphs-u63781.

Haines, Douglas William. "Left Out/Left Behind: On Care Theory's Other." *Hypatia* 32, no. 3 (Summer 2017): 523–39. https://doi.org/10.1111/hypa.12336.

Hakim, Catherine. "Erotic Capital." *European Sociological Review* 26, no. 5 (October 2010): 499–518. https://doi.org/10.1093/esr/jcq014.

Halford, Macy. "Was Holly Golightly Really a Prostitute?" *New Yorker*, 7 September 2009. https://www.newyorker.com/books/page-turner/was-holly-golightly-really-a-prostitute.

Hall, Stuart. "The Rediscovery of 'Ideology': Return of the Repressed in Media." In *Culture, Society and the Media*, edited by Michael Gurevitch, Tony Bennett, James Curran, and Janet Woollacott, 52–87. London: Routledge, 1982. https://doi.org/10.4324/9780203978092.

Halley, Janet E., Prabha Kotiswaran, Chantal Thomas, and Hila Shamir. "From the International to the Local in Feminist Legal Responses to Rape, Prostitution/Sex Work and Sex Trafficking: Four Studies in Contemporary Governance Feminism." *Harvard Journal of Law & Gender* 29, no. 2 (2006): 335–423.

Hallgrimsdottir, Helga Kristin, Rachel Phillips, and Cecilia Benoit. "Fallen Women and Rescued Girls: Social Stigma and Media Narratives of Sex Industry in Victoria, B.C, from 1980–2005." *Canadian Review of Sociology/Revue Canadienne de Sociologie* 43, no. 3 (August 2006): 265–80. https://doi.org/10.1111/j.1755-618X.2006.tb02224.x.

Hallgrimsdottir, Helga Kristin, Rachel Phillips, Cecilia Benoit, and Kevin Walby. "Sporting Girls, Streetwalkers, Inmates of Houses of Ill Repute: Media Narratives and the Historical Mutability of Prostitution Stigmas." *Sociological Perspectives* 51, no. 1 (March 2008): 119–38. https://doi.org/10.1525/sop.2008.51.1.119.

Hanna, Kathleen. "Getting in on the Action." *Kathleenhanna.com*, 14 August 2013. http://www.kathleenhanna.com/getting-in-on-the-action (site discontinued).

HappyCool (@HappyCoolOfficial). "Loretta Devine (The Client List) Interview." YouTube video, 8:21. 5 April 2012. https://www.youtube.com/watch?v=aiLSfwE3E1c.

Harcourt, Christine, and Basil Donovan. "The Many Faces of Sex Work." *Sexually Transmitted Infections* 81, no. 3 (June 2005): 201–6. http://dx.doi.org/10.1136/sti.2004.012468.

Hargreaves, Steve. "Deadbeat Parents Cost Taxpayers $53 Billion." *CNN*, 5 November 2012. https://money.cnn.com/2012/11/05/news/economy/unpaid-child-support.

"Harmful Consequences of Sex Work Criminalization on Health and Rights, The." Sex Workers and Allies Network, June 2020. https://law.yale.edu/sites/default/files/area/center/ghjp/documents/consequences_of_criminalization_v2.pdf.

Harris, Shani (@binsidetv). "The Girlfriend Experience Steven Soderbergh Interview." YouTube video, 7:47. 23 May 2009. https://www.youtube.com/watch?v=07QqpkQAhZ8.

Harvey, David. *A Brief History of Neoliberalism*. Oxford: Oxford University Press, 2005. https://doi.org/10.1093/oso/9780199283262.001.0001.

Haskell, Molly. *From Reverence to Rape: The Treatment of Women in the Movies*. New York: Holt, Rhinehart and Winston, 1973.

Hays, Sharon. *The Cultural Contradiction of Motherhood*. New Haven, CT: Yale University Press, 1996.

HBO. "Meet Darlene | The Deuce (HBO)" Facebook video, 24 September 2017. https://www.facebook.com/HBO/videos/meet-darlene-the-deuce-hbo/10155917978243933.

Heiman, Julia, Leslie LoPiccolo, and Joseph LoPiccolo. *Becoming Orgasmic: A Sexual Growth Program for Women*. Englewood Cliffs, NJ: Prentice-Hall, 1976.

Heineman, Jennifer, Rachel T. MacFarlane, and Barbara G. Brents. "Sex Industry and Sex Workers in Nevada." The Social Health of Nevada: Leading Indicators and Quality of Life in the Silver State. Las Vegas: UNLV Center for Democratic Culture, 2012. https://digitalscholarship.unlv.edu/social_health_nevada_reports/48/

Heins, Marjorie. "Sex and the Law: A Tale of Shifting Boundaries." In *Pornography: Film and Culture*, edited by Peter Lehman. New Brunswick, NJ: Rutgers University Press, 2006.

High Voltage Software. *Leisure Suit Larry: Magna Cum Laude*. Vivendi Universal Games and Sierra Entertainment, 2004.

Hill, Marilynn Wood. *Their Sisters' Keepers: Prostitution in New York City: 1830–1870*. Berkeley: University of California Press, 1993.

Hinckley, David. "TV Review: *The Client List*." *New York Daily News*, 6 April 2012. https://www.nydailynews.com/2013/03/07/tv-review-the-client-list.

Hirschman, Elizabeth C., and Barbara B. Stern. "Consuming Beings: A Feminist Perspective on Prostitution in American Film." *The American Journal of Semiotics* 11, no. 3–4 (1994): 223–83.

Ho, Rachel. "A'Ziah King Hopes *Zola* Will Inspire More Authentic Sex Work Stories in Hollywood." *Exclaim!*, 30 June 2021. https://exclaim.ca/film/article/aziah_king_hopes_zola_will_inspire_more_authentic_sex_work_stories_in_hollywood.

Hochschild, Arlie Russell. *The Managed Heart: Commercialization of Human Feeling*. Berkeley: University of California Press, 1983.

Hodge, P. "Massage Parlour Boom: Sex Spots Proliferating in the Capital." *Washington Post*, 30 May 1975.

Hoggard, Liz. "Melissa Gira Grant: 'I Got into Sex Work to Afford to Be a Writer.'" *The Guardian*, 15 March 2014. https://www.theguardian.com/society/2014/mar/15/melissa-gira-grant-sex-work-afford-be-writer.

Holden, Stephen. "Review: In *She's Lost Control*, Crossing Boundaries in Pursuit of Intimacy." *New York Times*, 20 March 2015. https://www.nytimes.com/2015/03/20/movies/review-in-shes-lost-control-crossing-boundaries-in-pursuit-of-intimacy.html.

Hollander, Xaviera. *The Happy Hooker: My Own Story.* New York: Dell, 1972.

Hopper, Tristin. "Public Libraries a New Hot Spot Risqué – and Risky – Erotic Webcam Performances." *National Post*, last modified 4 March 2015. https://nationalpost.com/news/canada/public-libraries-a-new-hot-spot-for-risque-and-risky-erotic-webcam-performances.

Horswill, Abbe, and Ronald Weitzer. "Becoming a Client: The Socialization of Novice Buyers of Sexual Services." *Deviant Behavior* 39, no. 2 (2018): 148–58. https://doi.org/10.1080/01639625.2016.1263083.

Hu, Caitlin. "Can the World's Oldest Profession Survive the Age of Social Distancing?" *CNN*, 25 May 2020. https://www.cnn.com/2020/05/24/us/sex-workers-coronavirus-intl/index.html.

Hubler, Shawn. "Actor Says He Got Call Girls from Fleiss on at Least 27 Occasions: Trial: Jury Views Videotape of Testimony by Fidgeting Charlie Sheen. Checks Totaled More Than $50,000." *Los Angeles Times*, 21 July 1995. https://www.latimes.com/archives/la-xpm-1995-07-21-me-26278-story.html.

"HunieCam Studio." TVTropes.com, accessed 30 June 2017. https://tvtropes.org/pmwiki/pmwiki.php/VideoGame/HuniecamStudio.

HuniePot (@HunieKyu). "HunieCam Studio Release Trailer." YouTube video, 2:06. 26 March 2016. https://www.youtube.com/watch?v=g48fRvaxaiM.

Illouz, Eva. *Consuming the Romantic Utopia: Love and Cultural Contradictions of Capitalism.* Berkeley: University of California Press, 1997.

Intelligence Squared (@Intelligence-Squared). "Pornography Is Good for Us." YouTube video, 1:25:23. 1 May 2013. https://www.youtube.com/watch?v=AASzf68w1JU.

International Professional Surrogates Association (IPSA). "What Is Surrogate Partner Therapy?" Accessed 3 June 2022. https://www.surrogatetherapy.org/what-is-surrogate-partner-therapy.

Internet Movie Database (IMDb). "The Client List." IMDb. Accessed 26 June 2022. https://www.imdb.com/title/tt2022170/?ref_=fn_al_tt_1.

"I Wasn't Really Naked. I Simply Didn't Have Any Clothes On." *Dance History Blog*, 11 July 2013. https://dancehistoryblog.wordpress.com/2013/07/11/i-wasnt-really-naked-i-simply-didnt-have-any-clothes-on.

Jackson, Crystal A. "Framing Sex Worker Rights: How U.S. Sex Worker Activists Perceive and Respond to Mainstream Anti–Sex Trafficking Advocacy." *Sociological Perspectives* 59, no. 1 (March 2016): 27–45. https://doi.org/10.1177/0731121416628553.

Jackson, Lynne. "Labor Relations: An Interview with Lizzie Borden." *Cinéaste* 15, no. 3 (1987): 4–9. https://www.jstor.org/stable/41687472.

Jacobs, Marion, Linda A. Thompson, and Patsy Truxaw. "The Use of Sexual Surrogates in Counseling." *The Counseling Psychologist* 5, no. 1 (Spring 1975): 73–7. https://doi.org/10.1177/001100007500500118.

Janos, Adam. "Why Are Sex Workers Often a Killer's Victim of Choice?" *AETV.com*, last modified 30 June 2022. https://www.aetv.com/real-crime/why-do-serial-killers-target-sex-workers.

Jean, Melissa, and Caroline S. Forbes. "An Exploration of the Motivations and Expectation Gaps of Mompreneurs." *Journal of Business Diversity* 12, no. 2 (July 2012): 112–30.

Jeffrey, Leslie Ann, and Gayle MacDonald. *Sex Workers in the Maritimes Talk Back*. Vancouver: UBC Press, 2006.

Jeffreys, Sheila. "Disability and the Male Sex Right." *Women's Studies International Forum* 31, no. 5 (September–October 2008): 327–35. https://doi.org/10.1016/j.wsif.2008.08.001.

– *The Industrial Vagina: The Political Economy of the Global Sex Trade*. London: Routledge, 2008. https://doi.org/10.4324/9780203698303.

Jenness, Valerie. "From Sex as Sin to Sex as Work: COYOTE and the Reorganization of Prostitution as a Social Problem." *Social Problems* 37, no. 3 (August 1990): 403–20. https://doi.org/10.2307/800751.

Jhally, Sut dir. *bell hooks: Cultural Criticism and Transformation*. Film transcript. Northhampton, MA: Media Education Foundation, 2005. http://www.mediaed.org/transcripts/Bell-Hooks-Transcript.pdf.

John-Fisk, Hena. "Uncovering the Realities of Prostitutes and Their Children in a Cross National Comparative Study between India and the U.S." PhD diss., University of Utah, 2013. https://collections.lib.utah.edu/details?id=196123.

Johnson, Eithne. "The Business of Sex: Prostitution and Capitalism in Four Recent Films." *Journal of Popular Film and Television* 12, no. 4 (1984): 148–55. https://doi.org/10.1080/01956051.1985.10661981.

Johnson, Zac. "Unveiling Figures: How Much Money Do Strippers Make in the US?" ZacJohnson.com, accessed 6 January 2024. https://zacjohnson.com/how-much-money-do-strippers-make.

Jones, Angela. "For Black Models Scroll Down: Webcam Modeling and the Racialization of Erotic Labor." *Sexuality and Culture* 19, no. 4 (December 2015): 776–99. https://doi.org/10.1007/s12119-015-9291-4.

– "'I Get Paid to Have Orgasms': Adult Webcam Models' Negotiation of Pleasure and Danger." *Signs: Journal of Women in Culture and Society* 42, no. 1 (Autumn 2016): 227–56. https://doi.org/10.1086/686758.

– "Sex Work in the Digital Era." *Sociology Compass* 9, no. 7 (July 2015): 558–70. https://doi.org/10.1111/soc4.12282.

Kaplan, E. Ann. *Motherhood and Representation: The Mother in Popular Culture and Melodrama*. London: Routledge, 1992. https://doi.org/10.4324/9781315001999.

Karen D. "A Survey of the Stripper Memoir." *The Rumpus*, 20 July 2009. http://therumpus.net/2009/07/a-survey-of-the-stripper-memoir.

Katz, A.J. "2017 Ratings: CNN Has Its Largest Audience Ever, but Sees Prime Time Losses." *TVNewster*, 27 December 2017. https://adweek.it/2w67LOW.

Katz, Sidney. "Body Rub Girl 'a Social Worker' at $300 a Week." *Toronto Star*, 11 December 1973.

Kempadoo, Kamala, and Jo Doezema. *Global Sex Workers: Rights, Resistance, and Redefinition*. New York: Routledge, 1998. https://doi.org/10.4324/9781315865768.

Kemsley, Tamarra, and Brad Hamilton. "Inside the $1 Billion Business of Erotic Massage Parlors." *New York Post*, 5 April 2015. http://nypost.com/2015/04/05/inside-the-1-billion-business-of-erotic-massage-parlors.

Kessler, Glenn. "Do Nine out of 10 New Businesses Fail, as Rand Paul Claims?" *Washington Post*, 27 January 2014. https://www.washingtonpost.com/news/fact-checker/wp/2014/01/27/do-9-out-of-10-new-businesses-fail-as-rand-paul-claims.

Kim. "I Work at the US Senate. I Shouldn't Have to Dance at Strip Clubs to Feed My Son." *The Guardian*, 5 August 2015. https://www.theguardian.com/commentisfree/2015/aug/05/us-senate-worker-shouldnt-have-dance-strip-clubs.

Kipnis, Laura. "How to Look at Pornography." In *Pornography: Film and Culture*, edited by Peter Lehman. New Brunswick, NJ: Rutgers University Press, 2006.

Kirkwood, Jodyanne. "Motivational Factors in a Push-Pull Theory of Entrepreneurship." *Gender in Management* 24, no. 5 (2009): 346–64. https://doi.org/10.1108/17542410910968805.

Kirshner, Lauren. "Shining a Light on the Labour of Sex Work." *Room*, 19 August 2019. https://roommagazine.com/shining-a-light-on-the-labour-of-sex-work-2.

Kishtainy, Khalid. *The Prostitute in Progressive Literature*. London: Allison and Busby, 1982.

Kissil, Karni, and Maureen Davey. "The Prostitution Debate in Feminism: Current Policy and Clinical Issues Facing an Invisible Population." *Journal of Feminist Family Therapy* 22, no. 1 (2010): 1–21. https://doi.org/10.1080/08952830903453604.

Kleinman, Alexis. "Porn Sites Get More Visitors than Netflix, Amazon and Twitter Combined." *HuffPost*, 4 May 2013. http://www.huffingtonpost.com/2013/05/03/internet-porn-stats_n_3187682.html.

Knox, Belle. "Tearing Down the Whorearchy from the Inside." *Jezebel*, 2 July 2014. https://jezebel.com/tearing-down-the-whorearchy-from-the-inside-1596459558.

Koester, Megan. "The New Normal: Why Television Has Chosen to Humanize Sex Workers," *The Guardian*, 14 November 2016, https://www.theguardian.com/tv-and-radio/2016/nov/14/television-sex-workers-porn-the-girlfriend-experience.

Koken, Juline A. "Independent Female Escort's Strategies for Coping with Sex Work Related Stigma." *Sexuality and Culture* 16 (2012): 209–29. https://doi.org/10.1007/s12119-011-9120-3.

Kolker, Robert. "The Botched Hunt for the Gilgo Beach Killer." *New York Times*, last modified 3 November 2023. https://www.nytimes.com/2023/10/19/magazine/gilgo-beach-killer-suffolk-police.html.

Labinski, Maggie Ann. "The Social/Political Potential of Illusions: Enthusiasm and Feminist Porn." *Porn Studies* 6, no. 1 (2019): 100–13. https://doi.org/10.1080/23268743.2018.1559082.

Larkin, Greg. "The Smartest Entrepreneur I Know Is a Stripper." LinkedIn, 5 October 2016. https://www.linkedin.com/pulse/smartest-entrepreneur-i-know-stripper-greg-larkin.

LaSalle, Mick. *Complicated Women: Sex and Power in Pre-Code Hollywood*. New York: St. Martin's Press, 2000.

Late Show with Stephen Colbert (@ColbertLateShow). "The Strange Intimacy of Emma Thompson's New Film, 'Good Luck to You, Leo Grande.'" YouTube video, 5:16. 16 June 2022. https://www.youtube.com/watch?app=desktop&v=fB6nsEKIYmQ.

Lauzen, Martha M., and David M. Dozier. "Maintaining the Double Standard: Portrayals of Age and Gender in Popular Films." *Sex Roles* 52 (2005): 437–46. https://doi.org/10.1007/s11199-005-3710-1.

Lee-Wright, Peter. *The Documentary Handbook*. London: Routledge, 2009. https://doi.org/10.4324/9780203867198.

Leigh, Carol. "Inventing Sex Work." In *Whores and Other Feminists*, edited by Jill Nagle, 223–31. New York: Routledge, 1997.

Lerner, Gerda. *The Creation of Patriarchy*. New York: Oxford University Press, 1986.

Lerner, Harriet Goldhor. *The Dance of Anger: A Woman's Guide to Changing the Patterns of Intimate Relationships*. New York: Harper & Row, 1985.

Levenson, Michael. "Judge Awards Nearly $13 Million to Women Who Say They Were Exploited by Porn Producers." *New York Times*, 3 January 2020. https://www.nytimes.com/2020/01/02/us/girls-do-porn-lawsuit-award.html.

Lever, Janet, and Deanne Dolnick. "Clients and Call Girls: Seeking Sex and Intimacy." In *Sex for Sale: Prostitution, Pornography and the Sex Industry*, edited by Ronald Weitzer, 85–100. New York: Routledge, 2000.

Levitt, Lauren. "Sex Work/Gig Work: A Feminist Analysis of Precarious Domina Labor in the Gig Economy." In *The Gig Economy: Workers and Media in the Age of Convergence*, edited by Brian Dollber, Michelle Rodino-Colcinco, Chenjerai Kumanyika, and Todd Wolfson, 58–72. New York: Routledge, 2021. https://doi.org/10.4324/9781003140054.

Levy, Ariel. *Female Chauvinist Pigs: Women and the Rise of Raunch Culture*. New York: Free Press, 2005.

L'Heureux, Catie. "Read Janet Mock's Empowering Speech on Trans Women of Color and Sex Workers." *The Cut*, 21 January 2017. http://nymag.com/thecut/2017/01/read-janet-mocks-speech-at-the-womens-march-on-washington-trans-women-of-color-sex-workers.html.

Liddiard, Kirsty. "'I Never Felt like She Was Just Doing It for the Money': Disabled Men's Intimate (Gendered) Realities of Purchasing Sexual Pleasure and Intimacy." *Sexualities* 17, no. 7 (October 2014): 837–55. https://doi.org/10.1177/1363460714531272.

Ling, Justin, and Tu Thanh Ha. "Killings in Toronto's Gay Community Highlight Dangers Faced by Sex Workers." *Globe and Mail*, 30 January 2018. https://www.theglobeandmail.com/news/toronto/killings-in-torontos-gay-community-highlight-dangers-faced-by-sex-workers/article37800442.

Lombroso, Cesare, and William Ferrero, *The Female Offender*. New York: D. Appleton and Company, 1898.

Lowman, John. "Violence and the Outlaw Status of (Street) Prostitution in Canada." *Violence Against Women* 6, no. 9 (September 2000): 987–1011. https://doi.org/10.1177/10778010022182245.

Lowrey, Annie. "In-Depth Report Details Economics of Sex Trade." *New York Times*, 12 March 2014. https://www.nytimes.com/2014/03/12/us/in-depth-report-details-economics-of-sex-trade.html.

Lowry, Brian. "The Client List." *Variety*, 5 April 2012. http://variety.com/2012/tv/reviews/the-client-list-2-1117947354.

Lucas, Ann M. "The Work of Sex Work: Elite Prostitutes' Vocational Orientations and Experiences." *Deviant Behavior* 26, no. 6 (2005): 513–46. https://doi.org/10.1080/01639620500218252.

Lutnick, Alexandra. "Beyond Prescientific Reasoning: The Sex Worker Environment Assessment Team Study." In *Negotiating Sex Work: Unintended Consequences of Policy and Activism*, edited by Carisa R. Showden and Samantha Majic, 31–53. Minneapolis: University of Minnesota Press, 2014.

M., Alexandra. "Why Stripping Isn't Empowering for Anyone." *Ravishly*, 8 September 2014. https://ravishly.com/2014/10/18/why-stripping-isnt-empowering-anyone.

Mac, Juno, and Molly Smith. *Revolting Prostitutes: The Fight for Sex Workers' Rights*. London: Verso, 2018.

MacKinnon, Catharine A. *Women's Lives, Men's Laws*. Cambridge, MA: Belknap Press of Harvard University Press, 2005.

Maine, Margo, and Joe Kelly. *The Body Myth: Adult Women and the Pressure to Be Perfect*. New York: John Wiley & Sons, 2005.

Marar, Ziyad. *Intimacy*. London: Acumen, 2012.

Margolis, Susan. "Taking the Bull by the Horns." *City Magazine*, 1 January 1973. https://iiif.lib.harvard.edu/manifests/view/drs:496223627$34i.

"Mark O'Brien: The Real Person behind *The Sessions*." *The Saratogian*, 24 October 2012. https://www.saratogian.com/2012/10/24/mark-obrien-the-real-person-behind-hollywoods-the-sessions.

Martin, Jess. "The Notion That It's Ok for Disabled Men to Pay for Sex Is Rooted in Misogyny and Ableism." *Feminist Current*, 11 November 2014. http://www.feministcurrent.com/2014/11/11/the-notion-that-its-ok-for-disabled-men-to-pay-for-sex-is-rooted-in-misogyny-and-ableism.

"Marty Hodas: King of the Peeps." *Rialto Report*, 29 June 2014. https://www.therialtoreport.com/2014/06/29/marty-hodas.

Mason, Richard. *The World of Suzie Wong*. London: Collins, 1957.

Massey, Alana. "A&E Completely Misunderstands the Reality of Sex Workers." *New Republic*, 2 April 2015. https://newrepublic.com/article/121445/aes-show-8-minutes-damaging-sex-workers.

– "Keeping Sex Workers Quiet." *Jacobin*, 2 November 2014. https://www.jacobinmag.com/2014/11/keeping-workers-quiet.

Masters, William H., and Virginia E Johnson. *Human Sexual Inadequacy*. Boston: Little, Brown and Company, 1970.

– *Human Sexual Response*. Boston: Little, Brown and Company, 1966.

McAteer, Amberly. "'Repeat after me: Do not pay women for sex': Why I Advise Readers to Avoid Prostitutes." *Globe and Mail*, 18 June 2014. http://www.theglobeandmail.com/life/relationships/repeat-after-me-do-not-pay-women-for-sex-why-i-advise-readers-to-avoid-prostitutes/article12634086.

McClelland, Mac. "Is Prostitution Just Another Job?" *The Cut*, 21 March 2016. https://www.thecut.com/2016/03/sex-workers-legalization-c-v-r.html.

McClintock, Anne. "Sex Workers and Sex Work: Introduction." *Social Text* 37 (Winter 1993): 1–10. https://www.jstor.org/stable/466255.

McLaughlin, Lisa. "Discourses of Prostitution/Discourses of Sexuality." *Critical Studies in Mass Communication* 8, no. 3 (1991): 249–72. https://doi.org/10.1080/15295039109366797.

– "Looking for Labor in Feminist Media Studies." *Television & New Media* 10, no. 1 (January 2009): 110–13. https://doi.org/10.1177/1527476408325363.

McNair, Brian. "Pornography in the Multiplex." In *Hard to Swallow: Hard-Core Pornography on Screen*, edited by Claire Hines and Darren Kerr. New York: Wallflower Press, 2012.

– *Striptease Culture: Sex, Media and the Democratisation of Culture*. London: Routledge, 2002. https://doi.org/10.4324/9780203469378.

McNeill, Maggie. "A False Dichotomy." *Honest Courtesan* (blog), 22 June 2011. https://maggiemcneill.wordpress.com/2011/06/22/a-false-dichotomy.

– "Quicker Than the Eye," *Honest Courtesan* (blog), 19 June 2013, https://maggiemcneill.com/2013/06/19/quicker-than-the-eye.

McRobbie, Angela. *The Aftermath of Feminism: Gender, Culture and Social Change*. Thousand Oaks, CA: SAGE Publications, 2009.

Mears, Ashley. "Aesthetic Labor for the Sociologies of Work, Gender, and Beauty." *Sociology Compass* 8, no. 12 (December 2014): 1330–43. https://doi.org/10.1111/soc4.12211.

Mears, Ashley, and Catherine Connell. "The Paradoxical Value of Deviant Cases: Toward a Gendered Theory of Display Work." *Signs: Journal of Women in Culture and Society* 41, no. 2 (Winter 2016): 333–59. https://doi.org/10.1086/682922.

"Meet the Team: 'Road Strip' Producer/Director Heidi Burke." Part2 Pictures, 30 October 2014. https://web.archive.org/web/20160427123704/https://www.part2pictures.com/news/meet-the-team-road-strip-producer-heidi-burke.

Mendes, Kaitlynn, Kumarini Silva, Ambar Basu, Mohan J. Dutta, Jennifer Dunn, Feona Attwood, and Karen Boyle. "Commentary and Criticism: Representations of Sex Workers." *Feminist Media Studies* 10, no. 1 (January 2010): 99–116. https://doi.org/10.1080/14680770903457469.

"Men Who Visit This Website Get a Grim Reminder and Eye-Opening Surprise." Women in the World, 29 June 2016. https://womenintheworld.com/2016/09/29/men-who-tried-contacting-the-escorts-advertised-on-this-site-got-an-unsettling-surprise (site discontinued).

Mermey, Joanna. "New York's 100 Kneadiest Cases." *Village Voice*, December 14, 1972. http://www.villagevoice.com/news/chasing-massage-parlors-out-of-times-square-also-a-fateful-kiss-ad-6708700.

Meulen, Emily van der. "Action Research with Sex Workers: Dismantling Barriers and Building Bridges." *Action Research* 9, no. 4 (December 2011): 370–84. https://doi.org/10.1177/1476750311409767.

Meulen, Emily van der, Elya M. Durisin, and Victoria Love. *Selling Sex: Experience, Advocacy, and Research on Sex Work in Canada*. Vancouver: UBC Press, 2013.

Miller, Madison. "Mug Shots Released of Nine Women Arrested in Prostitution Sting in Beaumont." *Fox4Beaumont.com*, 7 October 2016. http://fox4beaumont.com/news/local/mug-shots-released-of-nine-women-arrested-in-prostitution-sting-in-beaumont.

Miller-Young, Mireille. *A Taste for Brown Sugar: Black Women in Pornography*. Durham, NC: Duke University Press, 2014. https://doi.org/10.1215/9780822375913.

Millett, Kate. *Sexual Politics*. New York: Doubleday, 1971.

Mills, C. Wright. *White Collar*. New York: Oxford University Press, 1951.

Mirk, Sarah. "More Sex Workers Are Killed in the US than Any Other Country." *Bitch Media*, 14 December 2014. https://www.bitchmedia.org/post/more-sex-workers-are-killed-in-the-us-than-any-other-country (site discontinued).

Mitchell, Cari. "Sex Work Should Not Be a Crime." *The Guardian*, 7 April 2010. https://www.theguardian.com/commentisfree/2010/apr/07/sex-work-crime-legislation.

Monagle, Matthew. "The Oldest Profession: Looking Back at Alan J. Pakula's *Klute*." *Film School Rejects*, 28 August 2015, https://filmschoolrejects.com/jane-fonda-klute/.

Monbiot, George. "Neoliberalism: The Ideology at the Root of All of Our Problems." *The Guardian*, 15 April 2016. https://www.theguardian.com/books/2016/apr/15/neoliberalism-ideology-problem-george-monbiot.

Morgan, Robin. *Going Too Far: The Personal Chronicle of a Feminist*. New York: Random House, 1977.

Mortimer, Caroline. "Amnesty International Officially Calls for Complete Decriminalisation of Sex Work." *The Independent*, 27 May 2016. https://www.independent.co.uk/life-style/health-and-families/health-news/amnesty-international-officially-calls-for-complete-decriminalisation-of-sex-work-a7050021.html.

"Mugshots (Orange County Jail Booking Blotter)." *Orlando Sentinel*, accessed 30 June 2017. http://mugshots.orlandosentinel.com/mobile.php (site discontinued).

Mulvey, Laura. "Visual Pleasure and Narrative Cinema." *Screen* 16, no. 3 (Autumn 1975): 6–18. https://doi.org/10.1093/screen/16.3.6.

Murphy, Meghan. "*Cam Girlz* Director Believes Male Fantasies about Women Challenge Social Norms." *Feminist Current*, 6 March 2015. http://www.feministcurrent.com/2015/03/06/cam-girlz-director-believes-male-fantasies-about-women-challenge-social-norms.

"Mutoscope." Wikipedia. Last modified 16 August 2023. https://en.wikipedia.org/wiki/Mutoscope.

Nagle, Jill. "Introduction." In *Whores and Other Feminists*, edited by Jill Nagle, 1–15. New York: Routledge, 1997.

Nead, Lynda, curator. *The Fallen Woman*. Organized and presented by the Foundling Museum, 25 September 2015–3 January 2016. https://foundlingmuseum.org.uk/event/the-fallen-woman.

Negra, Diane. *What a Girl Wants? Fantasizing the Reclamation of Self in Postfeminism*. London: Routledge, 2008. https://doi.org/10.4324/9780203869000.

Nel, P., Alex Martin, and Onnida Thongprovati. "Motherhood and Entrepreneurship: The Mumpreneur Phenomenon." *International Journal of Organizational Innovation* 3, no. 1 (2010): 6–34.

Newcomb, Horace M., and Paul M. Hirsch. "Television as a Cultural Forum: Implications of Research." *Quarterly Review of Film Studies* 8, no. 3 (1983): 45–55. https://doi.org/10.1080/10509208309361170.

"New Subjects in Sprocket Films and Mutoscopes." *Film Historiography* (blog), 15 March 2007. https://wp.nyu.edu/filmhist/tag/peep-shows.

Nicholls, David A., and Julianne Cheek. "Physiotherapy and the Shadow of Prostitution: The Society of Trained Masseuses and the Massage Scandals of 1894." *Social Science & Medicine* 62, no. 9 (May 2006): 2336–48. https://doi.org/10.1016/j.socscimed.2005.09.010.

Nichols, Bill. *Introduction to Documentary*. Bloomington: Indiana University Press, 2001.

"Notable People." Decriminalize Sex Work, accessed 15 January 2024. https://decriminalizesex.work/why-decriminalization/notable-people.

NPR. "Pioneering *Masters of Sex* Brought Science to the Bedroom." *Fresh Air*, 30 July 2013. https://www.npr.org/2013/07/30/206704520/pioneering-masters-of-sex-brought-science-to-the-bedroom.

– "Strippers in the U.S. Want Better Work Conditions. Some Are Trying to Unionize." *Consider This*, 16 September 2022. https://www.npr.org/2022/09/14/1122937491/strippers-in-the-u-s-want-better-work-conditions-some-are-trying-to-unionize.

Nussbaum, Martha C. "Objectification." *Philosophy and Public Affairs* 24, no. 4 (1995): 249–91. https://doi.org/10.1111/j.1088-4963.1995.tb00032.x.

O'Brien, Mark. "On Seeing a Sex Surrogate." *The Sun*, May 1990. https://www.thesunmagazine.org/issues/174/on-seeing-a-sex-surrogate-issue-174.

O'Hara, Mary Emily. "How Sex Workers Dominated the News in 2015." *Daily Dot*, last updated 27 May 2021. https://www.dailydot.com/irl/2015-sex-work.

Okeowo, Alexis. "The Fragile Existence of Sex Workers during the Pandemic." *New Yorker*, 21 May 2020. https://www.newyorker.com/news/news-desk/the-fragile-existence-of-sex-workers-during-the-pandemic.

O'Neill, Maggie. *Prostitution and Feminism: Towards a Politics of Feeling*. Malden, MA: Polity Press, 2000.

Oullette, Laurie, and James Hay. *Better Living through Reality TV: Television and Post-Welfare Citizenship*. Malden, MA: Blackwell, 2008.

Paglia, Camille. *Vamps and Tramps: New Essays*. New York: Vintage Books, 1994.

Panofsky, Ruth. "'This Was Her Punishment': Jew, Whore, Mother in the Fiction of Adele Wiseman and Lilian Nattel." In *Textual Mothers/Maternal Texts: Motherhood in Contemporary Women's Literatures*, edited by Elizabeth Podnieks and Andrea O'Reilly, 95–111. Waterloo, ON: Wilfrid Laurier University Press, 2010.

Parish, James Robert. *Prostitution in Hollywood Films: Plots, Critiques, Casts, and Credits for 389 Theatrical and Made-for-Television Releases.* Jefferson, NC: McFarland, 1992.

Pase, Iris. "Tips for Reporting on Sex Work." *International Journalists' Network*, 19 February 2021. https://ijnet.org/en/story/tips-reporting-about-sex-work.

Patel, Suraj. "We Must Repeal SESTA, a Deadly Law That Does Nothing to Help Trafficking Victims." *Vice*, 21 May 2018. https://www.vice.com/en/article/xwmdkk/repeal-sesta-fosta-sex-work-suraj-patel.

Pateman, Carole. *The Sexual Contract*. Stanford, CA: Stanford University Press, 1988.

Patterson, Troy. "Ultra-Soft Porn." *Slate*, 6 April 2012. http://www.slate.com/articles/arts/television/2012/04/client_list_jennifer_love_hewitt_s_call_girl_drama_reviewed_.html.

Paul, Pamela. "What It Means to Call Prostitution 'Sex Work.'" *New York Times*, 17 August 2023. https://www.nytimes.com/2023/08/17/opinion/prostitution-sex-work.html.

Paulas, Rick. "Sex Workers vs. the Internet." *Longreads*, 14 June 2018. https://longreads.com/2018/06/14/sex-workers-vs-the-internet.

Pelisek, Christine. *Grim Sleeper: The Lost Women of South Central*. Berkley, CA: Counterpoint, 2016.

Pendleton, Eva. "Love for Sale: Queering Heterosexuality." In *Whores and Other Feminists*, edited by Jill Nagle, 73–83. New York: Routledge, 1997.

Penley, Constance, Celine Parreñas Shimizu, Mireille Miller-Young, and Tristan Taormino. "Introduction: The Politics of Producing Pleasure." In *The Feminist Porn Book: The Politics of Producing Pleasure*, edited by Tristan Taormino, Constance Penley, Celine Parreñas Shimizu, and Mireille Miller-Young, 9–20. New York: The Feminist Press at the City University of New York, 2012.

Pesta, Abigail. "Exclusive: Diary of a Call Girl Turned Teacher, Part 1." *Marie Claire*, 6 December 2010. https://www.marieclaire.com/culture/a5670/melissa-petro-exclusive-interview.

Petersen, Anne Helen. "Scandals of Classic Hollywood: The Many Faces of Barbara Stanwyck." *The Hairpin*, 13 March 2013. https://thehairpin.com/scandals-of-classic-hollywood-the-many-faces-of-barbara-stanwyck-a1dbaf8648a2.

Petro, Melissa. "The H-Word: She Works Hard for the Money (So You Better Treat Her Right)." *Bitch Media*, 28 October 2011. https://www.bitchmedia.org/post/the-h-word-she-works-hard-for-the-money (site discontinued).

– "I Did It ... for the Money: Sex Work as a Means to Socio-economic Opportunity." *Research for Sex Work* 9 (2006): 25–8.

– "Life after Sex Work." *Daily Beast*, 14 July 2017. https://www.thedailybeast.com/life-after-sex-work.

Petroff, Alanna. "It's Getting Even Harder to Be a Woman." *CNN Money*, 2 November 2017. http://money.cnn.com/2017/11/02/news/gender-gap-inequality/index.html.

Pettinger, Lynne. "'Knows How to Please a Man': Studying Customers to Understand Service Work." *Sociological Review* 59, no. 2 (May 2011): 223–41. https://doi.org/10.1111/j.1467-954X.2011.02005.x.

Pheterson, Gail, ed. *A Vindication of the Rights of Whores*. Seattle: Seal Press, 1989.

– "The Whore Stigma: Female Dishonor and Male Unworthiness." *Social Text* 37 (Winter 1993): 39–64. https://doi.org/10.2307/466259.

Phoenix, Joanna. *Making Sense of Prostitution*. New York: St. Martin's Press, 1999.

Podnieks, Elizabeth. *Mediating Moms: Mothers in Popular Culture*. Montreal: McGill-Queen's University Press, 2012.

Pollard, Tom. *Sex and Violence: The Hollywood Censorship Wars*. New York: Routledge, 2015. https://doi.org/10.4324/9781315632162.

Pomerantz, Dorothy. "Hollywood's Highest-Paid Actors." *Forbes*, 11 October 2011. https://www.forbes.com/sites/dorothypomerantz/2011/10/11/hollywoods-highest-paid-tv-actors/#741460634d5b.

Power, Nina. *One-Dimensional Woman*. Winchester: Zero Books, 2009.

Pressler, Jessica. "The Hustlers at Scores: A Modern Robin Hood Story: The Strippers Who Stole from (Mostly) Rich, (Usually) Disgusting Men and Gave to, Well, Themselves." *The Cut*, 27 December 2015. https://www.thecut.com/2015/12/hustlers-the-real-story-behind-the-movie.html.

Purcell, Natalie. *Violence and the Pornographic Imaginary: The Politics of Sex, Gender, and Aggression in Hardcore Pornography*. New York: Routledge, 2012.

Queen, Carol. "Sex Radical Politics, Sex-Positive Feminist Thought, and Whore Stigma." In *Whores and Other Feminists*, edited by Jill Nagle, 125–35. New York: Routledge, 1997.

Queen, Carol, and Lynn Comella. "The Necessary Revolution: Sex-Positive Feminism in the Post-Barnard Era." *Communication Review* 11, no. 3 (2008): 274–91. https://doi.org/10.1080/10714420802306783.

Rackham, Annabel. "Stephen Bear: Revenge Porn Prison Sentence 'Sends Clear Message.'" *BBC*, 3 March 2023. https://www.bbc.com/news/entertainment-arts-64799815.

Radakovich, Anka. "The Real-Life Girlfriend Experience." *British GQ*, 29 March 2012. http://www.gq-magazine.co.uk/article/gq-girls-anka-radakovich-on-the-girlfriend-escort-experience.

Ravishly. "Is Sex Work Empowering Or Enslaving? 12 Experts Weigh In." *HuffPost*, last modified 6 December 2017. https://www.huffpost.com/entry/is-sex-work-empowering-or-enslaving_b_5825882.

Raymond, Janice G. *Not a Choice, Not a Job: Exposing the Myths about Prostitution and the Global Sex Trade*. Washington, DC: Potomac Books, 2013.

– "Prostitution Is Rape That Is Paid For." *Los Angeles Times*, 11 December 1995.

Razack, Sherene. "Race, Space, and Prostitution: The Making of the Bourgeois Subject." *Canadian Journal of Women and the Law* 10, no. 2 (1998): 338–76.

Reuben, David R. *Everything You Always Wanted to Know about Sex (But Were Afraid to Ask)*. New York: D. McKay, 1969.

Richtel, Matt. "Intimacy on the Web, With a Crowd." *New York Times*, 21 September 2013. https://www.nytimes.com/2013/09/22/technology/intimacy-on-the-web-with-a-crowd.html.

Ridley, Jane. "Secrets of Sex Surrogates." *New York Post*, 25 October 2012. http://nypost.com/2012/10/25/secrets-of-the-sex-surrogates.

Ringdal, Nils Johan. *Love for Sale: A World History of Prostitution*. New York: Grove Press, 2004.

Rivers-Moore, Megan. "But the Kids Are Okay: Motherhood, Consumption and Sex Work in Neo-Liberal Latin America." *The British Journal of Sociology* 61, no. 4 (December 2010): 716–36. https://doi.org/10.1111/j.1468-4446.2010.01338.x.

Roach, Catherine M. *Stripping, Sex, and Popular Culture*. Oxford: Berg, 2007.

Roberts, Nickie. *Whores in History: Prostitution in Western Society*. London: HarperCollins, 1992.

Roberts, Ron, Teela Sanders, Ellie Myers, and Debbie Smith. "Participation in Sex Work: Students' Views." *Sex Education* 10, no. 2 (May 2010): 145–56. https://doi.org/10.1080/14681811003666507.

Rogers, Tim. "Can Camgirls Be Feminists?" *Splinter*, 16 July 2015. https://splinternews.com/can-camgirls-be-feminists-1793849204.

Ronai, Carol Rambo, and Carolyn Ellis. "Turn-Ons for Money: Interactional Strategies of the Table Dancer." *Journal of Contemporary Ethnography* 18, no. 3 (October 1989): 271–98. https://doi.org/10.1177/089124189018003002.

Rosen, Marjorie. *Popcorn Venus*. New York: Coward, McCann & Geoghegan, 1973.

Rosenbaum, Talli, Ronit Aloni, and Rafi Heruti. "Surrogate Partner Therapy: Ethical Considerations in Sexual Medicine." *The Journal of Sexual Medicine* 11, no. 2 (February 2014): 321–9. https://doi.org/10.1111/jsm.12402.

Ross, Daniel. "Sex on Yonge: Examining the Decade When Yonge Street Was the City's Sin Strip." *Spacing*, 9 March 2017. https://spacing.ca/toronto/2017/03/09/sex-yonge-examining-decade-yonge-street-citys-sin-strip.

Ross, Lynda R. *Interrogating Motherhood*. Edmonton: Athabasca University Press, 2016.

Rottenberg, Catherine. "The Neoliberal Feminist Subject." *Los Angeles Review of Books*, 7 January 2018. https://lareviewofbooks.org/article/the-neoliberal-feminist-subject.

Rubin, Gayle. "Thinking Sex: Notes for a Radical Theory of the Politics of Sexuality." In *Pleasure and Danger: Exploring Female Sexuality*, edited by Carole Vance, 267–320. New York: Routledge, 1984.

Samuelson, Robert J. "The Rise of Downward Mobility." *Washington Post*, 5 August 2018. https://www.washingtonpost.com/opinions/upward-mobility-is-a-myth/2018/08/05/bb960ce4-972c-11e8-80e1-00e80e1fdf43_story.html.

Sanders, Teela. *Paying for Pleasure: Men Who Buy Sex*. Cullompton, UK: Willan Publishing, 2008.

- "The Politics of Sexual Citizenship: Commercial Sex and Disability." *Disability & Society* 22, no. 5 (2007): 439–55. https://doi.org/10.1080/09687590701427479.
- "Researching the Online Sex Work Community." In *Virtual Methods: Issues in Social Research on the Internet*, edited by Christine Hine, 67–79. Oxford: Berg, 2005.

Sanger, William. *The History of Prostitution: Its Extent, Causes, and Effects throughout the World*. New York: Harper & Brothers, 1858.

Sanofka, Jasmine. "From Margin to Centre: Sex Work Decriminalization Is a Racial Justice Issue." Amnesty International, accessed 15 January 2024. https://www.amnestyusa.org/updates/from-margin-to-center-sex-work-decriminalization-is-a-racial-justice-issue.

Sante, Luc. *The Other Paris*. New York: Farrar, Straus and Giroux, 2015.

"Sasha Grey, the Dirtiest Girl in the World: The Story behind the Story." *Rolling Stone*, 29 April 2009. https://www.rollingstone.com/tv-movies/tv-movie-news/sasha-grey-the-dirtiest-girl-in-the-world-the-story-behind-the-story-63211.

Satz, Debra. "Markets in Women's Sexual Labour." *Ethics* 106, no. 1 (1995): 63–85.

Sawicki, Danielle A., Brienna N. Meffert, Kate Read, and Adrienne J. Heinz. "Culturally Competent Health Care for Sex Workers: An Examination of Myths That Stigmatize Sex Work and Hinder Access to Care." *Sexual and Relationship Therapy* 34, no. 3 (February 2019): 355–71. https://doi.org/10.1080/14681994.2019.1574970.

Scherstuhl, Alan. "Sex-Surrogate Therapy Drama *She's Lost Control* Is Shot with a Vigorous Chilliness." *Village Voice*, 18 March 2015. https://www.villagevoice.com/2015/03/18/sex-surrogate-therapy-drama-shes-lost-control-is-shot-with-a-vigorous-chilliness.

Schlussel, Debbie. "Suzy Favour Hamilton: Former Olympian I Knew Uses Bipolarity as BS Excuse for Being a Hooker, Slut." *Debbie Schlussel* (blog), 11 September 2015. http://www.debbieschlussel.com/79722/suzy-favor-hamilton-former-olympian-i.

Schweitzer, Dahlia. "Striptease: The Art of Spectacle and Transgression." *Journal of Popular Culture* 34, no. 1 (Summer 2000): 66–75. https://doi.org/10.1111/j.0022-3840.2000.3401_65.x.

Seelye, Katharine Q. "Margo St. James, Advocate for Sex Workers, Dies at 83." *New York Times*, 20 January 2021. https://www.nytimes.com/2021/01/20/us/margo-st-james-dead.html.

Senft, Theresa. *Camgirls: Celebrity and Community in the Age of Social Networks*. New York: Peter Lang, 2008.

Sepinwall, Alan. "David Simon and Emily Meade on What Lori Means to *The Deuce*." *Rolling Stone*, 22 October 2019. https://www.rollingstone.com/tv/tv-features/deuce-lori-season-3-episode-7-david-simon-emily-meade-interview-900235.

"Sex Surrogates Seem like Prostitutes but Are Helping Hands." *ABC News*, 1 August 2011. http://abcnews.go.com/Health/sex-surrogates-prostitutes-helping-hands-therapists/story?id=14207647.

"Sex Workers in the Recession." *The Economist*, 6 February 2009. https://www.economist.com/free-exchange/2009/02/06/sex-workers-in-the-recession.

Shakespeare, Tom. "Disabled Sexuality: Toward Rights and Recognition." *Sexuality and Disability* 18, no. 3 (2000): 159–66. https://doi.org/10.1023/A:1026409613684.

Shaver, Frances M. "Sex Worker Research: Methodological and Ethical Challenges." *Journal of Interpersonal Violence* 20, no. 3 (March 2005): 296–319. https://doi.org/10.1177/0886260504274340.

Shepard, Benjamin. "From Emma Goldman to Riot Grrrl: Sex Work, Public Space and the Transformation of Streets." *New Political Science* 37, no. 3 (2015): 424–8. https://doi.org/10.1080/07393148.2015.1056626.

Shepard, Susan. "Taking the Boom out of the Boom-Boom Room: Why Are Strip Clubs Banning Rap?" *Complex*, 4 December 2013. http://ca.complex.com/music/2013/12/strip-clubs-ban-on-rap.

Shteir, Rachel. *Striptease: The Untold History of the Girlie Show*. Oxford: Oxford University Press, 2004.

Simmons, Melanie. "Theorizing Prostitution: The Question of Agency." In *Sex Work and Sex Workers*, edited by Barry M. Dank and Roberto Refinetti, 125–49. New Brunswick, NJ: Transaction Publishers, 1999. https://doi.org/10.4324/9781351306683.

Sloan, Lacey, and Stephanie Wahab. "Feminist Voices on Sex Work: Implications for Social Work." *Affilia* 15, no. 4 (Winter 2000): 457–79. https://doi.org/10.1177/088610990001500402.

Sly, Savannah. "Good Work (If You Can Get It): Job Discrimination against Sex Workers." Woodhull Freedom Foundation, August 2022. https://www.woodhullfoundation.org/wp-content/uploads/2022/08/Savannah-Sly-Good-Work-If-You-Can-Get-It.pdf.

Smaill, Belinda. "Documentary Investigations and the Female Porn Star." *Jump Cut: A Review of Contemporary Media*, 2009. https://www.ejumpcut.org/archive/jc51.2009/femalePornstars/index.html.

Smith, Clarissa. "Reel Intercourse: Doing Sex on Camera." In *Hard to Swallow: Hard-Core Pornography on Screen*, edited by Claire Hines and Darren Kerr, 194–214. New York: Wallflower Press, 2012.

Smith, Clarissa, and Feona Attwood. "Emotional Truths and Thrilling Slide Shows." In *The Feminist Porn Book: The Politics of Producing Pleasure*, edited by Tristan Taormino, Celine Parreñas Shimizu, Constance Penley, and Mireille Miller-Young. New York: The Feminist Press at the City University of New York, 2012.

Snow, Aurora. "Naughty Nerds: College Grads Do Porn." *Daily Beast*, 1 January 2015. http://www.thedailybeast.com/articles/2015/01/31/naughty-nerds-college-grads-do-porn.

Sola, Katie. "This A&E Reality Show Promised to Help Sex Workers. It Just Made Their Lives Worse." *HuffPost*, 5 May 2015. https://www.huffpost.com/entry/sex-workers-8-minutes_n_7213182.

Spector, Jessica, ed. *Prostitution and Pornography: Philosophical Debate about the Sex Industry*. Stanford, CA: Stanford University Press, 2006.

Stacey, Clare L. "Finding Dignity in Dirty Work: The Constraints and Rewards of Low-Wage Home Care Labour." *Sociology of Health & Illness* 27, no. 6 (September 2005): 831–54. https://doi.org/10.1111/j.1467-9566.2005.00476.x.

Stadiem, William. "Behind Claude's Doors." *Vanity Fair*, 22 August 2014. http://www.vanityfair.com/style/society/2014/09/madame-claude-paris-prostitution.

Stanford Center on Poverty and Inequality. "20 Facts about U.S. Inequality That Everyone Should Know." Accessed 8 November 2023. https://web.stanford.edu/group/scspi/cgi-bin/facts.php.

Statista. "Unemployment Rate in the United States from 1990 to 2022." Accessed 2 May 2022. https://www.statista.com/statistics/193290/unemployment-rate-in-the-usa-since-1990.

Stein, Martha L. *Lovers, Friends, Slaves ... The Nine Male Sexual Types: Their Psycho-Sexual Transactions with Call-Girls*. New York: Putnam, 1974.

Sterry, David Henry, and R.J. Martin, Jr., eds. *Hos, Hookers, Call Girls, and Rent Boys: Professionals Writing on Life, Love, Money, and Sex*. Brooklyn: Soft Skull Press, 2009.

Strega, Susan, Caitlin Janzen, Jeannie Morgan, Leslie Brown, Robina Thomas, and Jeannine Carriére. "Never Innocent Victims: Street Sex Workers in Canadian Print Media." *Violence Against Women* 20, no. 1 (January 2014): 6–25. https://doi.org/10.1177/1077801213520576.

Sundahl, Debi. "Stripper." In *Sex Work: Writings by Women in the Sex Industry*, edited by Frédérique Delcasote and Priscilla Alexander, 175–80. London: Virago, 1988.

Szasz, Thomas. *Sex by Prescription*. Garden City, NY: Anchor Press/Doubleday, 1980.

Szeman, Imre, and Susie O'Brien. *Popular Culture: A User's Guide*. 3rd ed. Toronto: Nelson Education, 2014.

Tanzi, Alex. "Side Hustle Nation: The Number of Americans Working Multiple Gigs to Just Pay the Bills Is Nearly Double What We Thought." *Fortune*, 6 February 2023. https://fortune.com/2023/02/06/side-hustle-americans-working-multiple-gigs-double-previous-estimates.

Tarrant, Shira. *The Pornography Industry: What Everyone Needs to Know*. New York: Oxford University Press, 2016.

TEDx Talks (@TEDx). "Why I Stopped Watching Porn Greenslade" YouTube, 15:57. 26 October 2013. https://www.youtube.com/watch?v=gRJ_QfP2mhU.

Templeton, David. "Bedside Manner: Margo St. James on the Power of Sex and Dangerous Beauty." *Sonoma County Independent*, 5 March 1998. http://www.metroactive.com/papers/sonoma/03.05.98/talk-pix-9809.html.

Terkel, Studs. *Working*. New York: New Press, 1974.

Thompson, Carolyn. "Windsor Has Been Canada's Most Unemployed City for More than Five Years." *Windsor Star*, 10 July 2015. https://windsorstar.com/business/windsor-unemployment-rate-falls-to-8-9-per-cent.

Thompson, Derek. "8 Facts about the U.S. Sex Economy." *The Atlantic*, 12 March 2014. https://www.theatlantic.com/business/archive/2014/03/8-facts-about-the-us-sex-economy/284376.

Thomson, David. "Francois Ozon's New Movie Makes Prostitution Look like an Yves San Laurent Ad." *New Republic*, 18 May 2014. https://newrepublic.com/article/117780/francois-ozons-jeune-belle-review.

Tolentino, Jia. "How 'Empowerment' Became Something for Women to Buy." *New York Times*, 12 April 2016. https://www.nytimes.com/2016/04/17/magazine/how-empowerment-became-something-for-women-to-buy.html.

Tonight Show Starring Jimmy Fallon (@fallontonight). "Jennifer Lopez Teases Super Bowl Halftime Show, Reacts to Changing Google with THAT Dress." YouTube video, 6:35. 6 December 2019. https://www.youtube.com/watch?v=YguJqGu52V0.

Topping, Alexandra, and Helen Pidd. "Police Offer Heartfelt Apology to Families of Peter Sutcliffe Victims." *The Guardian*, 13 November 2020. https://www.theguardian.com/uk-news/2020/nov/13/police-offer-heartfelt-apology-to-families-of-yorkshire-ripper-peter-sutcliffe-victims.

Tron, Gina. "In Netflix's *Crime Scene: The Times Square Killer*, Who Was 'Porno King of NYC' Marty Hodas?" *Oxygen*, 23 December 2021. https://www.oxygen.com/true-crime-buzz/in-crime-scene-the-times-square-killer-who-was-marty-hodas.

Twigg, Julia, Carol Wolkowitz, Rachel Lara Cohen, and Sarah Nettleton. "Conceptualising Body Work in Health and Social Care." *Sociology of Health & Illness* 33, no. 2 (February 2011): 171–88. https://doi.org/10.1111/j.1467-9566.2010.01323.x.

Urback, Robyn. "Peter McKay Still Hopes Bill C-36 Will Eliminate Prostitution in Canada. Good Luck with That." *National Post*, 8 July 2014. https://nationalpost.com/opinion/robyn-urback-peter-mackay-hopes-bill-c-36-will-eliminate-prostitution-in-canada-good-luck-with-that.

Valenti, Lauren. "In Honor of Audrey Hepburn's Birthday, We Got Holly Golightly Highlights." *Marie Claire*, 2 May 2014. https://www.marieclaire.com/beauty/a9490/holly-golightly-costume-audrey-hepburn-style.

Van Brunschot, Erin Gibbs, Rosalind A. Sydie, and Catherine Knull. "Images of Prostitution: The Prostitute and Print Media." *Women & Criminal Justice* 10, no. 4 (1999): 56–78. https://doi.org/10.1300/J012v10n04_03.

Vance, Carole. "Pleasure and Danger: Toward a Politics of Sexuality." In *Pleasure and Danger: Exploring Female Sexuality*, edited by Carole Vance, 1–27. New York: Routledge, 1984.

Van De Griend, Kristin M., and DeAnne K. Hilfinger Messias. "Expanding the Conceptualization of Workplace Violence: Implications for Research, Policy, and Practice." *Sex Roles* 71, no. 1 (July 2014): 33–42. https://doi.org/10.1007/s11199-014-0353-0.

Vanstone, Gail. *D Is for Daring: The Women behind Studio D*. Toronto: Sumach Press, 2007.

Van Syckle, Katie. "Riley Keough on Her Sexy, Disturbing New Show *The Girlfriend Experience*." *Cosmopolitan*, 8 April 2016. https://www.cosmopolitan.com/entertainment/tv/q-and-a/a56560/riley-keough-the-girlfriend-experience-interview.

Veblen, Thorstein. *The Theory of the Leisure Class*. New York: Macmillan, 1899.

Vednita, Carter, and Evelina Giobbe. "Duet: Prostitution, Racism, and Feminist Discourse." In *Prostitution and Pornography: Philosophical Debate about the Sex Industry*, edited by Jessica Spector, 17–39. Stanford, CA: Stanford University Press, 2006.

Velarde, Albert J. "Becoming Prostituted: The Decline of the Massage Parlor Profession and the Masseuse." *British Journal of Criminology* 3, no. 15 (1975): 251–63.

Velarde, Albert J., and Mark Warlick. "Massage Parlors: The Sensuality Business." *Society* 11 (November 1973): 63–74. https://doi.org/10.1007/BF03181022.

Venkatesh, Sudhir. *Floating City*. London: Allen Lane, 2009.

Vertueux. "Would You and/or Have You Ever Dated a Sex Worker?" Reddit, 19 January 2015. https://www.reddit.com/r/AskMen/comments/2t05p1/would_you_andor_have_you_ever_dated_a_sex_worker.

Victoria's Friends. "Statistics." Accessed 18 May 2022. http://www.victoriasfriends.com/statistics (site discontinued).

Villiers, Nicholas de. *Sexography: Sex Work in Documentary*. Minneapolis: University of Minnesota Press, 2017.

Vine, Katy. "She Had Brains, a Body, and the Ability to Make Men Love Her." *Texas Monthly*, January 2005. http://www.texasmonthly.com/articles/she-had-brains-a-body-and-the-ability-to-make-men-love-her.

Wald, Elissa. "Notes from the Catwalk." *Creative Nonfiction*, 2000. https://creativenonfiction.org/writing/notes-from-the-catwalk.

Walsh, Katie. "Review: *Control* Is a Quiet Triumph with a Distinctive Voice." *Los Angeles Times*, 30 March 2015. https://www.latimes.com/entertainment/movies/la-et-mn-shes-lost-control-review-20150327-story.html.

Walters, Suzanna Danuta, and Laura Harrison. "Not Ready to Make Nice: Aberrant Mothers in Contemporary Culture." *Feminist Media Studies* 14, no. 1 (2014): 38–55. https://doi.org/10.1080/14680777.2012.742919.

"Webcam Market Size and Trends Analysis Report, 2021–2028." Grand View Research. Accessed 1 August 2021. https://www.grandviewresearch.com/industry-analysis/webcams-market.

"Webcam Model Streaming Sex Show at Library Caught in Act." *CBC News*, 4 March 2015. http://www.cbc.ca/news/canada/windsor/webcam-model-streaming-sex-show-at-library-caught-in-act-1.2981531.

Weitzer, Ronald. *Legalizing Prostitution: From Illicit Vice to Lawful Business*. New York: New York University Press, 2012.

– "Prostitution as a Form of Work." *Sociology Compass* 1, no. 1 (September 2007): 143–55. https://doi.org/10.1111/j.1751-9020.2007.00010.x.

– "Resistance to Sex Worker Stigma." *Sexualities* 21, no. 5–6 (2018): 717–29.

– "Sociology of Sex Work." *Annual Review of Sociology* 35 (August 2009): 213–34. https://doi.org/10.1146/annurev-soc-070308-120025.

"What Is Feminist Porn?" Feminist Porn Awards, accessed 19 July 2022. https://www.feministpornawards.com/what-is-feminist-porn-2.

Whisnant, Rebecca. "'But What about Feminist Porn?' Examining the Work of Tristan Taormino." *Sexualization, Media, & Society* 2, no. 2 (2016). https://doi.org/10.1177/2374623816631727.

White, Michele. "Too Close to See: Men, Women, and Webcams." *New Media and Society* 5, no. 1 (March 2003): 7–28. https://doi.org/10.1177/1461444803005001901.

"Why Decriminalization of Sex Work?" Decriminalize Sex Work, accessed 15 January 2024. https://decriminalizesex.work/why-decriminalization.

Widom, Cathy Spatz, and Joseph B. Kuhns. "Childhood Victimization and Subsequent Risk for Promiscuity, Prostitution, and Teenage Pregnancy: A Prospective Study." *American Journal of Public Health* 86, no. 11 (November 1996): 1607–12. https://psycnet.apa.org/doi/10.2105/AJPH.86.11.1607.

Williams, Linda. "Generic Pleasures: Number and Narrative." In *Pornography: Film and Culture*, edited by Peter Lehman. New Brunswick, NJ: Rutgers University Press, 2006.

– *Hard Core: Power, Pleasure, and the "Frenzy of the Visible."* Berkeley: University of California Press, 1989.

Williams, Raymond. *Marxism and Literature*. Oxford: Oxford University Press, 1977.

Willis, Ellen. *Beginning to See the Light: Sex, Hope and Rock-and-Roll*. Minneapolis: University of Minnesota Press, 1992.

– "Lust Horizons: Is the Women's Movement Pro-Sex?" *Village Voice*, 17 June 1981.

Wilson, Julie, and Emily Chivers Yochim. *Mothering through Precarity: Women's Work and Digital Media*. Durham, NC: Duke University Press, 2017. https://doi.org/10.1215/9780822373193.

Winnicott, Donald. *The Child, the Family, and the Outside World*. New York: Penguin, 1964.

Witt, Emily. "After the Closure of Backpage, Increasingly Vulnerable Sex Workers Are Demanding Their Rights." *New Yorker*, 8 June 2018. https://www.newyorker.com/news/dispatch/after-the-closure-of-backpage-increasingly-vulnerable-sex-workers-are-demanding-their-rights.

Wolkowitz, Carol. "The Social Relations of Body Work." *Work, Employment and Society* 16, no. 3 (September 2002): 497–510. https://doi.org/10.1177/095001702762217452.

Wollen, Peter. *Signs and Meaning in the Cinema*. Bloomington: Indiana University Press, 1973.

Woods, Sean. "'The Last Word: David Simon on Twitter Trolls, Trump and Making *The Deuce* in the #MeToo Era." *Rolling Stone*, 8 September 2018. https://www.rollingstone.com/tv-movies/tv-movie-features/david-simon-interview-deuce-hbo-719397.

Worstall, Tim. "Services, the Only Important Part of the U.S. Economy, Growing Nicely – PMI to 57.1%." *Forbes*, 5 October 2016. https://www.forbes.com/sites/timworstall/2016/10/05/services-the-only-important-part-of-the-us-economy-growing-nicely-pmi-to-57-1.

writermaia. "*This Is Life with Lisa Ling*: Storyline." IMDb. Accessed 11 June 2022. https://www.imdb.com/title/tt4071576/plotsummary?ref_=tt_stry_pl.

Yanek, Cheryl. "The Real New York City: Friendship, Sex Work and Beyond." Self-published zine, 2001.

Zeisler, Andi. *Feminism and Pop Culture*. Berkeley, CA: Seal Press, 2008.

Zelizer, Viviana A. *The Purchase of Intimacy*. Princeton, NJ: Princeton University Press, 2005.

Zilbergeld, Bernie, and John Ullman. *Male Sexuality: A Guide to Sexual Fulfillment*. New York: Bantam Books, 1978.

Ziplow, Steven. *The Film Maker's Guide to Pornography*. New York: Drake, 1977.

Zola, Émile. *Nana*. Translated by Douglas Parmée. Oxford: Oxford University Press, 1992.

Zulkey, Edward J. "The Ladies Everleigh." *Chicago Tribune*, 21 January 1979.

Index

Page numbers in italics refer to illustrations.

ableism, 196. *See also* disabilities, people with
Academy Awards, 3, 5, 6, 25, 32, 157, 183, 190, 191, 281n4
ACLU (American Civil Liberties Union), 260
activism, sex worker: in the 1960s, 240–1; critical of prohibitionists, 289n102; decriminalization and, 10–11, 241–2, 254, 290n3; depicted on screen, 240, 242–3; feminist porn and, 228, 230; labour movement, 11, 24, 290n3; transgender activists, 10–11. *See also* rights movement, sex workers'; *individual activists and organizations*
Acton, William, 28
adult stores, 6, 9, 11, 223, 238, 328n25
adult theatres, 22, 120, 213, 218, 226, 244, 248
Aella (*Cam Girlz*), 128, *129*, 130, 131
aesthetic labour, 43, 255; of call girls, 164–6, 319n42; definition of, 44; of erotic dancers, 56–9, 69, 77, 82; make-up, 44, 57, 77, 104, 123; of porn performers, 235; rewards of, 106; sartorial strategies, 155, 314n36; of webcam models, 128, *129*, 130, 135,

144, 314n36. *See also* conspicuous consumption; costumes; display work
affective labour, 40
Afternoon Delight, 20, 48, 53, 70–5, *73*, 82–3
After Porn Ends, 217, 236, 330n62
agency: dismissal of, 33, 62, 210, 238, 245–6, 265, 295n57; empowerment paradigm and, 27, 34, 130; in feminist porn, 213, 227–31, 234; labour paradigm and, 35–9; as leitmotif, 63, 67, 99, 101, 112; of people with disabilities, 198–9; sexual, 88, 91, 106, 130; and structure, 38, 145, 235, 243, 246, 259; of webcam models, 118, 122, 125–8, 148. *See also* "choice" discourses
Agony of Love, 158
alienation: result of care work, 202, 206–7; result of emotional labour, 21, 44, 61, 119, 137–8, 167–9, 177, 255; stigma and, 108, 110. *See also* emotional labour
Allow States and Victims to Fight Online Sex Trafficking Act (FOSTA), 260
Amelia Twist (*Cam Girlz*), 131
American Civil Liberties Union (ACLU), 260

American Dream, 50, 63, 67–70, 76, 83, 157, 248, 305n86
American Gigolo (film), 266
American Gigolo (TV series), 336n45
Amnesty International, 10, 37
ancient Greece, 153, 215
anger, female, 79–80, 97, 111, 179, 182, 242, 257–9
anti-loitering laws, 256
anti-porn movement, 213, 215–17, 228, 245–6, 330n65, 332nn84–7
anti–sex work feminism. *See* prohibitionist paradigm
anti-trafficking organizations, 260
Antonia ("Road Strip"), 54, 56, 58, 59, 60, 61
Apple, Fiona, 3, 77
Arrowsmith, Anna, 35
Arthurs, Jane, 15, 53, 259, 286n65
Ashford, Annaleigh, *189*
Atlanta, 17, 20, 47, 48, 63, 68
auletrides, 153
Australia, 10, 210
auteurs, 214, 232–5
"authenticity," 43, 255; call girls and, 152, 156, 160–3, 166–7, 314n36; client desire for, 44, 60–2, 126–8, 136, 156, 163, 166–7; erotic dancing and, 58, 60–2; webcam modelling and, 21, 118, 121, 124, 126–8, 130, 133–7
autonomy: bodily, 7, 24, 34, 230, 253, 269; fear of, 88, 142–3; financial, 13, 34, 39, 47, 50, 90, 102, 125, 159, 253, 320n66; sexual, 33–5, 91, 253
Ava-Lynn (interviewee), 17–18, 23
Avenging Angel, 316n60

Baby Face, 34, 76, 157
Backpage, 163, 259–60
"backstage" labour, 21, 43, 57, 64, 69, 152, 160, 163–4. *See also* aesthetic labour
Baise-moi, 249

Baker, Josephine, 62
Baker, Sean, 261
Baldwin, Margaret, 31
Baltimore, 10
Barbie, 48
Barry, Kathleen, 31, 294n52, 294n54, 295n57
beauty ideals, 57, 69, 82, 113–14, 131, 164–5, 182, 199. *See also* aesthetic labour
Beauvoir, Simone de, 34, 57, 162, 164, 285n45
Bechdel test, 143
Behind the Green Door, 189, 226
"Being Washed" (O'Brien), 197
Belgium, 10
Bell (*Cam Girlz*), 124–5, 131
Belle de Jour, 158
Bernstein, Elizabeth, 19, 38, 41, 120, 144, 155–6, 334n6
Best Little Whorehouse in Texas, The, 34
Beyond the Pole, 53, 82
Bildungsroman, 142–3. *See also* Künstlerroman
BIPOC sex workers: anger taboo, 258–9; collaboration among, 63–5, 67; depictions on screen, 14, 62–70, 75–6, 78, 82, 101, 222, 238–40, 261–2; discrimination against, 82, 148, 239, 256–7; erotic dancers, 62–70, 75–6, 78, 82; performance in porn, 234, 238–40; racist sexualization of, 69, 238–40, 307n18; stereotypes of, 14, 101, 225–6, 239–40, 307n18; treatment by police, 37, 101, 239, 256; violence against, 17, 222, 238–9, 265; webcam models, 148. *See also* racism
birth control, 24
Birth of the Pearl, 12
Blac Chyna, 48, 62
Bloom, Brooke, *203*
Blue Angel, The, 157

body positivity, 131
body work, 43; "body awareness" exercises, 193, 205; definition of, 45; of massage parlour workers, 103–4; of sex surrogates, 192–4, 198–9, 204–5; types of, 301n140
Boogie Nights, 216
Borden, Lizzie, 23, 35–6, 318n42
"bounded authenticity," 156, 162, 170. *See also* girlfriend experience (GFE)
Bourdieu, Pierre, 43, 155
Boyle, Karen, 15, 58
branding, personal, 43, 118, 126–8, 152, 163–4
Breakfast at Tiffany's, 5, 14, 21, 156, 157–8, 169, 172
Breathing (O'Brien), 197
Breathing Lessons: The Life and Work of Mark O'Brien, 190, 194
Brewer, Madeline, *139*
Bromwich, Rebecca, 85
brothels, 9, 153, 156, 185, 215, 281n5
"brown paper bag stores." *See* adult stores
Bruckert, Chris, 57, 111, 333n4
Burana, Lily, 38, 48
Bureau of Labor Statistics (United States), 53
Burke, Heidi, 55
burlesque: BIPOC dancers, 62; erotic dancing and, 20, 48, 55–6, 58, 62, 64, 83; history of, 49–50, 54, 59
burnout, 44, 105–6, 118, 134, 137–8, 141, 152, 182, 236. *See also* emotional labour
BUtterfield 8, 157, 158, 281n4

Cactus Flower, 14, 157
Cali (*P.O.P.*), 64
Call Girl, The (Greenwald), 155
call girl agencies, 9, 120, 155, 158, 318n42
"call girl mania," 153, *154*

call girls: aesthetic labour of, 164–6, 319n42; "authenticity" and, 152, 156, 160–3, 166–7, 170; challenges of, 167–9, 175, 319n42; conspicuous consumption and, 154–5, 164–6, 174; economic motivations of, 159, 173; emotional labour of, 151, 156, 160–3, 167–8; empowerment and, 151, 165; as entrepreneurs, 152, 153, 163–4, 166, 318n40; history of, 152–3, 163; kissing and, 152, 156, *161*, 162; in older pop culture, 14, 21, 25–6, *26*, 31–2, 35–6, 153, *154*, 156–8, 159–60, 318nn41–2; performativity of, 154–5; personae, 151, 165–6, 174; personal accounts of, 151, 153–5, 268–9, 318nn39–40, 320n66; personal branding, 163–4; precarity of, 152, 165–6, 320n66; review websites, 163, 164, 168, 170, 265–6; services of, 156; stereotypes of, 152, 156–9, 319n42; transactional intimacy and, 9, 21, 25, 152, 154, 156, 160, 166–7, *171*, 171–2, 175–7. *See also* girlfriend experience (GFE)
Call Off Your Old Tired Ethics. *See* COYOTE (Call Off Your Old Tired Ethics)
Calvert, Casey, 249
Calvert, Misha, 319n43
Cam, 21, 118–19, 135–42, *139*, 145, 148–9, 259, 261
Camgirl (Mazzei), 135
cam girls. *See* webcam models
Cam Girlz, 21, 36, 118–19, 123–34, *129*, 142, 145, 148–9, 265, 314n36
Campbell, Russell, 13, 96, 195, 285n49
CamsCreative, 122
CamSoda, 122
Canada, 36, 118, 268
Canadian Union of Public Employees (CUPE), 11
Candice, 213, 217, 229–30

capitalism: American Dream and, 67–70, 76, 248; critiques of, 3, 29–30, 75–81, 169, 182, 214; employment relations under, 9, 40, 100, 112; exploitation under, 7–8, 30, 75–81, 124, 174, 214, 220, 247–8; marriage and, 29–30; sex work and, 14, 29, 35–6, 75–81, 133, 148, 167, 181–2, 246–7; transactional intimacy and, 7, 9, 21, 102–3, 152, 159–60, 166–7, 172, 177, 181, 254; unequal distribution of wealth, 75–6; women and, 7, 29, 39–42, 148, 247–8, 311n87. *See also* financial crisis (2007–8); late capitalism; neo-liberalism; patriarchy

Capote, Truman, 157

"Captain Save-a-Ho," 71–2, 75

Carchietta, John, 142, 145

Cardi B, 62

care work, 21–2, 43, 45, 184ff, 255, 266–7. *See also* surrogacy, sex

Carroll's. *See* Earl Carroll Theatre

cash, 36, 48, 68, 70, 145, *147, 161*, 162

"casting couch" trope, 168, 329n46

Cathouse, 52

CBC News, 117

censorship, 48, 157, 215–16, 251. *See also* Hays Code

Ceratonin (*Cam Girlz*), 117, *129*, 130

Chambers, Marilyn, 188–9

champagne room, 78, 302n21

Chanel ("Road Strip"), 54, 58

Chapkis, Wendy, 34, 195, 206

Chaturbate, 117, 122, 132

Cho, Margaret, 10

"choice" discourses: labour perspective, 24, 99–100, 125, 127, 138, 241, 254; neo-liberalism and, 22, 37–8; overemphasis on, 64; post-feminism and, 141; prohibitionist perspective, 25, 31, 326n15; sex-positive feminism and, 34, 71

Chyna ("Road Strip"), 54, 56, 58, 60, 61–2

"classiness," 152, 155, 165–6, 174

classism, 15, 51, 71–4, 75–7, 79–80

Client List, The (film), 20, 87, 93–8, *97*, 101, 104–5, 111

Client List, The (TV series), 20, 85–7, *86*, 98–115, *103, 109*, 256–7

clients, sex work: ability to screen, 19, 153, 260; desire for authenticity, 44, 60–2, 126–8, 136, 156, 163, 166–7; with disabilities, 45, 184, 188, 196, 324n71; emotional attachment to, 170, 175, 179, 200–1, 207; emotional support for, 156, 196, 308n19; motivations of, 198–9; treatment of "johns" vs sex workers, 98, 111, 311n83; unequal power dynamic with, 20, 79, 179, 239

Club 90, 228

Cohen-Greene, Cheryl, 183–4, 190–1, 196, 199–200, 209–11

Comstock, Anthony, 215

Confessions of a Brazilian Call Girl, 335n44

conspicuous consumption, 43, 44, 67, 154–5, 164–6, 174, 255

consumerism, 152, 165, 169, 172

costumes, 44, 57–8, 69, 104–5, 123, 128, *129*, 130, 135–6, 144, 294n52. *See also* aesthetic labour

COVID-19 pandemic, 9, 17, 42, 118

COYOTE (Call Off Your Old Tired Ethics), 24, 241–2, 290n3

Craigslist, 163, 260

Crane, Antonia. *See* Antonia ("Road Strip")

creative entrepreneurship, 43, 68, 123–4, 125–8, 148, 300n127

Crimes of Passion, 35

"Criminal" (Apple), 3, 77, 269

criminalization: challenges to, 77, 111, 185; definition of, 36; depicted on screen, 15–16, 22, 108, 204, 207–9, 222, 242–3; financial burden of, 37; impact on violence

against sex workers, 10, 32, 37, 108, 111, 207–9, 222, 242–3, 255, 259–60; prohibitionist model, 32, 36–7, 111; recent legislation, 259–60; stigmatization and, 11, 35, 37, 108, 111, 169, 177, 207, 255, 264; in the US, 5, 33, 259–60, 281n5. *See also* decriminalization; "Nordic model"; police
Crystal Cat (*Cam Girlz*), 125
CSI: Crime Scene Investigation, 52
cultural capital, 43
CUPE (Canadian Union of Public Employees), 11
customers. *See* clients, sex work

"dad bods," 114
Damiano, Gerard, 225
Daniels, Stormy, 249
dating. *See* intimate relationships, personal
Daughter of the Streets, 316n60
Davina, Lola, 37, 320n66
Dawn, Amber, 287n73
Dawn: Portrait of a Teenage Runaway, 316n60
"Death of a Porn Queen" (*Frontline*), 237
death trope, sex worker, 13, 14, 31, 52, 74, 87, *89*, 91, 106, 140, 146, 156, 158–9, 160, 253–4
De Boer, Tracey, 183, 198, 324n71
decriminalization: in Australia, 210; definition of, 37; goal of COYOTE, 241, 290n3; opposed by prohibitionists, 30, 33; public opinion on, 12; and reducing stigma, 35, 169, 265–6; support for, 10–11, 35, 209, 211, 254; tenets of, 37. *See also* legalization
"deep acting," 44, 60, 79, 104–5, 160–2, 175. *See also* emotional labour
Deep Throat, 23, 213, 216, 225, 226, 230
DeJong, Monique Marie, 85
Deneuve, Catherine, 158

Despentes, Virginie, 249
"Desperate Housewives effect," 313n96
destigmatization, 7, 9, 35, 45, 70, 82, 92, 255, 266. *See also* stigmatization
Deuce, The, 22, 34, 214, 217ff, *219*, *221*, *229*, *233*, 256–7, 259, 261, 329n55
Devil in Miss Jones, The, 226
Devine, Loretta, 101, *103*
Diamond (*Magic City*), 47, 69
Dickens, Charles, 29
Dietrich, Marlene, 13, 157
digital piracy. *See* piracy
disabilities, people with, 184, 186, 188, 191, 194, 196–9, 210, 324n71
disassociation, 44, 104, 141, 174, 294n52
display work, 43, 255; definition of, 44, 126; of erotic dancers, 56–9, 64–5, *66*; of massage parlour workers, 103–5; of webcam models, 126–30, *129*, 144. *See also* aesthetic labour
DIY culture, 121, 126–7, 128
DJ Esco (*Magic City*), 70
documentaries: expository, 52–3, 54, 58, 61; impact on real life, 16–17, 53; "infotainment," 52; observational camerawork, 53, 61–2, 68, 123–4; personal portrait, 20, 53, 54–5, 61, 63, 66, 69–70, 123–4, 133, 148; vérité approach, 63. *See also individual named documentaries*
"docu-porn," 15, 53, 56, 58, 124, 286n65
domestic labour, 42, 90
Donovan, Basil, 45
Downer, Ivy, 62, 64
Downward Path, The, 31
doxxing, 133, 315n47
Dressed to Kill, 158
Dunne, Sean, 123–4
Dworkin, Andrea, 25, 31, 38, 105, 179, 213, 216, 234
dysfunction, sexual, 105, 183–6, 188–9, 196. *See also* surrogacy, sex

Earl Carroll Theatre, 50
East of Eden, 5, 281n4
Easy Alice, 230
eating disorders, 312n96
Ebert, Roger, 26
economic mobility, entrepreneurship and, 102, 112–13; erotic capital and, 43, 50, 63, 69, 77, 82, 100–1; erotic dancing and, 47, 48, 50, 56, 63, 67, 69, 77; motivated by, 7, 36, 50, 67, 82; rise of downward mobility, 334n6; webcam modelling and, 123, 124–5, 135
Edison, Thomas, 48, 326n6
education, sex, 131, 183, 188, 197–8, 205, 210, 213, 230, 266
Edwards, Blake, 157
8 Minutes, 263–4
8 mm loops, 216, 224, 239
Ellis, Havelock, 28
emotional labour, 43, 315n51; alienation, 21, 44, 61, 119, 137–8, 167–9, 177, 255; burnout, 44, 105–6, 134, 137–8, 141, 152, 182; of call girls, 151, 156, 160–3, 167–8; challenges of, 105–6, 134, 136–8, 151, 201–2, 206–7; definition of, 44; of erotic dancers, 56, 60–2; linked to maternal nurturing, 105; and loss of self, 31, 134, 135, 137–8, 167, 176–7, 207, 237; of massage parlour workers, 103, 104–6; minimization of, 95; rewards of, 106, 200–1; service work and, 41, 130, 134, 168, 247–8, 298n109; of sex surrogates, 184, 193, 195, 200–2, 206–7, 210; Stanislavski technique, 160; of webcam models, 133–8, 141–2, 148
emotion management strategies, 44, 58, 65, 104–5, 133–4, 195, 200–2, 207–8, 316n51. *See also* emotional labour; separation of "self" from "role"
empowerment: of call girls, 151, 165; definition of, 148; erotic dancing and, 47–9, 56, 57, 59, 62, 70, 74, 83; "ho chic" aesthetic and, 286n61; of massage parlour workers, 106, 308n19; of porn performers, 34–5; rhetoric of, 6, 38, 53, 70, 132–3, 148, 246, 256, 299n112, 332n86; self-representation and, 24, 27, 53, 241–2; of sex surrogates, 204, 210–11; sexual objectification and, 31, 34, 122, 133, 331n82; sexy body as site of, 95, 113–14, 119, 133, 165, 176, 256–7; webcam modelling and, 21, 117–19, 123–6, 130–3, 148. *See also* "post-feminist sensibility"
empowerment paradigm: and agency, 27, 34, 130; position on sex work, 25, 27, 33–5; and sex positivity, 34, 72
Engels, Friedrich, 29–30
entrepreneurship: call girls and, 152, 153, 163–4, 166, 318n40; creative entrepreneurs, 43, 68, 123–4, 125–8, 148, 300n127; economic mobility and, 102, 112–13; erotic capital and, 8, 43–4, 55, 82; erotic dancers, 47, 53–6, 63, 65, 67–8, 82; glamourization of, 112–14; impediments to, 37; indoor sex work and, 19; massage parlour workers and, 85–7, 94, 100–1, *103*, 104; neo-liberalism and, 9, 41–2, 55, 83, 112–14, 126, 148, 169, 181–2, 299n112; webcam modelling, 21, 118, 122–8, 135, 148. *See also* "mompreneurs"
Equal Employment Opportunity Commission (United States), 82
Eros (website), 163
erotic capital, 8, 20, 95; burlesque artists, 50; definition of, 43–4; erotic dancers, 48–9, 55, 63, 67, 77–8, 82–3; limits of, 82–3, 236, 257; and stigmatization, 7, 43–4, 67, 97, 227; upward mobility and, 100–1

erotic dance clubs: in 1990s pop culture, 51–2; backstage, 57, 69, 77; cash and, 68, 70; champagne room, 78, 302n21; distinct physical areas of, 57; gender inequalities within, 56–7, 61–2, 70; owners/managers of, 59, 68, 69–70, 78, 82–3; as place of creative synergy, 63, 67, 68; racism within, 82; in the US, 9, 48, 51; work conditions of, 59–60. *See also individual named clubs*
erotic dancers: aesthetic labour of, 56–9, 69, 77, 82; BIPOC dancers, 62–70, 75–6, 78, 82; display work of, 56–9, 64–5, 66; economic motivations of, 47, 50, 53–6, 63–4, 67–70, 77, 82, 260–1; emotional labour of, 56, 60–2; as entrepreneurs, 47, 53–6, 63, 65, 67–8, 82; erotic capital of, 48–9, 55, 63, 67, 77–8, 82–3; male gaze and, 50–1, 58, 67, 69, 77; as mothers, 54–6, 63, 69, 78, 305n86; musical artists and, 63, 68; in older pop culture, 5, 48, 51–3, 83; personal accounts of, 38, 47, 56, 59, 64–9, 253, 260–1, 305n86; public opinions about, 52, 66; stereotypes of, 5, 47–8, 51–2, 61, 65–6, 71, 77, 79, 302n21; stigmatization of, 47–8, 55, 65–7, 80; unions and, 11, 59, 83
erotic dancing: "authenticity" and, 58, 60–2; capitalism and, 75–81; challenges of, 59–60, 61–2, 78–9; creative entrepreneurship and, 68; empowerment and, 47–9, 56, 57, 59, 62, 70, 74, 83; history of, 48, 49–50, 59; idealized femininity and, 57, 58, 61–2, 69; pole work, 3, 4, 47, 54, 57–8, 63–7, 66, 68, 77, 269; precarity of, 54, 59, 62, 78–9; profits of, 9, 48; racism within, 82–3; "stripper culture," 48; training, 47, 49, 63–5, 66. *See also* burlesque
Erotic Review, The (website), 164, 265–6
Escort, The, 158

escorts. *See* call girls
ethnographies, 39, 95, 154–6, 308n19, 314n36, 320n66
Everleigh sisters, 153
exploitation: compounded by criminalization, 32, 37, 138; gamification of, 265; outside the US, 148; under patriarchal capitalism, 7–8, 30, 75–81, 124, 174, 214, 220, 247, 289n102; in popular culture, 51, 102, 235–6, 238, 250, 286n65; prohibitionist narratives of, 31–2, 33, 56, 123, 125, 198, 210, 228, 241, 289n102; within the sex industry, 31, 43, 52, 138, 168–9, 214, 238, 247, 293n40, 327n18; stereotypes of, 6, 14, 31–2, 47, 51–2, 71–5, 88, 109, 143, 146, 237–8, 255. *See also* trafficking, sex
expository documentary, 52–3, 54, 61
Eyes Wide Shut, 33

Facebook, 126, 315n47
factory workers, 26, 28, 30, 50, 55
fallen woman trope, 12, 23; mothers and, 20, 86, 90–1, 93–4, 96–8, 97, 101, 106, 110, 114; origin of, 106; qualities of, 5–6, 113; repudiation of, 100, 101 104, 112–14, 176; in the Victorian era, 29, 87, 91, 96, 97
Family Business, 52
family life, depictions of, 54, 56, 107–8, 123–4, 202
Fatima's Coochee-Coochee Dance, 48
Feel, 93
Feminine Mystique, The (Freidan), 88
femininity, idealized: features of, 29, 57, 69; performance of, 44, 57–8, 61–2, 154, 182; rejection of, 130, 175; repression of intelligence and, 61–2
feminism: binary thinking of, 8, 13, 53, 67, 72, 74–5, 216–17, 251; "choice" discourses, 22, 24–5, 31, 34, 37–8, 71, 125, 141, 241, 254, 326n15; collective

feminism (*continued*)
  action and, 8, 83, 114, 119, 132; debates about pornography, 213–14, 216–17, 228, 326n11, 332n85, 333n4; debates about sex work, 7, 17, 19, 25, 29–30, 48, 71, 118; digital feminist subculture, 121; first-wave, 13, 29; influence on pop culture, 30, 158, 254; neo-liberalism and, 9, 39, 81, 132–3, 332n86; "rescue industry," 27, 29, 37, 38, 71–5, 216, 242–3, 326n15; second-wave, 142, 240–1, 258; sex wars, 8, 22, 25, 72, 214, 216, 218, 245–6; third-wave, 17, 182. *See also* empowerment paradigm; labour paradigm; pornography, feminist; post-feminism; prohibitionist paradigm
Feminist Current, 118, 198
Femme, 329n46
femme fatales, 5–6, 12, 32, 136
Femme Productions, 228, 230
Film Makers Guide to Pornography, The (Ziplow), 223
financial crisis (2007–8), 75, 78–9, 87, 93–5, 98–9, 112–14, 159, 305n79, 312n87
financial independence, 13, 34, 39, 47, 50, 90, 102, 125, 159, 253, 320n66
Fire Down Below, 32–3
first-wave feminism, 13, 29. *See also* feminism
Fishback, Dominique, 240
"fishing," 80
Fitzgerald, Juniper, 92
Flashdance, 51
Fleiss, Heidi, 178
Flynt, Larry, 216
Folies Bergères, 62
Fonda, Jane, 25–6, *26*, 281n4
Fordism, 40, 152, 218. *See also* post-Fordism
FOSTA-SESTA, 260
"Four X." *See* Wolfe, Bob
Freedom Network USA, 260

Free Ride, A, 326n7
Freidan, Betty, 88, 332n86
friendship, depictions of, 64–5, 67, *76*, 94, 100
"frontstage" show, 43, 50–1, 160–3
Full Metal Jacket, 88
Future (rapper), 68

Gay, Roxane, 258–9
gender: common dynamic in sex worker films, 73–4; inequalities within erotic dance clubs, 56–7, 61–2, 70, 79; inequalities within sex industry, 15, 29, 213, 246; traditional gender roles, 27, 34, 90, 107, 253; wage gap, 83, 112, 114, 311n87
Gere, Richard, 5
gig economy, 9, 40–2, *41*, 78, 87, 137, 159, 166, 173, 254. *See also* capitalism
Gigi (*P.O.P.*), 47, 63–7, 255
gigolo trope, 266
Gilbert, Shannan, 17
Gill, Rosalind, 14, 30, 42, 114, 119, 132–3, 165, 176, 256. *See also* "post-feminist sensibility"
Ginger (*Cam Girlz*), 134
girlfriend experience (GFE), 21, 151–2, 156, 159–63, 170–2; mutual suspension of disbelief, 156, 161–2. *See also* call girls
Girlfriend Experience, The (film), 2, 152, 158–72, *161*, *171*, 177, 181–2, 249, 266
Girlfriend Experience, The (TV series), 21, 36, 151–2, 158, 172–82, *180*, 255–7, 261
Girl in Trouble, 51
Girl Next Door, The, 217
GirlsDoPorn scandal, 327n18
Girls Gone Wild, 6
Girls of Paradise (media campaign), 264–5
global financial crisis. *See* financial crisis (2007–8)

Globe and Mail, 71
Godard, Jean-Luc, 44, 159, 167, 249
Goffman, Erving, 16
Golden Age of Porn, 22, 213, 216, 218, 226, 228, 238–9, 244, 251
Goldman, Emma, 30
Good Luck to You, Leo Grande, 266, *267*
Grand Theft Auto V, 52, 265, 302n21
Grant, Melissa Gira, 38, 137, 180, 263
Grant, Shauna, 237–8
Great Recession. *See* financial crisis (2007–8)
Greenfield, Lauren, 67
Greenwald, Harold, 155
Grey, Sasha, *161*, *171*, 249
Grey's Anatomy, 183
Grierson, John, 52
G String Divas, 52
Guardian, The (newspaper), 305n86
Gyllenhaal, Maggie, 220, *221*, *229*

Hahn, Kathryn, *73*
Hakim, Catherine, 8, 16, 43, 50, 95, 101, 257
Hamilton, Suzy Favor, 16, 177–8, 320n69
Hanna, Kathleen, 38
Happy Endings?, 93
Happy Hooker, The (film), 34
Happy Hooker, The (Hollander), 158, 318nn39–40
Harcourt, Christine, 45
Hardcore (film), 216, 316n60
Hard Core (Williams), 225
Hart, Veronica, 228, 251
Harvey, David, 40, 112, 298n105
Haskell, Molly, 8, 16, 19, 157
Hays, Sharon, 21, 87, 107
Hays, Will, 13
Hays Code, 13–14, 157, 307n18
hetaerae, 153
History of Prostitution (Sanger), 28–9
"ho chic," 14, 286n61

Hochschild, Arlie, 8; "authentic experiences," 126, 130, 156, 163; emotional labour, 60–1, 105, 133–4, 201–2, 315n51; "role" and "self," 134, 138, 148, 160, 167–8, 176, 192, 207; "surface acting" and "deep acting," 44, 60, 319n45; the "unmanaged heart," 61, 128, 149; women's feelings, 178, 257
Hodas, Marty, 223
Hollander, Xaviera, 158, 318nn39–40
homophobia, 143, 146
"Hooker's Ball," 290n3
hooks, bell, 19
House of Cards, 158
Houston, 82
Houston Chronicle, 255
How Mamas Love Their Babies (Fitzgerald), 92
Huffington Post, 255
human rights, 10, 196, 254, 269
Human Sexual Inadequacy (Masters and Johnson), 185, 188, 206, 322n25
Human Sexual Response (Masters and Johnson), 185–6
HunieCam Studio, 265
Hunt, Helen, 183, 191, 193, *195*
hustler: definition of, 81; neo-liberal capitalism and, 3, 9, 39–42, 75, 80–1
Hustler (magazine), 216
Hustlers (film), 3, *4*, 20, 48, 53, 75–81, *76*, 82–3, 257, 269
"Hustlers at Scores, The" (Pressler), 75
Hyde, Sophie, 266

I, Daniel Blake, 335n44
Iman ("Road Strip"), 54, 56, 58
ImLive.com, 122
incarceration, sex worker, 5, 81, 96, *97*, 100, 108, 111, 157, 318n39
individualism, 87, 107, 152, 176; detrimental to collective empowerment, 8, 14–15, 81, 83, 114,

individualism (*continued*)
119, 132; neo-liberalism and, 40, 81, 132–3, 148, 259; sex-positive feminism and, 200. *See also* neo-liberalism
indoor sex workers, 19, 255, 256, 260, 264–5
Industrial Revolution, 28, 90
Inherent Vice, 93
Instagram, 126, 266
"intensive mothering," 21, 87, 107–8, 113
International Committee on Prostitutes' Rights (ICPR), 34
International Professional Surrogates Association (IPSA), 188, 192
International Union for Sex Workers (IUSW), 11
internet, 6, 9, 102, 118–21, 163–4, 260, 266
intersectionality, 9, 39, 111, 214, 256, 261
intimacy, commodification of, 9, 152, 154, 156, 167, 171–2. *See also* transactional intimacy
"intimacy coaches," 231, 330n55
"intimate labour," 45, 190. *See also* surrogacy, sex
Intimate Life: Sex, Love, and My Journey as a Surrogate Partner (Cohen-Greene), 191, 200
intimate relationships, personal, 110–11, 167–8, 170, 175–6, 179, 206–7, 240
IPSA (International Professional Surrogates Association), 188, 192
Irina Palm, 335n44
Irma La Douce, 5, 14, 157
IUSW (International Union for Sex Workers), 11

Jack the Ripper, 294n54
Jeanne Dielman, 23 quai du commerce, 1080 Bruxelles, 300n112
Jeffreys, Sheila, 104, 192, 293n40, 294n55, 332n86
Jenkins, Artemis, 63, 65

Jenkins, Patty, 32
JenniCam, 121
Jerry Springer, 5, 51, 52
"johns," 16, 31, 311n83. *See also* clients, sex work
Johnson, Eithne, 318n41
Johnson, Virginia E., 183, 185–7, 193, 206, 322n25
John TV, 16
Joint United Nations Programme on HIV/AIDS (UNAIDS), 10
Jones, Angela, 9, 122, 130, 148, 314n36

Kael, Pauline, 42–3
Kanai, Akane, 42, 114
Keough, Riley, 151, 172–3, *180*
Khyla (*Cam Girlz*), *129*, 132
Killing, The, 158
Kinetoscope, 215, 326n6
King, A'Ziah (Zola), 3, 253, 261
"King of the Peeps." *See* Hodas, Marty
Kinsey, Alfred, 185
kissing, 152, 156, *161*, 162
Klute, 25–6, *26*, 158, 281n4
Knox, Belle, 34–5
Koester, Megan, 253
Kubrick, Stanley, 88
Künstlerroman, 214, 220. *See also* Bildungsroman

La Bare, 336n45
labour: depicted on screen, 42–3; part-time, 40–1; precarious, 9, 24, 36, 40–2, 43, 54, 59, 62, 63–4, 78–9, 112, 137–8, 141–2, 165–6, 305n86, 312n87; rights, 7, 11, 16, 35, 255; social dimensions of, 39; unions, 11, 37, 59, 83, 241–2; unpaid, 42, 90, 107, 174. *See also* *individual types of labour*
labour paradigm: goals of, 27, 35; opposed to prohibitionists, 35; position on sex work, 35–7; sex

positivity and, 72; support for
decriminalization, 37, 255, 290n3
La donna delinquente (Lombroso), 28
Lana Rose (*Cam Girlz*), 126
Lancet, The, 10
lap dancing, 50, 58, 60, 61–2, 78–9.
See also erotic dancing
late capitalism, 60–1, 103, 107, 126, 130, 156, 172, 256, 312n96
Law & Order, 158
League of Exotique Dancers, 53
Leaving Los Vegas, 33, 74
Le Chabanais, 153
Le Coucher de la Mariée, 12
Lee, Gypsy Rose, 50, 54
Legal Aid Society of New York, 256
legalization, 30, 196, 296n83. See also decriminalization
"legal prostitution," 29–30
Leigh, Carol, 11, 18–19, 23
Leisure Suit Larry: Magna Cum Laude, 52
Le Mouvement du Nid, 264
Lerner, Gerda, 13, 96
Lerner, Harriet, 79–80
Levy, Ariel, 133, 176, 332n86
Lewin, Ben, 191
Leyla (interviewee), 17–18, 47
liberation, women's, 23, 29, 51, 88, 200, 218, 226, 240–1, 289n102, 307n18
Liddiard, Kirsty, 196, 198–9
"Life as a Truck-Stop Stripper," 53
Lifetime (network), 85, 98
LillSecret, 117–18, 149
Ling, Lisa, 53–62
Little Girls, 143, 144
"Little Red Riding Hood," 232–4
Live Nude Girls Unite!, 83
Live Sex Acts (Chapkis), 34
Lombroso, Cesare, 28
London, 28, 29, 35
loop machines, 23, 223, 225, 238–9.
See also Mutoscope

loops, film, 23, 119, 213, 223–6, 229
Lopez, Jennifer, 3, *4*, *76*, 269
Los Angeles, 11, 48, 83, 85, 153, 250, 302n21
Lost Girls, 17
Love Hewitt, Jennifer, 85–6, *86*, 93–4, 98–9, *103*, 114
Lovelace, 217
Lovelace, Linda, 223
Lovers, Friends, Slaves (Stein), 156
Lovers, The, 215
low-wage jobs. See "McJobs"
Lucas, Ann, 43, 153, 163, 265, 320n66
Lumière brothers, 12
Lust, Erika, 213, 249

Mac, Juno, 15, 289n102
Madame Claude, 155
Madam Kelly, 153
madams, 88, 94, 153, 155, 174, 318n40
Mafia II, 52
Magdalene, Mary, 74, 90, 106
Magic City, 20, 48, 53, 67–70, 82–3
Magic City (Atlanta), 47, 63, 68–70
Magic Mike, 266
Maguire, Gigi. See Gigi (*P.O.P.*)
make-up, 44, 57, 77, 104, 123, 155, 165.
See also aesthetic labour
male gaze, 7, 50–1, 58, 67, 69, 74, 77, 118, 122, 130, 144–5
"male sex right," 31, 34, 79, 82, 265
male sex workers. See sex workers, male
Malle, Louis, 215
Manhattan, 48, 75, 155, 158, 159, 165, 218, 318n40, 318n42. See also New York City
Marissa Frost (*Cam Girlz*), 131
Marked Women (Campbell), 13
marriage: former sex workers and, 110–11; as "legal prostitution," 29–30; non-commodified intimacies of, 156; trope in pop culture, 5, 13, 18, 74, 140, 157, 253–4; violence within, 37

Married ... with Children, 92
Martins, Millie, 315n47
Mary Tyler Moore Show, The, 25, 43, 227
Mason, Richard, 307n18
Massage Parlor Murders!, 88, *89*
Massage Parlor Wife, 88, *89*, 135
massage parlours: history of, 87–90, 306n11, 307n16; legality of, 88; in New York City, 88, 218, 307n16; profits of, 9; services of, 94–5; stereotypes of, 102
massage parlour workers: body work of, 103–4; display work of, 103–5; emotional labour of, 103, 104–6, 308n19; empowerment and, 106, 308n19; entrepreneurship and, 85–7, 94, 100–1, *103*, 104; legal status of, 88, 102; moral outrage about, 88–9, 307n16; in older pop culture, 88, *89*; personal accounts of, 85, 309n19, 311n80; stereotypes of, 20, 88, *89*; stigmatization of, 311n80; transactional intimacy and, 87, 102–3; violence against, 17
massage therapists, 45, 301n140, 307n11
Masters, William H., 183, 185–7, 193, 206, 322n25
Masters and Johnson Institute, 186
Masters of Sex, 183, 187–8, *189*
Matilda; or, the Dying Penitent (Reynolds), 106
mature sex workers, 118, 132
Mazzei, Isa, 135, 138–9, 141, 261
McClintock, Anne, 289n102, 295n57
"McJobs," 20, 36, 41, 55, 63–4, 69, 99, 108, 124–5, 173, 312n87. *See also* service work
McLaughlin, Lisa, 13, 39, 114
McNair, Brian, 48, 216
McNeill, Maggie, 155, 268–9
Meade, Emily, 330n55
media campaigns, prohibitionist, 264–5, 330n65

media studies, 9, 39
Meese Commission, 251
memoirs, sex worker, 3, 38, 56, 135, 153–4, *154*, 158, 183–4, 188, 191, 287n73, 318nn39–40
mental illness, 32, 158–9
mentorship, depictions of, 63–5, 100–1, *103*
method acting. *See* "deep acting"
Michelle (interviewee), 17–18, 85
Middles Ages, 27–8
Mildred Pierce, 300n112
Miller-Young, Mireille, 238–9
Millett, Kate, 25, 327n19
Mills, C. Wright, 298n109
Minsky Brothers, 49–50
misogyny, 174, 257; within porn industry, 22, 214, 216, 217, 225–6, 236, 243–4, 250, 328n36; and revenge porn, 177–81, *180*; sex work and, 105, 111, 170, 326n15, 327n19; and violence against women, 17, 32, 79, 294n54, 315n47, 328n36
Mme. Olga's Massage Parlor, 88, 100
Mock, Janet, 10–11
Moguls, The, 217
"mompreneurs," 20, 85–7, 101–3, 107, 112–15
Money on the Side, 31, 158
"money shot," 214, 223, 225, 226, 231, 235
Monster, 32, 294n53
Mother Deposits Her Child at Foundling Hospital, A (O'Neill), *97*
motherhood: body work and, 104; challenges of, 99; depictions on screen, 92; idealized, 86, 90–2, 95–6, 97, 105, 106, 107, 113; "intensive mothering," 21, 87, 107–8, 113; maternal nurturing, 95, 105, 107; "mompreneurship," 102; "new momism," 113–14; as performance, 103; virgin–whore dichotomy and, 90–1, 96, 98, 105–6, 107; "yummy mumminess," 114

mothers, sex worker: depictions of, 12–13, 54, 56, 63, 78, 85–7, 91, 93–115, 97, 103, 220, 335n44; as fallen women, 20, 86, 90–1, 93–4, 96–8, 97, 101, 106, 110, 114; loss of custody, 91–2, 108, 264; motivations of, 36, 55, 69, 78, 93, 99, 102, 108; personal accounts of, 47, 56, 64–5, 67, 92, 124–5; prevalence of, 86; public opinions about, 92; stigmatization of, 12–13, 21, 86–7, 90–2, 96–8, 107–11, 236. *See also* "intensive mothering"; "mompreneurs"
Moulin Rouge!, 6
Mrs. Fletcher, 217
Much Loved, 335n44
Mulvey, Laura, 122
music industry, 63, 68–70
Mutantes: Punk Porn Feminism, 217
Mutoscope, 119, 120, 326n6
MyRedBook.com, 260
My Surrender, 329n46
My Therapist, 188–9, 190

Nana (Zola), 3, 28
neo-liberalism, 7, 8, 151; in 1990s pop culture, 51; in 2000s pop culture, 14–15, 113; definition of, 40, 298n105; entrepreneurship and, 9, 41–2, 55, 83, 112–14, 126, 148, 169, 181–2, 299n112; feminism and, 9, 39, 81, 132–3, 332n86; ideal neo-liberal subject, 112, 137–8, 148, 259; "intensive mothering" under, 107, 113; rise of, 24, 40, 218, 298n107; success narratives, 85, 94–5, 98, 112–14, 248. *See also* capitalism
Nevada, 281n5, 296n83
"new momism," 113–14
news media, 10, 11, 16, 41, 77, 88, 179, 311n80
New South Wales, 210
New Wave Hookers, 244–5

New York (magazine), 10, 11, 75, 77
New York City: call girls in, 153–6, 157, 318n40, 318n42; early burlesque scene, 49–50; formation of Club 90, 228; massage parlours in, 88, 307n16; move towards decriminalization, 10; porn industry in, 213; sex workers in 1800s, 28; sex workers murdered in, 222–3. *See also* Manhattan; Times Square
New York Daily News, 86
New Yorker, 42
New York Times, 10, 42, 119, 184, 241, 258–9, 315n47
New York Times Magazine, 10, 11
New Zealand, 10
Nichols, Bill, 53, 55, 61, 63, 133
Night at the Follies, A, 51
Night Shift, 158, 318n41
9 to 5: Days in Porn, 217
"Nordic model," 33, 36–7
North America: cultural changes in, 6; economic changes in, 40–1, 59; massage parlours in, 88, 307n16; prostitution arrests in, 111
Norway, 36
Not a Love Story: A Film about Pornography, 216, 326n15
novels, sex worker, 3, 87, 153, 154
Nuts, 32, 158

objectification: definition of, 315n39; in "docu-porn," 54, 58; empowerment perspective, 34, 106, 176; prohibitionist perspective, 27, 31–3, 133, 331n82; racism and, 69, 239, 256, 307n18; subversion of, 69, 82, 122, 128, 130, 145, 193; of teenage girls, 142–3; in traditional pornography, 128, 216, 224, 227, 326n11; in video games, 265, 302n21. *See also* "self-objectification"
O'Brien, Mark, 183–4, 190–1, 194, 196–200

obscenity laws, 213, 215
observational camerawork, 53, 61–2, 68, 123–4
Of Human Bondage, 157
One-Dimensional Woman (Power), 39
O'Neill, Henry Nelson, 97
OnlyFans, 9, 42
"On Seeing a Sex Surrogate" (O'Brien), 191, 197–8
"oppression" paradigm. *See* prohibitionist paradigm
orgasms, 130–1, 133, 163, 185, 187–8
Oscars. *See* Academy Awards
"Other," 5, 12–13, 285n45, 289n102, 307n18
Ovidie, 333n90

Paglia, Camille, 60, 213
Parent, Colette, 111
Paris, 62, 153
Pateman, Carole, 28, 79
patriarchy: challenges to, 27, 57, 58–9, 77, 106, 241; dismissal of women's feelings, 178, 257–8; double standards of, 7, 22, 24, 27, 34, 67, 90, 97, 106, 109, 114, 174, 177–8, 181, 218, 220; economic control of women, 39–40; idealized woman, 12–13, 256; "male sex right," 31, 34, 79, 82, 265; objectification of women, 27, 31–3, 82, 95, 142–3, 170, 216; sexual repression of women, 27, 33, 59, 67, 77, 90–1, 130–1, 142–3, 145, 200, 229, 253, 255, 285n49; sex work and, 8, 12–13, 14, 25, 27, 29, 31, 32, 169, 181, 253. *See also* capitalism; misogyny
peep shows, 9, 117–18, 119–20, *120*, 128, 213, 215, 218, 223, 326n6, 327–8n25
Pelecanos, George, 22, 214, 231, 329n55
Pendleton, Eva, 34, 59
People vs. Larry Flynt, The, 216
Perfect Ending, A, 158

performance, 19, 43, 103–5; as art, 118, 123, 124, 128, *129*, 130, 136–7; of "classiness," 155; dangers of, 134–7; of feelings, 44, 61, 136–7, 152, 160–3, 167, 255; of femininity, 44, 57–8, 61–2, 154, 182; of lesbianism, 144–5; separation of "self" and "role," 44, 104–5, 134, 135, 137–8, 142, 160, 162, 167, 174, 176–7, 192, 201, 316n51; of sexuality, 34, 53, 59, 67, 70, 74, 144–5, 149; of submissiveness, 62, 69–70, 133, 175; of violence, 128, 133, 136, 140–2, 145, 238, 250, 328n36
performativity, 154–5
personae, 43–4, 49, 57–9, 62, 77, 104–5, 126, 128, 134, 135, 137, 151, 165–6, 174, 237, 294n52
personal portrait documentary, 20, 53, 54–5, 61, 63, 66, 69–70, 123–4, 133, 148
Perversion for Profit, 215
Petro, Melissa, 255
Pheterson, Gail, 108, 241
Philadelphia, 10
"phoniness," 44, 126, 136
Phyrne, 153
Pineapple Project, 249
Pinki Pixie (*Cam Girlz*), 125, 127, 134, 138
piracy, 133, 138
Playboy, 127, 157, 215, 330n65
Players Club, The, 51
Pleasure (film), 217, 250, 257, *258*, 259
pleasure, sexual: commodification of, 133; feminist porn and, 213, 227–8, 230–2, 234, 329n46, 332n85; privileging of male pleasure, 224, 226–7, 328n33; self-discovery and, 106, 130–1, 266–7; sex surrogacy and, 186, 192, 196, 198, 210. *See also* empowerment paradigm
Podnieks, Elizabeth, 92
pole dancing, 3, 47, 54, 57–8, 63–7, *66*, 68, 77, 269. *See also* erotic dancing

Pole Fan Addicts, 47, 63–5
police: discrimination against sex workers, 16–17, 140, 222–3, 241–3; fear of, 10, 32, 80, 108–9, 111, 208, 222, 255; systemic racism and, 37, 101, 239, 256–7; treatment of "johns" vs sex workers, 98, 111, 311n83. *See also* criminalization
"politicized whores," 34
"polymorphous paradigm," 39, 297n94
Poor Things, 3
popular culture: in the 1960s, 14, 51, 88, 142–3, 152–3, *154*, 157–8, 159–60; in the 1970s, 25–6, *26*, 43, 88, *89*, 102, 135, 158, 188–9, 216, 226, 316n60; in the 1980s, 43, 158, 188–90, 216–17, 237–8, 244, 316n60, 318nn41–2; in the 1990s, 5, 14, 51–2, 83, 121, 190, 216, 316n60; in the 2000s, 6, 14–15, 52–3, 113, 217; common gender dynamics in, 73–4; creative involvement of sex workers, 261–3; definition of, 19; depictions of work, 42–3; in early twentieth century, 12–14, 51, 52, 156–7; feminist influence on, 30, 158, 254; glamourization of sex work, 14–15, 18, 48, 69, 94, 106, 112–13, 157–9; impact on real life, 15–18, 53, 92, 213, 253–4, 260, 268–9; lack of racial diversity in, 62, 67, 82, 101, 302n21; about male sex workers, 266–7, 336n45; outside the US, 335n44; post-feminist media, 14–15, 81, 95, 113–14, 119, 132–3, 141–2, 148, 165, 176, 268; about transgender sex workers, 261–2, *262*. *See also individual named media*
porn cinemas. *See* adult theatres
PornHub, 217
porn industry: in the 1970s, 213, 223–4, 225–6, 238–9; as microcosm of capitalism, 246–8; problems within, 217, 236, 243–4, 327n18; profits of, 9, 223, 226; street-based sex workers and, 214, 223, 233, 239
"porno chic," 14, 216–17
Pornocracy: The New Sex Multinationals, 217, 332n90
pornography: alt porn, 6; faux empowerment and, 223–7, 243–4, 246; feminist debates about, 213–14, 216–17, 228, 326n11, 332n85; as a genre, 223–7, 326n7; glorification of submission, 128, 137, 145, 213, 216, 226, 229–30, 328n36, 332n86; history of, 119–20, 213, 215–17, 223–4, 244, 326nn6–7, 327–8n25; internet and, 6, 9, 120; legalization of, 23, 215, 226; mainstreaming of, 59, 120, 216, 293n40, 332n86; misogyny within, 22, 214, 216, 217, 225–6, 236, 243–4, 250, 328n36; objectification within, 128, 216, 224; in older pop culture, 216–17, 237, 244; power dynamics of, 118, 122, 225, 232, 239, 329n46; privileging of male pleasure in, 224, 227, 328n33; public opinion on, 216, 217, 226; racism within, 22, 214, 217, 225–6, 238–40, 249; sexual "education" and, 213, 230, 329n46; stereotypes about, 216, 237, 247, 251; in twenty-first century, 249–50, 332n90; visual codes of, 121, 124, 128, 130, 137, 148, 226–7, 231; vs webcam modelling, 118, 121–2, 124, 126, 128, 130, 148. *See also* anti-porn movement; Golden Age of Porn; revenge porn
pornography, feminist: aesthetic of, 231; film-makers, 35, 228, *229*, 230, 244, 249; goals of, 230, 329n46; history of, 227–30; labour conditions of, 227, 231; as "locus of politics," 228, 230; narrative focus of, 35, 213–14, 227–8, 230–1, 329n46; sex positivity and,

pornography, feminist (*continued*)
216, 217, 230; in twenty-first century, 249. *See also* auteurs
porn performers, 22, 122; in the 1970s, 223–4, 238–9; aesthetic labour of, 235; agency of, 213, 238; BIPOC performers, 234, 238–40; Club 90, 228; empowerment and, 34–5; limits of erotic capital, 236, 257; personal accounts of, 34–5, 228–30, 237, 249, 251, 329n46, 333n90; public fascination with deaths of, 330n65; stigmatization of, 230, 236–8
porn star experience (PSE), 156
post-feminism: "choice" discourses and, 22, 141–2, 256; "empowerment" and, 8, 113–14, 133, 148, 165, 176, 256–7, 331n82; individualism of, 81, 119, 132–3; post-feminist media, 14–15, 133, 148, 165, 268; sexy body ideal of, 95, 113–14, 119, 133, 165, 176, 256–7
"post-feminist sensibility," 8, 14, 119, 133, 256–7. *See also* Gill, Rosalind
post-Fordism, 7, 8, 9, 40, 102, 152, 159. *See also* capitalism; neo-liberalism
poverty: part-time workers, 41; reframed as opportunity, 42, 112; single mother-led families and, 87, 112
Power, Nina, 39, 299n112
Power of Pussy (P.O.P.), 20, 47, 48, 53, 62–7, 66, 82–3, 255
precarity, 7, 21, 40, 59, 63–4, 78–9, 112, 137, 141–2, 152, 165–6, 182, 217, 305n86, 312n87, 320n66
Pressler, Jessica, 75
Pretty Baby, 316n60
Pretty Woman, 5, 6, 8, 14, 18, 32, 33, 71, 73–4, 94, 158, 162, 166, 240
Princess Hunny (*Cam Girlz*), 123, 131
Private Practices: The Story of a Sex Surrogate, 189–90
Profumo, John, 153

prohibitionist paradigm: anti-porn position, 213, 216–17, 228, 245–6, 326n11, 330n65, 332nn84–6; challenges to, 25, 34, 35, 71–2, 75, 123, 125–6, 145, 192, 210, 225, 246, 251, 255, 289n102, 294n55; criminalization model, 32, 36–7, 111; critiques of sex worker films, 8–9; on dangers of disassociation, 44, 104, 174, 294n52; erotic dancing and, 48, 57, 67; exploitation narrative of, 31–2, 33, 56, 123, 125, 198, 210, 228, 241, 289n102; goals of, 33; hegemony of, 27, 245, 251, 287n73; language of, 31; media campaigns, 264–5; position on sex work, 15, 25, 27, 31–3, 58, 104, 179, 181, 332n86; sex surrogacy and, 198–9; webcam models and, 118, 123, 125–6
prostitutes. *See* sex workers
prostitution. *See* sex work
prostitution laws, 24, 27–8, 29, 98, 108, 111, 152, 186, 257, 268, 281n5, 311n83. *See also* criminalization
pseudonyms, use of, 58–9, 74, 104, 111, 146, 165, 174, 294n52
public opinion polls, 12, 52, 196, 303n23
Punternet, 164
P-Valley, 53

Queen, Carol, 33
Queen of Versailles, 67
queer narratives, 71–5, 119, 142–7, *147*, 149

racism: depicted on screen, 14, 88; in policing, 37, 239; in pornography, 22, 214, 217, 225–6, 238–40, 249; within sex industry, 82–3, 101, 148; sexualization and, 69, 238–40, 307n18; against sex workers, 82, 148, 239; stereotypes, 14, 101, 225–6, 239–40, 256, 307n18; systemic, 15, 51, 101, 238; and violence against

sex workers, 17, 222, 238–9. *See also*
    BIPOC sex workers
radical feminists. *See* prohibitionist
    paradigm
Rain, 13
rap artists, 62, 63, 68, 70
rape, 31, 32, 90, 128, 216, 226, 229–30,
    238, 242
"raunch culture," 14, 176
Reagan, Ronald, 251
Reaganism, 40, 158
reality TV, 5, 51, 92. *See also* talk shows
Reddit, 110–11, 266
Red Umbrella Project, 11, 250
relational rewards, 106, 200–1
"relational work," 45, 190. *See also*
    surrogacy, sex
Reproductive Biology Research
    Foundation, 186
"rescue" narratives: pop culture trope, 5,
    142–3, 233, 253, 316n60; prohibitionist
    perspective, 27, 29, 36–7, 38, 216, 263–4,
    326n15; rejection of, 71–5, 135, 140
Retail, Wholesale and Department Store
    Union (RWDSU), 11
revenge porn, 177–81, *180*
review websites, call girl, 163, 164, 168,
    170, 265–6
Reynolds, George, 106
rights movement, sex workers': fight
    against stigmatization, 91, 210, 241;
    growth of, 10–12, 24, 241–2, 290n3;
    human rights and, 10, 254, 269;
    impediments to, 6, 8, 83; language of,
    19; self-representation and, 241–2;
    symbol of, 234. *See also* activism, sex
    worker; unionization
rights movement, women's. *See*
    liberation, women's
Rikers Island, 81, 157, 222, 318n39
Ringley, Jennifer, 121
Ripper, The, 16–17

Risky Business, 158, 318n41
"Road Strip" (*This Is Life with Lisa Ling*),
    20, 48, 53–62, 82–3
Roberts, Julia, 5
Robinson, William J., 185
Rocco, 336n45
Rodriguez, Kitana Kiki, *262*
Roe v. Wade, 23
Rolling Stone, 237, 249, 251
Rosie (*Cam Girlz*), 127
Ross, Lynda, 113–14
Rottenberg, Catherine, 55, 85
Royalle, Candida, 213, 220, 228–30, 235,
    244, 251, 329n46, 330n60
Rubin, Gayle, 12, 213, 253, 332n87
RWDSU (Retail, Wholesale and
    Department Store Union), 11

Sadie Thompson, 13
Sakura, Nichole, *147*
San Francisco, 83, 199–200, 241, 331n74
San Francisco Sex Information (SFSI), 200
San Francisco Sex Worker Film and Arts
    and Festival, 261
Sanger, William, 28–9
Sarah ("Road Strip"), 54, 59, 61
sartorial strategies, 155, 164–5, 314n36.
    See also aesthetic labour; costumes
"saviour" trope. *See* "rescue" narratives
Scarafia, Lorene, 75
Scarlet Letter, The, 177
Scarlet Road, The, 210–11
Scarlot Harlot. *See* Leigh, Carol
Scott, Catherine, 210
Scott, Valerie X., 188, *190*
Seattle, 32
Second Coming (festival), 228
second-wave feminism, 142, 240–1, 258.
    See also feminism
Secret (*Magic City*), 68
self, loss of, 31, 134, 135, 137–8, 167,
    176–7, 207, 237

self-commodification, 43, 65, 125–6, 133, 152, 181, 182, 220, 227, 245, 249, 299n109

self-determination, 23, 27, 46, 74, 142, 240, 260, 265. *See also* agency; autonomy

self-discovery, sexual, 124, 130–2, 143–5, 149, 266–7

"self-objectification," 14, 122, 133, 142, 332n86

self-representation, 254; barriers to, 287n73; denied by prohibitionists, 33, 210, 245, 295n57; empowerment and, 24, 27, 53, 241; online, 43, 126, 153, 163–4, 249, 266; in popular media, 261–3; rights movement and, 241–2

Senft, Theresa, 121

separation of "self" from "role," 44, 104–5, 134, 135, 137–8, 142, 160, 162, 167, 174, 176–7, 192, 201, 316n51

serial killers, 16–17, 88

service work, 21, 24, 39, 40–2, *41*, 44, 59, 61, 78, 96–7, 102, 108, 124–5, 130, 134, 168, 246–7, 298n109, 305n86. *See also* "McJobs"

Sessions, The, 21–2, 183–4, 190–202, *195*, 209–11

SESTA (Stop Enabling Sex Traffickers Act), 260

sex industry, 7; exploitation of women, 31, 43, 52, 138, 168–9, 214, 238, 247–8, 293n40, 327n18; gender inequalities within, 15, 29, 213, 332n87; growth during COVID-19 pandemic, 9, 42, 118; internet and, 6, 9, 120–1; profits of, 9, 48, 118, 282n18; racism within, 22, 82–3, 101, 148, 256

sexism, 15, 51, 213, 220, 255, 322n87. *See also* misogyny

sexologists, 28, 183, 185, 209

sex-positive feminism, 23, 25, 33, 48, 67, 83, 130–1, 200, 227, 230, 234, 332n85. *See also* empowerment paradigm

sex positivity, 34, 54, 67, 72, 130–2, 142–3, 234

sex shops. *See* adult stores

sex surrogacy. *See* surrogacy, sex

sex surrogates. *See* surrogates, sex

"sexual inclusion," 183, 198

sexuality: as basic human right, 196; changes in the 1970s, 23–4, 187, 213, 307n18; commodification of, 14, 99–100, 125–6, 133, 220, 227; fear of, 88, 142–3; of men, 105, 234; motherhood and, 13, 86, 90–2, 97, 106, 113–14; performance of, 34, 53, 59, 67, 70, 74, 144–5, 149; politicization of, 12; popular attitudes towards, 6, 9; repression of, 27, 33, 59, 67, 77, 90–1, 130–1, 142–3, 145, 200, 229, 253, 255, 266, 285n49; self-discovery and, 124, 130–2, 143–5, 149, 266–7; and sense of self, 31, 133

Sexual Politics (Millett), 25

sex wars, feminist, 8, 22, 25, 72, 214, 216, 218, 245–6

sex work: benefits of, 36, 37, 41, 99, 117–18, 122, 124–8, 254; binary thinking about, 8, 13, 53, 67, 72, 74–5, 216–17, 251; definition of, 18–19; glamourization of, 14–15, 18, 48, 69, 94, 106, 112–13, 157–9; hierarchy of, 187, 209–10; history on screen, 12–15, 51–3; linked to sin, 15, 87, 94, 96, *97*, 102, 234, 332n84; medicalization of, 185–8, 324n71; neo-liberal capitalism and, 14, 29, 35–6, 75–81, 133, 148, 167, 181–2; occupational diversity of, 39, 45; vs "prostitution," 10, 268; public opinions about, 12, 29, 52, 66, 88, 92, 196, 253, 290n3, 307n16, 333n4; scholarship on, 13, 39, 45, 291n25; as "tool of patriarchy," 8, 12–13, 25, 27, 31, 57; as "tool of reappropriation," 33–4, 59; as work,

6–12, 18–19, 25, 26, 35–6, 39, 104, 123, 174, 254–5, 260, 266–7, 294n55, 318n42. *See also* activism, sex worker; criminalization; decriminalization; destigmatization; legalization; stigmatization; *individual types of sex work*
Sexworkerfest.com, 261
sex workers: collaboration among, 63–5, 67, 76–7, 80–1; creative involvement in popular culture, 261–3; deaths on screen, 13, 31, 52, 74, *89*, 158, 160, 222, 237, 242–3; economic motivations of, 19, 28–9, 36, 42, 47, 50, 53–6, 63–4, 67–70, 77, 82, 94, 99–100, 108, 124–5, 144–5, 159, 173, 260–1, 263–4, 327n19; as entrepreneurs, 7–8, 42, 43, 254; fear of being "outed," 16, 18, 108–11, 177–8, 255; as feminist radicals, 27, 175; friendships among, 64–5, 67, *76*, 94, 100; incarceration of, 5, 81, 96, *97*, 100, 108, 111, 157, 318n39; indoor, 19, 255, 256, 260, 264–5; marriages on screen, 5, 13, 18, 74; mature, 118, 132; as metaphor, 22, 289n102; moral outrage about, 88–9, 117–18, 119, 149, 307n16; as "Other," 5, 12–13, 285n45, 289n102, 307n18; outdoor, 5, 32, 264–5, 289n94; "politicized whores," 34, 241, 331n74; vs "prostitutes," 18–19; public support for, 10–12, 254; social history of, 27–9, 49–50, 59, 119–22, 152–3, 185–7, 223–4, 228–30, 322n25; teenage, 18, 21, 32, 51, 118, 121–2, 131, 236, 316n60; as "threats" to public safety, 16, 37, 88, 307n16; transgender, 257, 261–2, 265, 336n45; as "victims," 6–8, 14–16, 22, 23, 27, 29, 31–3, 47, 51–2, 67, 71–5, 88, 255. *See also* BIPOC sex workers; mothers, sex worker; rights movement, sex workers'; self-representation; stereotypes; violence against sex workers; *individual named sex workers*
sex workers, male, 266–7, 289n94, 336n45
sex workers, personal accounts of, 6, 10, 17–18; call girls, 151, 153–5, 268–9, 318nn39–40, 320n66; erotic dancers, 38, 47, 56, 59, 64–9, 253, 260–1, 305n86; massage parlour workers, 85, 308n19, 311n80; mothers, 47, 56, 64–5, 67, 92, 124–5; porn performers, 34–5, 228–30, 237, 249, 251, 329n46, 333n90; sex surrogates, 183–4, 191, 200, 210; street-based sex workers, 262, 264, 287n73; Victorian era, 28–30; webcam models, 42, 117, 121, 123–8, 130–5, 138–9, 141, 261, 315n47
Sex Workers Alliance of Toronto (SWAT), 250
Sex Workers Project, 11
SFSI (San Francisco Sex Information), 200
Shanghai Express, 13, 157
Shattered Innocence, 237
Shauna: Every Man's Fantasy, 237
Sheen, Charlie, 178
She's Lost Control, 21–2, 183–4, 202, *203*, 204–11, 255
Shiva Baby, 158
Shortbus, 183
Showgirls, 51
Shteir, Rachel, 49–50
Simon, David, 22, 214, 237, 248, 251, 329n55
Simone (*Magic City*, *P.O.P.*), 64, 65
sin, 15, 87, 94, 96, *97*, 102, 234, 332n84
16 mm loops, 23, 213, 225, 239, 249
Slate, 86
Slixa, 163
"slut" label, 22, 33, 35, 59, 66–7, 70, 106, 109, 117, 146, 191, 320n69

Smith, Molly, 15, 289n102
Smoking Gun, The (website), 16, 177
Snack Pack dancers, 63–7, *66*
social death, 311n80
social inequalities, 14–15, 21, 29, 49, 51, 64, 69–70, 71–4, 75–6, 79–81, 83, 101, 112, 114, 133, 144, 214, 305n79
social media, 43, 126, 153, 249, 266
social stigma. *See* stigmatization
Soderbergh, Steven, 152, 159–63, 165, 172, 249
Solomon, Barbara Bryant, 148
Soloway, Joey, 70–2, 74
Sophia (*Cam Girlz*), 123
Sophie (interviewee), 17–18, 151
Sopranos, The, 52
Spare Rib (magazine), 289n102
Spears, Britney, 51–2
Sprinkle, Annie, 228
Stacey, Clare, 106, 206
stage names. *See* pseudonyms, use of
stag films, 215, 239, 326n7
Stanford Center on Poverty and Inequality, 311n87
Stanislavski, Konstantin, 160
Star 80, 330n65
Star Garden Topless Dive Bar, 11, 83
St. Cyr, Lili, 58
Stein, Martha, 154, 156, 185
Steinem, Gloria, 25
stereotypes: in advertising, 91, 286n61, 312n96; call girl, 152, 156–9, 319n42; challenges to, 34–5, 54, 56, 63, 65, 67, 71–5, 77, 82, 108, 135, 294n53; as criminals, 15–16, 28, 77, 96, *97*, 100; erotic dancer, 47–8, 51–2, 61, 65–6, 71, 77, 79, 302n21; exploited victim, 6, 14, 31–2, 47, 51–2, 71–5, 88, 109, 143, 146, 237–8, 255; femme fatale, 5–6, 12, 32; internalization of, 109–10, 319; massage parlour, 102; massage parlour worker, 20, 88, *89*; of men, 198, 225–6, 234; in news media, 10, 16, 77, 88, 117, 311n80; in older pop culture, 5–6, 12–15, 31–2, 46, 51–2, 88, *89*, 102, 123, 156–8, 198, 253–4; of people with disabilities, 197; about pornography, 216, 237, 247, 251; prohibitionist, 32, 71; as psychologically damaged, 25, 32, 79, 117, 158; racist, 14, 101, 225–6, 239–40, 256, 307n18; sex worker "nurse," 45, 195; teen sex worker, 51, 142–4, 146. *See also* fallen woman trope
stigmatization: barrier to self-representation, 287n73; criminalization and, 11, 35, 37, 108, 111, 169, 177, 207, 255, 264; definition of, 16, 139; erotic capital and, 7, 43–4, 67, 97, 227; of erotic dancers, 47–8, 55, 65–7, 80; fear of, 16, 18, 74, 80, 108–11, 169, 177–8, 255, 311n80; fight against, 33–4, 35, 55, 91, 140, 210, 311n80; functionalization of, 80; intersectionality and, 111; and job loss, 16, 138–9, 177–8, 182, 241, 255, 264; of massage parlour workers, 311n80; of people with disabilities, 324n71; of porn performers, 230, 236–8; of sex worker mothers, 12–13, 21, 86–7, 90–2, 96–8, 107–11, 236; as "sluts," 33, 59, 66–7, 70, 106, 109, 117, 146, 191, 320n69; of webcam models, *139*, 139–40. *See also* destigmatization; stereotypes; whore stigma
St. James, Jacky, 249
St. James, Margo, *24*, 24–5, 241–2, 290n3, 331n74
Stone Age, 185
Stop Enabling Sex Traffickers Act (SESTA), 260
Stoya, 249, 333n90
Stratton, Dorothy, 330n65
Streep, Meryl, 14

street-based sex workers, 5, 32, 214, 223, 233, 239, 260, 262, 263–4, 289n94, 336n45
Streets, 316n60
Streetwise, 32
Streisand, Barbra, 158
strip clubs. *See* erotic dance clubs
"stripper culture," 48, 51–2, 67
strippers. *See* erotic dancers
Strippers (film), 335n44
striptease. *See* erotic dancing
Striptease Girl, 51
Strut, 158, 319n43
subjectivity, 23–4, 27, 34, 75, 145, 193, 228, 231, 254
Suck (magazine), 227–8
sugar babies, 9, 289n94
suicide: depicted on screen, 31, 160, 237; of fallen women, 91, 96; stigmatization and, 16, 110, 178
Suicide Girls, 6
Sun, The (magazine), 191, 197–8
Sundahl, Debi, 47, 58
Supreme Court (United States), 23, 215
"surface acting," 44, 60, 160, 319n45. *See also* emotional labour
surrogacy, sex, 18; challenges of, 201–2, 206–9; class dimensions of, 187–8; goals of, 184, 186, 191; history of, 185–90, 322n25; legality of, 183, 186, 206, 207–8, 209–10; links to medical science, 185–8, 192, 209–10, 324n71; people with disabilities and, 184, 186, 188, 196–9, 324n71; prohibitionist position on, 198–9; relational rewards of, 200–1; triadic nature of, 186, 205; as vocation, 184, 191, 201, 209. *See also* care work
surrogates, sex, 21–2; body work of, 192–4, 198–9, 204–5; care work of, 186, 190–4, 198–9, 204–7; compared to other sex workers, 188, 191–2, 209–10; criminalization and, 204–5, 207–9; emotional labour of, 184, 193, 195, 200–2, 206–7, 210; empowerment of, 204, 210–11; in older pop culture, 188–90; personal accounts of, 183–4, 191, 200, 210; services of, 183–4; stigmatization of, 188, 207, 210
Surrogate Wife: The True Confessions of a Sex-Therapist (Scott), 188, *190*, 199
Sutcliffe, Peter, 16–17
SWAT (Sex Workers Alliance of Toronto), 250
Sweden, 36
Sweet Potato (*Cam Girlz*), 131
"switching," 103, 154

Taken, 33
talk shows, 5, 51–3, 83, 197
Tangerine, 259, 261–2, *262*
Taormino, Tristan, 230, 249
Taxi Driver, 5, 316n60
Taylor, Elizabeth, 158
Taylor, Mya, *262*
Teenage Cocktail, 21, 118–19, 142–9, *147*
teenage sex workers, 18, 21, 32, 51, 118, 121–2, 131, 142–9, *147*, 236, 316n60
Temple, Juno, *73*
Texas, 93
Texas Monthly, 94–5
Theory of the Leisure Class, The (Thorstein), 155
Therese, Fabianne, *147*
Theron, Charlize, 32
third-wave feminism, 17, 182. *See also* feminism
35 mm films, 216, 226, 244
This Is Life with Lisa Ling, 53–62, 183, 303n34. *See also* "Road Strip" (*This Is Life with Lisa Ling*)
Thompson, Emma, 266, *267*
Thyberg, Ninja, 250
Time (magazine), 25

Times, The (London), 29
Times Square, 88, 218, *219*, 220, 223–4, 248, 307n16, 327–8n25
tokens, webcam, 21, 117–18, 136
Toronto, 17, 88, 307n16
Toronto Reference Library, 267–8
Touching Base, 210
Tracy (interviewee), 17–18, 117
Traffic in Souls, 33
trafficking, sex: anti-trafficking legislation, 260; conflated with sex work, 33, 260, 263; definition of, 288n90; distinct from sex work, 19, 35, 37; sex industry blamed for, 217
transactional intimacy: call girls and, 9, 21, 25, 152, 154, 156, 166–7, *171*, 171–2, 175–7; euphemized, 21, 151, 156, 157, 162, 166, 172; features of, 103, 156; massage parlour workers and, 87, 102–3; neo-liberal capitalism and, 7, 9, 21, 102–3, 152, 159–60, 177, 181, 254; normalization of, 7, 9, 21, 102, 151, 160, 166–7, 173, 181–2, 254; subversive nature of, 34, 175
transference, 195
transgender sex workers, 257, 261–2, 265, 336n45
Tressler, Sarah, 255
Trinh Thi, Coralie, 249
Trump, Donald, 217, 260
tube sites, 217, 249, 332n90
Twitter, 3, 10, 126, 261, 266

UNAIDS (Joint United Nations Programme on HIV/AIDS), 10
unemployment, 75, 85, 93–4, 98, 112, 118, 159
unionization, 11, 37, 59, 83, 241–2
United Kingdom, 16–17, 36, 178
United States: adult theatres in, 226; criminalization of sex work, 10, 33, 108, 186, 209; discrimination against BIPOC sex workers, 256–7; economic changes in, 9, 40–1, 59, 218, 298n107, 298n109, 311n87; erotic dance clubs, 9, 48, 51; gross domestic product, 102; introduction of internet, 120; legalization of pornography, 23, 215, 226; massage parlours, 87–8; new businesses in, 87, 112; obscenity laws, 215; recent legislation affecting sex workers, 259–60; sex industry, 9, 48; sex surrogate groups in, 188; sex workers' murdered in, 16–17, 222–3; single mother-led families, 87, 112; support for decriminalization, 12; unemployment in, 85, 112. *See also* financial crisis (2007–8)
"unmanaged heart," 44, 61, 149, 163. *See also* emotional labour
US Prostitutes Collective (US PROS), 36

Vance, Carole, 90
Vancouver, 287n73
Variety (film), 217
Variety (magazine), 86
Veblen, Thorstein, 155
Vera (interviewee), 17–18, 183, 208
Vera, Veronica, 228
vérité, 21, 63, 159–60, 162, 250, 318n42
Veronica Chaos (*Cam Girlz*), 128, 130
VHS porn, 237, 244
Victor, Roberta, 151
Victorian era, 3, 28–9, 87, 91, 96, *97*
video games, 52, 83, 265, 302n21
Village Voice, 88, 208, 222, 223, 307n16
violence against sex workers: criminalization and, 10, 32, 37, 108, 111, 207–9, 222, 242–3, 255, 259–60; depicted on screen, 79, 88, *89*, 128, 140–1, 142–3, 146, 208–9, 222, 238, 250, 263–5, 294n53; impact of pop culture on, 15–16; in the Middle Ages, 27–8; misogyny and, 17, 32, 79, 294n54, 315n47; murder, 16–17, 52,

88, 222–3, 242, 294n54; on-screen
deaths, 13, 31, 52, 74, *89*, 158, 160,
222, 237, 242–3; prosecution of,
16–17, 209, 222–3, 242; racialized,
17, 222, 238–9, 265; transgender sex
workers, 261, 265; in the Victorian
era, 29. *See also* rape; suicide
Violet October (*Cam Girlz*), 125
virgin–whore dichotomy, 12–13, 15, 34,
51–2, 77, 83, 87, 90–2, 98, 105–6, 111,
114, 156, 180, 268
Virgo (*Magic City, P.O.P.*), 64, 65
virtual rooms, 118, 127–8
visual codes, pornography, 121, 124, 128,
130, 137, 148, 226–7, 231
Vivre sa vie, 44, 159–60, 167

wage gap, 83, 112, 114, 311n87
Wall Street bankers, 75–6, 79–81
WAP. *See* Women Against Pornography
(WAP)
Washington, DC, 82
Waterloo Bridge, 31, 73–4
webcam industry, 118, 132–3, 135,
137–8, 148
webcam modelling: "authenticity"
and, 118, 121–2, 124, 126–8, 130,
135–6, 314n36; benefits of, 117–18,
122, 124–8, 131–2; challenges of,
117–18, 133–4, 136–8; condemned
by prohibitionists, 118, 123; creative
entrepreneurship and, 123–4,
125–8, 148; DIY culture and, 121,
126–7, 128; doxxing and, 133, 315n47;
empowerment and, 21, 117–19,
123–6, 130–3, 148; history of, 119–23;
as performance art, 118, 123, 124,
128, *129*, 130, 136–7; piracy and, 133,
138; power dynamics of, 118, 122;
precarity of, 137–8, 141–2; private
setting of, 121–2, 126–7; profits of, 9,
118, 124, 282n18; range of services,
126–7; and sexual self-discovery, 124,
130–2; vs traditional pornography,
118, 121, 124, 126, 128, 130, 148
webcam models: aesthetic labour of, 128,
129, 130, 135, 144, 314n36; agency of,
118, 122, 125–8, 130, 148, 265; BIPOC
models, 148; burnout, 118, 134,
137–8, 141; display work of, 126–30,
129, 144; diversity of, 118, 131; early
cam girls, 121–2, 126; emotional
labour of, 133–8, 141–2, 148; as
entrepreneurs, 21, 118–19, 122–8,
135, 148; male gaze and, 118, 122, 130,
144–5; motivations of, 124–5, 132,
144–5; online personae, 126, 128, *129*,
130, 134, 135, 137; personal accounts
of, 42, 117, 121, 123–8, 130–5, 138–9,
141, 261, 315n47; personal branding,
118, 126–8; stigmatization of, *139*,
139–40
websites, sex worker, 9, 43, 117–18,
120–2, 127, 132, 138, 163–4, 259–60,
266. *See also* review websites, call girl;
tube sites
Weitzer, Ronald, 39, 45, 156, 204,
294n55, 297n94
well-being, sexual, 22, 196, 211, 266
We're the Millers, 53
West, Desiree, 239
West Yorkshire Police Department, 17
What the Butler Saw, 119
WHISPER (Women Hurt in Systems of
Prostitution Engaged in Revolt), 33
White Lotus, The, 3
"white slavery," 31, 33
white supremacy, 69, 226, 234, 238,
256–7. *See also* racism
"whorearchy," 209–10
whorephobia. *See* whore stigma
whore stigma, 108–12, *109*, *139*, 140,
146, 172, 177–81, *180*, 222, 236–7,
255, 320n69. *See also* stigmatization

Williams, Linda, 224, 225, 226–7, 232–3
Willis, Ellen, 34, 71
Windsor, Ontario, 117–18, 149
Wolfe, Bob, 223–4
Wolkowitz, Carol, 45, 301n140
Wollstonecraft, Mary, 29
women: double standards for, 7, 22, 24, 27, 34, 67, 90, 97, 106, 109, 114, 174, 177–8, 181, 218, 220; expression of anger, 79–80, 97, 111, 179, 182, 242, 257–9; "good" vs "bad," 5, 13, 16, 23, 25, 67, 87, 90–2, 96, 233; idealized, 12–13, 86, 90–2, 256; objectification of, 27, 31–3, 34, 54, 58, 69, 82, 95, 122, 128, 130, 133, 142–3, 170, 216, 224, 307n18, 331n82; as "Other," 285n45, 289n102; patriarchal capitalism and, 7–8, 29, 39–42, 90, 148, 227, 247–8, 311n87, 318n41; sexual repression of, 27, 33, 59, 67, 77, 90–1, 130–1, 142–3, 145, 200, 229, 253, 255, 266, 285n49; subjectivity of, 23–4, 27, 34, 75, 145, 228, 231, 254; unpaid labour of, 42, 90, 107, 174; violence against, 17, 141, 328n36; working-class, 50, 59, 79–80, 83, 305n86. *See also* fallen woman trope; liberation, women's; sex workers; virgin-whore dichotomy

Women Against Pornography (WAP), 228, 245–6, 332n84
Women Survivors of Pornography, 33
Wonderland, 217
Working Girls, 8, 23, 35–6, 158, 318n42
World Health Organization, 10
World of Suzie Wong, The (Mason), 307n18
Wotton, Rachel, 210
Wrestler, The, 53
Wu, Constance, 76
Wuornos, Aileen, 32, 294n53
WUSA (film), 73–4

X (formerly Twitter). *See* Twitter

"Yorkshire Ripper." *See* Sutcliffe, Peter
Young, Madison, 249
YouPorn, 332n90
YouTube, 19, 63, 67, 261, 302n21, 311n81
"yummy mumminess," 114

Zack and Miri Make a Porno, 217
Zeisler, Andi, 256
Ziplow, Steven, 223
Zola (film), 3, 261
Zola, Émile, 3, 28

Printed and bound by CPI Group (UK) Ltd, Croydon, CR0 4YY
06/07/2025

14698938-0001